TONY BENN

TONY BENN

JAD ADAMS

MACMILLAN

First published 1992 by Macmillan London Limited,
A division of Pan Macmillan Publishers Limited,
Cavaye Place, London SW10 9PG
and Basingstoke

Associated companies in Auckland, Budapest, Dublin,
Gaborone, Harare, Hong Kong, Kampala, Kuala Lumpur,
Lagos, Madras, Manzini, Melbourne, Mexico City, Nairobi,
New York, Singapore, Sydney, Tokyo and Windhoek

ISBN 0 333 52258 2

1 3 5 7 9 8 6 4 2

A CIP catalogue record for this book is available from the
British Library

Phototypeset by Intype, London
Printed and bound in Great Britain by
Billing & Sons Ltd, Worcester

FOR MY MOTHER AND FATHER,
AMY ADAMS AND ANDREW ADAMS

Contents

List of Illustrations

Anthony, David and Michael Benn, 1930.
The family at Stansgate, 1932.
Evacuated schoolboy, 1941.
Pilot Officer, 1945.
Flying Officer Michael Wedgwood Benn, 1943.
Family reunion 1946.
Oxford Debating team, 1947.
Electioneering, 1955.
The Benn family at play.
H-Bomb National Committee, 1954.
The Benn family complete.

On the set of 'The ABC of Democracy', 1962.
'Winds of change' (Cummings), 1961.
Excluded from the House of Commons, 1962.
By-election triumph, 1963.
Postmaster General, 1965.
Priests of the new technology, 1966.
Concorde test flight, 1970.
'Who activated him?' (Garland), 1968.
Shadow Industry minister at Upper Clyde Shipbuilders, 1971.
Industrial discontent in the 1970s.
'He actually believes in miracles!' (Emmwood), 1974.

Picture Acknowledgements

The author and publishers would like to thank the following for their permission to use copyright sources:

The Tony Benn Archives: plate section I pages 1 above and below, 2 (inset), 3 above and below, 4, 6 and 7; plate section II pages 1 above, 3, 4 above and below, 5, 6 below; plate section III page 2 above.

Daily Express: plate section II pages 1 below and 7 below; plate section III page 2 below.

Daily Mail/Solo: plate section II page 8.

Nicholas Garland © *The Daily Telegraph* plc: plate section II page 6 above.

Philip Jones Griffiths/*Observer*: plate section II page 2.

Hulton Picture Company: plate section I pages 2 and 8.

The Independent: plate section III page 6 above and below.

Eddy de Jongh: plate section II page 7 above.

News of the World: plate section III page 1.

Press Association: plate section III pages 3, 4 and 5.

Caroline Rees: plate section III page 8.

Syndication International: plate section I page 5.

The Times (Richard Willson) © Times Newspapers Ltd 1984: plate section III page 7.

Every effort has been made to trace all copyright holders but if any have been inadvertently overlooked, the publishers will be pleased to make the necessary arrangement at the first opportunity.

Introduction

Few people can remember a time when Tony Benn was not playing a leading role in politics. He has served more than forty years in the House of Commons, having been elected fifteen times, more than any other living parliamentarian.

He spent eleven years as a minister of cabinet rank and has been thirty years on Labour's National Executive Committee. These facts alone give him a better record of service than any other current member of the Labour leadership.

Benn has also been responsible for more constitutional change in Britain than any other politician excepting some of those who became Prime Minister. His successful battle to renounce his peerage represented a fundamental statement about the relationship between the Lords and the Commons and the primacy of elected authority. His campaign for a referendum on membership of the Common Market meant a constitutional door was opened which can never again be closed. The reforms he supported in the Labour Party for re-selection of MPs and a wider franchise for the election of the party leader have had far-reaching effects in other parties and other organisations. Equally penetrating has been his questioning of the nature of political power in Britain, his criticism of the way the power of 'the crown' is concentrated in the hands of the Prime Minister and appointed officials, bypassing the Commons.

Yet he is widely seen as a failure as a politician, someone who almost became leader of the Labour Party. In the late 1960s he was not only tipped for the leadership within a decade, there seemed to be no one else in the race. However his enemies tried to marginalise him, he was always back with his quick wit and his moral superiority. Yet he stood for the leadership twice and twice, equally unsuccessfully, for the deputy leadership. Despite his acknowledged political skill, the positions he adopted made him unacceptable to his colleagues. Some would say Benn simply 'backed the wrong horse' in leading the left wing in the 1970s, and that he mistakenly believed it was a winning strategy. This biography challenges that view, showing that in the context of the rest of his life his move to the left was not a sudden leap but a natural working out of ideas. It was also in the tradition of the best role model he had: his father.

The Labour MPs would not back him as a socialist in the 1970s and 1980s; but neither did his parliamentary colleagues give their fulsome support in the preceding two decades. The underlying fact is that the Labour Party is a conservative party which is rather more efficient in undermining radicalism in its own ranks than in political combat with the Tories.

This biography offers an understanding of what makes this enigmatic man interesting as a politician, of his strengths and his weaknesses. It attempts an all round survey of the man, for the controversy surrounding his political stance has unfairly diverted attention from a full appreciation of his talents. He is one of the greatest orators of the second half of the century – admittedly a period in which the art of oratory was in decline. He has written the most extensive published political diary of his times. He has also kept what are probably the best records of any politician. This book relies heavily on material from the Benn Archives and I am deeply indebted to Tony Benn for permitting me access. I am also indebted to the Benn family for tolerating me with such good humour. Likewise Tony Benn's staff. His secretary Kathy Ludbrook also gave me the benefit of her extensive knowledge of the Labour Party.

There can be few editors who have had every piece of their work traced back to source as Ruth Winstone has, with my going through the unedited volumes of the Benn Diaries in her office. This she bore with equanimity, and despite my attempts to catch her out on errors of detail, I was never successful. She also gave patient advice at every stage of my work, over a three year period. Tony Benn himself was generous with his time, allowing me twelve lengthy interviews. He described them as 'a bit like the day of judgement without actually dying'.

Many of the people who were good enough to consent to be interviewed are mentioned in the references. Sometimes former colleagues of Tony Benn were prepared to see me at some discomfort to themselves. Meeting people in hospital rooms or talking to those who were clearly in the final stages of illness made me feel as if I were plucking history from the very jaws of death.

All errors and omissions are my responsibility, but the following people have been so kind as to read the manuscript, or large parts of it, and make comments: Andrew Adams, David Benn, David Butler, Richard Coopey, Harold Hewitt and Michael Zander.

Finally, but most importantly, my profound thanks to Julie Peakman, for her practical and moral support while I was working on this book.

November 1991

1

Childhood and Family

'When I was born in 1925,' Tony Benn reflected while in his sixties, 'twenty per cent of the world was ruled from London. In my lifetime I have seen Britain become an outpost of America administered from Brussels.'

The young Benn was able to observe Britain's changing role in world affairs from the vantage point of an intensely political home. His first coherent political memory is of visiting Oswald Mosley, then a Labour MP, at his home in Smith Square. He remembers thanking Mosley for his hospitality in what he has described as his first speech. When he was five in 1930 he went to see the Trooping of the Colour from the back of 10 Downing Street. He was more impressed with the chocolate biscuits than with meeting Ramsay MacDonald, the Prime Minister. A deeper impression was made by the gentle yet strangely dressed figure of Gandhi, in London in 1931 for the second Round Table Conference, which Benn's father had convened when Secretary of State for India.

What made a lasting impression on Benn was the knowledge that the powerful talked, walked and ate like everyone else, lived in houses just like him, were accessible. Schoolmates later talked of his self-assurance, of his confidence in his own position. He could respect the mighty as people but he had learned as automatically as he learned to speak that they were just other folk doing a job. When he was later to challenge prime ministers and sit with the Queen discussing stamps he was not tongue-tied. Inoculated by minute exposure from an early age, he had developed an immunity to awe.

Tony Benn was the second son of William Wedgwood Benn and Margaret Benn, later Viscount and Lady Stansgate. He was named

1

Anthony because Sir Ernest Benn, his uncle, had bought a painting depicting a Sir Anthony Benn who had been a courtier in Elizabethan times. The portrait shows a dark, sombre-looking man with no obvious connection with the latterday Benn family. Mrs Benn saw the painting for the first time in Sir Ernest's dining room when she was carrying the baby and decided, if it was a boy, to call him Anthony. 'We nearly didn't,' she said, 'because I said it will be sure to be shortened to Tony and I dislike the name Tony very much.'[1] Ernest Benn left the portrait to his nephew in his will but sold it when Tony Benn joined the Labour Party on his seventeenth birthday. The picture re-entered the family when the new owner sold it to Tony Benn's wife Caroline.

Baby Anthony received as his second name Neil, because his mother wanted to remind him of his Scottish ancestry. The name Wedgwood is a direct reference to his father. William Wedgwood Benn had been so christened in 1877 because his maternal grandmother, Eliza Sparrow, was a distant cousin of the pottery family. Tony Benn's debt to his father is clear from a tribute he wrote in 1977, 'His inherited distrust of established authority and the conventional wisdom of the powerful, his passion for freedom of conscience and his belief in liberty, explain all the causes he took up during his life, beginning with his strong opposition to the Boer War as a student, at University College, London, for which he was, on one occasion, thrown out of a ground-floor window by "patriotic" contemporaries.'[2]

Wedgwood Benn was the youngest person in the new Parliament in 1906 when at the age of twenty-eight he was elected for St George's in the East and Wapping, with a 'No Tax on Food' slogan. This was the first election which his future wife Margaret Holmes could remember. She was then only eight years old but had been born into a Scottish Liberal family, so the party's landslide was a significant feature of her childhood. The 1906 election produced the first great radical government of the century, which, with its Liberal successors, went on to introduce old-age pensions, national health and unemployment insurance and curbed the power of the House of Lords.

Before the election Wedgwood Benn had been working in the publishing business which his father had built up and had been supporting various trade union causes in the East End of London. He was already a radical, arguing for Home Rule for Ireland, for a Jewish homeland and for the protection of trade union funds, which had become liable to seizure as a result of the Taff Vale judgement by the House of Lords in 1901.

He became a junior Whip and junior Lord of the Treasury in 1910. One trait of his which was also to be apparent in his son's make-up was a love of gadgetry. He arranged for the installation in the Whips' room of telephones, a counting machine and a pneumatic tube to carry messages to and from the front bench. In the Whips' room he was in an ideal position to see how Parliament functioned. He was fascinated by the way the constitution and parliamentary procedure and democracy all fitted together to form part of the machinery of government, an insight which once led him to call Parliament a 'workshop'. It was this understanding, founded on sympathy, which prompted Lord Halifax to describe him as '[one of] the best Parliamentarians of my time in the House'.[3]

In 1914 he felt compelled to serve in the war, even though his age (he was thirty-seven) and his occupation as an MP exempted him. He joined the Middlesex Yeomanry, a mounted regiment for which he was eligible only because a fellow Liberal MP gave him a polo pony and groom. He served in the Dardanelles, then his individualistic talents found alternative means of expression. Joining the Royal Naval Air Service, he participated in the bombing of the Baghdad Railway. He was rescued from a sinking aeroplane in the Mediterranean and showed great bravery in the evacuation of an improvised aircraft carrier when it was ablaze after coming under attack from shore batteries. He commanded a unit of French and British sailors in guerrilla fighting against the Turks then went to Italy after training as a pilot. He was seconded to the Italian Army for whom he organised the first parachute landing of an agent behind enemy lines. The agent later named his first son after Wedgwood Benn. By the end of the war he had been twice mentioned in dispatches and had been honoured by three countries: Britain appointed him to the DSO and awarded him the DFC; France made him a Chevalier of the Legion of Honour and awarded him the Croix de Guerre; and the Italians awarded him the War Cross and the bronze medal for military valour.[4] While this was the stuff of which *Boys' Own* yarns were made, Wedgwood Benn's own account in his book *In the Side Shows* (1919) reveals how this sensitive man discovered 'what militarism really means: its stupidity, its brutality, its waste. . . . Is there anyone, now, who will deny that, step by step, warfare degrades a nation? The low appeal succeeds the high. The worst example prevails over the better.'[5]

While in the services he had refused invitations to return as joint Chief Whip under both Asquith and Lloyd George and had also declined the job of parliamentary secretary to the Munitions Department. His own constituency had been lost in boundary changes under the Representation of the People (Amendment) Act 1918 and, as he was not prepared to accept endorsement by the Liberal–Conservative coalition of Lloyd George and Bonar Law, those party chiefs were not going to find him a new seat. Eventually the Liberal Party in Leith invited him to stand against the coalition candidate there and he became one of twenty-nine non-coalition Liberals returned to the House.

Several of these, finding their position exposed, soon went over to the coalition, leaving the 'Asquithian' Liberals and the fledgling Labour Party as the only opposition to Lloyd George's rule. It was in this position as chief organiser of the independent Liberals, or 'Wee Frees', that he was able to court his future wife, Tony Benn's mother.

Margaret Holmes was from a Scottish Liberal nonconformist family. As so often, strength of character showed itself in early rebellions and solitary achievements. She was always a feminist and, against the wishes of her father, would go to meetings of Emily Pankhurst and Millicent Fawcett. Somewhat adventurously for a girl before the First World War, she began smoking at fourteen. Then, in 1941, when it might be thought there was more reason to smoke, she decided to stop and did so immediately. No less impulsively, she was inspired to learn Hebrew, when on a trip to Palestine in 1926 she heard Jewish pilgrims singing psalms. Despite the difficulty of the language, she learned it well enough to impress David Ben-Gurion after the founding of Israel and, in recognition of her scholarship, a library in the Hebrew University on Mount Scopus was named after her in 1975.

Her father, Daniel Turner Holmes, was elected for Govan at a by-election in 1911. Margaret Holmes was sitting in the Ladies' Gallery, visiting her father at the House of Commons, when she first saw Wedgwood Benn, then a junior government Whip. 'He was very alert and lively, with very fair hair,' she remembered.[6]

Eight years later he was helping her father at a North Edinburgh by-election of 1920, Holmes having lost his Govan seat because he had refused, like Wedgwood Benn, to accept the coalition 'coupon' which would guarantee victory. But he was defeated in North Edinburgh and moved to Seaford with his family. Wedgwood Benn visited them there on his bicycle, then invited the family several times to the House of Commons. The first time he was alone with Margaret, the forty-three-year-old bachelor proposed in his usual, practical style: 'Well, we could live near the House in Westminster and you could have a chop at the House every night.'[7] Margaret did not like chops, but she was taken with the proposition and they were married on 17 November 1920 before a congregation packed with leading Liberals, but from which Lloyd George was conspicuously absent.

The marriage was witnessed by Asquith. On the marriage certificate Sir John Benn was described as 'Baronet', a title he had been given in 1914; Daniel Holmes's 'rank or profession' was noted as 'Gentleman'. The one demand Wedgwood Benn placed on his new bride was that she should become teetotal, like him, because he wished their children to be brought up teetotal. His sister had made a similar demand on her fiancé in 1912. It was a peculiar feature of Liberalism's close connection with the nonconformist movement that many people in both the political party and the religious denomination had a deep abhorrence of alcohol. David Benn, like his brother Tony a 'non-proselytising teetotaller', remarked that being against alcohol in the early part of the century was rather like being against narcotics in the latter part. It was a principled but unremarkable position.

After a honeymoon at which they attended the inaugural meeting of the League of Nations in Geneva, they returned to live in rented accommodation in Westminster. Their first child, Michael, was born on 3 September 1921. 'He's going to be a great friend of mine,' said Wedgwood Benn. The family moved in November 1924 to 40 Grosvenor Road, on the river. It was here that Tony Benn was born on 3 April 1925. 'Isn't it wonderful, it's a boy!' said Wedgwood Benn. 'It would have been just as wonderful', Margaret Benn remarked dryly, 'if it had been a girl.'[8]

Margaret Benn gave to the boys, in Michael's words, 'the precious gift of religion'. Bill Allchin, a schoolfriend of the Benn boys, remarked that it was in their household that he first heard the phrase 'ordination of women', one of Margaret Benn's great passions. As a member of the League of the Church Militant she was summoned to Lambeth Palace to see Archbishop Randall Davidson. She explained to him, 'I want my boys to grow up in a world in which the Churches will give women equal spiritual status.'[9] She became an Anglican at the age of twenty, before her marriage.[10]

The twin pillars of religion and politics run through the Benn ancestry up to the earliest-known Benn, the Revd William Benn of Dorchester. A dissenter, he was one of 2000 Anglican clergymen exiled from their livings by the Five Mile Act of 1665, one of the retributions which followed the restoration of the monarchy after the English Revolution.

Wedgwood Benn, often known affectionately as 'Wedgie', was involved in the early 1920s in a tenacious struggle as he and a handful of colleagues kept the flag of radical Liberalism flying in an increasingly conservative House of Commons. He used to take three copies of *The Times*, one for Margaret and two for him to mark up and file. For these two he bought the 'royal edition', costing sixpence and printed on rag paper, which did not age. Using the information in his *Times* files, by lunchtime he had issued a bulletin on all the major subjects of the day with which his colleagues could challenge the government. They called it 'Benn's Blat'. Because of it, and because the Liberal dissidents were by nature challenging souls rather than voting fodder, the wee frees had an influence in Commons debates out of all proportion to their number.

Lloyd George was still the leading Liberal, despite abandoning his early radicalism. The first two years of Tony Benn's life were therefore a time of hectic activity for his father, who was attempting to prevent Lloyd George from becoming leader of the Liberals. With the party at last reforming after the divisive years of the coalition, Lloyd George was the obvious leader, and Asquith moved to the Lords to accommodate him. What he saw as Lloyd George's lack of principle, and the personal political fund he brought with him back to the Liberals disgusted Wedgwood Benn. 'I cannot put my conscience in pawn to this man,' he said. 'I will have to be a Liberal in the Labour Party.'[11]

He had long co-operated with the Labour Party, many of whose policies were identical with those of the radical Liberals. Crossing the floor of the House was difficult, for he had too much integrity simply to announce a change of party allegiance in mid-Parliament. Margaret Benn watched from the Gallery as he walked in to the Commons chamber on 14 February 1927 and sat down on the Labour benches. He then went to shake hands with the Speaker before leaving the chamber to resign. He joked in later life that the only political job he had ever asked for was the Chiltern Hundreds, the non-existent post which the British constitution allows a member of Parliament to apply for but which entails automatic disqualification as an MP.

This was a decision of great bravery. It may be noted that only one of the SDP MPs who left the Labour Party in 1981 had the integrity to resign his seat and let the voters decide whether they still wanted him. Wedgwood Benn was leaving the safe seat of Leith, for which he had been returned in four general elections (1919, 1922, 1923 and 1924). Leith Labour Party already had a candidate, so there was no future for him there. He was losing his MP's salary (back-benchers had been paid £400 a year since 1912) and had no wish to return to work in the family publishing firm of Benn Brothers, which his brother Sir Ernest had made his own domain. Wedgwood Benn could survive on his £500 per year pension from Benn Brothers but he was far from well off in relation to others of similar social status. Most importantly, Wedgwood Benn at the age of forty-nine and with a wife and two young children, had cut himself off from the Liberal Party, without having any alternative power base in a constituency or in the trade union movement.

The decision was a momentous one for the family. His brother Ernest, afraid that his talk of joining the Labour Party showed he had lost his mind, promptly sent Wedgwood and Margaret Benn on a Mediterranean cruise, hoping that a holiday would help him recover his senses. Expecting the trip to last only a few weeks, they left the two boys with their uncle, but Margaret was eager to see the Holy Land, so they disembarked at Haifa, then spent three months travelling through thirteen countries. They had reached Moscow when they heard news of the British General Strike in 1926, and only then were they at last prompted to return. Sir Ernest, fearing revolution, closed his London house and sent his nephews Michael and Tony to the country.

His uncle was a major influence on Tony Benn, for his maintenance of his political principles when all seemed against him. Two years older than William Wedgwood Benn, he stood at the opposite end of the Liberal Party spectrum. Wedgwood Benn was so concerned about public welfare, believing fervently in planning and in state intervention for the public good, that he was virtually a socialist even while he was a member of the Liberal Party. Ernest Benn, on the other hand, was the complete laissez-faire capitalist. He believed that wealth and public benefit could be achieved only by the absolute economic freedom of the individual. In 1925, two years before his brother joined the Labour Party, he wrote *Confessions of a Capitalist*, in which one chapter was entitled 'Making £1,000 in a Week'. He formed short-lived organisations like Friends of Economy and the Society of Individualists to promote his economic ideas and became a significant public figure on radio and on the lecture circuit. 'He totally disapproved of the way the country was going,' said David Benn. 'He thought the Labour Party was bringing the country down. He would have felt entirely at home in the Britain of the 1980s, though he would not have approved of a woman Prime Minister.'[12]

Tony Benn always had an affection for his uncle, despite their differences, and the Benn family in general had reason to be grateful to him. It was he who transformed Benn Brothers from a publisher of commercial journals into a major publishing house with a list which included H. G. Wells, Joseph Conrad and E. Nesbit. He was an enlightened capitalist; his firm was one of the first two to introduce a five-day working week and introduced a bonus scheme which related an increase in shareholders' dividends to an increase in salaries for his workers. It was thanks to Sir Ernest that Wedgwood Benn could afford to buy the lease on 40 Grosvenor Road and he always invited the whole family to enjoy the hospitality of his home at Christmas.

Tony Benn's mother, admittedly a somewhat partial witness, gave this account of his early childhood: 'He was a most delightful little boy, an unusually friendly little boy, awfully interested in people. He was very companionable – he would sit and play and talk to you and if anybody wanted an errand run you didn't have to ask him, he was there to do it. He showed for a child such an unusual interest in people. If somebody was ill he was concerned and asked after them. I thought to myself, "Here's a boy who's going to make an East End parson." ' [13]

Margaret Benn remembered Tony learning to speak very early, managing complete sentences almost (or so it seemed) at once. She especially recalled him speaking volubly one dramatic night when the Thames burst its banks and flooded the basement of 40 Grosvenor Road. This was on 6 January 1928, when he was three months from his third birthday. Margaret Benn was awoken in the early hours of the morning by her cook shouting, 'The Thames is in the house!' When she looked out of the window she saw that the road had disappeared under the rising water. Two tides had been held back by the wind and there had been a freeze further up the river which had now melted. The tides and the melted ice had met outside their house, so it was here that the Thames burst through, flinging the stone blocks of the embankment aside like toy bricks. She picked up the telephone and the operator advised her to go to the highest rooms and to be prepared to climb on to the roof. 'I got the children out of bed and Anthony was most interested in everything. He wanted to look out of the window and at the water in the house. I remember our nanny having to tell him he couldn't have ginger beer even though it was one in the morning.' [14] Beatrice and Sidney Webb lived next door and Tony Benn vividly remembers seeing a trunk of theirs floating out of the house on the flood water.

The house was uninhabitable for some time, so the family moved to Scotland, where Wedgwood Benn had been selected as Labour candidate for West Renfrew. Before a general election could be called, a by-election was held in North Aberdeen and the West Renfrew constituency party allowed him to stand. He was returned as a Labour MP for North Aberdeen on 16 August.

The family applied to the Norland Institute for a qualified nanny. They sent Nurse Olive Winch, a charming woman of twenty-eight, who was nicknamed Bud, who was to stay with the Benns for twelve years and to remain a family friend for the rest of her life – the next generation, Tony Benn's own children, were devoted to her. Margaret Benn said, 'Anthony was brought up under the influence of someone making him want to do what he ought to do and enjoy doing it. I think it's made a tremendous difference to his whole life.'

Wedgwood Benn called Tony 'the serving brother', on account of his eagerness to be of help to others. The Liberal–Christian tradition of life as a service was further encouraged in the children, doubtless unwittingly, by household games. Margaret Benn explained: 'They used to pretend they were workmen called Bill and Jim – Michael was Bill, Anthony Jim. Nurse Olive made them working clothes and they used to come and ask for jobs and I used to give them little jobs and pay them.'[15] This game gave Tony Benn the name his family was always to use, his parents humorously making the name more dignified by extending it to James.

The third Benn brother, David, was born in Scotland on 28 December 1928. Soon afterwards the family returned to London. Anthony's first school, in September 1931, was Francis Holland, a girls' school in Graham Street near Sloane Square which took boys in their nursery class. Miss Morison, the head, taught him scripture and before long declared that he was the most interesting little boy she had ever taught: 'To tell you the truth, when I begin he begins.' This was a reference to Anthony's eagerness to show off his scriptural knowledge – a knowledge somewhat coloured by his use of political terms to describe religious events. 'The Sinai pact' was one of these. Margaret Benn remarked, 'He was a very religious little boy. I remember when my husband and I set off for a long journey, when we went round the world in 1933, all three boys gave us something to take with us. Anthony gave us a little book of prayers which he wrote himself, for his father and mother in all sorts of circumstances on our travels. I keep it in my jewel case.'[16]

Congregationalism, the strand of nonconformism which William Wedgwood Benn protested, is distinguished by the emphasis on each congregation making its own decisions about its affairs, admitting of no higher temporal authority. Anyone brought up in that tradition receives the democratic message by a process of spiritual osmosis. Tony Benn also absorbed the militancy of the religious message. He said, 'I was brought up on the Old Testament, the conflict between the kings who exercised power and the prophets who preached righteousness. Faith must be a challenge to power.'[17] In the 1970s he was to describe early British socialist thought as deriving, in the first instance, from the Bible.

In 1934 he went to Gladstone's School, run by a descendant of the great Liberal Prime Minister, which later moved and was renamed Eaton Place Prep School. His early school reports suggested that he 'talks too much' and was 'too excitable', but they revealed nothing exceptional.

The boys' pastimes were unremarkable for middle-class children at the time. Tony was devoted to his elder brother and they spent a great deal of time together. Not surprisingly, these two sons of an RAF pilot who were each to become RAF pilots themselves liked to make model aircraft, which they flew in Victoria Gardens. At home the family enjoyed decidedly Victorian evenings, singing along to gramophone records while the young Tony wound up the motor of the machine.

He did not share the dream of most small children to become an engine driver or a policeman. As Margaret Benn said, 'He has only ever wanted to be in Parliament. It was his only ambition. He used to go to the House of Commons when he was a little boy and sit in the Strangers' Gallery and watch the debates. And he would say to me, "Dad seems to be very angry with those men." '[18]

The general election of 30 May 1929 was the first Tony Benn could remember. As a Labour MP with considerable parliamentary experience, Wedgwood Benn was picked out to become a member of Ramsay MacDonald's cabinet when the Prime Minister formed his minority government. In the event he was made Secretary of State for India, a difficult office for he had to drive a middle course between those Labour colleagues like Fenner Brockway who wanted Indian independence immediately and the imperialist right, led by Winston Churchill.

Throughout his years in Parliament the house in Grosvenor Road was dominated by Wedgwood Benn's work. The whole basement was taken up with his political office, which expanded to take more rooms as he engaged more staff and as the files increased in number. His procedure for cutting and filing *The Times* according to a decimalised system was soon fully mechanised. Tony Benn used to delight in watching as the marked-up newspaper pages were cut into columns by a guillotine, then rolled by a conveyor to another guillotine which cut at right angles, separating out the articles. They rolled on to be backed with glue and then stuck down on plain paper. Tony used to work in the office on Sundays and developed an enthusiasm for collecting and filing information. Perhaps, he later mused, his father spent too much time as a librarian and too little writing up his own experiences. Tony Benn was not to do the same. He made his first efforts at diary writing when he was nine, and fragmentary journals continued until 1963, when a day-to-day diary began.

The family were close and spent time together more often than might be supposed considering the weight of Wedgwood Benn's responsibilities and the amount of travelling he and his wife undertook (they travelled abroad in 1932, 1933 and 1934). In fact they probably saw more of their children than comparable middle-class families because they did not send them away to school. Nor was Wedgwood Benn prone, as many other politicians were, to spending his time in the drinking clubs of Pall Mall. Moreover the family always ate together. Margaret Benn said, 'The children did not have separate meal times, except breakfast, which they ate earlier. They had meals with us and the conversation at meal times was all politics, politics, politics.'[19]

It was a genuinely happy childhood, despite the rising horror of militarism in Europe and the Far East with the concomitant pusillanimity of the democracies. The family talked often about developments such as the persecution of Jews in Germany and the brutal Japanese invasion of Manchuria. The use of gas against Abyssinian tribesmen was an event so immediate to the family it might have occurred in the next street. International affairs were given an urgency for the children, imbuing them with a sense of world community which would never leave them.

There was a substantial age difference between Wedgwood Benn and his children. On one occasion, when he was arguing with his two eldest sons in public, a woman who felt that the old man needed some support remonstrated with his sons, advising them to do as their grandfather told them. It may have been because of this age difference that Tony Benn speaks and acts as if he is the product of a Victorian rather than a twentieth-century upbringing. The family was high-minded in a Gladstonian way, committed to ideals of service, of self-improvement, of elevated dinner-table conversation. Politics and religion were the constant subject of discussion; humour was present, but it was somewhat jocose. David Benn remarked that his father was 'not at all remote, an extremely lively and vigorous man. He found leisure very depressing. He had a way of overworking and collapsing. He got very keyed up when he was to make an important speech and then he would collapse.' Wedgwood Benn was one of those men who had no internal mechanism telling him to stop work. He would literally work till he dropped and he would berate himself if he had not used up the last ounce of his strength.

'His vision was strictly political and rather limiting therefore. We had an extremely good political upbringing but rather a poor cultural upbringing. We never went to the theatre, for example,' David Benn remembered. They were regular churchgoers and the children said their prayers at night, but religion was not a separate, doctrinaire aspect of life. Rather, life was suffused with Christian sentiments. In David Benn's words, 'Politics was not a morally neutral profession.'[20]

The boys' schoolfriend Bill Allchin remembers Wedgwood Benn's injunction 'The requirements of a moral life are to keep a job list and a cash book.' Wedgwood Benn tried to encourage his sons to live by these precepts. Tony Benn could receive his pocket money for the week if he accounted to Wedgwood Benn's secretary for expenditure the previous week. His father encouraged him to keep a time chart showing the way each day was spent. On this he would mark in different coloured pencils the amount of time spent on work, sleep, discussion and other activities. When the lines were joined up it would be a graphic demonstration of the productive use he had made of the hours in a day, a spur to do better in the future. This was a habit he was to keep up until his marriage. As a student, writing about himself in the third person, he described the system which had been started in boyhood: 'He attempts to organise his life with three mechanical devices. A petty cash account (to keep him economical), a job list (as a substitute for an imperfect memory) and a time chart (to give him an incentive to work).'[21] Tony Benn always was a maker of lists and keeper of records.

John Benn, the children's grandfather, who had died in 1922, had built a cottage at Stansgate in Essex as a holiday home but had sold it again in 1902. Wedgwood Benn had always been happy there, so he bought it back in 1933 for £1500. It was there that the family gathered for the birth of Margaret Benn's fourth child in 1935. Sadly the child, named Jeremy, was stillborn. That night six-year-old David fell ill with bovine tuberculosis. At the time, there was no cure except for rest. He was looked after by Nurse Olive at Stansgate, at her own home in Harlow, Essex, and in Bexhill, where it was believed the air would be good for him. His illness lasted more than three years.

Wedgwood Benn had lost his seat at the general election of 1931, but he remained with the Labour Party, which had lost office, in opposition to the national government of Ramsay MacDonald. For four years he had no constituency to nurse, until he was selected to stand for Dudley in 1935. The November 1935 election was the first in which Tony Benn could remember working. He campaigned for Kennedy, the Labour candidate in Westminster, distributing a pamphlet called '50 Points for Labour' which he was later to compare favourably with the result of the Labour Party's policy review in the 1980s. It seemed to him unremarkable that he should be working for the Labour Party, though he remembers calling a cheery socialist message to a workman unloading coal as he walked to school and being struck by the man's surprised reaction to this young toff's allegiances.

Wedgwood Benn lost the election, once again finding himself with no constituency to sustain him, though he was now fifty-eight. He could easily have become a man content in late middle age to reminisce, relying on his earlier prestige. He spent some time putting his papers in order and going on lecture tours for the British Council, but it was not enough for his restless energy. Fortunately for him, less than two years later he was selected to fight Gorton in Manchester for Labour at a by-election. He was returned in February 1937 to play his part in the battle against Chamberlain and the appeasers.

14

2

Westminster School

Tony Benn entered Westminster School in the autumn of 1938. Some boys were awed by going to school in a collection of buildings with a history stretching back five centuries, over the road from the Mother of Parliaments and round the back of Westminster Abbey. Tony Benn found it much more natural. 'It was my local school,' he said. 'I wasn't a boarder, I walked there and back every day. The Abbey was just where you went for prayers, Parliament was round the corner, where my dad worked. I'd been there in 1937 after he had won a by-election. I met Attlee and Lloyd George that day. It was my local village really.'[1]

The Westminster day started with a procession into the Abbey for prayers from 9.00 to 9.20, where the day boys would meet the main school in that mausoleum of famous men. There were the customs and rituals common to public schools: the tombstone in Westminster Chapel floor across which boys must not walk, the gateway where scholarship boys must stand guard while Latin prayers were conducted, the requirement that the first-year boy learn the lore and language of Westminster on pain of punishment, not to himself but to the second-year boy who taught him. One whimsical tradition was the Latin play, a comedy by Plautus or Terence, during which a master would sit with the tanning pole, the stick used to beat boys, on this occasion tied with a pink ribbon to render it less fearsome. When a joke was made on stage this instrument would be waved balefully from side to side to cue laughter.

Michael, three and a half years older than Anthony, was already at Westminster. He was a handsome, popular boy, both athletic and studious and with a deep moral sense, the very specimen the public

15

schools of England wished to produce. Neville Sandelson, a contemporary of the Benns, used to cox for the team in which Michael rowed. He said: 'He was quiet, modest, personally diffident. He was good. He emanated a quality of goodness which made an impression on me then and which I thought about in later years.'[2] Michael certainly made more impression in the school records than his younger brother. He was the one who rowed for the school and acted in school plays. In the words of the school archivist, Tony was 'overshadowed by his elder brother'.[3]

Physically Benn minor made a strong impression. Various sources remark that, whereas many boys looked idiotic in their top hat and high collar, Tony looked the part of a young aristocrat. Neville Sandelson said, 'I remember him as being a very good-looking young boy. He had a childish pink complexion – I think of him primarily in terms of pink and white. He was ebullient, garrulous, a little bumptious, a quality I admired enormously.'[4] Peter Ustinov in his memoirs called him a 'joyous little gnome'.[5] This garrulous cherub immediately became involved in argument and agitation about international affairs. Donald Swann's first recollection of Tony Benn is of him distributing leaflets. 'He had an influence on all of us because he was so full of conviction,' he said. 'The balls were in the air. It was obvious Tony was on the brink of a whole lot of things he was going to do with his life.'[6]

Patrick MacMahon, who was to remain in contact with Benn over the first decades of his life, said of the schoolboy: 'There was nothing remarkable about Anthony except that he was argumentative. He liked arguing and when an argument turned against him he turned it into a personal matter – he tried to get at the person he was arguing with.'[7]

There was ample opportunity for argument at Westminster, despite the school's traditions. Donald Swann remarked, 'It was a very outspoken, literate school. It was possible to have socialism and pacifism openly discussed. It resembled a university rather than a school.'

Tony was keenly aware of the international events which dominated 1938, the year he entered the school: the Anschluss of Austria by Germany in March and the Munich conference on the future of Czechoslovakia in September. The failure of old-style politics to

16

deal adequately with the great international problems of the 1930s gave heart to young radicals. The atmosphere of political debate in public schools at the time was unequalled in the twentieth century until the school revolts of the 1960s and 1970s. The school's United Front of Popular Forces, of which about a quarter of the pupils as well as nine masters were members, had collapsed under the weight of its own idealism a few months before Tony Benn joined the school. Its first manifesto statement, 'Uncompromising Resistance to Fascism, Conservatism and War'[8] offered a sample of the wealth of contradictions which progressive forces might embrace in the 1930s.

There were clear divisions in the school which were reinforced by the masters. The last period of every day was reserved for 'Occupat' ('let him be occupied'), in which the boys had a choice of doing officer training, physical education or the scouts. Tony Benn joined the scouts, which were led by a pacifist called Godfrey Barber. Benn said, 'The scouts were anti-militarist. The difference between the scouts and the officer training corps was really a political difference. When the war broke out I left the scouts and joined the Air Training Corps, which had just been set up, and this was seen by Godfrey Barber and some others as a betrayal of a political position, because of their distrust of the uniformed people who were preparing to go into the services as officers.'[9]

Almost as soon as Tony joined the school there was talk of the first evacuation from London in preparation for the coming war. Europe, it was felt, was sure to go to war over Hitler's demands for the absorption into the Reich of the German-speaking and heavily industrialised northern segment of Czechoslovakia. Because it was widely feared that devastating aerial bombardment would be the likely first consequence of a declaration of war, the school boarders were evacuated on 28 September to Lancing College on the Sussex coast, whose headmaster Frank Doherty was a Westminster Old Boy. Homeboarders like Tony and Michael went down the next day. Their mother remembered that Michael and Tony took evacuation badly – it was the first time they had ever been away from home.

The Munich agreement of 30 September 1938, signed by the British, French, Italian and German governments, supposedly

17

guaranteed the remainder of Czechoslovakia against aggression, once the Germans had taken a third of the population, together with the territory they occupied. Meanwhile Poland and Hungary enjoyed border adjustments at Czechoslovakia's expense. The Conservative Prime Minister Neville Chamberlain returned home believing he had obtained 'peace for our time', and the international situation was deemed safe enough for the return in two shipments of Westminster boys, on 1 and 3 October.

Whatever the international morality of what Sartre called 'the reprieve', it was the occasion for the first public acclamation of Tony Benn's talents as an orator. The Junior Debating Society held a meeting in October 1938 on the motion 'This house supports the government's attitude towards the present international situation'. The school magazine reported that 'The government's condemnation by 11 votes to 9 [was] largely the result of an excellent speech by a new member, Wedgwood Benn.' The minutes are less generous but still attest to the thirteen-year-old's oratorical fluency: 'Mr W. Benn gave a flowing and loud speech on various policies.'

Older boys also showed limited faith in their representatives' judgement. In the Senior Debating Society the motion 'This house approves of the government's solution to the Czechoslovak problem' was lost by a two-thirds majority. The seriousness of these debates should not be underestimated. Some of these boys would soon be asked to pay with their lives for the vacillation of their elders across the road in Parliament itself. They knew it very well. As Tony Benn said: 'When the war came there was an element of relief about it, it was something that we had expected for years.'[10]

The slide towards total war continued in 1939. Germany and Hungary took the rest of Czechoslovakia in March, and Hitler was given his final warning. School life continued. Tony's reports show a spread of academic achievement from good to average. In his School Certificate examinations in July 1941 he achieved similar results – Very Good in History, a Credit in English Language, English Literature and Elementary Maths, and a Pass in Latin, French, Maths and Science. The curriculum was conventional except for Monday morning's Current Affairs period, which was a subject in which he excelled. Benn was later to complain that in all his years of expensive education, he had never heard of the Levellers. This is no particular reflection on Westminster; schools in general show a reluctance to put the English Revolution on the History syllabus, in marked contrast to the syllabus in France, where the study of their revolution is the key by which other events are comprehended.

Both Tony and Michael loved rowing – they came home in a state of exhaustion on 'water' days, their mother remembered. Tony enjoyed fencing and also boxed, though not especially well. Neville Sandelson, who gathered a number of trophies for his amateur boxing, had no difficulty in beating Benn in a 'gnatweight' final. Benn later remarked, 'He was a very fine boxer, tremendously powerful, short and very sharp. I remember him winning easily and effectively.'[11] Benn reminded him of that final in 1971 after he had responded from the front bench to Neville Sandelson's maiden speech after the former pugilist had won Hayes and Harlington for Labour. He said, 'I have known him for many years: in fact, I had a fight with him thirty-three years ago and I must warn Hon. members that his mild manner is very deceptive.'[12] It surprised Sandelson that 'a distinguished political figure should remember a two-minute bad-tempered piece of fisticuffs between two boys, neither of whom was old enough to shave. There was an element of obsessiveness that revealed a good deal about Tony.'[13] One version of this event has it that Sandelson beat Benn in the ring, Benn accused his opponent of cheating and the fight continued under less control in the school courtyard, with Sandelson again winning. Neither man has a clear memory of this sequence of events, though both say it is possible. It would certainly be a characteristic Benn predicament to find himself fighting a superior opponent for a second time because of some alleged injustice in the first bout.

Success was more likely in the Junior Debating Society, where Benn was on the winning team arguing against 'a policy of friendship with Italy and Germany' to ensure Britain's security; against capital punishment; and, in February 1939, in favour of intervention in the Spanish Civil War, truly a lost cause for Madrid fell the following month. As in the wider world, the discussion about the state of Europe was rather more complicated than a two-cornered fight from which one side or the other must emerge victorious.

Tony Benn had been elected to the committee of the Debating Society on 23 January 1939 and soon progressed to secretary. The

Junior Debating Society met in the homes of members on Saturday afternoons. When Tony hosted the meeting they met in the long library at 40 Millbank (the name had been changed from Grosvenor Road in July 1932) called the Green Room. The ground floor of the house next door had been rented and the dividing wall removed, so the boys were meeting in the very room where Sidney and Beatrice Webb had once written. When he last wrote the Society's minutes on 16 June 1940, Tony (as secretary) signed himself Wedgwood Benn, but, because he was sitting in as chairman, signed in that capacity as Anthony Benn. The name he used himself, and that used of him by the school authorities, seems mutable during his school days. In his family he was, and would always remain, James. To his friends he was Anthony.

In August 1939, with a declaration of war imminent, the school moved back to Lancing College and to its sister school, Hurstpierpoint. Evacuation was easier given the dress rehearsal of the previous year. 'War melted all reservations away,' said Tony. 'All sorts of things you never contemplated before became absolutely natural. You were told you had to move and you moved.'[14] The epilogue to that term's Latin play featured the actors in gas masks.

The time for talk was long gone, the debating societies fell into decline. Debates with Lancing boys were more frivolous than they had been in the shadow of the Palace of Westminster. As a sage old before his time remarked in March 1940 in the school magazine: 'With considerable noise we decided that colours should be awarded for work as they are for games; with even more noise and with some colour, we resolved to encourage originality in dress; and we refused aid for Finland by four votes to three with hardly any noise at all. A sad falling off. . . .'

The scant Debating Society records show that when there was a subject of gravity sufficient to move Benn to contribute, his political thinking was already displaying the breadth which characterised it in later years. Moreover, he was not merely retailing the raw material of international affairs which he had learned at home. Thus in attacking Conservative policy for the previous twenty years on 14 March 1940 he is said to have 'countered with a speech defining the socialist policies, and criticised the post-war governments. He argued against many odds and was heckled by all.' He clearly made no effort to court popularity with his audience. His last contribution was a condemnation of the English public schools as 'the breeding ground of snobbery', in which he concentrated his fire on the fagging and monitorial systems.

This period of evacuation was the last time Tony was able to spend long periods with Michael, who was to join the Royal Air Force in the summer of 1940. He was staying in Shoreham, not in the boys' dormitories in Lancing as Tony was. The brothers would go out together when they had an afternoon off, walking in the country, then retiring to a tea shop in town.

On the morning of 4 June 1940 the gardens and fields around the school were crowded with exhausted soldiers brought back from Dunkirk. France had fallen only two weeks after the German attack. The only cause for celebration was this evacuation from the Continent of 338,226 men of the British Expeditionary Force. But moving the school to safety by the sea had actually taken it into danger – the South Coast was looking to be in the front line of a Nazi invasion. 'All of a sudden the war became deadly serious,' Tony Benn said. 'The Phoney War from September 1939 was happening somewhere else, people didn't quite believe in it. Then a great fear spread through people that the German army might arrive.'[15]

Lancing had not, in any case, been a perfect choice as an evacuation home. The town lay beside a civilian airport and the school's magnificent chapel window was a perfect landmark for enemy aircraft: there were frequent air raids. 'We spent a good deal of our time in the crypt of the chapel,' said Patrick MacMahon.

Westminster School therefore moved to Reed and Mardon Halls, two halls of residence at Exeter University. This location saw the first Flanders and Swann revue. The strikingly handsome Michael Flanders, known for his prowess in the Senior Debating Society and school plays, teamed up with the gentle Donald Swann, a small, alert boy who composed the music for the revue they wrote together. It took as its theme Minister of Home Security Herbert Morrison's slogan 'Go to It'. It was full of skits and songs on contemporary events, like the 'Slaves of the Food Office' dance. Michael Benn was stage manager, with Tony as an assistant.

After the school had broken for the summer holidays it was agreed that it should return to its Westminster home. The Tory politician and Old Boy, Lord Davidson, was one of those advising a return: 'The defences of London are increasing in strength every day and, unless the Hun goes completely mad, it seems incredible that he would be so foolish as to attempt large-scale bombing.'[16]

On such advice the school resolved to resume business in Westminster after the summer holidays. *Go to It* had been so successful that its progenitors had found a way of staging it in London in the first week of term, at the Moreland Hall, Hampstead, and the Rudolph Steiner Hall off Baker Street. Despite assurances to the contrary, the Luftwaffe's Blitz began that week, on 7 September. Thus *Go to It* was one of only two shows running in London (the other was the Windmill Theatre's nude variety). During air raids the family went from Millbank to the basement of nearby Thames House, which was their nearest shelter.

David, now aged ten, was also staying at Millbank and it was decided to remove him and Tony to the safety of Scotland. They were packed off by night train on 13 September 1940 to their maternal grandparents, who were living in the Columba Hotel in Oban. Grandmother and Grandfather Holmes had settled down to an itinerant lifestyle, and had been living in hotels since they had sold their house in the 1920s. The boys were not easy for the old couple to manage. David remembered, 'My brother and I were both very resentful at being sent out of the danger zone. All the action was in London and we had just been sent away. We were rather sullen and recalcitrant. My mother had to come up to reassure the grandparents that there was nothing wrong.'[17]

Tony immediately volunteered for Civil Defence work in Oban, where hasty preparations against air bombardment were being made. His experience was much in demand: though he was only fifteen, at least he had been in an air raid and could tell them what it was like.

Nineteen-forty was an eventful year for the Benn family. Nurse Olive left to do war work, in an orphanage in Bournemouth. Michael left school and joined the RAF at the age of eighteen, and, more surprisingly, Wedgwood Benn himself joined up at the age of sixty-three. It was, said his widow, the only decision in their married life on which he did not consult her. He asked her to meet him at St James's Park station, offering no explanation. When she arrived, there he was in his pilot officer's uniform with five rows of medals from the First World War. She said, 'I married a public servant – a member of Parliament in peace, in war he was off to the front.' When she asked about his constituency he said, 'I hoped you would look after that.'[18]

She did indeed, and found the work of advising the electors of Gorton very therapeutic. He went to work in the Air Ministry, moving a camp bed in and seeing his family at weekends when they were near enough.

Tony and David received a telegram from their mother simply saying, 'All well,' which was alarming because they knew no reason why all should not be well. There had, in fact, been a particularly serious raid on London. Soon there was a letter giving details of it and, sadly, news of a serious fire at 40 Millbank. The fire did not seem to have been started by a bomb and Tony speculates that poor wiring, some of it installed by himself and Michael, coupled with the movement caused by bomb blasts, may have been the culprit. Whatever the immediate cause, the family was now homeless and, what was worse for Wedgwood Benn, the collection of papers spanning his entire lifetime was seriously damaged. Margaret Benn salvaged what she could from the wreckage, and at a later date Tony and Michael collected what was left of their father's papers in a rented truck and took them down to a disused slaughterhouse at Stansgate. (The family house had been requisitioned.) Tony remembers his father's gratitude and the long hours he would spend up to the end of his life, attempting to put the remnants of his archives into some kind of order.

Tony Benn spent some time with his family in London during the Blitz. He remembers the bomb in 1941 which hit the church the family used to attend, St John's in Smith Square. In recollecting those nights he said: 'We would sleep in the basement of Thames House and in the middle of the night we might creep up to the door to see what was happening. We could see docklands ablaze – the lights were so bright it brought the skyline of the south bank into relief. We would wake up in the morning and see all the air-raid wardens and repair squads going round assessing the damage. We got to know each other very well. There was one old lady who used to sleep near us. On one particularly bad night we were worried

23

about her. When she came in we asked what it was like and she said, "Oh, it's a terrible night, pelting with rain – look at my umbrella." London during the Blitz was really something.'[19]

The head of Westminster School, John Christie, was meanwhile involved in a desperate search for empty buildings which were not being used by the military, where the school term could commence. Eventually a group of buildings was found in a six-mile radius of Bromyard, Herefordshire, Tony Benn staying in a farmhouse called Buckenhill. The boys changed their top hats and tails for shorts and open-necked shirts and dug for victory every afternoon in the large allotment, becoming self-sufficient in vegetables. Lessons were held in two locations and each day half the school had to bicycle to the farther site. They used to time how fast they could cycle from the main school building to the church in Bromyard, where they were going to defend the village against the Germans. When the war was nearing its end Christie wrote to parents, 'Few schools can have been so healthy for over two years as we have been.'[20]

As a member of the Home Guard Tony wore battledress and participated in military exercises with live ammunition. One memorable occasion was observed by a venerable soldier, a Colonel Blacker, who had invented the Blacker Bombard. This was a primitive mortar, a piece of piping with a spike at the bottom. Colonel Blacker was not impressed by their martial abilities but he was obliged to restrain his criticism as the Blacker Bombard was one of the failures of the day and the military man found himself gingerly divesting his device of one unexploded shell in front of the boys and elders of Bromyard.

Tony Benn also joined the Home Guard in Oxted in Surrey, where Margaret and David Benn settled in the house which had been Sir Ernest Benn's before the war. It was now a girls' school, but the Benns, as a homeless family with some historical connection with the place, were allowed to live there. Margaret Benn taught theology to the girls. Tony would go out at night with a loaded rifle watching for enemy parachutists, who might well be in disguise. He said: 'We were told they might arrive dressed as nuns. Fortunately I didn't see a nun or I would undoubtedly have opened fire on her.' The German invasion of Russia in June 1941 prompted the recall of all firearms for despatch to the Eastern Front. Tony's rifle was taken away and he was left to defend the nation with a pike, a bayonet stuck in a piece of tubing. For all its absurd aspects, the mobilisation of all available men with whatever weapons they could lay their hands on was, as Benn said in reflecting on it, 'a real defence policy. The only way you can really defend a country is when you are prepared to put your own body between the enemy and the village you live in.'[21] The result of the alternative, of leaving defence to the armed forces alone, had been seen in France the previous year.

It was at this point that an event occurred which was to dominate Benn's life for the next twenty years and which would eventually lead to an enhancement of his standing as a national figure. Churchill was ruling in coalition with the other parties, with an electoral pact in place which maintained political stability in the Commons. But Labour was embarrassingly under-represented in the Lords, so Churchill set about making some of the older Labour members into noble lords. Wedgwood Benn scorned the honour but, as always, was pleased to be of service. As his widow recalled, he said to Churchill, 'I'll go if you make it plain it's not an honour. I'm going up for a duty.'[22] The citation declared that the title was specifically 'to strengthen the Labour Party in the Upper House, where its representation is disproportionate, at a time when a coalition government of three parties is charged with the direction of affairs'. Wedgwood Benn consulted Michael, who as his eldest son would receive the title on his death. Michael felt that the peerage would be no encumbrance to him in his chosen career as a clergyman. Tony Benn discovered his father's elevation when he read about it in the *Daily Herald* in December 1941. 'I was very angry,' he said. 'Father later said I "roundly abused" him. He hadn't told me because, he said, I was a chatterbox and there was a convention that you don't tell anyone if you are offered a peerage. They don't give it to you if it leaks out before the official announcement. We didn't have a row – I didn't have rows with him – but I was upset that at the age of sixteen I hadn't been told.'[23] In January 1942 Wedgwood Benn entered the House of Lords as the first Viscount Stansgate, the name being borrowed from the family's holiday home.

Michael got his wings in 1941 at RAF Kidlington. Tony had been to visit him from school in his Air Training Corps uniform on 11 August and Michael took him up for a flight around Oxford. This infuriated their parents, who doubtless felt there was enough danger without courting it. Later the event was written into Tony's flight logbook, recording that he had experienced steep turns, air navigation and map reading. Michael himself maintained a contact with Westminster School – he had formed a small prayer circle there and he wrote to its members from wherever he happened to be stationed.

On 3 April 1942 Tony Benn was in London for his seventeenth birthday. He walked to Smith Square to join the Labour Party, which was based at Transport House, the headquarters of the Transport and General Workers' Union. There he met Will Henderson, the Labour Party press officer, who declared that of course the coalition government must be kept going after the war: country must be put before party. It was hardly an encouraging remark to make to someone who had just made a declaration of faith in the Labour Party. For Benn it was the first step towards the realisation of a series of ambitions. At the age of sixteen he had drawn up a list of things he wanted to do: to become an RAF pilot, to become an MP, to get married and to have children. All were to be achieved within ten years.

3

The Oxford Union and War Service

Benn was impatient to leave school. 'I was anxious to do something,' he said. It was a frustrating time for young men: they were too old for school but too young to fight, more than schoolboys, less than men. For those who had set their sights on university, there was the opportunity to attend for an intermediate year, filling in the time before they were able, and required, to enter the services. Patrick MacMahon, not the most ambitious of boys, had not considered going to university until Tony suggested it to him. Discussing the options which Oxford offered, they decided not to go to Christ Church, 'because all the Westminster people went there', and settled on New College. They both went up for an interview and entrance examination, Benn applying for the course in PPE – Politics, Philosophy and Economics. When asked his father's occupation at the interview, he said he was an RAF officer. 'Nonsense,' said the interviewer and mouthed 'Peer of the Realm' slowly as he wrote it down, which Benn considered very pretentious.[1]

MacMahon recalls an overheard conversation on that day: 'I was walking underneath a don's window and I heard them discussing us, so I stopped and listened. Because of his background – his father was so well known – they automatically said Anthony would be accepted, but they weren't sure about me. I went away thinking, "It's all right for the privileged." '[2] But Patrick MacMahon, a sea captain's son, was also chosen.

Benn went up to Oxford in December 1942, rather than at the start of term, because he had had a painful operation on a bone in his foot. Like many men who are driven to work long hours, Tony Benn is reticent about minor illness, as if being ill is unworthy of

27

him. Minor health problems occur in the unedited version of his diaries but are one of the features which do not make it to the printed page.

The PPE course, like all others, was structured according to a peacetime timetable, with a requirement of two or three essays a week. It quickly became obvious that this was impossible, so the academic regime was relaxed as the young men went into university divisions of the services. Benn joined the university air squadron and MacMahon the naval equivalent. Patrick was thrilled to receive a telegram on his birthday reading 'GREETINGS TO THE OLD SEA DOG' and signed 'EMDEN', which was the name of the commander of the Naval Cadets, a pompous and somewhat distant man who had not previously indicated that he was aware of MacMahon's existence. MacMahon immediately dashed off a letter of thanks, only to find that the telegram had been sent by Benn, who had no difficulty remembering MacMahon's birthday because it was two days after his own.

Benn joined the Oxford Union, paying the entrance fee which prevented less affluent students from joining. The public school atmosphere and the convention that the main speakers wore evening dress for debates also tended to make the Union a select club. Its function has been described by its historian David Walter: 'Within a university for the elite, the Union caters for an inner elite, ambitious to shine in politics, the law, the church, diplomacy, the media and the arts,' and he quotes with relish Barbara Castle's remark that it is a fine training ground for Parliament because both are dotty, out-of-date gentlemen's clubs.[3] Tony Benn later said, 'The good socialists didn't particularly like the Union people. It was looked down on because it was thought to be where the careerists went.'[4]

Socialist puritans presumably believed that the only real platform was a soapbox at a street corner. Benn, throughout his life, always accepted whatever platform would put him in contact with the maximum number of people. In Oxford this was the Union, not the University Labour Club with its endless splits and factional arguments (he was nonetheless always a member of OULC, once standing unsuccessfully for office).

Benn spoke at the Union for the first time on 21 January 1943 in a debate at whose start the President 'invited honourable members to gather closely round the stoves'. The debate itself generated considerable heat, with altercations between the visiting speakers matching in intensity the heckling from the floor. The motion was that 'planning of social security by the state must involve the loss of liberty and initiative for the individual',[5] the sort of subject on which Sir Ernest and Wedgwood Benn would have found themselves in complete polarity.

The *Oxford Magazine* reported, 'In a satirical maiden speech the Hon. A. N. Wedgwood Benn showed the wider implications of the motion, which made the Beveridge Report itself seem irrelevant.'[6] (As the son of a viscount, Benn was entitled to call himself the Honourable, but he never did and was embarrassed when others did.) It is interesting that he chose to make a satirical speech on this subject, given that for almost all of the rest of his Oxford Union career he was criticised for being too didactic. Indeed, later in the year he was warned to 'avoid treating the House as a class or a Salvation Army meeting'.[7] During this period Benn was certainly experimenting with different debating styles, but the subject matter of the debate was probably just as important. Britain was so hungry for social reform that it was outstripping the capacity of socialists to guide it. The Beveridge Report was the most obvious focus of this enthusiasm.

Sir William Beveridge's report, *Social Insurance and Allied Services*, was one of the few fruits yielded by the war to a people who were determined not to be betrayed, as the previous generation had been by Lloyd George's spurious promise that 'a land fit for heroes' would arise after the First World War. This time they wanted it in writing.

When the report was published on 1 December 1942 it seized the imagination of a nation already fired by two great successes. The Nazi advance had been halted at El Alamein in North Africa in July 1942 and turned into a retreat in October. This was the first great British victory, as opposed to a successful defence like the Battle of Britain. No less significant was the effect of the Soviet defence and then victory at Stalingrad in October and November. Stalingrad may have been even more telling than El Alamein because it was easier for the public to imagine the scale of the battle: the defence of a city literally room by room, the fight for possession of ruins by people armed with knives and pieces of twisted steel. The Soviet action was heroic, by the standards of any battle in history, but it was in defence of a nation ruled by a socialist system which the British public had long been taught to fear and despise. Co-operation with Russia increased interest in socialist thinking and therefore in programmes of social reform.

The BBC immediately realised the potency of the Beveridge Report and from dawn on the day of its publication broadcast to occupied Europe in twenty-two languages the message of the welfare state as a proof of the superiority of democratic culture over that of the Nazis. Resistance movements adopted a welfare state programme as one of their post-war aims. The report proposed a flat-rate compulsory insurance contribution by working adults which was to pay benefits for sickness, unemployment and old age. The report also recommended that family allowances for every child after the first were to be paid out of general taxation, that there should be a national health service and that mass unemployment should end.

Churchill's reaction to the report was to underestimate its force and bungle the government's approach. He wrote testily in January 1943, 'A dangerous optimism is growing up about the conditions it will be possible to establish here after the war.'[8] It was indeed dangerous to him and his party. As Benn later said, 'Everyone was much further left in those years. In the 1940s you really felt the spirit of change in the air. We weren't going back to the old world, that wasn't what soldiers had fought the war for.'[9]

The atmosphere at the Oxford Union reflected the increasing radicalism of the country with the January 1943 motion being lost by 128 votes to 89. The House of Commons' lukewarm acceptance of the report 'in principle' in February 1943 was the occasion for a revolt of back-bench Labour MPs against the government, the greatest challenge to its authority throughout the war.

Further evidence of the radicalism of the nation was the success of a motion in the Union, albeit carried only by the President's casting vote, calling for widespread nationalisation. This motion was moved by Benn with Sir Richard Acland as third speaker. Acland was a West Country Liberal MP who had founded the Commonwealth Party in 1942 to contest by-elections in which reactionary candidates would not otherwise be opposed because of the wartime electoral pact between the major parties. Commonwealth won three seats during the war but, rather more importantly, it helped foster a spirit of debate in which the Labour Party showed itself the moderate and credible party of government. During the war years the political centre of gravity shifted leftwards; it was no longer a battle between left and right but a debate in the socialist camp with the choice of being either left or further left. Benn maintained a spirited correspondence with Acland over several years and later worked with him on the H-Bomb National Committee and in similar organisations.

Benn's speech on 4 March 1943 in the nationalisation debate was described in the *Oxford Magazine* as 'the evening's best under-graduate speech, excellently delivered'.[10] He did a great deal of research for his speeches, far more than he ever did for essays. At this time he tended to write speeches out in full but would expand on the text while on his feet. The text can still, however, give some flavour of the times:

Restriction of output is the mark of monopolistic capitalism – maximum output must be the order of the day. Private firms advertise unduly now to escape excess profits tax – even when paper economy is a national necessity. They want exclusive rights to patented inventions when only a pooling of all the best ideas can do the job. The minds of these giant industrialists are on present and future gain, whereas we need a spirit of selfless co-operation to carry us through. Common ownership is the only way to achieve that. For the spirit of brotherhood will be aroused when work done in factories is not for the personal gain of one owner – who is probably never seen – but for the immediate wellbeing of the community.[11]

This example shows a style of construction which is characteristic of Benn throughout his life: first there is a statement which is not supported by any evidence, but before there is time to understand and question the statement, along comes an irrefutable truth: indeed post-war reconstruction will require maximum output. Two examples follow, both easily appreciated and clearly visualised dem-onstrations of a rejection of the common interest in preference for personal gain. An appeal to the higher emotions rounds it off. There is no marshalling of arguments, but the audience should feel – for there is enough to think about as the examples and paradoxes tumble out – that the conclusion follows logically from the previous statements. That is, an audience which wants to experience the warmth of brotherhood and common responsibility which is on offer should feel it has been brought to this emotion by ineluctable reason. The emotion of socialism, which after all is what really convinces, is given a foundation of economic fact and of revulsion for the contemptible behaviour of self-seeking capitalists. The conclusion does not flow from the premises, but this is a speech, not a lesson in logic.

Another Benn characteristic showed itself in the Union in this period before his war service: a tendency to stand for election. He stood for the Library Committee, the first step towards high office in the Union. He was obviously popular for he topped the list of eighteen candidates with fifty-eight votes.

On 24 July 1943 he volunteered for the Air Force, enlisting near the zoo in Regent's Park as an aircraftman second class, though with the white stripes indicating that he was a pilot cadet. He was posted to the Initial Training Wing at Stratford-upon-Avon for basic services discipline training, then to the Elementary Flying School at Elmdon in Birmingham, later the city's municipal airport. The winter of 1943–4 was spent in a cold and miserable Nissen hut at Heaton Park in Manchester while the RAF attempted to organise his future. On 11 January 1944 he sailed on the troopship *Cameronia* from Glasgow to South Africa. Owing to the limited airspace for training and the poor weather conditions over Britain, pilots were being trained in Africa under the Empire Training Scheme. There trainee pilots could get their wings, then return to Britain to gain experience by flying in more turbulent weather.

During the month on the *Cameronia* Benn and a former trade union official called Whitehead addressed the troops on the subject of war aims, Benn's first public meeting. When it was announced the commanding officer for troops called him in and said, 'I hope, Benn, this meeting on war aims isn't going to be anything to do with politics.' 'Oh no, sir, it's just a general discussion about what will happen after the war,' Benn said.[12]

The British establishment had some difficulty in reconciling the defence of democracy against Fascism with the hierarchical and class-ridden structure of the services. The inescapable fact was that too much democracy would prevent a return to the pre-war world. It was in an effort to forestall dangerous talk on post-war Britain that Churchill had withdrawn the Army Bureau of Current Affairs pamphlet for December 1942, because it contained a detailed account of the Beveridge Report. In fact this suppression gave its contents greater currency among the troops. 'For the serving officers it was a war against Germany,' Benn later remarked. 'For me it was a war against Fascism. Joining the air force was a political act, it wasn't a yearning for the uniform.'[13]

The troopship picked up a 'pathetic bunch' of Italian prisoners of war at Dar-es-Salaam, an apparent indication that the war was nearing its end, much to the frustration of Benn, who wanted to see action. From Durban, where the ship docked, Benn went to the Initial Training Wing of the Rhodesia Air Training Group at Bulawayo, before moving on in May 1944 to the Elementary Flying Training School in Gwelo. Much of the work here appealed to the technical side of Benn's nature – he found it no hardship to undertake routine exercises like dismantling and understanding parts of an aeroplane's ignition system. He progressed through the range of aeroplanes – from the tiny Tiger Moth he had flown in the UK to the American Cornell he learned to fly in Rhodesia, and then to an Oxford, a twin engined plane. The manoeuvres executed on each practice run were faithfully recorded in his logbook, and before long he was noted as being proficient in taking off into the wind, approach and landing, stalling, instrument reading, aerobatics, night flying and other skills. He took his first solo flight on 14 June 1944.

His stay in colonial Africa was a profound experience. He wrote an essay, 'The Matabele and the Mashona', about the two major tribes of Rhodesia. His account is full of anthropological and social details; information about African place-names and marriage rituals is followed by statistics about the poverty of Africans compared to Europeans. The Revd Percy Ibbotson, a missionary, took him to a native reserve outside Bulawayo where he saw the conditions in which black miners were living. Benn wrote: 'Bug ridden and dirty huts, pools of stagnant water, the nearness of houses one to another, and to rubbish dumps, all these factors are helping to undermine the health of the native.' He opposed the territorial segregation of Africans into native reserves, remarking that 'their continuing backwardness is likely to be a drag-factor hindering any general attempt to raise the standard of life, health and education'. He thus foresaw the effects of apartheid, even when presented at its most benign as 'separate development'.[14]

He made friends with J. B. Auld, an organiser for a whites-only trade union whose daughter was a nurse. She took him to a native hospital, which he described: 'There are many more patients than beds and the overflow of sick people were sleeping under the beds on the concrete floor, on strips of felt' – yet 100 yards away there was a brand-new, well-equipped European hospital. He later said it was his experience of inequality in Africa which made him devote so much of his time to the anti-colonial movement in the 1950s. At this point he argued 'for the complete political, economic and social equality of all Africans and Europeans in South Africa'.[15]

'The treatment of the blacks was appalling,' he later said. 'Here was I, an aircraftman second class and I had a guy who cleaned my room and did my laundry. It was my introduction to the real world after having had such a limited education. There were people there from all over the place – I had lots of political discussions, discussions about the war and about religion and its relationship to politics. It was a much better education than I had at New College. I learned an enormous amount which I couldn't have learned if the war hadn't occurred. It was my comprehensive school.'[16]

His main recreation in Africa was talking with his colleagues, though he would sometimes go to the cinema. Perhaps surprisingly for someone who has made words his metier, Benn has never read a great deal, preferring to pick up information from experience and discussion. 'I find taking things from the printed page quite difficult,' he said. 'Obviously if you have to you have to and I would get down to it, but it would not be by choice.'[17]

Tobacco was a halfpenny an ounce and it was in Rhodesia that he picked up his habit of smoking a pipe, as his father did. Being teetotal did not deprive him of the fun of mess life. He said: 'When there was a party I was the only one who was ever sober, so the next day they would ask me, "What did I do?" and I would tell them they had swung from the chandelier or something. People did get very tight and there were a few fights, which I didn't care for very much. But I found being a teetotaller was quite an advantage – you didn't get into a scrape. Although I was a bit gutless: I used to have ginger ale, which looked like a whisky and soda.'[18]

Michael Benn climbed into the cockpit of his Mosquito at 11 p.m. on 22 June 1944 and took off from RAF Tangmere, Sussex, on his last mission over occupied Europe. He had not flown far before he realised the air-speed indicator was not working – in fact the cover had not been removed from the Pitot tube, under the wing, which measures air speed. He radioed base to report his problem and was ordered to drop his bombs in the sea and return immediately. With no check for speed, the plane overshot the runway at Tangmere and crashed. Michael's neck was broken.

He was taken to St Richard's Hospital, Chichester, and Margaret Benn was telegrammed. She said: 'I was called to his bedside – I was with him the last twenty minutes. I think he knew I was there. He had discovered he had a vocation for the Christian ministry and was going to Pembroke College, Cambridge, to take the first steps in training. The technicians had failed to check his plane – they were terribly upset about it.'[19] It is characteristic of Margaret Benn that she should feel sympathy for the unhappiness of the technicians whose negligence had caused the death of her son.

Lord Stansgate was at that time an air commodore working in Italy for AMGOT, the Allied Military Government of Occupied Territories. Always an emotional person, the old man was riven with grief by the news of Michael's death. Without seeking permission he went to an RAF station and boarded the next flight to London. Because of his rank he was not questioned. It says something for the esteem in which he was held that his commanding officer, Admiral Ellery W. Stone, covered up for him and was prepared to take full responsibility for his disappearance. Years later, Stone met Tony Benn and explained the story when Benn was Postmaster General and Stone was European manager of an American electronics concern.[20]

As usual, Tony Benn went to his morning class for an hour of technical instruction. It was customary for letters to be distributed before this class, and in Benn's mail was a telegram telling him of Michael's death. Benn, just nineteen, was obliged to sit through the class before he could be alone. 'I was very distressed about it. I was very close to him and it knocked me out for quite a long time. I vividly remember in January 1944 I had stayed with him. I have a recollection of seeing Michael with his bicycle as the train pulled out and thinking I might never see him again, and I never did. But it also increased my resolve to complete training and get into action.'[21]

Michael had left a letter addressed to his family to be opened in the event of his death:

> So may I now take my leave of you.
>
> Father, from whom I inherited those qualities which I hoped would play their part later in my life and who was always a friend I could trust and who was everything a friend could be.
>
> Mother, from whom I inherited the precious gift of religion. Time alone would have shown what I intended to do with that.
>
> James [Tony], who would have been a helping friend and who shared so many interests with me. We might have done great things together.
>
> The little prof. [David], to whom I am devoted. Take care of him.
>
> To you all I say au revoir.
>
> It was my dearest wish to see us all united after the war. I wanted then to settle down to do what I could to prevent the suffering of another war from descending on the lives of our children. How I longed to see a world when people could be as free and happy as we were in our family. The toast is then 'The Future'. God bless you all.[22]

Forty years later Tony Benn published extracts from Michael's letters. Like his conversation with his family, his letters were full of religious and political insights. He had been a first-class pilot, winning the DFC for actions over North Africa and Europe. Yet inner conflict raged: 'Of one thing I am sure, you cannot reconcile Christianity to the war. Christ said – turn the other cheek, not go and bomb them four times as heavily as they bombed you . . . in my opinion war is unChristian and . . . the Church ought to say so, and not compromise with public opinion'.[23] To be a night fighter-pilot and be plagued by the certainty that what you do is against your deepest principles, yet to have at the same time the equal certainty that it must be done: that is the perfect allegory for man in the twentieth century. Michael Benn was a true spiritual leader, who had impressed others from boyhood with his gentle intensity.

Tony Benn never completely recovered from the death of his brother. 'It still moves me,' he said almost fifty years later. 'I was talking to my mother about it yesterday, thinking how old he would have been. He'd probably be a retired bishop by now. It was the biggest thing that happened in my life up to that time and for some long time afterwards. Losses of that kind are very bitter for a while, then in the end they mellow and sweeten. I was devoted to him.'[24]

Once back in London their father had himself posted around to air gunnery training schools, where he was assigned to give lectures and where he persuaded the instructors to put him through the gunnery course. He then had his lectures arranged so that he was with active squadrons, and at the age of sixty-seven he was back on active service, flying on operations behind a machine gun in the rear gun turret. He was found out only because he was mentioned in dispatches. He was then ordered to stop.

Tony Benn got his wings on 9 March 1945 after 313 hours of flying. He nearly did not make it, for the Oxford in which he was acting as navigator six days before had crash-landed with a load of practice bombs on board. It was a low-level bombing mission whose route was listed as 'Base – Croc Valley – Ruby Ranch – Gado – Kabanga'. They were to drop four bombs – these would be magnesium flares at night, smoke by day – and photograph the effects. Benn was to joke during the Rhodesia crisis which followed the Unilateral Declaration of Independence in 1965 that he was the only man in the cabinet who had bombed Rhodesia and would happily do so again.

After getting his wings – a source of immense pride – he was posted to Egypt in March 1945. There was very little for servicemen to do by this time. Two months later he was on leave in Palestine with some colleagues. Landing from the Sea of Galilee, they were approached by a Jew who announced, 'War finished.' They had an ice-cream to celebrate. Benn had told the Jewish Agency for Palestine that he wanted to visit a kibbutz. The Agency was suspicious but finally it welcomed him and he spent Victory in Europe Day, 8 May, at Shaar Hagolan. He later wrote light-heartedly about it in the Oxford University magazine *Isis*: 'Jews of all nations did their traditional folk dances and finally the three English officers were asked to do an English national dance. Boomps-a-daisy is said to be still popular in the Sea of Galilee area.'[25]

'I very much wanted to go to the Far East, where the war was still on,' Benn said many years later, 'and other pilots wanted to go too, so we drew lots – but I lost and I was sent home. I remember being very disappointed.'[26] Returning to Britain (where a general election had been called) on the troopship *Carthage*, he heard Churchill's first election speech on 4 June. The Prime Minister so demeaned himself as to claim that the Labour Party 'finds a free Parliament odious' and that 'No socialist government, conducting the entire life and industry of the country, could afford to allow free, sharp or violently worded expressions of public discontent. They would have to fall back on some form of Gestapo.' The support for Labour on the ship was overwhelming.

Tony Benn was returning to his family nearly a year after Michael's death. Regulations covering the movement of troops prevented him from telling his family where he was until HM Troopship *Carthage* docked in Scotland on 10 June 1945 and he could telephone them. His mother and David met him in London, stepping off the train in his pilot officer's uniform. It was a homecoming made more poignant by the absence of Michael. But Tony Benn did not intend to come home for good. 'He was afraid he would miss any sort of war service,' David Benn said. 'The war in Europe was over. In order to improve his chances of fighting in the Far East, he transferred to the Fleet Air Arm, where they still needed pilots.'[27]

Tony Benn was twenty at the time of the July 1945 election, a year too young to vote. 'I didn't think we'd win,' he said, underestimating – as many did – the desire for change in the country. Coming from such a political family and having such a clear idea of his aims, he was already in the running to stand for parliament. John Parker, Secretary of the Fabian Society, asked him if he would be available as a candidate even before he was eligible to stand.

He helped Jeremy Hutchinson, Labour's candidate in the Westminster (Abbey) constituency, whose wife was (then) the actress Peggy Ashcroft. Benn used to drive her around to the Peabody Buildings to talk about the need for a national theatre to women leaning out of their windows with their hair in curlers. Whether this gained any votes is questionable but it evoked the spirit of progress: now that the people's right to housing, education and health care had been fully accepted, the arts should also be available to all.

Still in RAF uniform, Benn went to the Labour Party head-quarters at Transport House to hear the outcome of the election three weeks after polling day – the pause had been arranged to allow the collection of votes from troops still stationed abroad. Everyone was assembled in a darkened hall where the results, as they were telephoned in from constituency declarations around the country, were written on smoked glass and projected on the wall by an epidiascope, a primitive overhead projector. 'Tory ministers were falling like ninepins,' Benn remembered, 'then the door opened and out of the bright sunshine came a little man blinking. It was Attlee. He had come straight from RAF Northolt, where he had flown in from [the peace conference at] Potsdam and he didn't know what had happened. He hadn't been able to follow the results. A BBC man came up to me with a microphone and asked, "Will you shout three cheers for the Prime Minister?" But I was too shy.'[28] William Wedgwood Benn was invited to join Attlee's government as Secretary of State for Air.

The Labour vote had increased by three and a half million over the 1935 figure. For the first time in its history Labour had an absolute majority, of an overwhelming 146 seats. The two-party system was restored with Labour at 393 seats, the Conservatives at 213 and the Liberals suffering a defeat from which they were never to recover, with only 12 seats. It was not just the scale of the Labour victory which amazed the leadership; they were astonished that there was a victory at all. Both sides had believed a Conservative victory to be most likely, and the loyalty of many Labour leaders to the coalition government had rendered them suspect in the eyes of party members, who scented an imminent betrayal in the style of 1931. Outsiders were shocked by the nation's abandonment of Churchill. He had truly been a great war leader, but for the voting public this did not cloud the memory of his deficiencies as a peace-time minister and of the Conservative Party's performance in the 1930s.

Apart from the election, it was a dull time. There was all the austerity but none of the excitements of war. After Tony Benn's transfer to the Fleet Air Arm as a sub-lieutenant, his first posting was to the Royal Naval College at Greenwich for 'what used to be called a knife-and-fork course. They didn't think RAF officers were gentlemen, so we had to train in etiquette'.[29] He was sent to a stone frigate in Cumberland, then spent some time on an aircraft carrier, HMS *Pretoria Castle*, in Portsmouth. He was in Cumberland, when he heard that the atomic bomb had been dropped on Hiroshima. He had read a novel by Harold Nicolson called *Public Faces* which forecast the development and use of the atom bomb. Benn understood its significance. The war in the Pacific was to be over in days.

Now that there was no need for pilots, either in the RAF or in the navy, Benn was sent on permanent paid leave. He went back to New College in January 1946, though he was not officially discharged from the Fleet Air Arm until 22 October. Some have accused Benn of inverted snobbery for saying in later years that he spent his time in the services as an aircraftman second class. In fact, of his two years in the RAF, twenty months were served in that rank. For the next three months he was in training to be a naval officer, then almost a year was passed, still as an officer, but on permanent leave as a student.

4

Touring the USA

Back at Oxford, Benn renewed his acquaintance with Bill Allchin. But the person who knocked on the door of his rooms in 1946 was very different from the self-assured schoolboy who had shone at the debating society. Allchin had been in Singapore at the time of the Japanese invasion in 1941 and he spent the duration of the war in the notorious Changi jail and on building the 'railway of death' from Siam to Burma. The experience turned him into a Quaker, pledged to eschew violence as a solution to human problems. He was physically and mentally shattered and quite unable to cope. He said, 'I was finding it difficult to adjust, I found it difficult to be with people. Tony would give me tea and toast and we used to talk. He helped me through that period. It took me a year to get over it.'

There was a bond between Benn and Allchin and the others who had gone through the war. Allchin said: 'We were counted as over-serious. We wouldn't have gone out for a good time in the terms that people now see it. Younger people who came straight from school were smoking black Russian cigarettes and drinking exotic drinks and trying to enjoy what they thought was the Oxford experience. We got on with our work.'[1]

Benn was elected secretary of the Union for the final term of 1946, and treasurer for the first term of 1947. His election as president for the second term of 1947 was virtually a foregone conclusion. He received 173 votes in the first ballot, almost twice the vote of his closest rival, the Hon. Gerry Noel. The correspondent for *Isis* thought it surprising that he should be elected in spite of the overwhelming Tory majority among Union members but remarked, 'If

Mr Benn has made a bad speech in the Union, we have yet to hear it. He has shown himself witty, courteous and forceful in debate and in private business. . . . His political opinions are not alarming to most people, nor are they insincere. Beyond question his success is well deserved.'[2]

But now there were no Tories in power against whom an adept moralist could fulminate; instead there was a Labour government which had to be defended. As later commentators have noted, however, in the period of the 1945–50 Labour administration it was possible to sound simultaneously left wing and loyal to the government, a satisfaction denied to later generations. Such loyalty was rapidly diminishing. The winter of 1946–7 exacerbated the problems of a country already suffering from war damage, shortages and virtual bankruptcy. Fuel shortages caused by the record low temperatures coincided with the nationalisation of the mines, which allowed opponents of the government to claim a causal connection. Certainly the workers who were sent home because factories had to close and the housewives cooking on low gas were in no mood to praise the government. That winter gave the Conservatives their first glimmer of hope that socialism was not invincible.

A symptom of this reassertiveness on the part of Tories was the barracking of the Attorney General Sir Hartley Shawcross when he spoke at the Union in support of a motion of confidence in Attlee's government which Benn had moved. According to contemporary accounts Shawcross handled the Union badly, and members did not take kindly to being condescended to. Their jeers and hisses were reported in the press the next day, making the students seem both childish and discourteous. In such difficult circumstances, remarked the *Oxford Magazine*, Benn 'must be congratulated upon facing a predominantly Conservative House in a fearless and admirable manner. Having gained the sympathy of the House by showing himself to be a master of the art of witty introduction, he then launched into a militant apologia for the government.'[3]

Three aspects of his work at the Union are significant because they show an early interest in matters which would preoccupy him later: he argued for a postal ballot of members for all Union elections, which would have greatly increased the number of people who voted. He also argued for admitting women as full members.

In neither of these was he successful. On the third issue, however, that of the Union's independence, he was. A report on traffic in Oxford had proposed the building of a road which would destroy the Union buildings. It was therefore suggested by the then secretary that the Union's assets should be transferred to the university in order to obtain the protection of the greater institution in the event that the compensation for the demolished buildings proved inadequate to reconstruct on the same scale. Benn argued that it was better to be independent with inferior premises than to be subject to the rules and regulations of the university. He won the day, and the road scheme was in any case dropped. Benn's arguments were those which he came to employ in the Common Market debate (after two changes of mind): ultimately, whatever the practical benefits of merging with the larger body, independence counts for more.

Kenneth Harris, an occasional speaker at the Union and later a journalist, has a memory of Benn at this time getting off his bicycle outside Blackwells the bookshop wearing a flat cap, with an army knapsack on his back and his pipe in his mouth. 'He was slim, golden haired, very attractive, especially when he laughed. He was a great giggler. He had a good sense of humour but it had to be stimulated. He was well known and respected as an outspoken, articulate supporter of the Labour Party, ambitious in the best sense of the word. Some would have said he was a bit of a bore and inclined to bang on about the Labour Party, though he wasn't a bore to me. He was obviously destined for great things.'[4]

He was also something of an eccentric, a characteristic exhibited during his time as president when he laid on a supper for the Union staff at which he and the other officers acted as waiters. But his enthusiasm for being of practical use was not always exercised tactfully. After a meal at the stately home of a fellow student he insisted that he and the other guests, also students, should do the washing up, the hostess protesting in vain that the servants would do it in the morning.

At Oxford Benn came into contact with a number of people who were to be significant figures in the Labour Party and in his life. The most important of these was Tony Crosland, who was seven years older than Benn but had graduated only in 1946 after serving for the duration. Crosland too was president of the Union for a term in that year, and it is in this period that Crosland made a well-known quip at Benn's expense. Benn made an intervention in one of Crosland's speeches to the effect that it was important for Labour undergraduates to discard the taint of intellectualism. Crosland replied that in order for the honourable gentleman to discard the taint of intellectualism it was first necessary for him to acquire it. This has frequently been repeated as if it were a mature judgement by one middle-aged politician on another, rather than an aside in an undergraduate debate. It later became a standing joke between Benn and Crosland.[5]

A gifted economist, Crosland stayed on at Trinity as an economics lecturer while seeking a safe Labour seat. As their letters show, he enjoyed an avuncular relationship with Benn, whom he was tutoring in economics, and he even took to calling him by the nickname Jimmy, a diminutive of his family name. It was in his rooms that Benn first met Roy Jenkins and a number of other current or future Labour leaders. Jenkins and Crosland had been allies since they were undergraduates and had together formed the Democratic Socialist Club in opposition to the Oxford Labour Club, which had maintained a pro-Soviet line even after the Russian invasion of Poland and Finland.

Crosland's behaviour at the time is chronicled by his widow Susan in her unsqueamish biography of him. Heavy drinking, gambling, sexual promiscuity and mere personal rudeness were his hallmarks. Benn suggested that Crosland's pose as 'a great bon viveur' was a reaction against his upbringing, for he shared with Benn a religious background of some rigour – his family were Plymouth Brethren – though Crosland's family were far stricter and more exclusive than Benn's. Both men were talented speakers and both young enough to feel that in 1940s Britain they were witnessing the dawn of a new type of society. The consolidation of the welfare state, large-scale nationalisation and the creation of the National Health Service were evidence of a bloodless revolution which would, they thought, bring about social change so profound that it could never be reversed.

Hugh Dalton acted as a talent scout for the Labour Party, as Rab Butler did for the Tories, seeking out gifted undergraduates of the appropriate political persuasion to steer towards the fast track to high office. Benn recalled meeting Dalton in Crosland's rooms.

'Have you met the Chancellor?' he said, introducing the visiting dignitary to another undergraduate. 'The ex-Chancellor!' Dalton boomed, and Benn was 'covered in confusion', having forgotten that Dalton had recently been ignominiously dismissed as Chancellor of the Exchequer for leaking information to a journalist before his Budget speech. In a self-deprecating account of himself written (in third person) at the time Benn remarks, 'He dresses scruffily, talks too much and is rather boisterous,' adding that he 'gets embarrassed rather too easily for comfort'.[6] His boyish looks and his tendency to blush at the slightest provocation were a spur to greater conviviality – as he could do nothing to alter these attributes he turned them to his advantage by making a joke of them. Thus he recounts the story of the time he was an orderly officer inspecting the kitchens when the cook, moved by his youthful appearance, gave him an orange to take away. 'Benn accepted this gratefully and fled, blushing furiously.'[7]

His position in the Union and his membership of the Labour Club brought obligations as well as introductions. He had been asked if he would join the speakers' panel of the Labour Party, and his first opportunity to take advantage of this came when he received a telegram from the 'Propaganda Office' asking if he could speak at a May Day rally in Worcester in place of Lord Pakenham (later the Earl of Longford). In this, his first speech to a Labour movement audience (which his father had helped him write), Benn emphasised international issues in deference to the international character of May Day, urging that 'the social democracy of our Labour movement is the only solution' which avoids the American and Russian extremes.[8]

The American Speech Association invited the Union to provide three speakers to debate in the US over four months from October 1947. Benn was obviously to go as president. Sir Edward Boyle, a leading Union figure and later a Conservative Education Minister, was given the second place. It was undesirable that the third speaker should also belong to one of the main parties, so Kenneth Harris, a competent, humorous debater, agreed to appear as a Liberal.

Kenneth Harris's book *Travelling Tongues* vividly recalls the thrill of this journey, during which the trio visited forty-three states in five months and held sixty debates. They crossed from a world of austerity in which chocolate and ice-cream were luxuries to one in which the only queue, as Benn remarked, was one at the post office to send food parcels to Europe. They sailed on a ship full of young people, many of them of a religious disposition, who had been doing voluntary service in Europe, effectively economic missionaries. Benn related in his own account how the ship approached the 'indescribable, unforgettable' lights of New York. 'This amazing scene symbolises all the strength and security and prosperity that one associated with peace,' he wrote. 'What a waste of electricity!' exclaimed a middle-aged Englishman beside him.[9] One of the economic missionaries, Libby, was to become a particular friend of Benn's and the three visited her at her parents' home near New York that Christmas. He also spent some time with the Christian theologian Reinhold Niebuhr, whom he knew through his mother's religious connections. When staying with Niebuhr he telephoned his host pretending to be a Scottish Presbyterian Minister, asking him to preach on a day when he knew Niebuhr was free. The great Christian moralist lied about his engagements to get out of the chore, much to the amusement of his family when Benn disclosed the prank to them all.[10]

The debaters were forever rushing from one location to another, often still in their dinner jackets, and were on one occasion mistaken for a comedy team. In Kenneth Harris's account, a hostess in Hollywood described the appearance of the debaters: ' "You looked so wonderful on that platform. So grotesque. Your hair down flat, and so long. Your suits, your shoes – boys! You were fabulous. Oh your suits! Those funny little lapels. Those vests, your tight jackets, your *collars*!" She threw up her hands and dissolved in helpless laughter. The Oxford debaters smiled wanly.'[11] Other cultural differences were less entertaining. After debating with a team at one of the negro colleges in a Southern state Benn asked the principal to have lunch with them in their hotel. He was shocked to be told that it was impossible: negroes were not allowed in white hotels.

They were pleasantly overwhelmed with American hospitality. In particular, coming from a small country, they were astonished by the distances Americans would travel as a matter of course. After a missed air connection a professor they had met only once was willing, despite their protestations, to drive them for five hours, between Chicago and Madison, Wisconsin, and then return alone. Benn found 'an engaging directness and commendable energy about Americans' and was impressed by their ability to stay up late and have fun. 'Is there a dance on tonight?' they asked, seeing couples on a perfectly ordinary dance floor in a hotel restaurant. It was difficult for them to understand that most young people in the US thought that life was for living. Benn found the young women at one meeting somewhat alarming. ' "Do you put it on?" asked one of my accent. "How do you heat your beer?" asked another, who had heard British beer was often warm.'[12]

They were forever having to bite their tongues and accept misrepresentations of Britain. Some were merely humorous, like the designation of them as 'royalty' because Boyle was a baronet (he had recently succeeded his father) and Benn an Honourable. Sometimes the misrepresentation was so great that there was no point in correcting it, as when the principal newspaper of Louisiana's state capital headlined one of their debates 'British Socialism versus American Democracy'. Austerity in Britain was widely considered to be deliberate government policy, and several times Benn lost his temper with what seemed to him to be simple American obtuseness in the face of the realities of life in Europe. His companions could tell from the other side of the room if he was going to engage in a spirited argument: his face would go white and a spot of red would appear on each cheek.[13]

Most perplexing was the way private enterprise was treated as a living faith, as an answer in itself rather than a means to an end. The American economic belief system eclipsed rational thought about other nations. 'One cannot speak admiringly of the technical achievement of the Dnieper Dam without running the risk of being called a "Red",' Benn wrote.[14] The intellectually paralysing effect of such a doctrinaire approach was depressing. They were told of a professor at the University of Minnesota who was investigated by the FBI, along with his students, because he was teaching them the principles of Marxism.

As leader of the group, it fell to Benn to organise the books, to ensure that they kept within budget, given the strict exchange control regulations at the time. 'One admired him for being so conscientious,' Harris said, 'but I sometimes felt we got more out of the trip than he did because his mind was on his administrative responsibility. I remember once going through Colorado when there was this marvellous mountain landscape and we said, "Come and look, Tony." But he was sitting on another seat working through the accounts. He still has those accounts.'[15]

He tried to give each member of the party a float which they would have to account for after they had spent it in order to have their expenditure reimbursed. He did not understand when both Boyle and Harris were appalled by this 'to each according to his needs' accounting. Harris argued that he would feel uncomfortable if he were spending more freely than the others because he enjoyed alcohol while Benn did not drink at all and Boyle very little. It would mean the other two were subsidising their colleague's drinking. After a struggle they were each given an allowance which they could spend on what they wished without accounting for it.

Benn, who never made judgements about the morality of alcohol, decided that Harris became more pleasant after he had been drinking, in contrast with people who became morose or truculent. Once in a bar in New England after a debate they were discussing drink and Benn mentioned the popularity of whisky in the US. 'Try some,' said Harris and offered his glass. Benn took a sip and said, 'Good Lord, is that what they all make such a fuss about?'[16]

One beneficial aspect of the need to explain every step of the arguments to apparently obtuse Americans was the effect this had on Benn's speaking style. Kenneth Harris remarked that on the ship going out they had all given a speech on party politics to entertain the other passengers and Benn's presentation had been long and dull, 'very pedestrian stuff, as if he'd got it out of some handbook. Within a month or so we had a very different Tony Benn when he got up to speak. He got funnier and funnier as we went on, he argued well, marshalled his facts well. After he returned from America I remember him giving one of the ablest and funniest speeches I have ever heard at the Union or anywhere else. His abilities were considerable before, but they were heavy, they could bore people. After America he was brilliant.'[17]

Benn later explained how studying the speaking styles taught in American universities helped him to do the opposite. 'The tradition of the Oxford Union was very stylised and mannered. In America the whole thing was forensic. They were training lawyers, we were training parliamentarians. Their presentation was stylised in a different way. It was not considered necessary in America to argue your *own* case which you believed in – you just took a case and developed it as if you had a brief. We decided to disregard that technique and do it in a much more informal way which was quite attractive to American student audiences. We were making jokes. I was putting things in a funny way to get them relaxed and then arguing the point.'

Benn was a fine-looking young man with obvious talents but, like many of his class and generation, he was ill accustomed to female companionship, having gone from a male school to the services and an all-male college. He wrote of his schooldays in *Isis*, 'He left utterly convinced of the desirability of co-education,' and in 1947 in a scripted BBC talk he argued, 'Since most of us are going to live the rest of our lives with a member of the opposite sex, it seems unnatural and unimaginative to compel us to spend the four or five most impressionable years in strict isolation from them.'[18] This awkwardness with women had doubtless been exacerbated by being brought up with two brothers and no girls. He felt the narrowness of his upbringing keenly when he saw the way American students behaved. He wrote, 'There is a social maturity about young Americans which contrasts favourably with the stiffness and inhibited reservedness of a tea party in St Hugh's. The embarrassed sweating and blushing which for so long plagued me in my early efforts is not commonly found among the fraternity brothers.'[19]

Isolation from women in early life induced in many men a tedious boorishness, but this was never a Benn characteristic. In 1947 he wrote that he believed 'in complete social and political equality as between the sexes'[20] and four years later showed that he understood the implications of such a statement for the division of labour. Asked by the *Daily Mirror* what he liked about the opposite sex, he replied: 'I admire most the sort of woman who can combine outside interests with domestic chores. This means that some responsibility lies with men to make it possible. Of course a woman wants her home and wants to be with her children, but that doesn't mean she should be saddled with all the dull and dirty work.' He was, it is true, saying this after he had met a woman who filled all his requirements.

5

Caroline Benn

Caroline Middleton De Camp was walking across the quadrangle at Vassar, New York, when she saw a piece of paper blowing along the ground. She picked it up and found that it advertised places in a summer school being run by Oxford University. To aid international understanding, two people from each of the major East Coast universities were invited to Oxford. Other students were invited from universities in Europe. Caroline applied and was accepted. In July 1948, five months after Tony Benn's return from his debating tour, she was sailing across the Atlantic.

Caroline came from a prosperous Cincinnati family of lawyers. They were church-goers, but not excessively so for an Ohio family in the 1930s. They were socially concerned without being explicitly political. On her father's side she was descended from a Huguenot family which had arrived forty years after the *Mayflower*, escaping persecution in France. One ancestor had fought in the War of Independence and had been given land in Ohio as a reward. His tombstone still proudly announces, 'Moses De Camp – Revolutionary'. During the Civil War the De Camps were fanatical supporters of the Republic. They helped run an underground network for smuggling freed slaves from the South. After the war the ten De Camp brothers visited President Lincoln and were proudly photographed with him.

Caroline was already socially committed as a child. She said, 'I was already on the left in the 1930s when I used to go on about the civil rights issue. It was not always appropriate, but I am glad I did it. You didn't have to know a lot, you just have to look around you to realise how bad it was. I was also very affected by the Depression, the people coming to the door looking for work.'[1]

She was intelligent and active as a girl. Her natural rebelliousness was sharpened by the Anglican girls' boarding school she was sent to. 'You had to be subversive in order to retain any individuality. The people were perfectly nice but the system was so oppressive.'

Caroline took a first class degree at Vassar and won a post-graduate fellowship. Other young women who were her contemporaries were the future Jackie Kennedy and Susan Crosland. When she found the fateful piece of paper on the quadrangle she was planning to go to Colombia to take a PhD in seventeenth-century English literature and to become a university lecturer.

When she arrived at Oxford she had a list of people to see which had been compiled by her Anglophile grandfather. It was quite a burden to be looking up her grandparents' friends, but happily she also had some names from one T. George Harris, a friend who had taken it upon himself to suggest some young men Caroline might like to meet while she was alone in Oxford. The first person she met through Harris she did not consider pleasant at all. The next on the list was Tony Benn, with whom Harris had debated at Yale. So as not to be alone with this unknown young man, who might turn out to be as disagreeable as the first one, she invited a number of people to tea on 2 August, including Benn. 'I was standing under the archway and I saw him come up the walkway. I thought, "I wonder who he is, he looks very nice." He *was* very nice, and after I started talking to him I was sorry I had invited all those other people.'[2]

Caroline was an alert, vivacious young woman with a manner which was at once humorous and serious. She was also extremely attractive – one of their contemporaries described her as 'ravishing'.[3] They saw each other every day thereafter and on the morning of 11 August at his rooms between the Banbury and Woodstock Roads she explained she was going to France and then back to America. They spent the day together, then walked down towards her room at Worcester. 'We sat down on a bench and I realised I would never see her again,' said Benn. 'Just after midnight I proposed to her and she accepted. We walked down to the bench on Magdalen Bridge and talked about what we wanted to do and agreed we wanted five children. Then I took her back to her rooms and the following day we had breakfast together. She went off to France then came back to see my parents.'[4]

Marriage meant a complete upheaval to Caroline. All her academic plans up to that point had to be abandoned; she would have to live in a foreign country and raise a family – something she had thought of only as a possibility before. 'I thought it would be a duty having children and in fact I found it was a pleasure,' Caroline said. 'Nevertheless, the division of domestic life was very uneven at that time. During the war people had been separated, a lot of people had been killed. There was a lot of pressure on women to stay home and raise families. We all fooled ourselves at that time that we were equal. Because we weren't like the Victorians we thought we had achieved equality and there was nothing else to do. The whole issue of who goes to work and who stays at home wasn't even discussed, not only between Tony and myself. It wasn't discussed at all.'[5]

As she was so soon to leave Cincinnati, which she loved, Caroline decided to use the next year to take an MA at the University of Cincinnati. She wrote her thesis on John Milton. Benn was to take his degree at the end of the year – Oxford degrees could be taken at two dates in the year at this time. Meanwhile the two young people corresponded voluminously about their families, themselves and their experiences.

Benn took his finals in November 1948 and in the new year Crosland sent him the marks for individual examinations which added up to his 'safe second'. He wrote back from 40 Millbank, 'They reveal me as a plodding all-round second-rater with a touch of inherited alpha from you in economics. . . . I too was delighted that the highest marks were in that subject, after all the effort you expended in trying to teach me something about it. It is no exaggeration to say that the results mattered far more to me because I didn't want you to feel you had wasted your time, than because I wanted a good pass.'[6]

Benn later called it 'a bit of a fraud degree really', because no one whose education had been interrupted by war service would have been failed.[7] His father commented that anyone who had been a sergeant for more than six months would be credited with Moral Philosophy and passed on the basis of that. His mother paid the fee to have the BA upgraded to an MA, a curious custom permitted by Oxford and Cambridge Universities, and the family drove down to the awards ceremony.

Tony Benn was now a graduate in search of an occupation. His cousin Glanvill Benn, twenty years older and chairman of Benn Brothers, asked if he would go to the US to solicit orders for their trade magazines. Sailing in January 1949, Benn was to learn the miseries of 'cold selling'. By night he would live in cheap lodging houses, by day he would look up the addresses of likely customers in Yellow Pages and call on them. The objective was to get North Americans to subscribe to *Hardware Trade Journal* or *Nursery World* or *Cabinet Maker*. It was not an endeavour likely to be crowned with success. 'They were of no interest to the Americans at all,' said Benn. 'They were skinny little publications because of the wartime paper shortage. And they had their own trade journals – they didn't need ours.'[8]

This was a miserable time for him. Benn wrote to Kenneth Harris, complaining that being a magazine salesman in the US was a very different experience from being a member of the Oxford debating team there. He learned the great truth of international commerce, that Americans are extremely difficult to sell to. Harris remarked that Benn was not a natural salesman, anyway: he liked to tell you things, not ask them of you.[9]

After a tour of the seedier hotels of Indianapolis, Chicago and Philadelphia, Benn obtained a room in a rundown boarding house in New York for $10 a week. He was there to be trained by the publishers McGraw Hill, with whom Benn Brothers were connected. He wrote a booklet for them on how to sell magazines and in return learned direct-mailing techniques and graphic layout, which later served him well in the production of leaflets and other political material.

He had met Caroline's family before he set off on his selling odyssey and she now joined him in New York in May 1949. She said her parents 'were a bit sceptical really. They thought I would never get married because I was too independent and I wanted a career. But they really liked him when they met him.'[10]

Caroline had been mildly curious about the difference between Tony Benn's name and that of his parents when she was introduced to them. 'He wasn't over-anxious to talk about it,' Caroline said. 'I suppose he could tell I instinctively wouldn't consider it one of his assets. It wasn't a selling point. When he explained it to me it was in a very matter-of-fact way – that during the war the government needed more Labour representation in the Lords so his father had been sent there. I still don't think I understood this thing about the second chamber that was hereditary. He said he wouldn't have to take it up. I was one hundred per cent behind getting rid of it.'[11]

They married on 17 June 1949 at the Church of the Advent in Cincinnati, where Caroline had been baptised and confirmed, and where her mother and her grandmother had been married. That afternoon Ohio was struck by one of its frequent cloudbursts which stop everything. Caroline and her father were obliged to wait in the car for twenty minutes until the rain subsided. The wedding was being recorded on disc for posterity, and the recording engineer did not wish to stop cutting discs for fear the bride would make an appearance when he was not rolling. He therefore recorded the organist vamping while waiting for the entrance, the sound of the rain and the shuffling congregation. After Mr and Mrs Benn were finally married they were presented with seven discs of such live action, with an eighth containing the ceremony.

Tony and Caroline Benn went to Lake Michigan on honeymoon, then to an international congress, the Summer Institute for Social Progress, at Wellesley College, Massachusetts. There Benn took part in a debate about the future of Europe with a Polish diplomat. Before leaving the US, Benn discovered that marriage in another country brought its problems. He learned that he had to pay purchase tax and duty on all wedding presents, which meant they could not afford a car. 'What is more, the customs will only give me three months to pay and after that they sell the stuff. I think that's a bit much even for socialist Britain.'[12]

In the event, when they arrived in England with the vast amount of luggage Caroline needed to start a new life, the customs officer smiled on the newlyweds and waved them on. At Waterloo station they were faced with the problem of moving the mountain of luggage to Millbank, but with characteristic Benn organisational flair the new husband commandeered an RAF van which took them to their temporary home. Soon they were to move to a flat in Hammersmith,

115 Stamford Court, at £114 per year. They could afford the car (Benn's first), a Ford Prefect.

If she wanted to work in education in Britain, Caroline realised she would have to have a British post-graduate degree. Accordingly, she started at University College, London, and began her thesis on the collaboration between Ben Jonson and Inigo Jones on the production of Jacobean masques.

Wedgwood Benn had hoped that his son would be employed by Benn Brothers, but Uncle Ernest vetoed this particular example of nepotism because Tony was a socialist. 'Father was absolutely furious,' said Benn. 'He had worked in Benn Brothers and felt it was right I should have the chance to do so. I was very pleased. I didn't want to do it and I was bracing myself to tell Benn Brothers that I didn't want to work for them and wanted to apply for a job in the BBC.'[13]

He had done a small amount of broadcasting for the BBC, on the basis of his position in the Oxford Union. He had been recommended by Derek Holroyde, a contemporary of Benn's at Oxford though a much older man. Holroyde had been particularly impressed by Benn's enthusiastic interest in the United States and, when he himself was moved to the general Overseas Service, he left a vacancy in the political and current affairs department of the North American Service. Benn was engaged at the BBC for £9 a week as a D Grade producer. The post-war BBC was not sensitive about referring to rank.

The BBC training school gave him the opportunity to use his creative imagination. One programme he devised had a typical Benn mix of wild originality and public participation in the media. Called *You the Star* it was a play broadcast with the leading part silent. The part would be printed in the *Listener* and members of the public could play the star role in the comfort of their own homes. Or perhaps they would find themselves without a copy of the magazine, listening to a very avant-garde radio play. Another idea he had was for a programme in which a mystery person would be asked questions by guests who had to guess that person's views on a major issue by hearing his or her views on unrelated topics. As a programme it would have been worthy even by the standards of the BBC Home

Service, though it did become the core of a programme Benn was involved with in 1960 called *In My Opinion*.

The Overseas Service of the BBC was funded by the Foreign Office but run by the BBC. The North American Service was a regional department within the English Service. It existed, as Derek Holroyde put it, 'to persuade the Americans of the needs of the British post-war world and the worthiness of the British war effort, to impress them with the Empire.'[14] There were also many British expatriates living in North America: emigrants to Canada and 'GI brides' in the US. The service existed to some extent to maintain their links with the mother country.

Programmes like the political flagship *London Forum* and Benn's own invention, *Let's Get This Straight*, taught other broadcasters that it was possible to put political figures in front of a microphone and ask difficult questions. Benn was able to meet yet more politicians, including members of the emerging generation in the Labour Party like Richard Crossman and Denis Healey. He also made the acquaintance of Conservatives, including Quintin Hogg (later Lord Hailsham).

At that time a producer did everything, from originating the idea to scripting it, finding the participants, interviewing them and editing the recordings. Recordings were made on 78 r.p.m. acetate discs which could be marked with a chinagraph pencil at the in and out points of a required quote. When the broadcast was made the disc was played between the two chinagraph marks. If more complicated editing was required, a section of a disc would be played on one machine while another machine cut a second disc. The waste made while discs were cut curled off into a swarf bucket. Tony Benn caused a panic one day when he knocked his pipe out into the swarf bucket and the thing went up in billows of smoke.

Any overt political involvement while he was at the BBC risked immediate dismissal. Benn's political ambitions had to be put into abeyance while he worked to keep his new wife and the family they soon hoped to have. It was a very happy time for the young couple, with Caroline working for her degree and Tony Benn taking the bus every morning to his office in Great Castle Street, near Oxford Circus. He could easily have stayed at the BBC, rising to any position he chose. His brother David made a career for himself in the BBC East European Services. The machinery had already been set in motion, however, which would take Tony Benn to the realisation of the last of his adolescent wishes.

6

Into Parliament with Bristol South-East

In February 1950, after almost five years in office, Attlee called a general election. Despite the years of austerity, the continuation of rationing and the failure of nationalisation to inspire the nation, Labour won with more votes than it had ever won before. The result of this election, fought on the slogan 'Fair Shares for All', was not the success the raw figures would imply. The Conservatives had received 45.5 per cent of the votes to Labour's 46.1, but the Tory votes had been better spread through the constituencies. The result was an overall majority for Labour of only five.

Tony Benn had helped the campaign of the Labour candidate in his own Hammersmith constituency, but because of the BBC ban he had not sought a seat, though he was on the B list of prospective candidates. He had been approached by Faringdon constituency in Oxfordshire but did not follow it through. In the summer of 1950 he was more receptive to the Constituency Labour Party in Northfield, Grampian. The MP, Raymond Blackburn, had left the Labour Party after winning his seat at the election. But he was still MP, so Northfield Labour Party were looking for a candidate who would fight the next election for them. Benn agreed to be nominated, a considerable step because had he been selected he would have had to resign his BBC job immediately, with no election imminent. But before the Northfield selection conference could conclude the process, Benn was distracted by events in the constituency of Bristol South-East.

The member for Bristol South-East was the Chancellor of the Exchequer Sir Stafford Cripps. A man of unassailable Christian principles, a teetotaller and a vegetarian, Cripps had established himself as a giant of politics through the moral ascendancy which his policy of 'austerity' achieved over the nation. His statement for the 1950 election suggests his tone: 'Neither I nor the Labour Party want to appeal to electors from the point of view of their own individual selfish interests. The nation and humanity at large require our services before we start to look after ourselves.'[1] He had replaced Dalton as Chancellor in November 1947, and his great triumph had been to hold back inflationary pressure by moral persuasion alone.

Cripps's health had long been poor, so the possibility of his dying in office or being forced to resign through ill-health was high. The future of his seat was therefore a subject of discussion among those like Tony Crosland and Roy Jenkins who were moulding the future of the Labour Party.

Mervyn Stockwood, later Bishop of Southwark, was at this time vicar of St Matthew, Moorfields, in Bristol. A close friend of Cripps, he even had a room in the Chancellor's house at 11 Downing Street. Through Cripps he knew Jenkins, now MP for Stechford, and Crosland, who had won South Gloucestershire. In April 1950 both MPs drove with Stockwood from Oxford to Bristol and used the opportunity to extol Benn's virtues as a candidate. His career so far had made both men 'anxious to see him in the House of Commons', as Jenkins later explained.[2]

Cripps finally resigned, both as Chancellor and as MP, on 20 October 1950, and the Executive Committee of Bristol South-East Labour Party were summoned to organise a selection conference. As Tony Benn said to a seminar in 1952 at the London School of Economics, 'As South-East Bristol is quite safe, the committee is all important – in short, as in the deep and solid South of the USA, the primary is everything.' To be put on the short list by this group would mean that the candidate would be invited to attend a selection meeting held before the General Management Committee, consisting of representatives from all the wards in the constituency plus the trade unions, co-operatives and other affiliated organisations. In a safe seat the real electorate consisted of the Executive Committee and the GMC. Of these the executive were more powerful, because a failure to receive their invitation would be the end of a hopeful candidate's chances. Moreover, the executive could also influence the decision negatively: they could fail to invite candidates who might impress the GMC, because they had a favoured candidate whom they did not wish to face strong opposition.

Benn described the members of the executive in the 1952 seminar: 'In policy they are left-wing, as all active individual members tend to be. They have been kicked out of the party twice and are waiting to be kicked out again.'

The seventeen members of the executive gathered in Unity House on 25 October 1950. They tended to be older members, many of them councillors with a lifetime of political service and skilled at political intrigue. Of the candidates, there were three people who had written soliciting support for themselves and five recommended from those around the table; Alderman Harry Hennessy reported recommendations he had been given by national and regional organisers of the Labour Party and by Mervyn Stockwood, who had spoken to Hennessy about Benn and written a letter in his support.

'Careerists,' someone said of the people who had written on their own behalf soliciting the nomination. That was enough to consign them to the rubbish bin. Stockwood later said, 'I don't think anyone else would have put Tony Benn up if it hadn't been for the very careful briefing I had from Roy Jenkins and Tony Crosland.'[3]

Councillor Kate Gleeson raised objection to Benn's candidature on the grounds that if he had Honourable in front of his name he was an aristocrat. Mervyn Stockwood said, 'She was a great character. She thought she was the only true socialist in the world – she would have been happiest if she'd been knitting at the foot of the guillotine. It was pointed out that a title didn't necessarily consign you to the flames of the socialist hell and she turned round.'[4]

The Labour Party's National Executive Committee had sent the national agent, Dick Windle. Windle, according to the minutes, 'hoped that members would pay regard to the fact that some candidates had lost their seats at the general election. He stated that the NEC would like to see Mr Creech-Jones returned to the House at an early date. Mr Jones had done a most useful job at the Colonial Office and the parliamentary party would benefit by his return.'[5] The five recommended candidates were shortlisted to three: Arthur Creech-Jones, Muriel Wallhead Nichol and Tony Benn.

Arthur Creech-Jones was a former Secretary of State for the

Colonies. He was the favourite for more reasons than one. He was an experienced politician, so the constituency would not be landed with an MP who turned out to be ineffective. He was born locally and his brother William was a member of the City Council. He was sponsored by a trade union, which would be able to make financial contributions to constituency funds. And he was supported by the party hierarchy, so a good deal of help with the election would be forthcoming. Benn had none of these advantages.

At twenty-five Benn had youth on his side; the constituency had experienced an old and ailing MP and would prefer someone younger. But this was a questionable benefit, for he looked so young and was so inexperienced, they might reject him for the opposite reason. They wanted someone young but not *that* young. Moreover, his career would end or at the very least suffer a hiatus with his father's death, so they might as well have been selecting someone of his father's age – seventy-three.

Muriel Wallhead Nichol was in many ways the ideal candidate. She was neither too old nor too young. She had the experience of five years in Parliament, representing Bradford. She was left wing and did not suffer the handicap of a peerage, like Benn, or close association with the errors of the government, like Creech-Jones. She did, however, have one overwhelming handicap: she was a woman. It was not impossible for a woman to be chosen as a candidate in 1950, but it was not easy. The most left-wing local party could still be highly conservative in its social attitudes and there was a long way to go before the average member of a General Management Committee was prepared to judge a woman candidate on her merits alone.

The *éminence grise* of the constituency was councillor Herbert Rogers; colleagues on Bristol City Council called him the Old Fox. 'Tactics,' he used to say, 'politics is all tactics. You've got to use tactics or you aren't going to win.' In him, Tony Benn found an able ally.

Rogers explained: 'I admired his father. I knew of him because he used to come to speak in Bristol and I knew he was prepared to stand up for a principle. When it came to finding a new candidate to replace Stafford Cripps there were two factors in my mind: we ought to find a young candidate, as Stafford had been an elderly man. Also I wanted to have a man with progressive ideals. I was very influenced by seeing his father and I thought he must have some progressive influence on his son. I telephoned Benn and I told him the type of constituency it was and also of course that we had continued to support Stafford Cripps when he was expelled. He was able to prepare his speech on the foundations that I told him.'[6] Benn freely acknowledges the debt to his father: 'The fact that I was his son gave me a huge advantage in opening the opportunity in Bristol, but it didn't get me the constituency – I had to fight my own corner at the selection conference.'[7]

The first time Tony Benn set foot in Bristol was for the selection conference on 2 November. He and Caroline drove from London, arriving at four in the afternoon. They walked around the centre of Bristol to pass the time and went to Kean's Café in Old Market Street. The General Management Committee met in the hall which used to be the headquarters of the St George Urban District Council at 84 Church Road. St George was a working-class area without grace or glamour. They drove to the hall and Caroline sat outside in the car. It was a cold November night and her proximity to a graveyard gave her no comfort.

Benn sat in a small anteroom with the other candidates. 'It was very embarrassing,' he recalled, 'because Creech-Jones was a very famous cabinet minister back in his home territory. Muriel Wallhead Nichol was a former MP.' When his time came he went into the General Management Committee room to find Alderman Harry Hennessy in the chair. He told Benn he would have ten minutes to speak and five minutes to answer questions.

Tony Benn's perfect fluency was the result of diligent work and training. The guileless asides and quick quips were carefully practised from drafts, which were revised and then revised again. From Herbert Rogers he knew the tone he should adopt and the sort of material which would be attractive to the meeting. For the construction of the speech he sought advice from MPs who had recently undergone the experience. He went to the House of Commons to consult George Darling, who had just been elected for Hillsborough, and his old mentor Tony Crosland.

He had a habit of using a typewritten speech with single words in the margin indicating the major points. He had prepared such a script for this speech but he knew it so well he hardly referred to it. First he jokingly engaged his audience's sympathy under the guise of updating the information about him sent by Transport House: 'I don't mean that Transport House is usually out of date – though some people might think they are. But since I gave them that "information" I have got married. My wife is sitting nervously outside. I am standing nervously here. We're not quite used to being apart.'[8]

As his greatest handicap was the peerage, he dealt with it head on. His father was in perfectly good health, he stated, relating the story of how his father had gone on operations as an air gunner in 1944. 'But the fact remains that though he looks as if he's going on for twenty years or more, one day I shall have to go to the Lords, unless by then we've done the sensible thing and abolished it. Whether this affects this selection conference is for you to decide. . . . I feel it would be an intolerable injustice if, as an active young socialist, I were to be debarred from going into the House of Commons for that reason.' He was claiming that voting for him would be striking a blow against the House of Lords.

Knowing there might be some prejudice against a young aristocrat, he stressed his socialist ancestry, his grandfather who went to work at eleven and campaigned with Tillett and Mann in the 1889 dock strike. 'I have been brought up in that same radical Christian socialist tradition. I never *became* a socialist. I've always been one.'

He appealed to the fighting spirit in the constituency, in a reference that harks back to the spiritual democracy of the Congregationalists: 'We don't want to be dictated to from above. Of course, I don't have to remind the South-East Bristol party about that. But the really important thing, as I see it, is that everybody in the constituency should play their part as a socialist *thinker* as well as being a loyal group of socialist *workers*. We've got so many problems to face that we need every bit of thought we can put into it.' It was an appeal to popular democracy which was both flattering to the immediate audience and challenging to the existing order, something which was going to become a Benn characteristic. He remarked on the importance of staying in touch with the constituency party and maintaining a personal relationship with the community; an MP should 'be as much a part of the community he represents as the local doctor and do many of the same things'.

With a pat on the back for the Labour Party's achievements since 1945 he urged further progress: fairer distribution of wealth, greater equality of opportunity, higher living standards. The sentiments so far expressed might have come from any Benn speech in the next forty years. It was in international affairs that he reflected contemporary anxieties rather than enduring verities: 'We still need to protect ourselves against the possibility of military attack,' he said. 'The lesson of Korea is clear – too much like Abyssinia and Spain. The Labour Party has always stood for collective security against aggression and we stand for that today. This means a certain amount of rearmament. Economic recovery and military preparedness must go hand in hand.'

In the peroration he urged, in what may have been a conscious echo of the style of Stafford Cripps, that a socialist policy was not 'a sort of Christmas stocking of a policy with a little bit for everyone. It is a faith and a way of life and a way of thinking that can find expression in every city and every community and every home. We are trying to build the sort of community where everyone counts for something and no one is neglected or left out, where "love your neighbour as yourself" finds practical expression. We must never get so bogged down by detail that we lose sight of that wider vision.'

'He swept the audience,' Herbert Rogers said, 'he was such a good speaker.' The speech alone guaranteed success: he was articulate and passionate and good-looking, a leader with youth and vigour. The candid way he answered the questions further disarmed the conference. One question was: If you are selected what money will you give the constituency? Benn replied, 'This is not a Tory selection conference. If I was going to give you any money I wouldn't tell you now.' There was spontaneous applause. Cripps had given them £500 a year before the war from his legal fees. Another question was: If we select you, will you live in Bristol? Benn said, 'I've just got married, I'm hoping to raise a family, I have to be in Parliament all week, London's 130 miles away. But I'll always be here when you want me.' This too received applause. These may not have been the answers which were calculated to purchase votes from the unknowns, but they were clear and they were honest. Bristol South-East liked that.

To his amazement, Benn was selected. He had forty votes to Creech-Jones's eleven and Muriel Wallhead Nichol's four. All the candidates were asked in to hear the announcement, a somewhat brutal procedure which must have been particularly unpleasant for Creech-Jones, who nevertheless made a short speech congratulating Benn. The young candidate went and retrieved Caroline, who found the hall hardly warmer than the car outside. For her it was the first of many freezing-cold Labour Party halls.

Besides his skill as an orator, the main point in Benn's favour was the National Executive's clumsy promotion of Creech-Jones. Dick Windle had boasted to Hugh Dalton that he 'had it all salted' for Creech-Jones in Bristol; in fact everything he did to help Creech-Jones's candidature damaged it, and the presence in Bristol of the party's national agent delivered the kiss of death to his own candidate. Additionally, the proud and independent members of the General Management Committee did not take kindly to the Creech-Jones camp's assumption that they had the nomination in the bag. Cyril Langham, who at that time was a young councillor starting on what were to become thirty-seven years on Bristol City Council, said there was another factor: 'The reason we picked Tony was because we thought rightly or wrongly Creech-Jones was veering to the right.'[9]

It is possible that a woman was chosen as the third candidate as a makeweight, the Executive Committee knowing that a woman's chances of selection were slim and that the race would be between Creech-Jones, who had been nobbled by his own trainers, and Benn. But Muriel Nichol was a fine candidate, and if Bradford North could choose her there was no reason why Bristol South-East should not.

If Bristol South-East Labour Party had been in any doubt about the dangers they were courting in selecting Benn, the *Manchester Guardian* soon disabused them: 'Mr Wedgwood Benn's main qualification would seem to be his youth. He is 25. But if the Bristol Labour Party hoped by choosing him they had a candidate for a very long period they may be frustrated. Mr Wedgwood Benn is Lord Stansgate's heir (and Lord Stansgate is 73).'[10]

The *Observer* was more generous, again remarking on his youth

– 'he is 25 and looks much younger'[11] – but at least gave him some credit for his political skill, declaring that he was the best undergraduate speaker the Oxford Union had had since the war. As this was a period of only five years it did not seem the most extravagant of compliments, but war service had delayed the education of so many that in this case the competition was between an unusually refined cohort of students.

He was always referred to in his brief press biographies as the Hon. Anthony Wedgwood Benn, educated at Oxford, an RAF pilot in the war and then a BBC producer. Mervyn Stockwood remembered that Benn 'came over as a very nice chap. He was what you'd expect: public school boy, Oxford, well mannered.'[12] He might have been applying for a job in a merchant bank. The idea that such credentials might not necessarily inspire the loyalty of Labour voters did not seem to occur to the party. Benn himself explained many years later that there was a tradition of educated young men like Cripps and himself finding loyalty from the working class, like the Eton-educated officers who went over the top with the infantry.[13]

Attlee wrote to 'The Hon. Anthony Benn' with what was probably for the most part a pro-forma letter sent to all by-election candidates. It gives some idea of the moral foundation upon which the government felt it rested: 'We have built up what is known as the Welfare State, the very conception of which was never dreamed of by preceding Conservative Governments. For the first time our economic life has been planned with the object of providing the material basis of a good life for all our citizens. Unemployment of the kind formerly accepted as inevitable has been abolished. Mothers and children are healthier than ever before and the fear of destitution has been banished. . . . You have youth, ability and high ideals, and I hope to welcome you to our ranks.'[14]

Cripps wrote to the electorate: 'I want all my friends and supporters in Bristol South-East to know how heartily I support the selection of Mr Anthony Wedgwood Benn as my successor. It is splendid to see Bristol South-East has another champion in the field – one who is as true a Socialist and who is as keen a Christian as I am myself.'[15]

Wedgwood Benn joked on his son's election that his own father, John Benn, had entered Parliament when he was forty-two, he himself had done it at twenty-eight, 'Now Anthony has been chosen at the age of twenty-five so the family seems to be getting more precocious from generation to generation.' He added, 'He is a very keen and active member of the Church.' These remarks about religion rather embarrassed Benn, who had not attempted to 'sell' his faith. He was, moreover, moving away from organised religion, retaining a fundamental belief in Christian principles without embracing the structure of Church dogma.

His speeches certainly contained far more Christian references in the early 1950s than they had earlier or were to do later. He told a meeting at Mervyn Stockwood's church hall that the precept 'love your neighbour' was not for Sunday only but for every day of the week. The pursuit of profit should no longer be the driving force of society, because the brotherhood of man was now a living reality: 'Don't you think when you lick your insurance stamp and stick it on your card that it's got nothing to do with the brotherhood of man; it's an example of the community as a whole accepting responsibility for its less fortunate members.'[16]

Socialism in Bristol had a strongly spiritual flavour. There were two vicars on the Labour side in the City Council during the 1950s and 1960s, but there was also another group whose members were primarily motivated by religion. Mervyn Stockwood said: 'They were outstanding men, seven or eight of them, deeply Christian. They had all been at some kind of Methodist mission in the early part of the century, some sort of course for people who had been converted. Instead of becoming Methodist ministers they decided to go into public life.'[17] Never less than two-fifths of the council turned up for prayers before meetings and a number of prominent members of Bristol South-East Labour Party were also active Church members or Methodists. Councillors and chief officers would meet at lunchtime in what was called the Christian Association in order, as one participant said, 'to discuss how religious ethics could come through in our work'.[18]

Beside the pervasive Christian atmosphere, there was a general belief in the worth of personal sacrifice for the public good. People like Kate Gleeson, for example, would walk to council meetings because they could not afford the bus fare and at those meetings would discuss the apportionment of tens of thousands of pounds and the welfare of people who were often better off than they were. Two long-serving Labour councillors, Cyril Langham and Charlie Smith, who became Lord Mayor, were both postmen. Because the Post Office was considered a civil service occupation, only workers at its humblest level were allowed to be involved in politics. No one overtly involved would receive promotion, though there was a suspicion that this rule was operated more rigidly against those in the Labour Party than against Tories. Thus Langham and Smith sacrificed the material comforts promotion might have brought in order to remain in unpaid public service.

Benn said, 'Scratch a trade unionist in Bristol and there's a lay preacher underneath. I felt very much at home there. The link between religious dissent and political dissent is in the best tradition of the radical left. It has always been about morality and not just about nationalisation.'[19]

In the short election campaign – he was selected on 2 November and elected to Parliament on the 30th – Benn was driven around Bristol to canvass and to address public meetings. He tried to meet as many people as he could, knowing that there would be curiosity about Cripps's replacement. Benn later came to believe that there was considerable unrest among the Creech-Jones camp, but he was shielded from it. Leading figures in the Labour Party came to support the young candidate, including some who would be important in Benn's later career: Michael Foot, Barbara Castle and Ian Mikardo.

Mikardo went down twice, once during the campaign and once on polling day for 'knocking up'. He knew Tony Benn's parents, because they shared his interest in Israel, but it was the first time he had seen the candidate. He said, 'What impressed me then was what always impressed me about Tony. He always had something original and thought-provoking to say. He would never talk for its own sake. He was always out of the mainstream and he always made you think.'[20]

Benn received 19,367 votes, almost exactly 10,000 less than Stafford Cripps's votes in February. He took the drop in the Labour majority personally and was deeply disappointed. By-elections are characterised by low turnouts, and this one was no different, though as a percentage of the votes cast he received 57 per cent compared to Cripps's 63. Voters are, additionally, more reluctant to show their support when the previous candidate has resigned.

Benn considered the reduction in his majority to have been in part related to President Truman's announcement at a press conference on the day of the election that the unstable General Douglas MacArthur, commanding the UN forces in Korea, had independent authority to command the use of the atom bomb. The time difference between the US and Britain meant that the wireless report of this announcement would have come late in the day, however, and could have had only a very limited effect. The impact on public consciousness of this slip by the President would be felt on the following day, as the major source of news for most people was the daily newspaper.

Nonetheless the atmosphere of world crisis which the Korean war had precipitated might well have had an adverse effect on Benn's share of the vote. Britain had backed the US in sending troops to South Korea in accordance with a United Nations Security Council resolution. But the American-directed troops had not stopped after driving the invading North Koreans back to their own border, but had crossed into North Korea, pushing far nearer the border with China.

The Chinese had countered with an invasion of North Korea from the north on 26 November, the event which caused Truman to make his ill-advised announcement about authorising his field commander to use the atomic bomb. With Sino-Russian relations still sound, an atomic attack on China might well have met a counter-attack in Europe by her ally the Soviet Union. Britain would undoubtedly have been a prime nuclear target, particularly because of the US bases in Britain, which America could use as she saw fit. Britain was neither asked nor informed when atomic-bomb components were sent to those bases on 10 July 1950. The crisis was such that within days of Benn's election Attlee flew to the US to see Truman to call for a British veto over the use of atomic weapons in Korea. As the newsreels pointed out, it was a trip grimly reminiscent of Chamberlain's flight to Germany twelve years before. The agreement reached was of similar value. The Americans agreed to 'consult' Britain over the use of atomic weapons.

Benn supported the United Nations, which meant in effect that he supported America. As he said at his selection conference, Britain had to resist aggression. He emphasised this view in an article for a Young Socialist magazine, 'WE ARE THERE BECAUSE THE NORTH ATTACKED THE SOUTH. THE WEIGHT OF EVIDENCE LIES HEAVILY THAT WAY and we shall have to leave to history the full story of mutual provocation and the many other factors that may have contributed to the aggression. I think we were right to go there and acknowledge the fact that the Americans have carried the greatest burden in casualties and cost.'[21]

The left of the party, including Cyril Langham, took an altogether different position: 'We weren't defending democracy,' he said. 'Both North and South Korea were dictatorships. It was the right against the left. We didn't think we should send troops to defend the right.'[22] This issue was the first on which Benn found himself standing on the establishment side facing a left opposition. It was not a comfortable feeling. Thirty years later it was to become one of his frequently reiterated themes that 'The judgement of the movement has been more correct than the judgement of its parliamentary leaders.'[23]

Winning the selection and then the election was one thing; winning the hearts and minds of the party members was a more arduous task. In a radio tribute to Stafford Cripps in 1951 Benn described the constituency's reaction to the arrival in 1930 of the aspiring candidate – it closely resembled the reaction to himself: 'Many of the trade union and industrial workers looked with suspicion at this intellectual, well-to-do, titled lawyer who sought to represent a working-class constituency. As a matter of fact, quite a few voted against his selection. Yet a few years later on they all stuck to him loyally when he was expelled from the party.'[24]

Benn suffered not only suspicion but also the disadvantage of comparison with his predecessor. Mervyn Stockwood said: 'Benn was very agreeable, though it was not easy for us in Bristol who had been accustomed to such a giant in Stafford Cripps. Tony came in as a young man who made a favourable impression. Most people saw him as no further left than Stafford, but being left or right wasn't the point. Stafford was a statesman of considerable experience. Stafford was like a god. There was no comparison with this young man.'[25]

7

New Boy at the House

He was an overnight sensation. Then he learned how quickly the bubbles go flat on the celebration of a by-election victory. He said a month later, 'I still feel very much a new boy at the House. I was given a locker to myself, I was photographed as the "new member" shaking hands with a blasé Westminster policeman. The next day he didn't even recognise me and shooed me away from the House.'[1]

Tony Benn had been married just over a year when he was elected. Caroline would call to see him in the Commons but she had to go through the same procedure as any member of the public, filling out a green card which would be conveyed to the Honourable member by a policeman. On one occasion under 'Object of visit' she wrote, 'A kiss.'[2]

Benn felt it was a great honour to be sitting on the back benches behind the Labour ministers who had achieved so much in the previous five years. The record of achievement could even be extended back into the war years, because only a socialist-style planned economy could have mobilised the country as it needed to be, and while Churchill ran the war the home front was under the direction of Home Secretary Herbert Morrison, Minister of Labour Ernest Bevin and Deputy Prime Minister Clement Attlee. Churchill might call Attlee 'a modest little man with a great deal to be modest about', but he was a far more effective peacetime politician than Churchill himself. More was achieved in his period of office than in any other five-year term. The implementation of the Beveridge Report and the 1944 Education Act, and the creation of the National Health Service were achievements which gave Britain the moral leadership of the world in the field of social policy. Abroad the government was a victim of its success. Had Ernest Bevin been a less commanding Foreign Secretary, Britain would not have been allowed to adopt the superior position which neither its wealth nor its overseas possessions justified and which was to cause so much misery in future years.

That was the wide-angle view of politics. Life on the hard green benches had a somewhat grittier pace. As Benn remarked in 1952 about his first day, 'On the day I was introduced there were two divisions. First I was told "this way" and I went, fuming. The second was a free vote and I couldn't make out what it was about. Then someone said: "Are you in favour of fun?" and I said, "Yes" and voted "aye".'[3] The vote was on whether to allow the Festival of Britain to open on a Sunday.

His restless nature quickly asserted itself, as he rebelled against the domination of business by the front bench. In a radio broadcast he said: 'I sometimes get the feeling, sitting in the House of Commons, that the two front benches are in alliance and the backbencher is left out of things.'[4]

He made his maiden speech in February 1951, just over two months after being elected, on the nationalisation of iron and steel. Industry and the Conservative Party were waging a furious campaign against the policy and it was creating difficulties for a government with a majority of only five. Steel nationalisation was, therefore, a highly controversial issue and Benn was breaking with the tradition which called for maiden speeches to be tepid affairs concerned with some constituency topic. Characteristically, he used this to maximum advantage. 'Conscious of the traditions of this occasion, I have chosen to speak in this very non-controversial debate.'[5] The issue was not, he emphasised, a controversial one because any reasonable person must agree that the government's position was in the national interest. There was agreement that the industry was essential to the nation, that it was in very few hands and that it was not competitive. Government direction of the industry in the past by Stafford Cripps had been beneficial. Now, particularly in view of the rearmament drive, the industry should be nationalised so that it could be run for public and not private benefit.

The House of Commons awards achievement, not effort. Had

Benn spoken badly in these circumstances he would have been somewhat coldly received. But he spoke with grace, wit and skill. As the Conservative Sir Ralph Glyn said, in speaking next, 'Not only does the Hon. member possess his father's gift of language, but he also has his courage. Very few members . . . would have got up to make their maiden speech in a debate of this sort. I am sure that all of us on this side, although we differ profoundly with him in our political views, will look upon the Hon. member as a colleague for whom we have great respect and whose future we shall all gladly cheer as he goes up the ladder of success in the House.'

Michael Foot, no mean orator himself, wrote in the *Daily Herald*: 'His speech was a model and almost every sentence was spiced with a touch of satire. South-East Bristol has every reason to be pleased with its new member. The tragedy is that some day, in what I trust will be a most distant future, he will have to be translated to the House of Lords, if that defunct body still continues to refuse to lie down.'[6]

The vote on iron and steel, narrowly won, was an occasion for rejoicing, but it was clear that a government with such a slender majority was living on borrowed time. The Conservatives kept up a relentless pressure, and the lame and the halt had to be wheeled in to vote. Benn's old friend Bill Allchin, at this time a house physician at Westminster Hospital, well remembers treating MPs like Tom Hubbard of Kirkaldy who had been called in by the Whips from their sickbeds to prop up the government.

A few months after his successful maiden speech, on 11 May 1951, the House saw the other side of Tony Benn. The occasion was a debate on a Bill designed to compensate former prisoners of war who had suffered in Japanese prison camps. Benn criticised it for its hypocrisy: 'If I were confronted with a Japanese at this moment and were asked to tell him that I believed that he was wrong in the treatment of those British prisoners in his hands, I could not but accept a similar criticism from him on the question of the atom bomb. . . . For every individual photograph that could be produced of a wounded and battered British prisoner of war in Japanese hands, I think one could find an equally horrible photograph of a victim of the atom bomb. (Interruption.) An Hon. Friend of mine says that the two things are not comparable. I do not myself believe that it is possible to draw any distinctions in war between the brutalities of both sides.'

He was frequently interrupted during this speech and called upon to justify himself, both by the Conservatives and by his own colleagues. He could either battle onwards against the opposition, continuing with his prepared speech, or he could recant and sit down, having made his point for the record. In what was to become a characteristic Benn position, he took the third option: against vociferous opposition he pushed the argument further, defying the howling crowd: 'What the Japanese did to our prisoners of war in the last war could be found in the annals of the British treatment of their prisoners in the far distant past. (Hon. members: "No.") War from the beginning has been horrible. I am sorry to disagree with so many Hon. Gentlemen here, but I strongly doubt whether in the last 400 years there have not been cruelties inflicted on prisoners held by the British similar to the ones inflicted on our men by the Japanese. (Hon. Members: "Where?") I think the massacres that took place in the Zulu wars were sufficiently horrible to be comparable in this respect.'[7] Challenged by a QC on the Opposition benches to substantiate his statement Benn was obliged to back down as he could not produce a satisfactory example of British cruelty.

This was the first time Benn was subjected to adverse criticism from press and public. He received critical letters himself, constituents wrote to the Bristol papers and there was some editorial comment. In a letter which shows rather more refinement from the press than he was to experience in later life John Carvel of the *Evening News* wrote: 'My dear Tony, I think I'd better warn you that I intend to attack you pretty severely in the leader column of this newspaper next Tuesday.'[8]

In retrospect Benn said, 'It was a very unpopular speech to make and I'm not sure I was right. I was insensitive about the suffering of the Far East POWs. I know it made me very unhappy because I hadn't got it right. I should have done it differently.'[9]

Some might say that in his maiden speech and in this one on the British prisoners of war was represented in embryo the whole of his future parliamentary career: oratorical brilliance applauded even by his opponents followed by a stand on a matter of principle which arouses indignation in equal measure. From Japanese compensation to the Gulf war, Benn refused to keep his head down on moral issues where a more calculating politician would simply stay silent and hope to pass unnoticed. His public morality never ceased to enrage his opponents but, more importantly for his own career, it also appalled his supporters.

His principal contact with the public was not through the House of Commons or reports of its activities but through *Any Questions?*, the first live, unscripted political radio show. This was an early assault by independent spirits in the BBC on the idea that the public should not be presented with political controversy. Each week the programme came from a different hall somewhere in the South Western region. Members of the invited audience would write out questions which would be vetted by the programme's staff then put to a panel of four people, mainly drawn from the field of politics. From its origins as a West of England regional broadcast it became a national programme in 1950 on the BBC Light (light entertainment) network. It was immensely influential, far more so than debates in Parliament itself, except on the most crucial issues. By 1953 there was a weekly listening audience of sixteen million, and the news-paper front-page stories on Saturday would frequently be what an *Any Questions?* panel member had said on Friday night.

The programme was somewhat limited by the existence of the 'fourteen-day rule', which prohibited broadcast debate on any subject which was to be discussed in Parliament in the next fortnight. The programme-makers' task was not lightened by the fact that parliamentary business was announced only seven days in advance.

The possibility of a broadcast prejudicing the business of Parliament was taken seriously. The very first question Tony Benn was asked on *Any Questions?* he had to decline to answer. It was about an MP who had passed a letter from a Sevenoaks vicar on to the man's bishop. The matter of whether a constituent might expect his MP to treat his mail with confidentiality was referred to the Commons' Committee of Privileges. Both Benn and his old Debating Society colleague Edward Boyle, also on the panel, felt bound as MPs to refrain from discussing a matter which was under judgement in the House of Commons. The other two panellists did comment and the producers of *Any Questions?* themselves were referred to the Committee of Privileges for permitting such a question to be asked on air, though no action was taken against them.

Benn was a member of the Select Committee which in 1956 successfully recommended the abrogation of the fourteen-day rule. He argued that it was impossible to bind everyone to the rules of the House and, if only MPs were bound by it, the rule discriminated against MPs and in favour of those who did not stand for Parliament or stood and were defeated, for they could comment as they chose. Benn cited the case of a Minister of Education who could not comment on *Any Questions?* on a particular issue, though one of his senior civil servants was able to do so in a letter to *Any Answers?* the following week. He argued for no restriction on debate outside Parliament at all on the ground that 'Any restriction brings little benefit at high cost in that it tends to make Parliament absurd in the eyes of the public.'[10]

Tony Benn was first invited on *Any Questions?* because he was the youngest MP and because the programme was always made from Bristol, where it had its origins, so as a Bristol MP he was a handy candidate. His original thinking and wit, combined with his natural courtesy to his opponents, made him as popular as a back-bench MP was likely to be with the public. Michael Bowen, producer of the programme from 1953 until 1977, said: 'Tony Benn was such an *Any Questions?* person. He was our automatic choice as the Labour MP on the panel. He built himself up as the star Labour man. When he knew he was going to be on the programme he would decide what messages he wanted to put across and he worked out a way to do it. No one knew what the questions were going to be but they were always topical, so there was a limited pool from which they could be drawn. Tony would arrive with a list of about fifty possible questions on every conceivable news story that might come up. He was better than us at anticipating what the questions would be.'[11]

His answers in the 1950s show him a supporter of the liberal causes of the day – against fox hunting, the colour bar and hanging. He was in favour of votes at eighteen, the televising of Parliament and, interestingly for a teetotaller, the liberalisation of Britain's restrictive liquor-licensing laws to permit all-day opening.

Caroline became pregnant early in 1951, which added to the

problems she faced at University College. 'They all thought that I would disappear,' she said. 'There were very few women, even fewer who were married. When I started getting bigger and bigger they kept thinking I was going to drop out. But I got the degree as planned. I took the viva a week before Stephen was born.' In anticipation of the birth and the need for more space they had moved to a larger flat in the same block at 91 Stamford Court. Stephen Wedgwood Benn was born at Queen Charlotte's on 21 August, the first of their four children.

Caroline had not been prepared for the absurdly unsocial hours of the House of Commons, which sits in the afternoons and evenings. When there were no sittings there would still be the round of party meetings and special-interest meetings, which anyone who wanted his name known would have to attend. 'It was worst at the beginning,' Caroline said. 'Over time I got used to being alone. It was more difficult at the beginning when I didn't have many friends. Then Stephen was born and I had a friend.'[12]

Tony Benn was also disconcerted at the hours of the House. He said, 'This is a central and wholly destructive part of parliamentary life. It was very difficult – there were many late nights and all-night sittings. I lived near, I had a car, so I could get backwards and forwards, I was much more fortunate than members who lived in their constituencies and didn't see their families at all. I used to see mine at breakfast every morning, which was something at least. However late I went to bed I always got up in time for the children. But at the weekends I was often away. It was really a very heavy price that the family paid, and I did too in the sense that I didn't see them grow up as I would like to have done. Their childhood had gone very quickly.'[13]

Over the years, Benn did make proposals for improving MPs' working conditions, including seconding a Bill on parliamentary reform in 1958, but there was no great progress. 'Labour governments are very nervous about making the changes which would be required,' he said, 'things like proxy votes, limits on speeches, timetabling motions, allowing people to put their speeches in Hansard without delivering them, as the Americans can do, arranging proper facilities. Also, government ministers of any party have never been interested in it because once they become ministers they are so privileged, they are exempt from having to treat the House of Commons as a place of work.'[14]

Benn had entered a sick House. Cripps had gone, Attlee was ill and Ernest Bevin was soon to die. Herbert Morrison was in the entirely unsuitable post of Foreign Secretary. Most damagingly, the Korean war and general rearmament had to be paid for. Cripps's successor as Chancellor, Hugh Gaitskell, brought in a Budget in 1951 designed to raise £4700 million through higher taxation. It included the imposition of health service charges on teeth and spectacles, a measure which led to the departure from the government of Nye Bevan, Harold Wilson and John Freeman on 10 April.

Benn abstained on the vote to impose charges. This was the second time he had defied the party chiefs. The first had also been on an issue connected with the Korean war, when he voted against the government's introduction of a 'Z reserve' scheme on 1 March. This was a plan to allow the recall of people who had recently been demobilised from the services on the basis that they were at least trained. Benn opposed it because he was in principle against conscription. He went through the 'no' lobby 'in fear and trembling, because the Whips were extremely stern'.[15] But there were no dire consequences of these instances of disobedience, perhaps because there were at this time no standing orders compelling Labour MPs to obey the whip on pain of reprimand. The only real penalty was the ultimate one: expulsion from the party. It could obviously be used only for serious or oft repeated offences. Benn was not prone to frequent voting against the Whips: 'I always took the view that what you said in the House is important, rather than the ritual vote. I'm not sure the vote against is the most effective form of left opposition. But there are occasions on which I would do it on a matter of principle.'[16]

Benn was by no means opposed to rearmament, indeed he accepted the prevailing cold-war thinking. At a Parliamentary Labour Party meeting after Bevan and Wilson had resigned, Benn said the rise in the defence estimates was less than he had thought it might be. 'Who is that very nice boy who just spoke?' said Ernest Bevin.[17]

Foreign affairs delivered a jolt to the already palsied grip of the government when the Prime Minister of Iran, Mohammed Mussadeq, urged the nationalisation of the property of the Anglo-Iranian Oil Company. This act of socialism was not to the taste of Foreign Secretary Herbert Morrison, who, advised by his service chiefs that military intervention was not possible, contented himself with naval demonstrations in the Persian Gulf. Neither were Mussadeq's emotional approach and his failure to comprehend the complexities of the oil market favourable to a settlement. The dispute dragged on until 1953, when an American-backed military coup restored the rule of the unpopular and increasingly repressive Shah.

Finally a balance of payments crisis and a round of wage increases undermined international confidence in the pound and the government felt it could proceed no further. Parliament was dissolved on 5 October 1951.

The Labour Party attempted to fight the election on the grim issue of imminent war. With world peace in such a precarious state, who should lead the nation in attempting to avert catastrophe? 'Whose finger on the trigger?' said the famous *Daily Mirror* headline, with the implication that Churchill was a warmonger. There was a rather crude equation put about by some Labour candidates that MacArthur plus Churchill equalled war. This was particularly impertinent considering Attlee's alacrity in committing Britain to Korea.

Benn expressed it more subtly: 'We are not, of course, accusing the Conservatives of wanting war. But what we do say is that by their ignorance of, and contempt for, those forces of nationalism at present rampant in the world, they could easily provoke a major conflict by the use of repressive measures that were all right in the days of nineteenth-century imperialism, but which are dangerous and wrong today.'[18] It was a prophetic remark, though whether the international situations which led to the disasters of the Suez invasion and the suppression of the Mau Mau uprising in Kenya would have been handled any better by a Labour government is an open question.

The real problem was not convincing the public of the government's competence abroad – British general elections are rarely won or lost on foreign policy. The problem was instilling any kind of fervour for domestic policy in the electors, particularly young electors. Benn wrote, 'it may well be that the welfare state in practice does not catch the imagination as vividly as the idea of it did when only dreamers dared to think it possible of achievement.'[19]

What caught the imagination was rather more mundane. Rationing continued and there were shortages of food and other goods. 'No beer, no stout, you put them in, you kick them out' was one rousing Tory slogan. Goods had been slowly derationed to ensure fair shares for all and to avoid overheating the economy with a flood of demand which could not be met. Conservatives played on the rationing issue as an example of unacceptable socialist intrusion into the lives of the people, but in the event the Conservative government maintained a similar policy, with some items not derationed until July 1954, less than a year away from the next general election.

In Bristol Tony Benn more than vindicated the party for selecting him by an extraordinary display of energy in the election campaign. The party in Bristol South-East was moving away from the public meeting and towards the loudspeaker, the door knocker, the shaking of hands. But the meeting was still a central political event. Clem Attlee came to address a meeting of 3000 people in Central Hall, Bristol, where he referred to Benn as a 'brilliant young man'.[20]

Benn was already sufficiently well known as an orator to be invited to address a similar rally in Bath for Victor Mishcon, later Lord Mishcon. 'Election meetings were real fun before television became widespread,' Mishcon recalled. 'Tony agreed to come over and we were pleased to have him. He was a very attractive figure, an intellectual in a party that consisted of all sections of society. Tony was an emotional orator, especially in those days. He almost sounded like a young lay preacher preaching a socialist faith. His peroration consisted of a story about three building workers on a building site. Each is asked what he is doing. One says, "I'm doing a lot of overtime," another says, "I'm chipping stone." The third one said, "I'm building a cathedral." My friends, "You have your choice on polling day: are you coming with us to build the cathedral?" The audience roared its applause.'[21]

Tony Benn had a full command of his audience by this time, even to the extent of handling hecklers efficiently, a skill few politicians develop. Frances Easton, the wife of Benn's constituency agent George Easton, said: 'He was good at dealing with hecklers – that's another political tradition which has gone, like the eve-of-poll rally.

Audiences are much more dignified these days. Tony would welcome the heckler, "If he's got a point, let's hear it" and then he would argue with him.'[22] Benn was to describe heckling as 'enthusiastic audience participation'.[23]

Benn's family stayed in Bath during the election campaign, and Caroline took Stephen to his first public meeting. Caroline herself had her first experience of how nasty politics could be when they went outside one night to their car, which was covered in Labour posters, to find that someone had slashed all the tyres. Despite the demands of motherhood and her studies, her sharp wits were quickly coming to terms with British politics. She was, admittedly, undergoing a crash course, sometimes attending three meetings a night. She was thus in a position to advise her husband on minor differences in delivery or reception: 'Just like if you work in the theatre and you hear the same play every night, but comment on the way the audience was a bit different.'[24]

On the eve of the poll he addressed five meetings, one in each ward, between 7.30 and 10 p.m. He then spoke at a mass outdoor rally in St George's Park. It would hardly have been possible to do more work than he did, and he was well rewarded. He had one of the highest votes he ever received, 30,811, which eradicated his feelings of inadequacy after his low poll in the by-election.

The Labour Party won almost fourteen million votes, more than any party has ever received in a British general election before or since. The bad news was that they lost. Part of the reason was the inherent bias of the distribution of constituencies: predominantly working-class urban areas were solid Labour seats where votes piled up far in excess of the number needed to win the seat – as in Bristol South-east, where Benn's majority was in excess of 14,000. The votes were much more evenly spread in Conservative areas. Moreover, Conservative administrative skill in organising postal votes was a major factor in many marginal constituencies.

The Conservatives won an overall majority of seventeen seats in a House in which the small parties were still further reduced. This was the heyday of the two-party system when, with the single exception of nationalisation, the parties vied with each other to do the same thing better. Housing was an obvious post-war priority, and Harold Macmillan was appointed to fulfil the Tory election promise to build 300,000 houses a year, bettering the Labour government's highest figure of 284,230 in 1948.[25] After initial opposition the Conservatives had settled down to acceptance of the health service. Though their welcome to the welfare state had been lukewarm, it was now irrevocably in place. Rab Butler's Education Act of 1944, providing secondary education for all, was the principal instrument of legislation for the following forty years. Rearmament was a Conservative policy which had been administered by the Labour government; likewise the support of the war in Korea. Now that Butler was Chancellor, and Gaitskell his shadow, *The Economist* coined the term Butskellism to describe the post-war consensus.

India had won her independence, and, after that, all else followed, as the diehards had predicted it would. The transition from Empire to Commonwealth was equally painful for both parties and it did the Labour Party no harm that the Tories were obliged to bear the brunt of reconciling the needs of European settlers with those of national liberation movements.

In his constituency visits Benn moved into a pattern which he was to follow for more than thirty years. He would visit every month, attending a public meeting on Friday, opening church bazaars and performing other functions of a public man on Saturday, then holding a constituents' surgery for two hours followed by a social, which would take place in a different ward each month. There was a meeting with party officers on Sunday. This would vary according to political requirements. Saturday, 31 March 1951, with an election imminent, found the party executive meeting with Tony Benn present. Benn, with characteristic enthusiasm, wanted to double the number of local party members with a membership drive linked to a 'Socialist Week' filled with evening meetings and other political events. He relentlessly struggled to cram more politics into an already packed schedule. 'There should be no reason', he said, 'why an evening meeting should not be fitted in before the Saturday social.'[26]

There were the speeches and street-corner meetings which took place whether or not there was an election. Perhaps surprisingly for a man so at home in front of an audience, it was the personal surgery meetings with individual constituents bringing their problems which were 'the side I prefer',[27] though he did not want to be thought of as 'a glorified welfare officer'. His mother said, 'His compassion for people as individuals is at the back of his politics. It's because he cares for people as individuals – he doesn't see them as a mass at all. He's got a pastoral soul. He enjoys his surgery work even more than he enjoys the parliamentary work.'[28]

His tenacity was astonishing. One battle with the Home Office took him eleven years. He was attempting to obtain British citizenship for a German refugee. After the first refusal from the Home Office he argued the case with every new Home Secretary as soon as he was appointed. When Benn himself became a minister in 1964 a Home Secretary was finally prepared to tell him the real reason why the Home Office had always blocked the naturalisation of his constituent. Benn was able to demonstrate that their refusal had been based on a civil servant's misunderstanding of the position. The man was naturalised.[29]

One piece of constituency work involved the call-up for the Z reserve against which he had voted, an act of disobedience which can hardly have endeared him to the War Office. He was approached by Bert Roach, a man in receipt of a disability pension from the army and obliged by crippling rheumatism to walk with a stick. He had been called up as part of the Z reserve scheme and ordered to a training camp in North Wales. He was physically incapable of doing any training and the damp would certainly worsen his condition. Benn pointed this out to the War Office but they would not accept the word of Roach's own doctor. Benn raised the matter in a question in the House, but to no avail. Finally he called the War Minister himself and persuaded him to telephone Roach's doctor. That did the trick and Roach received a telegram from Benn on the very day he was to report for call up: the War Minister had officially exempted him.[30]

Tony Benn had developed a particular style of making contact with an audience. He endeavoured to reduce the distance between speaker and listeners by a number of physical signs. He would take his jacket off and roll up his sleeves to give a 'Let's get down to business' air to his presentation. He would make a few self-deprecatory opening remarks to help the audience feel at ease with him. He would physically reduce the distance from his audience. Joyce Rogers, Herbert Rogers's daughter-in-law, recalled, 'In a public meeting he would sit on the edge of the stage or on a table and you got the impression he was part of the meeting – he was with the people he was talking to, not separate from them.'[31]

Women in particular found him spellbinding. One former MP remembered his wife being captivated by the young Benn addressing a meeting. A young woman at Transport House described Benn to a reporter as being 'typically English, fair, with a flawless complexion'.[32] He was, of course, everything an English screen idol of the 1950s was: tall, fair, aristocratic and an RAF officer. That he was also personally charming and held his beliefs passionately ensured that for women already committed to Labour he was an intensely romantic figure.

More of a problem was the working-class nature of the constituency and Benn's lack of life experience. 'He was quite a lightweight politically,' Joyce Rogers said. 'He was a young man who was feeling his way in a working-class area. But he was always very popular because he was a very friendly and open man.'[33]

Not all meetings were frictionless. At one General Management Committee meeting he was forced to defend attitudes the Labour Party had taken and was obliged to resort, in the words of Irving Rogers (Herbert's son and Joyce's husband), to a 'hierarchical' argument: 'He said there is an ascending scale of responsibility and I am telling you what our leader said. We must have regard for what the people who have been forced to take responsibility have to say. In effect he was saying the message came from on high and we'd better accept it.'[34]

Benn was severely shaken by the level of criticism of the Labour government and of his opinions at his first General Council meeting. He was so taken aback he asked for a vote of confidence. 'It was a silly thing to do,' he said, looking back, 'but I said, "This has been very harsh, do you really want me?" I felt under very heavy pressure. A lot of the left-wing criticism which exploded when Nye Bevan resigned was already apparent in the constituency.'[35]

Cyril Langham said, 'We were an out-and-out socialist party and Tony was a new person in that atmosphere. He came into closer contact with poverty and deprivation in Bristol than he had before. He could see the evils of capitalism.'[36] In later years Tony Benn tended to agree. 'There's no doubt that the instinct of Herbert

85

Rogers and Cyril Langham and Harry Hennessy was right. I was new and young and inexperienced and didn't really know what it was about, and they did. They were very kind, but they were also very clear and plain about what they wanted. This was my education.'[37]

The dissent in the party following the 1951 defeat was unparalleled until that which followed the 1979 defeat. Benn remembered: 'From then on the party became absolutely polarised and that polarisation continued from 1951 to 1957 when Nye came back into the fold with his "naked into the conference chamber" speech. So my first six years in Parliament, apart from the first few months, were spent observing this polarisation. It was very unpleasant – I hated it. Party meetings were just one slogging match after another. Clem was both leader and chairman of the Parliamentary Labour Party – it was only later that Wilson divided the two jobs. So poor old Clem used to have to take the chair and I would see him there with his hand shaking as he had to keep order and give judgements as leader. There was Nye and the firebrands; then there were the old right-wingers who were always weighing in and calling for expulsions; then there was Arthur Greenwood, who would come in at the end of the party meeting and appeal for calm. I used to describe myself as a member of the "keep calm" group with strong radical tendencies.'[38]

Tony Benn had been a member of the Labour Party since 1942, but the war and university and the demands of marriage and a new job meant he had never seen the Labour Party at work at close quarters until his own election. He had been a member of Oxford University Labour Club, which had split and split again in the manner of student politics. He had been a member of South Hammersmith Labour Party, though not a very active one because of the BBC political ban. His political precociousness meant he had not fought a safe Tory seat in his first election, as is customary. Likewise he had not enjoyed a period in local government in which to sample the rough and tumble of party politics, as his son Hilary was to do. Benn stood in the middle ground in this difficult period of the 'fifty-seven varieties' of socialist, named after the fifty-seven MPs who for their own reasons had opposed the Conservative government's rearmament motion in defiance of the Labour Party leadership. Benn was new enough and cautious enough to avoid excessive attachment to any faction. 'I didn't burn any bridges,' he later said.

Disagreements in the Parliamentary Labour Party were not all over major matters of policy. Frequently mere spite and pettiness dominated behaviour. At one PLP meeting in October 1951 Benn voted for the right-wing James Milner as Speaker, not because he sympathised politically with him but because he felt the man had been poorly treated by Herbert Morrison. Jennie Lee, Nye Bevan's wife, came up to Benn and his father, who were sitting together, and said to Benn senior, 'You really must do something about your son. He's turning into a proper little Tory.' Tony Benn was extremely upset, not realising that for many gratuitous insult is the small change of politics.[39]

Benn never voted for expulsions from the party – he always maintained that expulsion is the wrong way to deal with dissent; on the other hand he did not join the Bevanites. He was invited to do so by Fenner Brockway, at Bevan's request, but he did not wish to be subject to a Bevan group whip within the party. He nonetheless enjoyed good relations with Bevan himself, dining with him once and sharing a platform with him several times. He found the great Welshman 'mesmerising'.

He said, 'Nye was favourably disposed towards me. I suppose that he would have thought of me as the soft left. The theory that I was ever a right-wing member of the parliamentary party is a complete illusion – I was always radically minded. I expect the Bevanite left thought I wasn't really a socialist and I daresay they weren't wrong in terms of socialist analysis. On colonial freedom and democratic issues I was always with the Bevan group, but I was never one of his acolytes.'[40] Under Attlee, Bevan was the leading left contender for the leadership, with Gaitskell the choice of the right. Bevan was the working-class, oratorical genius, architect of the National Health Service, twice expelled from the Labour Party, the favourite bogeyman of the press and the Labour right wing. Gaitskell was the middle-class intellectual favoured by the press and even admired by the Tory Party, an administrator rather than a politician, a 'desiccated calculating machine', architect of the £4700 million rearmament Budget, scourge of the left and friend of the

USA, the very spirit of social democracy. When Attlee resigned in 1955, Benn voted for Gaitskell because he 'wasn't quite sure what would happen to the party under Nye. And I knew Gaitskell quite well.'[41]

Benn spent a great deal of time in his first two years in Parliament trying to understand the nature of the political machine and the place of dissent in it. He was struggling towards some way of reconciling the potential of the passion for reform in the Labour Party with the demands of managing the instruments of state. 'Life is more complicated than a battle between the visionaries and the realists,' he told Poole Labour Party. 'It is the balance of advantages.'[42] He described the inner policy conflicts as a creative and regenerative force. 'The Labour movement is a great combination of forces – trade union, socialist, co-operative, working class and intellectual. Its dynamism and power come from its disagreements, its strength from its loyalty.'[43] Here he approaches the idea of loyalty to the Labour movement rather than the Labour Party, an issue which was to recur in later years.

He was pondering the perennial question which has always troubled democrats: to lead or to follow? As Tony Benn said to his father in a BBC interview, 'You and I both owe our jobs to public opinion, and public opinion is a very funny thing. You want to know what it is, but obviously you don't want to go all the way to conceding it, because a politician is presumably intended to do some leading.'[44]

The only parliamentary group which he joined – and one which did not have its own whipping system – was the Bing Group, a back-bench ginger group comprising members from the right and left of the Labour Party: Geoffrey Bing, Ian Mikardo, Leslie Hale, Fenner Brockway, Reginald Paget and himself as 'a very junior member'. They met daily and worked on using procedure in the House to raise political points, rather as his father had at the time of the 'Wee Frees' after the First World War. It was here that Benn received the training in procedure which made him a respected parliamentarian all his career, always able to find a way of raising a topical issue. 'You don't get many opportunities as a back-bencher,' Benn said. 'The front benches dominate the agenda, whether with government business or Opposition Supply Days. My training was to find an opportunity and to use it politically. My dad always said to me, "Learn the rules, make friends with the clerks." The clerks were very conservative people but they were always happy to advise a young member. They were very helpful to me a few years later, in the peerage case.'[45]

8

The Cold War and Colonial Freedom

While still at the BBC in spring 1950 Benn had written to
Herbert Morrison offering to put his experience of broadcasting at the service of the Labour Party. It was a way of staying
in contact while not breaking the BBC's ban on open political
involvement. Morrison asked him to see Eddie Shackleton, his
parliamentary private secretary, who later set up a Technical Broadcasting Committee of which Benn was made a member. The establishment of this committee was a recognition that broadcasting was
too important to be left to the broadcasters alone; previously it had
been felt sufficient to entrust the technical side to the BBC (which
had a monopoly of broadcasting at this time) while the Whips dealt
with the political input. Above this committee was the Joint Broadcasting Committee comprising the leader, the Chief Whip and a
representative of the National Executive. There was, and continued
to be, a dispute between Westminster and Transport House over
who controlled broadcasts on behalf of the Labour Party. The parliamentary party regarded the broadcasts as their own property, the
National Executive as advertisements for the party.

The BBC had a different view. As Benn said later, 'The BBC
offered these broadcasts to political parties. We did not have them
as a right, and the theory was that if ever you pressed your luck
they would withdraw the invitation.'[1]

Through the broadcasting committees Benn had direct contact
with the higher reaches of the Labour Party, the sort of people a
back-bencher can usually see only with an appointment or not at
all. He helped Gaitskell with his first television broadcast as Chancellor and Bevan with his first broadcast. Hugh Dalton gives a

characteristically gossipy and gnostic entry in his diary about his session: 'Yesterday and today preparing broadcast (Party Political) with help of Tony Benn (very useful, moves through life like a cat, attractive, has reserves and sense of humour, but not quite to be trusted).'[2]

Benn later became secretary of the Technical Broadcasting Committee, then chairman of the Broadcasting Advisory Committee, basically the same committee in a new incarnation. He was obliged to give this up in 1964 when he became Postmaster General, as he was the minister responsible for broadcasting and there was an obvious conflict of interests.

Throughout the 1950s Benn was involved in international affairs to a far greater extent than he was in the future. One of the most celebrated issues he took up was the Seretse Khama case.

Seretse Khama was an African who on his father's death had become the chief of the Bamangwato tribe in Bechuanaland at the age of six. In his minority the tribe was ruled by his uncle Tshekedi Khama. Seretse was educated at Oxford and while in England he met Ruth Williams, an English office worker, at a London Missionary Society dance. They fell in love and married in 1948. This led to something of a conflict between Seretse Khama and his uncle, who wished to continue to rule. The pretext was that Khama had married without the tribe's permission and had therefore behaved in a manner not appropriate to someone of his rank. That a white English woman, knowing nothing of the mores of a southern African tribe, should be its queen was also at issue. This was felt to be an unacceptable state of affairs in England too and Ruth was sacked from her job at Lloyd's, ostracised by her family and besieged by the press.[3]

Khama returned to Bechuanaland, a British protectorate, and succeeded by his dignity and force of personality in persuading the tribal council to accept him as its chief with Ruth as his queen. All that was required was the consent of the British authorities.

The Labour administration was in some difficulty. It had been struggling to create a Commonwealth out of the Empire. A surly and reluctant member of this association was South Africa, many of whose people had a long-standing animosity towards the British, and whose government was erecting the legal framework of apartheid: the Group Areas Act restricting different races to different areas; the Mixed Marriages Act making mixed marriage illegal; the Immorality Amendment Act making sexual intercourse between different races an offence. The prospect of Seretse and Ruth Khama ruling a country on their borders was less than welcome.

There was another reason why the Labour government found it necessary to placate South Africa. This was the Bomb. There were large uranium deposits in South Africa which could, if South Africa would only sign them over, make Britain independent of the USA and capable of exerting some leverage over her ally, who had recently withdrawn atomic co-operation from Britain as a result of the McMahon Act.

A way had to be found of denying Seretse and Ruth Khama the right to rule in Bechuanaland, whatever the wishes of the tribe. The difficulty was that no one wanted to admit the true reason for excluding them: that it was unacceptable for a black man and a white woman to marry. Creech-Jones, the Secretary of State for the Colonies, whom Tony Benn was to defeat at the Bristol South-East selection conference, hoped to get the whole thing settled on 'administrative grounds' and strenuous efforts were made to demonstrate that the tribal council which had selected Seretse as chief was not properly established or that he was not a proper person to be chief. Unfortunately for Creech-Jones and his colleagues, a public inquiry set up to investigate these matters found no reason to exclude Seretse Khama except that South Africa was opposed to him. Its findings were therefore not published.

Ruth joined Seretse in Bechuanaland, where she was welcomed, but the British government found a way of enticing Seretse back to London and pretended that he would be allowed to return to his country. Eventually they were both exiled from Bechuanaland in August 1951.

Soon it was one of the problems faced by the new Conservative government. In his first major speech from the Opposition benches Benn moved an adjournment debate on 27 March 1952 on the question of the deposition of Seretse Khama and his exile in London. It was not easy to defend the previous government's record, though Benn loyally, if not very convincingly, tried to demonstrate that the situation was now altered and that what might have been just in the past was now an outrage. He was able to deliver a telling rebuke to the government when he quoted the words uttered when in opposition by Lord Salisbury, the Secretary of State for Commonwealth Relations: 'In the past an individual, unless he had committed an offence, was not only secure against the deprivation of his civil rights and liberties, but he was entitled to the protection of the law. Now it seems, in Bechuanaland at any rate, that that is no longer true.'[4]

Benn was seconded by the veteran anti-colonialist Fenner Brockway, who remarked that Benn had shown himself 'a very worthy son of his father', himself 'still standing for the ideals of liberty of which he was such a great champion in this House'.[5] The two men formed the Seretse Khama Defence Council, later merged with the Movement for Colonial Freedom.

Seretse and Ruth became good friends of the Benns. Seretse became godfather to Melissa Benn, born in 1957, and the Khamas called their son Anthony. Benn remarked that he would now know what to do if his daughter wanted to marry a black man: 'I should ask her godfather to have a stern talk to her.'[6] Sitting up very late after a party in 1956 Caroline and Ruth entered into a pact never to smoke cigarettes again unless the other had been informed first. Neither of these strong-willed women has yet informed the other that she wishes to give in.

The Khamas lived in Croydon, south of London, where Seretse continued his studies in the law. They were eventually permitted to return to Bechuanaland as 'private citizens' in 1956, and as a private citizen Seretse Khama set up the Democratic Party, which was returned in a landslide victory in the first elections in the newly independent Republic of Botswana in 1966. Seretse Khama became the country's first Prime Minister and was knighted.

The Seretse Khama case was only the most prominent of a vast range of colonial issues to which Benn addressed himself during the 1950s. By far the greater part of his time in Parliament was taken up by colonial matters. In the five years from February 1951 to November 1956 he asked 133 written parliamentary questions of ministers. Sixty-five were on the colonies, seventeen on foreign affairs and four on Commonwealth relations. Another eight questions to the Home Office concerned 'aliens'. Over the same period he asked seventy-two oral questions, of which fifteen were on the colonies, eight on Commonwealth relations and seven on foreign affairs.[7] Out of twenty-six speeches made and articles written in 1953, eighteen were on foreign affairs or some issue closely connected like 'Trade with China' or 'The Labour Party, Asia and World Peace'.

The Movement for Colonial Freedom was inaugurated on 8 March 1954 with veteran anti-colonialist Fenner Brockway elected as chairman and Tony Benn as treasurer. Through the MCF Benn took some part in every nationalist movement in the late 1950s. To detail the various strands of African independent movements would be beyond the scope of this book, not least because Benn was involved in a supportive role in each rather than playing a leading part in any single one. It was even difficult for him to keep track of the changing pattern of claims for independence, and in characteristic Benn style he drew up a list of all the anti-colonial movements in the world with their addresses and leaders.

His own appointments book reads like a Who's Who of Third World politics. Throughout this period he was meeting politically or dining with the future leaders of Africa. Among his contacts at this time Kenneth Kaunda became President of Zambia; Kwame Nkrumah became President of Ghana; Dr Hastings Banda became President of Malawi; Julius Nyerere became President of Tanzania; Cheddi Jagan and Forbes Burnham both became Prime Ministers of Guyana; Joshua Nkomo became President of the (then Rhodesian) African National Congress. As chairman of the Middle East Committee and of the Goa Committee, he was involved in meetings and agitation over Algerian independence from France and Goan independence from Portugal. He was also involved in the long battle for democracy in Portugal itself.

This was not an area which excited the general public. Indeed, if anything there was an undercurrent of working-class imperialism which resented the loss of the Empire and was mistrustful of foreigners to the point of xenophobia. Racism was soon to become a potent political force and Bristol was to experience a colour-bar scandal which split the local Labour movement.

With typical Benn defiance of what he considered ignoble attitudes, he was not prepared to yield to public opinion. Rather, he would attempt to change it by confronting it with a morally superior position. Thus in his 1951 election manifesto he wrote: 'We must preserve a proper balance between rearmament, economic aid for our poverty-stricken brothers in Asia and Africa, and our social defences at home.' By the 1955 election he wanted to be far more explicit about political power at Westminster and the struggling colonies: 'Don't forget that you are really casting two votes in this election. One is your own. The other is for some African or Malayan or West Indian – one of the sixty million colonials whose future depends on Parliament just as much as yours does.' He told a Bristol audience: 'Don't forget that when you go to the poll there stands behind you the shadow of a coloured man to whom the return of a Labour government means a great deal.'[8]

Why did he pay such attention to colonial affairs? Partly it was his father's influence – the former Secretary of State for India had always been an international politician. Like many of the positions he adopted, it was not necessary for Tony Benn to weigh up the issues and establish an opinion. He was automatically on the side of the independence movements. 'I had anti-imperialism in my bloodstream,' he said, 'the old left–liberal position. My interest was aroused when I was in Africa and the Middle East during the war. Colonialism had to end, though every struggle was resisted by the Tories and by our people not wanting to appear unpatriotic. It wasn't a very popular cause to take up except with the constituencies.'[9]

The constituency parties were Labour's rank and file, the people who turned out for canvassing and the rallies and demonstrations. They were invariably ahead of public opinion on civil liberties issues and their votes controlled seven seats on Labour's ruling body, the National Executive Committee. Anthony Sampson, at this time in Africa editing the magazine *Drum*, said, 'The Movement for Colonial Freedom was representative of part of the soul of the Labour Party. The fiery left had a straightforward enemy to attack – the colonial administration, the governors, the army, the civil service. There was no mileage in terms of votes from the public but there was in terms of party supporters – votes at the party conference.'[10]

It was certainly an interest which brought Benn into contact with the most radical wing of the party, and he found himself more in the company of Fenner Brockway, Michael Foot, Barbara Castle, Ian Mikardo and other Bevanites than with Gaitskell supporters.

The autumn of 1952 found Tony and Caroline Benn on the high seas, taking baby Stephen to see his grandparents in the United States. They frequently made the journey in later years, in an increasingly chaotic cabin as more children were added. There is a radical tradition among sailors, and Benn used to be invited down to the engine rooms for organised political discussions with members of the crew.

Nineteen-fifty-two was a particularly fruitful time for a politician to be visiting the US: during the previous five years America had steadily extended her role at the expense of a dwindling Britain. American military involvement in world affairs after the Second World War had much to do with Britain's inability to maintain an imperial peacekeeping force, leaving a power vacuum which the US felt obliged to fill. The winter of 1946–7 convinced Attlee and Bevin that they could no longer afford the luxury of policing other countries.

Benn did not appear as an opponent or even a critic of American foreign policy. In 1952 he wrote: 'Even in 1940, when Britain's survival was in question, not even President Roosevelt could bring America into the war to save us. Yet since 1945 President Truman has brought the nation to a full awareness of the global responsibilities that must accompany her overwhelming power. He rushed through the Truman doctrine and the Marshall Plan, and NATO. He sent American troops to Europe to give NATO teeth and took the decision to resist aggression in Korea.'[11] Nonetheless, he was concerned about the potential for abuse which America's vast power gave her. 'Negotiation from strength is all right so long as there is negotiation,' he told the Cincinnati Women's International Forum. 'We face the danger that comes from a position of strength in which negotiation is unnecessary.'[12]

Lord Stansgate, Tony and David Benn took part in a debate together at the Oxford Union in January 1951 on the motion that the government's foreign policy in the Far East displayed too great a dependence on that of the United States. Tony Benn remarked, 'It is absurd to describe the great record of Anglo-American co-operation since the war as dependence,' and the membership of the Union narrowly agreed, the motion being lost by 294 to 289.[13]

Caroline Benn's insistence on remaining American, meant that she was subject to surveillance under the Aliens Restriction Act. It is an example of the paranoia of the 1950s that this absurd piece of legislation was rigorously enforced. Caroline, staying with Benn at the family's house in Stansgate, Essex, opened her door one day to a policeman, who questioned her about why she had travelled more than twenty miles from London. The policeman was satisfied by her answers, though had he not been the Act provided for immediate deportation without recourse to the courts.

Benn raised the issue in the House of Commons when the renewal of the Aliens Restriction Act was debated. Tory MP Sir Herbert Williams was unsympathetic: if Mrs Benn were an alien, he said, that was her fault; a woman who marries an MP should accept his nationality. An irreverent Labour MP suggested that the Queen should become a Greek subject as she had married a Greek, but the jibe had no effect. The Act was renewed for another year.[14] It was allowed to lapse at the end of 1955.

In 1952 the family moved to a four-storey house in Holland Park Avenue in west London, which they obtained for £4500. The mortgage was a burden, as was the cost of renovating the old house, but financially the family was now secure. Tony Benn received an MP's salary of £1000 a year, plus whatever he could make from his journalism and a dividend on his 1560 shares in Benn Brothers. Buying a large, expensive house was a gamble, because Benn's father might die at any moment and Benn would be excluded from the Commons, thereby losing his salary. He embellished his new house with a purchase from Oxfordshire County Council: for £10 he bought the park bench on which he had proposed to Caroline and had it installed in the garden. All four Benn children grew up in this house. Another boy, Hilary, was born in 1953; Melissa arrived in 1957 and Joshua in 1958.

Benn soon set up his office at the top of the house. He was dealing with only 100 letters a week in his first years as an MP, a tiny amount by later standards. There was far less support, however, and he was obliged to pay for one or two mornings of secretarial help a week from his own pocket, 'and the rest of the letters I do by long hand'.[15] He had to pay his own postage and his own secretarial expenses, which he could claim against tax. MPs were later given allowances for secretarial help, but these never approached the level which Benn observed on a visit to the US Congress, where members were provided with an office and secretarial and research assistance. The nearest thing to an office a British MP normally received was a locker too small to accommodate a briefcase and access to telephone kiosks. With such tools the legislators of Britain grappled with the complexities of international politics.

The great issues of the time were the cold war and Britain's position in the world. They were linked by Britain's atomic bomb, whose secret development Attlee and Bevin had taken such care to continue. That Britain should have atomic weapons was unremarkable, as she had been involved in their wartime development; they had, moreover, ended the war with Japan. Early reactions to them were wonder and uncertainty, rather than terror, but in September 1949 the Soviet Union tested its first atom bomb. Now the fear of the cold war breaking into open fighting, already a miserable enough prospect, was joined to the fear of destruction on an unparalleled scale. The American hydrogen bomb test of 30 November 1952, with its power so many times greater than that of the atom bomb, added to the unease, particularly as its existence was revealed when the memory of America's mismanagement of the Korean war was still fresh. Russia's announcement in August 1953 that she too possessed the hydrogen bomb gave the impression that civilisation was locked in a downward spiral.

Among the educated middle class there was a terror of nuclear destruction which was almost pathological. Benn was a determined optimist, convinced that human destiny was driven by individuals who could change it if they only had faith in themselves. Yet at this time even he was given over to a fatalistic view of humanity's future. 'I have a grandfather of 93, a father of 71 and a four-month-old son,' he was reported as saying. 'On present reckoning I would say that the expectation of life for all four of us is just about the same.'[16]

Repeated tests of nuclear weapons, along with coverage of the injuries suffered by those who strayed too close to the test sites, served to keep the image of Armageddon in the public mind. It was obvious to those who had been watching the sequence of events that Britain was either producing a hydrogen bomb or contemplating doing so. In fact the decision to manufacture a hydrogen bomb had been taken in 1952 but, following the lead of the Labour government, the Tories decided not to tell Parliament. Benn, ever the parliamentarian, was more angry about the procedural violation which he currently suspected was occurring than about the nature of the weapon. 'We did not say ban the hydrogen bomb,' he told a meeting in Bristol in May 1954, 'or even that it should not be produced, but that it should not be produced without authority.'[17]

He formed the H-Bomb National Committee on 11 April 1954 with Sir Richard Acland, Fenner Brockway, Anthony Greenwood (Labour MP and son of Arthur) and the Methodist minister Donald Soper. This was in response to Attlee's call on 5 April for a summit of nuclear powers for arms-reduction talks. 'Time is not on the side of the survival of civilisation,' Attlee said. 'Every month increases the danger. Great civilisations have gone down while men said: "The worst may not happen; there is plenty of time." The Opposition believes that the time for action is now.'[18]

The H-Bomb National Committee was one of those extra-parliamentary organisations which Attlee instinctively distrusted and Benn instinctively found inspiring. The intention was to raise signatures for a petition supporting Attlee's motion. It proceeded with meetings and rallies until the end of December when a petition of 357,000 signatures was presented to 10 Downing Street by Benn, Anthony Greenwood and the Labour MPs Sydney Silverman and George Thomas. A third of a million is certainly a respectable number of signatures, but the achievement was somewhat diminished by their previous announcement of an intention to obtain fifteen million.

Finally, in February 1955, a Defence White Paper announced that Britain was developing an H-bomb. Nye Bevan and sixty-two others, including Benn, abstained on the vote after the defence debate. Making the hydrogen bomb was to prove an expensive decision which increased rather than decreased Britain's dependence on America. The atomic information-sharing agreements between Britain and America interested Benn all his life and were to be of central importance in his thinking in the 1980s. The secret Quebec Agreement reached in 1943 between Britain and the US was made public in 1954. Using the codename 'Tube Alloys Project', the agreement noted that the US had provided the lion's share of resources for the development of the bomb and should therefore make its own terms regarding the 'post-war advantages of an industrial or commercial character'. As far as the 'finger on the trigger' was concerned, the agreement stated that neither would use the bomb against a third party without the other's consent.

This worked well enough during the war, but then Senator McMahon – who knew nothing of the agreement – sponsored the McMahon Act (1946), which prohibited the exchange of nuclear know-how with other nations. Senator Hickenlooper in 1948 had the Quebec Agreement cancelled in his capacity as chairman of the Congressional Atomic Energy Committee. His concern was not the issue of nuclear know-how but that it was 'unwarranted' and 'unthinkable' that the US should obtain Britain's agreement before she could act in her own defence.

Churchill berated Attlee for having allowed the Americans to get away with an abrogation of the treaty while he was Prime Minister. As this charge was made during the debate on the hydrogen bomb on 5 April after Attlee had made his appeal for a summit, it all seemed a little too much like parliamentary sleight of hand: the Prime Minister produces a secret but obsolete document, the Prime Minister attacks the Opposition. While watching the fireworks Honourable members were failing to notice the real trick. Benn spotted this and pursued the Prime Minister on it on 8 April. The White House had emphatically stated that the Quebec Agreement covered the atom bomb, not the hydrogen bomb, which had been only a possibility at that time. Churchill should withdraw his slur on Attlee. Moreover, Benn said, 'May I further ask whether, in view of the importance he attaches to the hydrogen bomb, the Right Hon. Gentleman himself has made any approach to the American government to negotiate an agreement, or for consultation?'[19]

Churchill declined to answer, saying that 'All those serious, complicated questions had better be set out separately on the order paper.' This might well have happened in the near future had not Benn next had a curious encounter with Attlee: 'Clem stopped me in the corridor and absolutely blew me up. He said, "You've no right to ask that question at all, you should have come to see me about it." His anger that a mere back-bencher could put a question about nuclear weapons in some way that he must have thought had embarrassed him made a big impression on me.'[20]

But the following year Benn was again worrying at the subject. Referring to a draft Anglo-American agreement on the exchange of nuclear information for defence purposes, Benn pointed out that the agreement would be subject to change by US legislation – which was what had happened under the McMahon Act. 'Is the Prime Minister really satisfied that the agreement specifically safeguards the right of the United States Congress to alter its terms unilaterally while no such provision is made safeguarding the rights of Parliament in this matter?'

Anthony Eden, who had now replaced the ailing Churchill as Prime Minister, replied, 'The Hon. Gentleman is not right. This provision allows for further relaxation in United States legislation and I hope, although we had better not say too much about it, that in the course of time there may be such further relaxation. There cannot be any relaxation in our legislation, because there is no such legislation.' He further urged his colleagues, 'In view of their delicate character and the very great importance of confidential work between the United States and Britain at this time, I hope I may ask the House to be temperate in its questions on this subject.' So now both the Prime Minister and the Leader of the Opposition had told him to shut up about it.[21]

Benn's libertarian approach to the cold war was best presented in a talk on the BBC North American Service in 1953:

You have to ask yourself what we are trying to protect from Communism. It is surely the democratic way of life. We believe that you can trust people to have good sense and good judgement if you leave them to make up their own minds and elect their own governments. We believe the genius of the human spirit is something that needs to be free from restriction and censorship and oppression. Well, then, to put it bluntly, why Senator McCarthy with his accusations and quizzings and screenings and investigations? Why do they go on? Like all witch-hunting through history it breeds on fear. People are scared stiff of the tiny minority of Communists in the United States. Fear breeds oppression and if you try to oppress anybody, be they Communists or Fascists or Christians, you strengthen the thing you are trying to stamp out and destroy the thing you are trying to protect.[22]

101

Benn was able to help a victim of McCarthyism in Dr Joe Cort, who contacted him in 1954. He had been a member of the Communist Party while a medical student at Yale. When the McCarthy's Un-American Activities Committee began its investigation into American schools and colleges he began to find life difficult. Four American universities which had offered him assistant professorships withdrew their offers. All he could do was to leave the country. He went to England with his wife Ruth, also a doctor, and worked in a research post at Cambridge University before obtaining a job at Birmingham University.

In the US he had been rejected for military service because of his residual polio and TB, serious allergic reactions and very poor eyesight. The US authorities, however, now wanted to recall him, ostensibly to subject him to a further examination to assess whether his exemption from military service on medical grounds was still valid. His defenders in Britain, including Benn and Michael Foot, believed that returning him to the US would only result in his persecution.

Cort sought political asylum, but the Home Secretary refused his request. Benn wrote in *Reynolds News*, 'The Home Secretary has become the unconscious agent for the McCarthy mood and the McCarran Nationality Law. At a time when Britain should be preserved as a haven for those who are buffeted about in this age of suspicion and intolerance, he is unwittingly co-operating with the witch-hunters.'[23]

As the Corts were Jewish, Benn tried to encourage Israel to accept them, but the Israelis, somewhat dependent on American goodwill despite their need for immigrants, declined. Eventually the Corts sought, and were granted, political asylum in Czechoslovakia.

After the Corts had accepted the offer, Benn still wanted to pursue the matter in order to oblige the Home Secretary to justify his actions. Benn raised the case in the House of Commons, ironically enough on the day when, in the US, Senator Ralph Flanders of Vermont was moving a motion of censure on McCarthy. His voice quivering with emotion, Benn read out the letter Cort had sent him announcing their decision to go to Czechoslovakia. He said that when he read the letter the utter absurdity of the Home Secretary's decision came home to him; 'Here is a man whose only offence was that he was a Communist as an undergraduate. Yet the apparatus of two modern states is turned on him to hound him out and hound him behind the Iron Curtain. . . . This is an unhappy story and to the extent to which this country and this government are responsible for making it an unhappy one, it is one of which the whole House should be ashamed.'[24]

Benn went to the docks to see Joe and Ruth Cort off. The Corts went to Prague, where Joe became a distinguished doctor, but he continued fighting his case in order to reclaim his passport, seized by the US government. The case went to the Supreme Court, where he was finally successful and he was able to return to America. He called on Benn in the 1980s, prosperous and reconciled to capitalism, now working for a private medical insurance company.

Another battle against McCarthyism, this time joined by Benn and his father, was the Paul Garland case, an almost comic example of the British establishment calling out the Home Guard to kill a mouse. Paul Garland was a nineteen-year-old boy scout from Brislington, Bristol. By all accounts he was an exemplary scout, but his father was a Communist and he became one too. Garland was ordered out of the Scouts and told to return his badges, including, he said dolefully, 'the coveted Queen's Scout badge which it had been my privilege and pride to wear since the time it was awarded to me'.[25]

There was no sympathy from some quarters. A *Bristol Evening World* writer was disgusted that Garland 'wants to continue a political association which is rank poison to everything scouting represents' and advised, 'let him remember his scouting vows and do the decent thing'.[26]

This farce took on decidedly sinister overtones when it became known that a BBC West of England regional broadcast on the subject was planned. E. F. Beckett, chairman of the North Dorset Conservative Association, leaped into action to combat this threat to liberty with a telegram to all Conservative MPs proclaiming, 'Strongly protest BBC invitation to Communist ex-Boy Scout broadcast West Regional tonight.' The rallying call stirred R. F. Crouch, Conservative MP for North Dorset, who contacted his party Whip, the assistant Postmaster General and the Director General of the BBC. The free world was saved, the Bristol boy scout was banned.

Tony Benn tried to shame the Chief Scout, Lord Rowallan, into discussing the issue but he refused: 'Regret impossible spare time for debate' ran the telegram. 'Overwhelming support since facts were known makes this unnecessary.' Benn commented, 'The argument that the debate is unnecessary seems to me to be bunk. I think people are generally divided on the issue. As for the Chief Scout not having time to debate the issue, when for the first time since the scouts were founded a person has been dismissed for political reasons, it is a disgrace to the movement.'[27] Viscount Stansgate did, however, challenge Rowallan in the Lords, condemning the imposition of political tests in the Boy Scout Movement as 'foreign to its character and purpose and repugnant to our national tradition of liberty of conscience'. Members of the establishment were thus obliged, in the course of four hours of debate, to attempt to justify their position, an exercise which at least made it more difficult for them to take such vindictive action in the future.

Garland became district secretary of the West of England Young Communist League, which doubtless had a more congenial atmosphere for him, and the issue died down. He later became a manager for the Co-op and a leader of the Great Western Marching Band, 'which would parade through Bristol on May Day', Benn remembered, 'with Paul and the rest of them dressed as matelots marching to an Alexander Ragtime Band version of the Red Flag.'[28]

Tony Benn and his father also gave support to the victims of McCarthyism. Father and son were both members of a committee which protested to the US government when the passport of Paul Robeson, the negro singer and actor, was removed because of his Communist sympathies. When Robeson visited England, Tony Benn showed him around the Commons, and his father was his guide in the Lords. 'He does more to popularise the United States throughout the world when he sings one song, than poor Mr Dulles [the US Secretary of State] does in a dozen conferences,' wrote Benn.[29]

Father and son were frequently able to act in concert on such subjects. They were the closest of confidants, to be found together to such an extent that when Tony Benn left the Commons chamber the policeman on duty would tell him where his father was without waiting to be asked. Viscount Stansgate was sometimes jocularly called Big Benn, but much more often he was called by the name by which he had been known all his parliamentary life, Wedgie. He was once referred to as 'a Bevan boy in ermine' and he was certainly closer to the Labour left than to the leadership. In the House of Lords this frequently put him in a minority of one, a fact he noted when, speaking on a motion for which he could not even find a seconder,[30] he recited a line from the nonconformist Sunday school hymn, 'Dare to be a Daniel, dare to stand alone'.

Wedgwood Benn's elder brother Ernest died in January 1954. *The Times* described him, not without affection, as 'an unrepentant individualist in an age when all parties accept the fundamental tenets of collectivism'.[31] It was a reminder that all mortals must perish and this included Wedgwood Benn, whose death would leave a peerage which it would be incumbent upon Benn to inherit.

9

A First Assault on the Peerage

Both the major parties fought lacklustre campaigns for the May 1955 election, though the Tory Party organisation was far superior to that of Labour, in addition to being better funded (as it always was). Both parties urged top-level meetings to discuss the parlous international situation, now that both NATO and the countries of the new Warsaw Pact were armed with the H-bomb and the cold war showed no signs of a thaw. The Conservatives offered more 'Butskellism' and continued economic improvement. Labour offered the same but with added nationalisation. The party leadership had never attempted to transmit to the voters any passion for nationalisation, and this election was no exception. For the first time in almost a century the government increased its majority at a general election. The Tory overall majority in the Commons was increased from seventeen in 1951 to fifty-eight. The Conservative poll was down by 400,000 compared with 1951, but Labour's vote had fallen by more than one and a half million.

This was the last of the 'old-style' elections before television took over as the primary source of political information. Benn made a proposal for a radical new format in election broadcasts, but it was ahead of its time and was rejected in favour of the old 'point and spout' method: a politician would be pointed at the camera and then talk for ten minutes. His proposals were substantially accepted at the next general election.

Benn mounted his usual energetic campaign in Bristol South-East. Boundary changes had altered the constituency. Hengrove ward had gone, but Benn gained Kingswood and Stockwood wards, so he had 21,000 new voters to become acquainted with. These changes produced a net loss of 3000 electors, however, which in part accounted for the reduction in his majority of 6209. In part, too, he was suffering from the national decline in the Labour vote and from the decline in the numbers of people voting – his was a 78 per cent turnout as compared with 84 per cent in 1951. He now had a 59.5 per cent share of the total vote cast, however, compared to 65 per cent at the previous election. Nonetheless, he had been returned to the House of Commons for the third time. Each time could be the last unless he were able to divest himself of the peerage, and in 1955 his father was seventy-eight. Father, son and their supporters had already made some attempts at reform.

The Labour Party did not approve of reform of the Lords, on the ground that the more absurd and anachronistic the institution was, the easier it would be to abolish it completely. Any reform which helped bring the Lords up to date would entrench it even deeper into the fabric of the constitution. Some stood out against this notion. Reggie Paget, Benn's colleague from the Bing Group, was a somewhat unconventional MP; few Labour members have been a Master of Foxhounds, as Paget was for thirteen years. Paget, who was himself to be ennobled in 1974, introduced a Bill on 11 February 1953 which provided that peers would be excluded from sitting in the Commons only after they had taken the oath in the Lords. This would have meant that they could sit in the Commons as long as they were re-elected and could choose when to go to the Lords. This Ten-Minute Rule Bill, though unsuccessful, was the first attempt at reform which dealt specifically with Benn's problem.

It was a problem he shared with eight other MPs, all Tories. Some Conservatives, like Lord Hailsham, who had reluctantly succeeded to a peerage in 1950, clearly saw in Benn a symbol of their own hopes. 'It is surely intolerable', wrote Hailsham in the *Daily Express* in 1954, 'that generations of young men, sincere and able like Mr Benn, should be deprived of their rights of citizenship and an equal opportunity to use their abilities in the service of their country.'[1]

Hailsham, an unlikely adviser on socialist strategy, suggested that Benn should mobilise the Labour Party to support an amendment which would allow peers who renounced their peerage for life to sit in the Commons. In a Machiavellian aside the future Lord Chancellor told Benn to tell the Labour Party, 'If you really want to weaken the House of Lords, let the able young peers try for the Commons. All the good ones will prefer this and the Lords will be left with the second-rate people.'²

Somewhere in the maze of constitutional law, Benn thought, there had to be a solution, just one loophole through which he could slip. He found a clue in *Halsbury's Laws of England* in a passage on peerage law. No one, it said, could refuse a peerage. But a footnote led him to an Act of 1917, which had embodied Parliament's feelings, during the First World War, that despite the close links between the British and German nobility, German peers should not continue to enjoy the benefits of sitting in the House of Lords. He based his own proposal on this Act and sought personal precedents.

Benn next spoke to Attlee about it, then let it be known to the press in December 1954 that he wished to renounce the peerage. The instrument of renunciation he had drawn up declared that his eldest son should become Lord Stansgate on the current Lord Stansgate's death. On reflection he realised that the burden of a viscountcy might be too great for Stephen's three-year-old shoulders and he altered it to have the title held 'in abeyance'. He signed the instrument of renunciation on 15 February 1955, witnessed by Clem Attlee, Nye Bevan, Roy Jenkins and Joe Grimond, the Liberal leader, another unlikely ally for Benn. Three days later he appeared before a Personal Bills Committee of the House of Lords bearing the Wedgwood Benn Renunciation Bill. This is a procedure, in fact open to everyone but rarely used, whereby an individual can ask the Crown for a Bill to be brought forward for his benefit alone.

Benn had spent three months preparing for this. Now in the Moses Room of the House of Lords, watched by his father and Caroline, Benn presented his case for ninety minutes. It is open to question whether his eloquence did him any good. It has been suggested that the six peers who heard the petition might have been reluctant to lose such a talented recruit, albeit a pressed man.

The principal precedent for his case was that of Lord De La Warr in 1549. He had no sons, so his heir was his nephew, William West, whom he took to live with him. William West had the opposite problem from Tony Benn: he was so anxious to accelerate his accession that he decided to poison his uncle. Lord De La Warr narrowly escaped with his life and successfully petitioned Parliament to have West excluded from the peerage. 'If you are anxious for me to follow precedents exactly,' remarked Benn, 'I could always attempt to poison my father.'

Caroline Benn too had to sign a consent that she gave up what many young women would consider a great honour. The case attracted attention to Caroline, which she handled with all the patience she could muster, but she found the situation ridiculous. 'Like most Americans I find the titled world just make-believe – it went out with the powdered wig and the buckled shoe,' she told the women's page of the *Sunday Mirror*. 'It is romantic and charming but slightly ludicrous.'[3]

The Lords rejected Benn's application. It was not a personal issue affecting him alone, they stated, but dealt with a vital constitutional matter. Therefore it could not go forward as a Personal Bill. It was not a popular cause in the Parliamentary Labour Party. George Brown took the time to tell Benn why. He approached Benn in the Commons tea room after the verdict was announced and said, 'I'm glad you've lost. You with you middle class . . . now you're paying the price and it serves you right. You would never have got anywhere without the advantage of being your father's son and it will do you good to suffer from the disadvantages.'[4]

Now Lord Stansgate introduced the same Bill into the House of Lords, though no longer referring to it as a Personal Bill. This was an avenue to which he had always had access, but it had been felt that tactically Tony Benn's lone appeal was more likely to gain support. Now there was nothing to lose. Benn senior pleaded his son's case in characteristically passionate oratory. The situation his family found itself in had 'heaped on to the unwilling shoulders of this young man honours which were going to bar him from all his ambitions. He cannot afford to come here and he wants to go on serving his constituents. He is not of noble blood. He is a commoner and wants to remain a commoner.'[5]

As a trump card Lord Stansgate produced a letter from Winston Churchill, who had himself refused a peerage because it might bar the political ambitions of his descendants. Writing to Tony Benn he had said, 'I am personally strongly in favour of sons having the right to renounce irrevocably the peerage they inherit from their fathers. This would not, of course, prevent them from accepting another peerage if they were offered one later on.' Tony Benn later saw Churchill in the Commons and thanked him for his support. It was a sticky moment for the young man. 'I thought he was going to fall over and I was going to have to catch him. I think he'd had a drop too much to drink,' he said.[6]

Yet neither the expression of opinion by the elder statesman nor support from all parties in the Lords could prevail upon the majority. Viscount Stansgate's motion was defeated by 52 votes to 24.

On the same day Tony Benn presented a petition in the House of Commons – really a ploy to attract attention to the issue, since the pace of the Commons is considerably more hectic than that of the Lords and there was no chance of there being time to debate it.

That exhausted the possibility of using Personal Bills to achieve renunciation. The tenacious Benn had already been preparing another line of attack. Not for nothing did the newspaper cartoons picture him being dragged kicking and screaming into the House of Lords by a crowd of coroneted and ermined peers.

The other people affected by this issue, apart from the Benn family, were the electors of Bristol. Why should they be prevented from choosing Benn as their MP? Benn had already laid the ground for this with his supporters in Bristol. Mervyn Stockwood, then Councillor the Revd Canon Mervyn Stockwood, moved a petition to Parliament at the Bristol City Council meeting of 8 February 1955. It prayed that legislation could be brought forward to enable Benn 'to renounce irrevocably his right of succession to the title of Viscount Stansgate in the county of Essex to which he is Heir Male and thus make him still eligible to serve in the interests of the city'. It was passed with no opposition, the Conservative side preferring to abstain.[7] Benn introduced the petition in the Commons on 29 April with no greater success than before, but it squeezed out of the issue a little more publicity. He had to keep the subject alive and he had to ensure that the people of Bristol understood the issue at stake, for their support would be needed.

Now that action in the House of Lords and the Commons had failed, he set about changing the House of Lords itself. First he had to explain to his colleagues what was necessary. His most creative offering was a pamphlet for the Fabian Society called *The Privy*

Council as a Second Chamber, published in December 1956. The Fabian Society, to which Benn belonged, was a group of intellectuals who shared the belief that, because socialism was the most just and efficient method of organising society, it would achieve pre-eminence by a series of slow reforms. This 'inevitability of gradual-ness' was symbolised by a logo of a red tortoise forging ahead, dumbly raising the reptilian equivalent of a clenched fist.

Benn argued that Privy Councillors, constitutionally the advisers to the monarch, could form a new, replacement upper chamber. All those Privy Councillors who were not peers would be appointed to the Lords and all those peers who were not Privy Councillors would be excluded – thus abolishing the hereditary principle but keeping a much needed second chamber for fine tuning of legislation, which is frequently rushed through the Commons in an inchoate state.

The arguments had first been presented in a *New Statesman* article and the reaction of Jennie Lee was typical. Benn had been tipped off that Lee was angry about the proposal so he asked if he could sit beside her at supper in the Commons canteen. He wrote in his diary:

> It was a typical talk with Jennie. She had not read my article except to convince herself by a glance that I must be saying the sort of things she would expect me to say. This was enough for her to set in motion her sacred socialist principle. She therefore began lecturing me in an intolerable way and I decided to hit back – and hit back hard. Her argument was roughly this: 'The Lords perpetuate class and snobbery. My scheme is just another sort of Lords reform. It is very unsocialist. It will give great patronage to the leader. I am playing the Tory game.'

Benn convinced her that his scheme involved the abolition of the House of Lords. 'The argument therefore proceeded from there in the technical case for a second chamber. She had said that Privy Councillors were snob appointments. I asked her why Nye [her husband, Nye Bevan] had taken one. She could not answer. She said that socialism meant selecting everybody and not appointing. I asked if she was in favour of an elected cabinet; she was not.'[8] Lee was partially convinced, but when the Fabian Society pamphlet came out she rejected it in an article in *Tribune*, the paper of the left wing Tribune Group, claiming that Benn's proposal would produce an overwhelmingly Conservative second chamber and that 'There is still only one answer for the Lords' – that is, straightforward abolition.[9] She accepted a peerage herself in 1970.

Nor was the right any more supportive, for they were in favour of keeping the Lords with improvements which would render it more acceptable. The improvements came. Provision was made for peers to receive expenses of three guineas a day in 1957. Soon the 1958 Life Peerages Act allowed life peerages to be conferred on the worthy and permitted the seating there of peeresses in their own right, thus revitalising the Lords with new blood from any field in society, while retaining all the worst aspects of the old hereditary system. Another Bing Group colleague, Leslie Hale, wished to know if the new life peers would have the same privileges as hereditary peers, including the right to be hanged by a silken rope, where appropriate.

Benn called these measures 'a piece of political repair work, designed to establish for the House of Lords the respectability which it lacks'.[10] Labour opposition even to discussing reform of the Lords had not prevented these measures but merely meant that the reform was carried out entirely on Tory terms. The Labour Party should have been more constructive over a reform which was anyway inevitable, given the Conservative majority.

The arguments against an entirely hereditary, male House which one had to be rich to attend were now gone. There was no reason why the House of Lords should not survive into the next century. Benn was disconsolate – reform had stifled revolution, as it has a tendency to do. 'Yet one must look on the bright side,' he wrote in his diary, 'and recognise that the Lords with pay are a little bit better than the Lords without. Anyway the battle is not yet finally lost.'[11]

Meanwhile Benn ploughed on with solid parliamentary work. He came first in the ballot for Private Members' Motions in June 1956. It is one of those aspects of the British constitution which are difficult to explain, particularly to foreigners, but fundamentally the procedure is this: once the government has occupied the House with its legislation and other business, there is not enough time left for everyone who wishes to raise issues which concern them. There is therefore a ballot for Private Members' Bills or Motions. Legislation thus has a chance of being passed not on the basis of merit or superiority over other legislation but because its mover has come first in a lottery.

The legislation has a real chance only if it enjoys government support, because the amount of time allotted to Private Members' Bills is insufficient and always requires an allocation of government time. Alternatively, with no government assistance, the procedure can be used to introduce legislation designed to draw attention to a major issue: it has no chance of success. Unsurprisingly, Benn chose the latter course. In a speech he called 'Can We Humanise the State?' Benn proposed a commission of inquiry to investigate the public relations of public authorities. He scourged the poor service which government offices gave to the public: the use of jargon where plain English would do, the shabby design of offices where the public were seen; the generally unhelpful nature of the civil service bureaucracy, which was, after all, paid by the public to serve the public. 'If we are to put flesh and blood on the democratic skeleton,' he said, 'we must look again at the whole question of the way the state treats the individual.'[12]

The speech certainly succeeded in stimulating discussion on the topic. Benn received glowing press reports in every paper, particularly for his inventive approach to the subject: he had written to twenty-eight public authorities to see how they would acknowledge a letter from plain Mr Benn, asking the Ministry of Labour for example how he could become a coal miner or the Home Office how he could become a British subject.

In another use of Commons procedure (in this case a 'Presentation Bill') to draw attention to an issue, he introduced a Human Rights Bill in February 1958 which would have conferred upon the Secretary of State for the Colonies the right to establish Human Rights Commissions in all British colonies and territories. This was only putting into practice the preamble to the Universal Declaration of Human Rights which Britain had signed in 1948. Such a Bill could proceed only if there were no opposition at all and a Conservative MP 'talked out' the Bill with ridicule. But the point was made.

Benn's most courageous action in parliamentary terms was a vote of censure on the Speaker. This was an audacious procedure for any member to adopt. For one of the youngest members of the House it was a shocking impertinence.

His action had its source in a major international issue. In June 1957 British land and air forces were sent to Muscat and Oman to help the Sultan to suppress a rebellion led by the Imam of Oman. Benn and several MPs attempted to discuss this situation in the House of Commons, calling for a debate under Standing Order 9, which allows for emergency debates on matters of urgent public importance. The Speaker ruled that he would not permit such a debate. Benn found this an unacceptable restriction of the rights of back-benchers. He put down a motion 'regretting' the Speaker's decision, in effect a vote of no confidence in the chair. As a motion of no confidence must be heard before anything else, as soon as he had declared he was putting it down the House was obliged to give it time, though it did so with very ill grace.

The *Spectator*'s parliamentary sketch writer, Bernard Levin, remarked, 'I never heard the Speaker less sure of himself than in rejecting Mr Benn's attempt to move the adjournment under Standing Order 9, but at the age of 32 one would have to be pretty pompous to announce the following day that one has in consequence put down a motion censuring the Speaker.'[13] The probability of ignominious failure was high.

Benn described it at the time: 'It's the most terrifying thing an MP can do. An ordinary speech is bad enough for getting butterflies in your stomach. But this is infinitely worse. You feel the whole House is against you. The Speaker frowns. Your legs turn to lead as if to hold you forcibly to your seat. Everything inside you says, "Sit down – let it go – you've done your best – it's not worth it." '[14] Nor were the voices only inside him; members on both sides were restless and irritated. 'He looked like foundering amid indifference and hostility,' one parliamentary correspondent wrote. When he announced, several minutes into his speech, that he did not even intend to vote for his motion himself, but would ask permission to withdraw it, the mutterings and groans of impatience were by no means confined to the Tory side. This young man was just a time-waster.

He embarked on a history lecture starting in 1882, when Gladstone first introduced limitations on the rights of members to move adjournment debates; he gave a lesson on the language of Standing Order 9 and the precise meaning of each word; he compared the Speaker's recent decision with these rigorous standards and found the Speaker wanting. 'It was', wrote Bernard Levin the following week, 'eloquent beyond the farthest reach of all but a hand-count of his fellow-members; it was witty, graceful, modest, learned, pointed and in some ways deeply moving.'[15]

'It is not the vote at the end of the day that limits our right,' said Benn to increasing Opposition cheers. 'It is the right of free thought and free speech that is left unfettered by the party system. If you, Mr Speaker, give a ruling which means that an individual back-bencher cannot raise a point, even within standing orders, without the support of his party, then you give to the party a power over the members which I believe would be an imposition on the rights of the House.'[16]

In the peer's gallery the tiny, white-haired figure of Viscount Stansgate watched proudly as the House cheered his son loud and long.

A list of Benn's glittering moments in the House of Commons implies that, whenever he stood up, he spoke and was listened to with rapt attention. Yet there was as much boredom and frustration in the parliamentary life of Tony Benn as in that of any other new member, as he himself explained in the *Bristol Evening World* in November 1957. Eager to speak in a debate on the future of Central Africa, for which country the British government proposed a constitution with forty-four seats in the Parliament allocated to the quarter of a million Europeans and only twelve to the seven million Africans, he spent the weekend working on his speech, putting in thirty hours' work in two and a half days. 'The family didn't get a look-in,' he lamented. 'At 3.30 on Monday afternoon I slumped exhausted into my seat in the House of Commons and I sat there for six hours or more without even going out for tea. Every time a member finished his speech I jumped to my feet clutching my notes and ready to divulge my wisdom to the House. And every blessed time the Speaker called someone else.'[17]

10

The Suez Campaign

Tony Benn enjoyed a relationship with the Middle East stretching back to his own wartime service and, beyond that, to his parents' familiarity with the area. Benn was well placed to understand the implications of the Suez troubles festering through the 1950s. He would have been better placed had he been able to go on a planned visit to Egypt in the 1953 Christmas recess. He was one of ten MPs who were invited to Egypt, with unofficial Foreign Office approval, by the then ruler General Neguib.

British troops had been on Egyptian soil for almost seventy-five years protecting British interests in the region. Their removal had been one of the major demands made by the officers who seized power from King Farouk in 1952. Negotiations over the withdrawal of the 83,000 troops were becoming increasingly acrimonious in late 1953 and Anthony Eden, then Foreign Secretary, requested that the all-party group should not follow through their acceptance of Neguib's invitation. The press too was bellicose, the *Daily Express* commenting, 'It is intolerable that any group should go off at the expense of a government with which Britain is involved in a bitter and critical diplomatic dispute.'[1]

The five Conservatives pulled out, leaving the Labour members to face increasing antagonism alone. Before long, they too felt obliged to withdraw. 'It was a rather gutless thing to do,' Benn said in later years. 'There was tremendous hostility in the press but I very much regret doing it.'[2] He did visit Israel, however, with Caroline, in April 1956. He was able to witness at first hand the preparations for war throughout that beleaguered country and the threats which Israel faced.

After enraging Egypt by her bellicose approach Britain had, of course, backed down and agreed to withdraw the troops, Anthony Eden having thus secured by diplomacy the worst of all possible worlds: retreat and ill-will. Benn described it in a BBC discussion after the Conservative Party conference in 1955: 'The Conservative Party still believes that there's a military and strategic answer to all these problems. And you know, all the experience of the last few years – indeed the last fifty years – shows that isn't true at all. Take the case of Egypt. We are going to be tough with Egypt, we stay in Egypt. The result is that in the end we are pushed out of Egypt, and Egyptians set their own independence and try to make arrangements with the Russians. . . . This is what makes the whole Conservative approach to foreign affairs such absolute nonsense. You are tough, and then you scuttle.' Prophetic words, though Enoch Powell's response was apposite, that listening to Benn, 'you'd think that the Labour Party had the secret of relations with the Middle East'.[3]

In Egypt a new coup brought Colonel Gamal Abdul Nasser to the fore with an even more aggressive approach to the nation's problems. Nasser, like Mussadeq, had learned the lesson of nationalisation. In July 1956 he nationalised shares in the Suez Canal to pay for the building of the Aswan Dam across the Nile. This was to have been built with British and American help, but both those countries had pulled out.

Suez was a particular embarrassment to the Labour Party. Almost everyone in the party agreed in principle with Nasser's act of nationalisation, but even Nye Bevan was so critical of Nasser that it was impossible for him wholeheartedly to oppose Eden. 'Nasser's a thug,' he said, 'and he needs to be taught a lesson.'[4]

In a speech of bitter denunciation on 2 August, Gaitskell compared Nasser to Hitler and Mussolini. He was wildly cheered by the Conservatives but heard in near silence by the benches behind him. Benn wrote in his diary, 'I felt so sick as I listened. I wanted to shout "Shame". I very nearly did buttonhole him afterwards and say that his speech had made me want to vomit.'[5] In his capacity as a member of the Labour back-bench Foreign Affairs Group he went to see Gaitskell on 3 August with similarly minded colleagues to encourage him to oppose the government on the issue.

Gaitskell wrote in his diary, 'I decided to ask this committee to come along partly in order to smooth them down and make them feel they had been consulted' that is, he was not consulting them. He went on to comment, 'Tony Benn, although talented in many ways, a good speaker and a man of ideas, had extraordinarily poor judgement. He is the last person in the world I would go to for advice on policy.'[6] That Gaitskell might even consider going to a man of thirty-one with no government or even front-bench experience for policy advice seems rather more remarkable than that he would decide not to do so.

The British and French governments, confident of popular support, started making plans to invade Egypt on 10 August. All they lacked was a pretext. The Egyptians had not stopped shipping; on the contrary, Egyptian pilots were running traffic on the canal with great efficiency. No one had even been hurt, let alone killed over the nationalisation. All it meant was that the revenue from running the canal would go to Egypt instead of Britain. Share owners would be compensated. For all the fury provoked by Nasser's tweaking of the old imperialists' noses, it would be hard to sacrifice the lives of Europeans, or even Egyptians, on a question of legality.

As tension mounted, Benn called a meeting of the executive of Bristol South-East Labour Party for noon on Saturday, 18 August, to make sure of their support. In a statement released soon after he said, 'The real issue is very simple. Egypt is a poor country which since 1882 has been fully or partly occupied by British troops. Now free, she is anxious to raise her living standards. Without the Aswan Dam she cannot succeed. In deciding to make full use of her few resources for the good of her country, she deserves the support of the British people.'[7]

He wrote to Gaitskell to strengthen his resolve, stressing the proper legal channels to which Britain had access in order to settle the dispute. It was the illegality of Britain's threatened action to which Benn drew attention in a Commons speech on Suez on 13 September after the Prime Minister had refused to rule out military force. The correct path would be to take the matter to the International Court of the United Nations, but this the government refused to do. Its belligerence was playing into the hands of the Communists: 'I am tempted to put a wreath on Karl Marx's grave tonight with the inscription, "With love from Anthony Eden." ' He could see no reason why, if Britain invaded Egypt, the United Nations should not move in, as it had done in Korea, to drive Britain out.

If Britain were to go to war over Suez, it would be 'a war without national unity at home and allies abroad prepared to support us in it. It would be a war without purpose and without hope and for all we know a war without end as well. I say quite sincerely to the Prime Minister that even if he succeeds in the short run, which is by no means certain, it can never succeed in the long run. I believe that it will bring disgrace, dishonour and possibly disaster to this country.'[8]

Mid-September also saw a march and a rally in Trafalgar Square against the threat of war. Benn spoke, but it was to no avail. Plans were far advanced and eventually a *casus belli* was found: the Israelis invaded Egypt on 29 October and a joint British and French force was sent to keep the peace.

In the meantime Benn's mind had been absorbed by another international crisis. Demonstrations throughout Hungary from 23 October had led to open revolt against Soviet domination. Many of their actions were symbolic: they removed the red star on the Parliament buildings and replaced it with the Hungarian flag; and they dismantled the statue of Stalin in Stalin Square. Fighting began to spread throughout the country, Hungarians attacking Russian tanks with their bare hands. Then Hungarian troops began to join the rebels. For a time it seemed they might break free.

Benn decided to try to get an adjournment debate on the matter. He worked most of the night of 28 October and the morning of the next day on it and called Gaitskell to ask him to take it up as a front-bench issue. Gaitskell summoned him and other Labour members involved in foreign affairs after lunch. The consensus was that they might not be successful in getting an adjournment and a failure might be interpreted abroad as a divided approach. Benn noted in his diary: 'They also feared that a debate might lead to the expression of damaging opinions from left and right extremists which again might harm our capacity to help. I greatly resented all this but on reflection they may well have been right.'[9]

Practical as ever, Benn asked the Foreign Secretary in the House to make provision for the British people to send blood, relief and money to show solidarity with the Hungarians. The Foreign Secretary's mind was on other things. Israel was launching her attack on Egypt.

The complete entry for Benn's diary on 31 October shows his range of contacts, his grasp of the possibilities for political action and his astounding energy:

> First thing this morning I made a list of jobs which seemed to require urgent action.
>
> 1. To get a meeting organised in Bristol by the borough party [the coordinating body for all five Bristol constituencies] so that the protest could be made forcibly and immediately. Bill Waring, the secretary, fell in at once with the plan and I promised him a national speaker in addition to the Bristol members. Later today I persuaded John Strachey to do it.
>
> 2. I rang up the United Nations Association and urged them to launch a national memorial addressed to the Prime Minister. I gather that this was set in hand and the General Council of the UNA this afternoon issued a statement of view in the strongest possible terms.
>
> 3. I rang the Movement for Colonial Freedom and asked them to book Trafalgar Square for a rally on Sunday afternoon. This they did at once and the meeting was handed over to the Labour Party the same day.
>
> 4. I rang the Propaganda Officer at Transport House, Ken Peay, and suggested that the Labour Party undertake a national campaign. Apparently this is under way. Certainly the Bristol and Trafalgar Square meetings are the first to have been arranged, which is most satisfying.
>
> 5. I began drafting a petition for general signature to be signed at these meetings and presented in the House.
>
> 6. I telegraphed the Arab Society in Cambridge whose meeting I had promised to address on Friday suggested that it be united with Kenneth Younger's meeting for the Labour Club and with any other societies who were willing to take part. This was agreed.

At an electrifying meeting of the Parliamentary Labour Party Gaitskell, finally spurred into action, announced a motion of censure on the government and a national campaign 'in complete and utter opposition to this war. He warned us that we would be vilified and attacked as traitors.'[10]

Mindful of this, Benn made sure in his speech in the House to go out of his way to praise the gallantry of the troops being landed or dropped into Egypt, but, he said, 'the one thing which our troops need, which they have not had, is an argument as to why they should be engaged in these operations. The reason why our troops are in this critical difficulty tonight is that from nobody, neither from the government front bench nor from the back benches opposite, have we had a coherent argument to encourage our troops which will stand up to even today's test, let alone the test of time. It is because my Right Hon. and Hon. Friends and I feel that to put troops in any illegal war of aggression is a crime against those troops that we have moved our motion of censure in the House tonight.' Benn thought it the best speech he had ever made, which was the more remarkable because, though it lasted twenty minutes, it was delivered with hardly any notes; he had had time to scribble only four headings on a piece of paper.

Earlier that day he had called the Egyptian Embassy to urge Cairo not to withdraw from the United Nations because of that organisation's failure to help her, as it had been reported she was to do.

Nor was his activity limited to the Labour or even the Egyptian side. Back-bench Conservatives, shocked at the shameful behaviour of the government, had asked Benn what they should do. Benn approached Sir Walter Monckton, who had resigned as Minister of Defence over preparations for Suez but had loyally given 'health reasons' for his decision.[11] Monckton, MP for Bristol West, a Christian and, like Benn, a friend of Mervyn Stockwood, was pleased to see him, greatly appreciating the sympathy which Benn extended even to opponents in times of such moral decay. But Monckton had personal loyalties too, to Eden and Macmillan, and could not bring himself to lead the back-bench opposition to Suez. It would have been profoundly embarrassing for him if the subject of this meeting had leaked out, so Benn spoke to nobody about it except Caroline and his brother David, who were his main confidants in all he did.

Also on 1 November Benn and five other members cabled the Israeli Prime Minister David Ben-Gurion in Jerusalem with the message: 'Undersigned six Labour MPs lifelong friends of Israel urge immediate public assurance that object of Israeli action limited to protection of Israeli frontiers and elimination of Egyptian

121

marauders and raiders and has no connection with British action about Suez Canal.'

It was particularly difficult for Jewish MPs like Sydney Silverman and Ian Mikardo to send such a message, and they deserved better than Ben-Gurion's reply:

> The Egyptian dictator has constantly violated the armistice agreement, has organised bands of murderers in his own and other Arab countries to attack our people, has maintained a blockade against us in Suez and the Red Sea contrary to international law, has organised military alliances against us and declared his determination to wipe us out. We still recall that there were leaders of the Labour Party who did not take seriously Hitler's threats physically to exterminate the Jewish race until it was too late. Six million Jews perished in the gas chambers of the Nazi dictator. I am sorry that you do not see the danger of the Fascist dictator of Egypt.'[12]

On Friday, 2 November, Benn turned his attention to the national campaign, for which he coined the slogan 'Law Not War'. He dictated the national petition and had it duplicated and distributed, then went out to buy yards of blue and white ribbon and hundreds of safety pins for making buttonholes in United Nations colours. That afternoon he travelled to Cambridge to address the Arab Society meeting, which had, at his request, been expanded to a general public meeting and was being held in the Cambridge Union building.

A graduate student of Benn's own age with family in Egypt cried throughout the dinner which preceded the meeting. Outside the hall a crowd thirty deep struggled to get in. Inside it was pandemonium; every foot of space in the chamber was occupied and scores of people piled up on the window ledges, on the arms of seats and on the floor. Opponents of the war were vastly outnumbered by students with 'Support Eden Not Nasser' posters who even stole the United Nations flag. The influence of the extreme right-wing League of Empire Loyalists was in evidence. The crowd prevented the chairman from speaking by singing 'Rule Britannia' and there was chaos for fifteen minutes when the overflow of students from outside broke through the doors and took up the already crowded space on the floor.

Benn wrote: 'The crowd of students laughing and screaming for war gave me an icy hatred of them. The uproar and noise and silly funny remarks when the world was on the brink of disaster was completely revolting, disgusting and shameful.' When he rose to speak he was showered with missiles and howled down. He was pelted with lavatory paper, stink bombs and rotten fruit, a deluge which swept away his notes. He bought time by promising to answer questions at the end and spoke for an hour. But it was a battle against the odds. The *Cambridge Daily News* reported, 'Amid this terrific row Mr Benn went on to level bitter attacks on Sir Anthony Eden for leading the country to be an aggressor on Egypt. . . . He concluded by saying he hoped that all the people of this country would unite and march solidly behind the blue and white colours of the United Nations in protest and in shame for what was going on in Egypt in the name of Britain.'[13]

On the international stage Britain was floundering. That day an American resolution demanding a cease-fire was passed at the United Nations by 64 votes to 5 and America began to plan economic sanctions against her two principal allies. President Eisenhower, in the last days of an election campaign, was angry because initially he had not been informed and then had actually been misled by the British. Moreover, this example of European imperialism in Africa distracted attention from Soviet imperialism in Europe. In the days before Vietnam, America could make some claim to a moral superiority which her allies were now betraying.

Gaitskell rang up Benn on the Saturday morning, 3 November. Gaitskell knew that Anthony Eden was to broadcast that evening and wanted Benn to arrange a reply the following evening. The BBC had long-standing arrangements for ministerial broadcasts in which the Minister of Transport would advise safe driving or the Postmaster General would recommend posting early for Christmas. If a ministerial broadcast were controversial, however, the spokesman of the Opposition would be given the right to reply. Up to 1956, however, it had not been felt necessary to exercise this right. Only the Chancellor's annual Budget speech was always subject to a reply.

Benn telephoned Harman Grisewood, chief assistant to the Director General of the BBC. Grisewood resented any assumption that the BBC would give the Opposition a right of reply to a ministerial broadcast. Benn was told to go through the usual channels, which were for the two Chief Whips to discuss the issue and for the Opposition to ask the government for the right of reply. The BBC would then broadcast the reply or would adjudicate if the government refused.

Benn explained to Grisewood that in the event of a government refusal, which was the most likely outcome of the 'usual channels', a BBC decision would have to be made late that night as they could not know the content of the broadcast until it had gone out. 'That is quite impossible; we shall all be in bed,' said Grisewood.[14] Benn insisted and Grisewood relented, doubtless realising the difficulty he would have in explaining that while cities were being bombed in an undeclared war he was stifling debate on it in the interests of a good night's sleep. He agreed to ask Sir Alexander Cadogan, the Director General of the BBC, to stand by on Saturday night, while Benn was to make hypothetical arrangements with the Television Service for a broadcast to be made on Sunday.

The Whips' discussion went as Benn had expected it would. Edward Heath, the government Chief Whip, would not consent to a right of reply automatically or make the Prime Minister's text available in advance so that discussion could focus on whether a response was appropriate. The most he would do was to be present at Downing Street at 10.30 p.m. to respond if they were to make a request by telephone. A courier would be stationed at 10 Downing Street to take the text of the broadcast to Gaitskell at his home in Hampstead as soon as it was released.

At Benn's suggestion the Labour Party put out a press statement about the government's refusal to grant them an automatic right of reply. The fact that their decision would be made in the public eye would put pressure on the BBC to behave fairly. Benn asked several people to watch Eden's broadcast and be ready for immediate consultation when it finished at 10.15 p.m.

Eden's fifteen-minute broadcast was described by Benn as 'an odious performance to me but effective'. He then received suggestions for the reply, then waited for Gaitskell to call to give the final decision. After half an hour Grisewood rang to find out the position: 'He was miserable and full of self-pity and wanted to go home to bed.' When Benn called the Whip he found that Eden had been keeping them all waiting, finally saying at 11.30 that the government regarded the broadcast as impartial but would not object if the Labour Party asked the BBC for a right of reply. Labour therefore asked Grisewood, who asked Sir Alexander Cadogan. Cadogan said it was too late to reach a decision that night.

Gaitskell was furious and insisted on having Cadogan's number, but his calls were unanswered. After 1 a.m., furious at such high-handed behaviour from a public broadcasting organisation over a fundamental matter of democracy, he telephoned Benn to explain.

The decision came the following morning at about nine o'clock, which denied the Labour Party the right to have its broadcast announced on the 8 and 9 a.m. programme parades. The party immediately issued a press statement and Benn, Woodrow Wyatt (the journalist and Labour MP) and Gaitskell met at Gaitskell's house to put together a text for the broadcast. 'I really felt that at that house at that moment I was in the centre of the world,' wrote Benn.

Benn stayed with Gaitskell through the studio rehearsal and the live broadcast that night. Gaitskell was able to rebut the claim Eden had made that Britain could not afford to wait for a UN Security Council meeting before invading Egypt. The Security Council had met and reached a decision before the British and French ultimatum to Egypt had expired, but the Security Council decision had been blocked by the British and French veto.

Gaitskell's speech got about as close as it could to saying that every single statement by Eden was a lie. 'The Prime Minister has said we were going in to separate the two sides. But you do not separate two armies by bombing airfields and landing troops 100 miles behind one side only. No! This is a second onslaught on a country which was already the victim of an attack. Now a new idea has been put forward. The idea that we are going in to make way for a United Nations force. Nothing was said about this in the ultimatum. Nothing was said about this at the Security Council. If this was the government's plan, why did they not put it forward before?'

In an appeal calculated to establish him as a national leader in this time of crisis he claimed to transcend party loyalties. 'This is not a Labour Party matter. It touches the whole nation – all who care for the rule of law in international affairs, all who put their faith in the United Nations and its Charter, all who care for the good name of our country.' Anthony Eden should resign and Parliament must repudiate the government's policy. But the Labour Party alone could not bring this about. 'The responsibility therefore rests with those Conservatives who, like us, are shocked and troubled by what is happening and who want a change. I appeal to them. Theirs is a difficult decision but I want to say to them that our purpose too rises above party.' He undertook to support a new Prime Minister in halting the invasion of Egypt and complying with the decisions of the United Nations.[15]

Benn noticed that the technicians, who usually were involved in their work or glancing at the sports pages of newspapers, had been listening with rapt attention, even to the rehearsal. After the broadcast Gaitskell signed his script with the words 'A thousand thanks' and gave it to Benn. Later he wrote to Benn, 'If it was effective this was largely due to you, both for the general plan which you suggested and for much of the drafting.' This was somewhat ironic considering his earlier comment on Benn's supposed lack of judgement.

It seems clear from this and from Benn's meeting with Monckton that the idea of an appeal to the Conservatives over the head of the government was Benn's. It was by no means mere rhetoric. As well as Monckton himself, Anthony Nutting resigned as Minister of State for Foreign Affairs when Britain opened fire on Egypt. He later published a memoir of the events, *No End of a Lesson*, which had implications for the publication of other ministerial memoirs, including Benn's own diaries.

Another Conservative Minister to resign was the Economic Secretary to the Treasury, Edward Boyle, Benn's old debating colleague and a man profoundly respected by all who knew him. He was, like Nutting, tipped to become a future leader of the Conservative Party. Benn's Bing Group colleague Reggie Paget said a friendly word in the Commons corridor to him after his resignation and the poor man burst into tears. 'Reggie had to stand very close so that three Tories going by wouldn't notice,' wrote Benn.[16] He and Caroline later sought out Boyle and spent time chatting to him. Boyle said he was sure history would prove him right. His Conservative Association later gave a unanimous vote of confidence to Eden, which meant, of course, no confidence in Boyle. His agent explained how he had disappointed them: 'Oh Sir Edward, it would have been so much easier if you had been in favour of hanging.'[17]

Sunday, 4 November, also saw the 'Law Not War' rally in Trafalgar Square addressed by Nye Bevan, who was careful to explain that, though Eden was wrong, that did not mean Nasser was right. The Labour Party was well aware of a groundswell of working-class conservatism which liked to see British gunboat diplomacy in action; indeed, one result of Suez was to increase the government's popularity. The rally was well attended, but outside the ranks of activists there was little involvement. The press was almost universally pro-Eden, and television, before the days of current affairs, was bland in its coverage. Public meetings were not well attended – 'ordinary people are not yet moved on the issue,' wrote Benn.[18] Perhaps he was simply observing, reflected in an international crisis, a continuous trend through the second half of the century: increasing reluctance by members of the public to attend meetings.

The petition against Suez was presented to Parliament on 5 November. This is a routine procedure attracting virtually no attention to the subject of the petition, but Benn's parliamentary skills were well honed by this time and he used the little-known Standing Order 92 to ensure that the petition was read out by the clerk and thus merited a full page in Hansard.

At David Benn's suggestion his brother obtained, via the House of Commons library, the texts of propaganda broadcasts to Egypt from the British radio station in Cyprus. He read to a shocked House of Commons the text of one broadcast: 'We are obliged to bomb you wherever you are. Imagine your villages being bombed. Imagine your wives, children, mothers, fathers and grandfathers escaping from their houses and leaving their property behind. This will happen to you if you hide behind your women in the villages. . . . If they do not evacuate, there is no doubt that your villages and homes will be destroyed. You have committed a sin – that is, you placed your confidence in Abdul Nasser.' Benn wanted to know if this was, in fact, the policy of Her Majesty's Government. The Foreign Secretary could not answer.[19]

British and French aircraft had bombed Egyptian airfields in a softening-up operation on 31 October. The first of 22,000 British and French troops arrived on 5 November and Royal Marine

127

Commandos began battling into the centre of Port Said in house-to-house fighting with Egyptian defenders.

The same day the government of the Soviet Union announced that it was 'fully resolved to use force to crush the aggressors and to restore peace in the Middle East'. This was a scarcely veiled threat that London and Paris might be the object of a nuclear strike. The Soviet Union was feeling bullish. That day a thousand tanks had thundered across the Hungarian border and crushed the uprising with utmost savagery. An estimated 20,000 were killed.

Eisenhower, now bolstered by an impressive election victory, used the full force of the strongest economic power in the world to lever Britain out of Suez. He threatened oil sanctions and engineered a run on the pound. Macmillan, now Chancellor of the Exchequer, was obliged to tell the cabinet that Britain's gold reserves had fallen by over £100 million in a week. Only a ceasefire would secure US support for the necessary loan from the International Monetary Fund.

The late nights, emotional strain and incessant action were taking their toll on Benn. He virtually broke down during speeches on 5 and 6 November, but mercifully this phase of the adventure was nearing its end. The British, French and Israelis agreed to the UN's call for a ceasefire on 6 November. The operation was not even a military success: the Israelis had exceeded their orders and had reached their objectives near the canal four days before the British and French forces arrived. Between 2500 and 3000 Egyptians were dead. British and French casualties were 32, Israeli 200.

Late in the night of 5 November Benn wrote that the battles in the House 'reminded me once more that politics is not a tea party, even in a parliamentary democracy. It is an orderly and disciplined struggle for power. The fact that the power changes hands according to a set pattern does not diminish the importance of that power nor weaken the bitterness of the struggle for it.'[20]

The fighting may have stopped in Suez but the troops were still in place and the government was still claiming moral justification. On 9 November Benn used more transcripts from the Voice of Britain broadcasts to penetrate the shabby subterfuge. The government had claimed that it had ordered the invasion to protect British interests after the Israeli attack. British and French forces were there as a peacekeeping force to separate the two sides. This was

above Three brothers: Anthony at five driving eighteen-month-old David with eight-year-old Michael Benn beside them on a summer holiday at Stansgate in 1930.

below The whole family at Stansgate in 1932: David, Anthony, Michael, Margaret and William Wedgwood Benn.

above The evacuated schoolboy in 1941.

left A Pilot Officer in the RAF in March 1945.

above Flying Officer (later Flight Lieutenant) Michael Wedgwood Benn and Air Commodore Lord Stansgate in 1943. Michael was to be killed on active duty the following year.

below The family reunited in 1946: twenty-one-year-old Tony, Lady Stansgate, Secretary of State for Air Lord Stansgate and David.

The Oxford Union debating team, Kenneth Harris, Tony Benn and Sir Edward Boyle on 23 June 1947, ready to take on the best debaters of American colleges.

Electioneering in Bristol in May 1955.

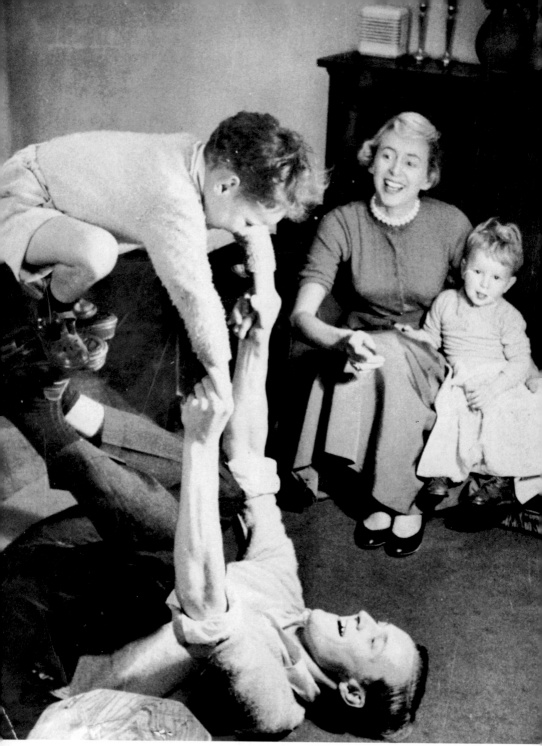

The Benn family at play.

Leading members of the H-Bomb National Committee in 1954: Fenner Brockway, Sir Richard Acland, Anthony Greenwood, George Thomas and Tony Benn.

The Benn family complete: Caroline holding baby Joshua; Tony holding two-year-old Melissa; Stephen, seven, standing behind five-year-old Hilary.

not believed to be true by anyone in possession of the facts, but it had to be demonstrated to be untrue. Benn told the Commons that he found it 'very curious that there is no record of the Voice of Britain broadcasting to Israel at any stage since the Prime Minister said that the intention of the ultimatum was to compel both sides to disengage. I think it is very odd – indeed more than odd – that at no stage has a transcript been received of a broadcast directed to the Israeli troops advising them to keep clear of the canal.'[21]

Point by point Benn compared the Voice of Britain broadcasts with statements by Eden. If the invasion were a police action, and had nothing to do with the dispute over the ownership of the canal, as the Prime Minister had told the British people, why was the Voice of Britain telling the Egyptian people: 'Oh Egyptians, this is the first blow which has befallen you. Why has this befallen you? First because Abdul Nasser went mad and seized the Suez Canal which is of vital importance to the world. . . . Accordingly the Allies shall continue taking measures with increasing force until peace is restored and the canal is placed above political and national ambitions on the understanding that we are in a position to apply further force to attain our objective and shall do so if necessary. Our fighters and bombers are now flying over you.'[22]

Not everyone was appreciative of Benn's efforts. 'Nasser's little lackey' one back-bench Tory called him.[23]

The Anglo-French force was withdrawn on 22 December and the Israelis left by 1 March 1957, but as early as the beginning of December it was obviously all over. Bob Boothby, a leading Tory Suez rebel, was mooching around the Commons smoking room complaining that the Conservative Party was finished for another ten years; at the other extreme, Benn noted, 'that old scoundrel Dalton was tight as a lord and cursing the wogs in the best Suez Group manner'.[24]

The texts of the broadcasts Benn had obtained proved that the British and French had been prepared for an attack and that the Israeli invasion was just a pretext. Evidence of long-term planning of the campaign also came from the propaganda station in Cyprus: requisition of the station had been planned as early as August. The psychological warfare unit had started work on 18 October – two weeks before the Israeli attack which was supposed to have sparked the Anglo-French campaign.

The final piece of evidence of collusion which Benn himself received came at his constituency surgery on 8 December. A young woman asked if Benn could get her husband home from Port Said for Christmas. He was in the headquarters ship HMS *Tyne*, which had sailed from Malta two days before the Israeli attack. What was not fully known until the publication of their memoirs by leading Conservative figures was the extent to which the British and French had actually planned, with Israel, an attack which otherwise might never have happened.

Even in April 1957 Benn was still presenting British involvement in the Israeli attack as foreknowledge rather than conspiracy. 'Eden was told of the Israeli attack two weeks before it happened and agreed to it so that when it took place it would give him an excuse to seize the canal,' he wrote in the *Bristol Evening World*.[25]

The most serious short-term result of Suez was the way it had wrenched attention away from the repression in Hungary. The pathetic calls from Hungarian radio for support from 'civilised peoples' in the name of justice and freedom met with no response. Civilised peoples were otherwise occupied.

David Benn had suggested writing to *Pravda* challenging the Soviet government to justify itself. The letter, signed by Benn and four other MPs, 'who in the past have always worked for a better understanding between our two countries', was sent on 27 December. It contained five questions and a comparison between Hungary and Suez: 'We protest against the Soviet intervention in Hungary, because we think it wrong for any great power to impose its will on a small country for strategic or any other reasons. For this very reason we condemned the Anglo-French attack on Egypt.' They urged withdrawal in accordance with United Nations resolutions.

The letter was not published initially, but when *Pravda* was told that the MPs would release it in the UK it was published, with a lengthy reply, on 10 February. The text was published in Budapest the following day.

Eden did not long survive his Suez adventure. He resigned in January 1957 and was succeeded by Macmillan. In May Macmillan announced complete capitulation to Egypt: British ships would use the canal on Egypt's terms and the dues would be paid in the currency of her choice. The cost of the seven-day operation against Egypt was estimated at £812 million, which includes loss of trade with Egypt and the loss of oil revenue.[26]

Suez was Britain's greatest diplomatic blunder of the second half of the century. It confirmed her inferior status and her inability to take action without the consent of the US. Although the credibility of the United Nations was enhanced, there was no doubt that it was US displeasure and, ultimately, US economic pressure which forced the withdrawal.

Paradoxically, the reliance on the US which Suez revealed increased the feeling that European federation was necessary; when even the more powerful of the small nation states, like Britain and France, were too weak for global activity, a larger union was necessary.

For Tony Benn's political career, Suez had been all gain. This was the first major political occasion on which he had been able to act upon events rather than be thrown and buffeted by them. It brought together all his skills as a broadcaster, as a speaker, as a political organiser. He had emerged as a champion of morality, his speeches bringing truth and light to the corners where government ministers had plotted lies and concealment. He was factually accurate, he was dignified and he was gracious to his opponents. If only all political events admitted of such clear divisions between right and wrong.

He had learned some personal lessons. One was to follow his instincts and not trust to the integrity of the Honourable Gentlemen opposite. The government would tell one lie supported by another, and even when it was found out it could still go on to win the next election.

Another lesson was to pay no attention to the press. The press was wrong in its support for a supercilious and then aggressive attitude towards Egypt. It was wrong to discourage a parliamentary visit at a time of increasing tension. Benn's best instincts told him this but he bowed to pressure and withdrew. If he ever needed one, Suez provided an enduring reminder of the folly of yielding to 'public opinion' as represented by newspapers.

11

Front Bencher

It was because of his good work on Suez that Gaitskell appointed Benn second spokesman on the RAF. He thus became one of seven front-bench spokesmen on the services – there were two for each service and one overall defence spokesman.

His first speech from the Opposition front bench, on 7 March 1957, was lyrically described by the *Reynolds News* correspondent: 'A slender, youthful figure rose to the Commons despatch box and glanced around at the half-filled chamber. . . . so competent and confident was Mr Wedgwood Benn that before he got down to the debate, he talked for a few minutes about the experience that faced him.'[1] It was a characteristic Benn opening. It had worked at the Oxford Union, all over the USA, in every church hall and party meeting in Bristol. He would establish himself as a person who could be trusted and liked, for every audience will approach every speaker with suspicion. Nothing can melt away suspicion as well as a joke and no joke is so effective as the one told against oneself.[2]

So accomplished was he by this time that he even managed to maintain his composure when he made an error early in the speech, referring to the wrong document and having to be corrected. 'Back to the back benches,' said an unkind Tory. 'I withdraw unreservedly anything I said,' declared Benn, 'the [House] is more than generous to those who make mistakes and withdraw. It sometimes pays to make mistakes so as to get the little round of cheering when one withdraws.'[3]

It was a typical Benn speech, full of common sense and argument about the rights of the House of Commons. He berated the service chiefs for living in the past. They still thought they had to keep all information about defence to themselves, not even sharing it with MPs, lest it fall into enemy hands. But atomic weapons were supposed to be possessed for deterrent purposes: 'in present circumstances our object is to reveal to the enemy our strength so as to avoid the necessity of defeating him in war by deterring him from starting it at all. . . . So far as I am concerned the more information about our services, if they are working properly, that is now in the hands of the Soviet Embassy, the more likely is the deterrent to work. I hope that the service ministers will take a little more intelligent view of this.' Pleas for open government, in particular those addressed to the defence chiefs, have long fallen on deaf ears in Britain. This was no exception.

Air was of particular significance at this time, because the only intercontinental means available for the delivery of nuclear bombs was aircraft, in Britain's case the ageing V-bomber force. This was soon to change when, in October 1957, the USSR launched the Sputnik satellite. It was a major event for anyone excited by technology, as Benn was. He was overcome with enthusiasm at a reception held in the Russian Embassy soon afterwards to celebrate the fortieth anniversary of the revolution and he wrote in the visitor's book 'Congratulations on everything.' 'Everything?' came the query from some members of the public, after the *Evening News* diarist had remarked on the entry. Not quite everything, Benn said in apology in the pages of the *Bristol Evening World*.[4]

At the Bermuda conference in March 1957 Macmillan attempted to patch up his relations with Eisenhower. After the disgrace of Suez, the US had to be placated. Whatever the Americans wanted, they could have. They offered to 'share' sixty Thor nuclear missiles with Britain in return for the right to site them on British territory. The missiles were marked with British insignia but the technology used to manage them was operated with two keys, one American and one British. There was really no doubt that the missiles were under American control.

As Benn said in the defence estimates debate on 9 May 1957: 'The Prime Minister has said that he had a better deal than Lord Attlee. I frankly doubt that. . . . The nuclear deterrents cannot be used without the permission of the United States, whereas under the old agreement the American deterrent could not be used without the permission of the United Kingdom.'[5] He stressed that the speed of nuclear warfare had removed the ultimatum from the machinery of power politics: an ultimatum backed by a threat of action if demands were not met would obviously meet with a pre-emptive attack. 'Since the man who strikes first has such a tremendous advantage, it is almost inevitable that a man seriously planning aggression would so plan his operations that the opportunity for retaliation is reduced to a minimum.'

In the Labour Party the long dispute over arms was crystallising into a major split on nuclear weapons. The party conference in 1957 was faced with 120 resolutions about the bomb, almost all of them calling for unilateral measures to rid Britain of nuclear weapons whatever other nations did. The Conservatives had been in power since 1951 and change was in the air, particularly because they were still in disarray.

This was seen to be one of the key issues for a forthcoming election: could the party present a united front on this issue? To the dismay of the constituency delegates their hero Nye Bevan, now shadow Foreign Secretary and speaking for the executive, lined up with the right. He renounced unilateralism, insisting that a British Foreign Secretary must be clad in the international agreements Britain had entered into while in the possession of nuclear weapons; he must not be sent 'naked into the conference chamber'. To disarm unilaterally would be to break these agreements and to send Britain into diplomatic purdah. 'If many had not been nearer to tears,' wrote Michael Foot, 'the whole place might have broken into uproar.'[6]

Bevan's speech was widely seen as a betrayal of principle for gain. With the government in a shambles, there was the probability that Labour would win the next election and he would be in a position to put together an anti-cold-war coalition to break the grip of the antagonism between the superpowers. But would the public vote for a unilateralist party? Could a unilateralist be Foreign Secretary? Bevan's mind was certainly influenced by discussions with members of the Labour right wing, such as the miners' union leader Sam Watson. Ian Mikardo, who also discussed the question with Bevan before the speech, felt that this was central: 'What Sam had said to him, had begged him to believe, was that the world needed Nye to become Foreign Secretary of Great Britain, and that this couldn't possibly come about unless Nye turned his back on unilateralism.'[7]

Speaking before Bevan, Benn made a mediocre speech calling for greater control over nuclear weapons. He was 'convinced as a practical matter that it would never be right or practical to use the hydrogen bomb' but was concerned that there was insufficient parliamentary control over nuclear weapons. 'Parliament no longer controls peace and war. . . . we are drifting towards disaster because we have not yet asserted popular control over the hydrogen bomb.'[8]

The announcement in 1955 that Britain was developing her own hydrogen bomb had given impetus to the unilateralist movement in the Labour Party. With Bevan's defection unilateralists knew that they had to seek a wider constituency. The Campaign for Nuclear Disarmament was born early in 1958 from the frustration of unilateralists with the inability of even the Labour left to maintain a principle. Benn did not join it, regarding the idea that Britain could renounce nuclear weapons and become the moral leader of the world as 'a typical bit of British self-deception. It wasn't going to make the world give them up.'[9]

Amid all the debate and despair Benn carefully considered his position. He was not a pacifist and had never been one, but he was morally unable to endorse nuclear weapons. Yet the Labour Party policy which he had to promote from the front bench was for a defence strategy of which nuclear weapons were an integral part.

'I sat and thought about it and I found there were no circumstances in which I could contemplate using them,' he said. 'I went to see Geoffrey de Freitas, who was the number-one air force spokesman. I told him in the spring of 1958 that I couldn't under any circumstances agree to the use of the weapons and I must resign, but I didn't make a big thing of it.'[10] So on 3 March 1958 Benn resigned. He had served one year on the front bench.

His discretion, at a time when Labour was healing its splits, with Bevan back in the fold, was much appreciated by the leadership. He did it so quietly, hardly anyone noticed he was gone. He said, 'When I came out as a unilateralist in 1974 in the cabinet Willy Ross said at the end, "At least you're consistent, you resigned over this in 1958." The only other person who remembered it was someone from the American Embassy who said, "You resigned, of course, over the question of nuclear weapons." '[11] The Americans obviously had keen reasons for needing to keep a close watch on the nuclear debate in Britain. Their nuclear technology was already on British soil and they would soon be pushing for a nuclear base which would not even be nominally British. A country which did not even want its own nuclear weapons would be unlikely to choose to be a repository for someone else's.

It is difficult to know exactly where Benn stood on nuclear weapons in the 1950s. He supported British possession of them but believed they were impractical and would never be used. He was more concerned that the development of weapons and the conditions under which their use would be threatened should be decided democratically. Whatever weapon was possessed, at least it should be possessed openly. Yet there was clearly no possibility of democratic control over American weapons based in Britain – even the Americans did not have that. What they had was a chain of command which went from President to Vice-President then through the military hierarchy. Moreover, the possibility of genuine democratic participation in the threat or the use of atomic weapons was an absurdity. In an international crisis events move so fast and the chosen strategy is so closely guarded that only a small committee of people can be involved in all decisions.

Benn's one contribution, later in the decade, to reducing nuclear tension was the suggestion that there should be inspection of nuclear bases by a United Nations inspectorate or by other nations. Someone had to go first and he suggested that Britain should unilaterally permit inspection of her nuclear installations. The idea was to create a climate of confidence and openness. It was never adopted as policy and it would have made but a small contribution to easing tension, though multilateral inspection did form part of the agreement reached between Presidents Gorbachev and Bush in 1989.

Benn's resignation as front-bench spokesman was the act of an honest man. He could not disagree, as a pragmatist, with the ownership of nuclear weapons, but he could not conceive ever using them himself. Someone motivated solely by ambition would have stayed in the job. After all, the second Opposition spokesman on the air force is not terribly likely to be called upon to press the button himself. However, he felt that, if in practice he was not prepared to cause civilian casualties on the scale which would occur during an atomic attack, he should not support the principle of doing so.

'Nuclear' was far from being the byword for evil it was later to become. Atomic was a synonym for modern. Benn made speeches with titles like 'British Socialism in the Atomic Age'.[12] It was particularly important for Benn the young technocrat to associate Labour with the smokeless future of atomic energy, the party having been so long linked with the dirt of industrial power. In response to a jibe from Anthony Eden about socialism and nationalisation being out of date, Benn hit back: 'The future lies with atomic energy in Britain. Mr Eden and ourselves recognise it. Atomic energy was launched by a socialist government in Britain, is being developed by a public corporation and, when we get it, it will be distributed by a nationalised industry. You can't be more up to date than that with atomic energy.'[13]

The oil embargo by the Arab states at the time of Suez intensified the programme for the development of nuclear power which was already under way. Calder Hall, Britain's first nuclear power station, was opened by the Queen in 1956. The scientist Jacob Bronowski on an *Any Questions?* broadcast demonstrated the enthusiasm atomic energy inspired: 'Calder Hall is one of the great British achievements of this generation. It's in the same class as the poems of Dylan Thomas and the novels of Graham Greene and the paintings of Graham Sutherland.'

Benn agreed with the enthusiasm, especially because it might prove possible to use cheap power to raise living standards. But he warned, 'We shall still need all the coal we can get out of this country. We haven't many raw materials of our own and coal is going to continue to be very important.'[14]

Calder Hall was on the Windscale site where the following year there was a fire, the investigation of which showed that for some time there had been serious radiation leakage. The matter was covered up by the new Prime Minister Harold Macmillan.[15] Its four Magnox reactors were designed to provide electricity for the national grid and plutonium for use in the production of nuclear weapons. It was not a swords into ploughshares programme; it was a swords *and* ploughshares programme.

*

Benn was now writing widely in national newspapers and had also started a 'New Sparkling Weekly Column' for the *Bristol Evening World* on 14 February 1957. The editor of the paper had told him he could use the paper to say whatever he liked but should not overload the column with politics. In seasoning it he gave many glimpses of his delight in the company of his young children, who numbered two by this time with Melissa soon to be born. Minor aspects of his life make an appearance here as they do not in his more political writing: the Anti-Smokers League fastened on to him as a prominent pipe-smoker to blast with their propaganda; he quickly picked up on the American invention of tea bags and began to use them for his six pints of tea a day.

He listed his recreation in *Who's Who* as 'staying at home'. The numerous family pictures from the time show him romping with the boys or sailing in a dinghy at Stansgate. Benn was normally up at 7.30 to help dress the children and to have breakfast with the family. He would work in his office at the top of the house in the mornings, often with Caroline present, then would go to the House of Commons in the afternoon and stay until the sitting finished, though all-night sittings were much more common in the 1950s than they were later to become. Apart from his long working hours and his weekend absences in the constituency, family life was idyllic. The Benns were an advertiser's dream family.

Caroline had originally planned to spend ten years having and bringing up children. The last, Joshua, was born in 1958, which meant that she spent the whole of the 1950s with small children. She returned to Cincinnati after each baby and Tony Benn would take the opportunity to talk to American audiences. Caroline's involvement in politics took the form of advice to her husband and in working on issues related to the Movement for Colonial Freedom, particularly connected with Africa.

They entertained other politicians but it was difficult for a young woman – they were all older than the Benns and some were considerably older. 'We would visit the Attlees', Caroline said, 'because they were friends of Tony's parents, but they were a much older generation. Even Nye was from another age.' The masculine atmosphere of politics was also unattractive to a lively young woman. Barbara Castle was often the only other female present and she was very much involved in a competition with the males. 'We girls have got to stick together,' her husband Ted said conspiratorially to Caroline one day. A frequent visitor was Tony Crosland, who never endeared himself to Caroline. 'He was just terribly rude,' she said. 'A number of other women I knew felt the same.' A number of men felt the same too, which accounts for Crosland's poor showing in leadership elections, though his intellectual capacity was sufficiently respected for him to be elected to the shadow cabinet throughout the 1970s.[16]

The autumn of 1958 found the Benn family in the middle of a battleground. Notting Hill had become a primary area of settlement for the Caribbean immigrants who had entered Britain looking for work and a higher standard of living. Not a few had received British encouragement in their own countries to emigrate to Britain to fill posts in the health and transport services.

Violence flared when white youths gathered outside a house occupied by black people a few hundred yards behind the Benn home. They taunted the Caribbeans with racist slogans; the blacks retaliated and missiles were thrown by both sides. Petrol bombs and milk bottles were hurled in running battles as sporadic rioting continued all night. The streets were strewn with broken glass and other debris.

The rioting continued night after night for two weeks. The family could hear the clanging bells and screaming tyres of police cars and ambulances as they rushed to the disturbances. Benn wrote at the time: 'In an area about one mile square, covering Shepherds Bush, Notting Hill and Paddington, it is not safe for a coloured person to walk before dusk until 2 a.m.'[17] Police would escort black families to their homes followed by hundreds of jeering 'teddy boys'. While some of the violence had obviously been an explosion of existing tension, the continuing attacks on black people and the movement of white youths from other parts of the city into Notting Hill were stimulated by Fascist organisations which also used the occasion for recruitment and the distribution of propaganda.

Every night, as Benn saw, crowds moved in either as participants or as spectators. When black people were seen out of doors they were attacked. Benn, among others, called for heavy sentences for the aggressors, and the judiciary was inclined to agree. Violence ceased when long sentences were publicised. On 15 September nine youths were jailed for four years each for attacks on black people.

No less shocking than the violence was the response of some right-wingers in mainstream politics who saw the black people rather than their white tormentors as the problem. 'Many voices are now raised calling for powers of deportation and the limitation of immigration,' wrote Benn. 'To give way on this now would be to encourage the racialists who are consciously demanding "a fight to keep Britain white". Are we to be asked for details of colour on our papers and passports? Is Britain . . . to deport them now so that the thugs may have no excuse for violence?'[18]

In other social thinking he was progressive, though he did not simply underwrite every reform. On the findings of the Royal Commission on Marriage and Divorce, which led to the relaxation of the divorce laws, he commented that a more humane way of stopping unsuccessful marriages would be to make marriage more difficult rather than divorce more easy. He suggested a longer notice period before a marriage could take place and medical and premarital education for the engaged couple.[19]

He was more circumspect about homosexual law reform. Homosexual acts between men were illegal, even in private. In 1957 a committee under Sir John Wolfenden recommended the decriminalisation of homosexual acts in private for those over twenty-one. Fierce arguments raged over whether its recommendations should be put into effect. Asked by the *Bristol Evening Post* in the run-up to the 1959 election whether he was in favour, Benn said, 'I think I am – though my mind is not fully made up. After exhaustive investigation it was the almost unanimous view of the Wolfenden Committee that certain changes should be made. Like the Archbishop of Canterbury, they distinguished between sin and crime. In Belgium, Denmark, France and Sweden experience has proved this can be done.'[20]

Benn became convinced of the value of television in politics after seeing the US presidential candidate on TV in 1952. He bought a television in April 1955 and it was not long before he was appearing on it himself. He was invited to present a Sunday afternoon programme called *Personal Column* which was 'a TV version of a newspaper "agony column"'. On it Benn would interview people

140

who had unusual requests: a sociologist who wanted 600 intelligent people for a survey panel; a beverage company wanting a tea-taster; a family wanting to find a good home for an heirloom which had proved 'unlucky' to them. Tom Driberg, one of the great behind-the-scenes fixers of the Labour Party, had already marked Benn out for greatness, 'Now that *Personal Column* is seen in London his growing stature will be more widely apparent,' he wrote in June 1957 when the series was successful enough to be shown nationally.[21] Driberg was a real fan, he wrote of 'the fragile, almost wistful charm of Tony Wedgwood Benn'.[22]

Benn wrote in the *TV Times* that the purpose of his interviewing method was to draw out from the interviewee what was within them. The precision of his approach is interesting because it gives an impression of how he weighed up people with whom he came into contact, in and outside a television studio, and ensured that they felt positively towards him: 'The principle is to put them at their ease. With an academic figure that may mean talking to him seriously about his subject. With an elderly person it may mean being extra-specially respectful. With a young person it probably calls for a bit of banter. But once the interviewer knows what he is trying to do, even if he fails to get a response, he can reduce the risk of failure.'[23] He was as attractive a performer on television as he was on radio, participating in three other television series of the time: *Sunday Afternoon; I Hear, I See*; and *In My Opinion*.

He had continued writing and speaking on the value to the Labour effort of good broadcasting presentation, in particular comparing the rather slicker Conservative campaign with its Labour counterpart in the 1955 election. He urged the message that in a few years the politician who had not mastered television would be as severely incapacitated as the politician who could not make a public speech.[24] Benn had suggested that the 1955 election broadcasts should be run like the popular BBC magazine programme *Tonight*, but his proposal had been rejected.

The first time he was allowed to use his skills was as producer of a radio broadcast on behalf of the Labour Party transmitted on 9 May 1956 just before local authority elections. For the first time a dramatic situation was introduced into a broadcast with a humorous sketch of a canvassing team getting the brush-off from a housewife.

The political meat of the programme was a series of quick interviews with councillors. Most adventurously, at the beginning and end of the programme Grimsby MP Kenneth Younger accompanied himself on the guitar singing a satirical song to the tune of 'Oh Dear, What Can the Matter Be?':

> They promised our standard of living to double
> Rab Butler won votes with a boom in a bubble
> It burst in the autumn and got him in trouble
> It's time that you told them to go.
>
> After they won all their whacking majorities
> They took a crack at the local authorities
> Cut down the subsidies, wrecked their priorities
> It's time that you told them to go.

It was a roaring success with enthusiastic press coverage and Labour increasing its share of the vote by 3.5 per cent over the previous local elections. As the general election approached Benn continued proselytising on the need for Labour to adapt to the electronic rostrum and crystallising the plans which he had formulated for the 1955 election. He won the battle to have a working television studio installed at Transport House so that people could be trained and ideas could be tested. He wrote widely about television, particularly wanting to put across the message to Labour supporters that in ten years the television public had grown from 80,000 to twenty-two million. 'Just as one hydrogen bomb packs more power than the total load dropped in World War Two, so one television broadcast more than equals a lifetime of mass rallies and street-corner oratory. Old methods of campaigning are as obsolete as conventional weapons.'[25]

He presented the Campaign Committee with a brilliant programme proposal, all the more remarkable because of the primitive state of television production at the time. He argued for the detailed construction of each programme, suggesting the style of music and captions, the set and the blending of style with political content. He even contrived an introduction to the programme which would counterbalance the presenters' announcement that there now follows a party political broadcast, which, he said, was an 'audience killer':

142

Therefore some buffer between them and our programmes must be our first objective. This can be done best by music and a picture. Both should be chosen with tremendous care to begin to create exactly the impression that we want. Suppose we decide that our theme is to be Land and the People. Then your opening film sequence should be an atomic power station under construction, seen across fields of waving corn. And your music should be 'Jerusalem' sung by a Welsh choir.[26]

One important feature of the broadcasts would be to build up the image of Hugh Gaitskell, who did not appeal as the most dynamic of leaders. He would have to appear often, and always in a specially created set. 'The desk, the table lamp, the crystal ashtray, the globe, the bust of Keir Hardie, the wallpaper and so on will all create the image of a Prime Minister waiting to take office. Only the leader himself must ever appear on the leader's set. Other leaders will have to use a different one.'

Of the other key figures he wrote:

It is no exaggeration to say that the success or failure of this whole idea will very largely depend on the person of the television chairman. He must have, or be taught to have, a complete command of the situation technically. He must be friendly but not smarmy. He must set the cracking pace without appearing to rush the important people with whom he will be dealing. He must be the friendly, warm symbol of the Labour Party today. He is the link between the party and the public – the impresario. He is in a curious way non-political. He does not make political points. If they have to be made he calls in someone to do it. He is the man who builds up the viewers' confidence throughout the campaign.[27]

In other words, it was Tony Benn.

He was given the task of introducing twelve television broadcasts (a thirteenth featured Gaitskell alone) between 21 September and 6 October, virtually a programme a day. In order to bear this load, he had to be excused from normal duties at Bristol South-East and it was a tense day when he came to ask the General Management Committee for permission to be away. He sweetened the request with a speech which showed how much in touch he now was with the rank and file. Victory in the election would mean a ban on nuclear tests, recognition of China, Britain's withdrawal from the cold war. He lamented that the government had said it was 'better

143

to have half a million unemployed than to allow prices to rise', thus using unemployment as the instrument for attacking the cost-of-living problem. A new Labour government would abolish the 11-plus examination and bring British education up to the standard of the USA and USSR. How could they refuse such a candidate anything?

Harry Hennessy remarked that Tony requesting to be absent was nothing new: Stafford Cripps used to go all over the country. 'If Tony has been asked to take charge – good luck to Tony.' They voted to let him go, with only one against.[28] When he did appear in the constituency during the election campaign he made the best use of his time, the *Bristol Evening Post* recording that he was attending seven meetings a night on the two days he was there.[29]

Some comrades were a little more suspicious than the General Management Committee in Bristol. Dick Crossman records how on 20 September he went with Benn to Gaitskell's home 'for a first talk about television shows, another matter which has been sedulously kept from me until this week. There was some tension in the air with those three stars – Benn, Wyatt and [Christopher] Mayhew – seeing Crossman at last getting in on their racket.'[30]

One of the broadcasts, 'Britain Belongs to You', opens with a stirring passage from *The Planets* Suite. Tony Benn is revealed seated in the 'Operations Room'. This was his idea, a set supposed to represent the Labour Party headquarters. It looks like a busy but spacious office with posters on the walls, telephones and papers on desks. From here any question can be answered, any Tory challenge repulsed. Benn is a slim, dynamic figure in a dark suit with prominent eyes and an accent just a little too clipped for public tastes in future decades.

He calls up graphics to demonstrate that the Tory slogan 'Life's Better under the Conservatives' is not true when Britain is compared to other European countries. The only aspect of life in which Britain leads is the cost of living index.

Has Britain never had it so good? In the Operations Room Benn introduces young journalist Woodrow Wyatt interviewing young economist Harold Wilson. Of course, says Wilson, things are better fourteen years after the war than they were immediately after the war. 'Of course there are more cars and television sets. The same is true in every other country and it isn't the government that's produced them. We'd have had the same number of cars and television sets if we had had a government of chimpanzees. Many other countries have had it much better.'

A cartoon sequence explains Labour's new pension scheme, then Benn introduces the stars of stage, screen and academia. Jazz musician Humphrey Lyttelton, philosopher A. J. Ayer, scientist Ritchie Calder and writer Compton Mackenzie line up to give their backing to Labour. Actress Jill Balcon sweetly presents a well-worded contribution on the nuclear dispute: 'I think that the most important issue for all of us is the bomb and I'm hoping that the Labour Party will make a most tremendous drive to achieve nuclear disarmament.'

Jim Callaghan expresses outrage at the Hola prison-camp massacre in Kenya where eleven African prisoners were clubbed to death by their warders in full view of the officer in charge of the prison. 'What happened to British justice? Is it reserved for white men only?' he demands.

Gaitskell is defensive about his 1951 rearmament Budget and shows no dynamism. George Brown is more forceful in calling on the Conservatives to give a pledge that if elected there would be no further increase in rents.

Benn appeals for volunteers to work in the Labour committee rooms and to make available their cars to help out on polling day, and adds that viewers should not think of themselves as spectators in politics but as participants in their own democracy.

'It was the best election campaign we'd ever had,' said Benn. 'Those election broadcasts were considered absolutely brilliant – they knocked the Tories for six.'[31] His opinion was shared by the Conservative press. The *Daily Sketch* said, 'If there is any ground for the belief, now widely held, that this is a TV election, then the Tories are in real danger of losing it.'[32] The *Daily Mail* said, 'The Conservative Party could lose this election on television technique.'[33]

The Conservatives were so concerned about their dismal television performance that they began accusing the BBC of bias – had the Labour Party got a better producer than they had? In fact Benn had said once again that he wanted the broadcasts to have the variety and pace of the *Tonight* programme, so his team had been given as their BBC producer Alasdair Milne, deputy editor of *Tonight* and later BBC Director General.

12

Breaking with Gaitskell

Benn was close enough to the party leadership to be called for consultation in Liverpool, where Wilson and Gaitskell were on the campaign trail six days before polling day. The campaign began in high spirits – they were certain of victory. Gaitskell was so eager to please, however, that on 28 September he announced that there would be no increase in income tax, despite having promised pension rises, hospital building and an expansion of public ownership of housing. No voter had to be a great political analyst to see that these things could not add up. Gaitskell was obviously lying about either his future spending or his future taxation.

Benn said, 'I was at the campaign committee at Transport House when he made that statement. It was as if somebody had put a pin into a balloon – morale totally collapsed. Then the Tories dug out some press release that Wilson had put out some weeks earlier and nobody had noticed saying there would be no increase in purchase tax. That made it even worse. Labour was trying to look absolutely harmless.'[1]

But this was only one blunder. In general, as well as the superior Labour propaganda, there were Tory deficiencies. Their economic policy was a quagmire in which they seemed directionless. Macmillan's Chancellor had resigned in 1957, normally considered a death blow for a ministry. Britain was lagging behind comparable countries in industrial production and living standards. Above all, the Tories were still the guilty men of Suez – only Eden had gone. Benn, with his good nature and willingness to put the best interpretation on everything, was only now coming to terms with the depth of lies and duplicity which had supported the Suez escapade. 'We know

147

now', he said in a newspaper interview, 'that the French and British governments helped Israel in her attack on Egypt. We know now that the French were supplying arms to Israel through Cyprus when Eden was calling on Israel to suspend operations. We know that he said he had consulted the Americans when he hadn't. We know that the figures of casualties given at Port Said were subsequently proved to be totally false, and what I object to is a group of people who are the same as they were at Suez . . . coming forward and claiming to speak for Britain because that is a disgrace which we cannot possibly overlook.'[2]

But overlooked it was. The Conservatives were returned for an unprecedented third term with an increased majority. They won 365 seats to Labour's 258, gaining an overall majority of 100. Labour's vote had fallen again, by 189,000, while the Tories had increased theirs by more than twice this amount.

In Bristol South-East Benn's vote was up by 1000 on the 1955 election, but his Tory opponent, Malcolm St Clair, had increased his by more than 3000, so Benn's majority was further reduced, to 5800. This was a third of the majority Stafford Cripps had enjoyed when he had last fought the seat in 1950. It was hardly even a safe Labour seat any more.

What had happened? Looking back on the election Benn said, 'Suez hadn't done the Tory Party any harm. Macmillan was a bit of a card, a very attractive figure. He was very pro-European, forward looking, had been a critic of Chamberlain. He had an affectation of senility but he was an extremely able, competent political leader. He'd only been Prime Minister two and a half years and there was still a certain honeymoon period. He was unbeatable. He lost a Chancellor in 1957 and he described it as a little local difficulty, although the great constitutional historians say that no Prime Minister can lose a Chancellor. He was the grandfather of the wets – his book *The Middle Way* says we must have a planned economy. The Tories said the right things. Macmillan said, "You've never had it so good." Butler said, "We'll double your standard of living in twenty-five years." They were a winning team.

'On our side, Gaitskell was just seen as a young technocrat. Gaitskell had been Chancellor in 1951, Attlee had called an election when he had a majority of six. Why did he go? They said he'd run away from an economic crisis. Gaitskell was the Chancellor who ran away. Wilson had been the President of the Board of Trade who had resigned from that cabinet, he was a rebel. Bevan had resigned against Gaitskell then become reconciled to him; he was the rebel who had repudiated his past. Barbara Castle was party chairman that year. The team didn't look very credible. It was a funny mixture. Though I suppose you could argue that it was the Labour Party as it always is and always will be.'[3]

So Bevan's sacrifice over unilateralism, and the virtual abandonment of nationalisation in the face of a massive industry publicity campaign against it, added up to nothing. As the Labour left was able to ask itself many times in the following decades, why should they make a sacrifice of principle to the right wing in order to win an election if the right wing could not win with or without the sacrifice?

Looking back, it is clear what had occurred during the 1950s. The Conservatives had reaped the rewards of Labour's post-war reconstruction of Britain. Had the Attlee government hung on for just another year after 1951, the results of its measures would have benefited Labour and not the Tories. Any party which was in power when the post-war boom started would win and win again. As Denis Healey said in his autobiography, just one more year and Britain would, like Sweden, have had a generation of socialist government.[4]

The profound conservatism of the Labour Party has made it far more difficult for it to bounce back refreshed after a major defeat. After 1931, 1959 and 1979 the party glumly wondered how the voters could be so misguided. The Conservative Party takes half the time of Labour to revive and regroup to face the challenge of a changing society. Benn was trying to modernise the party but it was slow work and could not be achieved under Gaitskell, who was, in Wilson's opinion, more of an administrator than a politician. He had a fine grasp of the mechanics of government, which was supremely useful when he was in government but, during his time as leader, he never was. This period, when diplomacy was most urgently needed, showed up his inability to comprehend politics – rather a serious failing in a politician. Most importantly, he did not understand the Labour Party itself. In particular he had no understanding of the feelings of the constituency members or the trade unionists and believed that his was an appeal which went over the heads of these activists to the country as a whole.

It was this grandiose belief that he alone was in contact with the mood of the nation which led him to his disastrous attempt to remove Clause 4 from the party's constitution. Clause 4, sometimes called the 'nationalisation clause', expresses an elevated aspiration in prosaic language: 'To secure for the workers by hand or by brain the full fruits of their industry and the most equitable distribution thereof that may be possible upon the basis of the common owner-ship of the means of production, distribution and exchange, and the best obtainable system of popular administration and control of each industry or service.' It had formed part of the constitution since the party conference of 1918, held in the heady atmosphere following the Russian Revolution.

Had Labour gone to the country intending to nationalise every-thing from the corner shop to ICI and been rejected on such a platform, Gaitskell might have had a point. Labour had done nothing of the kind. Nationalisation was pinpointed in the National Executive Committee meeting after the 1959 election as one of the issues on which there was uncertainty about Labour policy in the minds of the voters, but the proposition that it was a vote-loser in itself was explicitly rejected. Clause 4 was, anyway, an expression of a desire for equality and fairness, not a piece of doctrine by which every industrial action should be measured. This was instinctively understood by party members at large, but it was alien to Gaitskell's instinct. As he struggled to understand what had gone wrong in 1959 he hit upon the notion that the Labour Party was too working class, too much associated with industry and 'labour' in the diction-ary sense. There was even talk of changing the name to rid the party of this stigma so that it might move to the centre and enjoy some of the sunshine of the current Liberal revival – short lived, as it turned out.

Gaitskell was confirmed as leader by the Parliamentary Labour Party, and Bevan was elected deputy leader unopposed, when Par-liament was reconvened. The short party conference at the end of November might have been the occasion for a unified front between left and right against the government. But, to the horror of dele-gates, who were incredulous that the party leader was opening such a wound for no good reason, Gaitskell insisted on calling for revision of Clause 4.

At the 1959 conference Benn was elected to the National Executive Committee for the first time, taking the place of Ian Mikardo as a constituency section representative. This was most unfortunate for Mikardo, who having been vice-chairman the previous year would otherwise have been chairman. Benn received 566,000 votes, coming just under Jim Callaghan, who received 606,000. Benn's appearances on *Any Questions?* and the election broadcasts had made his name a household word among Labour members.

The National Executive Committee disembowelled Gaitskell's proposals over Clause 4. The clause stayed and Gaitskell was left feebly adding to the 'Party Objects', of which Clause 4 was a part, a twelve-point 'statement of aims'. He was not allowed to be at peace even with this: NEC members insisted on going through it in full committee line by line and adding amendments – one suggested by Benn – which strengthened it.[5] No one mentioned the statement of aims again. Gaitskell later admitted to Tony Benn that this had been the great mistake of his career. Surprised at the unprecedented self-criticism, Benn asked him to expand. No, Gaitskell said, attacking Clause 4 wasn't the mistake; failing to get the block votes of the trade unions behind him before he attacked Clause 4, that was the mistake.

Benn supported retention of Clause 4 but argued for party modernisation, something few could disagree with. He had been writing speeches for Gaitskell and was associated with him in the minds of his parliamentary colleagues, but he had not been party to Gaitskell's manoeuvrings on Clause 4, which he had first read about in the press, and he was feeling increasingly dissatisfied.

He took to NEC work with a determination to modernise which did not excite all he spoke to. 'His enthusiasm is, for me, the reverse of infectious,' noted Crossman.[6] Benn was on the Commonwealth, the Finance and General Purposes, and the Publicity and Political Education Subcommittees. He wanted to expand the Research Department and form a new Information Department; to develop a model design for the layout of constituency rooms; and to decide on a common logo for all Labour Party letterheads. Michael Foot later wrote of this work, 'No one in Labour Party history – not even

Herbert Morrison in his heyday – applied his mind and energies more assiduously to the work of the Executive.'[7]

He was also able to learn from other members of the NEC, particularly the trade unionists. It was Walter Padley, Labour MP and president of the Union of Shop, Distributive and Allied Workers, who introduced Tony Benn to the Levellers and Diggers, heroic figures of the English Revolution with whom Benn's expensive education had not acquainted him. Padley launched a violent attack against Gaitskell's attempt to abolish Clause 4, saying that the idea of common ownership went back to the Diggers, who had argued that the earth was a common treasury. Benn's interest in these early theorists of English socialism was fired, though he was not to incorporate their rhetoric into his own until the 1970s.

He was five votes short of being elected to the shadow cabinet (for which the electorate was the parliamentary party alone) – the closest he had come since he had first stood for a position in 1953. Denis Healey entered the shadow cabinet for the first time this year.

Outside the shadow cabinet jobs, other shadow ministerial posts were in the gift of the leader, and Gaitskell made Benn shadow transport minister on 12 November 1959. Clearly his resignation over nuclear weapons had not blotted his copybook with the leadership. Discretion had indeed been the best policy. At thirty-four he was the youngest shadow minister. As might have been expected, he took to his brief with a commitment to public transport and a flair for original thinking.

There was a good deal of dissent over his appointment because the parliamentary party had no shortage of trade union MPs with transport experience from the Transport and General Workers' Union and the National Union of Railwaymen. These members met as what was called a 'subject group', of whom the chair and vice-chair were customarily the party's spokesman and deputy spokesman. But they had not been consulted about the appointment of Benn and his deputy, Bermondsey MP Bob Mellish, so the subject group decided not to elect them. The Transport Minister thus found himself discussing Commons business with two obscure transport union-sponsored MPs instead of Benn and his deputy. The revolt was short lived. Benn met the subject group and charmed them into accepting him.

He was, anyway, becoming successful in the Commons through many hours of homework and the creative use of the fruits of his labours. He found, for example, that Prime Minister Macmillan had once been a director of the Great Western Railway. The company was doing well when he was appointed but by the time he ceased to be a director at the end of the 1930s the Great Western was bankrupt. This sort of detail of the performance of transport under private industry was guaranteed to produce shrieks of delight from his own side and embarrassed shrugs from the government.

In his maiden speech as shadow transport spokesman he argued for a Commissioner of Metropolitan Transport to take responsibility for bringing some kind of order to the chaos of London's traffic congestion. The Commissioner would be responsible for more road-building and the organisation of a body of parking inspectors, whom Benn did not particularly wish to have called traffic wardens – 'a mixture of shelter marshal and game warden' – but would prefer the name London Motor Patrol.[8] More controversially, he wished to give the Commissioner powers to tax companies which refused to stagger the working hours of their staff, producing massive congestion when all employees were discharged at exactly 5.30 p.m.

The Transport Minister Ernest Marples remarked, 'If he continues to make speeches like that I will steal all his bright ideas and claim credit for them.'[9] Something like this did happen. Benn argued for compulsory seat belts, harsher penalties for drunken drivers, annual roadworthiness tests for vehicles, analysis of the cause of accidents and imaginative road-safety programmes, all of which became law or public policy in future decades.

He also argued for a comprehensive transport policy to replace the approach which had always prevailed of treating every means of transport as a distinct entity to be scrutinised by the ministry in isolation. He was not successful and Britain has never had an integrated transport policy, planned in the public interest. Different means of transport competed on the same profitable routes while no public transport existed for other locations. Public transport continued to struggle for want of adequate subsidies, driving people to private means of transport which were less cost effective.

Tony Benn was better known in the party and nationally than ever before: his file for speeches and articles in 1960 is twice the size of that of earlier years. Now that he had entered the NEC, he was at the height of his prestige in the Labour Party. Being a front-bench spokesman gave him the best parliamentary platform he had yet had.

His international sympathies, however, were attracting attention from those who were presenting him as the blue-eyed boy of Labour's streamlined image. In an otherwise eulogistic piece the *Observer* commented that Benn was 'a little too enthusiastic, per-haps, about the FLN in Algeria'.[10] But history was on his side. Soon most of the objectives of the Movement for Colonial Freedom would be met.

In January 1960 Harold Macmillan embarked on a tour of Africa, ending the following month in Cape Town. There he told the South African Parliament, 'The most striking of all the impressions I have formed since I left London a month ago is of the strength of African national consciousness. In different places it takes different forms, but it is happening everywhere. The wind of change is blowing through this continent and, whether we like it or not, this growth of national consciousness is a political fact. We must all accept it as a fact, and our national politics must take account of it.'[11]

It was, of course, no thanks to Harold Macmillan or the Conserva-tive Party that Africans were winning their freedom, though it was a considerable act of statesmanship to recognise the inevitable and pronounce it so clearly in the face of right-wing objections at home and abroad. Britain is deserving of respect in Africa not because of the action of its governments but because of the relentless support of liberation movements by the rebels like Harold Laski, Fenner Brockway, Aneurin Bevan and Tony Benn, support which left them open to charges of treachery by their more 'patriotic' kin.

Tony and Caroline Benn had visited Tunisia in 1959 as guests of the government. Then in January 1960 Benn went there again as an official observer at the All African People's Conference, meeting again some of his old colleagues from the Movement for Colonial Freedom in this most exciting year for African politics.

Benn celebrated the anti-colonialists' success in Tunis, from where he wrote, 'I have just seen the "wind of change" blowing through a huge conference hall where delegates from all over Africa have been hammering out their future. Listening to them, I could come to only one conclusion. Within five years – perhaps less – the whole of Africa will be free.'[12]

At Nice airport on the way back French police detained him and attempted to confiscate documents he had brought from the conference, but he stood firm and eventually they desisted. The game was played out, anyway, and the old imperial powers were in retreat. Benn was right about majority rule for Africa, with the exception of South Africa, which maintained intractable opposition until the military and economic imperialism of the superpowers supplanted the nineteenth-century imperialism of the Europeans, and South African whites found a new security in playing one side off against the other.

In 1960 there was yet hope that sufficient peaceful pressure would compel South Africa to transfer to majority rule. Benn urged a boycott of South African goods. This was no empty gesture: the UK was by far South Africa's largest customer, taking a quarter of her total exports in 1959. Tony and Caroline Benn were both involved in a seventy-two-hour silent vigil outside Lancaster House, the venue of the Commonwealth Prime Minister's Conference, which was discussing South Africa's racial policy. South Africa had become an independent nation and was deliberating whether to rejoin the Commonwealth in her new status. Eventually it was decided the atmosphere was not welcoming and no application was made.

The extent to which a member of Parliament should toe the party line at the expense of his own conscience was ever a Benn theme. In 1960 it became a major issue for Richard Crossman. The left-wing intellectual journalist had been appointed Opposition spokesman on pensions. He was happy to promote party policy on pensions but was not prepared to support the right wing on nuclear weapons. The official Opposition amendment to the Defence White Paper supported the government's general policy but criticised its in-efficiency in carrying it out. Crossman abstained on the Opposition amendment, despite there being a three-line whip on it, and suffered a rebuke from Gaitskell.

As he noted in his resignation letter, Crossman felt unable to accept this 'extension of the doctrine of collective responsibility from the twelve members of the Shadow Cabinet to a numerous Shadow Administration [which] means that no less than 59 members of the Parliamentary Labour Party are now only permitted to express in private any deep-felt criticisms they may feel of the present Party line'. The next morning Benn rang him, 'terribly alarmed about his own position in the Shadow Administration'.[13] Benn was worried not because he agreed with Crossman over the defence amendment – he had not taken part in the rebellion, which had included forty-three MPs – but because of the implications for freedom of conscience for anyone who was an Opposition spokesman.

At the PLP meeting of 17 March 1960 Benn, 'white-faced and with much feeling', urged Gaitskell to reverse his decision to accept Crossman's resignation. Gaitskell reminded him that he had the right to appoint and dismiss any front-bench spokesman. Benn said he 'would have been reluctant to join the front bench as a spokesman on transport had he known that this would inhibit him from expressing his own views on any other matters of policy'.[14] It was to no avail in the case of Crossman, but Gaitskell, and future Labour leaders, were given a warning that they could not expect unalloyed adherence to every aspect of party policy, at least not from Tony Benn.

The increasing frequency of his appearances in Crossman's diary show how Benn was moving out of the orbit of Gaitskell and into that of the left. Crossman notes on 20 September 1960 that Benn was 'now discussing quite openly how to get rid of Hugh because, with him as Leader, we can't get anything done'.

The curse of the bomb fell again upon the Labour Party conference of 1960 at Scarborough. The question was whether Britain should remain in NATO and whether Britain should have independent H-bombs. A statement drawn up between the NEC and the Trades Union Congress said Britain should not develop its own H-bomb, should remain in NATO but should campaign to change NATO's dependence on the nuclear threat.

Another position was put by the 'awkward warrior' Frank Cousins, leader of the Transport and General Workers' Union, the largest union in the Western world and the most powerful single force at the conference. His Resolution 60 stressed the rejection of nuclear strategy but did not call for Britain to leave NATO.

There was, as Benn saw it, very little between the positions and no reason at all for a split in the party. George Brown wrote an article in the *New Statesman* suggesting that everyone at the conference could cheerfully endorse both statements, because they were not contradictory. Benn felt that agreement between the two sides might have been reached earlier, but they could still come to some accord if only they would talk about it. He obtained the endorsement of his constituency in Bristol to an attempt to bring about a reconciliation between them.

If this were not possible, at least the conference could be presented with an explanation of where the difference lay between the two sides. Did Cousins intend his motion to mean that Britain should leave NATO? Did Gaitskell's policy mean that Britain should not buy Skybolt, the missile the Americans had offered to Macmillan that year?

After a week of activity, urging peace and reconciliation, Benn went to see the two leaders in their hotels the day before the conference started. Dora Gaitskell recollected Benn's approach in Gaitskell's rooms in the Royal Hotel: 'I remember him trying to persuade Hugh not to press with his argument but to seek a compromise. He begged Hugh to change his mind. Well, perhaps in that sense Hugh was inflexible. But he would not compromise on what he regarded as a matter of great principle. Nor did he have any illusions about what was at stake.'[15] Perhaps understandably, Benn's recollection of the event is less sympathetic. 'He roasted me for trying,' he said. 'He told me Frank Cousins's wife was a Communist and all that sort of awful rubbish.'[16]

Benn received an even less enthusiastic welcome at Cousins's door. 'He thought I'd come at Gaitskell's request. He said, "It's no good you thinking you can come here as an agent for Gaitskell," and he tore me off a strip. I concluded there was a sort of death wish. They didn't want to agree a common policy, and one way of treating it would be to try and draw attention to the absurdity of this.'[17]

The executive meeting on 2 October was held in the basement of the hotel. This year was the high point of support for the Campaign for Nuclear Disarmament, and thousands of CND marchers tramped past the hotel with the repeated, insistent slogan 'Gaitskell Must

Go'. NEC members had to shout to make themselves heard across the room, so loud was the chanting.

Benn proposed that a new approach should be made to Cousins and the executive of the TGWU 'to ascertain and clarify the points of difference' between their resolution and the joint NEC and TUC statement on defence which was accepted by the leadership. Benn lost by five votes to fourteen – members felt that the compromise had come too late and was anyway too similar to the George Brown formula whose wisdom had not prevailed.

Benn shouted that he must resign. Other members did not take him seriously, and he stood and walked out, much to their surprise. Had he planned it? He said, 'I did have in mind that resignation was the one way I could draw attention to this. It was a most dramatic time with the chanting outside while we sat in that basement.'[18] The NEC were incredulous. Should they do anything? Their standing orders stated that if there were a resignation the place should be taken by the person who had come next in the original ballot, but Ian Mikardo was outside with the demonstrators and he might be difficult to find. Moreover, there was only one day to go before the election of a new NEC. They decided to leave it.

The air of spontaneity about Benn's resignation was somewhat spoilt by his calling a press conference immediately afterwards and reading a prepared statement. He said,

> I have resigned because it is the only way in which I can warn the conference of the great danger in which the party stands. What we are facing is a crisis of confidence and of leadership. Mutual distrust has reached such a point that some leaders will not even agree to meet each other. It is a terrible reflection on the state of the party that so many of its leading figures can view the prospects of split with apparent unconcern.
>
> No one single statement of policy on defence or anything else can possibly satisfy everybody or do justice to all the different traditions which have come to enrich our movement. But if we are to gain strength from unity there must be leadership that transmits our sense of common purpose in a pulse that can be felt at every level of the party.

Clearly he saw no reason to be subtle about the message that something was wrong with the leadership. 'My generation is not just prepared to sit by and watch this great party commit suicide. Our battle is not a battle for compromise, but for common sense. We are not the soft centre, we are the hard core, and at this conference we mean to be hard.'[19]

They were fighting words, but Benn was not able to follow up with fighting actions. The NEC opposed Cousins's Resolution 60 by thirteen votes to seven and conference went on to support it. This would have caused the split which Benn knew would take place, except that a split on a more massive scale was already shifting the ground from under their feet. Another motion, from the powerful Amalgamated Engineering Union, proposed complete unilateral disarmament and was carried at the conference with Frank Cousins's support. Benn's attempt at reconciliation and his gesture of resignation were irrelevancies swept aside in the earthquake. His speech to conference was 'mildly barracked' and he received 'a sympathetic, though not enthusiastic, round of applause' when he argued for an end to the cold war, the strengthening of the United Nations and more honesty with the public when presenting policy.[20] He had stood for election to the NEC again but was unsuccessful, Ian Mikardo taking his old seat back.

Newspaper coverage showed Benn's standing at the time. He was on the front page of every national, including the tabloids like the *Daily Sketch*, whose headline, 'LABOUR STAR QUITS IN ARMS RUMPUS' sums up the type of coverage his gesture received. 'By the action of one tall, handsome young man,' the *News Chronicle* had it, 'the conference becomes not only a testing ground for Labour's defence policy, but a mass jury which will either reaffirm Mr Gaitskell as leader or direct him towards the political wilderness.'

Not for the last time Caroline Benn found herself receiving telephone calls from the press about events she had played no part in. Benn had tried to explain it to her from a telephone box in the conference hall after the resignation but the scene was too hectic and he told her to watch it on the news. Apart from suggesting a certain faith in the credibility of news reports which was lacking in later years, this demonstrates that Benn had not agreed the resignation with Caroline, though they would have discussed his general intentions. Benn's mistakes have tended to be made when he did not take Caroline's advice.

For mistake it was. 'I regretted having done it immediately and I felt terribly miserable for a long time,' said Tony Benn. 'I over-estimated my own influence and the role I could play, but I was tremendously angry that the party was splitting quite unnecessarily. It was impulsive, ill thought out and didn't have the effect it was supposed to have.'[21]

It did, however, have the effect of making Benn think about the role of resignation in political action. He learned a hard lesson, but at least it had been learned and he never again made the mistake of resigning as a political gesture. It was a lesson that some people, notably George Brown, never learned.

Benn had also secured support from his loyal party members in Bristol. He was in good odour with them. The party sent him a telegram supporting his action in resigning.[22] At the next Bristol South-East General Management Committee he explained that Gaitskell and Cousins should have been brought together for the sake of party unity because their division was based on a poor argument and not a genuine issue of principle. The minutes recorded, 'He asked whether Mr Gaitskell really thought the nuclear bomb was a deterrent and whether Mr Cousins really thought Britain not having the nuclear bomb would encourage others to get rid of it.' He received a unanimous vote of confidence.[23]

He explained his feelings about NATO, probably the first time he had demonstrated his irritation at the domination of British foreign policy by the NATO alliance. He said: 'Until multilateral, comprehensive and controlled disarmament is brought about, any country must be free to make and retain alliances which appear to give it temporary security. NATO was conceived as such an alliance. It must not, however, be allowed to dominate foreign policy.'[24]

Gaitskell's defeat over unilateralism at the conference was not his only setback. He was defeated by two to one on the resolution that, though day-to-day tactics in Parliament were the job of the Parliamentary Labour Party, 'Labour policy is decided by the party conference, which is the final authority.' He had previously been defeated by eleven votes to ten in the executive on support for this resolution. This was not simply a matter of right versus left; in his failure to admit any possibility that he might be wrong in any respect, Gaitskell's autocratic style was alienating many of his previous sup-porters. His keynote speech to the conference showed how. 'I do not believe the Labour members of Parliament are prepared to act as time-servers. I do not believe they will do this and I will tell you why. It is because they are men of conscience. People of the so-called right, so-called centre, have every bit as much justification for having a conscience as people of the so-called left. . . . Do you think we can simply accept a decision of this kind? Do you think we can become overnight the pacifists, unilateralists and fellow travellers that other people are? . . . We may lose the vote today and the result may deal this party a grave blow – it may not be possible to prevent this – but there are some of us who will not accept that this blow need be mortal. There are some of us who will fight, fight and fight again to save the party we love.'

Benn was appalled. He wrote to Bert Peglar (the chairman of his constituency party) about Gaitskell, stressing the supremacy of conference and 'collective responsibility', which he saw as being responsibility to the collective views of the Labour Party as expressed by the conference, not just to the views of the shadow cabinet. He added that, though he was a multilateralist, he could not support Gaitskell, 'because this campaign pledges us not only to defy the Scarborough vote but every future conference decision with which we do not agree and will therefore inevitably develop into a general attack on the policy role of conference. Second: because it establishes a precedent for any member of the shadow cabinet who may disagree with any future conference decisions and thus it undermines the idea of collective responsibility.'[25]

Bristol South-east Labour Party was now roused to fury and wanted to go in for the kill, putting forward a motion demanding a change in the party leadership. Benn showed how much he had developed as a politician by successfully requesting that the motion be withheld in order to be replaced by a motion of his own devising which delivered a more refined rebuke to Gaitskell. On this motion, the meeting 'condemns any idea that the Parliamentary Labour Party should "fight" annual conference decisions and deplores all personal attacks, both of which will inevitably weaken the party and divide it from its real task'.[26]

Bevan had died of stomach cancer in July 1960, so the left had lost its champion. There was no obvious successor. Castle was female; Mikardo lacked the ambition, Foot the charisma, Crossman the

161

common sense to become leader of the left faction. The mantle fell on Harold Wilson. Wilson had been even more of a boy wonder than Benn, having been appointed President of the Board of Trade at only thirty-one in 1947, the youngest cabinet minister of the twentieth century. The son of an industrial chemist, he took an Oxford first in economics and became a don before entering the civil service. As well as being a fine economist he was a superb parliamentary tactician. It may well have been an ascendancy of tactics rather than socialist principle that led Wilson to the left of the party, there being more space for an ambitious young man at the top of that faction than on the right where Gaitskell, Jenkins, Crosland, Callaghan, Brown and Healey rubbed shoulders.

Wilson first stood against Gaitskell as leader in November 1960, getting 81 votes to Gaitskell's 166. Benn voted for Wilson and stuck his neck out rather further by issuing, at the suggestion of Crossman, a public letter of support for Wilson. It was a principled stand, for at any time Benn might need the support of the party leader in ridding himself of a peerage. Gaitskell looked like being that leader for a long time to come.

Benn came first in the ballot for Private Members' Motions in November 1960 and intended to bring in a Motion which would call attention to the urgent need for a new initiative in British foreign policy, to work for peace with neutral nations at the United Nations and against the cold-war blocs. Also in November, Benn was thirteenth in the ballot for shadow cabinet members, which would have automatically given him a place on the twelve-man shadow cabinet should one of its members die or leave the Commons. In fact the twelfth candidate, Alf Robens, left the House of Commons to run the Coal Board, accepting a peerage on the way. Benn would thus have been able to enter the shadow cabinet. But he had also been tipped as a leader of the House of Lords, for the time fast approached when he would have to give up his seat and be told to put on a coronet.

Lady Stansgate, although she maintained her religious zeal, had left the Anglican Church in 1949, irritated by its rigidity towards the ecumenical movement and the ordination of women. She had been a founder member of the inter-denominational Society for the Ordination of Women and was a member of the executive of the

Council of Christians and Jews. After leaving the Anglicans her new spiritual home was with her husband's church, the Congregationalists.

Lord Stansgate had been Secretary of State for Air in the early part of Attlee's administration before the services were reorganised and a younger man replaced him. In 1947 he was elected world president of the Inter-Parliamentary Union and spent the next eleven years travelling the world with his wife and often with their son David.

He attempted to develop this association of parliamentarians into a real forum for international co-operation. 'He fought hard against the division of the world, and especially the division of Europe, into two warring blocs, advocating peaceful coexistence and detente at least twenty years before it was politically respectable to do so, and was one of the first to campaign for the admission of China to the United Nations.'[27] When he retired from the Inter-Parliamentary Union, in 1957, he was nominated by the Americans and seconded by the Russians for the position of President of Honour, an honour indeed at the height of the cold war.

The lease on their house in Millbank had expired in 1958 and they had moved to a small flat in Great Peter Street, very close to the Houses of Parliament, where Lord Stansgate continued to be a regular attender. He had suffered a fall in the summer of 1960 and, at eighty-three, was not in the best of health, though he maintained the rigorous lifestyle he had always enjoyed.

He rang Tony Benn early on the morning of 16 November. He had, as usual, been up since 5 a.m. analysing *The Times*. He said, 'I see there's a list of candidates for the shadow cabinet' – the candidates endorsed by Gaitskell had their names starred. 'I'm very glad to see there isn't an asterisk against your name. I'm so pleased you are not an approved candidate.' Those were the last words his father ever spoke to Tony Benn. 'It is rather typical of my father, that he should have noticed that and been pleased,' he said.[28]

Later that day Tony Benn was sitting in a committee room when a message came from the Lords to say that his father had been taken ill. He had collapsed while waiting to speak in the debate on the proposed constitution of Rhodesia and Nyasaland, which he opposed.

When Tony Benn arrived, his father was sitting up in a small room off one of the long corridors. He had had a sudden heart attack. An ambulance had been called. Tony Benn, with the help of Lord Amulree, took him outside and went with him in the ambulance to Westminster Hospital, where his old schoolfriend Patrick MacMahon was able to help. He was now secretary of the Board of Governors of Westminster and was able to arrange for the family to stay in the hospital with Lord Stansgate for his last hours. They sat up with him all night and, the following afternoon, he died with his wife beside him. It was the fortieth anniversary of their wedding.

The accolades came in from all over the world, as well they might for a statesman whose last speech had been a plea for preserving the friendship between Britain and India, and who had been a radical on an international stage.

Other great fathers of Wedgwood Benn's generation had overshadowed their sons, who had found themselves unable to compete and found their lives disappointing. The most important gift which Wedgwood Benn gave to his son was the freedom to develop as he wished. It is his greatest tribute that Tony Benn did develop in a way which was so like his father. As he later wrote, 'I was, and still am, greatly influenced by my father's ideas and by his example. I am profoundly grateful to have started my life with, and learned my politics from, such a teacher, such a father and such a friend.'[29]

When Tony Benn walked out into the chill winter air of St John's Gardens that afternoon there were other feelings beside grief for his beloved father. He looked towards Parliament and saw the light in the tower of Big Ben burning to indicate the House was still sitting. He would have to take decisive action to prevent his career from dying with Lord Stansgate.

13

Expelled from the Commons

The procedure for evicting an MP whose father has just died and left a vacant peerage was brutally curt. The day after his father's death Benn received his national insurance cards from the House of Commons with 'Lord Stansgate' on the envelope. The Speaker gave an order that he was to be kept out of the Commons chamber, his copies of Hansard were stopped and his travel warrant was withdrawn with a warning that if London Transport were reluctant to refund the unused portion of it, he would be charged.[1] His parliamentary salary stopped immediately, with 'not even a week's paid leave after ten years in Parliament'.[2]

Lord Stansgate's sudden death upset the plans which father and son had worked on. Benn explained in 1961 that they had a tacit understanding that, during what they could assume to be a protracted period of illness prior to his father's death, they would be able to plan their strategy. He said, 'He and I both knew the rather macabre situation might arise of literally going from his deathbed to the Commons and taking it up immediately.'[3] The idea was that Benn would go to the Commons and take his seat immediately after his father's death, taking part in a debate and thus setting a precedent, breaking the magic spell. In the event he did not have the heart to go through with it, which was no loss to his campaign for such apparently callous behaviour would have lost him support.

He had a plan of action marked out day by day with different tasks: press releases, contact Bristol, see Leader of the House and so on. In the circumstances the plan was modified to cope with the number of arrangements which needed to be made and the weight of his own distress. That night as he looked through the files he had collected through years of research on the peerage he was 'terribly sad and upset and very, very lonely. The one man who could advise me wasn't there to do so.'[4]

His priorities were to support his mother and to make sure his political friends understood his predicament and were prepared to help. Far from being an unwelcome intrusion for Lady Stansgate, she reacted as one might expect of a woman who had lived always close to the centre of political life. 'My mother found the battle which began then the thing that really kept her going,' Tony Benn said.[5]

Among the callers offering condolences over the weekend was Barbara Castle, who mentioned that Benn's old colleague Geoffrey Bing was in town. Bing, the brilliant parliamentarian, had become Attorney General of the Ghanaian Parliament but retained a flat in Great Portland Street in London. Benn went to see him there, and watched him pace about in his shirtsleeves and braces, smoking one cheroot after another. Bing suggested a variety of different creative approaches by which the rules of the House might be used to attract attention to Benn's case. It was his suggestion that they draft an instrument of renunciation, something Benn had decided against because he had done it in 1955 without success. That was the point, said Bing; Benn had to draw attention to that 1955 renunciation. So they created another one which stated that, as Benn had renounced all claims to the peerage before his father's death, he could not even be considered the innocent victim of a peerage which had descended on him. He had already repudiated it, he had never been a peer.

Back in the Commons on Monday he started a punishing series of meetings with the most senior members of the House, while in the corridors he was tormented by well-wishers whose sympathy and commiseration he found almost unbearable. His first call was on the Speaker, who opened with the inauspicious pronouncement, 'I have made an order, my Lord, that you are to be kept out of the chamber.'[6]

Gaitskell was no more accommodating to Benn's needs. 'You can't expect the party to make a fuss over you,' he said, adding that it was just as well he was joining the Lords as the Labour Party needed some young peers. 'It's all very well you saying we need some young peers but what am I going to live on?' Benn exploded. 'Well, I hadn't thought of that. I suppose there is some difficulty in this,' Gaitskell answered, pursing his lips, and could only stare when Benn explained that he was not going to apply for the writ of summons which would establish him as a peer and was going to call on the House of Commons to decide the issue.[7]

It was understandable that Gaitskell should show a certain irritation with Benn. His resignation from the NEC over nuclear weapons was fresh in the leader's mind, though not in that of Benn, who had a short memory for political vicissitudes, even without a bereavement intervening. Gaitskell might well have borne a grudge too, because Benn, whom he had promoted to shadow transport spokesman, thereby incurring the wrath of the trade union group, had only two weeks previously been canvassing for Wilson in the leadership election.

Paradoxically, the liberal Tory Rab Butler, now Home Secretary and Leader of the House, received him with rather more sympathy, though Benn was later to discover that this was Butler's natural graciousness of manner rather than a specific sympathy with him. 'Very interesting case,' he said when Benn had finished explaining how he would like to renounce the peerage. 'By the way,' he said, 'one thing – would your scheme permit Quintin to come back?' Benn said it wouldn't; Quintin Hogg had already accepted the letters patent and had been Lord Hailsham for ten years; his ideas covered only people like himself who had not accepted a peerage and did not wish to. 'Ah well, that's all right,'[8] said the Home Secretary. The question of whether the ebullient Quintin could return as a contender for the leadership was a principal theme in Tory Party thinking on the peerage, but it was by no means the only theme or even the most predominant.

Benn's great obstacle was the Prime Minister. He had long believed that Macmillan was against him. In 1959 when he was soliciting support for legislation which might allow unwilling heirs to remain in the Commons he had written to Macmillan and, somewhat impudently overstepping the boundaries which should be observed between a young Opposition MP and the Prime Minister, had remarked, 'When you come to contemplate "the Earldom which is your right" I hope you will spare a thought too for the Member for

Halifax'[9] – who was Macmillan's son Maurice. Macmillan replied on the same day with a typewritten letter ruling out any possibility of introducing legislation to help Benn and adding a handwritten note: 'I slightly resent your last paragraph. Nothing would induce me to do what you suggest' – that is, to take into account personal considerations on a matter of public policy.

Benn restrained his impulse to send a sharp letter back. 'I did form the opinion', he said in 1961, 'that Macmillan was the real enemy on all this. I'm sure he's been the real enemy all along. Rab had said that he thought the Prime Minister was very much against the Life Peerage Bill. I think there's no doubt that Macmillan's a snob and it's just as simple as that.'[10]

The round of political interviews was augmented by arrangements with members of the fourth estate. With characteristic Benn insouciance, as if calling in at the office of the local paper, he went to see the editors of *The Times* and the *Daily Telegraph* and spoke with the editor of the *Manchester Guardian*. Later he also spoke directly with the editors of the *Daily Mirror* and the *Daily Herald*. He had press releases already written but felt it proper to wait until after his father's obituaries had appeared before he distributed them. The story of his intended renunciation was becoming popular gossip before it was propitious for it to be released, so on the Tuesday after his father's death he spoke to parliamentary correspondents on a 'lobby basis', which meant they could not quote him, a way of gagging them. By Thursday he was ready for a full press conference. Most of his actions in these first days were holding measures, to stop the escalator (as he put it) from moving him from one end of the building to the other. Most importantly, he had to distance himself from the viscountcy – he could not be taken seriously if he were to accept any aspect of the peerage. He returned to Buckingham Palace his father's letters patent, the two-foot-square parchment fixed with the Great Seal which conferred the honour. Benn argued that until he received a writ of summons from the Lords he was not a lord. He could only receive such a writ if he first produced the previous lord's death certificate and his own birth certificate, which he had no intention of doing.

He explained these points to the press, describing himself as 'a persistent commoner' rather than the tag they had taken to using, 'the reluctant peer'. He told them he had urged upon Gaitskell and Butler the virtue of setting up a Select Committee to look into the question of disclaiming peerages.

There were three new reasons why Parliament should allow him to remain a commoner. First, he had the day before signed his instrument of renunciation, a step which had a long lineage but which had been discontinued by the House of Lords in 1678. Could their Lordships' decision bind the action of a member of the House of Commons? Secondly, Benn had watched quietly and made no comment while the House of Common (Disqualification) Act went through in 1957. It prescribed that no MP should be forced to accept an 'office or place' which disqualified him from office. Benn now submitted that a peerage was 'a place' and he should not be coerced into accepting it. Thirdly, he argued that the Crown did not have the right to interfere with the Commons by preventing a member from taking his seat. He finally offered a threat that he might stand repeatedly for election as others barred from their rightful seat had done, until the law was changed to permit him to take his seat.

Benn was the front-page lead in almost every paper. The editorial opinion, moreover, was almost entirely positive. He cultivated the press assiduously, though he was always irritated by facetious remarks about a young aristocrat held back by privilege. He resented the focus on human interest in the newspaper stories. For him the point was the constitutional implications of the battle, not the obvious subject to inspire the reader of a popular newspaper. Caroline and Tony Benn simply accepted the personal coverage as the cost of press support. 'I'm not complaining about the press,' Benn said in 1961, 'because honestly the press was very sympathetic and without a sympathetic press we could have suffered terribly. They misquoted us occasionally but that's pretty regularly done. I have regarded the press all along as my friend.'[11]

There was a parliamentary breathing-space because the writ for a by-election caused by the seat being vacated for whatever reason is customarily moved by the party which previously held the seat. The Labour Party would at least hold off moving the writ until the case had been discussed in the House of Commons.

The Lords and Commons were now on hold and the press was aware of the situation. Benn had to see his constituency Labour

169

Party. He telephoned Herbert Rogers five days after his father's death. That he had not done so earlier was his most serious mistake of this period. 'An awful lot had started there that I had to reverse,' said Benn. 'I kicked myself for allowing it to slide, because they had accepted the inevitable in their minds, and the machine had already gone straight to work to pick the new candidate.'[12]

On 28 November at an Executive Committee meeting Benn explained the two points which were the basis of his fight to remain in the Commons: the right of a constituency to choose whom they wished to represent them and the right of an elected MP to serve in the House of Commons. The chairman Bert Peglar reported that there was no guidance from head office: 'matters were to be considered by a higher authority' – presumably the National Executive Committee. Benn suggested at this meeting a petition of all electors in Bristol South-east, mentioning that he had the support of Churchill, Gerald Nabarro and the Liberal Jeremy Thorpe and that supporters of other parties in the constituency would rally round.[13] This was agreed but Benn realised they would need a great deal of coaxing. 'They were utterly defeatist about it,' he said a few months later. 'They didn't believe for a moment that you could throw off 400 years of tradition. And the way in which tradition does press down upon people and make them feel there is nothing they can do about it was the first political lesson from a battle that has been as politically interesting as it has been constitutionally interesting.'[14]

It was not only an issue of high politics, however. As Herbert Rogers said, 'There was some opposition to Tony Benn and they were prepared to fasten on to the pretext of disqualification in order to get rid of him. They were trade union elements who wanted to get their own people in.'[15] There was certainly some following among the traditionalists in the party for the idea that Benn should simply be abandoned. After all, they had had ten years out of him, which was a reasonable time. The right of a peer to stand for the House of Commons, what *The Times* called 'the cause of the over-privileged politician',[16] was not the most obvious clarion with which to summon the masses.

There was also a characteristic trade union fear of matters outside their own experience. Les Bridges, the secretary of the borough party, representing all five constituencies in Bristol, 'really exploded in irritation' according to Benn. 'He hoped it was absolutely clear that what I was doing wasn't in any way to attack the system of hereditary peerage.' Bridges remained an opponent and told Benn, 'It's a pity that you're upsetting the selection procedure for a new candidate for Bristol South-East.'[17] Traditional party officials could not comprehend the point of the manoeuvre. Putting up a disqualified candidate was the opposite of everything their training and experience had taught them. An additional concern was that a by-election would distract attention from the municipal elections in May and so cause Labour to lose control of the City Council. At least the executive agreed to hold off the selection procedure until after the House had debated the matter.

On 29 November, the day after the Bristol South-East executive meeting, former Labour Solicitor General Sir Lynn Ungoed-Thomas presented a petition to the Commons on Benn's behalf, urging that the case should be sent to a select committee. Benn had prepared the personal petition, containing the legal points he had picked up over the years.

Rab Butler was probably entrusted by the cabinet with the final decision on whether Benn's petition should be referred to a committee of privileges, which would examine Benn's case alone, or a select committee, which could look at the whole issue of renunciation and make recommendations for changes in the law. Butler plumped for a committee of privileges. The House accepted this without discussion, largely because Butler gave an assurance that there would be a debate on the committee's recommendations.

Benn had scant hope that the committee would help him to achieve his object, but at least it stopped anything else from happening. While the committee sat no writ was issued for the by-election. This suited Benn, for he had a long way to go in persuading Bristol South-East Labour Party that they should select him as a candidate.

Benn had a further difficulty in that he had arranged before his father's death to go on a lecture tour of the USA. Despite his own changed circumstances, he could not let down the organisers, a commercial company based in New York. Moreover it was now his only source of income. He therefore had to tell Bristol South-East General Management Committee on 19 December that he was off to America for six weeks. It was a moment requiring considerable diplomacy. He had just asked them to put themselves out on a limb for him; now he was going abroad while the work got under way. It was a situation not lost on his opponents, who worked against him with the Labour Party regional officials. This was a more promising route than attempting to influence individual party members in the constituency, who were solidly behind him.

Leaving the UK was a particularly traumatic event for Tony Benn. He had not been parted from Caroline and the children for so long before and he was now leaving them, and his mother and brother, in that time a few weeks after bereavement when emotional support is particularly important. He left with uncertainty about his future in Bristol and the House of Commons and with enemies on his own side in both places.

His talks had titles like 'A Britisher Looks at the American Revolution', 'Britain Without an Empire' and 'Is There a World Opinion?' They were delivered to businessmen's lunch clubs and women's current affairs societies all over the country. It meant many lonely days and nights in motels, a situation which called to mind his experiences a decade before when he had been selling trade magazines.

The one advantage was that he was freed from the treadmill of meetings and planning and the now incessant attentions of the press. He was able to examine his own situation. Viewed from the standpoint of a more modern society, the issues in the peerage case became far clearer. Benn was embarrassed at having to explain to people in the US that he was no longer an MP because he had inherited his father's title. The whole thing was ridiculous. It went with the UK's drowsy image of olde-worlde cottages, the Beefeaters, pageantry and quaint customs, while France, Germany, Italy and Japan's image was of being ahead of the times.[18] Benn made two important decisions in the US. The first was 'To take this particular constitutional absurdity as a symbol of a deeper malaise in Britain today: our failure to adapt ourselves to modern life, our fear of the future and our nostalgic preference for living in the cosy afterglow of past glories.'[19]

The other campaign strategy came out of the meetings he had with politicians and ordinary people in the US. He took the opportunity of meeting prominent figures in public life including the economist J. K. Galbraith and the crusading journalist Ed Murrow. He was in Congress when Kennedy delivered his State of the Union message. Everything about Kennedy had a profound effect on Benn and he wrote a laudatory report for the *Bristol Evening Post* about him.[20] Most importantly, he was impressed by Kennedy's ability 'to mobilise all the creative people in the US to work for him' and to summon cross-party support for an ideal of courage and social development.[21]

Benn determined that part of his campaign strategy would be to invite distinguished speakers to use the election as a platform to argue their own case for bringing Britain up to date – scientists, architects, educationalists. He would write to a variety of eminent people in all walks of life and they would project on to the peerage case their own disappointments and frustrations arising out of life in Britain today. He would create a campaign which would appeal to all who were radical and forward thinking, attracting Liberals, radical Tories and the non-political as well as Labour voters.

While Benn was away in the US the Bristol petition was being prepared. Luckily, Herbert Rogers was in place as full-time constituency secretary, now a paid post with a salary of £5 a week. The idea was to involve the people of Bristol in the argument, and to convince them that it was not a matter personal to Benn alone or a national issue: 'This is first and foremost a Bristol matter.' The leaflet which accompanied the petition continued: 'This petition asserts the right of the electors to choose who they want to be their MP and not to have to lose him because of some old customs that have little meaning today. It asks Parliament to correct this absurd situation in whatever way seems best.'[22] Benn returned from America on 19 February and the petition was ready to be circulated six days later.

Benn's supporters in the Commons had moved quickly to prevent the issue turning into a party-political matter. Barbara Castle for Labour, Jeremy Thorpe for the Liberals and Gerald Nabarro for the Conservatives sent round a private all-party whip to every member calling on them to support Benn. Sir Lynn Ungoed-Thomas circulated a draft of a Private Members' Bill, the Peerage (Renunciation) Bill, which would enable any peer to renounce his peerage for life. It was supported by five Tories, five Labour members and two Liberals, giving the maximum of twelve sponsors.

Of his supporters, Gerald Nabarro was probably the most surprising. With his handlebar moustache and Rolls-Royce (its registration number NAB 1), the MP for Kidderminster would not have seemed the most obvious friend of Tony Benn. Nabarro was a self-made man, the sort of individualist who would have delighted Sir Ernest Benn. The more conservative of Labour and Tory MPs judged people on their background: Tories rated their colleagues according to which public school they went to; for Labour members the proudest boast was to have been the son of a miner. People like Benn and Nabarro disconcerted them by refusing to be categorised so simply. Gerald Nabarro was orphaned at an early age, went to an elementary school then spent ten years in the services, leaving in 1937 as an NCO and entering industry as a foreman. The Second World War gave him a chance to join the officer class and marry a colonel's daughter. Back in industry he made the best of post-war reconstruction. By 1950 he was a Tory MP. A passionate advocate of private enterprise and an opponent of high taxation, he was the scourge of prevaricating Treasury ministers. He introduced six Private Members' Bills himself, four of them with success. Tony Benn considered Nabarro 'the best back-bencher in the House'.[23]

Even before Lord Stansgate's death Nabarro had offered to help Benn on a Bill to renounce the peerage. He had already been involved during the passage of the Life Peerages Act, when he had tried to bring in an amendment which would allow hereditary peers to renounce, but he had been frustrated by the Whips.

Nabarro, rather more worldly-wise than Benn, realised that they had a lot more to fight than the issue of principle alone. He remarked, 'A lot of members of both parties do not like you personally, as indeed so many of them dislike me personally. They regard us as extroverts, swank-pots politically, and lots of other nasty things which we are certainly not, but they think we are.'[24]

Benn travelled to Bristol on 6 March 1961 to seek the endorsement he needed from the General Management Committee. Thirty-eight members attended to hear Benn present the case against himself. He said a nomination for him might be declared invalid even before the election and the Tory would get in unopposed; he might be defeated in the election when voters were confronted with one candidate who was disqualified to sit and one who clearly was not; even if he were to win the election there would be a petition to an election court and the court might decide that the Tory should have the seat or that there should be a fresh election. 'The question you'll have to decide is – is it worth it?' he asked. There was really very little reason to support him, except for the courage and the vision of a new Britain which Bristol would place before the nation. Of course, they loved him for it. Comrade after comrade stood to bear witness: 'This is a moral issue and it's unthinkable not to go ahead with it. We have supported Tony Benn up till now and we're not going to drop him'; 'All the facts have been laid before us. Of course it's worth it'; 'I was dampened by the difficulties but now I see the principles that are involved'; 'If 85 per cent of those approached signed the petition, of course we will win an election.'[25]

Benn later considered this the turning point of the campaign. Once the constituency was behind him, no opposition from the party machine or the Labour hierarchy or the government could bend him. The General Management Committee made the unanimous decision 'to back Anthony Wedgwood Benn in a by-election fought on the issue of his disqualification from serving as an MP for this constituency'. But Benn did remark that he would accept nomination only if the NEC endorsed his candidature.[26] The next day, 7 March, he wrote to leading figures in the Labour Party, including Gaitskell, Wilson, Brown and Crossman, to explain the position in Bristol South-East.[27]

The prospects for success within the House of Commons were meagre. The Committee of Privileges had spent eleven long meetings hearing witnesses and receiving documents. They had seen Tony Benn but had largely limited his contribution to factual matters. He was by no means treated as a House of Commons colleague. The Attorney General, Sir Reginald Manningham-Buller, 'bullied and hacked at me as if I was a man who had been caught red-handed in the act of rape and was then pleading mistaken identity. He really behaved in a most unpleasant and hostile way. I discovered from lawyers afterwards that this is his normal manner.'[28] He was told nothing of the committee's deliberations, though George Brown did indicate that things were not going well for him. In fact there had been a straight party divide on all the most important issues, the very worst development for Benn's campaign. The sole Liberal voted consistently with the Conservatives. The Tories were led by Rab Butler, while Labour were headed by Hugh Gaitskell, the presence of such leading figures making it certain that the debate on the report would follow party lines in the event of a disagreement. When the report was published on 21 March it found that Benn's instrument of renunciation was invalid; that the House of Commons Disqualification Act could not be used to allow him to renounce the peerage; that whether or not he had a writ of summons was immaterial; and that they could not recommend a Bill to cover Benn's case alone. The only even mildly positive note was that the committee chose to express no view on whether general legislation was desirable to permit the renunciation of peerages. At least that left the door ajar.

The decision not to introduce legislation to aid Benn was agreed by five votes to five, one Tory voting with the Labour side, and the issue being decided by Rab Butler's casting vote as chairman. This did not please his progressive supporters in the Conservative camp, nor did his announcement that when the report was to be debated on 13 April it would be subject to a whip. As a number of Conservatives had already associated themselves with Ungoed-Thomas's Bill, this was a move which was particularly resented and which was virtually an open call for rebellion. Benn's response was to declare that the report, 'far from being the end of the matter, marks the beginning of a campaign in favour of common sense, personal freedom and democracy'. He had developed a tactic of jumping back up after he had been dealt a blow so as not to demoralise his supporters.[29]

The report pointed out that Mr Justice Doddridge in 1626 had said a peerage is 'a personal dignity annexed to the posterity and fixed in the blood'. That seemed to them a sensible view, Benn remarked glumly. He was no more impressed with another remark quoted with approval, 'The question really is narrowed to this: "Had Roger le Bygod the legal right to make a valid surrender of the Earldom of Norfolk in 1302?" ' Benn felt this would not go down well in Bristol.[30] He was angered that the committee had treated the whole subject as a matter of peerage law and had not addressed the democratic question: should the electors of Bristol be denied their choice of representative?

He had been forced to become something of an expert on peerage law and was able to cite on request the degradation of the Duke of Bedford or the curious parliamentary life of Viscount Dudhope. Taking his father's advice to make friends with the clerks, Benn had long cultivated those in the Lords, though initially the reception had been frosty. 'They were very insulted that anybody didn't want to be a peer,' he said. 'If I had arrived with a string around my trousers and a choker scarf and said I was a dustman but thought I had a strong claim to be the Earl of Dundee I think they would have treated me with more respect.' Eventually they warmed to him because he took an interest in the peerage, 'much as someone who collects toy soldiers is delighted if you go along and offer to rearrange them in a new way'.[31]

The people who knew most about the peerage were those whose duty it was to protect the institution. Benn used the technique of approaching an enemy and asking his advice. Thus he wrote to Garter Principal King at Arms asking how he should divest himself of a peerage. Garter (as he liked to be called) replied that the whole matter was 'unthinkable'. If a duke elected to renounce his peerage, what would happen to his son, or his duchess, 'both of whom would presumably suffer social demolition by his action'? Perhaps trying to seduce Benn into acceptance of his lot, Garter cajoled him with an appeal to loyalty to the monarchy: 'One must reflect also on the theory that the peerage as an institution adds lustre and support to The Crown; anything which is harmful to the peerage is, according to this theory, "kicking away the props".'[32]

Spending his time on such matters increased Benn's feeling of injustice that his career had been stopped so abruptly. Gaitskell had been kind enough to permit him to remain shadow transport spokesman even after he had been excluded from the Commons chamber, but after a few weeks he had to write to Benn, 'It seems clearly that the issue is not likely to be settled very quickly. In the circumstances created by your absence the Officers have felt obliged to invite another colleague, George Strauss, to undertake the Front Bench responsibilities in connection with transport which you discharged so ably last session.'[33] It was hardly unexpected. Benn replied, 'The support of the parliamentary party, which you expressed, is a tremendous comfort at this lonely time for me.'[34] The support of many members of the Parliamentary Labour Party was lukewarm, at best; he needed all the comfort he could get.

The best chances of his career were slipping away from him. He had been the runner-up for a shadow cabinet position in 1960, which meant he should have a seat if one were vacated. But when Alf Robens, a member of the shadow cabinet, left the House of Commons to head the Coal Board, Benn was unable to take his position. He would have been a shadow cabinet member at thirty-five, a rare honour and one for which he had worked – unlike the peerage. 'Indeed are the virtues of the fathers visited upon the children,' as Gaitskell told the Commons in April 1961.[35]

Gaitskell was not enthusiastic about the case, which he saw as having limited electoral appeal. Indeed, he never summoned up any personal interest in it, rudely continuing to sign letters and order his papers when Benn came to speak to him.[36] The turning point for Gaitskell came when his fellow Leeds MP Charlie Pannell lobbied him on the subject during a four-hour train journey on 25 March.[37]

Gaitskell refused to meet Benn to discuss strategy while the Committee of Privileges was meeting, for fear it might prejudice the committee's deliberations. He then criticised Benn for trying to 'railroad' the party into supporting him in a by-election without discussing it. Benn had not, however, gone out of his way to canvass all shades of opinion on whether he should seek election in a by-election if the committee's report went against him. He canvassed support from those whose ideas were most likely to concur with his own. Thus he asked Barbara Castle whether he should first obtain NEC permission before going to Bristol for their support. 'Don't be so damned public school and middle class and ask our permission,' she said. 'Thank God you're in the fight and the instrument chosen to wage it. Go in and do it.'[38]

Pannell was Benn's most valuable supporter in the Parliamentary Labour Party, particularly because he came from the trade union group, who were unsympathetic to a campaign on an issue with so little relevance to the working class. Additionally they were against Benn 'on personal grounds, because they disliked me very much indeed . . . and it was the inverted class feeling which is very strong in the Labour Party'.[39] Pannell was able to act as Benn's shop steward and reassure his colleagues of the moral basis for Benn's fight. He was himself a 'fitter's bench to Commons floor' MP, a self-taught working-class man with an impressive grasp of parliamentary procedure and a powerful sense of justice.

Events began to move faster as Benn's supporters agitated to keep the issue alive. Pannell asked if Benn could be allowed to speak from the bar, a line opposite the Speakers' chair from which non-members were sometimes given the opportunity of addressing the House. The Speaker deferred his decision and announced five days later that it was not an issue for him but for the whole House, which must decide on a motion put down by one of Benn's supporters. Lynn Ungoed-Thomas introduced his Renunciation Bill on 24 March. Its purpose was to attract attention to the subject; it was not expected to be given parliamentary time. On 28 March the shadow cabinet declared support for Benn and the next day the Parliamentary Labour Party did so too, after a two-hour meeting with just fifty MPs present. A number of newspapers came out with positive editorials, including the Conservative *Daily Telegraph*. The day before the Committee of Privileges report was to be debated, the petition from Bristol was presented by Will Wilkins, Labour member for Bristol South, who lived in Benn's constituency. That morning all Conservative MPs received a copy of the letter from Winston Churchill to Benn supporting his case.

On 13 April, the day of the debate, the Speaker announced that he had a letter from Benn asking for permission to speak from the bar. Hugh Gaitskell moved that he should do so, saying 'There is no single case in the history of the House of Commons where a member, whose right to sit is in dispute and who has asked leave to address the House, has been refused.'[40]

Speaking before the bar was in fact a relatively common procedure. Four journalists had spoken at the bar since the war. In the nineteenth century Daniel O'Connell and Charles Bradlaugh had both done so, the former being excluded from taking his seat because he would not swear the oath of supremacy, the latter because of his atheism, which precluded a religious oath. The previous century John Wilkes, who had been in a similar position to

Benn in that he had a seat but was not being allowed to take it, had addressed the House from the bar.

Rab Butler, replying with an unhappy lack of generosity, pointed out that the Committee of Privileges report came about as a result of a personal petition from Benn. The procedure of allowing *petitioners* to speak from the bar was last used in 1837 and he had no wish to revive it. Comparison with the cases of other MPs denied their seats was inappropriate because Benn had ceased to be a member on the death of his father. 'It has been settled law since 1895 that one cannot renounce a peerage.' This was exactly the point at issue, of course, but Butler made it clear that he had already decided it.

George Brown summed up the feelings of many on both sides of the House when he said, 'I have rarely heard a debate in which there has been so little convincing, or even half-convincing, argument adduced for the course the government are inviting the House to take.' He pointed out that the Clerk of the House had already stated that, if the Commons felt that the 1895 interpretation of the law was wrong, it was at liberty to change it.

After three hours of debate the vote was 221 to 152 against Benn speaking. But the defeat operated in Benn's favour because it increased sympathy for him: here was a court which destroyed a man's career and took away his livelihood without even allowing him to say a word in his defence. This courtesy could have been extended in a fraction of the time taken to do him such a disservice. Benn's speech thus attracted more attention when he distributed it as a press release than it would have done had he been allowed to make it in the House.

The result of the debate on the Committee of Privileges report was now a foregone conclusion. The government had a two-line whip on and a clear majority. A further vote on the setting up of a joint committee of both Houses to review Benn's case was rejected by 207 votes to 143 and the whole report was accepted by 204 to 126. The one positive sign was that Rab Butler said, 'It may well be that one case leads to another, and it may well be that as a result of this case we are led to a further consideration of the future of the Upper House. That may well arise, but I am not prepared to go any further with it tonight.'

Butler was the Tory least likely to be drawn in the character of a villain. His distaste was explicit: 'The debate through which we have just passed I have found one of the most disagreeable in the whole of my time in Parliament, and I am sorry that it had to take place.'[41] Why did he behave as he did? The best explanation is that he just dithered. He had had five months including the intensive inquiry of the Committee of Privileges sessions to consider the issue, yet he was still, minutes from the vote on 13 April, 'refusing to amend the constitution by pulling out a brick here and there so as to make the wall collapse without knowing what we are doing'. As Lord Home of the Hirsel (the former Sir Alec Douglas-Home) said thirty years later, 'Faced with some decision he would go around asking everybody what to do and not actually taking any advice. He was consistent in confusing people over what he thought, none of his friends knew what he was going to do on any issue. He could never say yes or no.'[42]

Rather more significant for Benn than the presence or absence of Tory support was the low Labour turnout. He did not realise it at the time but thirty-five Labour members were absent unpaired from the first vote. A significant number of members of his own side had voted against him with their feet, even while the Tories were applying a whip.

As he walked away from the Palace of Westminster with Caroline and Stephen at midnight on 13 April 1961 Benn feared that this was the end of the road. The moment he had managed to delay for four months was upon him. They had shut him out and locked the door.

14

___

Challenging the Constitution

No one could doubt that the battle would continue. There would have to be an election and it was obvious that Benn would stand. Nabarro had urged that the Tory Party should not put up a candidate and hoped that Benn would be returned unopposed. Benn took comfort from the fact that a constituency had never been beaten on a point of principle – the House always gave in, as it had in the similar cases of John Wilkes, Lionel Rothschild and Charles Bradlaugh.[1] He could also reassure himself that this was the tradition in which the radicals of Bristol South-east were only too keen to find themselves. Now he must concentrate on the constituency.

A Special Executive was called for 17 April and the Labour Party's national agent and deputy general secretary Len Williams told them that the NEC had decided to support Benn's candidature if the local party decided to run him. This meant that the constituency would receive financial support, a significant issue because it was £3000 to £4000 overdrawn.[2]

The writ for the election was issued on 18 April 1961. The Tories would have been better advised to let Benn stand unopposed, exposing the event as a sham, and then unseat him with a petition to the electoral court. But they put up a candidate, Malcolm St Clair, a thirty-four-year-old dairy farmer from the Cotswolds who had stood against Benn in 1959, obtaining a very reasonable 20,446 votes to Benn's 26,273. Sir Lionel Heald, QC, MP for Chertsey, in Bristol for the by-election, denounced Benn's candidature as a 'stunt which would rightly receive the strongest possible public condemnation'.[3]

Almost immediately it began, the ecumenical nature of the campaign Benn proposed ran into difficulties with the traditionalists.

Nabarro had been forced to back down from his offer of campaigning for Benn but Peter Bessell, a former Liberal candidate, and Viscount Lambton, Tory MP for Berwick on Tweed, were still prepared to attend the first meeting of the campaign. The Liberals were not standing a candidate so there was no conflict of interests on their side, but considerable pressure was placed on Lambton to withdraw. Lambton had an obvious personal interest in the matter: he too was the son of a peer, so he would be in exactly Benn's position when his father died (the viscountcy was a courtesy title, like Benn's 'Honourable').

It was reported to Benn that Dick Crossman had buttonholed Hugh Gaitskell and George Brown and insisted that the Bristol campaign must be 'torpedoed' before it did the party any more damage: a Tory must not appear on a Labour platform.[4]. The traditionalists in Bristol did not like the idea any more than those at Westminster. Benn was miserable that in winning support from the other side he had lost the support of the party. However, the adoption meeting served its purpose of embarrassing the Tories, though Lambton declared that he agreed with Benn on no issue other than this one. He was nervously hustled from the station to the meeting, the dark glasses he wore because of his weak eyesight heightening his conspiratorial air.

The campaign was daily buoyed up by letters of support which Ben had solicited from famous friends or simply from people who he thought would back him, including those who had not previously taken a keen interest in politics. The theatre critic Ken Tynan, an old Oxford debating colleague of Benn, wrote an affectionate letter, and the playwright John Osborne wrote in the style of Jimmy Porter, 'By all means you can have my support, for what it's worth. Frankly, I should think it would decrease your majority considerably.' Other sponsors from the arts included Augustus John, Sir Basil Spence, Benjamin Britten, Henry Moore, Graham Sutherland, Arnold Wesker and Cecil Day Lewis. From the sciences or academia were Professor A. J. Ayer, Jacob Bronowski, Ritchie Calder, N. W. Pirie and C. P. Snow. Journalists Robin Day, Malcolm Muggeridge and James Cameron also gave their support, Day apologising in a telegram from Moscow that he could not be there in person.[5]

It was in politics that the Bristol campaign truly excelled, however.

In a series of meetings over two weeks, Benn had all the rising stars of the Labour movement in Bristol. The most complex task was to fit Benn himself into this schedule, for he attended every meeting, carefully timing the start and end points of his speech so that he could rush to the next hall. On the evening of 1 May he addressed four meetings, on 2 May six. Among many others, Harold Wilson spoke on his Four-Year Plan for Britain, Barbara Castle on the United Nations, Richard Crossman on the future of the left and Michael Foot on the reform of politics.

Above all, the campaign showed Benn giving of his seemingly unlimited energy. He would address bus queues at 6 a.m., attend works canteens at 8 a.m. and press conferences daily at 11 a.m., and spend his afternoons among his canvassers with a loudspeaker. Every evening at 6 p.m. he would telephone Caroline before the punishing round of meetings. After those, he could be found with other evening speakers at the Grosvenor Hotel with groups of thirty to forty young people discussing politics. He would often go on to midnight canteen meetings for shift workers, getting to bed at two or three in the morning. At the crack of dawn he would start again.[6] Throughout he was taming the press corps. Journalists, regarding it all as a publicity stunt, started cynical but were gradually won round to an enthusiasm for the campaign, almost against their own judgement, even becoming involved in the late night seminars at the hotel.

Benn's old colleague Sir Edward Boyle, now a junior Treasury minister, spoke at the by-election for St Clair as he was expected to. He made a speech on the budget which avoided the peerage issue, then joined Benn and his seminar group in the Grosvenor Hotel.

A short way into the campaign it was revealed that St Clair too was an heir to a peerage via a Scottish cousin. 'Where I could really dish my opponent is by murdering his cousin,' Benn mused, for this would have put both Benn and St Clair on the same footing.[7]

The Benn camp distributed 10,000 copies of the letter of support Churchill had sent him. Effectively this meant that the greatest living Conservative backed the principle on which the Labour candidate was standing. It was a particular embarrassment to Malcolm St Clair, who had been Churchill's private secretary. The Conservatives were not pleased. Exciting though the campaign was, the older Labour supporters looked glum when Benn talked of modernising Britain.

Meanwhile the government was backing down in an effort to save face. Rab Butler announced in the House of Commons on 26 April that a select committee would be set up to look at the question of surrender of peerages and the composition of the House of Lords. Gaitskell declared it a victory for Benn and the Liberal leader Jo Grimond suggested that Butler should send Benn a telegram of congratulation. While the announcement may have made the Tories at Westminster feel better, those in Bristol were livid. The president of Bristol Conservative Association, George MacDonald, was said to have come close to resignation, feeling that the government had conceded the whole issue.[8]

The Conservatives were not without creativity. On 25 April they issued a leaflet in the form of a legal proclamation. In copperplate script and in cod-legal jargon they set out the peerage case and said: 'Now take notice that all votes given for the said Anthony Neil Wedgwood Benn, said Viscount Stansgate of Stansgate at the said election will, by reason of the said incapacity and disqualification, be thrown away and be null and void.' It was signed by St Clair and Lieutenant Colonel C. P. B. Moggridge, his election agent.

The document was raised with Benn at his morning press conference. He brushed it off with 'We expected something like that,' in keeping with the principle of never letting the other side know they've hurt you. In fact he was very worried.[9] St Clair's supporters were planning to post their quasi-legal document at all polling stations. Over the next four days Benn consulted lawyers and politicians with a legal background like Lynn Ungoed-Thomas. Eventually the Benn camp produced a special edition of his campaign newsletter the *Bristol Campaigner* demonstrating that anyone could make a series of statements sound legal: 'Now take notice that . . . stating as a fact what can only be his private opinion upon a complicated question of law still to be determined may, in my opinion, render him guilty of the corrupt practice of using undue influence on the electors and, if so, he will be liable to criminal penalties and might for ten years be incapable of being elected to and sitting in the House of Commons for any constituency.'

Benn was genuinely concerned that the effect of St Clair's notices would be to turn the voters away. On his own authority he placed an advertisement, in the terms of his own statement, in the *Bristol Evening World*. The *Bristol Evening Post* wisely decided not to print it.

There were six eve-of-poll rallies. Benn spoke at all of them, then went to a mass rally in St George's Park in the centre of Bristol. Cars were drawn up around the park, shining their headlights on to a platform. The crowd thickened as the speakers mounted the stage. George Brown gave a magnificent performance. Benn was pleased the deputy leader had seen the level of excitement about the issue among ordinary constituents. After the rally Brown told Benn to come to his hotel room. 'I've been sent down by Hugh because you've become a guided missile,' he said. 'From now on, this goes back to the PLP.' Brown sternly outlined the strategy they would follow when Benn won the election, a strategy which would include Gaitskell moving in the House of Commons that Benn should be allowed to take his seat.

Brown explained that there were thirty to fifty members of the Parliamentary Labour Party who were against Benn and added, 'I may as well tell you, I'm dead against you myself. I would strongly object to you fighting the seat again. I didn't want to come down here to speak in this by-election, but still, I was asked to do it and this is my job.'[10] There was little warmth in Brown's approach, but at least it could be seen as a welcome back to the Parliamentary Labour Party, however grudging.

On polling day Benn was up at 6.30 a.m. to find that it was raining, always a bad sign for Labour, whose voters are, on the whole, not so strongly motivated as Tories and can more easily be deterred by rain. They are also poorer and less likely to have a car to drive to the polling booth. Benn went round the districts with his megaphone, calling on the voters. The weather cleared. The first sign that this would be an unusual election came at midday, a time when Tories generally come out to vote while few Labour voters do. This time there was nobody at all. The polls were deserted. The Tories were staying away. Benn started to get cheerful.

At four o'clock Benn went back to his hotel to find the national

186

agent Sara Barker sitting in the lobby looking grim. 'I've just come down to tell you,' she said, 'that in your speech tonight you're going to make no reference whatsoever to the future. I've been asked by the NEC to come down specially to say this to you. It's going to be particularly important if the result is better than we expect. The NEC will not support you further, in any election fight.' Benn was pained and grievously insulted that he should receive this rebuke on such a day and without Barker even being so gracious as to wish him luck. His victory would be just another problem for them.

'You could have sent me a postcard to tell me that,' he said.

He left her, hurt and resentful. Even if he won, he would have to face an election court and would have to pay the costs of the case, possibly for both sides. He would clearly get no support from the Parliamentary Labour Party or the National Executive Committee. His victory was starting to feel barren of meaning even as he held it in his grasp.

The same day he received the devastating news that St Clair had issued a writ for libel over the *Bristol Evening World* advertisement. Benn and Herbert Rogers were named. Now, he felt, he had involved Herbert too in a stupid action which would drain away money, without even producing political results.

On top of all the other problems, this was too much for Caroline, who had joined him for the end of the campaign. There had been no money coming into the household since Benn's US lecture tour in January. How could they put the bill for an election court and the bill for a libel action? How could they possibly afford it? Their only asset was their house. They both felt he had risked their future for a political gesture.

They went in silence out into the darkened streets to do the last-minute knocking up. It was pouring with rain and the town was deserted. There seemed to be no one going to vote from eight till nine. They drove slowly through the glistening streets, Benn's voice through the loudspeaker echoing back from the buildings. He shouted louder in an almost desperate attempt to persuade people to come out and vote. Eventually his voice gave out under the strain of this extra effort on top of weeks of speaking.[11] Now was the great

187

orator without a voice, about as much use as a disqualified electoral candidate, or a husband who has lost the family home. It was Tony Benn's darkest hour.

After the close of polls, while the ballot boxes were collected and taken to the count, Tony and Caroline Benn sat in Temple Meads station nibbling apples and drinking tea. At last they drove thoroughly dejected to St George's Grammar School, where the count was already under way. Banks of television lights were trained on the school buildings. They made their way through the crowd gathering outside. As soon as they entered there was a surge of excited voices. 'It's a landslide!' people said. 'It's four to one!' They had never seen a victory like it. As soon as the votes started to be counted, it was obvious Benn was getting vastly more votes than St Clair, from all areas not just the solid working-class neighbourhoods. The Benns' despair turned into the most glorious celebration. They walked about amid the piles of voting slips, chattering and laughing with the party workers.

Benn had given no consideration to what he would say when he won, so he sat down at a child's desk and composed a short victory speech. When the town clerk made the declaration Benn stepped forward and announced that the House of Commons was no longer dealing with him alone, but had the authority of the constituency to contend with. As the count had progressed, the crowd outside had increased in size, and shouts of 'We want Benn!' could be heard. He stepped out into the blaze of television lights, which were turning night into day for the crowd of 2000 mainly young people. He and Caroline stood on the steps of the school while the crowd cheered and cheered. His voice was still hoarse and he pushed it to its limits to give a shrill speech saying they would go on until they had removed all privilege from Britain.

St Clair, who had also come out, went forward but the crowd shouted him down and would not desist until Benn held up his hand for silence. To boos and hisses St Clair said it was not the end of the fight, obviously meaning that he was going for an election petition.

When he had finished Benn was taken up by the crowd and carried shoulder high to a jeep. He stood up in the back thanking his supporters as he was driven very slowly through the masses of people who were blocking the entire main road.

Benn received 23,275 votes against St Clair's 10,231, a majority of 13,044. He had won almost 70 per cent of the vote.

15

The Election Court

They drove back to London the next day to find their house under siege from the press, who were waiting to picture the conquering hero returning to his four devoted children. Press coverage of his victory had been lavish. Unmoved, Conservative Party Central Office put down a petition in St Clair's name to unseat Benn on the morning of 8 May – the day Benn was going to take his seat. The whole issue would now have to go before an election court.

The plan which Benn had discussed with George Brown on the eve of the election now went into effect. Benn had written to the Speaker, Sir Harry Hylton-Foster, saying he wished to take his seat or speak at the bar. He delivered the letter personally in the early afternoon of 8 May and asked what the Speaker would do. Hylton-Foster said he could not come beyond the door.

'Have you ordered that force should be used to keep me out?' asked Benn.

'Why do you ask that?' said the Speaker.

'Because I am not prepared to stay out for any purpose other than to avoid a scuffle.'

Hylton-Foster was taken aback. He could not decide, he would have to think about it.

'Well, this is quite clear,' said Benn. 'If I'm ordered to stop I shan't stop. But if you intend to stop me you must give orders that force is to be used to keep me out. That is the only condition under which I'm prepared to bow to your authority.'

Hylton-Foster was very upset. 'I had no idea you were going to put it like that,' he said.

Benn put the case again. He had been elected by a large majority and he was coming into the House. The Speaker must take full responsibility for barring him from his duty. Hylton-Foster was nonplussed, but finally said he understood how difficult it was for Benn.[1]

The well-planned incident went as anticipated. Benn, tailed by the usual twenty to thirty members of the press, attempted to gain admission to the House of Commons accompanied by Bill Wilkins from Bristol South and the Labour Chief Whip Herbert Bowden. Benn proffered his election certificate but the doorkeeper said that on the Speaker's instructions he could not enter. Was the door-keeper instructed to prevent his entering by physical force? Benn enquired. Yes, he was. So Benn went off with Caroline and nine-year-old Stephen to listen to the debate from the Distinguished Strangers' Gallery, greeting with silent disdain a suggestion that he should use the Peers' Gallery. The only time he became angry publicly in the course of the entire business was during this debate when he went to the corridor to smoke. This is a privilege reserved for MPs, and one of the Commons messengers told him that as a non-member he must put his pipe out.

It may well have had something to do with his encounter with Benn that in this debate the Speaker made the only courageous decision he was to make in the whole affair: that a debate could take place even though the matter was to go to an election court (by convention the House of Commons does not discuss cases which are to be heard in the courts).

It was a more highly charged re-run of 13 April: down to the discomfort of the government, the Tory defections and the brilliant Opposition speeches. No, Benn could not be heard at the bar, by 250 votes to 177. No, he could not take his seat, by 259 votes to 162. Yes, everyone sympathised with him. The debate lasted almost seven hours.

Benn's intended speech before the bar on 8 May 1961 was already printed for distribution to the press: He did not intend to speak as a man pleading to taste the fruits of compromise: 'I come now not as a supplicant for special favours but as the servant of those whose will must be sovereign . . . Are the people of Bristol South-East to have the right to choose their own member or is this right to be usurped by the government of the day, using its parliamentary majority under the discipline of the whips?'

One difference from the 13 April debate was the tone: Labour felt they had the Tories on a rack and could use the suggestion of improper motives to tighten the ratchet. Thus Gaitskell quoted the Tory *Daily Express* in seeking the motive for the government's behaviour and finding it 'in the able, brilliantly attractive, roly-poly figure of Lord Hailsham, Lord President of the Council . . . Could it be Hailsham, rather than Benn, whom the government is seeking to suppress?'[2]

Benn was not laughing. He had come to the end of the line. He sank into a depression interspersed with periods of frustrating activity. He couldn't get up in the mornings and, when he did, often could not work for days on end. When he did think about the case, it was entirely negatively. He was now facing two court cases and the opposition of the hierarchy of both parties. How far was he going to take this? Would he still be there in twenty years' time standing outside the House of Commons with a sandwich board complaining that Parliament had done him a disservice? At what stage does resolution cease to be admirable and become stupid stubbornness? Knowing the state he was in, Michael Zander, who was giving him legal advice, wrote to Caroline, urging her to get Benn to instruct solicitors to fight the petition.[3] Zander was an academic lawyer seven years younger than Benn himself and who later was to become Professor of Law at London University. He had spent four years studying, at Harvard and Cambridge, and was only at this time taking his articles to qualify as a solicitor.

Benn was inclined not to contest the petition in the court, principally because the government had already succeeded in its motion to debar him from taking his seat on 8 May. It had therefore already made the substantive decision on the only issue on which the election court would rule. Michael Zander stirred Benn's taste for battle by telling him, 'Morally, I think that you are committed to fighting on every front to the last breath. . . . Even if the chances of success were nil this would still be true – the commitment to fight and fight and fight and to ask and give no quarter.'[4] Zander's instincts were right. The Tories were raising the stakes in an attempt to push

Benn out of the game. Zander was advising the correct strategy: unrelenting resistance.

He had another opportunity for intransigence when he again saw Rab Butler on 16 May. 'I got you a Select Committee,' said Butler, 'this was very difficult, the Attorney General was very much against doing anything for you at all.' Benn decided to use the election court as a weapon against him and explained to Butler that he would summon him to the court to explain why he had put the whips on to stop a free vote on whether Benn could take his seat. He said if the election court found against him, he would fight Bristol again.

Butler was uncomfortable, he tried flattery, 'Well, you did very well in the election and our chaps are politicians you know. Remember we're all politicians and we noticed the result and it influenced us.'

Butler became pained and defensive about the issue, much to Benn's surprise. '*The Times* was quite wrong to say I fumbled this,' he said, as if seeking support for his behaviour from the man he had wronged.

Benn left the meeting, anyway, with some security: St Clair would not resign even though he wanted to, to seek a real seat before the next election. Butler would put pressure on him to 'do his duty'.[5]

St Clair sitting in the House of Commons would be, according to Benn at the time, 'a constant reminder of what this law really means. This is one weapon that I've had against them, and indeed the only weapon. It is to compel them to take the law to its own penal absurdity. This is what it really means: a man who has got only just over a third of the votes is now in Parliament. Now by going on and on and on we are courteously forcing them to go to the very end.'[6]

He had started with great faith in the Joint Select Committee, believing it would bring to light further evidence of the absurdity of the law and compel a reform. Unfortunately for him, and contributing to his depression, Labour and Conservative leaders had become locked in a dispute about the committee's terms of reference. Labour wanted the terms of reference to be virtually restricted to Benn's case, the Tories wanted to widen them to include further reform of the Lords, thus rendering it less of an absurd anachronism. The Labour belief was that Butler had deliberately drawn the terms of reference wide in order that Labour would reject them. No progress was made or looked possible and the setting up of the committee was deferred indefinitely on 11 May. At the beginning of June Benn records himself as being 'suicidally depressed'.[7]

Benn did at last instruct solicitors to contest the petition in the electoral court: Ashurst, Morris and Crisp, the City firm with whom Zander was articled. He asked specifically that Zander should work with him. By the intercession of Charles Pannell the Speaker gave permission for them to use the Commons Library during preparation for the trial. Benn and Zander were given a tiny, dark room with a small window through which they could just see the Thames below. Using an ingenious filing system of Benn's devising they constructed a compendium of case law relating to disqualification from the Commons. Whenever their case needed adjustment, they could cast a new thread through the precedents and arguments they had assembled in individual files and produce a new argument, or an argument approaching the subject from a new direction.

Michael Zander noticed admiringly that Benn had one of the prime attributes of a barrister – the ability to master a brief very quickly. This was just as well because one of his problems was that Benn wished to represent himself. Zander advised against it: the case was extremely complicated, he had no courtroom experience, the judges would not listen to him. The most eminent Labour QCs in the country, Elwyn Jones, Gerald Gardiner and Lynn Ungoed-Thomas, offered to represent him gratis but Benn was adamant.

In the event it was an articled clerk, a layman and his wife who took on an eminent silk with his retinue of juniors and instructing solicitors. Tony Benn with Stephen and Hilary had moved the ninety reference books he required from the Commons Library to the Victorian edifice of the Royal Courts of Justice the day before the hearing and Benn had taken the opportunity of sitting for an hour in the panelled courtroom to absorb the atmosphere. So this was what it was like.

Sir Andrew Clark, QC, instructed by Conservative Party Central Office, opened the case for St Clair. Because he spoke first, he had no knowledge of what Benn would say, and so spent a great deal of time proving a point which Benn had no intention of contesting – that the electors knew Benn was disqualified when they voted for him. He even called witnesses in support. Rather more to the point, Clark argued that a peer was disqualified upon succession whether a writ of summons had been issued or not. The rights and duties and disqualifications of the peerage relied on the letters patent which conferred the peerage, not on the writ of summons to appear in the Lords.

When Benn stood to speak it was to a court full of curious onlookers. How was this elegant young man to perform, now that the eminent QC had put his case? He had never been in a courtroom before this, let alone presented a case. Of all the observers the most nervous was Michael Zander, who had argued so strongly that Benn should not go on. He described the scene: 'People came in because he was a prominent personality, it was a peepshow. Gradually word got around the Temple that this was a serious argument going on here, it wasn't a joke. People came to listen to him and they stayed. The court was absolutely packed hour after hour, day after day. People sat or stood fascinated. It was astonishing, inspired. It was a flawless performance from start to finish.'[8]

Benn spoke for twenty-two hours, during which he dealt with 650 interventions from Clark and the two judges. As he expounded more than seven centuries of peerage law it became clear that Sir Andrew Clark, QC, did not know his case. He was ponderous and heavy and Benn 'ran rings round him'.[9] Benn's case was far more sophisticated than the Tories', arguing from the origins of Parliament in the thirteenth century, taking in Scottish and Irish peers who had sat in the Commons in the sixteenth and seventeenth centuries and analysing the nature of and reasons for disqualification. Very simply put, Benn and Zander argued that the basis of the disqualification was not, as had been thought, blood or succession but rather the incompatibility of duties in the House of Lords and the House of Commons. A peer had duties which made it inconsistent for him to sit in the Commons. Yet a peer who already had a seat in the Commons might consider that he had to balance two incompatible duties and so quite sensibly decide he would stay in the Commons.

The crucial point was that an heir to a peerage could not enter the Lords without personally applying for a writ of summons; he could not have one foisted upon him. No writ had been issued for

500 years except on the application of the peer himself. The rule adopted by the Commons in disqualifying him was therefore contrary to the basic equitable principle that you cannot punish a man for something until he has actually done it.

The judges described Benn's performance as 'magnificent' and were kind enough to remark that if he needed a job in the future he could always practise law at the bar. They then retired for a week to consider their verdict.

Gaitskell called Benn to the Commons late at night on the eve of the election court decision and asked for a promise not to seek renomination except in a general election or after legislation to legitimise his position. Benn had been expecting this. He gave the promise. There was little else he could do, faced with the unrelenting hostility of the leadership and the NEC to his position. Now he had to hope that the election court would not order a new election. More likely was that the decision of the court would go against him but St Clair would promptly resign, calling Benn's bluff by forcing another by-election. That would be the worst scenario, for Benn would be left exposed.

In the event, the election court played safe and decided against Benn. The judges held that while the hereditary system was retained it could not be modified by the courts. Benn was disqualified, ergo the seat must go to the only qualified candidate, Malcolm St Clair.

Tony and Caroline Benn stepped out of the great building to meet the press. They smiled and posed and gave interviews, much to the delight of the press, who contrasted pictures of the combatants. 'Who won?' asked the headline above the smiling Benns. 'We did!' said the headline above the glum St Clairs.[10] By his skill in court and his gracious but defiant manner after the judgement, Benn turned the occasion into a propaganda victory. 'The most brilliant defeat of Benn's campaign,' as Zander described it.[11]

Malcolm St Clair was in a difficult position, obliged to be the beneficiary as his allies bullied another man out of his rightful prize. St Clair was a man of honour and he wanted to get out of the whole rotten business. But he was locked into the machinations of the Conservative Party and of Tony Benn himself. St Clair offered to stand down if Benn would agree not to stand for Bristol South-East. Benn felt able to rub in the humiliation:

I can well understand Mr St Clair's embarrassment at the position in which he now finds himself. Following his defeat at the by-election he deliberately chose to get into Parliament by means of an election petition. It has now been explained to him that an MP ought to be elected on a majority vote – the very point on which the Bristol election was fought.

He now asks me to solve his problems for him by abandoning the whole campaign so that he can withdraw from the difficulties into which the government have led him. But it is not for Mr St Clair or the Conservative Party to decide who the Labour candidate at the next election in Bristol shall or shall not be.

He suggested that St Clair should seek a pledge from the government that the law would be changed and resign when the change was implemented.[12]

St Clair did, in fact, support a change in the law but would not campaign for it. He would continue to sit for the constituency – 'At least 10,000 people want me as an MP and presumably they are satisfied,' he said lamely. When he took his seat it was the occasion for a walk-out by nearly 100 Labour MPs led by Bob Mellish. Only the front bench stayed in place.

The judges had rejected a plea that each side should pay their own costs. They also had the option, because the case was of such obvious constitutional importance, of recommending that the Crown should pay the costs. Nevertheless, costs of £7518 were awarded against Benn. St Clair's libel writ against Benn was never pursued.

The indispensable Michael Zander had already urged on Benn the idea of an appeal to pay the costs. Asking people for money was against all Benn's instincts. Zander argued that the Benn family should not accept this crippling burden alone and should welcome the willingness of others to contribute to their cause in a tangible way. Finally accepting such good advice, Benn empowered Zander to set up the Bristol Fund at the end of July. Its sponsors were the usual range of glitterati from politics, science and the arts. Lord Attlee, Gerald Nabarro and Jo Grimond represented the three parties. Other areas of life were present in the forms of Augustus John, Sir Compton Mackenzie, Dr Jacob Bronowski, Sir Charles Snow and Lady Violet Bonham Carter. Contributions came from all his colleagues, many with touching messages like that from Barbara Castle. 'Dear Wedgy,' she wrote, 'When bankruptcy stared Ted and me in the face as the result of our libel action, your letter and generous cheque was the first thing we received to raise our morale. I shall never forget how we felt when we received them, realising as we did that you yourself were up to your eyes in your own troubles. You are indeed a good and generous comrade.'[13]

The honest Sir Edward Boyle, soon to achieve his first cabinet post as Minister of Education, wrote, 'The older I get, the less I like the idea of adopting a reverent attitude towards institutions. . . . I hope that perhaps you'll regard my contribution as atoning – to some degree anyway – for my views on democracy at Seattle in 1947. One lives and learns.'[14] He sent the extraordinary sum of £500 to the Campaign. Churchill sent £5, which demonstrated his continuing support. Many other politicians made similar gestures. Dick Crossman, consistently inconsistent, sent five guineas. The response was so good that by 25 June 1962 Benn could tell the Bristol South-east executive that the election court legal expenses had been paid.[15]

After it was all over, and against the advice of the long-suffering Michael Zander, Benn insisted on trying to pay the money back to those who would take it. This was rather akin to the behaviour of his great-grandfather, the Revd Julius Benn, who was left owing £300 in 1863 after a business venture had failed through no fault of his own, but who insisted on paying back every penny, over seventeen years.[16]

16

Political Limbo

With the excitement of the election court over, Benn plunged back into an even worse depression. He did not work for two or three days at a time. His condition was not eased by the constant sniping from the Labour Party hierarchy, who felt that he was now out and with little hope of return. On 5 June 1961 Benn had been nominated by Bristol South-East for the NEC and as a delegate to the national conference in Blackpool. The constituency party was particularly shocked when Transport House rejected his nomination on the ground that he was neither an MP nor a member of the constituency. Herbert Rogers tried again, asking the NEC to use their perfectly adequate powers to permit Benn's nominations 'in these exceptional circumstances'.[1] Len Williams gave the reply to Benn after the NEC had met on the issue: 'you cannot be a delegate to the conference for the South-East Bristol CLP, a nominee for the NEC or ex-officio member of the conference' (as MPs were). This meant, of course, that the Labour Party had decided he was not an MP. This was the point at issue, after all. They had rendered the by-election, the Commons debates and the election court void; they had made the decision themselves.

Benn had no doubt it was Crossman's pernicious influence again. Crossman was chairman of the party that year and so had considerable sway with the NEC and with full-time officers. Benn was, however, invited to the conference as a guest, though that did not give him speaking rights. Crossman said to the historian David Butler, 'At the conference for the first time I really did something dirty to Anthony Benn. I really damaged him.'[2] Probably this was the manipulation of the response to protests that Benn had not been allowed to be a delegate. Len Williams gave the NEC's response: 'Mr Wedgwood Benn can attend this conference as an ex-officio member if he is a member of the Parliamentary Labour Party, but unfortunately Mr Wedgwood Benn has not applied for membership of the Parliamentary Labour Party.'[3] As members of the PLP were either MPs or Labour peers, this actually meant Benn had not gone to the House of Lords, though expressed in the NEC's terms it looked as if Benn's plight had occurred as a result of some procedural oversight on his part. They thus denied him a platform at the place and time where it would have been most valuable to him.[4]

The conference had received many motions, including one from Bristol South-East, drawing attention to Benn's case and calling for reform or abolition of the House of Lords. These were boiled down to two resolutions, one for the relief of Benn and the other to abolish the hereditary element in the Lords. Benn lamented that nothing would create the impression of a real assault on the class system so much as a plain statement that a Labour government would remove hereditary peers from the House of Lords, but no one attended to him because they thought he was only fighting his own battle.[5] The NEC speaker, Anthony Greenwood, stressed the importance of the other policies they wished to put into effect, the very full legislative programme a new Labour government would have, 'and the question I think all of us have to ask is whether we want to clutter that timetable up further with constitutional legislation of the kind proposed in these resolutions. In the first year or so of Labour government it could completely block the advance of Socialism.'[6] Thus was the impetus of the Bristol Campaign deliberately run down.

Benn settled into his limbo of 'wait and see' whether the wheels of reform would again overcome inertia. The personal nature of the peerage question meant that his household was caught up in the waves of publicity on the issue. Coming from a family which had occasionally featured in the society columns of Mid-Western newspapers, was all Caroline Benn had ever known of press coverage. She was not used to the reporting of gossip being taken as seriously as it was in the UK, with reporters working for days on a variety of ingenious ruses to discover trivial personal information. She quickly tired of telling gossip columnists what her husband ate for breakfast[7] and anyway considered the peerage question so unimportant that it should have been settled in ten minutes. 'They thought every woman, especially an American, wants to be titled. . . . They thought I was either being loyal or very stupid because I didn't know how marvellous this thing could be.'[8]

Rather more distressing were reporters waiting outside for the Benn children to appear and asking them questions. Caroline exploded when one *Daily Express* reporter took Stephen aside at the time of one of the Commons debates: 'I overheard him say, "Now you really would love to be a viscount and wear a big crown, wouldn't you?" '

Caroline's function in the peerage case was to keep Tony Benn's optimism within realistic limits so that he did not have so far to fall when he failed. He said he needed a degree of optimism to keep him going, while she would provide the realism. Her down-to-earth style could be rather disconcerting to those who did not know her. The Tory MP Julian Amery turned to her at a dinner party during the peerage battles and said: 'What fun you must have had during the last year.' 'The first year I spend in hell,' Caroline replied, 'will be the next year that's nearest to the last one.'[9]

The most pressing question was: what were they going to live on? Caroline explained to the press early in the peerage battle. 'We are living on our savings. Luckily we have been able to put something by in the last few years. But of course, our savings can't last for ever.'[10]

Proof that the family was not enriched by ancestral wealth came with the publication of his father's will. Viscount Stansgate had left an estate of £37,837 to his widow. One decision was to let the house at Stansgate. Benn's income as a freelance journalist and lecturer was uncertain, but MPs were so poorly paid in comparison with the professions that it was not difficult for a talented speaker like Benn to earn more than his parliamentary salary, which had been £1750 inclusive of expenses.

His first lecture tour, at the beginning of 1961, had brought him about £1000, funding him over the period of the election and the election court. The battle over the title saw him gain in celebrity as far as Americans were concerned, so he was rather more in demand. His next tour took place from 4 January to 24 February 1962, when he returned with £1500; he made another tour, later that year, which raised a further £1000.[11]

He was also undertaking Foyles lectures, which he did not enjoy, and was increasingly in demand as a journalist. From January 1963 he contributed the Labour voice to a column in the *Sunday Citizen* which subjected issues of the day to the scrutiny of the three parties. He began writing a weekly column in the *Manchester Guardian* in November 1963. The *Guardian* pieces were later collected under the title *The Regeneration of Britain* and published by Gollancz as his first book in 1965.

He continued to make radio appearances as a political commentator and produced a series of programmes for Associated-Rediffusion in 1962 called *An A–Z of Democracy* in which the Tory MP Norman St John-Stevas and Jeremy Thorpe took part. He was offered a job as a producer by Granada at the impressive salary of £3000 a year but turned it down, feeling that any permanent post would prevent him from putting his all into his political work.

The Benns' financial difficulties were greatly eased because, as a matter of temperament rather than resources, the family had never gone in for extravagance. There were no expensive wardrobe and no large cars to maintain. Benn's lack of pretension was genuine, not a persona adopted for the cameras. Michael Bowen remembers Benn staying at his home outside Bristol after an *Any Questions?* broadcast. He said, 'I vividly remember him going off down the road to hitch a lift into Bristol with his beret on and his RAF haversack over his back.'[12] Both Caroline and Tony Benn found their entertainment in cerebral rather than material things. Benn even treated food with disdain, saying he 'regarded meals as "an interruption between two pipes" '[13] and that he 'yearned for America where eating has become much more mechanised. You can go into a clean Wimpy bar and get a hamburger or you can get chocolate malted milk. You can eat quickly and nourishingly at a reasonable price.'[14]

Nevertheless, denied the infusion of political minutiae, Benn was simply bored much of the time. So he had the opportunity to collate and file the correspondence and the documents relating to the campaign, which means they are the best presented material in the archive. In every respect the peerage case dominated his life, the petty issues being in many ways more upsetting than the major ones. He had a teeth-gritting battle with Sir William Haley, editor of *The Times*. He wrote to the few newspapers which had taken to calling him Lord Stansgate and explained that he really did prefer the name Anthony Wedgwood Benn on the ground that the name by which someone prefers to be known is a matter of courtesy to them rather than objective fact: both Beatrice Webb and Bertrand Russell were always referred to as such despite their ennobled state.

Sir William Haley replied that his was a newspaper of record and 'an election court has declared quite unequivocally that you are Lord Stansgate and it is for that reason that you cannot sit in the House of Commons. It seems to me that if *The Times* were to go on referring to you as Mr Wedgwood Benn it would perpetuate a fiction.'[15] In vain did Benn remark that the election court had called him Anthony Wedgwood Benn throughout and that a peerage supplements but does not remove a man's name. Haley was unmoved. Benn therefore paid for an advertisement in *The Times* on 28 December 1961 which stated: 'Caroline and Anthony Wedgwood Benn are continuing to use these names and would like to be known as such.'

Having the passport and electoral registration office call him Benn was a victory. The BBC would call him Anthony Wedgwood Benn but not MP. *Any Questions?* had particular problems with it, but eventually took to calling him 'for many years the member of Parliament for Bristol South-East'.[16] Dick Crossman, inevitably, delighted in calling Benn Lord Stansgate.

Foreign travel, paid for by his hosts, gave him some respite from the tedium of London without Parliament. In October 1961 he was invited to India for a conference on Portuguese colonialism in his capacity as chairman of the Movement for Colonial Freedom's Goa Committee. In April 1962 he went to Königswinter for the annual Anglo-German Conference. The Königswinter Conferences, set up after the Second World War and dedicated to brotherhood and co-operation between European nations, were highly influential in winning over Labour MPs (including Benn) to British entry into the Common Market. He went to Israel for a seminar in January 1963, at which he argued that time was not on the side of the Israelis and suggested linking the further immigration of Jews with the return of Palestinian refugees on the same ratio. He was called to meet Foreign Minister Golda Meir, who gave him 'a very stern talking to'.[17]

Some of his time in Britain was consumed in protest and agitation. The Benn family was pictured on vigils and demonstrations on the anniversaries of the March 1960 Sharpeville massacre in South Africa. Later, in June 1964, he was to join the protest outside the South African Embassy when Nelson Mandela was sentenced to life imprisonment in the Rivonia trials.

Even in the midst of the peerage case, when it might have been more judicious to avoid controversial subjects, he was involved in race issues. In January 1962 he proposed a motion in Bristol protesting against the government's Commonwealth Immigrants Bill, 'which legalises colour prejudice and places Commonwealth citizens in a worse position than aliens'. The motion went on to call for 'measures to make racial discrimination and incitement illegal' and urged the government to seek co-operation with other Commonwealth governments to 'abolish poverty in their own lands', which would obviate the need for immigration.[18]

The trade union lobby in Bristol, which was already somewhat suspicious of Benn, was not mollified by his support for the West Indian side in the Bristol colour-bar scandal in May 1963. The Transport Holding Company which ran the bus service in Bristol had imposed a colour bar and employed whites only, receiving tacit support from the Transport and General Workers' Union in the area. A young West Indian called Paul Stephenson organised protests against the policy. When Benn became involved, the regional committee of the TGWU angrily told him that Stephenson was a Communist (which was not true), an agitator, unrepresentative of the West Indian community, and that the trade union had been working for years behind the scenes to have the bar removed. Benn defended his position and even went so far as to persuade Harold Wilson to condemn the practice in a speech. Within days of the TGWU's attack on him, the bar was officially abandoned.

Benn was able to write to tell Gaitskell that Labour had done 'sensationally well' in the May 1961 municipal elections.[19] Even Crossman telephoned to congratulate Benn on the result, which was gracious of him given that the fear of a detrimental effect on the municipal elections had been one of his principal reasons for opposing the Bristol Campaign.

Even in Bristol, however, the faithful were feeling the detumescence which follows excitement. To tap some of the reforming energy he had unleashed in his seminars at the Grosvenor Hotel, Benn set up the New Bristol Group in June 1962 along with some of the enthusiastic young professionals who had supported him. They issued papers on housing, shopping, traffic planning, investment, marriage and family guidance, consumer protection, race relations and local government reform, thus anticipating many of the preoccupations of the 1960s. It was not a popular organisation with the traditional Labour patriarchs of Bristol, because it was a policy-forming group which was not under the control of the party or the council hierarchy.

Benn continued to visit the constituency at weekends, to attend meetings and give surgeries, where he dealt with problems from the public. Bristol City Council at first treated his intercessions with respect but, inevitably, the officials became bored with responding to him after a time.

The Bristol South-East Constituency Labour Party letter paper proudly stated: 'Elected Representative – Anthony Wedgwood Benn'. The party was steadfast, their defiance fuelled by the indignity of being represented by Malcolm St Clair. Benn said, 'The constituency party made an amazing sacrifice – for three years they were prepared to accept a Tory MP rather than give up. It was an astonishing act of political consistency and personal loyalty – it absolutely wedded me to that area. They were very kind to me and I was enormously grateful. I can never repay what I owe to the left in Bristol.'[20]

In July 1962 he invited Charles Pannell down to Bristol to debate the Common Market which Britain had applied to join in July 1961. Pannell was in favour and Benn at the time against. Though he was by no means a convinced anti-marketeer, he believed that the Market would contribute to cold-war thinking and would make British planning impossible because of the movement of economic decision-making to Brussels. Most importantly, he wanted the issues to be properly discussed by the public.

Benn had determined not to face the treatment from the National Executive he had received the previous year. He rented accommodation in the Bristol South-East constituency, got on to the electoral register, joined the local Labour Party and voted in the municipal elections to demonstrate his political presence as a member of the party. He was nominated as a conference delegate and for the National Executive. He was therefore present at the 1962 conference in Brighton at which Gaitskell, after wearing himself out fighting, fighting and fighting again to reverse unilateralism, actually succeeded in doing so. Benn also won back his seat on the National Executive, coming fourth in the constituency section behind Wilson, Greenwood and Castle, with Callaghan and Healey topping the list of those not elected. Dick Crossman came fifth. From being sent out shivering into the political wilderness, their rival had returned in triumph.

17

Back Victorious

On 18 January 1963 Gaitskell died after a short illness heralded by the acute onset of an auto-immune condition. 'Nobody realised how serious it was,' Benn recorded in his diary.[1] Gaitskell had gone for a check-up in November 1962, explaining that he might be Prime Minister soon and it would be wise to be sure he was in the best of health. It may well be, of course, that he knew he was unwell but wanted a reason for seeing a doctor which did not announce his fears to the world. The hospital identified the breakdown in his immune system.

Benn was not in the best of health himself. His overwork, fatigue and refusal to eat properly manifested themselves in recurrent attacks of bronchitis, the complaint suffered by his father. He underwent a bout of this which kept him in bed during a visit to Poland for the Jablonna Conference, an East European copy of the Königswinter Conference, at the end of January 1963. He came back in time to see, and applaud, the Parliamentary Labour Party make its choice in the leadership election. Wilson was declared leader on 14 February, having won 115 votes to George Brown's 88 in the first ballot and 144 to Brown's 103 in the second.

It was a particularly welcome choice for Benn. Wilson at that time represented the progressive forces which he had harnessed in the Bristol by-election and, most importantly for Benn, Wilson wanted to make use of him. Benn's diary for the period is full of positive references to Wilson and to Wilson's use of his talents, allowing him to assume a position next to the leader which Jenkins and Crosland had enjoyed next to Gaitskell. In December 1963 Wilson asked Benn to be his speechwriter and to co-ordinate the work of other contributors. It was an honour, but one which kept Benn out of the limelight and soaked away some of his best ideas, which he would otherwise have used in his own speeches or his *Guardian* column, the writing of which he invariably found trying.

Wilson also showed a little more interest in the peerage case. While Benn was keeping himself occupied and fighting to maintain his position in the party, the machinery of reform was slowly easing itself round. Iain Macleod's replacement of Butler as Leader of the House of Commons in October 1961 had lubricated the process. Macleod wished to make a gesture to demonstrate that he was now the hope of liberal Tories, a mantle Butler had in part repudiated by his shabby treatment of Benn. There were other reasons why he wanted to see the matter settled: it was unfinished parliamentary business; there was some pressure from long-time Benn supporters on his own benches; the public were overwhelmingly for reform and the presence of St Clair on the Tory benches was an intense embarrassment. Eventually Macleod let it be known that he would go ahead with the Joint Select Committee without Labour being represented. At the same time, the impediment to Labour's representation, that they wanted no part of a general reform of the Lords, disappeared under a combined assault. The Tory proposal for a select committee to examine the composition of the Lords as well as other anomalies had been sunk by a combination of opposition from Labour and from the Tory hereditary peers, one side fearing too little reform and the other too much.

Macleod asked to see Benn in December 1961. Benn sat miserably in the lobby with his khaki parachute bag of documents, never having felt more out of place in the House of Commons. Despite this feeling, when he saw Macleod, a Tory intellectual and a man of some integrity, he realised he was well on the way to success. Macleod wanted the Select Committee to deal with the obvious anomalies like the position of peers wishing to renounce; Scottish peers who were disqualified from the House of Commons even when they had no seat in the Lords and hereditary peeresses in their own right who could not sit in the Lords. Macleod assured Benn that he wanted to see him back in the Commons – it was his home. The interview was going extremely well until Benn raised the question of St Clair.

'I know he wanted to resign after the election,' he said, 'but Rab [Butler] persuaded him to stay. If we are now so near a solution to the problem, I naturally hope very much he doesn't resign.' St Clair's resignation would obviously mean that Benn, while still a peer, would have to stand again for his constituency just when a solution to the whole problem was being sought. It would be far more sensible to keep the whole thing on hold.

'Well,' said Macleod, 'I had no idea that you had any notion of keeping up with Bristol South-East. We've never regarded Bristol South-East as having anything to do with this committee whatsoever. I've never heard anything so arrogant in my life, that you should be sitting here thinking you can hold the constituency and the government up to ransom. Change the law so that you can go back! You can get a seat some other time, somewhere else.'

Benn's eyes filled with tears at the injustice of it. 'I'm sorry that you should think it arrogant,' he said, 'but what do you mean? What could I do? I'm out of Parliament, I may be out for life. I was only expressing my hopes as to how the thing might end. I can't force you to do anything about it at all.' His great fear now was of Macleod taking umbrage and letting the whole issue of Lords reform go by default. St Clair wanted to resign, Macleod told him, he might even go in the Christmas recess. It is possible they could hold him until spring. Why couldn't Benn accept St Clair's pledge that he would resign if Benn agreed not to fight the seat? Benn replied, 'Over the last year my relations with my constituency have been the only thing that really mattered. This year, beginning with the bereavement and losing my job and being thrown out of Parliament, then having an £8000 bill to pay, these chaps have stuck absolutely firmly by me. I'm not prepared to give up. I'm not prepared to desert them.'

Macleod then apologised for calling Benn arrogant, and no decision was made on the future of Bristol South-East. In fact Benn was in control: pressure was now put on St Clair to hang on to the seat he had won by such unconventional means.[2] St Clair was trying to find another seat and applied for Cheltenham on 22 January 1962, though presumably without the blessing of the party leaders. St Clair had a somewhat miserable time in the Commons, where he was notable for the Benn case rather than for his own attributes.

He made a maiden speech about the need for more radio sets for territorial army units.

Benn later explained his strategy: 'I kept saying, "The Labour government when it comes to power will abolish the Lords if you don't do this", but it was all bluff. The best-kept secret of the peerage case was how little support there was in the Labour Party hierarchy. If that had come out I'd have been dished.'[3]

With Macleod as midwife, the Select Committee was set up on 28 March 1962, with Labour representation, and had its first meeting on 16 May. Benn kept his head down on the advice of Charles Pannell, among others, because any further publicity around the subject at this time might have had an adverse effect. Pannell showed Benn documents from the Select Committee (as gross a breach of privilege as might be found) and Benn drafted a memorandum stating exactly what was required to solve his problem. Pannell then circulated this document to Labour members under his own name. By the end of the drafting procedure the only person the Bill did look like helping was Benn. 'This is going to be a Wedgwood Benn enabling Bill,' said Lord (Herbert) Morrison.[4] Fortunately for Benn, the popular Tory Viscount Hinchingbrooke (the 'Viscount' was a courtesy title, like Lambton's, and did not disbar him from the Commons) became Earl of Sandwich on the death of his father in 1962. Now both sides had favourite sons who required relief and Tory members felt much happier giving it to 'Hinch' than to Benn.

The report was published in December 1962. It was only narrowly – by eleven votes to ten – that the proposal that the right to renounce should be retrospective had been passed. That is, people who had already been peers would be able to renounce, rather than only those who would become peers after the law had been passed. Had retrospection not been recommended, it would have been incumbent upon Benn to go through another legal argument to prove that he never had been a peer.

After learning from Edward Boyle when the cabinet was going to consider its position on the report, Benn decided to put some pressure on the other cabinet members he knew. He telephoned Enoch Powell, the Minister of Health, a personal friend but an ultra-traditional Tory who did not support reform of the Lords; John Hare, the Agriculture Minister; Bill Deedes, Minister without

210

Portfolio; and Hailsham, who was away. As well as recommending this popular reform to them as a measure which should receive all-party support and would enhance the government's standing with the public, he made two threats: first, if this reform did not go through then a Labour government would go a good deal further in dealing with the Lords. Secondly, there was pressure on him to fight Bristol again: he had nothing to lose by doing so as he was out of Parliament anyway. He was actually waving an unloaded pistol at them but, as he wrote in his diary, 'These threats are much easier to make than to carry out.'[5]

At last, on 30 May 1963, the Peerage Bill was passed by the House of Commons. But the struggle was not over yet. In the form in which it was passed in the Commons the provision for renunciation would not come into effect until after the next election. The Tory leaders were blatantly attempting to block the passage back into the Commons of Home and Hailsham, who would then be in a position to stand for the leadership of the party. Their Lordships' House was not happy with this treatment of them and on 16 July passed an amendment, identical to one which had been rejected in the Commons, making renunciation possible from the day the Bill received the Royal Assent. It was the revolt of the peers. The government was defeated by 105 to 25.

Given Macmillan's opposition, Benn wrote, 'It did give me special personal pleasure when I had the satisfaction of watching a government over which he still presided introduce the very Bill which he had so resolutely announced he would not introduce.'[6]

He wrote to Pannell as the end came in sight, 'Life is very sweet for me at the moment as I contemplate the possibility of a reprieve emerging from your committee. I feel a little like a channel swimmer when he gets his first clear view of the white cliffs of Dover. It is nice that you should be in the motor boat bringing me over.'[7]

It was not an entirely smooth ride, however. At a public meeting in Bristol that July week he felt weak during his speech and collapsed in a chair when it was over. Party members looked for a doctor and finally Herbert Rogers drove him to the casualty ward of nearby Cossham Hospital. He felt better for the sedation and a night's rest. The following day he was given tests while Caroline, still in London, cancelled his engagements for the next few weeks and set off to join him. They spent Sunday together walking in the hospital garden in the sun and sitting on the grass, feeling they had 'stolen a little time from the hurly-burly of daily life'.[8] He spent four days in the hospital. Learning that it was due to close, he made use of his time by having a guided tour and later successfully lobbied for the hospital to stay open and receive more resources.

One of the enduring memories of party workers in Bristol is Tony Benn's victory party at the House of Commons, to which they travelled by coach on 29 July 1963. Some 400 people attended what was for them a symbolic event: the people of Bristol were entering the House of Commons having won the right to choose their own MP. Benn's speech was appropriate to the occasion – he held up a phial of aristocratic 'blue blood' which he had persuaded a doctor at Cossham Hospital to draw for him. Soon he would have commoner's blood and this would be all that remained of his peerage.

Tony Benn, Caroline and Lady Stansgate went to the Lords to hear the Royal Assent given to the Peerage Act on 31 July. As soon as the reading clerk had said the words of enactment, 'La Reyne le veult' ('The Queen wishes it' in Norman French) the Benn group left the gallery. As they left, the door slammed shut with a crash, so everyone knew that Benn was quitting the House of Lords. They raced along the corridor and down the stairs as if worried that Parliament would snatch his prize away from him unless he redeemed it immediately.

Downstairs one of the black-and-gold-clad badge messengers escorted them to the office of the Clerk of the Crown, where the Clerk himself presided in a full-bottomed wig. Benn had to hand in an instrument of renunciation, much as he had planned almost ten years previously. In the presence of the Clerk he had to put his right thumb on a green seal and say, 'This is my deed and my act'. Benn's name then went in as Number 1 in the newly created Register of Renunciation. It was fully expected that many more peers would renounce. In fact only fifteen peers took advantage of the Act in its first twenty years. The Act, moreover, did not permit permanent extinction so the sons of renounced peers were able to assume the titles. In Benn's case it meant that though he was no longer a peer, David Benn was the younger brother of a peer and Stephen was a peer's son who would himself inherit the peerage unless he were to renounce it of his own accord. Benn joked about the mumbo-jumbo of it – that he could reproduce peers from within himself but was 'statutorily immunised' from being a peer himself.

Malcolm St Clair resigned the Bristol South-east seat when the Bill became law, as he had said he would. 'I want to congratulate Mr Wedgwood Benn on achieving his object,' he said, and said that he wished reform of the Lords had come earlier.[9] Now there would have to be another by-election. Nabarro dissuaded Conservative Central Office from putting up a candidate and the Liberals maintained the position they had in the previous election of not standing. Absurdly, the question of the Labour candidate remained open.

On 27 May 1963 Bristol South-East had sent a resolution to the National Executive indicating that they did not wish to go through the procedure of nominating a candidate, because they already had one. The NEC pedantically insisted on the constituency having a selection procedure even though Benn had been adopted and endorsed in October 1959 and April 1961. 'My God, the Labour Party makes you sick,' Benn wrote.[10]

The General Management Committee sat on 4 July 1963 with twenty-two nominations for Benn in front of them but none for anyone else. He had been nominated by all the affiliated organisations and by every ward except Brislington, which had always been the enclave of a small anti-Benn faction. Instead of a proper selection conference, he gave a half-hour speech on the tasks ahead and was duly selected, surprising no one but satisfying the NEC.

For the people of Bristol he could do no wrong. He was that enviable entity, a prospective MP who was known and talked about in every home in his constituency. He was treated like a pop star – people wanted to be seen with him, wanted his autograph, boasted of having once spoken to him. Three 'anti-socialist' candidates stood. The only serious one was Edward Martell, head of a far-right pressure group which wanted to divert the Tory Party from its 'pink socialism', abolish family allowances and disenfranchise electors unable to pass an intelligence test.

After a short holiday in France with the family Benn returned alone on 11 August to campaign. He evolved a technique of bus canvassing at this election: he would board a bus, meet everyone on the top and bottom decks, then alight and catch another. 'It has suddenly hit me like a shaft of light,' he wrote to Caroline, 'that there are such public meetings criss-crossing my constituency all day just waiting to be addressed.'[11] He was not without his anxieties, but as he wrote to Herbert Rogers after the election, 'There has never been a polling day when I haven't been worried, and never been a result when I haven't realised how needless the anxiety was.'[12]

Benn received 20,313 votes, over 15,000 more than Martell, who saved his deposit with 4834 diehard Conservative votes. Benn was carried shoulder high from the count, then driven slowly through the crowds to make the customary speech at the Walter Baker Memorial Hall. 'We are a constituency', he proclaimed, 'that has discovered its own strength, and we must use that strength to show the world that underneath the musty pomp, cheap glitter and decaying façade of Tory Britain there is a new dynamic generation coming into its own.'[13] After three hours' sleep he drove to London airport and returned to Nice for the last three days of the family holiday.

18

The Tories in Decline

Benn's battle had far more profound implications for the Conservative Party than for his own side. The reasons for this were tied up with the recent constitutional convention that a peer could not be Prime Minister. Holding a peerage had been no bar to the office in previous centuries but with the ascendance of the Commons over the Lords it came to be considered unacceptable that someone from the hereditary House should hold the position. This was exacerbated by the disproportionate representation the two leading parties had in the two chambers from the 1920s. The constitutional ruling against peers was established in 1923 when Lord Curzon was passed over in favour of Baldwin. King George V remarked that since the Labour Party was the official Opposition in the House of Commons and was almost unrepresented in the House of Lords, the objections to having a Prime Minister in the upper chamber were insuperable.[1]

Whether Benn could become Prime Minister as a peer was certainly seen by contemporary observers as an issue, lyrically put in William Douglas-Home's skit, one verse of which ran,

> What is the matter with Wedgwood Benn?
> He is perfectly sane and the nicest of men
> And why SHOULDN'T a peer live at Number Ten?
> What is the matter with Wedgwood Benn?[2]

Benn has always denied an explicit intention to aim for the premiership. His intention in staying in the Commons was not to obtain a government job, because he would have had a far greater chance of a ministerial post as a Labour peer than as a Labour MP

– there were rather fewer able Labour peers than Labour MPs and there was a constitutional obligation to have both Houses represented in the government. Benn said, 'The only advantage that could have accrued from being in the Commons would have been the right to be Prime Minister. Now, with the best will in the world, I never really imagined that that was where I was going to end up.'[3] Long-term friends of Benn, who had observed his career since the Oxford Union, might question whether this was an entirely candid remark. Nevertheless the premiership was the only objective of the two Tories who renounced.

Unfortunately for the Tory Party, Benn's victory coincided with Harold Macmillan falling ill just prior to the 1963 party conference at Blackpool. Macmillan then resigned. Lord Home and Lord Hailsham, like butterflies turning into caterpillars, prepared to lay down their ermine robes and emerge as Tory MPs. The future Sir Alec Douglas-Home was more restrained than his rival, waiting for supporters to approach him before declaring his intentions. The future Quintin Hogg actively sought support by declaring his intention to renounce and by the vulgar creation of what would come to be called a 'photo-opportunity', making a display of feeding his baby in the foyer of the conference hotel. Rab Butler, the obvious contender, showed no greater ability to seize the moment than he had in 1956, when Eden had resigned.

Even with Home and Hailsham as candidates in addition to Butler, the Conservative Party did not have the widest possible choice: all three contenders were 'men of Munich'. The passing years had shuffled through the pack until the Tory Party had for its leader a choice between three appeasers. Home had actually gone to Munich as Chamberlain's parliamentary private secretary; Hogg had famously fought the 1938 Oxford by-election on the issue of appeasement; Butler as late as 1940 was asking the Swedish Ambassador to sound out the Nazis on the possibility of a compromise.

Benn remarked that Home would be the candidate most favoured by the Labour Party as leader of the Tories: 'His qualities are completely overrated by his own party and are preserved in the public mind by the fact that he is not subjected to cross-examination [in the Commons].' Crossman was his usual self on the issue: 'Of course, the price we pay for having you is having Hailsham as the leader of the Conservative Party,' he said to Benn. Hailsham certainly was the leader most feared by Labour but Benn considered faith in his abilities misplaced; he seemed a superlative politician in the subdued atmosphere of the House of Lords, where an able man had no competition, but in the Commons – like Home – he would lose his lustre.[4]

After a 'magic circle' selection procedure (neither the Chancellor of the Exchequer nor the Leader of the House of Commons had any idea it was happening), Home was chosen to succeed Macmillan.[5] He was asked to form a government, as Prime Minister, by the Queen on 18 October and held that office as a peer until the 23rd, when he renounced and became Sir Alec Douglas-Home, to preside as Prime Minister for sixteen days neither in the House of Commons nor in the Lords until he won a by-election at Kinross on 8 November. The journalist James Cameron wrote scornfully about 'this five-ringed circus of middle-aged political acrobats' who were practising 'government by witch doctors'.[6]

Sir Alec Douglas-Home's experience of returning to the Commons confirmed Benn's feelings about the difference between the two Houses. The difference between being Foreign Secretary in the Lords and Prime Minister in the Commons was, he said, 'Exchanging a placid life for one facing the mob. I'd been away for eight years. When I got back and I rose to speak my knees knocked with the shouting and yelling and the opposition.'[7]

Benn returned to take his seat on 24 October 1963, after the summer recess. Harold Wilson was waiting behind the Speaker's chair to congratulate him. Labour members cheered him. Disconcertingly, the Conservatives cheered too, waving their order papers to celebrate Home's appointment as Prime Minister, made only six days previously. 'What should have been the celebration of a clear defeat of the Lords by the Commons looked like a victory by a hereditary peer over the dignity and privileges of the Commons,' Benn wrote.[8]

He was discomfited and decided not to speak at all, but Charles Pannell persuaded him to. The House was almost empty by the time he rose but he showed that he had lost none of his skill, charging the Tories with using the prerogative of the Crown for party ends.

Constitutionally, he maintained, the prerogative could be used only on elected advice. Here the prerogative had been used to pick a Prime Minister on the advice of the departing Prime Minister alone. 'The fount of our honour is the ballot box,' he declared.[9]

The peerage case, which had made Benn a national figurehead of radicalism and even, to a small extent, internationally known, had not impressed parliamentary colleagues. In the election for the shadow cabinet in 1963 he attracted eighty-two votes, only three more than in 1960. The electorate was the same body of Labour Party MPs, of course, for the Parliament had not changed while he had been out of it, so it is clear that his support in the party and in the country as a whole was not reflected in support among his colleagues in the House of Commons, a problem which was to dog him throughout his career.

At that year's party conference in Scarborough Benn came third in the constituency section election for the National Executive, with only Anthony Greenwood and Barbara Castle ahead of him. He was enthusiastically received by the conference, particularly because he had been selected by the NEC to announce the pledge that a Labour government would act to ensure publication of Conservative Party finance contributions by industry and that political donations would need the direction of shareholders. There had been such control of political donations by trade unions since 1913.

It was at this conference that Harold Wilson in his keynote speech spoke of 'redefining and restating socialism in terms of the scientific revolution. . . . the Britain that is going to be forged in the white heat of this revolution will be no place for restrictive practices or out-dated methods on either side of industry'. This was a speech to gladden the heart of Tony Benn, the party's leading technocrat after Harold Wilson himself. What could be done, Benn pondered, to redefine industries already under public control? The General Post Office was a science-based industry in public ownership. He therefore prepared a seven-page development programme for the Post Office to enable it to 'serve as an example of what can be done, and demonstrate how public enterprises can actually meet the needs of the community in an imaginative way'.

Imaginative it certainly was. Some of the ideas, like telephones on fast inter-city trains, were not implemented for another twenty-five years. Most of the ideas, however, were simple and obvious and should have come into effect years before, like coding to allow the mechanical sorting of letters and an extension of Post Office banking.[10] Benn sent the proposals to Harold Wilson on 30 October 1963. He was frequently writing speeches for Wilson now and had long had an association with him through his work as chairman of the Broadcasting Committee. As a result of this memorandum, Benn feels, Wilson decided to make him Postmaster General if Labour won the next election. Benn learned of this from Dick Crossman in July 1964, with the additional proposal that he would be moved to the Ministry of Transport, a cabinet post, after eighteen months. Wilson said as much to him himself while they were attending the Durham Miners' Gala on 17 July. 'My real cabinet will be made in 1966,' he said, 'just as Clem's was made in 1947.'[11] Benn therefore stopped studying transport policy as he had been up to now and concentrated on the Post Office.

Another memorandum did not have such happy consequences. He wrote a paper for the NEC's Home Policy Subcommittee, on which he sat, advocating the reform of the honours system. Hereditary honours are wrong in themselves, Benn argued, because they confer status and privilege merely by virtue of birth but with no demonstration of merit. What was really wrong with the honours system, however, was the use of titles which buttress the class system by dividing people into social categories built on the idea of superior and inferior human beings. Benn additionally criticised the awards for public service and decorations for gallantry in that they were awarded on the basis of the status of the person who had performed the service rather than the quality of service or the courage shown. The best system would be for a Labour Prime Minister to discontinue the hereditary parts of the system and not recommend anyone for the Orders of Chivalry. Instead, Benn suggested a new type of honours system based on the old one but which would 'provide a simple and dignified way of rewarding merit and courage that is more in accordance with the needs of our time.'[12] If Benn's proposals had any chance of success it should have been now, just after Macmillan had made his doctor and public relations men baronets and his private secretary a peer. As was to be seen, however, Macmillan was not the only Prime Minister who enjoyed the honours system.

When the NEC discussed the paper it was without enthusiasm; at length George Brown said they had spent too long on an unimportant subject and the paper was 'noted'.[13]

Schooling presented a problem for a socialist in the early 1960s – the Benns had a choice of sending their children to a public school, a bastion of elitism, or to the deplorable and equally class-ridden state system, which Labour were pledged to do away with. By 1963 all four children were at private schools, despite the opposition of both parents to such institutions and despite Benn's own precocious vow when he was still at Westminster that he would never send his own children to a private school. The Labour solution to the crisis in education would be to abolish the invidious testing and grading of children at eleven years and develop the comprehensive system, which accepted pupils of all abilities and all classes. Grammar and secondary modern schools would be done away with.

What should Tony and Caroline Benn do in the meantime, however?

In the spring of 1964 they were actively working on removing their children from private schools. When they began looking into the issue they decided a comprehensive school was what they wanted. Nearby their home in Holland Park a comprehensive had been built whose first intake was now in the fifth year. In May 1964 the Benns visited and Tony Benn noted that it was 'new and vigorous and active, and we were much impressed by it'.[14] They arranged that the two older boys would start the following September. The two younger children were to move to the local state primary school shortly after.

The Benns told the staff and head of Westminster Under School of their decision regarding the two older boys. The staff were taken aback, Caroline recalls, as they assumed a comprehensive was some sort of trade school, and that the boys would have to abandon academic education.

In the event, all four of the Benn children attended Holland Park. The whole family was committed to the school and, in the years that followed, defended it and the comprehensive system frequently. Caroline was co-opted as a governor in 1968.

Tony Benn had been keeping a diary sporadically since childhood.

It had always been his ambition to keep one, and early fragments of diary exist, including one during his time in the services, where diary-keeping was forbidden for security reasons so he put key words relating to places or equipment in code. In the 1950s he began keeping a political diary and wrote at least some parts of a diary for every year from 1953. The emotional shock of his father's death and the peerage case stopped his diary writing in 1961 and 1962 but, with victory in the peerage case in sight, he resumed it on 15 January 1963. This was not because he felt moved to record great events: the first occurrence he notes is a dinner with his friend Enoch Powell and their wives.

Benn thereafter managed to maintain a daily diary despite the pressures of office, which often had him up till the early hours of the morning. His own dogged self-discipline and stubbornness obliged him to continue with the diary once he had started but there were two contributing factors which helped. The most obvious was the development of a small portable tape-recorder, which allowed him to dictate a fragment of diary while also dictating letters for his secretary. His frankness may have been curbed by dictating to another person but it does not appear so. He managed to dictate gnostic remarks like 'I have made the office buy me an egg-timer for my desk. They will just have to get used to the way in which I work',[15] and 'To the office where I found an invitation waiting for a sherry party at Buckingham Palace. This is what I have been dreading.'[16] But to think of an individual forming the audience for Tony Benn's diaries is to misunderstand the nature of the man. The diaries are the spoken word; they reflect his gifts as an orator rather than a writer.

When in 1966 he took to dictating the diary and storing the tapes so they could remain confidential, he did not know when he would transcribe them, or indeed if they would be transcribed in his life-time. This leads to the second reason why he was prepared to maintain a habit of diary-keeping which sometimes added two hours to the working day: he was moved by the idea that maintaining a record of this nature mattered for the people of the future, the idea that he was contributing to history. The historian David Butler said that the diaries are Benn's 'attempt to hijack history. The historians of the future are going to use his diaries because they are a much more complete and precise record than they will have from anyone else. He will have an odd, magnificent triumph in the long light of history and will have earned it, when you think of all his nights spent writing.'[17]

But historical objectives aside, we still have in Benn a man obsessed with diary-keeping and the collection of personal memorabilia. Indeed it is something of a misnomer to think of the Benn diary. There are, in fact, several strata of Benn diaries – the daily political diary is only the most complete. This was originally based on ring-bound note-books which Benn habitually carried, but from 1966 he evolved a system of writing diary notes on the minutes of meetings he was attending, sometimes five a day, or on letters he had received. These notebooks and diary notes were also maintained in what was coming to be the Benn archive. This expanding office plus repository moved to the basement of the Holland Park house in January 1964.

Benn also kept a private five-year diary noting family events, and a pocket diary of appointments which related back to the desk diary kept by his secretary. Occasionally, notably in the peerage case, he would construct a 'chronology' of the main events in a separate loose-leaf book.

A more adventurous and characteristically Benn artefact was the creation of a 100-year diary which has a page for every year from his birth until 2025 with the main events written in. Some of these events, like the birthdays of his family, he would write in prospectively. Elections and political events in which he was involved would be added as they occurred.

One reason for the meticulous note-keeping was simply that he had a love of accuracy for its own sake: 'If you do keep a record it has to be accurate.' The diary obviously has a use as an extension of memory. 'I can't remember things that happened yesterday if I don't write them down. If I go out of a meeting I can't remember what was decided, let alone what was said, unless I've scribbled it down.'[18]

The many causes of the Tory fall from office in October 1964 are outside the scope of this book, but three factors deserve some attention because they were to be major themes in Benn's own

career: Common Market entry; the failure of Skybolt and conse-
quent reliance on American nuclear technology; and the relationship
between the secret services and government.

Edward Heath had been struggling for months to reach an agreement for British entry into the Common Market which would give
some kind of protected status to the Commonwealth. In December
1962 Macmillan travelled to see President de Gaulle of France and
failed to persuade him to lift his veto on British entry. The veto was
confirmed in January 1963.

The failure of the Common Market negotiations confronted
Britain with a dismal prospect of isolation. America had long been
saying that Britain had better find a role for herself in Europe; there
was no place for Britain beside the US on the world stage – she
must go and join the chorus. The public political snub was bad
enough, but with a worsening economic situation marked by low
economic growth and a growing balance of payments deficit, the
Tory government was brought face to face with its own political
bankruptcy. Nothing it could do would alleviate the economic
situation; the Common Market had been a last hope of economic
recovery. Rab Butler told Benn in February 1963, 'You know the
Common Market breakdown was a much bigger shock for us than
your chaps realised.'[19] Politically the Tories were fortunate that their
turn-of-the-year crises happened with the Opposition leaderless or
uncoordinated.

Macmillan's government had signed an agreement with the US in
1958 which overruled the McMahon Act and therefore permitted
the exchange of nuclear information between the two nations. The
government was keen to develop its own nuclear arsenal but also
required the means to deliver these bombs. The US was developing
Skybolt, a long-range air-to-ground missile with its own guidance
system. Britain was offered a chance to buy this missile, in return
for which she would provide the US with a deep-water base for its
Polaris submarines. The Americans were obliged with Holy Loch,
off the River Clyde, perilously close to Glasgow. Thus Scotland's
most populous city was turned into the first target for a nuclear
strike, whether pre-emptive or retaliatory. Macmillan was reassured
by Eisenhower that 'In the event of an emergency, such as increased
tension or the threat of war, the US will take every possible step to

consult with Britain and other Allies.'[20] Then the Americans cancelled Skybolt at the end of 1962, which meant that they had something for nothing. At a summit at Nassau in the Bahamas Macmillan
insisted that the new President, John F. Kennedy, should give Britain the Polaris missiles at knock-down prices. Against considerable
opposition at home, Kennedy agreed, and Britain's 'independent'
nuclear force was thus inextricably linked to American technology.

Benn saw the dangers – 'Buying US weapons will not strengthen
our bargaining power with them' – and uttered the complaint which
was to be heard in many Conservative circles, that the cost would
make the UK neglect the maintenance of conventional forces. He
argued for 'a new and realistic policy for Britain based on the
abandonment of any attempt by us to remain an independent nuclear
power'.[21]

The ineptitude and questionable loyalty of the secret services put
an additional burden on the relationship with the US. One spy
scandal followed another: the uncovering of the Portland spy ring,
of George Blake, Kim Philby and John Vassall, all gave the
impression of a nation which had no secrets from its enemies –
though a great deal was kept secret from the British public. Confidence in the intelligence services was not reinforced by the decision
to imprison two journalists, from the *Daily Sketch* and *Daily Mail*,
for refusing to disclose their sources for stories on the Vassall case.

Such actions reinforced the feeling that the public were deliberately being kept in ignorance about matters which may have had
very little to do with national security. As Benn wrote, 'The overwhelming majority of so-called secrets are of little or no value.
Governments use them to cover up their failure – especially the
failure of their weapons and the ghastly waste of money in defence.
Eighty per cent of material now kept secret should be declassified.'[22]

Worse was to come for the Macmillan administration when the
Profumo affair burst upon a startled public. John Profumo, the
Secretary of State for War, lied to the House of Commons about
his relationship with Christine Keeler, a young woman who enjoyed
a similar friendship with a Russian naval attaché. The press began
to get their own back for the martyrdom of two of their number
during the Vassall case. Everything the government did now was
incompetent, outmoded, a whiff of fusty air from the Edwardian

wilderness. Underneath it all, so the Profumo affair testified, the ruling class was irredeemably decadent. The Profumo case did not bring down the government, but its coverage lubricated the ramp on which the government was skidding.

In keeping with his general tendency to avoid such matters, Benn refused an invitation to discuss the affair on television and remarked in his weekly column in the *Sunday Citizen*, 'We must avoid the temptation to win support by stirring up the dirt. There's a lot of wisdom in the saying "Don't wrestle with a chimney sweep." '[23]

Macmillan's resignation and his replacement by Sir Alex Douglas-Home did nothing to inspire confidence, and 1964 was an election year. The cartoonist Franklin pictured Wilson and Grimond on the track ready to race while the third contestant, Home, held the starting pistol to his own head. Eventually Home could put it off no longer and the election was announced for 15 October 1964. Despite the Tories' widespread unpopularity, a Labour victory was by no means a foregone conclusion. The party's poor organisation, particularly over postal votes, and its lower level of funding compared with the Tories, tended to deaden the message.

The effect of racial prejudice, stimulated by fears of continuing Commonwealth immigration, was also felt to be a factor operating against Labour, who were believed to favour unrestricted immigration. The first draft of the Labour manifesto contributed to this suspicion by not mentioning immigration at all. In order to remedy this, Benn wrote a draft drawing attention to the party's determination to make racial discrimination a criminal offence, offering help to local authorities in areas of high immigrant settlement and accepting the necessity for immigration control. The draft was accepted and Benn congratulated himself on killing immigration as an issue during the campaign. Racial prejudice, encouraged by some Conservative supporters, was probably the deciding factor only in the Smethwick constituency.

Caroline Benn suggested for the title of the manifesto, 'The New Britain', but it was thought too catchy for a political document so it was encumbered with 'Let's Go with Labour for the New Britain'.

Benn continued to work on the party broadcasts during the election, including a nerve-racking occasion when the film to be broadcast was made so late the technicians did not have time to cement the joins. Benn was therefore put in the studio in front of a camera while the film was transmitted. If it broke the vision mixer was to cut to him and he would improvise as best he could until they put on a new lead and rethreaded it. Fortunately the film held.

Benn won in Bristol South-East with a majority of 9835. The national result was not so obvious. Indeed, the result was so close that Benn, listening to the results on the car radio as he drove home from Bristol, could not be sure Labour had won until midday. They had an overall majority of four.

19

The Modernising Postmaster General

Like a hundred or more Labour MPs Tony Benn waited by the telephone over the weekend, watching his colleagues on the television news bulletins turning up at 10 Downing Street to receive their ministerial appointments. He had almost given up hope and was mapping out a new career for himself when the telephone rang at 4.45 on Sunday afternoon and he was told to stand by. He stood by until 2 a.m., when he retired anxiously to bed. The next day, 19 October, he was up early and had again almost given up hope by late morning when the telephone rang and he was summoned to Downing Street.

He found the new Prime Minister in the Cabinet Room. Wilson said he was sorry about not appointing Benn Minister of Transport. By way of consolation he said that Benn might be a Privy Councillor, – he had not yet established if it were customary for Postmasters General to be so appointed.[1]

Benn's first act after leaving Number 10 was to find a call box and telephone his mother. He then returned home and called Post Office headquarters. 'Happy birthday,' he said to the Director General, Sir Ronald German, having learned from the extensive background reading he had done on the Post Office that 19 October was German's birthday. German had read Benn's *Guardian* piece on the Post Office and knew he would be in for some changes. He had a lunch appointment, anyway, but would see Benn afterwards. Benn asked for a car to take him to his office immediately.

In a short time a huge black limousine with a uniformed chauffeur drove up and out stepped Henry Tilling, Benn's principal private secretary. He was a tense and pale man who sat with Benn in the back of the car as they drove to St Martin-le-Grand in the City and attempted to make small talk. Tilling told the Postmaster General that his great interests were heraldry and orders and decorations. The Postmaster General realised he was going to have a long, uphill task.

Postmaster General was by no means a poor start for a man who was not yet forty. Attlee's first government job was head of the Post Office, 'and a very antediluvian set-up he found it too,' his biographer Kenneth Harris remarked.[2] Tony Benn was to have a similar reaction to his new job. Anthony Sampson dismissed it in parenthesis, referring to the Ministry of Works as 'the most despised and unsought-after of the departments (with the possible exception of the Post Office)'.[3] With a third of a million workers and a nationwide network of post offices operating as selling outlets, it was more of an industry than a government department. It had more than twice the staff of ICI, for example, and in size and income ranked third among state-owned ventures after the coal and electricity-supply industries. It was not an industry, however, but a department run by civil servants, whose entrepreneurial skills were limited.

The Post Office empire covered the mail service; the telecommunications network of telephones, morse and the nascent satellite systems; the Post Office Savings Bank, which was the biggest bank in the world in terms of its holdings; and all television and radio broadcasting. Benn's job was vast; as a US newspaper explained, 'He is a combination of what in America would be the Postmaster, general president of the Bell Telephone Company and the chairman of the Federal Communication System.'[4] He liked to think of it as a Ministry of Communication, 'working on a wide front to give Britain the communications system it needs to develop its economic and community life to the full.'[5]

Making him Postmaster General was one of Wilson's more inspired appointments. It used Benn's creative energy in a department which yearned for creativity and hardened his approach by driving his boyish enthusiasm up against the worst civil service inertia. At thirty-nine, he was the youngest minister. As one report said, 'his close-cropped hair gives an impression of youthful zest'.[6] Another newspaper put it less agreeably by calling him the Scoutmaster General.[7]

228

Whatever he was going to be called, Benn knew the great truth of government, that in the first ten minutes the civil servants decide whether the minister is going to run the department or the department is going to run the minister. Benn started to take control almost as soon as he walked through the door, held open for him by a man in a red frock-coat and a top hat. He told the Director General to send him all the heads of departments in the Post Office at ten-minute intervals throughout the afternoon. He introduced himself to each and questioned them about their work. This was indeed where the pattern was set for the next two years, for Ronald German could not stop the Postmaster General speaking to his staff if he so wished. But he could frustrate the manoeuvre simply by staying in the room while the anxious officials were quizzed. It would have been impolite for Benn to have told him to get out, so he was faced with people who were unwilling to speak frankly in front of their boss. To ease the situation Sir Ronald took to talking about each of them in their presence.

All the diarists and memoir writers of the period record the chilly welcome afforded to the incoming Labour government, which was not expected to last past the first crisis. Underlying it was a philosophical rejection of Labour's ideas, manifested in mere pettiness or dumb insolence from the civil service. Marcia Williams records how staff at 10 Downing Street would not tell Wilson's staff the correct postal procedures, how they tore pieces of headed notepaper out of press officer Gerald Kaufman's hands because they considered he was not permitted to use it. In a piece in the *Daily Mail* titled 'How Whitehall Is Beating Wilson' the writer commiserated with 'Poor Mr Benn, a twentieth-century product if ever I saw one, trying to do it all in Hackney-carriage material of nineteenth-century vintage.'[8]

Within the next few days senior civil servants in the Post Office underwent the novel experience of having the Labour Party manifesto drop on their desks with the passages which related to the Post Office underlined. Unlike his predecessor, Reginald Bevins, Benn decided he would attend the office every day. This was a shock to the civil servants. 'We'll see you when the recess is over,' one of his staff said when Parliament broke up. 'Not at all,' said Benn, 'you'll see me in the morning, and every other day except for normal working holidays.'[9] He worked in his shirtsleeves with frequent infusions of tea from the pint mug he brought in from home. Benn was not an obvious candidate for a job with such a range of ceremonial functions but fortunately his assistant Postmaster General, the former miner Joe Slater, was only too happy to cover the more formal functions.

Benn insisted on visiting the whole administrative building, 'even those places where a Postmaster General had never gone before,' said the man who was later his private secretary, Donald Wratten. 'He ate in the canteen for the manual staff on the bottom floor, what was called the Cleaner's Arms, before he had eaten with the management. The establishment didn't know what to make of him. They weren't a very bright bunch on the whole and here was this brash politician trying to overturn 300 years of tradition at a stroke.' Sir Ronald German would come in after an ample lunch, sink into an armchair in Wratten's office and say, 'What has that young man been up to today?'[10]

None of the real work seemed to flow through the Postmaster General's office. Decisions had always been taken elsewhere and ratified by the PMG. Benn was shocked to discover that there were no files in his filing cabinet – it was just for show. As a step towards rational management via the Postmaster General he therefore re-established the Post Office Board, originally a creation of one of his Tory predecessors, the energetic Ernest Marples. Under this system the Director General and the top people in the department would meet Benn weekly to report on their activities.

The Post Office was a difficult service to run, because the public is never satisfied: one lost letter or wrong number is one too many. This was compounded by a somewhat supercilious attitude on the part of Post Office officials towards their customers. Overall, the department was in a poor state with deficit budgeting, a below-standard service on both posts and telephones and low staff morale. It became clear that one cause of its inefficiency was its structure. Benn said, 'I discovered when I got there that there was no one in charge of the telephone service and no one in charge of the postal service. There was the engineering chief, who ran the network of telecommunication links, and there was the man who was in charge of the administration of post offices. But neither of them had full control over the full range of services they were running and there was no provision for cost accounting.'[11] To the civil servants' under-standable dismay he called in a firm of American Management consultants, McKinsey and Company. Someone was disposed to spread disinformation about the appointment for Benn was criticised about it in the House of Lords, a Tory peer claiming that McKinsey's had taken Benn for an expensive business lunch and that he had been won over by their salesmanship. In fact, McKinsey's had been suggested by George Brown and, in true Benn style, he took the consultants to the Post Office canteen, where he gave them a three-shilling (15p) lunch each, for which he paid personally.

The Postmaster General was, as Wilson had supposed, a Privy Councillor, so Benn was called to Buckingham Palace to receive this honour and to be formally appointed minister. Traditionally the Privy Council is made up of the coterie of ministers who advise the monarch, and membership of it is an honour which is not relin-quished on leaving office and which confers parliamentary advan-tages: in particular that the Speaker normally gives preference to Privy Councillors who wish to speak in debate. The Privy Council is in theory the supreme body of government, and the Cabinet is a committee of the Privy Council.

When called to the Palace, ministers had to take the oath of their ministry, then kiss hands and bow before the Queen. Those not already Privy Councillors had to listen to the Privy Council oath as it was 'administered' to them. Benn chose to affirm rather than swear, despite his religious beliefs, because he disapproved of a religious oath for any but religious purposes. Anthony Greenwood, also a believer, regretted that he had not affirmed, as it was 'a lot of mumbo-jumbo and only rogues need to swear an oath'.[12] Benn was disgusted with the ceremony: 'I left the Palace boiling with indignation and feeling that this was an attempt to impose tribal magic and personal loyalty on people whose real duty was only to their electors.'[13] Dick Crossman remarked, 'I don't think anything more dull, pretentious or plain silly has ever been invented.'[14] Even Wilson boasted of having circumvented the procedure: he did not kiss hands as Prime Minister but was then exempted from kissing hands as First Lord of the Treasury because it was assumed he had done so as Prime Minister.[15] Even so, he was not prepared to modify these archaic procedures.

As soon as the Labour ministers received reviews of Britain's current financial situation their worst fears were confirmed: the entire economy had been disastrously mismanaged. Indeed, the economic problems of the next twenty years can be ascribed to the failure of investment in industry and the absence of planning in the 1950s, which could have ensured economic growth comparable to that of other European countries. The muddle of economic policy, crowned by the ludicrous stop–go pattern of growth, had produced a balance of payments deficit of £800 million. At the Post Office the problems Benn inherited were those of inertia and a fumbling failure of management. Some of the immediate problems were caused by the Tories' reluctance to take three unpopular decisions prior to a general election. It therefore fell to Benn to increase postmen's pay; to raise postal charges; and to announce to the House of Commons the projected budget deficit. All three were to cause him difficulties.

'When I became Postmaster General I discovered that the postal service was losing money at the rate of £50,000 per day and the BBC were down by £40,000 per day,'[16] Benn explained in 1965. The loss in the current financial year on postal services was likely to be £16 million and the loss in 1965–6 £21 million. By 1967–8 the cumulative deficit was projected at £120 million.

In keeping with the principle of the impartiality of the civil service, papers relating to the decisions of previous PMGs were removed from the files before Benn received them, though as the information about the projected deficit was part of a current position statement, this was available to Benn. It became apparent that his predecessor had known about the projected deficit.

Benn referred to this in his first position statement to the House of Commons, on 10 November 1964. A back-bench Labour member pushed the Postmaster General to blame the Conservatives, and Benn obliged: 'If Mr Bevins had told the House of Commons of the position, that would at least have been an advantage. As late as 25 July, after the accounts had been published, in reply to a question . . . he said he had no intention of raising postal charges, despite these facts.'[17] The Tories quickly discovered that this was an error and put down a motion of censure: Bevins had said no such thing on 25 July 1964. Benn had misled the House. In fact Bevins had said exactly that on 25 July 1963, but had used the words

'I have no plans for increasing postal charges' a year later on 28 July 1964. So Benn's inaccuracy was a minor slip.

The motion of censure against him took place on 30 March 1965. It was a fine Benn performance. Speaking with casual confidence, he delayed the answer to the main Tory criticism until he had been speaking for half an hour, then justified himself comprehensively, including a criticism of Bevins for excising embarrassing paragraphs from the Post Office accounts. Bevins explained that these had been cut out because they were 'too verbose'.[18] Benn used the occasion for a review of the department and of his plans for the future from satellite communications to a new fellowship in stamp design. A parliamentary correspondent reported, 'It may take Mr Wedgwood Benn six days to carry a parcel a mile and a half across Watford, but when it comes to performing in the House of Commons the Postmaster General is no sluggard.'[19] After the debate he took the Director General and some other members of his staff, who had been watching, to the tea room, where they were joined by the Prime Minister. It was the sort of experience which endears civil servants to their political bosses.

The postal charges had to be put up, which would not be a popular move because it contributed to wage and price rises. In theory, cash to bail out the postal service could come from telecommunications, which made a profit, but to do this would be to starve the telephone service of vital investment capital at a time when growth was all-important. So Benn proposed new charges but, to his horror, the cabinet decided against. He telephoned Barbara Castle, his closest confidante of cabinet rank, to find out what had happened, asking conspiratorially, 'Is your phone scrambled?' When she said it wasn't they proceeded to talk 'in hieroglyphics'.[20] She explained that the real question was when the election would be: if the government were to fall soon, a rise in postal charges would help the Tories. That is, they wanted to delay the price rises for the same reason the Tories had. Moreover, it was by no means easy to secure the agreement of cabinet for an increase at a time when George Brown was promoting his prices and incomes policy. Faced with these impediments to his policy, Benn was obliged to put in six months of hard lobbying, but at last the new prices were agreed.

When they were introduced there was found to be an embarrassing shortage of 1d stamps. These were essential because the basic letter rate had risen from 3d to 4d and many people would have supplies of 3d stamps which would now be useless on their own. It was a particularly infuriating predicament for Benn to cope with and was made no easier by his having to defend a huge £109,000 advertising campaign about which he had not even been consulted. A *Guardian* political columnist commented, 'Hunting the Post Office, with which is associated the subsidiary sport of bullying Mr Benn, has become one of the leading Tory exercises in the Commons.'[21] The stamps had in fact been printed and were at the supplies department, but unofficial strike action there had stopped them from being distributed to the post offices. This was not good enough and Benn was labelled as the man who presided over a service which simultaneously raised prices and failed to have the goods ready for sale.

The last of the challenges with which Benn was obliged to deal in his first months was the problem of postmen's pay. The Post Office was a labour-intensive business: 70 per cent of its costs were absorbed by pay. With wages therefore having an immense effect on overall costs, pay had been kept low, and postmen's wages had not kept par with those of factory workers, leading to a decline in recruitment, staff shortages and an extremely high rate of overtime – some postmen could work overtime of forty hours a week.

Benn was obliged to head the negotiations with the Union of Post Office Workers, led by Ron Smith. Benn had a somewhat idealised view of the trade unionists, having previously encountered only the most politicised at May Day rallies or individually in the Commons or on the National Executive. Now he was to deal with trade union-ists who did not care whether or not he was a socialist: he was the employer and they would make it as awkward for him as possible. 'I was expected to be very tough and they were very tough. I felt uneasy and inexperienced and got much criticised afterwards for the way I'd handled it.'[22]

The negotiations began at 10.30 a.m. on 15 April 1965, in a somewhat ritualistic fashion, because all the points Ron Smith and Tony Benn were now putting to each other had been rehearsed over previous days between the union and the Director General of the Post Office. The negotiation followed the balletic – or perhaps one should say operatic – style of these things, with each new proposal from the Post Office meeting with mock horror by the unions and union proposals being greeted with mock alarm by the Post Office. At the end of these performances there would be a reconciliation scene in which both sides would express their willingness to reach an agreement and their commitment to the public. Then another act would start with the management wooing and the unions sniffing their proposals with disdain.

This went through seven acts, during which Benn twice rang the Chancellor, Jim Callaghan, and gained agreement for increases in the offer. After the seventh act Benn 'got rather angry and banged the table and said I hoped it had not come to this point but I was not prepared to give way any further'.[23] After this they rejected the seventh proposal. Benn rang Ray Gunter, the Minister of Labour (Callaghan was travelling and unobtainable by this time) and he suggested that, rather than risk a strike if there was no agreement, to adjourn the negotiations until after the weekend.

It was clear that Ron Smith himself wanted to accept the proposals but his more militant colleagues were voting him down. Benn tried one last attempt, the eighth. He recited all the proposals he had made so far, to show how reasonable he was, and made one final token offer, of an extra shilling a week from 1965, but not backdated through 1964. At almost 9 p.m. the UPW negotiating committee returned and accepted. There was a scene of reconciliation and harmony and Benn and Smith presented a finale to a press conference. It had been a very long day.

The negotiations had profound repercussions, not least on George Brown's lame prices and incomes policy. This had already been breached by settlements for railwaymen and nurses, who had received increases above the advised 3 to 3.5 per cent, steelworkers and coal miners having already proclaimed their intention to do the same. Benn's pay award, however, meant that postmen's wages would have increased by almost 20 per cent between the beginning of 1964 and the beginning of 1966. Additionally, there was a reduction of working hours from forty-two to forty a week.

Over the next few weeks venomous pieces began to appear in the press. The most offensive was in *The Economist*. It was headed 'Mr Brown's incomes policy starts under the worst possible auspices:

largely because the Postmaster General has kicked it in the teeth'. Benn had given in 'at the first whiff of pressure. . . . the glad word has gone around the post office that the union is bargaining with a politically ambitious weakling. . . . Mr Wilson should immediately have dismissed Mr Benn from ministerial office.'[24]

At the end of May during an all-night sitting at the House of Commons, Benn and a group in the tea room were joined by Brown, who was drunk as usual. Brown said to the other MPs, 'Can't you make the Postmaster General go away. I don't like him at all.' Benn thought it was friendly banter until Brown turned on him and said, 'You have wrecked my incomes policy – you know that, don't you? . . . As soon as the Commies started shouting at you, you gave way.' Benn suggested they discuss it in private, in Brown's room, but Brown wanted to stay and shout. He became more offensive and made several untrue references to Benn's conversations with Gunter and Callaghan during the negotiations, using phrases which came straight out of the press, presumably, as Benn surmised, because they were the phrases he had put into the press in the first place.[25]

People who knew Brown and his moods told Benn he would get an apology – Brown always apologised after such outbursts. Benn wrote a letter to him putting the record straight, with a copy to Callaghan and Gunter. In response he received a letter in Brown's own handwriting: 'Tony, Your letter has never been out of my mind. Although I do feel strongly about the matter I have absolutely no defence on the issue you properly charged me with. I'm only too well aware that a private apology for a public wrong isn't very satisfactory! But there's little else I can do. I'm very sorry, yours, George.'[26]

The government's precarious majority almost toppled into disaster during the passage of Jim Callaghan's first Budget on 2 June 1965 when three Labour members failed to vote on the Corporation Tax clause and the result was a 281 tie. Benn was the only one of the three who was a minister, so wrath was concentrated on him. During the vote he had been with Caroline, showing some visitors the Crypt at the House of Commons, and had relied on the man who unlocked the gate to tell him if there was a division because the bell could not be heard from the Crypt. When he emerged and continued the tour he learned from a policeman that there had in fact been a division. He ran into the members' lobby but it was too late. The vote was held again and the government won, but endangering the government by such a silly error was courting criticism. The press evidently thought they were on to an even juicier story because, though Benn had told the lobby correspondents he had been with his wife, when Caroline returned home at midnight she found reporters in the garden trying to check whether Benn really had been with his wife and hoping for scandal. The extent to which Benn was identified in the public mind with his family is demonstrated by a cartoon which appeared that Sunday in the *Observer*; it depicted Benn asleep, with Joshua and Melissa standing by his bed with a bell, daring each other to wake him with it.[27]

The criticisms of Benn were much the same in all quarters. They were most succinctly put in the *Daily Express* Cross-Bencher column:

Consider the remarkable treble he has lately pulled off.

In April he made a fool of Mr George Brown. By agreeing to a 20 per cent pay increase for postal workers which drove a coach-and-four contemptuously through Mr Brown's incomes policy.

Last month he made a fool of himself. By increasing the letter-post rate – and omitting to have sufficient stamps ready to meet the changed demand.

And this month he made a fool of the whole government. By getting lost in the crypt during a crucial division and so exposing them to the humiliation of a tied vote.[28]

Ben did attempt to bat criticism by inviting newspapers who had attacked him to send a reporter to get his side of things, and the *Daily Sketch* at least printed an interview with him in response to such an invitation. Benn confided to his diary, 'The Post Office is not an efficient organisation – it is something that the press like to attack. The Tories have a deliberate political reason for trying to spotlight the failures of public enterprise. Nobody in the party or government ever seems to come to my support and I am very much on my own.'[29]

In his dealings with the unions, Benn was assisted by his parliamentary private secretary, Charles Morris, MP for Openshaw and himself a member of the Union of Post Office Workers. He had spent his life in the Post Office and had studied the American equivalent with the aid of a Ford Foundation scholarship. The Director General had told Benn that it would be undesirable for him to appoint someone involved in a Post Office union and warned him against getting too close to the unions. Benn said he could not believe that Mr Bevins had been advised not to get too friendly with the head of businesses which dealt with the Post Office. He appointed Morris and told the Director General he had considered his advice but had rejected it.

One difficulty his officials had was that Tony Benn insisted on treating both the trade unionists and the senior civil servants as equals. They had never encountered such a notion before and they found it profoundly disconcerting. But Benn went further and cultivated a positive relationship with the unions. He spoke at the conferences of the Union of Post Office Workers and the Post Office Union. He was the first Postmaster General to be a guest at the headquarters of the UPW and he started having 'tea and sandwiches' lunches for trade union officials. He spent a great deal of time simply talking to staff about what they were doing, visiting them at work and showing an interest. 'Never before have I seen a politician with such skills of diplomacy and communication,' Charles Morris said.[30]

It was a measure of Benn's success as a business manager that by the time the accounts were made up for the year 1965–6, there was a profit of £40 million and both telecommunications and posts contributed to it. The decline of the postal service had been halted.

Having settled the problems of price increases and postmen's pay by the spring of 1965, Benn began to notice, rather than gratitude or even respect from his officials for his efficiency, a 'woodenness' bordering on non-co-operation. He wrote in his diary, 'I think the reason for this is that having achieved the tariff increase which they desperately wanted for the sake of the department, and having got the highly generous UPW wages settlement which they wanted just in order to get peace and quiet, they have more or less lost interest in me and are deliberately slowing down all the things I wanted to get moving.'[31]

'I already hear from Tony Wedgwood Benn how utterly isolated he feels in his ministry.' Crossman's account of his own experiences in these first months focuses on his struggle to prevent himself being 'swallowed up' by the civil service machine. His isolation was shared by other new ministers of Harold Wilson's first administration who felt that the civil service was treating them as temporary guests: one need make no changes for them, they won't be staying long.

Only a month after the 1964 general election while he was still struggling to establish himself at the Post Office, Benn was shocked to discover a new threat to his career: there had been an overspend on his election expenses, a serious offence. There would have to be another election court. Benn was distraught. He had been out of Parliament for three years and had already faced one election court – was his parliamentary life cursed? His grandfather John Benn had been in a similar position after winning St George's in the East and Wapping in 1895. Two minor infringements of electoral law led to his being forbidden to stand for that seat for seven years and left him with legal costs of £6000. Such injustices were part of Benn family lore. When examined in detail it became clear that the 1964 overspend had been £59 9s over and above the total permitted budget of £838 8s 9d. An astute Liberal had noticed it and reported it to the police.

Coming so soon after the peerage case, the thought of going through it all again floored him. He wrote in his diary, 'Carol and I were so depressed at the thought that we might be caught by the law again that we decided to emigrate if I was unseated on a technicality. How I hate the law.'[32] The faithful Michael Zander returned to the Benn household for more nights of poring over legal tomes.

It transpired that Herbert Rogers had made an error in his calculations. Benn decided that Herbert, who was almost seventy, would have to go. He told key people on the Executive Committee that he did not want Herbert as agent again. The constituency chairman Bert Peglar and the rest of the executive supported Rogers and he stayed to fight another day – many more days in fact: he was still active twenty-five years later.

In a hearing lasting less than half an hour the election court recognised that both Rogers and Benn had acted in good faith and exempted them from the consequences of the illegal electoral practice in which they had been involved. The only penalty was the payment of court costs of £1347 13s 10d. These Benn dealt with.

The fortunes of his ministerial colleagues seemed no happier. The first disaster of Wilson's premiership came indirectly as a result of the racist campaign directed in the run-up to the 1964 general election at Patrick Gordon Walker in Smethwick. Following this campaign, with its unofficial slogan, 'If you want a nigger neighbour vote Labour', Gordon Walker lost his seat. Wilson nonetheless appointed him Foreign Secretary, and contrived a vacancy for him in Leyton by persuading the sitting Labour member to take a peerage. At the Leyton by-election which followed in January 1965 Gordon Walker lost by 205 votes, thus reducing Labour's majority to three. On the same day at a by-election in Nuneaton, where the Labour candidate was Frank Cousins, general secretary of the Transport and General Worker's Union, there was a drastic drop in the party's vote. Wilson wanted Cousins as Minister of Technology so a seat had been found by the identical ploy of moving the sitting member to the Lords.

How Wilson could have been such an adroit politician at the level of Westminster yet treated the voters and constituency party workers with such contempt is a mystery. It was the behaviour of Wilson, more than anyone else, which stimulated the revolt of the constituencies which culminated in the constitutional changes of the early 1980s.

A certain resistance to reform of the structure of government was one of the weaknesses of Harold Wilson which set him at variance to his Postmaster General, but they had a positive relationship based on the mutual benefit of their acquaintanceship. Benn was asked to contribute to a stand-by obituary of Wilson; he paid tribute to his leader's intellectual gifts: 'In this country we don't like clever people and we tend to write intellectual ability down. Harold Wilson could not only read documents like a flash but he could understand what you were trying to explain to him as quickly as you could say it. This saved such an enormous amount of time, it made it such a joy to go and see him. In the sense that he could get to the heart of a thing, one was a bit frightened of him. His interrogation when you'd

explained your problem – his interrogation to s(
it – was always rather frightening.'[33]

Wilson enjoyed his power over men and wo(
them. His secretary Marcia Williams (late)
described how Wilson asked her to bring the I
to him urgently. They were at a hotel in Brightc
party conference which followed the general e
Williams rushed off. When she had found Ben: —— ....
Prime Minister wanted to see him. 'What about?' Williams did not
know but it was urgent. They rushed down the corridor and Benn,
all enthusiasm, bounded into Wilson's room. 'Want to see you,
Postmaster General, rather urgently,' Wilson said, and continued
without laughter, 'It's my father's eightieth birthday – and I want
to make absolutely sure that the telegram I send him gets there. I
know what the Post Office can be like.'[34] Not long after this Benn
suggested a parliamentary award for industry and export as a means
of stimulating much-needed growth in exports and advances in technology. Wilson teasingly told him that the Queen is the fount of
honour, and later launched the hugely successful Queen's Award
for Industry.[35]

The Gordon Walker affair left Wilson with the Foreign Office
vacant, so Michael Stewart was appointed there, to perpetrate the
long misery of the Wilson government's Vietnam policy. This move
obliged Wilson to reshuffle his cabinet. Benn stayed where he was,
but Tony Crosland was moved from Brown's Department of Economic Affairs into the cabinet as Secretary of State for Education,
after Roy Jenkins had turned it down. Four of Benn's near contemporaries were in the cabinet already: Barbara Castle was Minister
for Overseas Development, Healey was at Defence, Callaghan was
Chancellor and Greenwood was Secretary of State for the Colonies.

Benn was not universally liked by his colleagues. One reporter
noted that 'his self-possession grated on some of the more sensitive
members who thought him brash, cheeky and arrogant'.[36] Probably
part of the resentment was directed as him because he seemed set
for even greater success. When Kenneth Harris interviewed Harold
Wilson for the *Observer* in September 1965, the newspaper wanted
some pictures taken in Downing Street before a cabinet meeting.
Wilson, ever eager to emphasise the youthful image of his govern-

241

nt, suggested that he be photographed with some 'up and coming' members of the government; he chose Benn and Dick Marsh.[37] At the National Executive constituency section election in that same month Benn moved one more rung up the ladder, coming second to Barbara Castle's first.

Benn did not achieve his success without an enormous expenditure of energy. He would be up at 6 or 6.30, and breakfast in his basement office. There he would work, dictating constituency letters, until 8.45 when his secretary would arrive and he would be off to his office in St Martin's-le-Grand.

A breathless article on the Benns at home entitled 'It's Go, Go, Go! All the Time' described their house as less a home than 'one of those disciplined-through-freedom boarding schools, or a well-run community centre. . . . The Benn's have a big living room which is exactly that – they eat there, talk there, meet there, pop group there [the children had formed a pop group] and cook in a kitchen alcove off it. . . . The furniture is comfortable and as tough as furniture in a school common room – refectory tables and wooden chairs and couches and old-fashioned easy chairs where kids can curl up without spoiling the upholstery.'[38] They certainly gave the impression of being a perfect 1960s family: like something out of an American situation comedy, they were living a hectic and invigorating but always family-based lifestyle.

The Benn children were again subjected to the unwelcome attentions of the press when a newspaper discovered that the elder boys had been moved to Holland Park. 'They said we were making our children suffer for the sake of our dogmatic principles,' said Caroline Benn. 'They said we had only done it for a political principle, not because we thought it was a good school.'[39] Having seen the Benns attacked for their decision, a number of educationalists and teachers who supported the comprehensive system got in touch to discuss how they could promote a campaign for comprehensive schools. The group, later to meet in the Benns' house, formed the basis of the Comprehensive Schools Campaign. At that first meeting, on 25 February 1965, Caroline sat next to Brian Simon, with whom she was later to write *Half Way There*, published in 1970, a progress report on comprehensives. She became editor of the journal *Comprehensive Education*, organised conferences on issues like the sixth form or streaming in comprehensives and also produced the *Comprehensive Reorganisation Survey* between 1964 and 1970. This was a directory of the progress of comprehensivisation in each local education authority. It showed the Department of Education and Science's lack of commitment that private citizens should be left to do such work, she commented.

By the time the children were all at school and Caroline was able to return to academic work, she found she was as interested in the nature of education and its availability as she was in her own subjects. This prompted her to start working for the National Extension College, a forerunner of the Open University in offering higher education to adults; and to teach London University extra mural students.

It has often been suggested that the Wilson government's position on Vietnam was the moral issue by which it should be judged. Benn's lack of involvement in Vietnam protest poses something of a question: why was someone who had been so caught up in international affairs in the 1950s so little concerned in the great international issues of the 1960s? Even before the Labour government took office there had been a decline in Benn's commentary on international politics, and the last of his wide-ranging articles, 'China – A Test for Labour', appeared in the *Sunday Citizen* in May 1964. It is not difficult to isolate the reasons for his narrowing horizon. First, the principal stimulus to his thinking about international affairs had been his father, and, with the spring of his daily conversation gone, Tony Benn's interest withered. Secondly, his principal activities had been on behalf of the Movement for Colonial Freedom and by the early 1960s old-style colonialism by the European nations was virtually dead: his task was completed. Most importantly, his duties at the Post Office left him no time to spend on any matters which did not touch directly on his work.

The former French colony of Vietnam was now divided between the Communist North and a right-wing dictatorship in the South, the latter propped up by the US against attacks from the Viet Cong, insurgents supported by the North. President Kennedy stepped up military and financial aid and increased the number of US 'advisory' military personnel. Finally, under President Johnson, the systematic bombing of North Vietnam began in February 1965, followed by the sending of US combat troops. The Soviet Union supplied weapons but not troops to North Vietnam.

Afraid of seeming unfriendly, the Wilson government refused to condemn US involvement in Vietnam, though Wilson claimed to be putting pressure on Johnson to seek a negotiated peace. We now know with what contempt those entreaties were received. 'I won't tell you how to run Malaysia and you don't tell us how to run Vietnam. . . . If you want to help us some in Vietnam, send us some men,' Johnson said in one diplomatic exchange.[40]

The Labour movement throughout the world was in uproar over the American attack on North Vietnam. The Labour Party in Bristol South-East was no exception and in Herbert Rogers the anti-war protesters had an assiduous champion. He was frequently berating Benn on the government's position, fearing that Britain would be induced to send troops to Vietnam as it had to Korea. On several occasions he led groups which lobbied Benn on the subject, on one occasion at the House of Commons.

As Benn's diary reveals, he was deeply discomfited by the war and used his influence with Wilson to impress upon him what the party was saying about Vietnam, for example when the Prime Minister invited him to Chequers for dinner on 7 June 1966. On that occasion, however, he found that Wilson 'was not prepared to say anything whatsoever that might divide him from the Americans'.

Marcia Williams notes him as one of the opponents of the war worth mentioning while the more vociferous opposition of, say, Foot, is not. The opposition to US behaviour in Vietnam was one of degree, as she writes, 'I would hazard a guess that there was almost nobody either in the Government or in the Parliamentary Labour Party who genuinely felt a hundred per cent support for the line which the Americans pursued, and which we ourselves confirmed in the attitude we took up. Ernie Fernyhough, Peter Shore, Thomas Balogh, Dick Crossman, Tony Benn and all of Harold's close friends became increasingly perturbed by what was happening and increasingly fearful of where the escalation might lead. All felt a distaste that a Labour Government was having to go along with this.'[41]

Benn struggled with a belief in collective responsibility. He was concerned for the fragility of Labour's majority, but he was already questioning how far conscience should be shackled for such purposes. He praised Harold Davies, a junior minister at the Ministry of Pensions and National Insurance, who made a well-received speech at the party conference in 1965 critical of the government's line on Vietnam. 'It was wildly cheered and was a very interesting speech because it represented a clear breach of collective government responsibility. I'm sure the Foreign Office will be absolutely furious about it but Harold Davies remained true to his own background and beliefs and I cannot see why, if you become a minister, you should have to pretend that you've abandoned all that you've ever stood for in pursuit of some vague constitutional doctrine.'[42]

20

Stamps and Pirates

Even with a tiny majority, the Labour government was able to preside over some liberal reforms. The spirit of the age was strongly in favour of social change and long-considered legislation had become inevitable. Benn missed a trip abroad to vote against hanging, terminated for a trial period in 1965 and never resumed. He had been involved in the debate since he had sponsored Sydney Silverman's Abolition Bill in 1955. He also voted in favour of Tory MP Humphrey Berkeley's Bill to legalise homosexual practices between adults in private, putting into effect the conclusions of the 1957 Wolfenden Report. 'This is how Rome came down,' said George Brown.[1] Benn himself was not the most enthusiastic advocate, writing that he was 'against the persecution of these people but I can't say that I regard it as the beginning and end of a socialist society'.[2] The 1965 Race Relations Act forbade racial discrimination, a long-overdue measure close to Benn's heart. Unfortunately the government bowed to pressure and removed the criminal elements of the intended Act, leaving discrimination in public a civil offence. It was a feeble measure compared to those which came later, but at least put a stop to the most extreme examples of prejudice.

In the Post Office Tony Benn was the very spirit of innovation. As Charles Morris said, 'Within a few months he dominated every aspect of Post Office thinking. He seemed to throw out ideas kaleidoscopically. He had the most incisive mind I have ever encountered.'[3] The kaleidoscopic approach to policy-making was not appreciated in all quarters, however. Benn wrote more than a hundred official minutes to the Director General in his first year at the Post Office on subjects as various as the design of pillar boxes and free telephones for the elderly. He did not realise, as Donald Wratten said, that 'he ground the department to a halt for days while they frantically handled every aspect of his enquiries. He just threw out ideas, expecting one in ten to be successful. They were used to treating an enquiry by the Minister as a message from God.'[4]

One successful intervention was his approach to the differential rates for letters (which were all posted at the same price) and printed papers. The latter could travel at a cheaper rate if the envelope was unsealed, allowing the Post Office to ensure that no letters were secreted among the printed paper and that the printed paper conformed to the Post Office definition, being at least 'five words of conventional meaning'. Under this system all letters were treated as urgent, though it was becoming clear that most material sent by letter was not: there was an increasing volume of advertising material, for example. Benn therefore inaugurated a first- and second-class letter system under which the customer decided whether the letter was urgent and whether it was therefore worth paying the extra halfpenny to ensure speedier delivery. A cumbersome bureaucratic procedure was replaced by consumer choice.

Benn was delighted to be in charge when the technological marvel of the Post Office Tower was ready to be opened as a telephone and TV aerial in October 1965 and as a tourist attraction in May 1966. The tower, 620 feet high with a viewing gallery and restaurant on the top, conformed precisely to his ideas for the image of the Post Office of the future. But attempting to instil enthusiasm into the Post Office was, however, 'like trying to resuscitate a dying elephant'.[5] Nonetheless by sheer tenacity he achieved his greatest imaginative contribution to the Post Office: the commemorative stamp. He was fascinated by the design aspect of stamps, remarking that they are the only art form available to everybody, and endowed a fellowship in minuscule design at the Royal College of Art.[6] When he took over there had been thirty-one special-issue stamps between 1924 and 1964, limited to royal or postal anniversaries or events of outstanding national or international importance. In December 1964 Benn expanded the definition to include British contributions to world affairs, the arts and sciences, the commemoration of any anniversaries and the development of minuscule art.

Britain invented the postage stamp and had never felt the need to place the name of the country of origin on them: the sovereign's image sufficed. This was all very well for the standard stamps, but if there were to be a series of designs on stamps, the Queen's head might be inappropriate on some. She might, indeed, prefer her head not to share space with some of the events which Postmasters General might wish to commemorate – the English Revolution, for example. Tony Benn wanted to remove the Queen's head from the commemorative stamps. As usual, there was no single motive. Benn did care passionately about stamp design but he also wished to have the sovereign removed for explicitly political reasons: edging the sovereign out of public life would prepare the way for a continuing erosion of royal responsibility and a concentration of powers in Parliament.

This was not a novel contribution to Benn thinking or even one which had been developed after he had been told he would have the Post Office. On 24 June 1963 he had produced a memorandum for Harold Wilson entitled 'War Book Project' which suggested that while in opposition the Labour Party should provide a day-by-day guide to what Labour would do when it came to power. The memorandum included some suggested publicity moves, 'deliberately made to create an atmosphere of excitement'. Among these were replacing the ministerial limousines with mini-minors, giving all British Nobel prize-winners life peerages, putting the ceremonial guard at the Bank of England in full battledress and 'Postage stamps bearing the Union Jack but not the Queen's face'.

Benn made the proposal of stamps without the Queen's head almost as soon as he was appointed Postmaster General. The first to hear of it were his staff, who reacted with horror. He then made a guarded statement to the House of Commons about encouraging new designs and asking for new subjects.

The next stage was to make proposals around the issue: he suggested very large commemorative stamps with a full-size standard stamp on the right-hand side so that on the envelope it would appear as if a stamp without the Queen's head had been stuck next to the definitive (a philatelic term for the ordinary, non-commemorative stamp). Benn thought of using a Winston Churchill commemorative stamp at the time of his death, to urge the issue on. It was known that the Queen would not share a stamp with anyone else's head, so one of them would have to go and it would be unattractive for her if she seemed to be denying the great man his honour.

An ally arrived in David Gentleman, a stamp designer who wrote complaining that the Queen's head interfered with his designs. Benn's office drafted a reply stating that there was no possibility that the Queen's head would ever be lost. Benn stopped the letter and asked Gentleman in for a breakfast meeting. The designer then submitted a Churchill stamp without the Queen's head and Benn asked for it to be submitted to the Stamp Advisory Committee which considered matters of stamp design. This did not happen. The civil service machine just crunched to a halt.

Benn was convinced the Post Office civil servants were working against him behind his back with the civil servants at Downing Street. Civil service sabotage was the constant talking point when-ever Labour ministers got together, as almost all diaries and memoirs of the period show. Benn would have to short-circuit the sabotage by dealing with the issue in person at the highest level. He arranged to see Harold Wilson, who agreed to ask the Queen whether she would be willing to see 'non-traditional designs'. She would, and Benn found himself at Buckingham Palace on 10 March 1965 equipped with all his charm and a portfolio of David Gentle-man designs.

He arrived wearing a black tie, because the court was in mourning for the death of Churchill, and was sent into the state apartments where the Queen was sitting. He bowed, shook hands and sat to give his carefully prepared speech. He explained the need to pro-mote Britain abroad by publicising national achievements through stamps, spoke of the quality of stamp designs and suggested a new definitive stamp which would have a more beautiful picture of the Queen. But the head, yes, the question of the head on the lovely new commemorative stamps. Some of these were just right for a monarch's head but some, unfortunately, were not. The United Nations wanted the same stamp all over the world, for example, so there could be no Queen's head on that one, and north of the border they wanted a Burns stamp: how could she share a stamp with the head of this Scotsman?

The real difficulty was that it was understood by the civil servants in the Post Office that the Queen herself had commanded that no stamps without her head could be considered. It was such an unfortunate situation because designers were full of new ideas but they could not be seen by her because of this head business. So the obvious thing to do was to come and ask her about it. She was clearly embarrassed, 'I have had no personal feeling about it at all,' she said.

Benn immediately jumped on this. It was all a misunderstanding and it was so ridiculous that there should be these lovely stamps available which she hadn't even been allowed to see. Would she like to see some now? He had some in his official box. She consented and Benn brought out David Gentleman's album of foreign stamps for comparison, then spread out twelve huge new stamp designs on the Buckingham Palace floor. Some were designs commemorating the Battle of Britain which bore no royal head but the words 'Great Britain'. He knelt on the floor and passed them up to the Queen one by one. After about forty minutes Benn left, thanking the Queen for being prepared to accept different designs for consideration.

Benn was delighted: the Palace determination to eschew controversy had left him ahead of the civil service. He decided that it was not the Queen herself who was the real enemy of progress but those surrounding her who used the Queen as a way of freezing out new ideas.[7] 'I never thought I would have to go down on my knees before my monarch in order to get a policy through,' Benn told Charles Morris.[8] He explained the meeting to Harold Wilson. 'Did she get down on the floor with you?' was the Prime Minister's only comment.[9]

To consolidate this phase of the campaign Benn now had to report it to the Commons, so he had a parliamentary question placed which would ask him about stamp design and he could reply including the magic formula, 'In future designers may submit any designs they wish.' This was too much for William Wolverson, Deputy Director General of the Post Office, who tried to modify the answer Benn had agreed with the Palace. Benn restored the original answer. Three days later when Wolverson came to finalise the question Benn discovered that he had changed it again, once more omitting the key phrase. He changed it back and the question and answer went through on 24 March 1965.

The next stage was to solicit public support so that the Palace would feel under pressure not to reject the headless stamps. He therefore met the Stamp Advisory Committee and secured agreement that he should be allowed to release rejected designs to the press. The civil service continued to obstruct. When he asked to see the instructions to artists working on new designs, he found them exactly as they had been before his meeting with the Queen. They specified: 'The Queen's head must be a dominant feature of the designs.' David Gentleman's Battle of Britain designs had also been excluded from the set to be sent to the Palace. He had them reinstated and recommended a block of six of which only one carried the Queen's head. His second recommendation was the same block of six with the Queen's head on each.[10]

This was a time of particularly vitriolic press criticism of Benn, some of it over the postmen's pay issue. Unwilling to take any more criticism, he had second thoughts about his recommendation to the Queen to accept the headless stamps. He knew that she was more or less constitutionally obliged to accept his advice, but if it emerged to the press that she was unhappy about it, he would be in for a tough time. He therefore telephoned the Palace to say he was equally happy with the block of Battle of Britain stamps with her head on each. It was a calculated retreat on his part: the principle had been assayed and the way marked for headless stamps in the future.

Over 140 million of the Battle of Britain stamps were sold, though they were not popular in all quarters. Some considered that the designs made the Battle of Britain look like an air-show spectacle rather than a great victory which preserved democracy in Europe. Others took offence at the swastika which appeared prominently on the tailfin of a Luftwaffe bomber. Benn explained that the tailfin depicted was not only shattered but was sinking in the Channel. This was by no means obvious, the grumblers asserted.

The story had not ended. The Palace staff also knew how to manipulate the political machine. Sir Michael Adeane, the Queen's private secretary, had a word in the ear of Derek Mitchell, the Prime Minister's private secretary, who wrote to Donald Wratten, the Postmaster General's private secretary. The letter explained the Queen's feelings about 'whether her effigy should invariably appear on commemorative stamps', or whether it should be replaced 'by an emblem of sovereignty'. The Queen, it was apparent, had strong views and, while she would keep an open mind, 'she would greatly prefer not to be faced with an unpalatable decision and one in which she might feel bound to reject the advice offered to her'. Then came the threat. If the Queen were to feel as strongly as this, the letter continued, 'it may be that a number of her subjects will have equally strong feelings. In other words there may be a political aspect to this to which the Postmaster General and other ministers will wish to give some thought.'[11] In other words, the Queen has many battalions of loyal supporters, probably more than your majority-of-three Labour government. Do you really want to make her call on them?

Benn prepared to do battle, penning letters to the Palace which threatened to cancel stamp policy in the face of royal opposition. On reflection, and on the advice of senior officials, he thought better of it and held on to the letters. His allies in the design camp meanwhile conceded that a silhouette of the Queen in the far right-hand corner of the commemoratives would be acceptable. What they really objected to was not a head but the obligation of having to incorporate into their designs the three-quarter profile which was the design of the definitive stamps.

Benn again went to see the Prime Minister. Wilson had spoken to the Queen about stamps and she wanted her head to stay. 'She is a simple and nice woman,' Wilson said, 'and you absolutely charmed her into saying yes when she didn't really mean it.' He did not want Benn to go back and argue with her again, because he was sure Benn would win, 'and she really wouldn't be happy'.[12]

Wilson went off to see the Queen that afternoon. When he came back to Downing Street, Benn was having dinner there with Marcia Williams and others of the 'kitchen cabinet'. Wilson told Benn that the Queen would accept a silhouette on all commemorative stamps, but a head of some description must appear. Benn had lost.

Matters were somewhat complicated by Wilson's need to remain on the friendliest possible terms with the Queen during the Commonwealth crisis which preceded Rhodesia's Unilateral Declaration of Independence in November 1965. Despite his realistic grasp of the situation, Benn was still bitter. 'I clearly can't make an issue of it,' he wrote, 'because it would be ludicrous to try to defy the Prime Minister on a thing like this and obviously I shouldn't succeed. But for the record, this is how the Palace operates, this is what is inevitably involved when you have a monarchy, and this is how the Queen exercises power to retain her own status. This is incidentally just one more example of why Britain is backward, why new ideas are rejected, and why it is such bunk to suggest that there is a clean breath of fresh air blowing from the Palace through the cobwebs of British industry. With its limited power the monarchy and all it stands for is one of the great centres of reaction and conservatism in this country.'[13]

It was a little naïve of Benn to think he could push through a measure which was clearly designed to marginalise the monarchy at a time when there was no groundswell of opinion arguing for a republic. The Palace was obviously well aware of Benn's political intentions riding alongside the design question. The two issues were interlinked, as design and politics so often are in Tony Benn's thinking, but both sides knew that the bottom line was whether the monarchy retained its central position in public life.

That said, the consequences of the stamp-design debate were entirely beneficial. In 1966 a silhouette of the Queen's head on commemorative stamps replaced the Dorothy Wilding studio portrait which had been used for thirteen years, and a new portrait was commissioned for the definitives. Beautiful stamps were produced celebrating the Salvation Army's centenary, Joseph Lister's discovery of antiseptic and the 900th anniversary of the foundation of Westminster Abbey. Even these stamps excited some opposition. Michael Clark Hutchinson, Tory member for Edinburgh South, asked, 'Why must we have this ludicrous number of new stamps?' and was told by Benn that for some Tories even one stamp was too many, reminding him that the Penny Black was described by *The Times* in 1840 as a disgrace and a discredit to the nation. He coined a new term, 'misatelists', to describe those who hated stamps.[14] The sale of colourful stamps by the Post Office's philatelic counter was an immense success financially. Benn judged that the measure had made him 'cost effective', because the profits from the venture had paid his salary as an MP and a minister thousands of times over.[15]

Benn had inherited a telephone service which had 800,000 would-be customers on the waiting list and a high level of misdirected calls which plagued those lucky enough to have an instrument. The problem was, paradoxically, an over-enthusiastic drive to embrace the technological revolution in the period prior to Benn's term of office. When he arrived the Post Office was in the middle of a disastrous experiment to replace the existing electro-mechanical exchange system with an electronic one which was not feasible at the early-1960s level of expertise. Unfortunately for his reputation, the change-over to an exchange system which would in the long run permit more numbers and greater efficiency, in the short term increased the volume of wrong numbers.

While the telephone system was straining under these pressures, there was also immense consumer demand: 30 per cent more in 1965–6 than in the previous year and 70 per cent more than in 1960–1. Amid these problems, development sections of the Post Office continued with their work in producing, for example, the new-design warbling trimphone and a car radiophone. This led to press criticism that the Postmaster General was obsessed with gimmicks while the service went from bad to worse. The failure of efficient supply for whatever rational reasons was deeply resented when set against the glittering publicity.

The arrival of all-figure dialling was heralded by a press conference on 26 July 1965. There were various reasons for the introduction of it, chiefly to help international communication, which would assist the all-important trade balance – very few countries used letter codes, and telephone codes had to be presented in terms which could be internationally understood. There was also the problem that if the Post Office continued to use letters from district names, they would soon come to the end of usable telephone numbers. There were 648 ways in which the letters on a dial could be arranged, but less than half of them could make pronounceable names. It might be easy enough to remember PARk (Benn's own code) but PSX, for example, would be no easier to remember than 678.

Bernard Levin thought the whole procedure redolent of conspiracy. He wrote, 'Others may suspect that it is not so much the technical advantages which have moved the Postmaster General towards internationalism as his party's relentless egalitarianism. No social cachet can attach to the owner of a telephone with the number London 352 0000 which effectively disguises the geographical and socio-economic differences between Chelsea and Bermondsey.'[16]

Benn also agreed to the introduction of an infuriatingly complicated post code incorporating two sets of both figures and letters. When he understood the way the civil service worked, he particularly regretted having allowed his officials to tell him that this was the only way; the pilot scheme had used this process; it would cost too much to stop its introduction now; and other such arguments. He later said, 'I capitulated, but I should have stuck firm and said, "Well you'll have to start all over again." '[17]

A Benn innovation which was long overdue was the introduction of a Giro bank at post offices. Fundamentally this was the setting up of a nationalised bank which could compete with other high-street banks. Post offices were open six days a week, unlike banks, and there were 23,000 of them, far more than the number of branches any one bank had. This should have ensured success for Giro and given rise to apprehension among the commercial banks.

The Post Office had had a savings bank since 1865. Giro additionally would be able to offer free banking and credit-transfer facilities. It was by no means a novel idea – it had first been established in the nineteenth century in Austria and at least forty-four countries already had the system.

One problem it was intended to remove was that of the wage snatch, the attack by armed gangs on pay packets in transit to places of work. Far more people in Britain than elsewhere in the industrialised world were paid in cash as a result of the Truck Acts, which stipulated that workers must be paid in coin of the realm to prevent embezzlement by employers. Payment by cheque was possible but bank charges and the delay between presenting a cheque and being able to draw money against it made conventional banking unpopular. Only thirteen million people had bank accounts, perhaps a quarter of the population, so most were not served by the commercial banks. There was an obvious market for what was being called

Benn's Bank, which was therefore welcomed by Parliament and press.

Giro would have been an immediate success had the government backed it fully from the start and directed the Treasury to transact all its business through Giro. The Treasury was cold about the idea and did not wish to disconcert the high-street banks by transferring business away from them. It also undermined Giro by denying it the assets of the National Savings Bank, which remained under Treasury auspices, ostensibly because it was believed that the Chancellor could have an influence on general interest rates by manipulating the National Savings interest rate.

Giro was launched in October 1968, with the largest computer centre in Europe being opened in Merseyside by Harold Wilson. After six months only 110,000 people had opened accounts. It made a loss until 1975 and then became popular, though it was never the glittering success which was originally hoped. In the late 1980s Benn was asked if he would appear in a commercial advertising Giro prior to its being sold off by the Thatcher government. He refused. Girobank PLC was sold in 1990 for £112 million.

Broadcasting was yet another area where Benn was beset by controversy. Because the Postmaster General had responsibility for radio and television transmissions, Benn resigned his position as chairman of the Labour Party's Broadcasting Committee. This was to avoid any accusations of a conflict of interests, though in fact his ministerial position gave him responsibility for everything except the content of the programme broadcast. He did, however, have powers to intervene in the case of lapses from good taste and general integrity which continued over a period. This was not lost on those who railed against the allegedly increasing turpitude of broadcasting. It was the right-wing who were the censorship enthusiasts in the 1960s. The supporters of Mrs Mary Whitehouse, a self-appointed guardian of public morality, were told, 'Make no mistake. A group of evilly dedicated people firmly entrenched inside the BBC are plotting to denigrate the morals of the nation.'[18]

In December 1965 various Tories called on him to ban television programmes of a low moral content, programmes criticising Her Majesty's Prison Service and programmes denigrating religion. One programme had featured a crucifix being used as a pipe rack. An outraged Tory wanted such programmes labelled 'Only suitable for atheists and not ordinary people'.[19] One Tory knight complained of 'the continuous socialist party propaganda which seems to be brought into every programme on both channels on every conceivable occasion.'[20]

Having attacked the BBC for taking the influential satirical series *That Was the Week That Was* off the air at the behest of Tory ministers, Benn was not willing to attempt to assert control over broadcasting content, either covertly or overtly. His personal contribution to the debate was given at the annual dinner of the Independent Television Authority in September 1965; 'Another problem is an undue emphasis on violence and crime. To say this is not to argue for censorship. Dramatists and writers have throughout history felt it to be their duty to reveal, explore, describe, analyse and discuss every aspect of the human condition. This process is bound to be disturbing, often distasteful and to some disgusting. But it is clearly the function of television to do it. . . . [But] violence and crime are not the only aspects of the human condition worth exploring. There is still poverty, inequality, injustice to be unveiled. And courage, dedication and determination are features of human life which would merit equally penetrating analysis.'[21]

Yet he introduced a ban on cigarette advertising on television without demur. Lord Hill, a former Tory minister, was now chairman of the ITA. Income for the independent companies came from advertising, so it might be expected that he would oppose a ban, but he had been a doctor before his political career, becoming famous as the 'Radio Doctor', and he put his ideas of public health before financial concerns. Moreover, the Minister of Health, Kenneth Robinson, was the son of a doctor and was passionately committed to the principle of public health. There was also a strong and well-organised anti-tobacco lobby, but no pro-tobacco lobby. On the other hand, Imperial Tobacco was one of the major employers in Bristol South-East, so there was some pressure against Benn bringing in the ban and it might have seemed a question of putting the national interest before his constituency interest. In fact he received no letters at all from his constituency complaining about his action. This reinforced his view that the public would be prepared to accept decisions which were against their own interests if they were seen to be for the benefit of the community as a whole.

The standard by which programmes were broadcast had to be changed to keep pace with higher-quality broadcasting technology, and which system was adopted – French, German or American – was ultimately his decision. The trade in television programmes and technology, including domestic television sets, would be easier with those who shared the system and correspondingly difficult with those who did not. It was one indication that he was looking towards Europe and not the US that he adopted the German-developed PAL (Phase Alternating Line) standard rather than the American NTSC (National Television Systems Committee).

The major problem was that of the licence fees. The BBC was funded by a charge on a television or radio licence. The Corporation was facing an accumulated deficit which was expected to rise to £125 million by 1968–9. The only solution was an increase in licence fees; this had to be agreed with the Postmaster General, who had to clear it with the cabinet. Again, as had been the case with postal tariffs, the cabinet was unwilling to concede an increase with an election on the way. This gave Benn an undeserved reputation for indecisiveness as it was injudicious to admit the real, political reason for the delay. While the decision was pending a number of other sources of funding for the BBC were discussed. Benn approved of advertising on the Light Programme of the BBC as an alternative to the BBC's demand for a continuing escalation of the licence fee. But there was too much opposition to the principle of advertising. In particular, it was assumed by the powerful BBC chiefs that, once advertising had been permitted, there would be no stopping it until there was a service totally funded by advertising. Eventually, in 1965 the fee was increased from £4 annually to £5, not to the £6 which the BBC had desired.

Benn was also responsible, with Jennie Lee at the Department of Education and Science, for setting up the University of the Air, later called the Open University. It was a means by which people who had not had the opportunity to enjoy further education could obtain a degree by completing a series of correspondence courses connected with television programmes broadcast on the recently launched channel BBC2. Caroline Benn was later also involved in this enterprise, teaching Open University preparation courses. Harold Wilson always considered the Open University to be one of the finest achievements of his government.

By far the most difficult aspect of broadcasting policy was the problem of the pirate radio stations. These unlicensed stations, operating from ships or disused forts mainly outside British territorial waters, were beyond British law for tax and copyright purposes. They played continuous pop music, their growth coinciding with the Mersey Boom of music and style most notable for producing the Beatles. By 1963 the audience for the pirates was thirteen million each day, their comparative popularity augmented by the BBC's refusal to play more than a limited amount of popular music and the Corporation's staid presentation.

Benn was told by his department that the pirates were interfering with wavelengths needed for the emergency services and were stealing wavelengths which had been allocated to European countries by the Copenhagen Plan in 1948. Additionally, the artists' representatives said they received no royalty payments, so they were stealing the musicians' work.

The outgoing Conservative administration had been worried about the pirate stations but had been unwilling to ban this clearly popular exercise in free enterprise. Bevins, the previous Postmaster General, had licensed a commercial station on the Isle of Man on 15 October 1964 and, had the Tories won the election, they would doubtless have licensed the pirates.

The only law which applied to them was the Wireless Telegraphy Act of 1949, which forbade people from receiving transmissions from stations not authorised by the Postmaster General. This Act, aimed at preventing people from listening to police and defence wavelengths, incurred a penalty of £10. Millions of otherwise law-abiding people were breaking the law.

The pirates themselves felt they were cheerfully providing a public service and making money. They had supplied an evident need and, happy to be legitimised, they patiently waited for the government to license them. The more respectable of them offered sums in lieu of royalty payments. Interestingly in view of his belief in open discussion as a means of settling problems, Benn never met the pirates or invited them to give their point of view. They were to be subject to legislation, but not to participate in its framing. The model the pirates were offering was one of public expectations being met by buccaneering capitalists: in this model the law is disobeyed, the public applaud it in their millions, and the law is changed, a victory for the people.

Benn did not see it that way. He regarded the eventual suppression of the pirates as one of his more substantial achievements, noting in the early 1970s, 'I did have the satisfaction of getting the Pirate Radio Bill [though that was not its name] approved by the cabinet before I left.'[22] With hindsight, it is difficult to see the attack on pirates as anything but a failure of imagination.

To be fair to the Postmaster General, the UK was a signatory to the 1965 European Agreement for the Prevention of Broadcasts Transmitted from Stations Outside National Territories, and this bound him to introduce legislation to make the pirates illegal. The point was how it should be done and what should take their place. The entire debate could have been settled by Benn licensing commercial stations. He did not do this for two reasons. The first was that he had a plan for local radio as a service for the community, which he therefore wanted to place in the hands of the BBC. He did not believe he had the extra wavelengths to allocate for both the BBC and commercial radio. More importantly, he was personally opposed to the pirates on the ground that they had broken the law by appropriating a wavelength and withholding royalty payments. They should not, Benn felt, be permitted to benefit from breaking the law by being handed a licence to print money.

This was understandable as a principle, but the cabinet is less interested in principles than in governing the country, and it is expected to balance the wishes of the people with what is practicable and what is judicious. The cabinet turned down Benn's proposal to have advertising on the BBC, which would have funded a pop channel. But they were also against legislation to ban the pirates. 'I didn't see any point in losing the votes of young people before the BBC had any real alternative,' Crossman wrote. Benn's intransigence on pirates did him no good at all with his colleagues. It was over this issue that Crossman mused,

It's a queer thing but I am not very happy about him now I see him at work. To begin with, on every single occasion when he is about to bring a plan to Cabinet a leak occurs giving the full details in advance [contrary to Crossman's suspicions, Benn was not leaking information, though he was probably unacceptably unguarded in his general conversation about his intentions]. In the second place, there is an odd hardness about him which makes him sometimes unattractive as a colleague. He has certainly got himself detested by the Tories – though that's nothing against him – but even among us in Cabinet he doesn't inspire conviction, partly because, although I doubt whether he is a believer, he has at times a kind of mechanical Non-conformist self-righteousness about him which seems to come out even more strongly in office.[23]

'The cabinet was worried,' Benn confirmed, 'and the managing director of one of the stations decided to broadcast appeals to me to lay off the pirates. One Sunday when I was listening to a pirate station I heard, "Mr Benn, you are a young man, you are a family man – surely you enjoy listening to popular radio. I appeal to you to allow us to continue." The phone rang and it was Wilson. He had been listening to the pirates too. "Have you heard that broadcast?" he said. I said I had, "Well, why do you keep pursuing them?" I gave him all the arguments about the wavelengths.'[24] In fact he could have circumvented the wavelength arguments if he had a mind to do so. What the cabinet and Wilson were experiencing was Benn stubbornness. It was a quality which had carried him through the peerage battle and more than one fight with his colleagues and civil servants: opposition strengthened him. He believed he was right and nothing would change him, not even the 2000 letters he received from members of the public on the issue, more than he had received on any other topic.

On this question the positive aspect of the conservatism of the civil service was seen. The Post Office had no powers to stop the pirates so Benn approached the Board of Trade, who were responsible for ships, but they fobbed him off: ships on the high seas were not within their jurisdiction. The forts in the Thames from which some pirates broadcast were owned by the Ministry of Defence, but they were not prepared to send a boarding party. Official obstruction was preventing Benn from taking action which was only questionably in the public interest.

Now that Benn knew the rules of the civil service game, he would play it himself. It was a good deal easier to have civil servants say what could not be done than what could, so he told the Director General in a minute to prepare a paper for the Cabinet Broadcasting Committee on local broadcasting, adding, 'Please add the reasons (needle time restrictions, etc.) why commercial stations could not operate a pop service.'[25] 'Needle time' payments were made for the broadcasting of recorded music.

It would be wrong to suggest that this combat was Benn versus the world. There were powerful interest groups who also wanted to see the pirates banned. Paradoxically, they were from the music industry. The Performing Rights Society (and Phonographic Performance Limited, responsible for payments to recording companies) wanted the pirates closed down over the royalties issue. The Musicians Union was actually against recorded music because it believed that the more records that were played the less call there was for live musicians. Of course, this implied a constant market for music, whereas in fact, with the expansion of ownership of transistor radios and record players, the market could expand almost indefinitely and with it work for musicians, producing an ever larger number of records. There was a growing interest in live-music concerts generated by the expanding music scene. The interest groups faced a choice between protecting a privileged position in a small market or taking the leap into a free market in an expanding music industry. In the battle over the pirates an opportunity was lost to instigate a reorganisation of the whole question of needle time – the government could have threatened that it would do nothing about the pirates unless the vested interests liberalised their position. But, though the Beatles were given MBEs by Harold Wilson for their contribution to Britain's exports, the government never did realise the export potential of popular music and musical equipment.

Benn's failure to comprehend the boom in youth consumerism and youth aspirations was disconcerting to his colleagues. As the *Daily Telegraph* noted,

> It seems only the other day that Mr Benn was the idol of the radical young, the Labour politician who could be relied upon to be with it when all his seniors were behaving like fuddy-duddy Victorians.

Yet, once a Minister, the radical and the rebel in him is tamed. To the dismay of some of the grey heads in the government who sit with him . . . Mr Benn wants to accompany a party campaign to give votes at 18 with a punitive action against the pirate radio stations that within the last year or two have become the warp and woof of teenage life.[26]

The association between Benn and youth was largely illusory, born of his youthful appearance. His political influence at such a young age did not give him a direct link with the aspirations of the young; quite the reverse – he was politically successful at a young age because he was exceptional, not because he was typical. He was of that generation of men who had served in the war. Old roués of the Conservative Party had far more in common with youth in the hedonistic 1960s than Tony Benn did. He was an establishment politician from his short haircut to his polished shoes. At this stage, the underground press, fringe theatre, pop music and situationist student politics were as nothing to Benn. He never had the passion for drugs and sexual licence which characterised youth in that decade and which was by no means unknown in the world of Westminster.

In June 1966 an event took place on one of the pirate ships themselves which caused establishment opinion to swing in Benn's favour. On the day of debate on pirate radios a rival group seized Radio City on Shivering Sands Fort and the managing director was shot and killed. It demonstrated a point Benn had been trying to get across through the discussions: there was something unsavoury about the pirates and they were open to manipulation by criminals.[27]

Finally the Suppression of Marine etc. Broadcasting Bill, to outlaw the pirates, was drafted for Benn. He was not pleased with the illiberal title and insisted on its passing into the statute books as the Marine Broadcasting (Offences) Bill, 'which at least sounded more reasonable.'[28]

The pirates were banned from August 1967. The BBC began broadcasting all-day pop music on Radio 1 from the following month. There need not have been a trade-off between local radio, commercial radio and a BBC national pop station – all three were possible. The BBC was given its local radio stations in the late 1960s and in 1971 the new Conservative government announced a plan for sixty commercial radio stations.

263

'I was misled about the wavelengths,' said Benn twenty-five years later. 'It now turns out there are thousands of wavelengths which could have been used, and I'm not sure it was even true they were stealing broadcasting wavelengths from Europe. There were bands which were being kept for defence purposes and that was one area I never realised at the time. I was caught in that and I learned a lot from it.'[29]

Wilson chose the date for the election well. The Labour Party had demonstrated that it could govern, so justifying the slogan 'You know Labour Government works'. There were no major crises and personal incomes were rising. On the other hand, the Conservatives were in no state for a fight, having only in August 1965 selected their new leader, Edward Heath, the first Conservative leader to be elected on a ballot of MPs. This was a procedure necessitated by the outcry over the selection of Sir Alec Douglas-Home. The Tories had little to offer, they did not fit with the reforming image of the decade and Heath was never as popular a figure as Wilson. The time was right for Labour. On 31 March 1966 Labour gained a majority of ninety-six over all other parties, the first time an outgoing Labour government returned with an increased majority. In Bristol South-East Benn increased his majority to 11,416 in a straight fight with the Conservatives.

After the election Wilson attempted the same trick of putting a vigorous young man in charge of a moribund department by asking Benn to go to the Ministry of Works. Benn refused, because it was not a cabinet post and so was no real promotion. Additionally, he felt that Dick Crossman's brief at Housing and Planning would make him ultimate overlord of Works and he had no wish to be under him. Wilson said he intended other moves; in particular he expected Frank Cousins to leave the Ministry of Technology, 'the real glamour job',[30] and, though he would not promise it to Benn, this was as broad a hint as anyone was likely to receive from the Prime Minister. Benn attempted to ensure that Wilson would remember his suitability for the post by speaking about his long-term interest in technology and about his experience of Japan, where he had seen considerable state support for industrial development.

Benn returned to the Post Office, where he explained that he had been offered a job elsewhere but had decided to stay on. The Director General was 'shaken to the core'[31] – the civil servants had thought they were rid of Benn for good and had been preparing briefings for his successor. Now they not only had him back, they had a Benn determined to complete his reorganisation of the Post Office. Any suggestion of a reorganisation had been fiercely resisted by the old guard until Donald Wratten, after much heart-searching, had risked his career by disobeying the Director General and revealing to Benn that there had already been a working-party report on reorganising the Post Office.

Equipped with the report, which Benn had had to obtain for himself from the Director General, and now in contact with its principal author, William Ryland, Benn was able to proceed. He proposed that the Post Office should become a nationalised industry divided into two corporations, one dealing with telecommunications and the other with mail and banking. Both would be run as industries in the public interest under a Minister of Communications. He explained to senior staff that with departmental status, 'too much power necessarily remains with the civil servants who are naturally not held publicly responsible for what they do', and as if to sweeten the pill he added, 'and are denied the credit for their achievement.'[32]

The division into two was effected on 1 October 1969 when the Post Office became a corporation and the Postmaster General at the time, the ill-fated John Stonehouse, became the Minister of Posts and Telecommunications. British Telecom was created from the telecommunications division in 1981, in preparation for its privatisation in 1984. The mail section was never privatised, it is said because of opposition from the Queen.

The Press Association writer Alfred Browne remarked that in later years when asked for his opinion of Tony Benn, Harold Wilson would say, after a moment's reflection, 'Tony made a very good Postmaster General.' Browne added, 'The second time one heard him say it, going through the same little act, that apparent moment's reflection, for one renowned for his memory, seemed a little contrived.'[33] It was still, however, a valid assessment. Benn could hardly be said to have succeeded with everything he touched at the Post Office, but everything he touched certainly bore his imprint.

The creation of the Giro and the establishment of the Post Office as a corporation, both of which happened according to his plans but after his term of office, were Benn's most enduring achievements. His accomplishments which took effect while he was still at St Martin's-le-Grand were more ephemeral but they endure in the affection with which he is remembered there. His energy and vision gave the Post Office a future (it was adequately provided with a past) and reversed the demoralisation suffered by staff operating a declining service in the face of incessant public criticism. The affection was mutual. 'Of all the departments I ever worked in, the one I liked the most was the Post Office,' he said. 'I liked the people, the inspiration, its history. It reflected all that was best and all that was worst in British society.'[34]

21

Technology Evangelist

Benn at last left the Post Office in July 1966, a move relating back to the government's pay and prices policy, which had caused him such grief in his first months as a minister. The difficulty inherent in any such policy was exacerbated by the Machiavellian scheming behind Harold Wilson's appointments. After the 1964 general election victory, George Brown, deputy leader and the man who had fought Wilson for the leadership after Gaitskell's death, had to be neutralised. He was given the new post of Secretary of State at the Department of Economic Affairs, set up in opposition to the Treasury. The Chancellor of the Exchequer, Jim Callaghan, thus found himself in perpetual combat with Brown. This prevented either of them turning on the Prime Minister, who, as First Lord of the Treasury and a brilliant economist himself, always let it be known who was top dog.

Another masterful Wilson manoeuvre which failed was his appointment of the country's leading trade unionist, Frank Cousins, to the cabinet as Minister of Technology. Wilson hoped to gain trade union support for his economic policies by fettering Cousins with cabinet collective responsibility. The other purpose of his appointment was to ensure that the unions did not sabotage his new industrial revolution, the transfer to technologically advanced means of production, which would certainly have major, and in some cases terminal, effects on employment. It was an unhappy appointment, and Cousins never felt at home in the Palace of Westminster. He felt that after he had worked a full day in his ministry, he should be free to go home, not be expected to stay until 10 p.m. to vote in a division. He was, moreover, a natural antagonist and was somewhat more accomplished at rebellion than management.

The opportunity for combat came over the prices and incomes policy of his former colleague in the Transport and General Workers' Union, George Brown. A National Board for Prices and Incomes had been set up to consider and report on price increases and wage demands as they were referred to it. It had no statutory powers, though proposals for these were eventually put forward. Brown himself was never in favour of them but was obliged to carry them through.[1] The suggestion that there should be advance notification of wage claims to a statutory body transgressed the hallowed precepts of free collective bargaining. Cousins had warned that he would resign from the cabinet if the legislation were forced through, and in July 1966 he did. The following month the Act was passed and George Brown left the Department of Economic Affairs.

Wilson sent for Benn, who waited in Marcia Williams's room, reading his horoscope in the *Evening News*. 'Follow your instincts,' it said. 'This is a lucky day for you.' In the Cabinet Room Wilson told him that on Cousins' resignation, in a few days, he would have Technology, the large and rapidly expanding industrial overlord ministry. It was the plum job of the technological revolution with all the creative opportunities of the age unencumbered by the limitations of the past. Wilson told Benn to spend six months learning about his ministry and to go easy on publicity until he had mastered it.[2]

Dick Crossman had dearly wanted the ministry for himself and believed that Benn had been given the post because Wilson needed the Post Office for his Chief Whip Ted Short, who was simply not up to handling a parliamentary party with a majority of almost a hundred.[3] This seems more like spite from his old rival, however, in the light of Wilson's statement to Benn after the election that he expected Cousins to leave and the hint that he was thinking of Benn for the job.

Benn was, moreover, a good choice for Technology Minister. He had been more closely associated with the image of progressive Britain and the fruits of technology than anyone else and, as Wilson later said, he had been a very technological Postmaster General.[4] He was also temperamentally suited for the post. Friends had always remarked on his love of gadgets, demonstrated by his passion for Biros in America after the war, his having a telephone-answering machine before other people even knew what they were, and his purchase of a photocopier, which he found limitlessly entertaining, in 1964.

The announcement of Benn's appointment was made on Sunday, 3 July, and the press and television crews arrived in his garden to find him, appropriately enough, playing with a model steam engine with Melissa and Joshua. The next day he was picked up at 7.30 a.m. and taken for the last time to the Post Office. His departure gave further examples of the way Benn was able to inspire devotion in the ranks of the less senior people who worked for him. His driver said, 'If I can ever do anything for you for the rest of my life, please let me know,' and his messenger clutched his hands and said, 'You're the best man I've ever worked for.'[5]

At 8.30 he was at the Ministry of Technology building, Millbank Tower, on the site of the house where he had been born at what was then 40 Grosvenor Road. Two hours later Frank Cousins came to welcome him to the ministry. Cousins reminded him that in 1960 at the time of Benn's resignation from the NEC he had said it would ruin Benn's political career. He was pleased to see he had got it wrong.

From his eleventh-floor office in the modern glass tower Benn could see the Houses of Parliament, Westminster School, the Post Office Tower and the church in Smith Square where his family used to worship. He truly felt at home here. He had arrived. He was at last a cabinet minister, though not quite the youngest, for he was forty-one and Dick Marsh at thirty-eight had been made Minister of Power three months previously. His salary was £9750 (inclusive of expenses), unchanged since the Post Office.

Benn spent much of the first years at Mintech (as he dubbed it) making speeches to rally industry for the battle and to inspire the nation with calls to training and productivity. 'The battle of Britain 1966 must be won on the parking lots of America,' he said;[6] 'Raise the school-leaving age to sixty-five'[7]; 'We've all got to learn to be a lot more impatient'.[8] Mintech could absorb enthusiasm endlessly – there was always a new group of workers to exhort or a new group of managers to chide, always a dinner of the Reinforced Plastics Conference or the International Welding Federation to address.

He developed a speech which he often made, ascribing Britain's industrial decline to imperialism, and thus marrying his 1950s preoccupation with the Movement for Colonial Freedom to his 1960s enthusiasm for technology. Britain had become the workshop of the world, he would say, between 1750 and 1850, when national efforts had been directed towards industrial development. In the century to 1950, however, Britain had gained an empire, and the highest respect went not to the engineers or producers of wealth but to the conquerors and administrators of wealth overseas. Britain had captured the markets, quite literally, with her troops. Now there were no more colonies and Britain must return to the development of industry, which had made the country powerful in the first place.

Another favourite theme, which was developed into a lecture he gave on BBC television, was about the rate of technological change. He took a subject, like transport or killing or communications, and explained how it had advanced since prehistory. In most cases there had been little change until the late nineteenth century. Thus the only communications advance on a single voice was the development of the megaphone in 1665. The invention of radio allowed general broadcasting; then the rate of change accelerated with bewildering rapidity with television, more powerful transmitters and finally the apogee, the Early Bird communications satellite, launched in 1967. Each of the high speed changes which had taken place since 1945 was delineated until the audience was presented with the hydrogen bomb, the computer, the space ship. Benn then made his characteristic contribution: a leap from technology to democracy. We must learn to take control of these advances, he argued, or the machines will be using us. We are trying to control a twentieth-century society with democratic tools fashioned in the nineteenth century.[9]

Sometimes Benn was making two major speeches a day as a technology evangelist. It was the perfect role for him, combining the visionary and practical elements of his personality. He once said, 'Technology serves a higher purpose than mere production. It offers us a hope for the future. It is the light at the end of the long, dark tunnel of poverty through which most of mankind has been journeying throughout the whole of human history.'[10]

Whether the Ministry of Technology was an adequate vehicle for this missionary task was another question. When it was established in 1964, or soon after, the ministry had responsibility for the Atomic Energy Authority, the National Research Development Corporation and 'sponsorship' of four 'key' industries: computers, electronics, telecommunications and machine tools. Mechanical and electrical engineering industries were later added, having been sheared off from the Board of Trade. The growth of the government management of industry continued with the Industrial Reorganisation Corporation being set up in January 1966 with responsibility for overseeing mergers between companies. It went to Mintech in 1969. Five months after he had taken over, and before he had had a chance to come to terms with the empire he already had, Benn's ministry was given responsibility for the merchant shipbuilding industry.

During this time of hectic speech-making and inspiring visits to the industrial front line, Benn was at his most vulnerable. Everything was so complex, and there was so much of it. He found it difficult to keep ahead of the decisions: 'Mintech is becoming a bit too much for me. All the decisions are so frightfully complicated and technical and I'm not really qualified to judge them.'[11] He had nightmares in which he had to see General de Gaulle about the future of Concorde and he had not read the briefing papers.[12]

He was also in a new league as far as the civil service was concerned. Civil servants in the Post Office might obstruct him with dumb insolence or by altering memoranda hoping he would not notice. The civil servants at Mintech were of a different calibre. As Benn noted in his diary after meeting Sir William Penney, who had worked on the atomic bomb during the war, 'It is difficult for a new and still relatively young minister to be dealing with these very distinguished people who had worldwide reputations when I was a student.'[13]

His permanent secretary, who had been at the Treasury but had joined Mintech at the same time as Benn, was Sir Otto Clarke, 'a very slick operator' according to Benn.[14] Clarke would 'boil like a kettle' during arguments with his minister, but Benn knew he could rely on him to manipulate the Whitehall machine to Mintech's advantage when they had decided on a policy. Benn's mature judgement was that Clarke was the best permanent secretary he ever had.[15]

He instructed Otto Clarke, in the face of his protestations, that it was essential that all papers on which he had to reach a decision should come to him with Professor Bruce Williams's advice on them. Williams, an academic and economic adviser to the ministry, had first met Benn via Wilson's economic adviser Tommy Balogh, with whom he shared a flat in Hampstead. He said, 'Tony Benn was a very exciting person to work for. He assumed policies were matters of rational thought and persuasion. If your argument won, you would have Tony's backing for your policy.'[16] Williams found, however, that this did not mean that the backing of the rest of the department would necessarily follow.

The Mintech years were the start of a period of government involvement with industry which continued throughout the 1960s and 1970s. Behind this involvement lay two principles: that bigger is better and that productivity is related to the percentage of wealth invested in research and development. Mintech's experience helped to throw doubt on these principles, but in 1966 they were sacrosanct. Benn presided over the acting out of the dream with the 'industrial reorganisation' functions of Mintech. Described as mergers, 'reorganisations' were more often than not thinly disguised take-overs when the predator company did not have the cash to carry its ambition through and had to appeal for government funds.

The major reorganisations included the merger between International Computers and Tabulators and English Electric Computers to form International Computers Limited (ICL); between Associated Electrical Industries and the General Electric Company (GEC); between Bristol Siddeley and Rolls-Royce; and between British Motor Holdings and the Leyland Motor Corporation to form British Leyland, combining the Jaguar, Daimler, Morris and Mini motor cars under one roof. It became the third largest European motor company, after Volkswagen and Fiat but ahead of Renault.

If the answer for Britain's poor industrial performance was to create larger industries, then Benn did more than anyone else to deliver that answer. If more capital was required, the government would provide it. The Industrial Expansion Bill, which Benn steered through in 1968, provided for the lending of government money to companies which could not raise capital and empowered the state to take shares in companies which had been so assisted.

above On the set of 'The ABC of Democracy' in 1962, Tony Benn talks to Jeremy Thorpe, with journalist Keith Kyle in the background.

below For Cummings of the *Daily Express* the peerage case showed Macmillan's 'winds of change' were blowing only in the Commonwealth. (8 May 1961)

Dr. MacJekyll and Mr. MacHyde

Disconsolate at his exclusion from the House of Commons in 1962.

Triumphant in the by-election following his renunciation of the Stansgate peerage, August 1963.

above The young Postmaster General keeping a watchful eye on the Prime Minister as they talk to President Lyndon Johnson to inaugurate the Early Bird communications satellite on 28 June 1965.

below Priests of the new technology. The Minister of Technology (fourth from left) visits Dounreay nuclear power station in October 1966.

Back in flying gear for a Concorde test flight on 10 April 1970.

above The *Telegraph*'s Benn is a disturbing but absurd techno-man, whose radical Llandudno speech is regarded with disdain by his ministerial colleagues. (27 May 1968)

below The Shadow Industry minister arm-in-arm with comrades at Upper Clyde Shipbuilders on 23 June 1971.

above The grim face of industrial discontent at a factory gate meeting in 1974.

below Cummings sees the Labour right wing speaking the truth while Harold Wilson is the leading militant. (27 September 1974)

DAILY EXPRESS Friday September 27 1974

"Mrs Williams! Mr Jenkins! If you utter that smear-word again we shall have to expel you, too, from the Union!"

'He's a pushover for the part, Sir Lew — he actually BELIEVES in miracles!'

The *Daily Mail* presents Benn as a deluded messianic figure. (2 August 1974)

The merger on the grandest scale, and the one which was the cruellest disappointment, was the creation of Upper Clyde Shipbuilders. Benn's Shipbuilding Industry Act of 1967 was designed to promote amalgamations and to give credit to shipowners via a Shipbuilders Industry Board. It was welcomed by the Tories, who showed no aversion, as a whole, to state investment in private industry. But shipbuilding was in decline and no amount of investment seemed able to stop it. In 1950 the UK launched 48 per cent of the world's ships, in 1966 6 per cent.

There were several reasons why shipyards on the Upper Clyde were no longer profitable. The industry was cursed with restrictive management and equally restrictive trade union practices, overmanning and low productivity. An additional curse was the narrowness of the shipping lanes in the Upper Clyde, which were inappropriate to the building of tankers and bulk carriers which the shipping trade now demanded.

The Upper Clyde would be saved as a shipbuilding area, however, because there were particular political reasons for saving it. On the Labour side, there were communities dependent on the shipyards, communities which solidly returned Labour MPs. The workers in shipbuilding, too, were represented in unions which funded the Labour Party. If these workers could not be protected, who could?

The Tories and civil servants had equally potent reasons for supporting this branch of heavy industry in particular, in addition to the mere class interest of identification with the shipyard owners. Britain was a maritime nation which had built ships from time immemorial. The building of a great ship was a symbol that Britain counted for something in the world. As Otto Clarke commented, 'If we can't make ships what can we make?'[17]

At the instigation of Mintech's Shipbuilding Industry Board, in summer 1967 four out of five shipbuilders on the Upper Clyde agreed to merge, forming Upper Clyde Shipbuilders from John Brown, Charles Connell, Fairfields and Andrew Stephen. It was a very public demonstration of the blessings of government intervention in industry.

The prize which Mintech offered Benn was membership of the cabinet. He had attended parts of cabinet meetings before as Postmaster General, invited in only to make a contribution on his departmental concerns. Now he was among these political titans as of right.

Admiration for the cabinet's abilities was not universal. Anthony Sampson said: 'I always thought it was extraordinary the way Wilson's cabinet was dominated by an over-donnish, over-confident, over-academic group. The lack of a mix, of an experience of how the world worked, was an important part of the failure of that government. They were an amazingly unified group in their lack of experience. Practically none of them had ever had to hire or fire anyone. Interestingly Tony Benn, who did come from an established, confident family background, was much closer to the roots of the Labour Party than Crossman or Crosland. I was always struck by his clear sense of what the grassroots were saying and doing.'[18]

It was indeed rule by intelligentsia. Rather like the nineteenth-century squires who believed they had a right to rule the country because they owned the country, people like Wilson, Jenkins, Crosland and Crossman believed they had a right to rule because they were very, very clever. For them, the art of government was the art of perfectly tuning a powerful machine. There was a right way to do it, and a wrong way. They would listen patiently to talk of a vision of the future and of inspiring a call for change in the hearts of the people, then they would remark that this was all very well, but how were they going to set the exchange rate?

Benn was despised as a non-intellectual and at the same time resented because he was so popular and so successful at putting his ideas across. Crossman said, 'Wedgy is brilliant at public relations and has enormous drive and ambition and even imagination, but he refuses to face the real difficulties because he has a second-rate intellect.'[19]

Harold Lever, soon to become Financial Secretary to the Treasury, felt differently. 'Tony was the wittiest member of the cabinet and that was very welcome,' he said, 'and he was very much underestimated for political ability by his right-wing opponents. They said, "He's only a boy scout." I said, "That boy scout runs rings around you." He was a tough negotiator and a ruthless pursuer of his ends, much better than his detractors.'[20]

Crossman would criticise 'the lack of success of the interventionist policies of Peter Shore [Benn's Parliamentary Secretary at Mintech then Secretary of State at the Department of Economic Affairs] and Tony Wedgwood Benn, young men who with carefree arrogance think they can enter the business world and help it to be more efficient',[21] though he did not give his suggestions for what would be effective if intervention would not, or what demeanour they should adopt to render the government's policies more appealing. Benn had his own criticisms of Crossman, describing him as 'an incredibly inadequate man, like Hugh Dalton'.[22]

Benn joined the cabinet at a time when Wilson believed it to be up to its neck in steaming conspiracy. Wilson was convinced in July 1966 that there was a coup being planned against him involving the right wing: Callaghan, Jenkins (now Home Secretary) and Crosland. They would replace Wilson with Jenkins and Brown with Callaghan.

Benn knew nothing about this until the next month. There may have been no more to the affair than senior politicians parading their ambitions, but the fear of a plot increased Wilson's paranoid tendencies and his reliance on the kitchen cabinet of Marcia Williams, Gerald Kaufman, George Wigg and Tommy Balogh. Benn and Crosland discussed the 'July plot' over lunch in September that year and came to the conclusion that there had been no conspiracy. This is almost certainly the case. Crosland would not have misled a colleague and old friend over such an issue: he had many faults but he was not devious. He grudgingly remarked that Wilson was 'as good a peacetime Prime Minister as this country ever gets'.[23]

Benn remained loyal to Wilson and was closer to him than most of his cabinet colleagues, but he despaired of the Prime Minister's lack of radicalism. Moreover, Wilson never seemed to hit quite the right note with Parliament or his Labour colleagues. After a number of Labour abstentions in the defence debate in March 1967 Wilson made one of his most offensive speeches when he told the Parliamentary Labour Party, 'Every dog is allowed one bite, but a different view is taken of a dog that goes on biting all the time. He may not get his licence returned when it falls due.'[24] The comparison with dogs was obviously offensive but, as Benn realised, the imagery gave an insight into Wilson's attitude towards his colleagues: they were there to support him and he licensed them in return.

22

The Common Market and Concorde

B enn was present at all the major cabinet meetings on Common Market entry and came to share the general belief that membership was inevitable – it was only a matter of the right time and the right terms. European Economic Community entry was, moreover, an issue well in keeping with those which motivated Mintech. If planning was desirable, was not planning on a continental scale even more so? Why should not agriculture too enjoy the benefits of the division of labour between nations and the economies of scale which held out such promise to industry?

At a day-long cabinet meeting at Chequers on 22 October 1966 George Brown spoke about a report of his own which was strongly in favour of entry, and it was finally agreed for himself and the Prime Minister to visit the six countries of the Common Market to sound out their reaction to another UK attempt at entry. On 30 April 1967, again at Chequers, the cabinet voted for entry, Benn making what Barbara Castle called a 'passionate speech in favour of a technologically united Europe'.[1] His position surprised both pro- and anti-Marketeers, for both sides had thought him more equivocal. Roy Jenkins, a leading pro-Marketeer, sent him a note welcoming him to the fold. Crossman considered he was a 'convert' to the Market.

Wilson insisted there should be no formal vote until the next meeting at 10 Downing Street, on 2 May, but it was clear what the decision was. Of the twenty-one cabinet members present, thirteen were for application and eight were either against or were for deferred application.[2]

Whatever the perception of Benn prior to this, he now became a convinced pro-Marketeer. He later described the decision to go for entry, though sincerely felt, as one of desperation for all concerned. He said, 'By April 1967 we were a totally demoralised cabinet. We had tried the National Plan and it had failed. We had tried to hold the pound and it had failed, we were going to have to devalue. We had tried everything. I thought we didn't have a choice. I also thought at that time that the only way you could deal with multinational companies was by multinational political structures.'[3]

In February 1967 Mintech absorbed the Ministry of Aviation, its staff increasing overnight from 8000 to 38,900. It made Benn responsible for 'the biggest state-directed complex of scientific and industrial power in Europe'.[4] Included in the take-over were Ministry of Defence procurement functions. It was something of a coup for Benn to take over the procurement of aircraft, guided weapons and electronic equipment. The Minister of Defence Denis Healey had laid claim to these when the demise of a separate Ministry of Aviation was discussed but Benn had obtained them, probably because Wilson wished to keep his ministers divided against each other, and the fostering of departmental rivalry was the best way to achieve this.

When Benn looked over his new empire he realised that waste and unwise investment were rife in the aircraft industry. He cannot have improved the digestion of members of the Society of British Aerospace Companies on 28 June 1967 when he told them at their annual dinner that aviation ministers financing the industry from public funds 'had run off with sums of money that made the Great Train Robbers look like schoolboys pinching pennies from a blind man's drum. . . . All right, I will consider your proposition, but you have really got to persuade me that any public investment has a real chance of producing an economic pay-off.'[5]

He was being somewhat restrained. The aviation ministers may have run off with the money but it was the manufacturers who had put it in their pockets. A committee of inquiry set up under Sir Roy Wilson found the Bristol Siddeley company had 'budgeted for and achieved exorbitant profits' on government contracts between 1959 and 1963. The conduct of the company's negotiating representatives had 'amounted to intentional misrepresentation' by which the government's representatives had been 'deceived'.

The company paid back almost £4 million of excess profits, but little else could be done, it seemed, to pursue the guilty. Witnesses to the inquiry had been assured of confidentiality, and the ability of future inquiries to get to the truth would be impaired if any of the witnesses were prosecuted after having received such an assurance. Benn worked late into the night preparing his statement to the House of Commons about the affair. It was a bitter pill but it had to be swallowed, much to the anger of Labour back-benchers, who were outraged to see a business get away with major dishonesty while private individuals were imprisoned for far less.

Benn sacked two chiefs of Bristol Siddeley, Sir Reginald Verdon-Smith and Brian Davidson, from three government advisory committees. The posts were all unpaid but it was the only mark of disfavour the government could offer to men whose evidence had 'fallen short of the accurate, complete and frank response to questioning which the committee were entitled to expect'. The Tory aviation spokesman Frederick Carfield called it 'vicious victimisation'.[6]

Some companies found more favour with Benn, including the Beagle Aircraft Company, which Mintech took over in 1969. It made a light military aircraft, the orders for which were cancelled when the Ministry of Defence found they could not fit the heavy equipment into it which they required. Benn felt that the cancellation, which led to the collapse of Beagle, was an error, but it was one of the battles he lost with the military. He succeeded in retaining the Harrier jump-jet, however, against Denis Healey's opposition. The Treasury also tried to cancel the Skyvan, manufactured in Northern Ireland by Shorts, but Benn won through. 'It was distressing really.' he later said. 'The designers always wanted something new, and a lot of money; the Treasury always wanted to cut things, and I was trying to sort out rational criteria to stick to a limited number of projects and see them through.'[7]

A run on sterling after the 1964 election had obliged Harold Wilson to go cap in hand to President Johnson, who insisted on spending cuts if he were to release a $4 billion loan. Britain could not, the Americans argued, be at once asking for money and spending on prestige projects. They should cut the TSR2 and Concorde.

TSR2, a tactical strike and reconnaissance aircraft, had been in development since 1959. The Americans wanted Britain to be a client for their new fighter-bomber F111; they therefore offered it to the UK at half the cost of the TSR2, with other trading advantages.

The building of Concorde, a passenger plane which would fly at twice the speed of sound, had been agreed as part of a deal between Macmillan and de Gaulle in 1962. As both nations were working on a supersonic air transport, it seemed sensible to combine efforts. Development costs were estimated at £190 million. The Americans had an interest in closing down the Concorde project because they were developing their own similar aircraft and the Anglo-French project was years ahead of their Boeing design. The Soviet Union were leading the supersonic race with their TU144.

The Wilson government was prepared to cut Concorde until it saw the small print on the contract. The agreements with the French to build Concorde jointly had been designed with fiendish skill to prevent the French from backing out. Any side which reneged on the contract would have to reimburse the other for all the money already spent on Concorde. So the Americans had to be satisfied with the sacrifice of the TSR2. Benn played no part in the TSR2 decision (he was Postmaster General at the time), though it was being built partly in Bristol.

The Ministry of Defence ordered fifty F111s, only for the cabinet to agree to cancel the order against the advice of Defence Minister Denis Healey. Healey said that, if Benn would support him on the F111s, he would not take a leading role in opposing Concorde. Benn voted against the F111s, with the majority of the cabinet, arguing that it would have been unacceptable to spend on defence while making cuts in social spending. Benn took the round of cuts badly. Barbara Castle remarked, 'Wedgie was nearly in tears at the suggestion that we should sacrifice £3m of his expenditure.'[8]

On 11 December 1967 the first Concorde was rolled out at Toulouse to the theme tune of the television puppet show *Thunderbirds*. They were five years ahead of their American rivals. Tony Benn himself decided that Concorde should be spelled in the French way,

279

with an E. There were few dissenters. As the *Daily Express* head-lined its double-page spread: 'Something to shout "Well done!" about'.[9] Even the Queen was romantic about it. 'You *can't* cancel Concorde,' she said to Benn at a later date, and she wished the test pilot could have seen the crowds around Buckingham Palace burst into spontaneous applause when Concorde roared over in a fly-past on her birthday.[10]

Concorde was the symbol of the technological future. For Benn everything about it impressed him: it was the biggest project in the world outside the US space programme, the biggest aircraft project, the most sophisticated international collaboration. 'It'll change the shape of the world, it'll shrink the globe by half. We're trying to build the T model Ford of the supersonics for the 1970s and 1980s. It replaces in one step the entire progress made in aviation since the Wright Brothers in 1903,' he said.[11]

Despite this enthusiasm for public relations purposes, Benn was realistic about Concorde. He considered it had to be a commercial proposal and refused to give an assurance, as he was requested to do in the House, that no financial difficulties would be allowed to stand in the way of its completion.[12] Benn attempted an agreement on a 'costs ceiling' with Jean Chamant, his French opposite number. The proposal was that they should agree a sum above which they would cancel. Benn spent eight hours in talks with Chamant, who was really only prepared to agree to recommend cancellation to his government if there were no firm orders for Concorde by the end of 1969.

The continuation of the Concorde project was based on the balance between the cost of producing it and the amount earned by selling it. A realistic projection therefore had to be arrived at for the investment it would require and the number which might be sold. Benn was advised that the cost would be between £500 and £1000 million, which was thought to represent the nature and size of the uncertainty in the programme. Benn thought that was too vague to announce to the House of Commons, so he said, 'It will not cost less than £550 million.'[13]

Such was the nature of the figures on one side of the balance sheet. The other side – the orders which might be expected – could not yet be filled in. One of the factors affecting the order book would be the volume and frequency of sonic booms when Concorde flew overland. These booms are a result of the two abrupt air-pressure rises which are created at the front and at the back of a plane flying supersonically. They are experienced at ground level like a clap of thunder but with a characteristic double sound.

As unknown quantities, the magnitude of the boom and the damage it could cause grew in the public imagination. There were fears it could damage the spires of ancient churches and make herds of cattle stampede.[14] Benn arranged a boom, by a military aircraft, during a cabinet meeting, but the boom issue remained central for Concorde: if public opinion in Britain prevented the plane from flying overland then there could be no expectation that any other nation would allow it to fly overland. That would prevent Concorde from flying the lucrative routes on the North American and European continents and reduce orders to an unacceptable level. But Concorde had to be built, and flown, before its 'boom signature' could be established and public reaction to it gauged. As Benn told the *Bristol Evening Post*, consciously addressing his constituents working on the aeroplane, 'I am trying to manage the project in a sensible, technical and economic way, and it is no part of my job to look into a crystal ball and venture my opinions. It is the facts that matter, and these have got to be kept under continual review.'[15]

The most expensive and least valuable of all the high-technology projects of the time was the 'hardening' of Polaris missiles, variously known in its later incarnations as the Antelope, the Super Antelope and the Chevaline project. This grew out of one of the major government decisions considered at the time: whether to replace part or all of the Polaris fleet with the larger and more fully armed Poseidon submarines which the US was developing. Cabinet decided against, but maintaining Britain's position in the arms race was still a hot issue, particularly as the Soviet Union was setting up anti-ballistic missile systems to defend against a nuclear attack. John Hill, the chairman of the Atomic Energy Authority, went to see Benn on 5 December 1967 to discuss the question of hardening Polaris missiles at the Aldermaston atomic weapons research centre, for which Benn was responsible. At the cabinet's Nuclear Policy Committee Benn was against the hardening of Polaris on policy grounds – he felt the money would be better spent elsewhere. He was not a unilateral nuclear disarmer, though it was this issue which was later to make him one. The Treasury opposed it on financial grounds while Denis Healey and George Brown, Defence and Foreign Secretaries, were in favour. Sir Solly Zuckerman, the government's chief scientific adviser, was against.[16] Lord Kings Norton was asked to set up a committee to look into the question of hardening. Lord Rothschild, Zuckerman's nominee on the Kings Norton committee, wrote a minority report disagreeing with a great deal of what was said and arguing that the nuclear weapons programme in Britain was totally unnecessary. Kings Norton reported in July 1968 suggesting some savings at Aldermaston but basically maintaining a high staff level. Healey wanted no firm decision made until the results of the Polaris Improvement Studies and he called Benn in and made this clear in his characteristic blunt fashion. 'I was told I was to have nothing whatever to do with it,' Benn said.[17] The division of ministerial responsibilities was that Mintech funded the maintenance of Aldermaston while the Ministry of Defence was the customer for its products. As two ministers were involved, both had to take part in decisions regarding nuclear developments. When the Conservatives returned to office they placed Aldermaston under the Ministry of Defence so there was even less reason for the Defence Minister to consult than there had been when Benn was at Mintech.

Because money for 'studies' was all that Denis Healey could supply, no real decision was taken to harden Polaris under this government. It was, however, Denis Healey who turned it into a working project which was available for the next government to endorse or reject.[18] Benn later said, 'I think the truth is that the project had been going on quietly at Aldermaston from 1967 or 1968.'[19] Why had he not been kept informed? One reason is given by Dennis Fakley, deputy chief scientist at the Ministry of Defence at the time: 'From the point of view of the nuclear weapons programme, Mintech was an irrelevance.'[20]

Benn had his personal enthusiasms like the Tribology Committee, which was trying to save industry £500 million by recommending better design and lubrication and so less wear on machinery. Benn's vigorous promotion of new ideas led to the sobriquet Hover Benn, with the implication that his feet were never on the ground. He certainly felt it his duty to promote a project with all the zest at his disposal when it had Mintech backing, but there were many projects which did not enjoy initial support or which were terminated under Benn. There was no end to the number of schemes into which scientists wished to siphon development money. Benn was in the unaccustomed position of having to restrain the exuberance of others.

The quest for power from nuclear fusion was one expensive high-science project which Benn did not feel able to back. It was believed that the experiments at Culham, Oxfordshire, could lead to sustainable fusion in a laboratory – duplicating the mechanism by which the sun creates power, the nuclear physicist's grail. Experimental physics, however, is distinguished both by being exciting and by requiring sums to sustain it which only governments can afford. Physicists therefore had to convince the Minister of Technology that the laboratory at Culham was worth investing in, whether or not it was producing results. Bruce Williams's counsel prevailed. He considered that too much investment was being put into research and not enough into application and marketing. 'Fast breeder reactors and Culham couldn't possibly have any effect on the economic generation of power until the 1990s at the earliest. If it was worthwhile for research it should be sent to the Department of Education and Science, not a ministry concerned with industry.'[21] Benn cut it back by 50 per cent over five years, not wanting to lose the expertise of the team assembled at Culham by axing it completely. The Atomic Energy Authority diversified and took on commercial work in order to keep Culham going.

Bruce Williams appraised various nuclear power station types and decided the only type which was likely to produce power economically was the Pressurised Water Reactor on which very little work was being done. He considers they were 'Badly misled by the nuclear physicists'.[22] The decision to make the mainstay of nuclear development the British Advanced Gas Cooled Reactor rather than the American Pressurised Water Reactor was made before Benn took over Mintech, though he always supported it.

Benn's diary is full of remarks about how tired he is and about the ill-health which is related to fatigue. He usually worked till two or three in the morning at this period and even abandoned the full diary from the time he was promoted. This was for two reasons. Initially it was due to the increased pressure of work. When he tried to catch up, however, and dictate the months July to September 1966 to a secretary, he felt it wrong to be dictating a diary dealing with cabinet matters to a person who was not in the cabinet. The diary then lapsed from September 1966 until 1 January 1968, after which date he adopted Richard Crossman's suggestion that he dictate it and store it, without having it typed up, thus ensuring confidentiality. When Labour was out of office in the 1970s Benn dictated entries for the missing period from his small five-year diary, which was just a list of the basic events of the day.

The technology proselytising, and latterly his ministerial responsibility for metrication, tended to make Benn a target for the right-wing traditionalists who were angered by change. *Private Eye* eschewed its customary humorous front cover to deliver a full-blooded attack on him entitled 'The Most Dangerous Man in Britain'.[23] Often the criticism was humorous or even affectionate, as in 'Next week Wedgbenn of Mintech on Hallucinogenics and Society: Living with Psychedelic Change'.[24] Even the most affectionate portraits, however, betrayed irritation with him. A positive local-paper feature headed 'Our Man in the Cabinet – A Go-Getter with Kennedy Style' still commented irritably: 'He seems to have an inherent notion that everything was wrong the day he came to this earth and must be altered with the minimum of delay before we all perish.'[25]

23

Radical Clarion

Britain's continuing economic problems were not alleviated, in the short term, by the devaluation of the pound, a policy Benn accepted. A number of men of industry began to consider leading a government of national unity themselves. It was a peculiar delusion, probably promoted by de Gaulle's example, though they did not seem to recognise that de Gaulle had emerged as a leader at a time of enemy occupation and had been called back by the nation at a time of civil war. The times were not so dire in Britain in the mid-1960s, nor were the men so impressive. People of the calibre of Cecil King and Lord Robens would have had to wait a very long time indeed at Colombey-les-Deux-Eglises before the call came to lead the nation.

Cecil King, of the Northcliffe dynasty but without a peerage, was a director of the Bank of England and chairman of the International Publishing Group, which controlled 40 per cent of national newspaper circulation and more than 200 magazines and had interests in television and the paper industry.

King's newspapers, which included the *Daily Mirror*, had supported Labour with varying degrees of enthusiasm. He was not happy without an intrigue, however, and according to Barbara Castle's account of a conversation with Wilson on 17 July 1966, King had been an influence in the 'July plot' of ministers against Wilson. All the diarists indicate that King showed animosity towards Wilson almost from the beginning. Wilson told Crossman that this was because he had offered King a life peerage and King had refused, holding out for a hereditary peerage, which Wilson had declined to give him.[1] King had once insisted on Benn's having lunch with him when Benn was Postmaster General. King had pressed the point that he wanted a seat in the cabinet and a peerage. Benn had said cheerfully, 'You can have my peerage – I don't want it!' which did not amuse the newspaper magnate at all.[2]

Benn's turn for a meeting at which King attempted to enlist him in the new plot came late in the round of conspiracy, in February 1968, which indicates how closely he was associated with Wilson. He was obviously not someone upon whose support and silence King could rely.

King gave 'the unanimous view of the City' that the economic situation was critical and there would be a second devaluation that year. He had the opinions of others to offer also: the former Governor of the Bank of England, the United States Ambassador and the permanent secretary of the Treasury were other non-politicians whose political views he put forward as being associated with his own. King felt there would be no time for an election when the government fell – immediate action would be required. Denis Healey was King's favourite for a coalition leader but, he said magisterially to Benn, 'There may well be a larger part for you to play.'

Benn thought King was unhinged. He discussed the conversation with Peter Shore, Secretary of State at the Department of Economic Affairs, then telephoned Wilson, who of course had been receiving intelligence about King's behaviour from other sources.[3] On 10 May the *Daily Mirror* came out with a front-page editorial written by King and headed 'Enough Is Enough'. In it King stated that Britain was 'threatened by the greatest financial crisis in our history' and called for 'a fresh start under a new leader'.

Benn turned up at a television studio on the evening of 9 May 1968 for a discussion on the local government elections and was obliged to talk about King's attack, which was available in early editions. There is no doubt that the government was in trouble. Between July 1966 and February 1968 the Labour Party lost control of over 100 local authorities and lost six of twelve by-elections. A second devaluation was threatened and was not assisted by King's casting doubt on the viability of the currency.

Ian Mikardo famously remarked that 'owning a newspaper doesn't give a man any more political qualifications or knowledge than owning a fish and chip shop'.[4] The result of the plot was a sharp increase in support for Wilson, demonstrated by his parliamentary colleagues rallying round and by readers of the *Daily Mirror* writing angry letters to the paper. Before the end of the month the board of IPC had sacked Cecil King. They had decided enough was enough. He never did get that peerage.

Just prior to the coup attempt Wilson had one of the reshuffles which he had every year to keep his colleagues on their toes. Benn was pressing his claim at the beginning of April for a different position. He would have liked to be Minister of Education, though it would have been difficult for Caroline to pursue her interests in promoting comprehensives if the minister she was lobbying was her own husband. The job he really desired was Leader of the House, about which he spoke to Wilson, but he came away thinking that the Prime Minister 'wanted someone who was a bit more genial and jovial and less worried-looking than me, someone with a trade union background who would drink in the bar all the time and be jolly. It may well be that he thinks me too stiff and Crippsy.'[5]

That night, his forty-third birthday, he went home despondent after the parliamentary sitting. He arrived home at 2.15 and talked to Caroline until 4.15. She thought he had missed out on promotion by keeping his head down and not making more radical political interventions and that he had not gained by being so closely associated with Wilson. In future he was going to talk more to the press, making his general political outlook known.

This was a position he had been coming to over some weeks in the spring of 1968. Two days earlier he had set out a deliberate programme in his diary: 'I'm going to make a series of speeches between now and the conference in which I really lay down quite clearly the direction in which I think the party ought to move.'[6]

Benn improved his position by a few notches in Wilson's reshuffle, though he remained at Mintech. He was made fifteenth in seniority where previously he had been twenty-first. He ascribed this to his lobbying of Marcia Williams and Harold Wilson. He felt shabby about jockeying for minor career advances, though he acknowledged that it was good for the ministry, and the civil servants were pleased that their minister had more power.[7]

The intention to become more politically vociferous was not only a question of personal ambition. Benn was dissatisfied with the direction the nation and the party were taking. He had the feeling that his natural radical conscience was being smothered by his ministerial career. As he remarked later that year when the government was being castigated by his old Movement for Colonial Freedom colleague Fenner Brockway, 'He really made us feel very uncomfortable, the way prophets must have made the kings of Israel feel uncomfortable.'[8] Benn certainly felt more comfortable as a prophet than a king. It disconcerted him too that he was losing contact with grassroots opinion in the Labour Party. In the NEC election of October 1967 he dropped to fourth place, losing 100,000 votes on the previous year.

For the whole of spring and summer 1968 he considered whether he should apply for the post of general secretary of the Labour Party, from which position he could transform the party into an instrument of radicalism. By rule the post of general secretary is not filled by an MP. In order to make the post desirable, and to imbue it with the power he felt it deserved, he believed it should be open to MPs and should automatically confer cabinet rank. This was less revolutionary than it seemed: Arthur Henderson in the 1929–31 government had been Labour Party general secretary and Foreign Secretary in the cabinet. Benn did not pursue his interest in the post as he could not persuade his NEC colleagues to have the rule changed back to that which had prevailed at the time of Henderson.

As for the post of Prime Minister, for which he was so often tipped, he said: 'In principle I should like to be Prime Minister, in practice I don't think about it much.'[9] He was certainly ambitious for his ideas and such an ambition cannot be dissociated from personal political success, for the only way he could increase the purchase of his ideas was to accrue more personal power.

Watching Harold Wilson's handling of power politics led him irresistibly to the conclusion that this was no way to run a country. At the same time, the rise of radical thought as demonstrated by pressure groups and student demonstrations was instinctively attractive. When students at Bristol University in June 1968 held one of the 'Free University' teach-ins, an alternative form of education popular at the time, Benn paid his shilling and sat and listened to the lectures. In order to remain inconspicuous he wore his spectacles and took off his jacket and tie. That night he wrote, 'I realised all of a sudden that for three and a half or four years I have done absolutely no basic thinking about politics.'[10]

The influence of his home was another factor. Caroline Benn and her colleagues used the downstairs office during the day for the Comprehensive Schools Committee, which made the place a dynamo of radicalism. The Benn children and their friends also acted as a force for change, now that all were of an age to be involved in discussion. In May 1968 Stephen was sixteen, Hilary fourteen, Melissa eleven and Joshua ten. Referring to his children in an interview he said, 'They argue with me, they are very critical, and if they see me on television or come to the House of Commons or if they come to my constituency or if they read anything that I've said or done, I find I am very sharply criticised at home and this is very good for me. Also, through them, I realise how very quickly you get out of date in the age in which we live.'[11]

Another politician who was ambitious for his ideas was Enoch Powell. A long-time friend of Benn since their first meeting on the set of *Any Questions?*, Powell was the very model of an independent thinker. A classically educated and isolated man, Powell's brilliant oratorical flights of fancy usually lacked the restraining influence of mere common sense. It would have been available at the cost of a short conversation with others, had Powell been a man who had developed better skills of communication on a simple personal level.

Powell was the most prominent Conservative to have taken up race as an issue. Events in Africa following the break-up of the British Empire had produced a volatile situation in which many Commonwealth citizens looked to Britain to aid them in times of persecution. In particular, in the late 1960s, Jomo Kenyatta of Kenya pursued policies which discriminated against Kenyans of Asian origin, who responded by making use of their rights to enter Britain as immigrants. The rights had been granted by Duncan Sandys when Commonwealth Secretary to safeguard the position of white settlers but were equally applicable to the Asians. Liberal thinkers, Benn included, seemed to find racial discrimination from a black politician to be less unpalatable than it was when coming from a white, for they were not vociferous in their condemnation of Kenyatta for creating the conditions in which Kenyan Asians were obliged to come to Britain in their thousands.

Nor was Powell concerned at this injustice. To him the influx of immigrants was a cause not for compassion but for dread as to what they might do to the host population. The speech Powell made to the annual general meeting of the West Midlands Area Conservative Centre on 20 April 1968 is sometimes rather heroically called the 'rivers of blood' speech. This is because Powell at one point in his vision of the future quoted the poet Virgil, who saw 'the Tiber foaming with much blood'.

He spoke of 'The discrimination and the deprivation, the sense of alarm and resentment' of the white population and he gave what purported to be an example. After he had spoken about race on a previous occasion, Powell received a number of letters. He paraphrased one which claimed to tell the story of an elderly white woman who kept a lodging house in a street in Wolverhampton. Other properties in the street had been taken over by immigrants, but she refused to let rooms to them. Powell quoted from the letter: 'Immigrants have offered to buy her house – at a price which the prospective landlord would be able to recover from his tenants within weeks or at most months. She is becoming afraid to go out. Windows are broken. She finds excreta pushed through her letterbox. When she goes to the shops, she is followed by children, charming, wide-grinning piccaninnies. They cannot speak English, but one word they know. "Racialist," they chant. When the new Race Relations Bill is passed, this woman is convinced she will go to prison.'[12] Needless to say, the best endeavours of Fleet Street reporters working for weeks failed to find any trace of either the besieged widow or the miraculous children who spoke no English but a three-syllable abstract word. Nor was the letter-writer available for comment.[13]

Benn immediately thought of the speech in personal terms, that it illuminated Powell's personality rather than any great truth about race in Britain. He wrote, 'Enoch is of working-class origins, he got a scholarship to a grammar school, did very well academically, became a professor at twenty-four and a brigadier at twenty-nine. But he has never been accepted in the Tory Party. . . . He has got to have someone to look down on and this is the way he does it.'[14]

The speech was made on 20 April, which, probably unknown to Powell at the time, is the high feast day of the extreme right wing: Adolf Hitler's birthday. The Fascists quickly saw their opportunity and organised a demonstration of support for Powell from among London's meat porters and Tilbury dockers, a few hundred of whom marched to the House of Commons. The tens of thousands of letters Powell received applauding him did, however, indicate a level of support for his view which was wider than that of the 'white trash' alone.

In establishment circles, across all parties and among all people of even average goodwill, the speech was considered despicable. This came as a surprise to Powell. He had spoken 'more forcefully' on race earlier in the year at Walsall and had told a Young Conservatives meeting in 1966 that immigration was one of the most important subjects the Conservative Party had to examine. These speeches had attracted little attention. But this time Powell was shocked by the response, and later referred to it as 'the earthquake speech'.[15]

Two other people who had earlier played a part in Benn's life now acted decisively against Powell. Sir Edward Boyle and Quintin Hogg telephoned Powell and told him they could no longer serve in a shadow cabinet of which he was a member. They must have told Heath the same thing for he later agreed with his Chief Whip, William Whitelaw, that he could not lose Boyle and Hogg for the sake of Powell. Heath had Powell summoned to a telephone to be sacked the day after the speech.

Tony Benn made the most dramatic speech of his career just a month after this, at Llandudno on 25 May 1968. The occasion was the annual conference of the Welsh Council of Labour. The political background showed a world which cried out for change. In the US rioting had spread through dozens of towns and cities following the assassination of Martin Luther King. In eastern Europe all eyes were on Czechoslovakia, where Alexander Dubcek was transforming hard-line Communism with liberal reforms. The North Vietnamese Tet offensive, which achieved the temporary capture of the American Embassy in Saigon, showed that capitalism was not invincible and gave a new impetus to Vietnam protests from Tokyo to London. In France the 'days of May' saw half the national workforce on strike, joining the students, whose barricades and street fighting in Paris produced the most enduring image of the period. If there was a month to be radical, at any time since 1945, this was it.

The atmosphere in the Winter Gardens in Llandudno was tense and security was high, for the night before the Welsh Office in Cardiff had been bombed by Welsh nationalists. Benn started his speech by announcing what he was not going to talk about – the economic system, which was an understandable obsession of politicians. Today he was going to talk about the decision-making process. If one did not get that right, he said, the economic system would never function. 'Much of the present wave of anxiety, disenchantment and discontent is actually directed at the present parliamentary structure. Many people do not think that it is responding quickly enough to the mounting pressure of events or the individual or collective aspirations of the community.

'It would be foolish to assume that people will be satisfied for much longer with a system which confines their national political role to the marking of a ballot paper with a single cross once every five years. People want a much greater say. That certainly explains some of the student protests against the authoritarian hierarchies in some of our universities and their sense of isolation from the problems of real life. Much of the industrial unrest – especially in unofficial strikes – stems from worker resentment and their sense of exclusion from the decision-making process, whether by their employers or, sometimes, by their union leaders.'

Clearly something was being said here which was different from anything said by a leading politician before. It was also, quite clearly, subversive. Benn gave six conditions which had to be met to ensure the redistribution of political power – to transfer power from institutions to the individual.

First, 'freedom of information' legislation on the Swedish model would permit public scrutiny of decision-making. Secondly, the government should know more about the people it was elected to serve via statistical services and the publication of more data. Ultimately the taxation and social security systems could be integrated: 'Then we shall be able to decide politically what to do about means and needs on a personal basis, entirely free from anomalies.'

The third requirement would be to hold referenda on real issues, perhaps starting with those subjects now decided by Private Members' Bills. Electronic referenda would soon be possible and with them would come 'a considerable uprating of the responsibility and understanding of ordinary people' – in other words, possessing the ballot itself leads to education in how to use it.

Fourth, Benn urged an opening up of the mass media to those with minority views. 'The day may well come when independent groups of publishers would be allocated so many hours of broadcasting a month and told to help those who have something to say, to say it clearly and well, to national audiences.'

Fifth, 'representative organisations' should be encouraged and promoted so that they could be consulted by government. Trade unions should be funded to help them to perform their duties in regard to industries which had already been amply supplied with government money. Pressure groups should be encouraged as a source of ideas for future policy. Finally, there should be devolution of power to regions and localities.

These, Benn said, were the main political issues which would be argued about in the 1970s and beyond. He ended on an apocalyptic note: 'In a world where authoritarianism of the left or right is a very real possibility, the question of whether ordinary people can govern themselves by consent is still on trial – as it always has been and always will be. Beyond parliamentary democracy as we know it, we shall have to find a new popular democracy to replace it.'[16]

It was his most successful speech to date in terms of press coverage. Benn was already an important figure, but this put him at the forefront of progressive thinking and, by induction from these views to others he might reasonably be supposed to have, it distanced him from the most reactionary behaviour of the Labour government.

The left were delighted with the speech and the right were perturbed. The most serious criticism, and one which was to dog Benn for the rest of his time as a minister and shadow minister, was that he was breaching cabinet responsibility – the obligation for the front bench to give the appearance of unanimity regardless of personal opinion. That criticism was misplaced, Benn remarked. He wrote in *Tribune* on 14 June 1968, 'Cabinet responsibility relates to what a Cabinet has done, is doing or is seriously thinking of doing. It does not limit the right to think about long-term future policy.'

Wilson nonetheless felt that an attack on the system of government was an attack on the cabinet because that body was responsible for the government, but this was a rather obscure line of reasoning and not even the Tory newspapers picked it up. The situation was complicated because the Home Secretary, Jim Callaghan (he had swapped jobs with Jenkins after the devaluation), had said in a speech that prices and incomes legislation would lapse at the end of 1969, thus pre-empting a cabinet decision. With Wilson unsuccessfully attempting to rebuke Callaghan in cabinet on 30 May, the heat was taken off Benn.

There was encouragement from all sides, most commentators relating the speech to unrest in France, some referring back to Powell. 'Could Britain too become embroiled in bloodshed and violence? Yes, said Mr Anthony Wedgwood Benn, Minister of Technology,' reported the *Sunday Express*, only to add with assailable logic, 'There is now no alternative. There must be an immediate general election.'[17] The speeches by Benn and Powell were compared by the cartoonist Garland. In his drawing a Benn robot bursts in on sober-suited Labour cabinet members to say, 'I too see the Tiber foaming with blood.'[18] The speech was reported as far afield as Hong Kong and New Zealand. The American news magazine *Newsweek* described Benn as 'The only European statesman who has so far made a public attempt to apply the lessons of the new French revolution to his own country.'[19]

His vision of the future was in some parts correct. The referendum on the Common Market and referenda on devolution were held in the 1970s, though referenda on anything but major constitutional issues have not been favoured. Official secrecy remained a major problem, while government increased the volume of information it held on the public. Decentralisation did not occur. Indeed, over the following twenty years local government suffered growing control from central government. Pressure groups, however, did begin to enjoy funding and co-operation with local and national government. A major development which Benn promoted, the issue of minority access to the mass media, became the driving force behind Channel 4 television.

Benn followed Llandudno with a series of dramatic speeches which maintained his position at the centre of radical thought – for example, on industrial democracy[20] and on the new politics (both in

November 1968).[21] In the latter he remarked, 'It is an encouraging paradox that at the very moment when technological pressures are supposed to be casting us all into the same mould, we are in fact all breaking out of the mould again and demanding a freedom of expression which is actually disintegrating the monoliths. This is a sort of political parallel to the permissive society. Individuals are demanding the right to renegotiate the social contract, on a personal basis, and are thus providing a completely new dimension and meaning to the phrase "government by consent".'

He referred to the new pressure groups representing tenants, consumers, black people, educational reformers and so on, all siphoning off political effort into direct action. 'This phenomenon of a myriad of political action groups is not really new. What is new is the realisation that they have now become an integral part of a new-style parliamentary democracy, and may, in the process, be undermining the monolithic character of the parties, and in part supplanting them.' He was saying that politics was too diverse to be left to political parties.

He wrote to Bristol South-East Labour Party on 6 June 1968 in terms which were to become common ten years later: 'The keynote of party reconstruction must start with a search for greater participation in decision-making. People today are not prepared to have policy handed down to them from on high – even from a Labour government.'[22]

Benn was keen on the idea of the Labour Party admitting its mistakes and talking honestly in public about the problems of government. An attempt by Benn to make the 1968 conference the occasion for a review of the first three years in power failed at the NEC in July that year. Both right and left attacked the principle of analysing the past and confessing to weaknesses. How could they possibly agree on what were the mistakes?, it was asked.[23] The practical value of the proposition was questioned by two cartoonists who had the same idea: that, given the Wilson government's poor reputation for veracity, admitting their mistakes would be futile because no one would believe them.

Benn's increasing radicalism showed in a hardening of his attitude to Vietnam. He argued in cabinet on 8 October 1968 that the government had to dissociate itself from the war, 'because [he noted in his diary] the rumours are that the Americans are going to stop the bombing in North Vietnam and I was afraid we would be the last government in the world that had come out against it'.[24] He was unsuccessful, and similarly so in arguing in cabinet for dissociation from US actions after their invasion of neutral Cambodia in 1970.

Through 1967 and 1968 Benn was seeing a good deal of 'the cabinet left',[25] Dick Crossman, Barbara Castle (Minister of Transport until April 1968), John Silkin (Chief Whip) and Peter Shore, often with the addition of Thomas Balogh from the kitchen cabinet, who would be able to report back to Wilson that no conspiracy was afoot.

Benn became more concerned about the interaction between technology and society and more interested in the trade unions. He told the Bristol South-east Labour Party he was planning to extend his contacts with the trade unions, 'so as to bring them more and more into the development of industrial policy'.[26] In a paper he wrote for the inner cabinet (known as the Management Committee) when he became a member of it in late 1969, he argued that ministers should be able to visit workplaces where there was an industrial dispute in order to conciliate. 'As a sponsoring minister who receives many direct appeals from harassed managements I find it hard to explain, let alone justify, my enforced silence.'[27]

The most controversial of his dramatic policy speeches in 1968 was an expansion of one of the 'preconditions for a popular democracy' from the Llandudno speech. 'The Role of Broadcasting in a Participating Democracy' was given on Friday, 18 October, to thirty-five people at Hanham in his constituency. As he had already circulated the text of the speech three days earlier via the Labour Party's Press Office, there was also a crowd of newspaper and television journalists waiting at the ward Labour Party meeting to see it delivered.

He started topically. Demonstrations like that soon to take place in opposition to the Vietnam war at Grosvenor Square (Stephen Benn was one of 100,000 people who took part) would receive extensive coverage, 'and they will trigger off a whole series of discussions among the usual panel of pundits who will talk absolutely predictably about their significance and the problems of law and order. But the one thing we shan't get, whether before, during or after, is any opportunity to hear, first hand, at length and in peace, the views of those who are organising these demonstrations.'

Similarly, despite claims that industrial disputes had lost the motor industry £48 million of exports, 'Neither the motor manufacturers nor the trade unions have been offered even an hour apiece to tell the public how they see it, or even to address their own management or members.' Coverage of such important issues was trivialised and simplified to the point of absurdity.

He specifically repudiated any notion of government control of the media and emphasised that he was not in this speech concerned with political 'balance'. The point was that there were thousands of organisations who were denied access to broadcasting. 'The BBC has assumed some of the role of Parliament. It is the current talking shop, the national town meeting of the air, the village council. But access to it is strictly limited. Admission is by ticket only. It is just not enough.

'Broadcasting is really too important to be left to the broadcasters, and somehow we must find some new way of using radio and television to allow us to talk to each other. We've got to fight all over again the same battles that were fought centuries ago to get rid of the licence to print and the same battles to establish representative broadcasting in place of the benevolent paternalism by the constitutional monarchs who reside in the palatial Broadcasting House.'

The Times, Telegraph and *Guardian* printed the speech in its entirety, an indication of the importance Benn now had as a political thinker. The speech was widely reported elsewhere and just as widely criticised. Most comment missed the point and quoted the line 'Broadcasting is too important to be left to the broadcasters' without the rest of the sentence, then went on to claim that Benn wanted government control of the media. Others interpreted the speech as a blatant attack on the BBC. Even commentators who got the point dismissed the idea of greater access to the media as calculated to produce hour upon hour of boring television.

It was the first time Benn had been so widely criticised and so grievously misrepresented. Paul Johnson in the *New Statesman* suggested that the reason was:

the need for people to have an envy-hate figure. Benn is young (worse, young-*looking*), handsome, immensely confident, able and articulate. He is a highly successful minister, who will quite possibly be PM one day. So, many people envy him and need to hate him; and in order to hate him in good conscience they have to make him do things, and say things, which he has not done or said. Benn did not say that the government should interfere with the BBC. He said exactly the opposite. But he might have saved his breath. A lot of people, in the TV world, the press and the Tory party, wanted to believe that Benn had advocated a government takeover of the BBC, and therefore what he actually said was brushed aside as totally irrelevant.

Not for the last time.[28]

Richard Crossman was furious about the speech because he intended to make one himself about broadcasting the following week and had even spoken to Benn about it. He attacked Benn at a dinner in Barbara Castle's flat for having got in first but apologised for his behaviour two days later. Perhaps he had realised that he needn't mind the competition. Benn's contribution made the public more aware and more receptive to Crossman's, so increasing rather than decreasing its coverage. Crossman's speech took the form of a Granada lecture after a dinner at the Guildhall, a big event for the upper ranks of media folk, 900 of whom were there to hear him. Before it was delivered, Sir Hugh Greene, Director General of the BBC, said that Crossman's speech would be on 'an entirely different level' from Benn's, which he described as 'silly, trivial rather than dangerous'.[29]

Yet Benn and Crossman were talking in entirely different traditions of media criticism, both of which were to bear fruit in different ways. Crossman had nothing to say about access to the media; his was a critique of television simplification which Peter Jay and John Birt developed and applied in the 1970s and 1980s. Benn's arguments for access, carried forward by others, notably Philip Whitehead and Jeremy Isaacs, led to the setting up of Channel 4, which started broadcasting in 1982. It was a national TV channel with a charter establishing it as a medium for minority interests with maximum viewer access.

Wilson felt the ministerial speeches had gone far enough and sent round a sarcastic memo warning his colleagues to restrain themselves. Whether or not Richard Crossman or Harold Wilson approved of Benn's speeches, the Labour Party certainly did. His increasing radicalism was reflected in popularity in the NEC election – in 1968 he came third in the constituency section election, a move up one place from the previous year, and in 1969 and 1970 he came second, with only Barbara Castle above him.

24

Technology Turns Sour

Tony Benn sat up with Joshua to watch the moon landing on 20 July 1969, an event which for the whole world was the high point of technology worship. But unease had already set in. A mood of uncertainty was entering public perceptions of technology, a mood which reinforced doubts about Concorde.

In January that year workers at Rolls-Royce in Bristol had jeered Benn when he came to tell them he would decide whether to continue with Concorde on the basis of the flight tests. Until then they would not go ahead with full production and there would be redundancies.

At the end of 1969, which was the agreed date for determining whether or not to proceed with the project, the French would still not agree to cancellation. Costs were escalating beyond all reason and there were still no firm orders. Benn argued at a meeting of the cabinet's Economic Strategy Committee that the project should continue for six months or a year, and at least the cancellation should not take place before the election. The committee accepted this.[1] 'It was fascinating to hear Wedgie admit that his enthusiasm for advanced technology ("never very great" – *sic*) was now much diminished,' Barbara Castle wrote of the meeting.[2]

Benn began to talk of the 'debit side' of technology: 'There's the danger of nuclear war, there's the possibility of pollution and noise; there's the fact that in order to have technology you have to operate on a large scale so decisions have to be taken more centrally.'[3] He asked rhetorically, 'What is the white heat of the technological revolution?' and answered, 'It's the unemployment of the miner. He's the guy who's burnt by the blowtorch of technological change, because you don't need mines, you've got nuclear power. Go to the docks where containerisation will reduce the demand for labour, and the white heat of the technological revolution is the docker going to the House of Commons to support Enoch Powell one week and Jack Dash the next.'4 The gleaming world that Mintech had built was already beginning to rust.

The new prestige liner *Queen Elizabeth II* was back in dock at Clydebank at the beginning of 1969 with a fault in her advanced turbine engines just when the commemorative stamps celebrating it were released. When Benn visited Clydeside on a bitterly cold February day in 1969 all 15,000 workers, everyone except those working on the *QE II*'s engines, stopped work in a jobs protest. The amount of money the government had to help them was limited, he had to tell them, they must rely on their own resources. Not for the first time, he had to explain that things would be tough for a while. The following month he told the same workers they must co-operate with management in achieving speedy delivery dates and working economically or there would be no further help from government.

The unions were advised in May 1969 of plans to save Upper Clyde Shipbuilders with considerable reductions in manpower. Eventually a cabinet committee agreed on 6 May 1969 to give more money in return for reduced absenteeism, better middle management, fewer unofficial stoppages and higher productivity. A 'final, non-negotiable offer of assistance' of £9 million was made two months later. This was their last chance. Another last chance came that December when, with an election looming, UCS was given an additional £7 million. Benn announced this to the House of Commons with the understatement, 'It was always realised the re-organisation on the Upper Clyde would present particularly difficult problems.'5

Enoch Powell was a lone voice in the Tory Party in rejecting such assistance, arguing that giving money to UCS was comparable to tourists giving food to the prairie dogs of North Dakota. In winter when there were no tourists the dogs would die because they would not have the ability to fend for themselves in the harsh natural climate. These ideas would take another decade before they became Tory policy in the form of Thatcherism. At this time, neither Tory nor Labour were prepared to have the death of the shipyards on their hands.

In industrial relations the state had often appeared as the big nanny in the form of Tony Benn, telling unions and management not to be so silly and to get on with the job. Management was chided for 'industrial amateurism, often a hereditary disease in family firms', and the unions for 'neo-Luddism, frowned on by the best trade unions'.[6] But it was on the unions that Labour's heavy guns were eventually trained. Barbara Castle's White Paper, *In Place of Strife*, of January 1969, attempted to bring strikes under legal control, recommending legal sanctions to enforce a twenty-eight-day cooling-off period before a strike could be called and a ballot of members imposed when a strike was threatened.

Benn supported Castle out of loyalty to her and out of a genuine feeling that unregulated strikes were seriously affecting British industry. He later said, 'Looking from a management point of view at the way British industry was being run, and being rather a corporate-state man, it seemed that what she was doing was sensible and I went along with it until it obviously precipitated a major breakdown in our relations with the unions and then I pulled back.'[7] By siding early with the unions, Callaghan had played a crucial part in ensuring Castle's failure.

At the cabinet meeting which sank the Bill as an instrument containing legal penalties, on 17 June 1969, Benn said, according to Crossman, 'We are in advance of the times. We only started talking about trade union legislation a year ago and it is too early to talk about a statutory obligation when we haven't yet had a process of education.'[8] The proposed Bill was replaced by a 'solemn and binding undertaking' that member unions would adhere to the TUC's guidelines on regulating unofficial strikes.

The government staggered from one disaster to another. Richard Crossman's attempts at reform of the House of Lords ground to a halt in April 1969 when his Bill for an appointed second chamber had to be dropped under the weight of time-wasting opposition. Benn had been on the House of Lords reform working group and had again suggested his 1957 proposal that the Privy Council should become a second chamber with hereditary peers losing all voting rights, but this had not been accepted. Crossman's Bill was defeated at the hands of what Benn called 'the conservatives of left and right',[9] an alliance of Enoch Powell and Michael Foot, who talked it out for the old reasons: on the right, that it went too far, and on the left that it did not go far enough.

Despite these political buffetings, life was good for Tony Benn and he did not tire of saying so. On their wedding anniversary in June 1968 he wrote in his diary of 'A very happy nineteen years of married life'. He praised Caroline's work on the Comprehensive Schools Committee and her work in teaching with the National Extension College. 'Quite apart from that, she advises me more directly and effectively than anyone else and I rely on her enormously.' With a happy marriage, the four children and his work, he considered himself to be 'a very, very lucky man'.[10]

Holidays would now again be spent at Stansgate, where the couple would relax by painting the house or doing other odd jobs. As his ministerial work became more testing, Benn had increasingly absorbed himself in carpentry during the holidays, building a lectern, several ladders and a seat to fit on the roof of his car, a regular feature of Bristol South-east electioneering.

It was one of Benn's great regrets that he did not have more time to spend with the children. He told a reporter, 'I talk to them a bit before they go to bed and I start work after that. I mention that as a hint to people to spare me from being invited to too many functions so I don't have any time with the family at all.'[11]

Benn was suffering increasing disenchantment with Wilson as the decade wore on, a disenchantment which was not lessened by confidential meetings with Wilson at which the Prime Minister tried to inspire Benn with enthusiasm for his new honours list. With his reliance on a kitchen cabinet of favourites at 10 Downing Street, his political mastery and his studied use of patronage, Wilson came more and more to resemble Lloyd George. There were echoes here of William Wedgwood Benn's rejection of Lloyd George after their close association early in their relationship. Even the underlying disdain for the Prime Minister's lack of 'honour' was a characteristic shared by father and son. At one time Wilson had warned the cabinet that ministers must stay in line or lose their jobs, then had leaked the whole warning to the press. As Benn wrote in his diary, 'It does reveal what a very small man he is, with none of the boy scout, public school virtues. Maybe I overstress these but there is a certain lack of character in him which I find increasingly annoying.'[12]

He was still dependent on Wilson's favour, however, a humiliating position for a proud man to be in. He called Wilson anxiously in July 1969 when the Sunday papers reported that responsibility for industry would be given to the Ministry of Employment and Productivity, to which Barbara Castle had been moved in April 1968. He need not have been concerned. Following a suggestion Benn himself made, Mintech became a ministry of industry and technology in October 1969, taking over the Ministry of Power and the nationalised boards responsible for electricity-generation, gas, coal and steel-production (steel had been renationalised in 1967). Responsibility for the remaining manufacturing industries, including textiles and chemicals, went over from the Board of Trade. Mintech was now the sponsoring ministry for 80 per cent of Britain's total manufacturing output still in private hands and for virtually all the state-owned industries. More power for industrial sponsorship was taken from the Department of Economic Affairs, which was at last allowed to die, with its head, Peter Shore, becoming Minister without Portfolio.

Mintech was one of two departments which were enlarged and restructured, the other becoming Local Government and Regional Planning, which was given to Tony Crosland. Benn had been offered this job and had refused it. He had suspected that Wilson wanted to get him out of the way in order to give the top job in a restructured Mintech to Healey, who now had nothing to do at Defence. Wilson's two new 'super ministries' followed the prototypes set down when the Department of Health and Social Security had been created in November 1968 and the Foreign and Commonwealth Office in October 1968.

Benn had thus moved a few more inches up the greasy pole. As the *Sunday Times* remarked, he was 'seriously thought of as the only possible contender for the party leadership a decade from now'.[13] He could be introduced on a television show as 'one of the three or four most powerful men in Britain'[14] and in his local paper as 'one of the most powerful men in Europe'.[15] Press comment, including that from traditionally unfriendly papers, was far more positive after this dizzying promotion – a promotion Benn might not have received had he not made himself into a more commanding national figure by his series of radical speeches. Wilson paid attention to these things.

Reg Prentice was appointed as a junior minister but resigned within three days, disappointed to find that he was in fact number three at the ministry and not number two. There were two ministers of cabinet rank: Benn himself and the charming and sophisticated financier Harold Lever, who was described as one of the cleverest half-dozen men in the House. There was talk that he had been appointed by Wilson to 'keep an eye on' Benn,[16] but years later Lever specifically denied that any such measure was necessary. Lever reflected, 'He wasn't doing anything that was dangerous – he was behaving intelligently and carefully. I never had a cross word with Tony. If he'd proposed anything mad I would have said so.'

Benn soon invited his new number two for a working breakfast at 7 a.m. Lever replied, 'I am convinced that there is such an hour, as there is a seven in the evening and I know it is a twenty-four-hour cycle, but I have not been acquainted with such an hour before and have no wish to be.' A working lunch, then, Benn suggested. Lever agreed, but on the condition that he could bring his own sandwiches. He had heard of Benn's simple fare before. He duly supplied the Mintech lunch with a Fortnum and Mason's hamper complete with champagne and smoked salmon.[17]

With all the power, all the talent and all the money of Mintech, what did it achieve? Depressingly little. There was the political will and the means to reverse industrial decline, but one by one, now or in the next decade, after Mintech had gone, British manufacturing industries collapsed.

The most extreme free-market approach would be to say that industry failed *because* of Mintech and the ideas it represented, because government intervention prevented industry from facing the bitter competitive winds of the free market and from cutting the excessive workforces or incompetent managements in order to compete more freely. Yet machine tools went down too.

There was little state intervention in the machine-tool industry, at a time when the American industry was in collapse and there should have been great export opportunities. It therefore provides a useful control model for the debate about whether state intervention was beneficial or damaging to industry. If there were ever an industry which should have grown strong in the bracing climate of competition it was this. The only major help machine tools received from government was a guaranteed purchase scheme whereby the prototype of a new machine had a guaranteed sale to the government – a means of ensuring that new lines were developed. Yet, despite the lack of government assistance, the industry, the largest in Europe, went down at a time when the Japanese and German industries were taking over the market.

Nor was industry in general acting as if government assistance were a scourge. As Benn wrote in July 1970:

> To take some examples, Alfred Herbert, Cammell-Laird, Swan Hunter, Joseph Lucas, Plessey and Vickers – each of which had contributed substantial sums towards the Tory Party and its front organisations to pay for posters and leaflets calling for an end to government intervention in industry – had between them received well over £18 million in funds or facilities from Mintech, IRC, the National Research Development Corporation or the Shipbuilding Industry Board. Nobody would have been more shocked than they to have discovered that a Conservative government really meant to leave them out in the cold to fight their own foreign competitors, many of whom were in receipt of substantial help from their own governments.[18]

The Japanese Ministry of Industry and the French Mintech gave assistance to their industry directly. In the US there was generous help to industry through NASA and Pentagon contracts.

Benn continued to be concerned about race relations, convinced that politicians should address a matter which so concerned the public. He was aware of the sensitive nature of the subject, however, and worked on at least one speech on immigration and assimilation which he did not deliver.[19] It was two years after Powell's inflammatory speech that Benn first responded, though he did not name Powell.

On 20 March 1970 he said at Huddersfield, 'The obscenity of racial hatred has been vigorously propagated over the last few years in Britain by frightened little men who sought to build up their own political position by playing upon the natural human anxieties which arise when people come up against something new. It is utterly revolting to hear the argument about the birth statistics going on – as if the new definition of being progressive is that you don't believe there will be many black babies and the definition of being conservative is that you warn against babies who are non-white. And it is equally revolting to hear people speak as if the nicest thing we could say to a black boy or girl is that when they have lived here long enough and behaved themselves we will treat them as if they are white.'

On 1 May 1970 Powell made an obsessive, highly detailed speech about the rates of birth of children to parents with one parent (not of UK descent) who was born in the New Commonwealth. This was a complex way of arriving at a figure for the 'coloured' population. Later that month an election was announced for 18 June. Benn would have left the race issue, having made his point, but Powell raised it again in his election address, published on 30 May, and Benn decided that 'When racialism raises its head, you should strike against it.'[20]

A decreasing proportion of Powell's support had come from respectable Conservatives. He was appealing more to the disaffected working class and to Fascists, for whom Powell was the first figurehead of any stature since Oswald Mosley. Press reports of a Powell meeting on 3 June record forty skinheads forming a bodyguard for their hero and declaring they would guard him throughout the thirty meetings he would be holding in the West Midlands.[21] Skinheads formed a working-class youth cult stressing violence and austerity. They were heavily politicised by Fascist organisations, primarily the National Front, which had been formed in 1967 by the amalgamation of three extreme right-wing groups.

The evening when Powell first enjoyed a bodyguard of such youths, Benn was speaking to a Students for a Labour Victory rally at Central Hall, Westminster. His speech was standard for the time: he presented them with some of the economic, industrial and social choices the election offered. He talked, as he increasingly was talking now, about 'leadership from below' and the accountability of power. In the middle of this unexceptional speech, he inserted ten short paragraphs which he had prepared as a press release at Transport House earlier that day and which had already been distributed.

He said, 'The smooth smile of Edward Heath is little more than a public-relations front for the harsh fanatical policies that Enoch Powell has developed.

'Those who want to know what a Tory Britain could be like should read the speeches of Enoch Powell. These are the policies which will be pushed on to a weak Mr Heath by the Tory Party if they are allowed to win this time. However distasteful they may be to him, he isn't strong enough to resist these pressures.

'The most evil feature of Powell's new Conservatism is the hatred it is stirring up, playing on fear, fanning suspicion. It has started with an attack on Asians and blacks. But when hate is released it quickly gets out of control. Already Powell has spoken against the Irish. Anti-Semitism is waiting to be exploited as Mosley exploited it before. Every single religious or racial minority can be made the scapegoat for every problem we face.

'The flag of racialism hoisted in Wolverhampton is beginning to look like the one that fluttered over Dachau and Belsen. If we don't speak up now against the filthy and obscene racist propaganda still being issued under the imprint of Conservative Central Office, the forces of hatred will mark up their first success and mobilise for the next offensive.'[22]

Wilson was furious and let the press know of his displeasure. Both major party leaders, concerned about divisions within the ranks of their own supporters, had been keen to keep race out of the election, and now it was an issue. Edward Heath called on Wilson to repudiate Benn. The Prime Minister would not go so far in public, but he said at a press conference, 'The words he used must be his own choice. I do not write my colleagues' speeches for them.'[23]

Benn was actually on the same side as Powell insofar as he wanted the race issue discussed. As the storm raged around him he wrote in his diary, 'I think that an issue as important as this can't be left out of an election because an election is a period when the public engages in a great debate about its future and race is one of the most important questions in the future and it is quite wrong to keep it out.'[24] He did have doubts about the precise language he had used, but all he could do was stand by it, for a repudiation of the terms employed would imply a repudiation of the sentiments. It was better to ride it out.

Moreover, Benn was not alone in feeling that Powell should be condemned in stronger language than that used for any common political difference. The effect on black people of a senior politician denouncing racism in such terms should not be ignored. The level of racist attack and racist abuse which could be associated with Powell's views was not appreciated for many years.

Some saw the situation differently. Cartoons pictured Benn fanning the flames of Powellism or putting a match to the touchpaper of the Powell rocket. The right wing of the Labour Party were the most concerned to ignore the race issue altogether. Michael Cocks, later Labour Chief Whip, wrote, 'Even today one can still sense the shudders that ran through politicians and Labour supporters at the extraordinariness of the language. Not only was it an offensive attack upon a politician, whose views one did not have to share but whose patriotism could hardly be challenged, it was inflaming racial tensions.'[25]

Politically the effect of Benn's speech was to force leading Conservatives into repeated denunciations of Powell (though they denounced Benn at the same time) and to destroy the possibility that racist remarks would become common political currency. No respectable politician ever again dared make remarks as extreme as Powell's.[26]

Benn did later regret his attack on Powell as a person. He said, 'I regretted having done it afterwards. I realised as soon as I'd said it because I've known Enoch very well and I didn't want to be very personal and I think I did go over the top with Dachau and Belsen. I felt uneasy at making it so personal. But it was a statement that came out of my stomach. I was so sick about it. I don't regret having tackled him on the question because his influence has been wholly pernicious.'[27]

Harold Wilson claimed that the attack on Enoch Powell cost Labour five seats,[28] though he never substantiated his claim. Nor do the figures bear this interpretation. Powell himself did not hold constituencies in his gift, so it is unlikely that criticising him would mean the difference between electoral success or failure. The most detailed study of the election results, David Butler's *The British General Election of 1970*, found that 'the Powellite Conservative candidates fared exactly as their party did nationally – an average swing of 4.7 per cent'.[29]

The same piece of research found, however, that the evidence that Powell helped the Labour Party by mobilising support for it from black people was extremely strong. In areas of a large immigrant population there was a higher turnout and a lower swing to the Conservatives than elsewhere. Benn's vigorous anti-racism can only have assisted this trend.

Labour had every expectation of winning the general election. The hard economic measures were showing results and the nation's books were finally balanced. The opinion polls were positive, giving Labour a large lead. This demonstrated one of the many deficiencies of opinion polls: they show what those questioned would do if they voted, not whether or not they are going to vote. The other thing the high opinion poll prediction did was to dissuade those whose commitment was lukewarm from voting. If Labour was going to win anyway, why bother voting? A low poll favoured the Conservatives. The startled Edward Heath emerged on 19 June with 330 seats to Labour's 287.

In Bristol South-East, boundary changes had weakened Benn's majority but the constituency was also showing the effects of voter lethargy. With a turnout the same as that nationally, 72 per cent, he had a majority of 5688, half the 1966 figure.

Looked at as a whole, the Labour government's period in office may have been a disappointment but it was not an unmitigated disaster. The 1960s were a time of great hope for the public – class barriers were being broken down and Britain was at the forefront of world culture in music and fashion. A series of liberal reforms, either promoted or backed by the government, were exactly right for the times. Equal pay for women and race relations legislation were significant advances which were not repudiated by later governments. The reform of laws on divorce, adult homosexuality, abortion and theatre censorship were in some places unpopular measures but they were not so with the general public. On the other hand, the government baulked at reforming the law relating to possession of cannabis and failed to consider reforming the laws on prostitution and pornography. This showed that, progressive though it was in some social legislation, the Wilson administration was not in the front league of reforming governments in the 1960s.

A deeper failure, and one which plumbed the shallow foundations of Wilson's administration, was the moral failure to confront the issue of Vietnam. This outraged Labour supporters the most, which meant the footsoldiers had no will to fight, not for those generals anyway. If they were apathetic about returning Wilson to Downing Street, how could the uncommitted be spurred to enthusiasm?

In Bristol South-East, Benn tried to cheer the despondent party workers when the result was announced in the early hours by telling them that Labour had been defeated but not routed. He and Caroline decided to return to London that morning, and set off at 5 a.m. Caroline took the wheel when Benn began to doze off. In London he decided to go straight to Millbank Tower and clean out his desk. By 8.35 a.m. there was no sign that anyone had worked in the eleventh-floor office of the Minister of Technology, and Tony Benn slipped out into the morning air.

25

'Citizen Benn'

The immediate response to loss of office was one of relief. On the Sunday after the election Caroline and Tony Benn went to a 'wake' at the Croslands'. Susan Crosland, who noted how cheerful they were, remembered her husband remarking that Benn was happier in opposition – it was only now he could make his move to become leader.[1] It cannot have helped Tony Crosland's view of Benn that he had a furious row with his old friend that evening: 'Crosland was coming out in favour of Enoch Powell, just to show off, and that was more than I could stand.'[2]

Certainly, it was the internal affairs of the Labour Party, NEC and shadow cabinet which were to preoccupy Benn for the next four years. During this time he had the advantage of being vice-chairman then chairman (in 1972) of the party, thanks to the 'Buggins' turn' process of giving the position to the next longest-serving NEC member in line.

David Butler probed Benn on his strategy in one of a series of detailed interviews in which Benn 'stressed the importance of having a position in the NEC or, when the party was in opposition, in the PLP. In dealing with the leader of the party you had to have an independent power base to be able to stand up to him most effectively.'[3] Butler was impressed by the conviction with which Benn wanted to be leader of the Labour Party and by his honesty in saying so, unlike Jenkins, Healey and Callaghan, who sidestepped the issue when questioned.

Benn spoke at this time not of wanting to be Prime Minister, but of wanting to be leader of the Labour Party. The distinction is more important for Labour than for the Conservatives. Only one twentieth-century leader of the Conservative Party in the House of Commons, Austen Chamberlain, failed to become Prime Minister. Twelve were successful up to the early 1990s. Ten chairmen or leaders of the Labour Party (the appellation changed in 1922) had failed to become Prime Minister in the same period and only four had become Prime Minister.[4]

The gossip columns were whispering that Wilson was advising his cronies that Benn would succeed him. He made no secret of this, at least to senior colleagues, even remarking to Benn himself about a difficult decision,[5] 'I've got to do this. When you have my job, you'll have to do it.' Given Wilson's methods, however, his apparent acceptance that Benn was certain to win may have been calculated to get a 'stop Wedgie' movement off to a head start in the Parliamentary Labour Party.

Viewed from some angles, the whole of Benn's political life to this point may be seen as the progress of a man ambitious for leadership. The evidence of his own diary, however, shows the leadership question occupying him hardly at all. This changes during the four years of opposition. He records on 22 May 1971 that he has 'decided I would like to be leader rather more consciously'. For a man of Benn's temperament, with his mixture of high ideals, showmanship and diffidence, what he most wished to happen would be that his admiring colleagues would thrust the crown upon him, by common consent that only he could bear it. This is a rare occurrence in politics, and the path Benn now took was more common: he established the leadership in his sights, and looked to ways which would propel him towards it.

Standing for the deputy leadership against Foot and Jenkins in November 1971 was a clear statement of his interest and not one he found easy to make. At the beginning of October he told Wilson he would stand, then spent the next six weeks agonising about it. Caroline was always doubtful, and almost every day Benn's diary entries show him wondering whether to pull out.

Benn used a strategy which was to become familiar in the following years: he appealed to the 'Labour movement' for its support. He issued a statement saying, 'The Labour movement is entitled to have its agreed policies properly presented in the Commons by its elected leaders and not absolutely ignored.' This may well be true, but as the Labour movement had no vote, the sole electorate being the PLP, it was not a rallying call likely to achieve its object.

With the Heath government pressing for Britain's entry into the Common Market, Europe was clearly the battleground on which the Labour Party leadership was to be won or lost and in the early 1970s Benn's approach – that only a referendum could commit Britain to Europe – was easily defensible in terms of democratic openness. Jenkins's attitude – join Europe at all costs – appeared contemptuous of the opinions of others, including those in his own party. The story of these two politicians in the first half of the decade is of how Jenkins smashed his own chances of becoming party leader against Benn's winning argument, and of how Benn, almost compulsively, snatched defeat from the jaws of victory.

The closer Benn came to power the worse were press attacks on him. In part this is because his political opponents were feeding information to the press in order to undermine him. The press were amenable to being so used, however. There was a vehemence to some of the attacks which was almost surreal in character. 'What is Mr Harold Wilson going to do about Mr Pipsqueak Benn?' asked the *Sunday Express*. 'Intellectually if he were to turn sideways, you would not see him. . . . Politically he is a zero – a pipe-puffer with nothing in his pipe . . . a miserable little squirt.' By contrast Roy Jenkins 'shines with the better qualities of Richelieu, Bismarck and Gladstone rolled into one'.[6]

The savage press attacks on Benn bemused him. He wrote, 'I had always thought that Harold Wilson was paranoid about the press but I can well understand how this could affect somebody,' and he asked for advice as to why the press were so critical. Bob Carvel told him his lobby correspondent colleagues 'liked people they could see through and the sea-green incorruptible teetotaller annoyed them'.[7]

David Butler reported that Benn was doubtful whether he had done the right thing in standing against Roy Jenkins, 'but in the long term it did good to stand up and be counted. After Wilson lost the next general election, as [Benn] was sure he would, Wilson would go and there would be a true leadership contest which he would have a more than even chance of winning.'[8]

While Benn was never popular with the majority of his colleagues in the Parliamentary Labour Party, this was not an insuperable obstacle to electoral success, as the performance of Denis Healey shows. The PLP members were perfectly capable of recognising ability. In 1970 Benn received 133 votes and fifth place in the shadow cabinet election, the highest position he was ever to achieve.

Benn felt the coolness towards him among his parliamentary colleagues during the deputy leadership contest and he feared a humiliating defeat. When the vote came out he had 46 votes as against 96 for Foot and 140 for Jenkins. Benn felt it a perfectly reasonable poll considering the circumstances, but it was still depressing. 'November and December [1971] were the lowest political period in my life', he wrote.[9] He had no emotional mechanism for dealing with failure. He would accept a blow, retire in silence to tend his wounds, then bounce back as if nothing had happened. He made no apparent effort to learn from his mistakes, which was one of the things which made advising him so infuriating for Frank McElhone, the popular Glasgow MP who had asked to be Benn's parliamentary private secretary. He was soon showing signs of regretting it.

Intellectually, Benn knew McElhone was right. 'I have got to think of the PLP as a constituency,' he wrote,[10] but practically he found it impossible to be tolerant and coddling to his colleagues. He had the radical back-bencher's fondness for demonstrations of principle. When the young editorial staff of *Oz* magazine were jailed for obscenity, Benn signed a motion protesting against the sentences. Frank McElhone told him he would lose fifty votes for the leadership by this gesture, which showed him siding with drug-takers and sexual libertines. Benn was unrepentant but wrote in his diary, 'This is the difficulty. If you are going to go simply for high office then you have got to be very cautious and I am not sure that I want to be. I would rather stand up for what I believe.'[11]

Benn considered that his time in opposition should be used in developing new strategies for the future of Britain. He remained an excellent parliamentarian, now on the front bench as shadow trade and industry minister, but the real work was the unfolding of his vision of increasing democracy in Britain. With his eyes firmly set on the horizon, in September 1970 he produced a Fabian tract called *The New Politics: A Socialist Reconnaissance*. It had been written

315

in just forty-eight hours. To a large extent he was reiterating the principles he had expressed forcibly in 1968. He argued for greater participation in government and for democratisation of the mass media. The new addition in this pamphlet was a proposal for workers' control of industry, something which was to dominate his thinking through the first half of the 1970s. He remarked that workers have 'negative power' in that they could strike and dislocate the system, but 'Workers' control – if it means the power to plan their own work and to hire and fire their immediate plant management just as MPs are now hired and fired by the voters – converts that existing negative power into positive and constructive power. It thus creates the basis of common interest with local managers struggling to make a success of the business and get devolved authority from an over-centralised bureaucratic board of management now perhaps sitting on them from above.'

It was calmly received, though a few were fired with enthusiasm for his ideas. The young MP for Bedwelty, Neil Kinnock, began to write what he himself called a 'confessional', to acquaint Tony Benn with his feelings. Several times he began letters to Benn but each time discarded them in frustration until finally he managed to blurt out, 'I must confess to a personal disappointment: the peculiar sense of depression which one feels when one finds that the personal, treasured and, above all, novel ideas which one thought to be an unique analysis have all been thought of by someone else.'[12]

In opposition Benn was free to develop his interest in radical causes. He was the first male politician to declare himself in favour of the women's liberation movement despite the derision it had attracted. 'Every struggle for rights by an oppressed group is exposed to ridicule by those who are frightened of the power it generates,' he told the Yorkshire Labour Women's Rally. 'It is also true that the leaders of a new movement for social change are always liable to be accused of being unrepresentative. How easy to dismiss them as a lunatic fringe commanding no real support amongst their own constituency of women. But just the same was said of the trade union and socialist pioneers or the Chartist agitators in a deliberate effort to separate them from a supposedly sensible body of people who, the public was told, were quite content with their lot.'[13] Melissa Benn, now fourteen, began to contribute to feminist strands in Tony

Benn's thinking. He showed her the first draft of the Yorkshire speech, which she substantially redrafted.

He also stated he would make an effort to apply his beliefs practically by helping with the housework. He wrote in his diary, 'My growing interest in the women's liberation movement had better begin at home because I don't think it's fair that [Caroline] should have to do as much as she does.'[14] Caroline herself was looked upon as a role model, being invited to a social gathering of women members in Bristol, 'with a view to creating some interest for a women's organisation'.[15]

The loss of a ministerial salary was a blow to Benn, who had come to enjoy a higher standard of living over the previous six years. A back-bench MP's basic pay was £3250 with £1750 in allowances. He had inherited some shares in the publishers Benn Brothers which brought in something less than £2000 before tax in the 1970s. He estimated he had to earn an additional £50 a week from lecturing and writing to keep himself going.[16] As well as the family expenses, with four teenaged children (Stephen at university), he had to maintain his home in London, a room in the constituency and the house at Stansgate, which had been enlarged over the years. Next door was a cottage used by David Benn and his wife, the novelist June Barraclough, and their two children, Frances and Piers.

Luckily for his bank balance, Benn found himself in some demand to address business conferences including an international businessmen's meeting in Trinidad, where he explained to the assembled industrialists that 'The biggest single issue of the seventies, eighties and beyond is the need for democratisation of power.'[17] He made an increasingly detailed critique of the power of multinational companies. These companies had to be negotiated with as if they were sovereign states. 'If you take General Motors, their turnover is greater than the Japanese budget and is growing more rapidly.'[18] He concluded positively: because multinationals wanted co-operation from governments, and public sector contracts, the argument between the companies and national governments was more evenly balanced than the bald figures would suggest.

As shadow industry minister Benn sat across the chamber from the new Trade and Industry Minister, John Davies, former Director General of the Confederation of British Industry. The industrial

317

principles of the new government were to be those of Selsdon Man, the proto-monetarist policies established at the Tories' Selsdon Park Conference, which declared the party in favour of more incentives for business, lower taxes, cuts in public spending, tougher competition and an end to public subsidies for private industry. In a phrase which was to haunt him, John Davies remarked that the government would not be supporting industrial 'lame ducks'.[19]

Davies started boldly. He abolished the Industrial Reorganisation Corporation and repealed the Industrial Expansion Act, wound up the Shipbuilding Industrial Board and declared there would be no more government help for shipbuilding. Such negative actions were easy. But some problems were beyond the influence of single governments – the ever increasing cost of Concorde, for example, aggravated by a decline in its commercial promise.

Benn went to the US on behalf of the Concorde workers of Bristol in an attempt to persuade the New York authorities to allow the plane to land at that city's airport. He was pitted against a lobby which contained a combination of anti-technologists who opposed the aircraft on environmental grounds and protectionists who opposed it because it was not American. At least now he could criticise the decisions which had brought Concorde into being, something he had had no free rein to do as a minister without appearing to argue with himself. He accused the Conservatives of incompetence over Concorde on four counts: failing to undertake noise tests before commissioning it; wildly underestimating the development costs; failing to include a let-out clause in the treaty with the French; and conducting 'no real public discussion' about whether it was sensible to commit such enormous sums of public money.[20]

Despite his misgivings, thousands of jobs relied on Concorde: he had to defend them and defend the aircraft. He said, 'Having now succeeded in producing an aircraft that can meet its performance requirements, it would clearly be foolish not to try to sell it hard to world airlines.'[21] His efforts were in vain. In January 1973 Pan-Am decided to cancel its options on seven Concordes, a decision TWA had already reached.

Opposition was Benn's metier, even if it meant he was now often arguing against policies he had promulgated while in office. Harold Lever said, 'I have heard Tony address two contrary arguments to the Commons and been cheered for both and not only by his own side. I told him if I was ever accused of a crime I'd like him to plead for me. When Rolls-Royce folded he made a brilliant speech then turned to me on the front bench and said, "I think the fox has shot the rider," because John Davies couldn't get him.'[22]

Benn had attacked the further £42 million being given to Rolls-Royce for the RB211 engine by John Davies in November 1970. Then he attacked Davies for allowing the company to go bankrupt in February 1971. Davies proceeded to have the most potentially lucrative parts of Rolls-Royce sold off to private bidders while Benn argued for nationalisation, believing the public should get something back for their investment.

Benn issued a statement condemning 'quick and easy profits at public expense' and reminding potential investors of the Labour Party policy 'to renationalise, without compensation, public assets which are sold off by the present Government'.[23] This was actually an annual conference decision which 'called on the next Labour government' to take such action. The press were outraged, regarding this threatened expropriation of private property as nothing but licensed theft.

Benn's enemies in the shadow cabinet made representations to Wilson while Benn, seeing a battle loom, contacted those like Foot and Shore whom he expected to support him. He was particularly angry because he had obtained Wilson's general consent for such a statement before making it. At the shadow cabinet he was the central player in a left–right masque which ended in a trade-off: Benn was to get a Supply Day debate on Rolls-Royce to put his position, and the shadow cabinet was to issue a statement which began, 'It is not the policy of the Labour Party that shareholders in the automobile section of Rolls-Royce should be dispossessed of their shares without compensation.'[24] Benn's position was popular with party activists, as usual, but more importantly in terms of his power base it was popular with the trade unions.

It was over the Upper Clyde Shipbuilders that Benn became the bridge-builder between the unions and the party, the role he had so coveted in 1960. The Clyde was finally dying as a shipbuilding area. The government considered there was no point in giving the shipyards any more money. Benn published a Bill for the nationalisation of UCS – a method which was to become his standard for publicising an issue – but it was a gesture. Though death was inevitable, the House of Commons was in uproar when John Davies pronounced the sentence on 29 July 1971. Some Scottish MPs were close to tears. 'This is a major tragedy,' said Benn to Davies, 'and it has been introduced by you without one single word of regret.'[25] Davies called Benn an 'evil genius'.[26]

But the parliamentary jousting was a sideshow. The real action was on the Clyde, where the workers took over the yards. They began a work-in on 30 July, the workforce having occupied one of the yards since the middle of the previous month. They had 'rediscovered their self-respect', Benn declared. He marched with up to 70,000 UCS supporters in August and addressed a mass meeting on Glasgow Green: 'We are seeing the birth-pangs of industrial democracy.' He was delighted. 'This is the stuff of which great events are made,' he said in the UCS canteen. He was euphoric with it all: the banners and the songs and the socialist determination, the strong men marching together in brotherhood. He was treated as a saviour, and not only by the footsoldiers: he received three standing ovations when he addressed a meeting of 400 UCS shop stewards in June.[27]

The establishment saw the work-ins as subversion by Communists, and the presence of Communist Party members like Jimmy Reid in the leadership reinforced their belief. They feared a complete workers' take-over, for UCS was just the most spectacular of these events. As a Trotskyist commentator later remarked, 'Occupations averaged one every fortnight from then on.'[28] In fact the Communist Party acted in this as in other social movements of the 1970s as a conservative force. 'The party line of the Communist Party shop stewards was that it was all "adventurist",' said Ken Coates, a leading member of the Institute for Workers' Control and later a Member of the European Parliament.[29] The Communist commitment to total, centralised revolution meant that anything short of that was to be dismissed as an infantile disorder.

Benn had made several visits to the shipyards in the summer of 1971 and issued a statement calling for workers' control, in keeping with the ideals of industrial democracy he had been promoting. His previous experience was with a proposed electrical factory work-in in Liverpool in 1970 which he had visited as Minister of Technology. That occupation did not get under way but it was here that Benn first encountered the Institute for Workers' Control, which was an important advisory force on the Clyde and with which Benn was to be associated for the next twelve years.

The association was not without its misgivings at first. Ken Coates described the suspicion among trade unionists for Benn at this time: 'He was not rated very highly, although he would be given credit for having done some good on the Clyde. He was felt to be too dodgy a customer by far. They thought he was a careerist, born with a silver spoon in his mouth, that he had got a position in the Labour Party because of his father. I brought them round to see that he represented a better left than the more conventional left, more adventurous, more dynamic, more liable to do things that we believed in.'[30]

In his support of an illegal occupation and in his urging of the Scottish TUC to lobby the Prime Minister, Benn was considered by Harold Wilson to be taking action which was unacceptable in a shadow minister. Wilson soon came to the view that Benn's instincts were right and he asked for a visit to the occupied shipyards to be organised for himself.

Eventually, in February 1972 a government subsidy of £35 million was granted to Govan Shipbuilders, and another £12 million was made available to entice an American company to take over the Clydebank and Scotstoun yards. The work-in petered out, the number of men involved dwindling until it was wound up in October 1972.

Benn had been seriously considering the role of the trade unions in the Labour Party ever since Eric Heffer had collared him at a party conference and berated him for his earlier support of *In Place of Strife*. Heffer said, 'I put a class-conscious, working-class point of view to him about solidarity with working people. If you bring in laws that are going to tie up the trade unions you actually undermine the working-class movement.'[31]

Heffer was surprised to find, as so many other people were, that Benn actually listened to arguments against his position. It was not a common trait in politics. Benn later remembered his discussion with Heffer as one of the most important of his political career. He recalled, 'I had never had a trade union experience, my life had never depended on collective bargaining for wages. It is something those who negotiate their salaries individually find it difficult to understand. What I began to realise was that wages were not just a matter of economic policy – they were also about power and the workers' relationship to power.'[32]

Benn had to have the backing of the unions, the power brokers of the Labour Party, to achieve anything. The unions, like other institutions in society, had become radicalised at the end of the 1960s with the result that three of the most powerful unions now had left-wing leaders: Hugh Scanlon led the Amalgamated Engineering Union from 1967, Jack Jones the Transport and General Workers from 1969, and Clive Jenkins the expanded Association of Scientific, Technical and Managerial Staffs (ASTMS) from 1968. They were all to give significant help to Benn as he began to emerge through the years of opposition as the principal parliamentary voice of the unions. In May 1971 *Tribune* made a most perceptive remark: 'Trade unionists who were never quite at ease with the Minister of Technology must get to know one of the few Labour leaders who left office more Socialist than when he went in.'[33]

The Conservatives were pledged to reform the trade unions, in particular to curb strikes. The Industrial Relations Bill would require registration and standardised rules for trade unions and it would set up a National Industrial Relations Court with the power to order strike ballots or to postpone a strike for sixty days in some cases. Strikes in certain circumstances, in defence of a closed shop for example, were to be banned, as was sympathetic industrial action. It would have been a far more politically dextrous act for the government simply to have reintroduced the *In Place of Strife* proposals, Barbara Castle's intended legislation, which would have had a similar effect on the trade unions but would have crippled the parliamentary opposition to it.

The Bill provoked a level of trade union solidarity unprecedented since before the war: 1.5 million workers staged a one-day strike against the Bill in March 1971, and the previous month 100,000 marched through London. Predictably, trade union resistance made the new legislation unworkable. In most cases unions simply refused to register. The route to opposition was clear: trade unionists had to force the government to create martyrs by actually using the draconian powers they hoped they need only threaten.

The NIRC was weakened by the failure of the Court of Appeal to uphold two of its major decisions. Then the showdown came. In July 1972 five dockers were arrested on the instructions of the NIRC for contempt of court. Incarcerated in Pentonville Prison, they were the living symbols of resistance to injustice, Benn finding it particularly easy to sympathise. He compared the Pentonville Five to the Tolpuddle Martyrs and said, 'Millions of people in Britain, whatever they may think of the rights and wrongs of the dockers' actions, will in their hearts respect men who would rather go to jail than betray what they believe to be their duty to their fellow workers and the principles which they hold.'[34]

It was a subject tailor-made for Benn. On one side were the unjust lawmakers with their political courts, on the other side were the courageous workers standing defiantly against them. Ahead was the principle shining brightly: that individual conscience has supremacy over the law. It was a principle Benn traced to the great prophets of Judaism. 'Let judgement run down as waters, and righteousness as a mighty stream,' he said, quoting the prophet Amos.[35] For Benn it was the continuous tradition of radicalism, which applied as well to religion as to politics, that 'our prime duty is to each other, and to what our conscience tells us to be right'.[36]

Amid rising unrest over the Pentonville Five, and with the threat by the TUC of a general strike, which Labour's NEC supported, the dockers were released on the intervention of the Official Solicitor, a government official with a fortunate remit for intervening when people have been committed to prison for contempt.

The Conservatives were outraged that anyone should defy the law with impunity, and still more outraged that a former government minister should encourage them to do so. No less outraged was the right wing of the Labour Party. Some of Benn's colleagues, including Prentice, Crosland and Healey, criticised him at a shadow cabinet meeting. Benn shrugged it off, confident of his support. He did not need to be lectured on the trade union movement by them, he said.[37]

Benn's comments on the Pentonville Five had provoked another series of press attacks on him. A closer association with the unions was certain to increase press venom, for the unions were particular hate figures to newspapers. Partly this must be for straightforward class-war reasons: newspapers understandably represented the interests of the wealthy individuals and companies which owned them. Another factor, however, was the experience of union behaviour on Fleet Street itself, which had some of the most reactionary trade unions confronting some of the most reactionary managements. The everyday running of Fleet Street was a procedural nightmare of restrictive practices and archaic agreements. The only unions newspaper executives knew much about were desperately in need of reform.

Benn knew that on the Industrial Relations Act what the newspapers were saying was not what the public were saying. He convinced Hugh Cudlipp, editor of the *Daily Mirror*, of this and received a double-page spread in the largest-selling newspaper. Headed 'Citizen Benn Replies', it covered the ground of industrial democracy and access to the media which Benn had made his own, starting with the injustice of the Pentonville Five case. 'According to the Prime Minister, Britain has been taken to the brink of anarchy because five dockers disobeyed the law,' he wrote. 'If that was true, the situation would be serious. But it is not true. No five men could undermine our country. What has really frightened the Cabinet is that millions of people who did NOT break the law expressed their sympathy and support for the dockers. One of them was me.'[38] *Mirror* readers demonstrated that Benn had been correct in his assessment of the situation and Cudlipp had been wise to listen to him: 11,000 people wrote in, supporting Benn's position by eight to one.

26

Party Chairman

In September 1971 Tony and Caroline Benn went to China, still in the throes of the Cultural Revolution, as the bullet holes in the wall near their quarters testified. Benn was the first major British politician to go there since Attlee in 1955 and the first British MP since the Cultural Revolution started. There was more than a hint in the visit of the 'fellow travellers' admiring Stalin's Russia of the 1930s, although, perhaps with that example in mind, the Benns tempered their expressions of admiration. In truth, there was much to admire, though the regimentation of the country and the cult of Chairman Mao were grotesque. One achievement, he said, could not be denied China, something which manifestly had not been done in Russia in the 1930s: the feeding, and housing, of the population.[1] The visit took place just before the UN Security Council gave China a seat, for which Lord Stansgate had argued so long. The time was now ripe because Nixon was losing the war in Vietnam and needed a Far Eastern ally to act as a counterweight to the Soviet Union and so enable him to retreat from Indochina.

It was at this stage that Benn began to use history more exactly to interpret the present. He had always had a fondness for historical analogies, but they tended to be drawn from general knowledge. His need for a model to interpret the confused world of early 1970s politics led him to the seventeenth century. He read the debates of the English Revolution and the Civil War, which all found their parallels in the turmoil over the Industrial Relations Act. The Agitators in the Revolution reflected the contemporary schismatic sects of the left; the right wing of the Labour Party had its counterpart in the rigid, doctrinaire Presbyterians.

Benn was so absorbed in the subject, and so aware of his own ignorance, that he asked fellow MP, former lecturer Jack Mendelson, if he would give him a private tutorial. So in the House of Commons tea room Benn's education was extended with an explanation of the Diggers and the Levellers and the nature of political debate in the Revolution. 'I had no idea', Benn wrote in his diary, 'that the Levellers had called for universal manhood suffrage, equality between the sexes, biennial Parliaments, the sovereignty of the people, recall of representatives and even an attack on property.'[2] The spiritual values which informed many of the revolutionaries made them immediately attractive to Benn and led directly to his work on Christianity and socialism, published as the first part of *Arguments for Socialism* in 1979.

He wrote two papers for the National Executive, 'The Challenge of Community Politics' and 'Labour and the Splinter Parties', in which he suggested that Labour should take up the discontents which had led to the phenomenon of proliferating parties and pressure groups.[3] Discussions with his family broadened his outlook, particularly now that his children were growing up.

Hilary proved to be similar to his father in many ways, including early devotion in romance. He was married to Rosalind Retey in 1973 at the age of nineteen. The early 1970s found him at Sussex University, with Stephen Benn at Keele. Melissa and Joshua were at Holland Park School. Throughout the 1970s Caroline Benn increased the range of her educational work, continuing to teach as well as to edit and write books on comprehensive education. In 1970 she was co-opted to the Inner London Education Authority and became chair of the governors of Holland Park. She also later became a member of the Education Section of the UK's UNESCO Commission and of the ILEA's Standing Advisory Committee on Religious Education. She particularly enjoyed the latter: 'It seemed to me an absolute miracle of democracy that you could get all the world's religions to co-operate on what you taught children about religion.'[4]

Lady Stansgate had continued with her religious interests, becoming an executive member of the Council of Christians and Jews and playing a leading role in the Congregational movement. In common with other Churches, the Congregationalists had seen a decline in their numbers during the 1960s and now it was felt by a majority that the only way forward was union with the Presbyterians. Lady Stansgate felt that this would destroy the Congregational principle of self-government but her faction in the movement failed and a private Bill was prepared to take all the property of the two Churches into the new United Reformed Church. A Bill of this nature would normally pass through without debate but Nigel Spearing, another Labour MP with Congregationalist family connections, put forward an amendment. This was supported only by Benn and, to their embarrassment, by the Unionist MP and Presbyterian Ian Paisley.

Lady Stansgate watched from the gallery in June 1972 while Tony Benn spoke in the Debate. He argued that any church wishing to stay out of or leave the new union should be able to do so, retaining its own assets. This was a labour of love but it was not one of those issues on which he could expect the support or even the understanding of his parliamentary colleagues. 'I never felt such absolute hostility in the House,' he wrote in his diary. 'It was the whole establishment gathered together against dissent. On the Labour side too, with the traditions of trade union loyalty and the feeling "one out we're all out, one in we're all in".'[5]

Lady Stansgate, unwilling to sacrifice the principle, went on to lead a breakaway group called the Congregationalist Federation, becoming its president, the first woman, with the exception of English queens, to head a Christian denomination.

With the Heath government determined to achieve Britain's entry into the Common Market, and likely to succeed now that President Pompidou had taken over from de Gaulle, Tony Benn sent a letter to Bristol South-East Labour Party on 14 November 1970 which was simultaneously released to the press. In it he made the case for a referendum on the issue. Nothing short of a decision by the whole population could be binding on such a question, he said. It was indeed a novel proposal, but as he put it on *Any Questions?*, 'We've never had a referendum before, but we've never signed an irreversible treaty either, which commits us in perpetuity to surrender our sovereignty?'[6]

The proposal was placed before the shadow cabinet to an unenthusiastic response. Only Jim Callaghan, more canny than most, remarked that 'Tony may be launching a little rubber life raft which we will all be glad of in a year's time.'[7] Neither public nor press nor party colleagues were supportive of Benn's proposal. When it came up at the NEC in April 1971 Benn was in a minority of one, without even a seconder. In true Benn style, he was undaunted by any defeat and simply plugged on with the next action in the campaign. He presented a European Communities (Referendum) Bill to the House of Commons, with himself as the only proposer. He anticipated that other potential backers would be anti-Europe and he wanted to promote the measure as a positive, democratic move, not as an anti-Market procedure.

Now it was time to appeal to the country and the party. He proposed that the NEC should hold a special conference on the Common Market, once again using a power base outside the Parliamentary Labour Party to out-manoeuvre the leader, who wished to keep the decisions within the PLP. In the event, the rather lacklustre conference on 17 July 1971 did not achieve its objective. Wilson outflanked Benn by using his influence to prevent a vote being taken at the conference, on the ground that the arguments must be heard without prejudice.

By the time of the Common Market debate in the Commons on 22 July 1971 Tony Benn was arguing against going in without an election or a referendum. He also argued in favour of entry for his usual reason: that a supra-national body was necessary to control the multinationals. The argument gave no comfort to Tory supporters of the Market.

The annual Labour Party conference of 1971 overwhelmingly rejected a motion proposing a referendum in favour of one calling for a general election. It was an uphill struggle for Benn, but an increasing number of people were coming to see the logic of his paradoxical argument that a referendum could permit dissent while also ensuring unity and at the same time come to a binding decision. No general election could be fought on the issue because both major parties were divided, but, if the public were to decide, their decision would be binding, and individual politicians could put their case to the people according to their own conscience, not according to a party whip.

How deep the party divisions were was demonstrated in the major vote on entry in the Commons on 28 October 1971: sixty-nine Labour MPs voted with the government to enter Europe, in defiance of a three-line whip which Labour had the poor judgement to impose. The Tories had a free vote.

Wilson was coming round to the proposal that a promise of a referendum could deliver an election victory. It was also, after all, a very European procedure: Denmark, Norway and Eire were planning referenda on their entry into the EEC; Switzerland had them on constitutional matters.

What finally swung his colleagues in Benn's favour was the announcement by the French on 16 March 1972 that *they* would hold a referendum on whether Britain could enter. The timing was benign for Benn, as he had unsuccessfully attempted the night before to persuade the shadow cabinet to table an amendment supporting a referendum in the Commons. There was no question of his being seen to be taking an opportunistic advantage of the French decision. The shadow cabinet finally, on 29 March, voted eight to six in favour of a referendum.

On the same day Benn himself had to choose the next general secretary of the Labour Party: two tied votes on the NEC had brought the chairman's casting vote into play. Benn chose Ron Hayward, the more left candidate, who was also anti-EEC. There was bitter feeling afterwards that he had 'imposed' his candidate on the Labour Party but criticism was inappropriate. After all, he had a duty to use his casting vote in the event of a tie.

With no prior warning, on 10 April Roy Jenkins resigned the deputy leadership of the party over the decision to support a referendum. He was followed out of the shadow cabinet by Harold Lever and George Thomson. The resignations were represented in the press as a disaster for which Benn was responsible, a charge which upset him because he had genuinely seen the referendum proposal as one calculated to promote unity while extending democracy.

When the vote was taken in the House of Commons on a referendum clause in the early hours of 19 April, there was a government majority against the proposal of forty-nine. Sixty-three Labour members abstained. Thereafter the legislative procedures ground on until 1 January 1973, when Britain formally entered the Common Market.

329

Tony Benn's changing attitude towards the Common Market at this time is one of the more troublesome thickets in a landscape of decision and revision. On 14 November 1970, with his letter to the constituency urging a referendum, he was in favour of entry. The Market had not emerged as a cold-war tool, which had been his early fear. Far from it, the Market could act to restrain international capitalism. He was not even reticent about his support for the EEC; on 20 May 1971 at the Itchen by-election he was speaking in favour of Europe.

In retrospect Benn explained that he turned against the Market after becoming a minister again in 1974, when he experienced the way in which he as an elected politician 'was a slave in chains in Brussels, and I loathed it when I saw what it was about'.[8] He was certainly influenced by his first visit to Brussels as a minister, in June 1974, yet before this, by 27 January 1974, he was 'hostile to it but content to let the people decide'.[9]

What had changed? It is probable that Benn, always sensitive to the influences around him, had simply moved into a circle where the predominant feeling was anti-Market. The effect of his increasing gravitation towards the left of the Labour movement, for a variety of reasons which had nothing to do with the EEC, had meant his thinking was being influenced only by left trade unionists and constituency activists. The argument to which he always gave the most prominence in the future – that membership of the EEC was an unacceptable sacrifice of popular sovereignty, was no new discovery for Benn. As already shown, he was using the sovereignty argument in 1970 as a reason for a referendum; in other words, he already had it in mind when he was pro-Market.

Not that Benn was the only one to do an about-turn on the Market. As Prime Minister, Wilson had set a date in 1970, just after the general election, for negotiations leading to entry. After losing the election, May 1971 found him discovering a principled opposition to the Market on the terms which had been negotiated by the Tories. Healey likewise miraculously saw the light of the anti-Market argument only months after he had been worshipping at the shrine of European union. Enoch Powell came out against the Market in 1969, having voted for entry in 1967.

Benn's manoeuvrings over the Market were seen by most of his colleagues as mere cynical manipulations to find the most effective vehicle for his ambitions. Neville Sandelson, who was pro-Market, said: 'He was strongly pro-Europe, then against it. It was a personal political ploy. He tried to work out in his mind what was going to have a great national appeal which would support him in his ambitions, because he was always an intensely ambitious politician.'[10]

The argument in Benn's favour, suggesting that his change of view on the Market was made for opaque but principled reasons, is that he chose the wrong side. It should have been obvious that the Marketeers were going to win. On the other hand, it may have been simply poor judgement: he believed the left represented the future, and opposition to the Market was a left policy.

Bristol South-East found it all acceptable. Celia Roach said, 'I heard him give his views on the Common Market when he was in favour of it and when he was against it. They were equally passionate speeches.'[11] David Langham said, 'It was a new thing to us all, but his views changed as he listened to what people said – he was always a good listener.'[12]

The equivocal approach to the Common Market adopted by both major parties (a foretaste of what was to come) caused enormous frustration among potential political allies in Europe. Dr Sicco Mansholt, President of the European Commission, wrote to Benn in his capacity as chairman of the Labour Party to say that he was 'ashamed to see my socialist colleagues adopting such a negative attitude'.[13]

Benn's referendum proposal was attacked by being taken to absurd extremes. In particular, patrician liberals like Roy Jenkins wondered whether homosexual, censorship, obscenity or abortion laws would have been reformed had the decision been left to the populace. We could not stop at one referendum, the argument went; we have a representative not a participatory democracy. What would happen if the British people were to decide on whether to admit the Ugandan Asians? Benn rose to the challenge, arguing that 'I am sure most people would respond sympathetically. . . . We would never shut our doors on these innocent people who have been robbed of all they have and expelled from their homes at gunpoint.'[14] It was a response which demonstrates the immense gulf between his

331

thinking and that of his fellows, on both the right and the left of the party. Tony Benn has a belief that deep, deep down, people are good. Given unbiased information, fairly presented, people will react in a philanthropic manner, even taking actions which would be against their own interests. This has been an underlying spring of his actions which led his colleagues always to describe him as naïve, from his youth to the time he was virtually the longest-serving MP in the House.

At a time when conflicts were most intense in the Labour Party, with the press and in the Commons, Benn considered whether he ought to 'strip myself off from what the world had to offer' and resign his Privy Councillorship, his MA and the four honorary doctorates he had been awarded in the previous few years. He realised this would appear ridiculous but he did decide to stop using his middle name. This is rather less remarkable than the fact that through some affectation or other he had decided to use it in the first place. Most people, after all, do not use their middle names. The resort to the name Wedgwood may, he later suggested, have been to differentiate between Lord Stansgate and Sir Ernest Benn's side of the family, the right and the left wing, so to speak.[15] Anyway, in August 1972 Benn finally decided to stop using Wedgwood. 'I have been Tony Benn in Bristol for a long time and I will be Tony Benn in Parliament,' he wrote in his diary.[16] He also dropped reference to his public school and Oxford college from his *Who's Who* entry. He told an inquiring journalist, 'As I get older the educational influence becomes less significant compared with the ways in which I have spent my years at work.'[17]

He was criticised, at the time and thereafter, for attempting to forge a spurious link with the working class, dropping references to his upper-middle-class origins so that he could pretend to be one of the lads. Such a criticism implies that Benn was actually a man of genteel and refined tastes who suppressed his delicacy of feeling in order to muck in with the workers. This is verifiably wrong. Benn genuinely drank a great deal of tea and was happier with a sandwich at his desk than with an invitation to a gourmet meal. He was also, somewhat to the exasperation of his family and staff, decidedly lowbrow in cultural taste. If he enjoyed drama at all it was sentimental, like the family film *The Railway Children*. He found nothing risible in remarking in his diary that he had watched the Eurovision Song Contest.[18] For some he had to be a demon of perfidy, feigning a taste for the ordinary things of life while secretly dining on caviar and claret. They refused to accept that with Benn you really did get what you saw. 'He drove a Ford Escort and bought his best suit from C & A,' the Labour MP Joe Ashton was moved to remark, irked by the insistence that Benn had to be possessed of great wealth.[19]

He did not make strenuous efforts to change the name – he simply stopped using the Wedgwood himself, though his cheques were still in the longer version of his name in 1990 and so was his Inland Revenue form, both still misspelled. In 1975 Hansard was still referring to him as the Rt Hon. Anthony Wedgwood Benn and so, perhaps more improbably, were Labour Party press releases, though press releases from his own department at the same period called him Tony Benn. He was still signing memoranda A.W.B.

He was clearly concerned at the time about his image. At the 1972 party conference at Blackpool, which he chaired, he wore spectacles, though he did not usually do so in public. It may have been to give him the appearance of greater maturity or, at least, make him look as if he were forty-seven years old. He still looked young for his years, not an asset in a man wishing to become a party leader. When people remarked on how young he appeared he would say, 'Yes, that's what Ramsay MacDonald told me in 1931.'

He was not considered to be a very successful chairman, being criticised for permitting too many points of order and for the shambles of having two votes on the same composite motion because the 'reservation' implicit in the NEC's acceptance of it had not been made clear the first time. 'Democracy is a rather messy business,' Benn remarked, in the understatement of the conference.[20] One Benn innovation, standard 'request to speak' cards to ensure that preference was not given to people who happened to know the chairman, was hailed as a great advance when the cards were next used, almost twenty years later. He made every effort to be available to delegates, going to eight engagements each evening and introducing a chairman's surgery in the early morning.

The conference was expected to be the occasion for a major

blood-letting, with the hounds of the left let loose on Jenkins and his pro-European supporters. Benn was expected to call for loyalty or damnation in his opening speech, but spectators were disappointed. In a gesture of moderation he gave notice that he would not use his chairmanship to attack the right wing, while affirming the importance of conference decisions for the guidance of the party, 'Conference never has and never will want to dictate to a Labour government, but they do expect Labour governments to take conference decisions seriously and not deliberately reverse or ignore them.' This speech increased his stature and was particularly well received by his enemies. Anthony Shrimsley in the *Sun* said, 'I felt like joining in the clapping for Mr Benn.' Predictably, it was not possible for most of the press to accept even this small triumph and it was said that Benn had a fire-and-brimstone speech prepared which he had modified at the last minute through cowardice. As the still extant notes of the speech show, this was not the case.

The conference voted for a statement that the party was still in favour of staying in the Common Market if the terms were right and subject to a referendum or a general election. The pro-Marketeers did not put up a fight, though Benn cruelly asked from the chair if Jenkins wished to speak, knowing he did not. Jenkins, furious, had publicly to declare he would not address the conference on the most important principle of his career, with the implication that he preferred to do his business behind closed doors. Such actions from Benn entertained those who were already his supporters but did nothing for the uncommitted and further embittered relationships with his opponents.

Benn's major error of judgement, which left an acrid taste after the conference was long over, was to fall into a trap set by Dick Taverne and *The Times*. Taverne, the liberal-minded Labour MP for Lincoln, was extremely pro-Europe. His constituency party was not and asked him not to stand at the next election. He resisted and appealed unsuccessfully to the NEC for assistance, which made the constituency more truculent. During the 1972 conference there were press reports from the Taverne camp that the MP might resign and stand as an independent. Taverne had been to see the editors of the *Guardian* and *Sunday Times* but his keenest supporter was William Rees-Mogg, editor of *The Times*, whose newspaper had, on the

Saturday before the conference opened, come out with a call for a new centre–left party. Benn was also aware that London Weekend Television knew that Taverne was going to resign and stand for election under a new banner at Lincoln, because Benn had been asked to take part in a programme about the forthcoming Lincoln by-election before Taverne had even stood down.

Taverne kept everyone guessing until the afternoon of the last day of the conference, when he knew his announcement could eclipse any conference news in the next day's papers. Benn was given a note about it as he chaired the last session, before making the closing remarks which are intended to send the delegates away inspired for the struggle ahead.

Instead Benn in his speech inflated the Lincoln by-election into a great battle between the forces of good and evil or, in this case, of the working class and the media. 'We are for the first time in the history of British politics fighting a political party invented by the press of this country. That is the significance of the Lincoln election,' he said. 'The television companies are now preparing the most massive campaign in support of the candidate Fleet Street is promoting in the Lincoln election. Television companies who have ignored working people, distorted what they have said and insulted them in so many of their programmes, have tried to suggest that our people are either apathetic or violent.' Harold Wilson was smoking his pipe furiously, unable to conceal his anger. Not only had Benn gone too far, he was going even further: 'I sometimes wish the trade unionists who work in the mass media, those who are writers and broadcasters and secretaries and printers and lift operators of Thomson House, would remember that they too are members of the working-class movement and have a responsibility to see that what is said about us is true.'[21]

Why didn't Benn wait for the by-election announcement and then utter an imperious and slighting put-down to the upstart Taverne, who thought he was bigger than the Labour Party? Probably because Benn was highly strung after four days of chairing the meeting; perhaps too he was carried away by the enthusiasm of most of the audience, who were certainly stirred by such talk. He had not discussed the speech in advance with Caroline, who later told him it had been a mistake.

335

Predictably, the press attacked Benn, on the Saturday and Sunday. On the Sunday Wilson let it be known that he would be issuing a rebuke to Benn, the warning of the rebuke being published on Monday and the attack itself on Tuesday, thus giving Wilson two anti-Benn press headlines for the price of one. 'The Labour Party is totally opposed in all circumstances to the use of industrial action for the purpose of impeding printing or dissemination of news or expression of views,' Wilson said.[22]

The last important battle between Benn and his colleagues in the opposition period was over the 'twenty-five companies' proposal. This was the issue of whether the proposal to nationalise twenty-five of Britain's top manufacturing companies should form part of the manifesto. A linked issue was the question of who had final say on the manifesto: the National Executive or the Parliamentary Labour Party.

After a day-long meeting on the topic on 30 May 1973 the NEC eventually supported the proposal by seven votes to six. Wilson immediately said that the shadow cabinet had a veto on manifesto proposals. When the shadow cabinet discussed the issue, even Michael Foot felt it was a losing policy. 'Are you really going for the twenty-five companies?' he asked Benn. 'Do you really want to win an election?'[23] The story was immediately leaked, with the next day's newspapers appearing with the headlines saying, 'Foot Leads Attack on Benn', 'Benn Rapped Over State Grab Plan' and 'Ex-Rebel Condemns Benn'. Foot was embarrassed and apologised to Benn, though the leak had not come from him. Benn used the press coverage of a shadow cabinet meeting as another argument in favour of their proceedings being made public. He was, of course, playing the same game as Wilson. The leader would summon support from the press, who he knew would back him. Benn wanted to let the wider Labour movement know what was being done, because he was sure they would support him.

The wrangling over the proposals continued right up to the NEC meeting at Blackpool on the Friday before the 1973 conference. Benn had had a struggle even to be allowed to speak on industry, as Wilson had been playing him off against Foot whom he had asked to wind up on the industry debate while he, quite acceptably as leader, introduced it. Wilson eventually conceded, though only after what was probably the only time Tony Benn simply lost his temper and shouted at him.

Wilson presented the delegates with a radical nationalisation programme involving building land, oil and gas, ports and docks, shipbuilding, aircraft production and parts of the drug, machine-tool, construction and road-haulage industries. It was not the 'twenty-five companies' proposal, but it satisfied Benn's basic requirement that the manifesto should not simply demand an extension of public ownership in general terms. It needed to be spelled out in great clarity.

Benn, in summing up, hit the keynote of the conference when he affirmed the commitment to 'a fundamental and irreversible shift in the balance of power and wealth in favour of working people and their families'. In the most memorable phrase of the conference he pledged that 'The crisis we inherit when we come to power will be the occasion for fundamental change and not an excuse for postponing it.'[24]

Under the retaliatory fire of the trade unions, and with manufacturing industry continuing on its seemingly inexorable decline, most of the Conservative government's industrial policy now became a patch-up and prop-up operation. It was conducted with rather less extravagance and sparkle than Mintech had been but the policies increasingly came to resemble those of the former incumbent.

The great U-turn took place on 6 November 1972. Selsdon Man was cut down like John Barleycorn with the announcement of a statutory incomes policy inaugurated by a freeze on prices, pay, dividends and rents. It was one of the most socialist measures of the decade. Enoch Powell raged in frustration at the apostasy: the government should not interfere in the market at all except in monetary policy. 'Although he held the House in his hands as he spoke,' said Benn, 'I can imagine the same speech being made for keeping the government out of health, education or housing.'[25] That time was yet to come.

The government had lost its grip. It had no solution. Ministers staggered from one crisis to another, governing a nation which genuinely seemed at some times to be descending into anarchy. When Benn rose to answer John Davies in a debate in August 1971

337

he began by commiserating with him for the bombing of his flat.[26] Previously there had been bombings of the home of Secretary of State for Employment Robert Carr and of the Miss World contest and a Knightsbridge boutique. Every new map of the political situation in Britain showed more people with bombs – the Irish Republican Army, the Angry Brigade, even Scottish and Welsh nationalists seemed to be able to obtain explosives, not to mention ephemeral organisations like Red Flag which waged a brief campaign and suddenly died.

The atmosphere of conspiracy and political violence at home was heightened by political instability abroad. The violent overthrow of the properly elected Marxist government in Chile by right-wing rebels, aided by the US, in 1973 further served to destabilise Britain. The left felt that the British establishment and the US would never permit a peaceful transition to socialism through the ballot box: they would be the first to use violence.

Whether world capitalism could be sustained was openly discussed. The left had maintained its momentum since 1968. What should be done about it? The US magazine *Fortune* in October 1973 placed Benn on its list of 'The Ominous Forces of World Socialism', along with leaders from other countries who also personified the radicalism which 'presents some serious threats to US business and US foreign policy'. Benn was probably a little more paranoid than most in the mid-1970s, but not a great deal so. He wrote, 'I half assume that all these people who come to see me now, particularly the Americans, are working for the CIA or MI5 or MI6 – I haven't any idea which.'[27]

His adversaries were generally more public, like Aims of Industry, a right-wing pressure group arguing for private enterprise, rather as the Institute for Workers' Control was a left-wing one arguing for co-operatives. Understandably, Aims found a ripe target in Tony Benn, though its members were angry when he hit back. Inadvisedly, he referred in the same sentence to Aims and the Watergate scandal, where political funds donated by business were used for illegal purposes. The occasion was the announcement by Aims that it was devoting £500,000 to an advertising campaign against the Labour Party. In general, Benn took objection to the fruits of industry being used for political purposes. Trade unionists were in a position to contract out of paying a political levy to the Labour Party while the directors of a company alone could make the decision to spend money supporting an organisation whose campaigns would help the Conservative Party.

Aims saw a report of the speech in the *Western Daily Press* and threatened Benn with a libel action. There was some question as to whether their intended action also referred to a time Benn had said a similar thing in the House of Commons so Benn took Aims to a Privileges Committee of the House, it being against parliamentary privilege to accuse an MP of libel. They were back in government by the time the privilege issue was heard and Benn lost. He eventually agreed to settle out of court, issuing an apology and paying the legal fees for Aims. His diary shows he was settling because he had no confidence in the courts to deal fairly with the case rather than that he felt he had defamed Aims. He had feared the courts and the concomitant escalating legal costs since the peerage case and the 1964 overspending case.[28]

The same spirit moved Benn in 1974 to start taping all speeches and interviews. He wanted to be able to demonstrate the correct version if he was misquoted, and he found that the presence of a tape recorder had a miraculous effect on print journalists' desire to be entirely accurate.

If Benn suspected a number of people he came into contact with of being spies, he was only expressing a common paranoia of the times. A greater social problem was presented by the delusions of the most conventional members of the establishment, civil servants and army officers, who had no experience of trade unions or small revolutionary organisations and even lacked the imagination to understand them. They imagined that 'militancy' was a homogeneous movement with trade union shop stewards, anarchist bombers, Opposition spokesmen and nationalist arsonists all linked to a great conspiracy to overthrow established order. They needed an insidious, 'enemies within' threat and were too unsophisticated politically to see that Communism as represented by the Communist Party of Great Britain was a conservative force by the 1970s and that the revolutionaries were confined to the tiny Trotskyist parties and their wilder splinters. They were as inimical to Benn as the far right were, both sides referring to him as Lord Stansgate.[29] As far as the extreme left were concerned, his co-operation with industry just made him a dupe of capitalism. In *Socialist Worker* a cartoon showed the Good Samaritan Benn coming upon an industrialist who has fallen upon hard times. He feeds and clothes him only to be beaten up and abandoned by the recovered industrialist, who mutters, 'Dirty Communist.'[30]

Nevertheless Mick McGahey, vice-chairman of the National Union of Miners and chairman of the Communist Party, served the purposes of the right, so they vastly exaggerated his importance as they moved into what both sides came to see as the great battle between government and organised labour. The confrontational Heath style of government did nothing to stabilise the country. Heath declared five states of emergency in his less than four years in office, compared to two in the previous twenty years.

Two of the major confrontations were with the miners, who were ultimately the agents of the government's downfall. The first, in January 1972, quickly led to power cuts with industry on a three-day week. The strike was remarkable for the organisation and flexibility of the miners. Two innovations were the development of 'flying pickets' and 'mass pickets', the latter used to great effect by Arthur Scargill, a little-known area officer of the NUM, to close the Saltley coke depot. Benn played his part in meeting NUM leaders and addressing meetings, inspired as he always was by the spirit of the miners. But his role was not exceptional in this conflict.

Less than two years later, a miners' overtime ban followed by a strike was built up by the government as a make-or-break conflict. Industry was put on a three-day working week almost six weeks before the strike began. It was clearly a political move to give the impression that the miners were destroying the economy.

Here Benn was able to use his political skill to further an industrial issue, showing the miners, the backbone of the working class, just how committed he was. In these few weeks he forged bonds with the miners which were to sustain him into the 1990s. In December 1973 Benn lashed the failing government: 'We know that the coal stocks at the power stations will last Britain through to the spring. . . . It is a deliberate act of psychological warfare directed against working people and the trade unions they created.'[31]

But Benn realised he could be most useful by organising a practical monitoring of the fuel crisis: what were the fuel stocks, where were they moving? He had a meeting with his advisers on 30 December. Michael Meacher, Hugh Macpherson of *Tribune*, Joan Lestor, Frances Morrell, Tony Banks and Ken Coates were involved in planning the campaign. Later Francis Cripps, a brilliant young Cambridge economist, was to contribute to the monitoring operation. These people (Macpherson excepted) were to be part of Benn's 'alternative cabinet' through to the end of the decade.

It was a high point of excitement for Benn, bypassing the media and the civil service to receive information directly from the workers in industry by means of a questionnaire. Who knew better than the power workers what fuel consumption was? Who knew better than the sewage workers whether the scare stories about the streets becoming flooded with waste were true? All the information he received demonstrated that coal stocks were well above the officially stated level. The three-day week was a fraud.

Suspicions were reinforced when the head office of ASTMS was given a copy of a note from a station superintendent saying that all information regarding coal stocks had been classified as secret by the Central Electricity Generating Board and must not be divulged to outsiders. Why should the Board want to keep the real facts secret unless they were lying to the public on government orders?, the Benn camp argued.

Even Wilson, at a low point of relations with Benn, conceded, 'You have helped to fill in a couple of rather thin news days and you have caught Heath off guard.'[32] The easiest way for the Tories to deal with it was to utilise press animosity towards Benn and claim that his was just a personal campaign. In these circumstances Benn's support from the unions was particularly important if he was not to be isolated.

'Wedgie only needs a dash of success to become uncontainable,' wrote Barbara Castle; he 'was positively bubbling with euphoria'. With all the support from the broad left of Labour, Communists and unaffiliated radicals, Castle considered, 'he seems to have appointed himself a one-man Popular Front.'[33]

The short-time working, with all the damage it did to the economy, continued into the New Year. With the coal strike imminent, Heath declared an election for 28 February 1974. The unofficial slogan was 'Who runs Britain?', with the implication that it mustn't be the unions.

Benn remarked at the time that it was the first national election in which not a single national paper supported Labour.[34] He was not alone in pondering on the power of the press to influence the course of political change. As Cecil King wrote in his diary after seeing Rupert Murdoch, 'He thinks Ted might win an election, as neither Rupert nor the *Mirror* could support Wilson, Benn and the Labour Party.'[35]

At constituency level, the negative press image of Labour exerted a discernible effect. David Langham in Bristol South-East said: 'There was a determination that when we got back in next time we were going to do something. That was when the press criticism came. When you just said it, and weren't going to do anything about it, that didn't matter.

'The loss of public meetings contributed. You would get fewer and fewer people. A politician only counted if he was on the tele-vision'.[36] The means of influencing the public had entirely passed from the party's own ground to the despised media.

Over the period of increasing unrest and the three-day week the attacks on Benn became even more hysterical. The scoutmaster's uniform in which the tabloid cartoonists had often depicted Benn became a Nazi uniform. In SS guise Benn ordered two trade union-ists in Gestapo gear to torture a cringing representative of the British public.[37]

Tony Benn had not neglected his constituency during the years of opposition. In April 1972 he sent out 50,000 letters to Bristol South-East (and to parts of the nearby constituency of Bristol Cen-tral which were to come to him under boundary redrawing), asking his constituents if they had any problems they wanted him to deal with. Benn and Labour Party volunteers produced the Community Action Index, which gave him an input to every community group in Bristol. This was obviously in keeping with the ideas of community involvement he had been developing even in the late 1960s, but there was a practical application to this work. He considered that new boundaries made the seat marginal.

Hundreds of people from outside the constituency offered help, including Welsh miners, for the first time embracing Tony Benn as one of their natural leaders. Yet his diary entries are full of gloom. The impression is conveyed, though never explicitly, that he might prefer Labour to lose rather than see it form a government and betray his hopes as the last Wilson administration had done.

Benn's thoughts were as close to revolutionary as a man's can be who is still standing for election for a major party. He was wooed by the far left but spurned them. At the other extreme, Enoch Powell declared he would not stand for the Conservative Party, and advised the nation to vote Labour because the referendum proposal offered the only chance of withdrawal from the Common Market. He followed his own advice and voted Labour, a devastating blow for Heath. Considering that the election was closely run in a great many constituencies, Powell's die-hard anti-Marketeers' votes were very well worth having. They were available only because of Benn's referendum campaign.

Benn's worries about the result were unnecessary. He emerged with a majority of almost 8000 over the Tory. Nationally Labour did less well, gaining 200,000 fewer votes than the Tories, but with 301 seats to Heath's 297. Heath unsuccessfully tried to form a coalition with the Liberals. After a tense weekend he finally conceded defeat and resigned.

27

'The Wedgie Man'

Back in government, Wilson played his usual trick of elevating his enemies just high enough to persuade them that they had too much to lose by opposing him. Barbara Castle got the massive Department of Health and Social Security, Michael Foot was given Employment, Peter Shore had Trade and Benn was given Industry. The other leading left-wing figure, Judith Hart, held the highest position outside the cabinet, that of Minister for Overseas Development. Thus the left had their place, but all the top positions went to the right wing of the party: Healey as Chancellor, Callaghan as Foreign Secretary and Jenkins as Home Secretary.

This time, to his satisfaction, Benn became a Secretary of State, the first time he had held that position, even though he now had a smaller department than in 1970. Indeed, his Department's size was a source of some resentment; Wilson softened the blow by giving him Posts and Telecommunications while they were in the process of being split up.

Crosland had been given the giant Department of the Environment, but the 'super ministry' which Benn might have expected to assume, Trade and Industry, had been split into three: Industry, Trade, and Prices and Consumer Protection. Energy had been removed from the department a few weeks previously. The chair of the cabinet's Industrial Development Committee, which Benn would have expected to have, was taken by Wilson himself.

In a move of great skill, instead of trying to control Benn by giving him right-wing ministers to work with, Wilson decided to push Benn so far to the left that he would propel himself over the edge. He attempted to staff Benn's department with left-wing or ineffective ministers and under secretaries. This would make life extremely difficult for Benn, because so much of his work required compromise and co-operation with businesses. As Benn wrote at the time, 'What I want is a nice right-wing guy trusted by industry and the City.'[1] He did not get his nominations but the result was not totally unsatisfactory. The most left wing of his ministers was Eric Heffer, a former carpenter who had an affectionate relationship with Benn.

Throughout this period of office Benn was haunted by the spectre of 1931 and the great betrayal which had cut down the Labour Party, giving the Conservatives the biggest parliamentary majorities in British history in 1931 and 1935. Benn felt a personal continuity between contemporary events and those of the 1930s; his father had been a member of MacDonald's cabinet up to the formation of the National government and the elder Benn always felt he shared some responsibility for those events. Tony Benn's warnings were not invariably well received. Foot snarled at him not to be so hysterical at a 'Husbands and Wives' left-wing dinner.[2] 'He never eats,' Caroline said at one of these dinners. 'He never used to sleep either, but he does that a bit more now.' Barbara Castle found the Benns' home 'just what one would expect: roomy, comfortable, shabby and littered with political mementoes and some pleasant cultural bric-à-brac. . . . I suspect [Caroline] and Wedgie normally get by on mugs of tea and bread and cheese.'[3]

The return to government meant a resumption of a punishing schedule of work for Benn. On 13 March he arrived home from the Commons at 11 p.m. and did not finish his red boxes and his diary until 3 a.m. Some of the diary entries have an insufferable air of bravado, however: 'Overslept and in fact wasn't woken until 5.15', for example, on 14 June 1974. He was also a prey to his good nature, never able to resist a request. At one time he had to be driven from his constituency early on Saturday morning to address a miners' gala in Barnsley at 11 a.m. and the miners sent a volunteer to drive him. The drive could have been achieved after a reasonable night's sleep but the driver successfully persuaded Benn to agree to be picked up at 4.30 a.m. so that he could take the cabinet minister home to have breakfast with his family.[4]

He was, as ever, the despair of his supporters. Frank McElhone was horrified that Benn was speaking to the Young Socialists – he really ought to be addressing the Institute of Directors if he wanted to be Prime Minister. Benn wrote, 'I think what he is saying is certainly sensible from a purely ambitious point of view but I am not that ambitious, not at that price. . . . I suppose I am ambitious for influence, not for power.'[5] It was not a political position Frank McElhone found it easy to comprehend. Later in 1974 he resigned as Benn's parliamentary private secretary, to be replaced by Joe Ashton. One of Benn's special advisers, Frances Morrell, tried to get him to foster better relations with his ministerial colleagues and to do what all the other leading politicians did and have lunches with newspaper proprietors. He did so with no apparent emollient effect on newspaper coverage of his activities.

His permanent secretary was Sir Antony Part, an urbane career civil servant who took objection to the proposed appointment of Sir William Nield to an Industry Department post because Nield's knighthood was of a higher order than those usually awarded to people in the home civil service. Benn remembered how much patience was needed in dealing with the civil service.

The civil servants had to deal with Benn's foibles too. Soon his office in Victoria Street was home to characteristic Benn artefacts: the mugs of tea; a blue and crimson silk trade union banner, with a male and female worker shaking hands over the slogan 'United to Obtain the Just Reward of Our Labour'; and the upside-down map which showed the British Isles with its rich and poor areas reversed – 'a new perception of an old problem,' he said.[6]

The first major problem was Concorde. At the end of their period of government the Tories had reached tentative agreement with the French to cancel the aircraft, since both sides were horrified by the increasing development costs and the empty order books. Benn's view was that having built it, however inadvisedly, it should be allowed to fly. Taxpayers would have something to show for their money, skilled workers would remain in employment, and the two nations would have a symbol of engineering excellence travelling the globe. There were also the issues that the cancellation would look bad for the government in power at the time; and that many of those jobs which were in jeopardy were those of voters in Benn's increasingly marginal constituency.

With Whitehall and most, if not all, of his cabinet colleagues against him, Benn had little room for manoeuvre. In a typical Benn outflanking operation he bought time in the cabinet and used that time to muster outside forces to support him. The Chancellor Denis Healey was his main opponent, eager for cuts to announce in his first Budget. Benn ingenuously suggested to the cabinet that if he told the public about the development costs of Concorde, which the previous government had failed to do, enormous political credit would accrue from such an exercise in open government. He argued that the government must 'open the books' and have the debate about Concorde's future in public. Also, of course, there would have to be consultation with the trade unions and with the French. Thus he sidestepped the Chancellor, who was left clenching his jaws on air. 'Wedgie has lived to fight another day,' wrote Barbara Castle.[7]

Benn was fortunate in that the Tory minister who had been responsible for Concorde, Michael Heseltine, was now the shadow industry minister. As Westminster correspondents frequently remarked, Benn had no difficulty in outclassing his opposite number in the House of Commons. In his detailed 'open books' exercise, he explained that the total projected cost was now £1070 million at 1974 prices, half of which the UK must pay.

In Bristol Benn mobilised the trade unions, telling them to bring grassroots pressure to bear and to get Jack Jones of the Transport and General Workers' Union to influence Harold Wilson directly. While his manoeuvres served his political purposes, they were not cynical. Benn genuinely wanted greater public participation in government decisions.

When Concorde had first been planned it was a participant in a race to develop supersonic passenger carriers. By 1974, however, the American and Soviet projects had been cancelled and Concorde was out there on the field alone, looking very isolated. The world in which British salesmen tried to sell the plane, moreover, had changed utterly. The high fuel consumption was objectionable in the wake of the oil-price rises following the 1973 Yom Kippur War. In a more environmentally conscious world, the noise of the plane prohibited it from being licensed for the lucrative trans-continental routes. Even the concept that reducing flying time would substantially decrease total travelling time became questionable. Time in the air became a smaller proportion of door-to-door travelling time because of increased airport congestion caused by the rise of the Jumbo and by tighter security necessitated by air terrorism. The only purchasers for Concorde were the British and French national airlines and they could see no possibility of using more than fourteen of them, two more than were on the production line.

Benn had now tried to save Concorde using open government, public consultation and the trade unions. It was time to play the French card again. The French decision-making machinery, mercifully for Concorde, had been delayed by the death of President Pompidou. After a meeting with George Edwardes, chairman of the British Airways Corporation, in June 1974, Tony Benn took him down the corridor and into the lift so that they could be alone. 'The cabinet have told me to suggest we discontinue,' he said urgently to his guest, 'but if the French insist on producing sixteen planes we shall go ahead. Therefore, without breathing a word that you have heard this from me, your job is to persuade the French to make such a demand and we shall have to build them.'[8]

George did his job. When Harold Wilson went to meet the new French President, Giscard d'Estaing, they agreed to produce sixteen Concordes. Denis Healey never forgave Benn this success, contemptuously referring to Concorde in his memoirs as one of only two monuments Benn's ministerial career had left behind. There was the Rossing mine (which is referred to in Chapter 29) and, 'an aircraft which is used by wealthy people on their expense accounts, whose fares are subsidised by much poorer taxpayers'.[9]

Healey had much to be smug about. He had managed to maintain such secrecy over his own equivalent of the Concorde, the Chevaline project (the 'hardening' of Polaris), that the cabinet never discussed it. No unauthorised member of the public ever saw it, even though it cost the British taxpayer more than Concorde and was rather less useful.

Secrecy had something of a pedigree in these affairs, the cabinet had been kept ignorant of the development of the atom bomb by Attlee and Bevin. It was left to Churchill to reveal that Attlee had built that bomb, and it was left to Thatcher to reveal that Chevaline had been made under the previous Labour government.

The Wilson government considered it only on 20 November 1974 and then in coded terms. Wilson introduced the subject as being about retaining nuclear weapons and carrying out 'certain improvements'. He was expecting trouble from nuclear disarmers but faced little resistance. The comments of the old campaigner Michael Foot 'were so muted as to be almost token' as Barbara Castle wrote. She herself said she could make better use of the money which was at that time said to be £24 million a year for ten years. This was as one might expect. Tony Benn coming out as a unilateral nuclear disarmer might also have been anticipated, given his increasing association with all things left. 'I have never been a unilateralist,' he said, 'I have never marched to Aldermaston, my instinct is to keep them.' But he went on to argue that they were expensive, unusable and ineffective as a means of defence – the only wars which had been won since 1945 were by guerrillas defending their own country. He also doubted whether there was any real political control over the military establishment. Perhaps worst of all, 'The retention of nuclear weapons misleads us about our influence. Somehow the bomb makes us feel powerful. There are many people in Britain who think that the Queen and the bomb are the only two things we have left. I don't think either of them are much use to us.'[10]

The cabinet voted to retain the weapons with the 'improvements', the person who should have been preventing them from taking such an economically reckless step being Denis Healey who later described it as one of his 'major mistakes' not to have cancelled Chevaline in 1974.[11] The project was never, even in such a masked form, presented before Benn again, though he was in the cabinet until the fall of the government.

Benn's relationship with his permanent secretary was never very sweet. Early in his period at Industry Sir Antony Part asked him if he really intended to go ahead with the National Enterprise Board, public ownership and planning agreements with industry. 'Of course,' said Benn. 'Not just because it is the policy but because I was deeply associated with the development of that policy.'

'Well, I must warn you', the permanent secretary said, 'that if you do it, you will be heading for as big a confrontation with industrial management as the last government had with the trade unions over the Industrial Relations Act.' 'I'm not going to jail any industrialists,' said Benn, 'I'm not going to fine them. We have just got to move forward.' Part said he would try to help if that was really what the Secretary of State wanted.[12]

Benn's habit of note-keeping, partly for use in his diary, was disconcerting to Part. He described Benn at work:

> He put a block of paper in front of him and drew a line down the middle. As the conversation proceeded, he noted my remarks to the left of the line and any comment or counter-argument of his to the right of the line. This did not make for a relaxed atmosphere and occasionally it was as though he were pointing a pistol at my head. Metaphorically, I would watch his fingers tightening on the trigger and when I judged that he was about to fire I moved my head to one side.[13]

Benn found more comradely support in his advisers, Francis Cripps on economic and Frances Morrell on political matters. He had successfully argued while in opposition that ministers should have their own advisers, appointed by themselves and not reliant on the patronage of the 'old-boy network' of Whitehall. Newspaper accounts report that Benn outraged the Society of British Aerospace Companies when he took Frances Morrell to their annual dinner because they felt unable to tell their traditional dirty jokes with a woman present.

The civil servants found allies in senior trade unionists. Lionel Murray, general secretary of the TUC, for example, was no more sympathetic to industrial democracy than Sir Antony Part.[14] After Benn had cajoled the Department of Industry to take note of the views of trade unionists, the trade unionists wanted only to speak with real Whitehall civil servants, not people like Frances Morrell, who were 'too political'.[15]

In pushing through his industrial policy Benn was the very soul of tact and diplomacy. Not even Part accused him of relaxing his calm, polite and determined manner. With his colleagues he was the same: 'Wedgie sat in the chair as if butter would not melt in his mouth,' wrote Barbara Castle of a potentially explosive NEC meeting, 'reasonableness itself on every point raised. He really is the most skilled political practitioner of us all.'[16]

The industrial strategy was to encourage participation between government, unions and management. This necessitated a free flow of information, particularly from the companies to the other agencies. It also envisaged an increase in public ownership, particularly by government purchase of shares in companies, and support for co-operatives and other workers'-control ventures.

Benn went for maximum support for the industry proposals by asking the NEC's Home Policy Committee to release a report of his plans even before they had gone to cabinet. It was a gesture calculated to stimulate support among the unions and party members, but it also, inevitably, stimulated the opposition of press, industrialists and cabinet colleagues. At one of the 'Husbands and Wives' dinners Barbara Castle attacked him for his lack of solidarity with his colleagues. 'The socialist virtue', she remarked, 'lies in knowing when to keep one's mouth shut.' Benn disarmed her by dropping the rhetoric and saying, completely naturally, 'But you are able to *do* things, Barbara. I am in a department where, at present at any rate, I can do nothing but talk.' She clutched his hand sympathetically – not for the first, or the last, time overwhelmed by his charm and vulnerability.[17]

Benn's first major nationalisation, to his great glee, arose because the owners sought that solution themselves. Court Line, which owned shipyards and holiday firms, asked Benn in June 1974 to take their sixteen shipbuilding companies into public ownership to safeguard employment together with the ships already on the order books. When John Davies tried to smear Benn with the failure of UCS, his former opposite number was able to parry smartly, 'Mr. Davies was the personal architect of the legislation I am using. I pay warm tribute to him.'[18]

The case trailed him unhappily, for he had given the impression that he was also saving the holiday firms Clarksons and Horizon, though the nationalisation of the shipbuilding sectors of the company merely relieved pressure on the holiday firms. Such subtleties were lost on the would-be package holidaymakers who stood to lose their money as well as their holidays when the holiday firms collapsed. The government felt obliged to refund them. Benn also introduced a Bill to nationalise British Leyland in May 1975 after it had been demonstrated in the Ryder report that collapse was otherwise inevitable.

Three workers' co-operatives were supported by Benn, all of them born out of the failure of earlier firms: KME in Kirkby, Meriden near Coventry and the *Scottish Daily News* in Glasgow. The chief problem was always that the co-operatives had to start with a history of the failure of an earlier enterprise. Additionally, the cabinet would not agree to fund them adequately. There were also what might be called ideological problems. The co-operatives, KME particularly, started to demonstrate not the merits of co-operation but the assertion of inegalitarian values: there were top people who dominated the co-operative as much as any management would have dominated the workforce. Benn had to fight desperately for the co-operatives with his own officials, the Treasury and his cabinet colleagues. He did manage to force financial support through cabinet but the Treasury still called them 'Benn's follies'.

Kirkby Manufacturing and Engineering, making an improbable mix of soft drinks, radiators and motor parts, lasted four years. The *Scottish Daily News*, set up by workers at the Beaverbrook newspapers in Scotland when publication of separate editions North of the border ceased, went down after six months.

The story of Meriden probably best demonstrates the difficulties of the workers taking over an existing plant, however much the product is in demand. The workers at the Norton Villiers Triumph plant at Meriden had blockaded the factory after they had been declared redundant, refusing to let components and equipment out. While it was an inspiring act of defiance, it created more than a little ill-feeling between them and the workers at the NVT plant in Birmingham, where those components were needed. The Birmingham workers were also defensive: a successful bike produced at Meriden would take the export orders they wanted. Benn went to speak to them. The local paper reported that 'he left to a continuing chorus of boos and jeers, with perspiration running down his face. Workers pressing around his car left him in no doubt that they wanted guarantees on their own job security before backing Meriden.'[19]

Ever enthusiastic, Benn proclaimed that the co-operatives were to start a new chapter in industrial relations in Britain. 'They can unlock a considerable productive potential that cannot be released by the present authoritarian system,' he said. 'This country could, with the same plant and equipment, produce a great deal more on a continuing basis if the energy now wasted could be released.'[20]

But this was not to happen at Meriden. The wrangling with fellow workers, the delay in obtaining the government loan to buy the plant, the delay in obtaining export credits, all combined to wound Meriden fatally before it had produced one bike. Productivity was high and wages were low with frequent periods of short-time working, but still Meriden could not make a profit. The Meriden co-operative could produce machines more efficiently than the factory did before, but the US export market had collapsed by the time the bikes could be shipped out.

Once he had proved the competence of his government, Wilson called another election, for October 1974. The election failed to achieve the desired result as far as Labour was concerned. There was an overall majority, but of only three seats. Benn did better than the national average, his majority rising from 7912 in February to 9373 in October.

At a breakfast meeting with David Butler during this campaign Benn emphasised his commitment to the unions. 'The impression he left was that if the Labour leadership was controlled by the trade unions, so much the better as far as he is concerned. . . . He did seem to be implying that the organised workers would and perhaps should take things into their own hands.'[21]

The working-class trade unionists never understood how sincere this convert was. His move to the left was interpreted as being inspired by careerism. 'We felt he was with us but not of us,' said Jack Jones, leader of the largest union, the Transport and General Workers. 'He never seemed to be attuned to the trade union outlook. He was a marvellous communicator but he had this innate ambition. If he hadn't been so ambitious he would have served the Labour Party better.'[22]

Following the election Benn was reappointed to the same post, though Wilson was not so courteous as to tell him, which demonstrates how far their relations had deteriorated. But there was some relaxation in the press onslaught. With the election over, there was no clear point to aim at, no sense in continually repeating that the electors would not put up for long with the antics of Wilson and

Benn. They clearly would – the papers were not in step with their readers. There was also a limit to the amount of abuse which could be slung at 'Bennery', 'Bennification' and 'Wedgwood Benthamism' and diminishing returns of mirth for 'Thin End of the Wedgie' headlines.

Paul Johnson in the *Daily Telegraph* was the first to question the 'anti-Benns' in the first week of January 1975:

> Anthropologists say that all societies in distress need an object, however innocent, on which to vent their impotent fury. Thus primitive peoples often kill their kings; and Italian peasants, in time of drought, have been known to stone statues of the Virgin Mary.
>
> We, it seems, have chosen Mr Benn. Whenever newspaper editors, or economists, or City slickers, or businessmen gather, to ponder the mess and exchange horror-stories of the latest national reverse, Mr Benn's name crops up and he is duly denounced.[23]

Even more improbably, Peregrine Worsthorne remarked, 'Such is his reputation at the present time that if he were to advocate the restoration of hereditary peerages it would be seized upon as marking the dawn of a new revolutionary age, hailed by the Left with enthusiasm and excoriated by the Right with indignation.' The piece ended, 'Benn or bust! That is the real choice. Why not let him have a go?'[24]

The publication of the Industry Bill on 31 January 1975 ended the brief respite Benn had enjoyed from otherwise unrelenting attack. Not all the attacks were nonsense, however; commentators repeatedly pointed out the inefficiency of companies already publicly owned, like the Gas Board. They asked in what way nationalisation was to help the aerospace or shipbuilding industries. Why, they asked, if there was no market for capitalist motor cycles, should one arise for co-operatively produced ones? They pointed out that Benn was:

> asking for powers to take over or otherwise interfere with any firm for almost any reason that takes his fancy such as:
> Because it is making a profit
> Because it is not making a profit
> Because it is so inefficient that foreigners are driving it to the wall
> Because it is so efficient that foreigners want to buy it.

It is characteristic of the tenor of the times that the intelligent, if somewhat shrill, article from which this quotation comes was given the headline 'Today Dictatorship No Longer Seems So Far Away for Britain'.[25] Benn's industrial policy, as Barbara Castle described it, was 'very simple: to defend what we have, even if its equipment is lousy, defend it if necessary behind protective walls and then reconstruct it with the help of workers in the industry and make it viable.'[26] The apparent contradictions and overall inadequacy of the policy can hardly be blamed on Benn or any other individual. The fact was that manufacturing industry was in decline under Labour and the Conservatives and nothing seemed able to stop it. A miserable stream of representatives from industries as diverse as typewriter, tights, toy and machine-tool manufacturers came appealing for help to Benn in his fifteen months at Industry.

As the Industry Bill went through its committee stage, attacks from industrialists and the City became more pronounced. It did not take them long to find that they had an ally in the Prime Minister. The Labour MP Jeremy Bray later explained that industrialists were going behind Tony Benn's back to complain to Harold Wilson about the disclosure provisions of the Industry Bill, which would have obliged them to divulge company information. Bray remembers Wilson entering the members' dining room, sitting down with some back-benchers and announcing with glee that 'he had been redrafting the disclosure provisions and making them so byzantine they could never be used to enforce disclosure'.[27] Ian Mikardo, at that time working on the Bill, recalled, 'The Prime Minister's intentions were clear in the drafting of a series of government amendments to the Industry Bill in committee. It was clear-cut: the Bill was being emasculated.'[28] The Prime Minister was positively asking his Secretary of State for Industry to resign.

Benn's increasing isolation in the cabinet put the civil servants in a difficult position. As Sir Antony Part wrote,

In such a situation a Permanent Secretary is liable to be faced with a dilemma. To whom does his loyalty lie – his Secretary of State or the Prime Minister? To reply that his loyalty lies to the Crown, whose servant he constitutionally is, does not provide a practical answer to the question. In my view his loyalty must lie to the former unless the Secretary of State is doing or contriving something that would be regarded by Parliament as improper.'[29]

Benn, however, never felt that Part's loyalty was fulsome.

In a procedure which was immediately leaked to the press, Benn was subject to an Accounting Officer's minute. This is a note from senior civil servants to the minister concerned questioning an item of expenditure. In effect, it is putting on record the civil servant's warning to the minister that he or she considers the expenditure goes beyond what the permanent secretary can accept. In this case the minute referred to the £10 million spent on the three co-operatives (out of a total of £800 million given to industry in 1974–5) and to a research grant of £20,000 to the Welsh TUC. Benn pointed out that there was never any complaint about giving money to private industry for research, only now when it was going to a workers' organisation.

Part made rather a mistake using this procedure against Benn. The Secretary of State argued back that there had been no Accounting Officer's minutes in the last government or the previous Labour government or even in the current government on projects which were clearly not viable, like Concorde, or on questionable projects like Rolls-Royce and Upper Clyde. The only issue on which the permanent secretary felt moved to issue such a minute was over workers' co-operatives. 'This is no coincidence, and in fact it is a matter of political judgement, not financial propriety.' 'I cannot accept that any civil servant is political,' Part said.

It was clear that, rather than taking his reprimand quietly, Benn was going to turn it into an instrument to plague his tormentors. 'I shall insist that in future all Accounting Officer's minutes take a special form, are explicitly numbered and circulated to everyone to discuss them,' he said. Part was clearly regretting the whole thing.[30] Benn then drafted a detailed letter demonstrating that each time Part had questioned one of his actions, Benn had adjusted the policy to take account of the objection. On the day Part received the letter, however, the permanent secretary had a (non-fatal) heart attack which ended the affair.

The press attacks reached an absurd pitch, with Benn portrayed as Viscount Dracula, sucking the lifeblood of British industry. The *Daily Express* printed a picture of him on which a Hitler moustache had been drawn, with a commentator remarking that he could 'see a considerable likeness between Tony Benn and another of fanatical disposition'.[31] It had become so outrageous that cartoonists on the papers themselves began parodying their own colleagues' excesses. The *Evening Standard*'s Jak had a mother telling her child to be good 'Or the Wedgie man will get you.'

Benn was subjected to the usual death threats from disturbed people, one of which he took more seriously. It was written to Caroline in the name De Camp (her maiden name) and warned that a group of ten businessmen called Defenders of Private Enterprise were contributing to a pool of cash to pay for an American hitman to kill him. Of course it was a complete invention designed to disconcert Benn; anyone really wanting to kill him would have done so rather than write letters about it. Moreover, the use of Caroline's name indicated that the writer was out to 'spook' the family: he (or she) wanted to do something sinister and frightening.

Caroline was the focus of attention when the press discovered she had gone to Greece on a yachting holiday with some of the children and her childhood friend Phyllis Lambert. They had always taken holidays together, sometimes in this yacht, which was owned by a member of Phyllis Lambert's family. There was further unwelcome attention when Caroline's mother died leaving a sum of money (which came to less than £45,000 each) in trust for the four children. The Benns usually ignored comments on their private lives, on the basis that any denial or justification in response to an accusation lent a spurious credence to those which were not denied. One wonders how some claims could be denied, anyway. It was frequently said that Tony Benn was married to a millionairess. This was not true, though going into print about it would only encourage further exaggeration about Caroline's background.[32]

The Benns could do no right. Caroline and Joshua, at some risk to themselves, rescued two people from drowning after their dinghy capsized on the estuary near Stansgate. They were criticised in the press the next day for not telling the coastguard so that the search could be called off, though they did not know that a search was taking place.

Sometimes the persecution was calculated. On one occasion Caroline was dealing with a Holland Park teacher's dispute. Some of the pupils had demonstrated in support of the teacher and this had attracted press interest. The absence of any semblance of riotous behaviour robbed the event of its value as a picture story. A team from one newspaper had come prepared, however, with a bag of tomatoes, one of which a reporter handed to a pupil as Caroline Benn approached. 'Throw it at that woman,' he said, but the boy declined and instead pelted the reporter, much to the entertainment of those who witnessed it.[33]

The times were such that it was exasperation rather than alarm which greeted the setting up of private armies. Two old soldiers were independently setting up bodies of trained volunteers in order to keep the country running in the event of a general strike. General Sir Walter Walker, formerly commanding officer of NATO's northern flank, was aiming at a membership of three million for his UNISON organisation. Colonel David Stirling, the founder of the Special Air Service, was setting up a similar organisation, to be called GB 75. One of the documents he sent out to supporters specifically targeted Benn:

> Wedgwood Benn's two-headed purpose, elaborately planned but naïvely camouflaged, of steady encroachment on the private enterprise system, together with the forcing of trade union members on to the executive board of public companies – and both these tactics running in parallel with growing inflation and the exercising at will of the political strike weapon – amount between them to a realisable threat of a magnitude this country has probably never faced before.[34]

The crude right-wing position was that Benn was advocating a state take-over on a Leninist model. Industrial democracy was not state control, of course, and the more sophisticated of Benn's detractors had to deal with this point. Michael Ivens in an Aims of Industry pamphlet called *The Ugly Face of Mr Wedgwood Benn* grappled with it: 'Syndicalism, the doctrine that an industry should be controlled by the workers in it and run in their interest . . . is totally at variance with socialism, which is a state managerial system. It is however a historical fact that syndicalism has been constantly fomented among industrial workers by the Communists as a means of seizing power, though they quickly forget such crackpot notions once they have seized it.'[35]

Michael Ivens later explained that he had attacked Benn because he was easy to tease and always rose to the bait. He was also honest, and said in public what other cabinet members said in private. 'He always said what he believed in,' said Ivens, 'we took him as the open and influential representative of the Labour Party.'[36] In fact all ministers were inclined to be rather more left wing in public where they were playing to their supporters, than they were in private where they had to grapple with the realities of wielding power. It was a persistent myth, however, that the government was packed with revolutionaries – a myth which forces rather more sinister than Aims of Industry strove to perpetuate.

Colin Wallace, employed by the army to circulate 'disinformation' about armed political opponents in terrorist groups, found that his job also included discrediting members of the government. It is evident that the objective was not to discredit the left alone because information was also manufactured about right-wing members of the government. Wallace would, for example, show gullible journalists a forged internal Labour Party document supposedly written by Benn, Healey and Stan Orme which was called 'Economics: Master or Servant of Mankind?' and expressed crudely Marxist views. A left-wing leaflet attacking the British army was accurately reproduced but the names of Benn, Merlyn Rees and David Owen were added.[37]

Even if some of what Wallace says is untrue (and at least some of it has been confirmed by various Secretaries of State under pressure from back-benchers), it enjoys corroboration from other former secret service personnel who have gone public: Peter Wright and Cathy Massiter.[38] It was certainly the objective of some members of MI5 to smear the Labour government in order to precipitate its fall.

The Security Service delusions about Harold Wilson being a spy and the IRA being under Russian control may have represented the extremes of lunacy, but they were consistent with the rest of right-wing thinking at the time. The role of Airey Neave, aide-de-camp to Margaret Thatcher, will probably never be fully understood. He was killed in 1979 in the House of Commons car park by a bomb planted by Republican terrorists. He had previously seen both Colin Wallace and former MI6 electronics expert Lee Tracey and according to Tracey his fears were that Labour would be re-elected and that Callaghan would soon retire leaving the way clear for Benn to become Prime Minister. Neave was allegedly putting together a team of intelligence and security specialists to 'make sure Benn was stopped'.[39] When confronted with this allegation, Benn explicitly rejected the implication that Neave would have used violence against him: 'I sat in parliament for many years with Airey Neave, talked to him on many occasions and do not for one moment believe such a thought would have entered his mind.'[40]

Benn was also the subject of attempts to smear him with indiscretions relating to drugs or sex, including an allegation of bestiality, but these were unsuccessful, and the rumours never gained public currency. In the 'Clockwork Orange' material which was supplied to Colin Wallace by MI5, the 'vulnerabilities' of various leading politicians were assessed, with Benn being shown not to be open to attack on either moral or financial grounds but to be vulnerable to political assault. Probably this means that ways could be found of undermining him with his own supporters, alleging that he was a hypocrite, for example, and enjoying the benefits of wealth while advising socialist values for the public.

One clear fact was that Benn's telephones were tapped for a period in the 1970s. He had two lines, one for business and the other exclusively for family use. Though these were separate lines, a crossed line on one was found to be accompanied by the same crossed line on the other – indicating that they were going through a system which linked them at one point.[41] More telling was the time Melissa Benn made a telephone call then picked up the other instrument to make another call and heard a recording of her previous call.[42] The tapping of the telephones of people involved in ordinary democratic behaviour – trades unionists and CND activists, for example – was a characteristic of the Security Service paranoia of the 1970s. Cathy Massiter, a former MI5 agent, was required to resign from the service for complaining of such behaviour.[43]

Joshua Benn, fiddling with a short-wave radio upstairs in the house, picked up his father's telephone conversation which was taking place below, suggesting that the telephone contained a transmitter. Who planted it is uncertain. It could easily be the same agency which bugged the telephone line, as a fail-safe measure, in case pressure was ever brought to bear on them to stop tapping the telephones of politicians. Joshua Benn did voice the possibility that given the right wavelength and a sufficiently powerful radio, a nearby telephone call could be picked up without the intervention of a transmitter.[44]

The family became suspicious about the rate at which their refuse was being cleared, so Joshua Benn rigged up an alarm system by placing the rubbish on a hinged board which rang a bell in the house when it was removed. Awoken by the bell, family members looked out of the window in the early hours one morning to see a man loading Benn family rubbish into a limousine.[45]

Benn was sometimes aware of Security Service observation, though at least some of it was for genuine security reasons: cabinet ministers were particular targets for terrorism and terrorism was rife at the time. His political work aside, Benn's days in the 1970s were dotted with near misses, 1973–4 seeing a campaign of mainland bombing by the IRA. A man was killed by a bomb around the corner from the Benn home in Kensington Church Street; a week later Benn missed by ten minutes a bomb which killed two at the Hilton Hotel. Benn had little to say about Northern Ireland. While in opposition he had come to the view that the government should set a date for a phased withdrawal of troops but, apart from saying this in cabinet and finding himself in a minority, he made no contribution to the politics of the province at this time.

Paranoia must be kept at bay, and it is important to remember that not everyone in the intelligence services was disloyal or plotting against the government. Neave, for example, was meeting with outsiders and the disaffected. One must also be cautious of taking at face value the testimony of people who, by their own admission, lived to lie. It is not the individual account which convinces, however, but the cumulative evidence. It is clear that this Labour government was threatened with subversion, at a level unparalleled in post-war history, and that Benn was a major target.

Benn felt that MI5 and MI6 should be more accountable to parliament, and wrote a paper for the NEC about the lack of accountability of the security services.

His attitude to secrecy in general was very much conditioned by his own open nature. His instinct was that if people in government wanted to keep secrets they were almost certainly up to no good. On one visit to the USSR as a minister he was taken to a bug-proof, sound-proof room by the Ambassador and told he could speak his mind freely. There was an awkward pause, 'I can't think of anything secret to say,' said Benn.[46]

28

Wilson Attacks

B enn's next campaign concerned the right of ministers to express their views independently of the cabinet. His colleagues tended to think of this as a maverick attempt to evade collective responsibility while striking political postures for public consumption. Nevertheless, he had an important point: the reins of collective responsibility should not be pulled in too tightly, or why have experienced politicians as ministers at all? As he wrote in a minute to his colleagues in June 1974, 'All ministers are individuals with personal convictions that have brought us into political life; and we have been elected and appointed *because* of our convictions and not in spite of them. In the end, it is our loyalty to what we believe that offers us the only ultimate safeguard on our conduct.'[1]

Harold Wilson merely felt that Benn was attempting to undermine his position. He warned the cabinet about collective responsibility after three ministers, Benn among them, voted at an NEC meeting to condemn the government for undertaking joint naval exercises with South Africa. The Prime Minister eventually elicited a statement from Benn that he fully accepted the doctrine of collective responsibility. Wilson warned that he might have to forbid cabinet members from offering themselves for election to the NEC. Wilson had more to worry about than Benn alone; he was also concerned by Reg Prentice (now Secretary of State for Education and Science) and Roy Jenkins making speeches condemning government policy from the right. The threat to party unity from the right was greater than that from the left – within seven years both Prentice and Jenkins had stood for election against the Labour Party, Prentice as a Conservative and Jenkins for the SDP.

Unlike theirs, Benn's speeches were always reported, and he also tended to attract attention in other ways. In the Commons one evening, when he was the only cabinet member present, he petulantly abstained on a Prime Minister's motion to 'take note' of various EEC regulations. The next day the cabinet was united in its exasperation; Barbara Castle, despite her policy agreements with him, was 'getting a bit sick of his clear determination to strike attitudes publicly whenever he can'. She added that Foot thought Benn 'obsessed with ambition'.[2] Wilson had him this time. 'No question of conscience could conceivably arise on a motion which was merely to take note,' he thundered. 'You will have seen in Cabinet today the indignation of your colleagues. Once again, it is simply not acting as a member of a team.'[3]

Yet his colleagues still stood in awe of the speed of his wit and the dynamism of his rhetoric. Barbara Castle records that even Harold Wilson was nodding in agreement with Benn during just another cabinet meeting when 'Wedgie gave one of his extraordinarily fluent tirades on democracy.' The petty squabbling and the terrifying tedium of the whole business of renegotiating the Common Market terms should not obscure the reality, that in Benn there was a champion of 'vivid and telling words' whose gifts anyone would be glad to have on their side.[4]

The conflict about collective responsibility came to a head over the Common Market, in an argument which Benn won without covering himself in glory. At a cabinet meeting in July 1974 he finally took the plunge and declared himself against remaining in the EEC. His colleagues were not amazed at the revelation.

Predictably, Tony Benn felt the need to be enthusiastically opposed to entry. He planned a strategy to give himself maximum coverage. Over Christmas 1974 he wrote a letter to his constituents in Bristol South-East attacking the Common Market for decisions which would 'make the United Kingdom into one province of a Western European state'. He criticised EEC membership as having degraded parliamentary democracy and subjected Britain to laws and taxes enacted by authorities not directly elected by the British people.

What it said, however, was secondary to what he did with it. In the last days of December he sent a copy of the 'letter' to all the daily papers, to the Press Association, to the two Bristol papers and, almost as an afterthought, to the Prime Minister. Within a few hours Harold Wilson's office called to ask whether copies had already gone to the press (and were therefore almost impossible to recall). Benn said they had, but perhaps Wilson's attention could be drawn to the fact that the letter had not dealt with renegotiation of the Common Market terms but only with the constitutional effect of membership. Benn tried to put across the impression that this kept to within cabinet agreements.

Wilson was not interested in engaging in a legalistic dispute about it. He was so angry that he would not even speak to Benn but instead had his private secretary tell Benn's private secretary that the Benn statement contravened a cabinet agreement that 'no one should be involved in private enterprise on these issues until the cabinet had collectively discussed how the matter is to be handled'.[5] Benn thought he might well be sacked.

His defence, that he had written as an MP to his constituents, explaining how the relationship between them would be changed, and not as a cabinet minister, was dismissed as 'dissembling' by others. Jim Callaghan wrote, 'One of Tony's blind spots was his inability to understand that for him to argue he was keeping within the letter of the law, when he clearly offended against its spirit, aroused hostility even among those of his colleagues who shared his opinions on the merits of the issue.'[6] Fortunately for Benn, the Bristol letter was followed by a statement by Roy Hattersley (a junior minister at the Foreign Office) that the loss of sovereignty was minimal, and a detailed response to this by Peter Shore; so indignation at Benn's outspokenness was diluted in the transgressions of others.

Eventually 5 June 1975 was set as the date for the referendum and cabinet decided, along the lines Benn favoured, that ministers would have the freedom to follow their own instincts on what they said to the public. Benn joined Barbara Castle, Michael Foot, Peter Shore and John Silkin as the 'dissenting ministers'. In March, launching the campaign against membership, they signed what Benn called a 'declaration' of opposition to the Market, Benn clearly intending it to have the historic resonance of the American Declaration of Independence. It had gone through several drafts by the time it was released and had lost the commitment 'We accept that the decision must be binding' which had appeared earlier.[7]

How did a minister, however acrobatic, represent the government's view on the Common Market while retaining an independent opinion? Asked whether the steel industry would get more or less cash under the EEC rules Benn explained to the House, 'I have nothing to add to the speech made in other parts of the country by my Right Hon. Friend the member for Bristol South-East.' It took a little time for members to get the joke.

The 'No' campaign consisted of a curious amalgam of the parliamentary right and left with their uneasy allies from the extra-parliamentary far right and far left. People who considered themselves 'moderates', both Labour and Conservative voters, tended to favour the Market. Their position was not modified by the exhortations of Tony Benn and his allies, probably the reverse. There is considerable truth in the historian David Childs's verdict: 'Many members of the "silent majority" felt that if Benn, Powell and the Communists were against the EEC, it must be a good thing.'[8]

They were united in their concern about the 'sovereignty' of Britain and British institutions. The vehemence with which this issue was addressed was peculiar to Britain. France, Greece and Denmark had had their qualms about loss of sovereignty, but nothing in those countries was as profound or long lasting as the Common Market battle in Britain. To the two wings of opposition to the Market, needless to say, the term sovereignty meant quite different things. For the right sovereignty was of value in itself – like the Queen and the Tower of London – while for the left sovereignty mattered because without it there could be no British road to socialism. Benn's 'alternative economic strategy' for example – with its tariffs, import controls and restrictions on the export of capital – could not function unless Britain was independent.

Benn was the undoubted star of the anti-Market campaign, touring the country in a blaze of publicity, facing adulatory audiences and a universally hostile press. When David Butler visited in early May 1975 he found Benn speaking of the meeting he had had in Birmingham the previous day: 'One thousand people marching and cheering him as he had never been cheered before.' Benn had no answer to Butler's observation that in his experience people were just not reacting like that, and that anti-Market Labour MPs were conceding defeat. Probably Benn genuinely believed his own propaganda – it was the only way to maintain the struggle against all odds. Butler observed, 'He struck me as being in a very exhausted and hysterical condition – very different from the calm figure I had seen two weeks earlier. He was drunk with his own oratory.'[9] It was unsurprising that he was carried away by his own performance: Benn was at his best, and at his best he could stand beside the greatest orators of history. Castle remarked at one meeting they both attended that 'the reception of Wedgie fell just short of idolatry: a standing ovation before he started and one afterwards'.[10] Michael Foot mused, 'the huge audiences addressed by Tony affected him maybe even more than he affected them'.[11]

Benn addressed 2000 in Cardiff, 1000 in Barnsley – not great figures in terms of mass-media audiences, but it was an impressive achievement to summon people in their thousands to a political meeting at all. His skill was the more remarkable because he spoke either without notes or with four or five pages of pencilled scribble. He felt excitement in giving people a sense that their own destiny was in their hands, that they were invested with power to change the future of the nation. In the process he may have presented 'a criminally over-simplified version of the facts', as Barbara Castle remarked.[12] He certainly made some statements which sounded magnificent but look a little more questionable in print. For example, the 1000-strong audience at Acton town hall broke into spontaneous applause when Benn said, 'Much of what is wrong with Britain is that those who have led us for so long have systematically sought to demoralise us because they have not found answers to the problems which afflict our society.'[13]

The religious overtones of his appeal were worked on by the cartoonists. In the *Daily Mail* a television producer spoke to Benn over a telephone, standing against a set rising to the studio roof like a Biblical epic: 'We've got the new seating arrangements fixed,' he said. 'Who do you suggest sitteth at your right hand?'[14] The *Evening Standard* had Benn depicted as Moses in a vast painting called 'Let my people go'. Benn himself was shown as saying to the artist, 'a trifle understated, but I like it.'[15]

Wilson became alarmed at the coverage Benn was receiving and asked the chairmen of the BBC and the IBA to ensure that a wider selection of anti-Marketeers was represented on television. This was to Barbara Castle's advantage, but she felt it was 'more anti-Benn than pro-Barbara'.[16] Wilson felt it was time to cut down Benn's career. The *Sunday Times* on 11 May carried a story which baldly stated in its first line, 'Mr Wilson plans to sack Tony Benn as Secretary for Industry immediately after the Common Market referendum on June 5, probably within a couple of days of the poll.' This was not a matter of supposition by a journalist; it bore all the marks of a briefing direct from Wilson himself.

At this stage Benn was exhausted by the combined effects of his speaking engagements, the pressures of running his department and the incessant attention of the press. The attacks from the Prime Minister were the end. When the newspaper articles arrived announcing that Benn would be sacked, he was ready to throw in the towel. He called Joe Ashton and told him he was going to clear his office at the department, taking down his trade union banner, to continue on a day-to-day basis, making no future plans. 'Don't be such a damn fool,' said Ashton. 'The word will spread throughout Whitehall that you are about to resign. You mustn't do it. You must fight. You are the only one we have got hope for.'[17] His counsel prevailed and Benn stayed on.

The only thing which could save Benn would be success for his side in the ballot: even Wilson could not victimise a winner. But Wilson knew that the 'No' side would not win. Almost all the money, all the newspapers and most of the politicians were in favour of the Market. The anti-Marketeers spent £131,354 on campaigning, the pro-Marketeers more than ten times that. Even the electorate's conservative nature tended to support a 'Yes' vote: they were not asked whether they wanted to go in, in which case they might well have resisted change, but whether they wished to *remain* in.

One significant event in the campaign was Benn's remark that the EEC had cost Britain 500,000 jobs. This was dismissed as a falsehood by Healey and led Jenkins to remark, 'I find it increasingly difficult to take Mr Benn seriously as an economics minister. It is this technique in which you just think of a number and double it and if challenged you pretend that you have not been challenged and react by thinking up some new claim.'[18] Wilson told ministers not to squabble in public.

The figure had been arrived at by Francis Cripps as part of 'a completely conventional calculation based on trade and industrial statistics'. Cripps said, 'I went to bed not expecting it to make any particular impact. When I woke up there was a newspaper headline saying "Minister of Lies". It was just bizarre, it was like living in another country. I never saw anything which took the figures I had presented in the press release and said what was wrong with them. The rebuttal took the form only of saying it was a lie – there was no analytical argument. I was really shocked by that.'[19]

Newspaper harassment reached a pitch at the time of the referendum campaign and was at its most malign in a story that one of the Benn children was in hospital. This had started in January 1975 with a reporter telling Caroline Benn that Joshua was in hospital after a car accident. He was upstairs at the time so she put it down to an honest case of mistaken identity. Journalists continued to call with the same story, and rang up Lady Stansgate and Hilary Benn's university tutor to report injuries to various Benn children. Then the story died, only to revive when the referendum campaign started. The *Daily Mail* began to pursue it again, although it had put a great deal of fruitless work into it in January and Tony Benn had telephoned to tell the editor it was false.

In May 1975 the Benn family and teachers at Holland Park School were repeatedly told by the *Mail* and other papers that various Benns, including Caroline, were injured or ill. Benn counted fourteen repetitions by the *Mail* alone by July 1975 and called the newspaper again to deny the story categorically.[20] The *Mail's* extraordinary persistence suggests that someone in a senior position on that newspaper had received a tip from a source whose tips had previously paid off. The newspapers, although hostile to Benn, were probably willing dupes of a manipulator rather than the prime movers. News management is the art of building up trust so as to profit the better by betraying it at a strategic point. The *Daily Mail* gained nothing and lost time and resources by sending reporters out after a story which could not stand up. The beneficiaries were elsewhere.

Another sign that the story was planted was that there was no interest in the health of the Benn children when they were genuinely ill. Hilary's hospitalisation with a serious sporting injury just prior to his wedding in 1973 and his wife Rosalind's fatal illness in 1978 and 1979 aroused no press interest at all.

Once the *Mail* had decided to go no further, the *Daily Telegraph* must have been fed with the story because it started checking it with the Radcliffe Infirmary in Oxford, where one of the Benn sons was said to be receiving private treatment. Other newspapers followed. The manipulators had more success with *The Times*, which ran the story unchecked on 2 August 1977. Tony Benn was alerted to it after the first edition came out and other newspapers began to ring to follow it up. After receiving Benn's call, the editor of *The Times* pulled the story from later editions and agreed to print a letter from Benn and an unreserved apology.

Someone had been waiting for the story to be printed, however, for postcards with a copy of the original (not photocopies) pasted on to them were posted to a variety of newspapers, magazines and individuals. They had all been through the same franking machine, which was traced to the office of the British European Movement, a body funded by the Common Market to promote a positive image for the EEC. The Movement's director denied the involvement of any of his staff but remarked that many voluntary workers also had access to the franking machine.[21] The fact that the story was still being planted after the Common Market referendum demonstrates that it was not just a dirty trick by the 'Yes' faction in the referendum campaign, but was an explicitly anti-Benn ploy operated by someone who was probably using the British European Movement as cover.

Most press attention had no such rounded conclusion – it was interminable. Joe Ashton said, 'He took a terrible, traumatic, personal bashing from the press at that time. They used to go through his dustbins every night, they used to come banging on the doors all night, they rented a flat opposite his house with a long-range camera, they followed his kids to school. He was beleaguered on all sides. You had to see it to believe it.'[22]

By polling day in the Referendum Tony Benn fully expected the defeat, though not the scale of it. Seventeen million voted to stay in, just over eight million to come out. He made a brief statement from his home on 6 June when the result was known: 'It is clear

369

that the British people have voted overwhelmingly for this country to remain in the EEC. All of us must accept that decision. I am very proud that the people had the right to vote in a referendum and will enter the community as free men and women and not as serfs taken in by their masters.'

Benn had lost, and was associated more than anyone else with that losing cause. The referendum had been his triumph of democracy but his advocacy of this unique solution to a national dilemma was lost in the arguments about the Market itself. It would have been in vain to have told Benn he should be a little more restrained on the Market issue and should reap the glory of the referendum without the opprobrium of defeat in the ballot. For Benn the path was either pursued with optimum enthusiasm or not at all.

The Common Market was the rock on which careers and parties foundered. Roy Jenkins had been deputy leader with a respectable majority over the left candidate. Had he stayed deputy leader he would have been the obvious choice for the top post when Wilson vacated it. But Jenkins threw away his chance of leading the Labour Party when he resigned over the shadow cabinet's endorsement of a referendum. His vote in the Parliamentary Labour Party leadership elections dropped from 140 in 1970 to 56 in 1976. In 1977 he went off to become President of the European Commission. When he had resigned over the referendum his acolytes had all stood around admiring his conscience as if it were a prize-winning bloom. They would have done better to examine his judgement. The principle of not giving the public a say in an issue was exactly the wrong thing to resign over. Its only effect was to damage him personally.

The referendum, as Harold Lever said, 'made it impossible to doubt that the majority of people wanted to be in Europe'.[23] This really should have been the end of the affair – Britain was in Europe for the foreseeable future and should make the best of it. The anti-Market cards had been played: they were a losing hand. Benn had no gift for accepting defeat, however, and was soon showing glimmerings of a desire to gather the smashed forces and fight again. Several weeks after the vote he told David Butler that he was encouraged that with only a dozen or so people really campaigning on the 'No' side, they still managed 8.4 million votes and that despite the support of all the press and broadcasting and the leaders of three main parties the 'Yes' side persuaded only 40 per cent of the electorate to register a positive vote in their favour.[24]

In retrospect, the saddest thing about the campaign was that it was so alien to Benn's nature to argue for a negative. He was a prophet of hope, of the future, of advance. Arguing for a retreat from one path, which he had previously advocated, in order to follow another was not the obvious message of a bringer of good tidings.

On 9 June Benn answered questions in the House. By chance, it was the first day Commons business was broadcast by radio. The public therefore heard Benn the statesman for the first time, not the wild-eyed orator of the news pages or the uniformed commissar of the cartoons. Even his enemies were impressed. 'Big Benn is the star of the air!' ran the headline on the *Sun*'s front-page story; 'Benn a hit in radio Commons' said the *Daily Telegraph*.[25]

But even as he left the chamber his fate was sealed. In the tea room he was asked to go in to see the Prime Minister at six o'clock in the Cabinet Room at 10 Downing Street. Wilson went straight to the point: he wanted to move Benn to the Department of Energy. He gave a run-down of the department. It was responsible for North Sea oil, soon to be on tap; for the miners, with whom Benn had a good rapport; for the nuclear industry, about which Benn knew a great deal. He gave him two hours to think about it; Benn asked for a longer period, so that he would have time to speak to Caroline. Wilson gave him until ten.[26]

Benn's first call was to his private secretary Roy Williams. 'Clear up the office,' he said, 'remove my banner, take everything out, as if I had never been there.' He then called the family. Hilary and Stephen agreed to come to the House and Melissa went to fetch Caroline from Holland Park School, where she was chairing a governors' meeting. Such was the nature of the times that Caroline's first thought was that her husband had been assassinated.

Benn summoned his supporters to his room and they began a long meeting in the stifling heat of the summer evening. Others came uninvited, so they could later say they had shown their face at the scene of lamentations. The line-up changed as people went on to other engagements but at some time that evening there were Caroline and the two eldest sons; Michael Foot; Barbara Castle and

371

her husband Ted; Judith Hart and her political adviser Tony Banks; Michael Meacher, a junior minister at the Department of Industry; Joe Ashton; Ian Mikardo, who was on the Industry Bill committee and was a link with the Tribune Group; Ron Hayward, general secretary of the Labour Party; and Benn's political adviser Frances Morrell.

When Barbara Castle arrived she found Benn sitting at his desk, 'a figure of tragedy, surrounded by a cortège of political advisers' and other figures she could not make out because the curtains were drawn against the sun. Castle was clearly relieved she was not for the chop herself and her communications with Benn were limited to consoling him, since she assumed he would accept the demotion.[27] Benn suspected her motives. Foot's primary contribution was acting as a go-between with Wilson to have the time limit extended.

Mikardo left early, finding the whole thing a shambles. He thought there were too many people and that the involvement of Stephen and Hilary was not helpful. Benn's motive in inviting them was probably that he did not want them to feel excluded from the major decisions, as he had been as a teenager. In fact, he was not well advised to mix family and MPs in this matter. Hard decisions such as this might well call for his colleagues to say things to Benn which could not be easily said in front of his sons.

There were only three choices: Benn could resign and mobilise support for the left outside the cabinet, which was Joe Ashton's advice. He could stay on and do his best in his new job, which was Frances Morrell's advice. Or he could rely on the strength of solidarity among the left wing inside Parliament and in the trade union movement to force Wilson to reinstate him, which was what Ian Mikardo wished to see happen.

Ron Hayward thought if he resigned it would be 'a two-day wonder and it would be forgotten the day after'. But Ashton argued, 'If you resign now, you will become the leader of the rest of the party in opposition to what Wilson is doing. If we lose the next election in 1979 you will walk it as leader of the Labour Party.'[28]

Benn was not a natural resigner. He had also worked out after the 1960 débâcle, when he had resigned from the NEC with no benefit to his cause but with a cost to himself, the terms under which he could resign. He said, 'I came to the conclusion that resignation was only justifiable if you found that the party of which you were a member was no longer the lesser of two evils. I argued it through that, if you resigned from the cabinet and there was a vote of confidence in the government from which you'd just resigned, you'd have to vote for the vote of confidence. If you didn't vote for the vote of confidence and there was a general election then you clearly would have to consider whether you could stand as a Labour candidate to re-elect the cabinet from which you had just resigned.'[29] Looked at in these terms, resignation was an impossibility in virtually every circumstance.

Benn was not known for his reticence, and Wilson would certainly have heard this line of reasoning, either from Benn himself or from someone who had heard it from him. It was held against him by some that he had not been prepared to resign long before. Eric Heffer, a veteran of many resignation threats, said, 'One of the problems was that Tony himself had never really, at any time, been prepared to make a stand and actually resign. Instead, when Wilson pushed him, he had written letters which gave way.'[30]

With hindsight Joe Ashton was even more convinced that the best policy for Benn would have been to resign. He said, 'It was a major mistake in his career not to resign because the right wing stuck it on him. Whenever he criticised the Labour government they said, "Why didn't you quit?" Whenever he said anything about nuclear energy they said "Well, you were the Secretary of State for Energy." '[31]

The main reason for holding the meeting in his room was to give the left a chance to demonstrate their support, which might have been used to considerable effect. As Ian Mikardo said, 'Wilson could not have stood up to it if the left in the cabinet had said, "If you emasculate the Industry Bill and if you move Tony and sack Judith Hart then we will all walk out." It would have been a mortal blow to Wilson – he could not have survived it.'[32]

The Judith Hart story was a genuine, though rather farcical, demonstration of this. She had been Minister for Overseas Development, the top position outside the cabinet. Wilson wished to demote Reg Prentice, the right-winger, from the cabinet in order to make his usual play of being even-handed. Roy Jenkins had gone to the Prime Minister and threatened resignation if Prentice were sacked from the cabinet. Wilson did a certain amount of juggling, which it would be tedious to recount, and ultimately Prentice was kept in the cabinet, appointed to Judith Hart's job as Minister for Overseas Development, which was made a cabinet post just for him.

Hart was offered a demotion, the Ministry of Transport, out of the cabinet. Benn, Castle and Foot rallied round, going to see Wilson late on 10 June, asking him to put Transport in the cabinet. They were all surprised when, the next day, before Wilson's reply to their entreaties, Judith Hart announced her 'resignation' from the government in the House of Commons.

So why wouldn't the left do this for Benn? This question is the central conundrum of Benn's political career: why could he stimulate devotion bordering on adoration from members of the public, yet fail to command sufficient respect among his closest colleagues to save his job? Their lack of solidarity was the more remarkable because Wilson might have been picking them off one by one – Castle herself felt in danger of the call to Number 10 for an abrupt word with the Prime Minister.

In the event, when she was called, she was relieved on arrival to find that it was to consult her about a reshuffle of her junior ministers. She told the Prime Minister, 'I must say your move for Wedgie was brilliantly cunning. . . . I told Wedgie he ought to accept,' for which Wilson told her she was a good girl.[33]

Some would say the comparison with Hart is unrealistic. Senior colleagues would be prepared to support a junior because, according to Michael Meacher, 'Judith Hart was not seen in the same light, she was not as senior, and Tony was more of a rival, and even a threat. The relations between the senior cabinet members, though ideologically friendly, were in personal terms based on rivalry and other considerations.'[34]

Michael Foot's comments on Benn bear out this interpretation. In the harshest passage of his bitter list of recriminations against Benn in *Loyalists and Loners*, Michael Foot writes,

> He did believe in open government; no doubt whatever, and he could conceivably claim that he had believed in it longer than anyone else. But he did also once believe in collective responsibility, particularly for the Cabinet. . . . But gradually his belief frayed; gradually his other loyalties

elbowed out this allegiance; gradually, from the point of view of his Cabinet colleagues, or even his smaller group of associates, he became – literally, it is hard to avoid the term – not to be trusted. This was the practical conclusion to which many who worked with him were forced.

Indeed there are no friends at the top.[35]

The solidarity of the trade unions, which Benn had assiduously cultivated, might well have been called into play. Jack Jones had appeared on television three days earlier to say that if Tony Benn were sacked from the cabinet it would be a grave affront to the trade union movement. But the first Jack Jones heard of the whole affair was the news that Tony Benn had accepted Energy. 'Nobody ever contacted us,' said Jones, 'and although I was concerned that he had been moved from Industry, I was relieved that he was still in the cabinet, and Energy was a very important post. We wanted him in. We did regard him as a friend of the trade union movement in the cabinet, and there were people in the cabinet who weren't very friendly to us.'[36] Wilson had also been clever in his choice of a replacement. Eric Varley, who had been offered Benn's job, was the current Secretary of State for Energy. He was a former miner who was MP for the mining town of Chesterfield. He was trusted by the trade union lobby, whose members might well have considered that he would be able to deliver industrial policy where the more controversial Benn could not.

Benn spoke to Varley during a division that evening. Varley was close to Wilson and he gave one explanation for the decision to move Benn: 'I think Harold entered into some commitments with the City or somebody, and he has to get rid of you.' Varley assured him he would not take Industry unless Benn took Energy. Benn encouraged him to take the job, clearly feeling by now that there was no option of staying on in his old post and that his current choice was whether to resign or to accept Energy. By the time he had returned home to dictate his diary, Benn's mind was made up: 'There is no principle in resigning over being given a different cabinet job.'

Joe Haines, Wilson's press secretary, wrote that Benn and Heffer (who had been sacked by Wilson in April over the Common Market) 'were scaring the wits out of some highly vocal sections of the City and of industry. . . . Only if Tony Benn was sacked, it was said, would the confidence of British industry be restored.'[37]

The next day the second eleven did go on strike in his support. It was one of the final committees on the Industry Bill. The Labour members said they would not proceed if Benn were sacked, but he gave them no encouragement. The battle was already lost. When he finally went in to see Wilson it was twenty-four hours after he had first been told he must move, most of which time had been spent in meetings. Wilson would amuse his friends by recounting how Benn gave him a lengthy lecture about the history of the Labour Party, particularly the betrayal by Ramsay MacDonald. He called up the spectre of his father and described his position in 1931 when Labour was hostage to the City and the international monetary organisations, just as the government was once again in 1975. During all of this the Prime Minister still did not know whether Benn was going to take the job or whether he would need another reshuffle. Wilson was still in the dark when they said goodbye, so he had to ask, 'Well, are you going to accept Energy?'

'Yes, of course,' said Benn.[38]

The press now swooped in for the kill. Outside the Benn house the next morning was a solid body of reporters, photographers, radio journalists and television crews. They surged forward and shouted questions as the door opened to let Melissa and Joshua out to go to school. The two Benn children ignored the press and some reporters shouted at them, 'You fucking well answer my questions,' 'You push off, you little shit.' They were followed down the road.[39] If Benn were to go out and remonstrate, it would be an ideal opportunity for them to take pictures making him look disturbed. The creation of a 'picture opportunity' of this nature was perhaps the point of harassing two teenagers on their way to school. Tony Benn had never considered that a life in politics would mean he would have to stand and watch the press abusing his children.

Tony Benn himself, for all his experience, was nervous when he left for the House of Commons much later that morning. It was a hot day and he went out in shirtsleeves with his jacket slung over his shoulder. He walked slowly down the drive, the cameras all on him and the microphones pointing. The journalists shouted questions and he ignored them. 'I just walked through them as if they weren't there,' he later wrote in his diary, 'and that made them wild. They had dehumanised me in the press, now I was dehumanising them by not acknowledging their existence.'

29

Secretary of State for Energy

Benn settled down at the Department of Energy, in his office at Thames House South, relieved to be free from the burden of press criticism. There was rather less about the job which was liable to arouse controversy than at Industry. In the opinion of Frances Morrell, who went with Benn to Energy, Wilson assumed, mistakenly, that all the important decisions had already been taken at Energy and that Benn was being consigned to a political limbo.

The feud did not cease – Wilson appeared to be on the look-out for other quarrels with Benn, even when the announcement of his resignation as Prime Minister was only weeks away. When the press reported in February 1976 that the NEC's Home Policy Committee, which Benn chaired, was looking into the honours system, Wilson demanded Benn's 'immediate assurance that you do not intend to proceed in this way'.[1] Benn coldly assured him that the press reports were wrong and he had merely referred the committee to his 1964 paper on honours, which was still available to them should they be interested. It was probably a sensitive issue with Wilson because he was working on his own resignation honours list in which his dubious selection of favourites damaged the honours system more than Benn ever could have.

One of Wilson's last acts before his resignation was to sack Joe Ashton as Benn's parliamentary private secretary because Ashton had voted with the Tribune Group against a spending-cuts package in March 1976. The announcement of Wilson's resignation was a surprise to almost everybody, though Benn had an inkling of it because he had been speaking to his driver, who had remarked some time before that Wilson had decided to provide cars for all ex-Prime Ministers, even for Anthony Eden, who did not want one. The opinion of the drivers' pool was that Wilson was soon to become an ex-Prime Minister himself. But there was no mystery about Wilson's resignation – it was typical of the man. He had no intention of losing an election or of being pushed out of the premiership; he wanted to resign while he was on top. He told Benn in 1970, after the election which everyone had thought Labour would win, that had he remained Prime Minister he would have stayed only three years.[2]

This turn of events made it more difficult for Benn to become leader. Had Wilson stayed on and then retired after losing the election, Benn would have had a far better chance of leadership with an older and more battle-weary Callaghan in no position to take up the baton. Healey, of course, would have been available, but the party traditionally moves left in opposition.

On the day of Wilson's resignation Benn decided to stand for the leadership, urged on by his family and by Joe Ashton, who became his campaign manager. Benn published a manifesto and sent out letters to the electorate of Labour MPs, urging that the election should be a time for discussing European policy, industrial democracy and open government. Individual MPs were also invited into Tony Benn's room to talk with him and Ashton about their problems and let them meet the candidate. It was the first election campaign in the PLP.

In the first ballot Foot came first with 90 votes followed by Callaghan with 84, then Jenkins with 56, Benn with 37, Healey with 30 and Crosland with 17. Benn immediately withdrew in favour of Michael Foot. He had done better than everyone had expected and it was particularly gratifying to have beaten the right-wingers Healey and Crosland and to have come close to Jenkins, who had for years enjoyed an adulatory press while Benn had been excoriated.

Benn had known he was not going to win, but he had acted with far more confidence than he had at the deputy-leadership contest five years before, even though in the event he received nine fewer votes than he had on that occasion. It was the old problem which had let him down, the fact that he was not favoured by backbenchers despite his parliamentary gifts and his standing in the party. Joe Ashton explained, 'He'd done a big U-turn in 1972 from

379

being the right-wing, establishment, up-and-coming MP into being a left-winger in about four or five years. They didn't quite trust him. The conversion time hadn't been long enough for some people. Old timers on the left thought he was too much of a careerist. Some back-benchers had very small majorities, and if it looked as if their seats were going to be in jeopardy, if you were rocking the boat or splitting the party, they didn't want to know. . . . That was when Tony began to think we'd got to have a better way of picking the leader or it would always be a play-safe right-wing leader of the PLP.'[3] Some thought Benn's chances were good; the bookmakers Ladbrokes gave odds of 3–1 on his becoming Prime Minister before 1985.

Benn got on better with Callaghan than he had with Wilson. Callaghan promptly sacked Barbara Castle, settling their old score over *In Place of Strife*, but apart from this he did not launch an attack on the left. He permitted Benn to reappoint Joe Ashton as his PPS but left him at Energy, even though Benn asked to be moved. Benn wanted to be Leader of the House, but that job had already been promised to Michael Foot. He would have taken Employment but that too had gone. Benn suspected a deal: Foot had demanded that Roy Jenkins be kept out of the Foreign Office and Callaghan had insisted that Benn be kept out of trouble. Foot had forged an alliance with Callaghan which was to last until after the general election.

Both Foot and Callaghan told Benn they believed he would go on to lead the party, Foot even making his declaration public. At a miners' gala at which Wilson and Callaghan were present he announced that they had on the platform 'Prime Ministers past, present and' – indicating Benn – 'future'.[4] Callaghan was less jocular, 'I can see you as leader of the Labour Party in opposition,' he said, 'and ten years in opposition you will be.'[5]

Despite his disagreements with other senior members of the government, Benn was becoming less confrontational. He had 'found a new way of dealing with the problems that face me as a member of the cabinet. So long as I don't criticise the cabinet or government policy I am free to argue the socialist case.' It was a discovery his colleagues would have liked to have seen him make rather earlier.[6]

Benn now had more time to develop his ideas of what a British socialist tradition was. He emphatically repudiated the right-wing accusation that it was a foreign political philosophy transplanted to Britain. He said, 'If you read what was said by the Levellers and Diggers in the seventeenth century you will find that the ideas of socialism in Britain anticipated by two centuries or more many of the things Marx said.'[7] He spoke at Burford Church where the Levellers were imprisoned after they were defeated by Cromwell's forces in 1649 following their refusal to go to fight in Ireland. Three were executed and Benn was asked to give their memorial address.

He remarked that their ideas had shown greater durability than the institutional changes Cromwell carried through. 'And so it will always be. For politics is really about education, and not about propaganda. It is about teaching more than management. It is about ideas and values and not only about Acts of Parliament, political institutions, and ministerial office.'[8]

It gave Benn much pleasure that the old master Fenner Brockway asked him to write a preface for his book *The First British Socialists*, which had been inspired by Benn's own comments on the Levellers.[9]

He had such success in proselytising the religious traditions of socialism that he was now frequently asked to address Christian audiences and even to preach sermons on subjects such as 'The Morality of Socialism'. 'The traditions of the Labour movement in this country begin with the Bible,' he would explain.[10] It was a milieu in which he felt perfectly at home. 'In our family religion and politics have always been the same thing really,' he said.[11]

His purely political thought is rather more difficult to quantify. If there was a historic role for the working class in Benn's thinking, it was not easily apparent from his speeches, nor was a reliance on the labour theory of value except in the most oblique ways. In middle age it was still true that the strongest influence on his political thought was not Marx or any other textbook socialists, but his father. The living person with the most influence on his political thinking was Caroline Benn and she decided he had better know some Marxist theory. Consequently he received a copy of the *Communist Manifesto* in his stocking at Christmas 1976. He read it on Boxing Day, realising how much he had in common with the Marxist analysis of the structure of society. He was also moved to

381

analyse his own development, concluding that up to 1968 he had been 'just a career politician' and had then started thinking of participation in society, an ideal which was not particularly socialist: his Fabian paper *A Socialist Reconnaissance* was 'almost anti-socialist, almost corporatist in character with a democratic theme – management and labour working together'. Up to the next period of government he moved to the left, then at the Department of Industry he 'learned it all again by struggle. . . . I have been driven further and further towards a real socialist position.'[12]

Even when he was not being criticised, there was a continuing media fascination with Benn. What was he going to do next? What really motivated him? Why was it, an interviewer once asked him, that in real life he was so witty, such good company, while when being interviewed on radio or TV he appeared earnest, waspish, abrasive? 'It's very difficult,' Benn replied, 'if you're put under heavy pressure, not to become a bit intense. It would be very nice to look all the time as if you hadn't a worry in the world but if you're fighting your corner, particularly on behalf of other people, where you have a sense of responsibility for them, you do get a bit tense.'[13]

When people saw the titan of the political stage they were often bemused, 'He looks a surprisingly frail figure beneath the TV arc lights,' one commentator said, 'in his crumpled, dark-grey lightweight suit, elegant dark-blue button-down shirt and distinctly ropey, much worn Labour Party tie.'[14] His eyes, with their 'look of perpetual surprise', were frequently referred to as hypnotic and were caricatured in cartoons. 'What does it feel like to *be* Tony Benn?' asked James Fenton.

'What's it like to wake every morning inside Tony Benn, to shave Tony Benn's chin, to eat Tony Benn's breakfast, to kiss Tony Benn's wife, to go to work in Tony Benn's car, to sit in Tony Benn's office twiddling Tony Benn's thumbs, to consult the charts on Tony Benn's walls, to be blamed for Tony Benn's errors of judgement, to be praised by Paul Johnson for Tony Benn's good qualities, to argue Tony Benn's case in cabinet and quite another case outside, to consult with Tony Benn's conscience about whether to resign – and to do all this not once or twice, but *all the time*, without ever letting up?'[15]

Benn's tea-drinking habits were a frequent source of entertainment. It was a jibe at his teetotalism and what were seen as his working-class pretensions that a nightclub called Wedgie's was opened in the King's Road in 1977. Appropriately enough, it failed to obtain a liquor licence in time for its opening.

The pound was worth more than two American dollars at the beginning of March 1976. It was over-valued and required the usual remedy of devaluation. Rather than devalue explicitly, a decision was made to let the pound find its own level: it would be allowed by the Bank of England to fall. Unfortunately, by chance, some major sales of the pound were made just as the Bank was selling pounds to adjust the value of the currency downwards. The effect of the two nudges downwards was to accelerate the fall and panic the money markets into selling fast. The gentle drift down of the pound was turned into a free fall.

World bankers were angry about the destabilising effect the clumsily manipulated fall of the pound would have on the other world currencies. They were also alarmed by the spending levels of what they saw as a profligate socialist government. Through the spring and summer of 1976, loans, interest rates, taxes and spending projections were manipulated. The pound sank further, to reach $1.55 by 25 October. The Labour Party's conference decision to nationalise the banks was not considered tactful.

Finally the proposal was stark: the nation needed a loan from the International Monetary Fund and would have to subject its spending programme to IMF scrutiny. That meant spending cuts. Knowing how unacceptable this would be, Callaghan gave his colleagues a choice: accept this path or come up with a better plan and convince your cabinet colleagues of it.

In a series of nine long meetings Callaghan skilfully guided the cabinet through the alternatives, basically divided between Benn proposing an 'alternative economic strategy', Healey proposing the IMF loan and cuts, and Crosland arguing that they should hold their course, correctly judging that the situation would stabilise itself.

Callaghan called on Benn to present his paper first. Benn had already helpfully circulated the minutes of the 1931 cabinet so his colleagues were aware of the historical parallels. He proposed selective import controls, guided industrial investment and compulsory planning agreements with industry: a reinvestment programme which could be presented to the IMF as an alternative to cuts to negotiate a loan from a position of confidence. This was always criticised as a 'siege economy'. Benn's reply was: 'We haven't an alternative to a siege economy. The difference between my siege economy and yours is that in my siege economy we'll have our allies with us, against the bankers. In your siege economy we'll have the bankers with us, and our supporters outside.'[16]

In the end Crosland was persuaded to support £2 billion worth of cuts, less than had been originally proposed, and Healey secured a reluctant majority for his IMF package.

Benn was convinced the Treasury had its own agenda and had already been converted to monetarism. He later said, 'The Treasury wanted to persuade the cabinet that we were bust, bankrupt, finished, in order to force their policies on us. I said the oil is beginning to bubble ashore, we don't have to capitulate. If we hadn't capitulated in 1976 we would have won the 1979 election and we would have had a Labour government using the oil for industrial renewal in the 1980s.'[17]

Whether wilfully or not, the Treasury had misled the Chancellor: the whole business was unnecessary. As Denis Healey wrote, 'The Treasury had grossly overestimated the Public Sector Borrowing Requirement, which would have fallen within the IMF's limit without any of the measures they prescribed. Later figures showed that we also managed to eliminate our current account deficit in 1977, before the IMF package had time to influence it.'[18] He drew on only half the IMF loan offered and had paid it back before he left office, but the Labour Party considered that their leaders had sold out a social programme to the demands of international capital.

Characteristically, Benn made the best of his new job. His first innovation was an experiment in open government, the creation of the Energy Commission. This was a body which met regularly and whose papers were published. The participants were the energy chiefs, large users like British Rail, environment analysts and ministers. 'We turned it into an energy parliament,' said Benn.

The chairman of the British National Oil Corporation was Lord

Kearton, a man well known to Benn from Mintech days when in an earlier incarnation as Sir Frank Kearton he had been head of the Industrial Reorganisation Corporation. The objective of BNOC, Kearton said, was 'To bring the oil companies to heel. They were treating us like an offshore Arab oil state.'[19] The British government wanted to license the right to search for oil, drill for it and bring it ashore. BNOC sought participation agreements with all the oil companies. Kearton said, 'Whenever we had a sticky one, half a dozen in about eighty complicated agreements, we brought Benn in and he solved it. He was marvellous. He was patient, persistent and logical. I never knew him to be unclear or discourteous, or to lose his temper.'[20]

Benn's achievement, via Kearton and BNOC, was to have a quarter of North Sea oil belonging to Britain within five years. The achievement should not be underestimated; as British manufacturing industry continued its decline, oil was the only large-scale economic development in the country. If it weren't for North Sea Oil, Benn observed in 1978, Britain would be £5 billion a year in deficit.[21]

The rows about the choice of the next nuclear reactor showed Benn at his best. Frances Morrell remarked on his 'great strength, strategic judgement and ability to stand up to powerful interests'.[22] He had the advantage that he had already dealt with the nuclear industry in the 1960s at Mintech, though he said he had never known such a well-organised lobby as that devoted to promoting nuclear power.

He submitted a paper to a cabinet committee called, 'Nuclear power – The case for a pause' in May 1977. He suggested talks with the US on reprocessing, waste management, fast-breeder reactors, fusion, nuclear accountability and uranium demand and supply. He mentioned 'growing uncertainties about the economics of nuclear power as compared to other energy sources. For example, studies in my Department now suggest that it is by no means certain that thermal reactors will be cheaper than coal-fired stations in the UK.' Additionally he noted 'a growing interest in the potential of alternative benign and renewable resources of energy as a serious option for consideration.'[23]

The major decision on reactor types had been taken by Frank Cousins, Benn's predecessor at Mintech. He had decided to go for the Advanced Gas-Cooled Reactor (AGR) despite the objections from his department, who had wanted a Pressurised Water Reactor (PWR). A principal concern of Cousins had been that the AGR was British technology while the PWR was American. The first AGR, Dungeness B in Kent, was started in 1965 and was intended to be operational in 1970. It was still being built when Benn visited it in 1978. Walking round the site made him reflect, 'I have to be very careful not to go ahead with more nuclear power stations than are absolutely necessary.'[24]

In 1973 the oil-price increase, imposed by the Arab states as a punishment for Western support for Israel in the Yom Kippur war, made the Central Electricity Generating Board feel they must replace oil-generated with nuclear-generated electricity. The department were still devoted to the idea of PWRs, and when Benn assumed responsibility they were asking to build twenty-two within ten years.

Benn later cut it down to two generators and stuck with AGRs for a variety of reasons. There were safety problems with PWRs; there was little experience of the large models which would be required for Britain; and Benn was suspicious of the reliance on American nuclear technology and the tie-in with the US nuclear industry which PWR development would entail.

Furthermore, Benn was appalled at the prospect of adding another type of power station to Britain's current array. Indeed, he endorsed the running down of one system, the Steam-Generating Heavy Water Reactor at Winfrith, which was allowed to continue production on a small scale but did not form the prototype for new stations. This left the Magnox stations, like Calder Hall at Windscale; the Advanced Gas-Cooled Reactors, two of which were already working well despite the problems over the construction of Dungeness B; and the fast breeder reactor, at Dounreay in Scotland. 'We were a small country. To add a fifth system seemed absolutely absurd,' Benn later said.[25] 'I have no doubt that what I did was right, even though we should never have gone even for the AGRs.'

A focus of particular concern was the fast breeder reactor, which 'bred' its own fuel by producing plutonium from uranium in the reaction, and which by the late 1970s was ready to go commercial. Benn decided there should be no commercially developed fast-breeder reactor until there had been public consultation on the matter. He was by now opposed to a further extension of nuclear power, and was unwilling to be seen as the Secretary of State who authorised the fast breeder. Concern centred on the tie-in of the newly 'bred' nuclear material in weapons production and the safety of the plant in general. In a conventional reactor only 2–3 per cent of fuel takes part in the reaction. In a fast breeder a quarter of the fuel is involved in the reaction so the chances for a disaster are vastly increased.

Benn had also become suspicious of the nuclear lobby and of the departmental officials who worked closely with them. He had been politically damaged and had been drawn into a net of deception himself in the Rossing affair. This was an example of how decisions made for speed or expediency in a previous government could come back to haunt him. The giant Rossing uranium mine was in Namibia, a territory illegally held by South Africa. Benn as Minister of Technology had agreed in 1970 that the UK Atomic Energy Authority could receive uranium from the British-owned mining company Rio Tinto-Zinc. Soon after the election the story began to leak out that the deal had been done for the Rossing mine, and that it involved the South African Atomic Energy Board, the UK Atomic Energy Authority and Rio Tinto-Zinc.

The AEA had been especially keen to get the deal through fast and quietly because there had been an election in the offing; possibly it had also been influenced by the imminence of a UN Security Council request to member states to refrain from dealings with South Africa which would recognise its authority to administer Namibia.

The question for critics of Benn was whether he knew where the uranium was coming from. The original agreement was for uranium from Canada via a Rio Tinto-Zinc subsidiary called Rio Algom. A cabinet agreement was made in 1968 for the purchase of the uranium, the contract to be negotiated by the AEA and finally authorised by the Minister of Technology.

When the papers came to the cabinet's Overseas Policy and Defence Committee, however, it was obvious that the uranium was to come from the Rossing mine, via another Rio Tinto-Zinc subsidiary called Rio Finex. There was some suggestion that the AEA had not kept the cabinet fully informed.[26] Benn asked the

Attorney General to look at the contract, which had already been signed by the AEA. He was advised by the AEA that it would cost £6 million to cancel it. 'I took it to the cabinet,' Benn later said, 'and I recommended that we had no alternative but to go ahead. What I didn't realise at the time was that, I think, the reason they shifted from Canada to South Africa was that Canada had an "end-use control" and it couldn't have been used for nuclear weapons. South Africa had no end-use control.'[27]

In opposition between 1970 and 1974 he arranged for a pledge to be inserted in *Labour Programme '73* to have the contract cancelled. It did not find its way into the manifesto, however, and the Foreign Office, paying more than usual attention to Labour Party documents, noticed this omission and declined to cancel it.

In 1975 Benn received a message, as Energy Minister, that more uranium was required from Rossing. He took it to cabinet in 1976, recommending that they cancel the contract and find the uranium elsewhere. He said years later, 'That was one of the nastiest meetings I had ever experienced. I was defeated and the contract went ahead. It is one of the things I look back on with shame because if I had been more alert or more courageous I would have recommended that we cancel in 1970.'[28]

Benn always had great affection for the miners. He somewhat idolised the working miner for his sense of community and dependence on his workmates, saying, 'Miners have to depend on the person next to them in case there is a flood or gas or roof collapse, and it breeds a formidable loyalty.'[29] He attempted to give the National Union of Miners a veto on pit closures. This was turned down by the union, which feared that it would be blamed for closures that were necessary.

Bruce Williams, now a professor working in Australia, would visit Benn on trips back to Britain. 'There was more to his job than coal mines, but you wouldn't have thought it to look at his office,' he said. 'He had gone native. His office was filled with miners' lamps and trade union banners.'[30] Lord Kearton considered Benn's respect for the working class was something of a character defect. He said, 'He was too idealistic where the unions were concerned. His Achilles' heel was that he thought anyone who was a union shop steward was a good man. Some would take advantage.'[31] Joe Ashton put the point differently: 'I had to turn round and tell him there were as many bastards in the working class as there were in the middle class.'[32]

He did not find the organised middle class, the civil service, so thrilling to deal with. Bruce Williams said, 'At Energy he kept complaining of being failed by the civil servants. It didn't occur to Tony that this was due to Harold Wilson. Tony's judgement had been questioned by him and by his cabinet colleagues and the civil servants were reflecting this.'[33] The mere impertinence of civil servants could be extremely crude. Benn had issued a statement virtually forbidding disconnections of the elderly for fuel debts during the winter. He was angry to find that the statement had been circulated with significant deletions. He ordered his officials to circulate the original text. 'Are you sure your colleagues will agree?' said a twenty-five-year-old civil servant to his Secretary of State.[34]

David Owen, hardly a Benn supporter, recalled, 'The civil service, sensing this disagreement among ministers, and the fact that Tony Benn was really an outsider in the cabinet, did tend to conspire against him, and you would find, in briefing notes for a cabinet meeting, "Mr Benn is expected to say the following, and you should argue against it . . .".'[35]

In February 1977 Benn's old friend Crosland died after a stroke. In political terms this meant that the right wing had lost its best intellectual. His memorial service featured quotations from his book *The Future of Socialism*, including his dismissal of 'total abstinence and a good filing system' as 'signposts to the socialist utopia', a jocular criticism of Benn from their Oxford days. Crosland was too clever and not nice enough – the mirror image of Benn.

The coalition of which Benn had warned now came upon them, hastened by the loss of the government's majority through by-election losses; two defections to Scottish Nationalism; and the unreliability of John Stonehouse. James Callaghan did a deal with David Steel, leader of the thirteen-strong Liberal group. The Liberals would support the government in return for consultation over legislation.

Benn was bitterly unhappy. To him the heart of the Labour movement was being betrayed. He discussed resignation with several people including Lady Stansgate but heeded her advice to stay put. Not only did he decide not to resign, but on Callaghan's threat to dismiss him, he withdrew support from a petition about the issue which was being taken round by Eric Heffer. Paul Johnson publicly called on Benn, as 'by far the ablest and most valuable politician in the Labour Party', to resign from 'the hideous shambles of the Callaghan government'.[36]

The crisis of government was keenly felt in the constituencies. From July 1976 to May 1977 in Bristol South-East there were five special GC meetings, in addition to the usual cycle, to discuss aspects of the political situation, and advise Benn. They were not poorly attended, one in March 1977 to discuss the Lib–Lab pact had fifty members present when regular GC meetings in the early 1970s often had less than twenty.[37] For whatever reason, Benn always had the support of his constituency members, who called on him to stay in the cabinet, as they would rather have him fighting from a position of power than outside crying in the wilderness.

Callaghan felt the opposite – he would rather have Benn under control in the cabinet than outside gathering power. Callaghan therefore frequently resisted the temptation to sack him. These urges would overtake the Prime Minister so often it was difficult to take them seriously. At one National Executive meeting, red-faced and isolated, Callaghan threatened to sack Benn if he appeared at a press conference to announce the newly decided manifesto for direct elections to the European Parliament.[38]

But Callaghan's method had its successes. At the 1977 conference, where the Lib–Lab pact might have been expected to be bitterly savaged, Benn made a speech supportive of the government. It was 'A real leadership speech' according to Callaghan, a plaudit which cheered Benn as much as did the Liberals coming up to ask for his autograph.[39] The Benn family were shocked: Caroline, Stephen and Hilary registered their disappointment; Caroline 'thought that I made a ghastly error, just failed to press the right button, missed a supreme chance. The conference was longing for something different and why shouldn't I give it to them?'[40]

At this conference Benn again came top of the poll for the constituency section election to the NEC, a position he held for a decade from 1974. He continued to use his power base on the

National Executive to challenge the government. In particular he could not leave Europe alone. June 1977 found him announcing that it was time for a debate about what the Market had meant to Britain, adding that Britain had 'a clear constitutional right to leave the EEC if parliament and public so decide'.[41]

He opposed the Bill to set up direct elections to the European Parliament on the grounds that 'When you establish a democratic structure in Europe – or semi-democratic – then you are setting up a double legitimacy, of the European and the British Parliaments. It would undermine the legitimacy of Parliament and was a major move towards a federal Europe.'[42] He was not alone in being concerned: the Bill was passed on massive Conservative support, only 127 Labour MPs voting in favour of it, with 124 against. There was little passion for the subject, however, and Labour's negative attitude was not attractive to the voters. In the 1979 direct elections, the Conservatives won sixty seats and Labour seventeen.

As a minister Benn had to deal with the Common Market, including a stint as President of the Energy Council of Ministers, but he was never happy in Brussels. 'I loathe the Common Market,' he wrote after one trip, 'It's bureaucratic, centralised, there is no political talk and officials control the ministers.'[43] He made his attempts at open government in Brussels, but the whole atmosphere was against it. When he was President he proposed having the meetings of the Energy Council open to the public, but every other minister found a reason why it should not be done.

Any Prime Minister would have found Benn a somewhat trying colleague even without his latest campaign: a direct attack on the patronage of Prime Ministers. With his characteristic love of statistics Benn worked out that 286,958 electors of Bristol South-East had given him his years in Parliament, yet for his job as a minister the electorate was one man – the Prime Minister. Taking Wilson as an example, he compiled the figures for his eight years as Prime Minister. 'He appointed or reshuffled 100 cabinet ministers, 403 ministers of state and junior ministers. He appointed 243 peers.' On and on the canticle of patronage went: chairmen of nationalised industries and royal commissions, bishops, judges and members of public bodies. 'And for none of these purposes was the House of

Commons or the electorate required to be consulted. No medieval Parliament would have given so much power to a medieval king.'[44]

One of Benn's brushes with patronage was over his parliamentary private secretary. The PPS is an unpaid, personal appointment by a particular minister but requires the approval of the Prime Minister. When Joe Ashton was given a post as assistant Whip he ceased to be Benn's PPS, so Benn wished to appoint Brian Sedgemore, a former civil servant and barrister. Callaghan did not like Sedgemore and refused, then relented and permitted Benn to appoint him, only to sack him in 1978 over the leaking of some Treasury documents to a House of Commons committee, an event which had nothing to do with Benn. Benn was advised after the event about the dismissal of his PPS and decided against having another one.

Benn maintained his position as one of the few politicians who were listening to what the most radical vanguard of society was saying. He gave active support to feminist campaigners defending the reformed abortion law which was threatened during the 1970s by Bills brought by various back-benchers. He also enjoyed a steady influx of feminist ideas at home. In a humorous parody Melissa (then studying for her finals at the London School of Economics) put up posters in support of the cause. She stood in the hallway in Holland Park Avenue and handed out leaflets saying 'End sexism in the Benn household'. The campaign called for a more equal distribution of domestic chores, since Caroline Benn bore almost all the burden of running the household. Tony Benn immediately rushed upstairs to prepare a counter-leaflet which he handed out. It criticised theoretical feminists who were engaged in debate while the hard work was being done by other women. They filmed the campaign on a home-movie camera. 'I used the language which would get me heard,' Melissa Benn said. 'It was a parody but the point was there.'[45]

Industrial decline brought unemployment, which had reached 1.5 million by 1977, a level unprecedented since the 1930s. With a general cynicism about the ability of traditional parties to reverse social and industrial decline came a recrudescence of Fascism and racism. Benn's instinct was always to confront racism while others counselled caution.

He spoke at an anti-racist rally in Birmingham against increased

National Front activity in the area on 24 September 1977. The National Front had pushed the Liberals into fourth place in two important by-elections in the Midlands. He did not, however, immediately support the Anti-Nazi League. This was largely the creation of the Socialist Workers' Party but it had an influence far beyond that Trotskyist group, harnessing popular music and design to attract young people and making it fashionable to be anti-racist. Benn was invited to address one ANL rally, in April 1978. Those he asked for advice, including Neil Kinnock, said he should not accept: for him to be associating with the far left would be giving the wrong signals and would stimulate criticism in the newspapers. He was ashamed afterwards that he had let the media frighten him. The next request, to speak at the vast Anti-Nazi League rally on 24 September 1978, he accepted. The *Financial Times* gave the crowd at 80,000, the BBC said 30,000. By his own estimation, at the time, it was the largest meeting Benn had ever addressed.

The Labour Co-ordinating Committee (LCC) was set up in 1977 by Frances Morrell and Michael Meacher and held its first meetings in the Millbank offices of Edmund Dell's Ministry of Trade, where Meacher was now a junior minister. Meacher later described it as comprising 'people who were disillusioned by the progress of the Wilson–Callaghan government and who supported Tony as a hope for radicalism and real change'.[46] Frances Morrell was quick to point out that it was not a vehicle for Tony Benn's leadership ambitions but was designed and organised 'to promote rank-and-file policy-making'.[47] Outsiders would be forgiven for failing to see the distinction, and considered the LCC a Tony Benn fan club.

LCC was specifically concerned with holding meetings, publishing papers and generally framing left policies. The Campaign for Labour Party Democracy, set up by Labour Party activists in 1973, worked for the minutiae of changes in the Labour Party rule book which would make Labour MPs and a Labour government more responsive to the wishes of the membership.

The movement for greater democracy in the Labour Party had been encouraged by Tony Benn and he was its most prestigious advocate, but it was by no means his show. The time had come for the people who worked to put a Labour government in power to be

393

consulted about what it did with that power. Detailed constitutional change was the only answer.

All over the country at ward Labour Party and trade union branch meetings, ordinary members supported the model motions framed by the CLPD for the mandatory reselection of MPs, for the leader to be elected on a wider franchise than Labour MPs alone, and for the manifesto to be under the control of the National Executive rather than the parliamentary leadership.

When the PLP discussed reselection of MPs in March 1978 the right-winger John Golding shocked the meeting by being honest about the current system. 'I could hold [my] seat by organising the GMC any time I like, by packing the delegates in. I have organised more selection conferences, and seen how they are packed, than anyone in this room except for Ron Hayward and Reg Underhill [the party's national agent]. The ideal method of selection under which people are chosen by the GMC is pure cotton wool – it doesn't happen like that at all.' The Chief Whip Michael Cocks said, 'He's right, you know, that's what actually happens.'[48] Benn felt 'utterly sick', as well he might. Within five years these two fixers were to be using their dubious skills against him.

Reselection was the great issue at the 1978 Labour Party conference, at which Hilary Benn spoke for the first time, to Tony Benn's great pride. The left were in the ascendant, evinced by the election of Dennis Skinner and Neil Kinnock to the NEC for the first time. This conference almost saw reselection become a reality, but Hugh Scanlon did not cast the engineers' union block vote, which he had been mandated to cast for the motion. To the left it was just another example of abuse of power by the old guard.

The stream of change rippling through the Labour Party also flowed through Bristol South-East. Members came increasingly to reject Herbert Rogers's dictatorial methods. He expected that his armies of helpers would do what they were told but the new young party faithful, sometimes disdainfully called the polyocracy, were no great respecters of experience and felt that authority must constantly justify itself. Herbert Rogers was respected for his past deeds but resented for his present tenacity in the position he had occupied for more than fifty years. 'His methods were fine in the 1930s' was a common remark. Dissatisfaction with Rogers was emphatically not a matter of a rising left wing criticising faithful old right-wingers. Rogers was, and remained into his nineties, as far left as a person could be while still remaining in the Labour Party. The removal of Rogers in Bristol South-East was part of the time-honoured conflict between young and old.

When the great battle came, a young teacher called Dawn Primarolo defeated Herbert Rogers for the secretaryship by twenty-six votes to twenty-four. 'Mr Rogers left the meeting,' the minutes record blankly. Benn suggested they set up a committee to consider how they could best express their appreciation of the lifetime of service Rogers had given; he had joined the Labour Party in 1912 and had served as secretary from 1918 to 1979.[49]

Other changes in the constituency endangered it as a Labour seat. There was a movement into Bristol of Londoners seeking lower house prices and a less hectic environment. The decline in traditional manufacturing industry was felt in Bristol as elsewhere; there were fewer jobs and so fewer trade unionists and fewer trade union affiliations to the party. In the urban constituencies a dissatisfied middle class, often with working-class parents, who felt excluded from wealth and position, threw in their lot with the oppressed. School teachers and local government officers, who felt they did not enjoy the status or salary their skills deserved, began to use their abilities to transform the Labour Party into a force which was responsive to their needs.

Concomitant with these changes, and representing one facet of the polarisation of British politics, was the high profile of the Militant Tendency in the constituencies. Militant was a largely young, working-class, male organisation which was structured around the *Militant* newspaper. Its historical roots were firmly in the Trotskyist revolutionary tradition. Puritanical, doctrinaire and deadly boring, Militant supporters could be said to drone their way to prominence. They had the stamina and dedication to stay at meetings and argue motions through while the less zealous would give up. They were not underhand, however. Benn's constituency was typical in that Militant had no exceptional influence except what they achieved by dint of hard work. The urgings of impatient revolutionaries left their mark on the minutes book. In 1977 Bristol South-East debated a motion which began with a statement of opposition to capitalism and ended 'The workers have no country – workers of the world unite', which gives little to social democratic compromise.[50]

The Labour Party Young Socialists, with one seat on the NEC, was the only Labour Party organisation which was ever under Militant control. When Andy Bevan, a Militant supporter, was selected as national youth officer the red barbarian was standing in the doorway as far as the right wing were concerned. A long bruising battle to remove him started, along with a widespread scare about 'entryism' in the Labour Party. This alleged that revolutionaries were entering the party in order to transform it into a vehicle for their own ends.

Benn felt that the people who wanted to expel Militant supporters were the same as those who had wanted to expel nuclear disarmers or Bevanites in the 1950s. He was also impressed by the proselytising zeal of Militant supporters; they did not push through motions by procedural means but wanted their issues discussed early in meetings so they could convert people in the discussion.[51] He had no political sympathy with them, however, and never himself used the Trotskyist analysis of society which Militant proffered. It was particularly courageous of him, therefore, to risk his own position further to defend Militant supporters and the existence of a Marxist school of thought in the Labour Party, arguing in an article in the *Guardian*, that Marxism had always been openly accepted by the Labour Party as one of its many sources of inspiration.

It was later the claim of the left (including Benn) that the Callaghan government had betrayed its own supporters with extended incomes policies against which the unions eventually had to fight. It was the claim of the right that trade union militants had brought down the government with excessive wage demands. Neither interpretation gave any comfort to those who believed that the government was under union control. Benn was opposed to any restriction on trade union bargaining, which he considered 'handcuffed labour while leaving capital free to do what it likes'.[52]

At the end of 1978 the trade unions were facing a fourth year of government-imposed pay restraint. The Chancellor's policy – a 5 per cent maximum – had already been rejected by the conference and the House of Commons voted down a proposal to permit legal sanctions against employers who breached it. The 'winter of discontent' had begun.

As Energy Secretary, Benn was most deeply involved in the tanker drivers' dispute, which took place at the same time as a lorry drivers' dispute. This gained him admittance to the Civil Contingencies Unit, chaired by the Home Secretary and meeting in the Cabinet Office. He was surprised to find that in spite of his lifetime in Parliament and many years in government, he did not recognise the civil servants who were handling this emergency.

Benn's role would be to go to Balmoral and ask the Queen to declare a state of energy emergency under the Energy Act. He could then requisition oil tankers, which would be driven by soldiers brought in from the army in Germany. This would permit the delivery of emergency supplies of fuel to hospitals and other essential users. After hearing their plans Benn said he could get better emergency cover by negotiating directly with the trade unions. 'Looking at their faces,' he said, 'it was as if I had suggested negotiating an easement of the blockade with Hitler during the war.'[53]

Benn went to Moss Evans, the general secretary of the Transport and General Workers' Union, who agreed to all the emergency supplies on the Civil Contingencies Unit list with the exception of the newspapers, which he did not consider to be in the class of essential users of energy. The agreement broke down on this point but Benn continued to urge the Unit to defer the decision to put the emergency plan into operation.

He wrote in his diary, 'There is a part of me that tells me I am just being sucked into this terrible military operation to hold the working class back. On the other hand, I have to protect emergency supplies and argue for a radical programme for the Labour Party. But there is no doubt I am compromised up to the hilt by remaining in this bloody awful government.'[54] Finally, without the emergency plan going into operation, the disputes were settled with a 13–15 per cent pay rise for drivers, which destroyed any semblance of a government-backed pay policy. The winter continued with selective local strikes by public service workers, calling for a £60 minimum wage. The rubbish began to pile up in the streets and the morgues filled with the unburied dead.

David Steel had withdrawn the support of the Liberals in the spring of 1978 and by 1979 the government was living from vote to vote. Finally it lost by one vote on a confidence motion on 28 March 1979, and the election was called. Labour's manifesto was rapidly assembled in late-night sessions, during one of which, in that mixture of table thumping and sentimentality which characterised that cabinet, all discussion stopped so that they could sing happy birthday to Tony Benn, as it had just passed midnight on 2 April.

Whatever the manifesto, the timing was wrong. Callaghan had made a serious misjudgement when he failed to call an election the previous autumn. Now it was too late. When the election came, on a freezing cold May day, the Conservatives had 339 seats to Labour's 269.

Benn had given the campaign his usual enthusiasm. He had been to thirty-seven constituencies to speak, and almost nothing had appeared in the press, though reporters were always there in force, waiting for him to slip up. In Bristol South-East he won the narrowest victory of his life, with a majority of 1890 over his Tory opponent. Only an MP as assiduous as Benn was in his constituency work could have held the seat with such a swing against Labour. Despite the cruel press campaign against him, his personal vote was vast. On one housing estate he visited while canvassing he discovered that one in three of the homes contained people he had helped. A study of his constituency work found he dealt with over 1000 cases a year involving over 5000 letters.[55]

The press attacks on Benn took their toll on his vote. Irving Rogers said: 'We picked it up on the doorstep. When I was canvassing I saw the effect of this appalling press campaign, even from people who were our supporters. They were saying, "I will vote Labour in the local election but not for Tony Benn because he's a Communist." I remember telling Tony, "We've got to do something about this," and I don't think he realised how serious it was. That was part of his naïvety about people.'[56]

30

The Battle for the Labour Party

After the election Benn was relieved to be free from the burdens of office. 'I'm much happier now than I've been for a very long time,' he said. 'The sweets of office, such as they are, they can have. I'm very happy because I actually don't want anything from anybody.'[1] He found opposition less of a spiritual strain than government and was quite spritely when he went to Buckingham Palace to tender his resignation. The Queen used a common conversational ploy of those who must speak to many people, and repeated to Benn what the previous outgoing minister had said to her, about the stress of all the changes in politics. Benn did not wish to miss the opportunity of explaining his current insight to a new listener so he remarked how useful it was to have a 'snapshot view' of the country when governments change. 'Whereas twenty-five years ago we were an empire, now we are a colony with the IMF running our financial affairs and the Common Market Commission running our legislation and NATO running our armed forces.' The Queen changed the subject.[2]

Benn had already decided not to stand for election to the shadow cabinet, in order to be free to 'study and analyse the experience of the last five years, especially the relationship which existed between the Labour government, the parliamentary party, the National Executive and the annual conference, so that we can apply the lessons learned to the future work of the party.' He was going to use the period of opposition to reform the Labour Party according to his own framework.[3]

The 1979 party conference saw a victory for reselection of MPs and for the proposition that the NEC should have a final say on the manifesto; and a defeat for the proposal that the leader should be elected by an electoral college of the whole party. Thus for the first time in post-war history the party was balanced between right and left. Neither side liked it, though the left did not threaten to leave the party if it was unsuccessful.

Benn's affection for the freedom of the back benches had a long lineage. In 1964 he was writing lovingly, 'On the back benches, stepped up sharply behind, there is an invigorating air that stimulates controversy and independence. Down on the front benches the atmosphere is muggier and the sluggish waters of the "usual channels" give off a faint odour of coalition that is far less exhilarating.'[4]

But he was front-bench material, wherever he sat. The jubilant Tories sent Keith Joseph forward to enunciate their philosophy of the market place. Labour's champion was still Benn, still the only one with both the parliamentary skill and the conviction of his own righteousness which a fighter must have. After he had spoken on the Queen's speech, people he had hardly addressed in years came up to congratulate him on his performance. His speech had correctly pinpointed what many Tory MPs had not yet understood: that the path upon which they had embarked was directly contrary to the paths of Churchill and Macmillan. Benn must have known – anyone must have known – even at this late stage, that all he needed was to steer a steady course and keep pleasing the PLP and he would be leader. Whatever their reservations, the PLP needed him.

Benn was ahead of the field in realising just how radical the new Prime Minister was. 'She is opening up guerrilla raids behind our lines to try to reopen questions that were settled 25, 50 or even 100 years ago,' he said.[5] Benn admired Margaret Thatcher for her vigorous approach and her presentation of clear alternatives to the electorate. She had been converted to radical Conservatism by the experience of the failure of consensus in the Heath years, where both parties had operated policies of government intervention in the economy; and by the ideology of Hayek, to which Keith Joseph had introduced her. It was a transformation similar to Benn's conversion to radical socialism in the light of his experiences in government and his introduction to an older socialist tradition.

Benn had said that in Britain, 'Democratic reform seems to come in roughly thirty-five-year cycles: 1832, 1867, 1906, 1945. If that is so we should be on the eve of another great period of reform.'[6] The reform was certainly coming, and it was to be a fundamental and irreversible shift of wealth and power. But it was not to be in favour of 'working people and their families'.

Benn was himself setting out his political philosophy. He now had a considerable body of published work. Between 1974 and 1980 he produced sixteen pamphlets with titles like *The Case for a Constitutional Premiership* and *Why America Needs Democratic Socialism*. Most were published by the Institute for Workers' Control and all were based on speeches which had been made at major occasions. When he was looking for an editor to assemble his speeches into a book, he was introduced to Chris Mullin. The book which Mullin edited for him, *Arguments for Socialism*, was published in 1979 to mixed reviews – one writer called it 'Arguments for Me' – but it was a great success with the public, eventually selling 75,000 copies in hardback and paperback.

The Benn family was rather more spread out now, with the three older children, all having taken degrees, now living away from their parents. Stephen Benn was studying for his PhD and took time off to work as an assistant to a Democratic Senator in Washington; Hilary Benn was working as a research officer for the union ASTMS; Melissa Benn was starting work as a journalist; Joshua Benn was pursuing his love for electronics which was to lead him into a career in computing when the personal computer revolution took place. All four children took an active interest in politics, two of the eldest standing unsuccessfully for council seats in May 1978. Then Hilary Benn successfully stood for a seat on Ealing Council at a by-election in September 1979.

A family as close as the Benns was inevitably devastated by the terminal illness of Hilary's wife Rosalind, who died of cancer in June 1979. The whole family gathered in Hilary's home the night she died. Benn's diary for the period is almost unbearably poignant. It is revealing of the value he placed on personal courage, regardless of the circumstances, that what he admired his son for was his eloquence at the funeral. He wrote, 'Then Hilary got up and went and stood facing the coffin, only a few feet from his beloved Rosalind, and delivered this beautiful address, absolutely without

401

any tremor in his voice or indication of grief. It was the best speech I have ever heard. It was amusing, perceptive, sensitive, tender, but it was at no stage sentimental, and on occasions was even funny.'[7] Characteristic too of the Benns was their videotaping of the funeral, to include these moments along with the happy times in the family archive.

The family always had a sense of occasion, taking care to celebrate birthdays and Christmas with time-honoured rituals, but also commemorating sad occurrences. More than forty years after the event Tony Benn and his mother went to the nearby church in Stansgate on the anniversary of the stillbirth of the baby who would have been Tony's brother. Stephen Benn played his own compositions on the organ.[8]

Press interest in the Benn family continued, with sporadic outbursts like an expensive *Sunday Times* investigation of Caroline Benn's family in the US, seeking evidence of great wealth which was, unsurprisingly, not found.

An investigation of Tony Benn's genealogy by Debrett's on behalf of the *News of the World* was more interesting. Benn obtained a copy and was pleased to learn that the family tree showed him to be of artisan stock: brickmakers, weavers and cabinet-makers. The *News of the World* published in January 1980 with the sole revelation that Tony Benn's great-uncle (his father's uncle) had been criminally insane and had killed his own father.

William Rutherford Benn had murdered the Revd Julius Benn in a boarding house in Matlock, Derbyshire, in 1883. Julius Benn had taken his demented son into the country in the hope that the rest would calm him. Unfortunately the young man started having delusions about his father and killed him while he slept by striking him on the head with a chamber pot. He then attempted suicide twice, once by cutting his throat with a penknife at the scene, then by defenestrating himself at the hospital to which he was taken. He was eventually incarcerated but years later was reunited with his wife and, dropping the Benn from their name, he became William Rutherford – his middle name was, in Benn family tradition, taken from the female line (it was his grandmother's maiden name).

No newspapers followed up the piece, probably considering it tasteless to resurrect a grim story 100 years old which had been given sufficient coverage at the time. But in June that year most newspapers did carry it when Debrett's, which had a new edition of its reference book to the peerage appearing, re-presented the story with a new introduction. This was that William Rutherford's daughter was Margaret (later Dame Margaret) Rutherford, the actress who had died in 1972. She was thus Tony Benn's first cousin once removed. This was no secret – she used to refer to him as 'Cousin Tony' and all the family were proud of their association with her. The public did not seem particularly interested in this expensively gained story. The only response which Tony Benn heard was from a taxi driver who said, 'Sorry to hear about your uncle, Mr Benn,' as if the event had happened that week.[9]

The mood of the Labour right wing was not improved by the special conference of May 1980. This endorsed a compromise document called *Peace, Jobs, Freedom*, which stopped just short of unilateral nuclear disarmament and withdrawal from the EEC. The conference was marked by a cool reception for Callaghan, an openly hostile one for Healey and Foreign Secretary David Owen, and a standing ovation for Benn.

Labour's procedural negotiations continued with a commission of inquiry at the ASTMS country club in June 1980, called to discuss the details of the electoral college which was to elect the leader and deputy leader of the party. The meeting reached a stalemate over what the proportions of the college should be. Benn favoured giving a third of the votes each to the trade unions, constituency parties and MPs, but later he changed his view to half for the trade unions and 25 per cent for the other two sections. It was a fatal mistake. Had he stuck to the three-thirds proposal he would have won the deputy leadership contest in 1981. 'The thing was very haphazard,' he said. 'I suppose at the time we were trying to say to the trade unions, "Look, the Labour Party was defeated because a parliamentary leadership that had no accountability to the movement introduced a policy that ended up with a punch-up with the trade unions. You had no power to do anything about it and as a result drifted into this confrontation and Thatcher came to power. You could have stopped it if you had had a greater vote in a leadership election."

You must remember also that at the conference the union vote was 92 per cent, so a drop to 50 per cent was substantial.'[10]

At this meeting he became involved in an argument with Michael Foot, lost his temper with him and shouted, 'For years the only thing you have answered to any question is "Rock the boat, bring in Thatcher, lose the power." You haven't thought about anything in ten years. What's wrong with you?" '[11] The consistent unhappiness in their relationship was due to a basic difference in approach: for Foot, at least in old age, loyalty to colleagues and collective responsibility were the most important things. For Benn the principles were more important, and loyalty was a dubious virtue.

The crowning achievement for Benn and the left was the 1980 party conference at Blackpool. Motions were carried calling for the removal of all nuclear bases, including the American ones, from Britain, and for withdrawal from the EEC without a referendum. 'This was above all the conference of Tony Benn,' wrote Philip Whitehead. 'He seemed to be everywhere, addressing fringe meetings three at a time, if the agenda was to be believed, and mixing a potent brew of instant socialism from the platform.'[12] Benn proclaimed that the next Labour government would introduce an Industry Act for common ownership, industrial democracy and controls on capital. It would withdraw from the Common Market and, in order to achieve these objectives, would have to abolish the House of Lords by creating a thousand peers. This proposal was rapturously welcomed by the conference but was particularly criticised as unrealistic by press and parliamentary colleagues. It was far from novel: the abolition of the Lords had been Labour Party policy since 1935 and, as Benn correctly stated in his defence, the precedence of the Commons over the Lords had been gained only in 1911 with the threat of 'swamping' the place with new peers, a threat which had been considered just as unrealistic until it was successful.

Benn made what he believed was the best speech of his life on one of the procedural motions – for the NEC to control the manifesto. To an accompaniment of spontaneous applause Benn castigated those leaders of the party who sat silently, voicing no opposition, while conference debated and passed motions, then killed the proposals by veto behind closed doors at a late stage. He hailed back to the one unrealised demand of the Chartists, of annual Parliaments which could be more accountable. He pleaded for the educational role of the Labour Party, 'an organisation designed to change people's perception'. He begged for conference to be given the power which should accompany responsibility. 'The route to unity in this party is not to lecture it to stop squabbling, but to start listening to the debate, to discuss the policy in advance of the movement, and go on discussing it year after year after year.'[13] Typically, his *tour de force* addressed the one motion beloved of the left which was expected to fail. He was always at his best when fighting against the odds. The motion was lost, but by just over 100,000 votes, far fewer than had been predicted.

Yet, just as he was deified by the activists, he was execrated by the PLP, who feared the assertiveness he was encouraging in their constituencies. Joe Ashton said, 'Where I fell out with Tony was when he started changing the rules of the party: how you elect the leader, reselection. He alienated a lot of people. Those two things were the ones that gave the SDP credibility. The Campaign for Labour Party Democracy insisted reselection had to be mandatory, so lots of people with no problems with their constituency had to jump through the hoop. It was a major own goal for Tony. Clem Attlee didn't need this to bring in a radical programme. It wasn't the left-wing policies – the PLP would have gone along with them – it was putting their jobs on the line that they couldn't stand.'[14]

Ashton fed the conference with unpalatable truths and they responded with a slow handclap. He said that if an MP was deselected and he walked away regarding it as hard luck, he would get no redundancy money. But if he was defeated in an election, he would receive redundancy payments from Parliament. There was every incentive to stand again. Why should MPs feel loyalty to the party if they believed they had been badly treated, often after long service? 'If Roy Jenkins wanted to form a party of twenty-five sacked MPs now in this Parliament, they could be in business in six months, and they would be backed by the media.' Twenty-seven eventually broke away, so Ashton's guess was not so bad.[15]

A procedure known as the Mikardo compromise, whereby reselection would go into effect only when a vote of no confidence was carried against an MP, was rejected. Tony Benn opposed it

because under this system 'You could not have a selection conference until you'd killed your sitting member. All the efforts of those
who favoured a different candidate had first to be devoted to the
destruction of the reputation of the sitting member and that would
be the worst thing that could happen.'[16]

The third Labour Party constitutional change, a wider franchise
for the leadership, was reaffirmed, but the precise structure of the
electoral college was deferred for decision by yet another special
conference in January 1981.

It had been a week of spectacular success for Benn but one thing
remained. The night before the conference ended he spoke at a
fringe meeting, calling for Irish unity in calm, measured tones. 'That
completes my last task at conference,' Benn wrote. 'I think I have
now reopened every issue that the establishment wants to keep
closed – the Common Market, defence policy, economic policy and
Northern Ireland. All these issues will mature and develop and in
time they will come right.'[17]

31

The Deputy Leadership Election

After four years of Callaghan's leadership, Wilson's boast that he had kept the party together seemed less empty. Callaghan had lost the respect of both sections of the party. The left was looking for a new leader, with Benn the top contender, and the right was looking for an exit. Callaghan had badly misjudged the election date; and his cabinet-making was remarkable for only two decisions: dropping Barbara Castle and promoting David Owen. Castle was loyal and able despite the Prime Minister's differences with her. She had plenty of political life left: she went on to lead the Labour Group in the European Parliament from 1979 to 1985. The appointment of David Owen as Foreign Secretary when Crosland died was a promotion above Owen's maturity and ability, which gave him a position of authority from which to assist in the launch of the SDP. Foreign Office mismanagement in the events leading up to the Iranian revolution caused serious, lasting damage to Britain's position in the Gulf area.

Callaghan's resignation after the 1980 party conference was accepted without regret, though the timing meant that the election of a new leader would have to be carried out under the old rules, with only the PLP voting. Had Callaghan resigned a few months after the January 1981 conference, the election could have taken place using the electoral college. Benn telephoned his supporters to discuss what he should do and they all felt he should not stand, partly because the system of election was discredited, partly because he would not win and risked getting a derisory vote which would damage his standing in future. Benn's advisers at the time, who used to meet on Sundays at his home, included Stephen and Hilary

Benn, Audrey and Valerie Wise, his secretary Julie Clements, Chris Mullin, Tony Banks, Frances Morrell, Jo Richardson, Victor Schonfeld, Vladimir Derer, Michael Meacher, Stuart Holland, Ken Coates and Reg Race. Not all of them would be present on any one occasion.

Foot had long been so closely associated with Callaghan that Benn did not consider him even to be left wing any more. Benn felt he could support Foot as a 'caretaker' leader until the new rules came in. He would be unlikely to remain long; at sixty-seven he was less than two years younger than Callaghan – hardly a young man stepping into an old man's shoes.

In the election in November 1980, Healey received 129 votes and Foot 139 in the second ballot. What might be seen as a narrow victory for the left is more complex when the motives of the voters are understood. The MPs who were to leave for the SDP as a result of the reselection decision were already planning their retreat and, as they thought, leaving behind a slow-acting poison in the Labour Party. Neville Sandelson, who was to leave just four months later, said, 'There was a collective move by [future] SDP MPs to wreck the Labour Party by voting for the more extreme characters. They deny it and they don't want their names mentioned – they will say this is Neville Sandelson and nobody else. I can assure you that is quite untrue and the number of votes in the Healey–Foot election were sufficient to tip the balance Foot's way. He was the man most likely to lead the crumbling of the Labour Party.'[1]

Benn now decided to stand for the shadow cabinet again, saying that he had gone to the back benches to campaign for reforms, all of which had now been carried through. He discussed with Foot the possibility of his being shadow Home Secretary when he was elected. His standing in the PLP had fallen so far that he came thirteenth, with eighty-eight votes; Neil Kinnock came twelfth with ninety. Even without a better endorsement from his colleagues he could have had a position, because it was in the leader's gift to appoint him as a shadow spokesman, but Benn declined an appointment based on patronage.

Benn did not speak at the January 1981 special conference, which agreed that the unions should have 40 per cent of the votes in the electoral college. David Owen and his supporters spoke a great deal to the press, not to the conference. The following day the 'gang of four', David Owen, Roy Jenkins, Shirley Williams and Bill Rodgers, announced the formation of the Council for Social Democracy, an alternative party being created within the Labour Party. They offered a 'realignment of British politics' and appealed for cash through newspaper advertisements. When they felt secure, in March 1981, they announced the formation of the Social Democratic Party to ecstatic media applause. Altogether thirteen Labour MPs and one Conservative defected to the SDP at this point.

Benn's view of Jenkins and Owen was that they were 'people who have failed to persuade the party to which they have given their lives that the course of action they believe in is right'.[2] As a result of SDP defections he was able to take his shadow cabinet place, as he was the highest runner-up and when Rodgers departed he could move in. Ten years later he still had not been re-elected to the shadow cabinet.

There should never have been any doubt that Benn would stand in the first elections which could be held under the new procedure, at the party conference of 1981. The 'Sunday group' was discussing his contesting the deputy leadership in January 1981, and as part of the strategy urged him to join the Tribune Group. 'Tony was coerced into joining the Tribune Group,' said Tony Banks. 'He hadn't done it before and said he didn't want to. We thought as it was the only left grouping in Parliament and he was the left candidate, he ought to be a member.'[3] It was probably unwise, for he now gave Tribune an implied control over his actions, a control he would resist at his peril.

Benn waited for the SDP defectors to leave before announcing his candidature for the deputy leadership – he did not wish to be accused of having precipitated their departure. He told Foot he was going to stand, and his supporters arranged for sixteen MPs, including some Tribune Group members, to sign a nomination. Other Tribune Group members started working to stop the candidature. Benn had not asked the Group as a whole whether he should stand because, he said, he had only just joined and did not want it to seem as if he were seeking support. Others would say he was concerned that they would urge him not to stand. Ian Mikardo felt that his failure to consult with them created bitterness against him which left the dissatisfied Tribunites free to abstain in the final vote.

During an all-night sitting on 1–2 April 1981 a group of Tribune MPs signed a letter urging Benn not to stand. Joe Ashton sought out Benn in the tea room and told him, 'You are going to get a letter asking you not to run and I'm asking you before you get the letter to think very carefully about it, because I don't think you can win. And also you won't do yourself any good and I don't think it'll do the party any good.'[4] This meant Benn had to move fast. In the early hours he sent out to all Labour MPs and to the press a statement declaring that he would be contesting the election. The campaign had become unstoppable.

When he next met the Tribune Group Jim Marshall, a Leicester MP, whispered to him, 'You know what this is really about, don't you? It's really about who is going to be the leader of the left and they don't want to concede it to you.'[5] Eric Heffer, no shrinking violet himself, accused Benn of a 'cult of personality'.[6]

It is easy to see how colleagues might see the deputy leadership as a distraction and a drain on energy. On 13 April 1981, for example, Benn attended three meetings about it: a Tribune meeting; a meeting of his Campaign Committee (basically the 'Sunday Group'); and a meeting of the Rank and File Mobilising Committee which consisted of the Labour Co-ordinating Committee, Militant, Socialist Action, London Labour Briefing, Independent Labour Party and the Campaign for Labour Party Democracy.

He also met with other members of the NEC prior to NEC meetings, something which led to the most furious row he ever had with Michael Foot. Benn protested to Foot that he was going 'all over the shop' to keep the right in the party but did not feel the same about the left. Would he be prepared to meet the left caucus on the executive? Foot protested that it would be better if there were no caucus meetings because they undermine democracy. Benn should 'stop the rigid prearranged votes which prohibited any real discussion, to give us a renewed chance to let the executive perform its proper function: to prepare to fight the Tory enemy.' As Foot described it, 'He shook his head as if to deny that any such effective caucus existed.'[7] Benn's diary note of the meeting records his saying that the caucus 'tried to reach a sort of general agreement about

410

things' and was no more subversive than the 'Husbands and Wives' dinners which used to be held at Foot's house during the 1974–9 Labour government. 'You're a bloody liar,' said Foot (something both accounts agree on) and Benn stormed out.

In fact Benn and the hard left on the NEC could not carry votes unless they had the support, following discussion, of the soft left, who did not attend caucus meetings. The caucus was not big enough, or powerful enough, to perform the function Foot ascribed to it. If Foot felt everything was going Benn's way in the 1979–81 period, it was not, as he suggests in *Loyalists and Loners*, because Benn was pulling the strings, but because Benn represented the mood of the times.

Healey claims he did not particularly want the job of deputy leader, which he considered 'disagreeable and which in itself was not worth having. I felt, however, that it was essential to deny it to Tony Benn.'[8] In the electoral college Healey could rely on the votes of the MPs and the right-wing trade unionists. He frequently met with Sid Weighell of the railwaymen, Frank Chapple of the electricians, Terry Duffy of the engineers, Tom Jackson of the Post Office Workers and David Basnett of the General and Municipal Workers. Benn had the support of the constituencies. The battle was over winning the uncommitted trade unions: chiefly the Transport and General Workers' Union and the National Union of Public Employees (NUPE).

Both Healey and Benn toured the trade union conferences seeking support. The trade unions had widely differing electoral methods, and the election had the helpful side-effect of highlighting the undemocratic nature of trade union decision-making. Often the leadership and the members disagreed. Clive Jenkins of ASTMS had an attractive china cup made for Benn, one side of which bore the motto, 'Elections can be poisoned chalices', and the other 'Don't do it, Tony'. Yet Jenkins's membership backed Benn.

The Labour Party had arranged a series of demonstrations to draw attention to the level of unemployment, which by 1981–2 had reached three million. Two of these, at Birmingham and Cardiff, were wrecked by Trotskyists, anarchists (increasingly to become a disruptive force on the left) and IRA supporters. Foot and Healey tended to believe that these scenes, which could be presented in the

411

press as caused by Labour Party supporters, were in some way a direct result of Benn's decision to challenge Healey. Healey even believed that disturbances were being orchestrated by Benn's campaign manager Jon Lansman, and claimed on television that he had seen Lansman directing hecklers at the meetings. In fact Lansman had been in Italy at the time of one of the meetings and in North Wales at the time of the other. Healey was obliged to apologise.

Certainly, Healey had a rougher ride than Benn, but he was the right-wing candidate and public meetings, even those without the revolutionary element, tend to attract the left. Healey remarked that Benn 'did nothing to discourage or condemn' the extra-parliamentary agitators.[9] Presumably this was because such condemnation would have had no effect and would therefore merely leave Benn looking ineffectual. Benn did not dictate the political temperature. The year was one of rioting in Northern Ireland and in Britain. In Liverpool tear gas was used on rioters for the first time on the mainland. It would have been foolish to imagine that violent discontent would not show itself in public meetings.

Nevertheless, the violence was associated with Benn by his enemies and his lukewarm friends, giving them a spurious reason to distance themselves from him. Others had genuine reasons for viewing the whole affair with distaste. Vladimir Derer, of the Campaign for Labour Party Democracy, said: 'The Bennite left ran for the deputy leadership like it was the presidency of the United Kingdom. They treated union meetings like election primaries. It came over on television simply as a naked power struggle.'[10] Derer had done as much as anyone to democratise Labour's internal procedures, but this was not what he had done it for. Undoubtedly, when they realised they could actually win (which was not anticipated when the contest started) Benn's supporters showed more enthusiasm than was customary in British political contests.

Nor was the bullying all on the side of Benn's supporters. As Michael Meacher said, the campaign 'showed how bitterly the right will fight. He was the first left-wing challenger since Nye Bevan. The sheer weight of what was thrown against him was enormous. There was never less than half a page of vitriol in the press per day and the source was the right wing of the Labour Party. They were feeding stuff into the press even though it did cataclysmic damage to the Labour Party. It was like a bombing raid flattening everything in sight. It was more a cause of the defeat in 1983 than the Falklands.'[11]

Michael Foot tried to stop Benn's candidature in his somewhat bookish style: he read out a twenty-four-page statement at a shadow cabinet meeting calling on Benn to stand against him for the leadership. Benn thought the gesture foolish and disloyal. He had supported Foot against Healey and, if Foot did not consider he could support Benn against Healey, the least he could do was to keep quiet. He reminded Foot that the leader had never in the past become involved in elections for Labour Party positions.

When Benn was stopped it was not a political opponent who stopped him. On 5 May 1981 he recorded a tingling feeling in his legs and hands; later he remarked on a deepening of his voice and unsteadiness in his gait. With further loss of feeling later in the month, he saw his family doctor, who correctly diagnosed a condition in his sensory nerves. He continued the punishing round of meetings while an appointment was made for him at the Charing Cross Hospital. By the beginning of June when he walked to the rostrum to address the railwaymen's conference, he was so unsteady on his feet that he was worried it would be picked up by the cameras.

Benn went into hospital for tests with considerable anxiety: a condition which had been merely curious was by now disabling. Several members of his family feared he had been poisoned. The neurological specialists thought that Benn might have a viral infection which had affected his nervous system, deadening the reflexes in his arms and legs. In the second week of tests they diagnosed a polyneuropathy called Guillain-Barré syndrome. The condition had been first defined in Paris in 1916 in almost identical terms to Benn's own, featuring progressive pins and needles and weakness of limbs without any preceding illness, and a delay in reflex muscle contraction.

An identifiable infection might precede the condition by a few weeks but in half the cases no such preliminary event is recognisable. Part of the diagnostic criterion for establishing that a condition is Guillain-Barré, and not some other condition, is to exclude a toxic cause.[12] This the specialists at Charing Cross did. So far as it is possible to tell, Tony Benn's condition was not caused by poisoning.

Letters of support (four to five thousand in total) and flowers poured into the hospital. Benn talked to the shop stewards in the hospital, who invited him to address a meeting, and made friends with the other patients, including a woman who had a similar condition to his own but had become completely paralysed and was in considerable pain.

When Benn's whereabouts were known, a twenty-four-hour media circus camped outside the hospital, eager for a sight of Benn and, preferably, a picture. A reporter tried to get in dressed as a doctor. A photographer was admitted to casualty pretending he had a pain in his leg; on examination, he was found to be concealing a camera. There were also attempts to bribe hospital staff, many of whom were low-paid workers much in need of the hundreds of pounds journalists were offering for a picture, yet no picture appeared. Benn later recounted how the hospital porters had evaded journalists by pushing him round on a trolley with a sheet over his face, as if he were a corpse.

In the worst cases, Guillain-Barré can continue to devastate the nervous system until death occurs. Much more frequently it is self-limiting and most of the sensory loss is recovered. After two weeks in hospital Benn's doctors decided his condition was not progressive. There was no cure; he was simply told to rest for three months. He cancelled all speaking engagements until September and enjoyed the enforced rest. Sensation eventually returned to his limbs, though not completely: his handwriting had deteriorated over the course of the illness and he did not recover sufficient sensation to bring it back to its earlier standard. He had lost some sensation in his feet but it was really only troublesome when he tried to walk on a moving train.

He began campaigning again in September and the press barrage resumed. The *Sun* warned of 'The Marxist Kingdom of Benn and Scargill',[13] while *The Times* was again obliged to apologise to Benn, this time for falsely claiming that he was 'a wealthy aristocrat' with a farm in Essex and investments in the form of a 'Stansgate Trust' in the Bank of Bermuda and that Caroline Benn was independently very wealthy.[14]

The *Times* smear, which appeared on the morning of the TGWU executive's decision about whom to back, was investigated by Chris

Mullin. He found that it was the result of an anonymous source feeding information to a journalist, who did not check it, but changed the (accurate) biographical details in another journalist's copy so that it contained the lies. This was done without the knowledge of the editor, Harold Evans, who did not see the story until after it was published. Evans said it was 'a professional error for which two people have been rebuked. . . . I was livid when I found out.'[15] Mullin rang the Bank of Bermuda to discover that not only was there no such trust, but no one from *The Times* had been in touch with them to ask whether there was. Mullin had no doubt it was 'MI5's contribution to the election campaign'.[16]

Chris Mullin said of the deputy leadership campaign, 'For the only time in my political career someone mobilised forces which posed a threat to the established order. 'Once you win, and the hatred dies away, the landscape changes: the established order does a deal. Tony said that he recognised that and his aim was to make the price of the deal as high as possible. The great strength of Tony was that having been on the inside for so long he understood how the ruling class operate and that's why they hated him. He had got behind the lines.'[17]

The most damaging press attack came from the unlikely quarter of *Tribune*. Neil Kinnock wrote a 3000-word article called 'Personality, Policies and Democratic Socialism' for the 18 September issue. In it he bitterly condemned Benn's decision to contest the deputy leadership, and denounced the tone of his challenge, which adhered to the 'betrayal theory of politics', alleging that the leadership had betrayed the policies of the Labour movement.

He wrote, 'I believe that Tony has fostered antagonism within the party, he has undermined the credibility of credible policies by over-simplification, he has not disowned those who insist upon support for his candidature as the test of loyalty to Labour policy.' The article made a personal attack on Benn, without extolling the virtues of Healey, and addressed not the real question – whom to vote for – but whether there should be a deputy leadership election, a question which now required no answer. The piece, coming out the week before the conference at which the decision would be made, probably did its work, however, in reassuring Tribune members that they could vote for Healey or abstain (which in practical terms had the same effect) in the second ballot.

The first ballot was to eliminate a third candidate, John Silkin, who received 18 per cent of the votes against 36 per cent for Benn and 45 for Healey. The question now was how the Silkin votes would be redistributed. Joshua Benn had worked out on his computer that the result would be within 1 per cent. In the event, after two recounts, Healey had 50.426 per cent to Benn's 49.574. Healey had won by 0.85 per cent.[18]

Joshua Benn calculated that Tony Benn would have won easily if each component of the college had a third of the votes, or even if the abstaining Labour MPs had been included in the equation, rather than the procedure which was followed, increasing the value of the remaining votes to make the *voting* MPs' votes worth 30 per cent collectively.

It was the thirty-seven abstaining MPs who gave Healey the result, seventeen of them from the Tribune Group and including Joe Ashton, Joan Lestor, Stan Orme and Jeff Rooker, as well as Neil Kinnock. Joe Ashton described his abstention as being more a vote against the times than against Benn. He said, 'I wasn't against Tony having it but the whole mood at that time: Livingstone and the so-called loony left in London, and Hatton in Liverpool, and Scargill. . . . We were going down a road which was leading us nowhere. And if Benn had become deputy leader it would have given a tremendous boost to the Owen mob. That's what they wanted. That was the main reason I didn't vote for him. Without Healey there to give us a bit of stability and pull towards the middle we'd have finished up in third place.'[19]

Ian Mikardo cites a number of reasons for the decision to give the contest to Healey rather than vote for Benn. 'By that time there were a lot of right-wingers in the Tribune Group – it was no longer a left-wing group. They would prefer Healey anyway. Also Kinnock saw in Benn an obstacle for his career prospects, and he had friends. And there were a number of people who did it because they were terribly angry that Tony hadn't spoken to them about standing, though I did vote for him.' Mikardo considered that, had Benn handled the individual Tribune Group members with more sensi-

Benn is a monster of ambition and Harold Wilson a placid administrator in the *News of the World.* (11 May 1975)

above Tony (third from right) and Caroline Benn on a visit to Bedwas Colliery in November 1975.

below Cummings presents the equally vigorous Thatcher and Benn as the true faces of the Conservative and Labour parties with their respective 'moderate' appendages. (27 May 1981)

Surrounded by young women on a school visit to his office, the Minister for Energy gives a coy smile.

Caroline and Tony Benn at the Labour Party conference of 1981 where his failure to win the deputy leadership left him undaunted.

A tense moment as Tony Benn observes the right wing beginning to take back the Labour Party at the 1982 conference.

above Defying the government's ban on the publication of *Spycatcher,* which detailed illegal actions by agents within MI5, Benn reads from it at Speakers' Corner in August 1987.

below Benn as a wasp – a frequent image in cartoons. Here a contemplative Kinnock is distracted by Benn's Chesterfield Conference. (23 October 1987)

Tony Benn as John Bunyan. (27 September 1984)

In the 'basement office' in 1987.

tivity, he could have reduced the rate of abstention to twenty MPs, which would have given him the result.[20]

Neil Kinnock was widely felt to have betrayed the left in order to advance his own ambitions. His fulsome support for Foot in the leadership election had appeared to be a playing out of an ancient truth: if you want the job for yourself, support the oldest man for it. Kinnock's ambitions had long been apparent, and the fact that he would end up fighting Benn had not escaped notice. As early as 1976 a commentator was remarking in an article on Benn that 'if Kinnock wants to inherit the mantle of the left, he may well find himself outflanked by someone who *has* in fact done the donkey work and is known as a capable minister'.[21] Kinnock was so obviously heading for the leadership that Chris Mullin in 1974 went into a betting shop, against his usual habit, and asked for odds on Kinnock becoming leader. The betting shop refused on the grounds that they had never heard of him.[22] Benn had always found Kinnock shallow, with too much style and not enough substance. He had almost recommended him for a job to Callaghan as having 'a very lively mind and good capacity for communication', but this remark did not survive to the second draft.[23]

For the right, it was virtually the culmination of a battle between light and darkness. Giles Radice wrote in his diary that night,[24] 'By beating Benn, however narrowly, Denis Healey has saved the Labour Party.'

As for Benn, he was pleased a contest had taken place, describing it as 'the best and most important debate we had ever had'.[25] He felt the result was a good one because if *he* had won by such a narrow margin, there would have been no peace for him in the post, while Healey had won unconvincingly – as soon as there were defections to the SDP, he would have the position but not the authority. Caroline Benn said with her usual perception, 'You've got popularity without power, which is what you want.'[26]

The next great battle in the Labour Party was the Tatchell affair, involving the press, the SDP, the leadership and the 'London factor' of radical Labour Parties in the south espousing issues which, it was claimed, lost traditional Labour votes. Among these issues was gay rights. Benn's position was unequivocal, at various meetings he argued for the civil liberties restrictions on homosexuals to be removed – the age of consent for male homosexuality was twenty-one, as against sixteen for all heterosexuals, and even this did not extend to the armed forces or the merchant navy, where homo-sexuality was still illegal.[27]

In November 1981 Bermondsey Labour Party held its selection meeting with six candidates to choose a replacement for the retiring MP Bob Mellish. Bermondsey duly selected Peter Tatchell, the twenty-nine-year-old constituency secretary who was known for his support for gay rights, though he and the Bermondsey party always maintained that his personal sexual orientation was not and should not be an issue in the election. The press and his right-wing opponents in the Labour Party thought otherwise. Additionally, Tatchell had in the past advocated 'extra-parliamentary action' by which he meant such things as mass demonstrations and civil dis-obedience to challenge the government.

Michael Foot was taunted by the SDP over Tatchell's selection and in the worst mistake of his career as leader, which was not otherwise error-free, he said Tatchell would never be endorsed as a member of the Labour Party as far as he was concerned. Tatchell was, of course, already a member of the party. He was not at the time endorsed as a *candidate*, and Foot later put out a statement claiming that that was what he had meant.

Endorsement of candidates by the NEC was largely a matter of form, designed to ensure that the procedure for selecting a candidate had been properly carried out. But Foot had made it into an issue. When the NEC meeting took place, on 16 December 1981, the first motion was for Tatchell to be permitted to address the meeting. This was lost, so Tatchell was not permitted to be present, nor was he told what the charges against him were.

Neil Kinnock showed the shape of things to come by treating the issue as one of confidence in Foot. Failure to support Foot over this would, he said, be throwing away victory at the next election and the chance for unilateral nuclear disarmament, the alternative economic strategy and withdrawal from the Common Market.[28]

Benn argued against the manifest injustice of not endorsing Tatchell: constituency parties must have the right to choose their own candidates; the NEC should not give in to the implied threat from right-wing MPs that if Tatchell stayed they would go. Ultimately, the attack on Tatchell would fail anyway, as similar attacks on Cripps, Bevan and Foot himself had failed in the past.

It was to no avail; the vote went against Tatchell by fourteen to fifteen, a straight left–right split. Kinnock's vote was considered to be the pivotal one which might have gone either way, for he was still regarded as being on the left of the party. He voted with the right.

Benn was distraught, and when he left the meeting and spoke to the press he made the tactical error of attracting attention to himself, saying he was 'speaking as deputy leader of the Labour Party because, of course, Denis Healey's entire majority has now defected to the Social Democrats'. He meant that the nine Labour MPs who had defected to the SDP in the two months since the conference, and who had voted for Healey, accounted for Healey's majority. This was true, but the point should have been made in a more considered and calm way. Saying it on the steps of the party headquarters (now in Walworth Road) gave the tabloid press licence to return to their 'loony Benn' jibes, and detracted attention from the real injustice which had been perpetrated that day.

Benn's emotion was understandable: he knew it was the end. If he could not win that vote, on such a matter of principle, it meant the left were in retreat. Benn was by nature a fighter, unable to concede defeat while he still had breath to deny it, but what he said next, a message to party members 'not to be discouraged but to go on fighting for peace and social justice' were not the words of a victor.[29]

He travelled to Bristol South-East and told his friends there that the meeting of the NEC that day 'was the saddest he had ever attended. . . . A man had been destroyed in public and then denied a hearing against all natural justice.'[30]

419

32

The Falklands War

The new generation of nuclear weapons gave rise to a new generation of protesters. The US Tridents and Soviet SS20s were an escalation of an existing arms race. More sinister weapons were the neutron bomb, which could flood an area with radiation while doing little damage to property; and Cruise missiles, which could travel below radar limits and so were an ideal 'first-strike' weapon which could be used to start a war. Part of the new wave of protests were the peace camps, most notably the women's camp at Greenham Common US air base, which Benn always praised as a heroic example of peaceful civil disobedience in the face of intimidation by the Ministry of Defence. 'You can't stop an idea by putting up a fence,' he reassured his supporters, 'and you can't stop an idea with a police force.'[1]

He addressed a vast CND meeting on 26 October 1980 in Trafalgar Square, in the company of Neil Kinnock, at this time a unilateralist. The following year in the wake of the strikes in Poland which were the first signs of the break-up of the Soviet empire, Benn told a CND rally of 150,000, 'The Poles have had the courage to stand up to the Kremlin. The British people must now stand up to the Pentagon and close all their nuclear bases here.'[2] His concern about undue US influence in British policy in the heightened cold-war atmosphere of the 1980s was increased by the bellicose statements of Reagan and Thatcher. Reagan's reference to the 'evil empire' of the Soviets and Thatcher's claim that they were bent on world domination gave exactly the wrong messages to the Kremlin while gaining nothing for the West.

Although never a pacifist, by the early 1980s it would be difficult to imagine a situation in which Benn would be prepared to support British participation in a war. Even the invasion of British territory, the annexation of the Falkland Islands by Argentina, left him arguing that any course but military intervention was preferable.

To be fair to him, Benn and the Callaghan cabinet had already conceded that there was little to be done about the Falklands. David Owen, as Foreign Secretary, had gone to cabinet with a sell-out proposal which had been rejected, but Benn reflected, 'The arms trade, the total spinelessness of the Foreign Office and the general decay of the British will combine to put us in a position where frankly it is not going to be possible to do anything about the 1950 Falkland Islanders. The Argentine is determined to get hold of them and there is nothing much we can do.'[3]

Nicholas Ridley, a Foreign Office junior minister, sought a solution on behalf of the new government and came up with a scheme to cede sovereignty to Argentina but lease back the islands to Britain in the same way that Hong Kong was leased to Britain. Lack of political backing led to Ridley's scheme being almost literally shouted down in the Commons. The security of the islands was further compromised by the announcement that HMS *Endurance*, which had been patrolling the islands, was to be withdrawn to save a paltry £3 million.

In Argentina General Leopoldo Galtieri took control of a regime of exceptional brutality, even by the standard of Latin American dictatorships. One of the few things on which there was general agreement in Argentina was that the Falkland Islands, or the Malvinas as they called them, were Argentinian property. Britain had claimed them in an imperial grab in the nineteenth century. A call to arms to liberate the islands would unite the nation, so that is what Galtieri did. On 2 April 1982 an Argentinian force invaded and captured the islands.

Thatcher's government had made the most disastrous mistake any government can ever make: through its own actions, it had lost British territory to a foreign power. If Thatcher hesitated in her response, it was not noticeable. She immediately ordered the enactment of contingency plans – the assembling of a forty-ship task force – and called a meeting of the House of Commons for the following day, the first Saturday meeting since Suez.

Benn had viral pneumonia and was too weak even to write his diary for the first fortnight after the invasion. He went to the Commons to hear the three-hour debate, during which the back benches from both sides of the House made it clear that no negotiated peace was acceptable. Michael Foot spoke of Britain's 'moral duty and political duty and every other kind of duty' to expel the Argentinians, a speech which reminded Benn inexorably of Hugh Gaitskell's speech about Suez on 2 August 1956, before Benn and his colleagues had managed to persuade the leader to oppose the adventure. Only George Foulkes, Labour MP for South Ayrshire, spoke against the military adventure. Benn did not speak but his entry for the day, written in retrospect, runs, 'I'm tempted to say before this exercise goes any further, let's consider some of the consequences. Someone has to say it.'

On the day the battle fleet sailed, 5 April, Benn drafted a resolution on the Falklands, proposing that the Labour Party refuse to support the government in its preparations for war, but instead urge the United Nations to take responsibility for seeking a settlement. Despite his illness, Benn dragged himself from meeting to meeting, from the Tribune group to the International Committee of the NEC, then to the NEC itself, without success. 'The purpose of the battle fleet is to recover Mrs Thatcher's reputation and the issue for us was the Labour Party position,' he wrote.[4] He despised Foot for failing to stand on an issue of principle because he was concerned about short-term unpopularity. There was an argument in the upper levels of the Labour Party which suggested that they should give tepid support to the government until the task force was defeated, then round on Thatcher when she was down.

To a barrage of Conservative shouts Benn spoke in the Falklands debate on 7 April, stressing the hazardous nature of an operation so far from home, in winter and in unknown territory, and against an enemy armed by Britain herself. 'This is an ill-thought-out enterprise and will not achieve the purposes to which it is put.'[5]

Benn's most serious mistake was his belief that the United States would not support Britain because of the importance of her relationship with Latin American countries, 'because American power rests on the rotten military dictatorships of Latin America'.[6] He was wrong for two reasons: America could not allow an important

NATO ally to be defeated by a Third World dictatorship; and there was a close personal friendship between Reagan and Thatcher. After attempted mediation had failed through the intransigence of Argentina, Reagan pledged American support for Britain on 30 April. The enterprise had become far less hazardous.

Margaret Thatcher now required a spectacular success, for the situation must not only be resolved, it must give her a victory parade. She had no interest in any kind of settlement which did not give full sovereignty of the islands back to Britain. It is unlikely a peace plan was possible to either side by this stage, but by personally ordering the sinking of the *General Belgrano* while it was outside (and sailing away from) the exclusion zone around the Falklands, she ensured there could be no settlement without a battle.

When the war began in earnest, and British ships were sunk, many more people came round to Benn's view that any kind of settlement was better than this. The letters he received rose to 2500 a week, almost all in support. But the letter-writers were not great demonstrators, and anti-war rallies on 9 and 23 May were attended by only a few thousand people. Still, in opposing the war and particularly the atmosphere of jingoism promoted by all the national media without exception, Benn was representing a large, thoughtful minority of the population. As was often the case with Benn, he represented moral reservations which people were glad had been expressed, but may not have wished to be the entire basis of national life.

Benn later said, 'There is a crisis of representation in Britain, there are millions of people who take a view which is not articulated by any of the front benches in Parliament and that is a serious problem of British democracy.'[7]

The war transformed Margaret Thatcher's standing. By the beginning of her third year as Prime Minister, in the spring of 1981, she was deeply unpopular, with the public and with many of her own party. She was attempting to operate monetarist policies with 'wet' cabinet ministers who doubted their appropriateness. The policies had begun to hurt, but not to pay off. Unemployment was rising to three million; total national output had not fallen so much in one year since 1931; industrial production was crippled. The sense of hopelessness engendered disorder, and the Brixton riots in April

1981 were thought to presage a complete breakdown of social order in the inner cities. 'It is not only General Galtieri for whom the Falklands war is a diversion from domestic failure,' Benn told the Commons.[8]

Once the Falklands were retaken, on 29 May, Thatcher's position was assured. She was the Mother of the Nation, the warrior heroine. She had dared to win. The Tory wets who had been prowling about her, waiting for her to falter, fell back in disarray. She was the principal victor of the Falklands war, which cost 650 Argentinian lives and 255 British. The junta fell and was replaced by an elected government. Taking a world view of it, the cost of just under 1000 lives might not have been too great a price to pay for the restoration of democracy in Argentina. The other effect of the Falklands war was that it drove the SDP from the news pages, where the nascent party had been receiving ecstatic coverage. By the time the war was over, SDP matters had slipped very far indeed down the list of newsworthy items.

The Labour Party conference of 1982 reaffirmed left-wing policies, including unilateral nuclear disarmament and the renationalisation of firms privatised by the Conservatives. But the underlying trend was to the right. The conference strengthened the right wing on the executive and passed the register of proscribed organisations which would permit the expulsion of Militant supporters. On the NEC Tony Benn was voted out of the chair of the Home Policy Committee, a position he had occupied since 1974, and was removed from nine key committees including the Campaign Committee and the TUC Labour Party Liaison Committee. His annual report to his constituency for 1982 said, 'I regret to report that most of the time of the new NEC is now occupied by the campaign to carry through a series of expulsions from the party.'

The repudiation of Peter Tatchell by the leadership of the Labour Party at the end of 1981 was followed by more than a year of press coverage and public harassment of Tatchell.

Bermondsey Labour Party had, unfairly, failed to shortlist several sitting councillors and one of them stood as an independent against the official candidate at the local elections in May 1982. Bob Mellish supported this candidate and himself resigned from the party before

424

he was thrown out: supporting opposition candidates is the one crime which everyone agrees merits expulsion from the party. Foot became more sympathetic to Tatchell now that his chief adviser on the matter of Bermondsey was gone. Mellish resigned as MP in November 1982, causing a by-election to be held the following February, in which he supported another Labour renegade. Though Foot had by now lifted his veto on Tatchell, he insisted on another selection conference, which Tatchell won by a vast majority. Meanwhile the attempt to expel from the Labour Party five members of the *Militant* newspaper's editorial board continued. On 23 February 1983 the NEC met and agreed, by nineteen votes to nine, to expel them. The 24th was polling day in Bermondsey, so the image in the voters' minds was of Labour Party members denouncing each other.

The Labour Party suffered an overwhelming defeat, losing a safe seat to the Liberal candidate. It came as the profoundest shock to Benn. He believed that Bermondsey had been lost because Foot had disparaged and the press had demonised the candidate. Benn felt that Tatchell 'came out of it with considerable courage and dignity', which to him was rather more important than winning.[9] This was a stage in one of the most important decisions in his life: to stay and fight in Bristol. The boundaries had been redrawn, his constituency would not exist at the next election, and he had every right to go and seek another seat. He had received offers of nomination for six other safe seats around the country,[10] but now he telephoned Pam Tatlow, the new secretary of his doomed constituency, and told her that someone had to make a stand – they could not keep running and let the press and the right wing of the party dictate the terms of politics.[11] Tony Benn had decided that the duty of a leader is to lead. 'The qualities of leadership required you to be there courageously holding the fort when things weren't going well as well as when they were,' he wrote in his diary on the day of the selection.[12]

33

Defeat in Bristol

It had been clear since December 1980 that the parliamentary Boundaries Commission would do away with the constituency of Bristol South-East altogether.[1] The plan was to reduce the five constituencies to four, splitting Bristol South-East three ways: to Bristol East, Kingswood and Bristol South, the latter being the constituency of Michael Cocks, Labour Chief Whip and no friend of Benn. Kingswood was unwinnably Tory; Bristol East was currently a Tory constituency, but whether it stayed that way depended on which parts of Bristol South-East were incorporated into it.

A key ward was the Labour-voting Windmill Hill. Its incorporation into Bristol East would turn a Tory into a Labour seat, but in Bristol South would only turn a safe Labour seat into a safer one. Obviously the Conservatives, who had an equal say in the apportionment of wards in the boundary changes, wanted the new Bristol East to be rendered winnable by the inclusion of Windmill Hill in Bristol South; what swung the balance was Bristol South Labour Party themselves arguing that they should have Windmill Hill.

The incoming activists from Bristol South-East were not given access to the membership lists of Bristol South but clearly there had been an extensive recruitment drive, for as Dawn Primarolo said, 'Suddenly all these new delegates arrived, membership back dated to the qualifying date for participation in the selection.'[2]

As Cocks explained it, 'Although delegates taking part have to have been Party members of the constituency for twelve months previous to the selection, members who select those delegates do not have to fulfil this requirement. They can be members for a day, or even less. With this in mind, between November 1982 and

February 1983 a number of known Cocks supporters living in Knowle and Whitchurch Park wards were quietly recruited into the Labour Party. Their applications were passed through the Bristol South CLP a few at a time.'[3] Another exercise was to have the rules for the new constituency fixed so that the number of delegates a ward had at the selection meeting did not closely reflect their membership, 'By this means the Southville and Windmill Hill wards with pro-Benn delegations could be kept down to a manageable size.'[4]

The trades unions were also involved in increasing the number of their delegates who would support Cocks. At a meeting at the Dragonara hotel in Bristol in November 1981, Roger Godsiff from the clerical union APEX, and John Golding, the MP who was also a leading member of the Post Office union, met with others from the electricians' and the Transport and General Workers' unions. Golding outlined a plan to increase the strength of right wing trade union delegates. It was stressed that, 'Trade Union representatives could be offered the inducement of not actually becoming actively involved in the Constituency Labour Parties but simply getting themselves registered as a Trade Union delegate and only attending the annual meeting of the GMC or selection conference as necessary.'[5]

Even on the day of the selection, it was possible for Benn to back out and there were those who felt he should. Pam Tatlow said, 'We had profound debates as to whether the [East] seat would be winnable. Some people thought it was more important that he should fight somewhere winnable than stay in Bristol – it was important to the future of the left.'[6] A secondary debate was whether, if he lost the selection at Bristol South, which they expected he would because of the Cocks organisational skill, he should go on to face the selection at Bristol East, a much less winnable seat. He was automatically shortlisted for both seats as an MP whose redistributed constituency fell into both areas. The two selection meetings were held on consecutive days, 7 and 8 May 1983.

At Bristol South's meeting at the Hartcliffe Labour Club there were 107 delegates, many of them people Dawn Primarolo did not know by sight, and Benn wondered whether many of them had been to a political meeting in their lives before.[7] As usual, Benn rose to adversity and spoke as if he were on trial for his life. 'It was an outstanding speech,' said Dawn Primarolo, 'which made it all the harder for us. It was rubbing salt in the wound, the style and ability they had rejected for nothing.'[8] The selection conference was irrelevant because Cocks had the votes before it started. Benn accepted the vote with grace, making a short, cheerful speech congratulating Cocks. In 1985 the activists had their revenge. By taking Windmill Hill ward Bristol South had gained Labour voters, but also Labour activists, and in 1985 they selected Dawn Primarolo in the place of Michael Cocks as parliamentary candidate.

On the following day, 8 May, Benn was selected for Bristol East. An election was clearly imminent, the government was buoyed up on the success of the Falklands campaign, it would be foolish to waste the enthusiasm. Margaret Thatcher called the election for 9 June.

The fact that he faced what was largely a new constituency was not the only problem for Benn. There had also been a change in the city as a whole. Manufacturing industry had declined in Bristol as it had over the rest of the country; trade union membership and trade union consciousness had diminished as unemployment rose. The high housing costs in London meant that young professionals who were not Labour voters had moved to Bristol, where they could afford better properties than in the capital.

The negative press Benn received also had a more significant effect in a constituency where he had not been in personal contact with the constituents by helping them individually. He had dealt with 40,000 cases in Bristol South-East, but not many of the people concerned now lived in Bristol East. David Langham said, 'Even when the press turned him into a bogeyman you still got the people who knew him and knew what he stood for. But people who didn't know him would quote from the tabloids and you could still see the quote marks around it when they were saying it – he said this, he said that, he's got millions put away.'[9]

Benn still had a vast number of loyal supporters. George Easton, one of the few old comrades who were in the new constituency, said, 'We were getting people coming to canvass from all over the country, from the Midlands, coachloads of miners from Wales. They were horrified that people weren't going to come out and vote for Tony Benn. They would come back to the committee rooms astonished at it – how could anyone not want to vote for Tony Benn?'[10]

The count was held at Brislington School, the largest comprehensive in Avon, set among vast playing fields. There was as large a press corps as Benn had ever had at a count: 'they had all come to be there at the killing,' he said.[11] Benn and his supporters arrived jubilant. One of them, Bob Glendinning, said, 'We started off quite confident. Our count was behind the rest of the country. I had a little radio and reported back the early results – they were met with incredulity. We didn't expect to lose nationally. We felt the gradual onset of depression. I don't think he expected defeat and he was quite devastated.'[12]

While the Bristol East returning officers took the pink tape from the black ballot boxes and poured out the votes on tables, Tony Benn sat watching a portable television. He was aghast at the enormity of the national defeat: it would be the greatest electoral disaster for Labour since 1935. Caroline Benn reported back on how his own votes were piling up. He was behind the Conservative, but not by much.

When the result was announced a great cheer went up from the Conservatives; there was a stunned silence from the Labour supporters. Tony Benn had lost by 1790 votes. The winning candidate, Jonathan Sayeed, was himself struck by the sense of occasion and paid tribute to Benn's service to Bristol, recognising that he could have gone to a safe Labour seat elsewhere but had decided not to desert the city.

Benn spoke of the Chartists and the suffragettes, for 'every election is a tribute to their strengths'. Secondly, he wanted to thank the people of Bristol, 'who over a third of a century have returned me to Parliament, and to say how glad I am that I stayed, since nothing but the decision of the people of Bristol would ever have induced me to leave this city'.[13] Following this speech, said Glendinning, 'There were great cheers but whatever he said would have been met with great cheers. He was comforting people who were shocked and upset. The younger ones were in tears, they couldn't comprehend it – how could it happen to Tony?'[14]

Benn spoke again to supporters crowding round outside the school, saying, 'I hope nobody will shed any tears for me, because

I am going to carry on my work.' No one heeded him for when he spoke again at the constituency headquarters the entire room was filled with people crying and a drunk young man repeated the refrain, 'Why did you do it, Tony? Why didn't you leave Bristol?'[15] The most common Labour Party view was that of Herbert Rogers:[3] that it had been a conspiracy by the establishment and the Labour right wing to eliminate Benn. 'The only way they could get rid of him was to get rid of his constituency.'[16]

Labour's defeat nationally had come after an exceptionally badly organised campaign, against an opponent superior in all tactical respects. Confidence and pride in Thatcher's leadership after the Falklands had brought the Conservatives out in strength to demonstrate their support. Lack of confidence in Foot and the disunity even of the Labour Party front bench over policy had weakened the Labour vote. As Benn said, 'In 1983 not only couldn't we persuade the public to support Labour policy, we couldn't persuade the leadership to support it. Jim Callaghan and Harold Wilson came out against it, the front bench didn't agree with it.'[17] The other major factor was the SDP splitting the anti-Tory vote. In the end Thatcher had almost 400 seats with just over 42 per cent of the vote. The Liberals had seventeen seats, their best result since 1935. The SDP had six seats. But the SDP and Liberals between them had 7,780,949 votes, close to the Labour Party's 8,456,934. Benn consoled himself that at least eight million people had been prepared to vote for a socialist programme.

Michael Foot was in disgrace for his disastrous electoral performance and, with Benn out of the way, there was no reason to delay his departure. He telephoned Neil Kinnock to ensure he was ready to assume the mantle, and worked out a strategy with Clive Jenkins of ASTMS. On 12 June in a prearranged call while Kinnock was waiting to appear on a national radio programme, Jenkins called him to nominate him for the leadership. The first other candidates heard that a contest was under way was the news that Kinnock already had a head start.

That day Tony Benn was meeting for an election post-mortem in Chris Mullin's flat with his leading supporters, including Stuart Holland, Jo Richardson, Frances Morrell, Ken Livingstone, Audrey Wise, Tony Banks, Reg Race and Michael Meacher. Without Benn, there was no realistic candidate. The sense of loss was so great that Tony Banks, newly elected for Newham North-West, offered to resign his seat so that Benn could fight it. Benn turned down the offer. The Bennites juggled around a slate involving Meacher as leader and Richardson as deputy but it was obviously hopeless, Kinnock so clearly had sufficient support in all three sections of the electoral college. The best they could do was to propose Michael Meacher as deputy leader, leaving the leadership to Kinnock.

Roy Hattersley contested the leadership from the right, as did Eric Heffer from the traditional left, but there was nothing in it. When the election took place at the conference in Brighton in October 1983, Kinnock received 71 per cent as against 19 per cent for Hattersley and 6 for Heffer. The deputy leadership was a more closely fought contest, but eventually Hattersley won 67 to Meacher's 27 per cent, despite Benn's active support for Meacher at rallies. The magic only worked for Benn in person – it was not transferable.

The London constituency in which Benn lived, North Kensington, sent him as a delegate to the conference, where he again watched others gathering the fruits of reforms he had worked for. He was mandated to vote for Eric Heffer in the first ballot and Neil Kinnock in the second, though he was not obliged to cast his vote a second time as Kinnock's first result gave him a clear majority. Neil Kinnock's remark about Tony Benn at the time, that he 'couldn't knock the skin off a rice pudding', says rather more about Kinnock's character than it does about Benn's.[18]

The NEC had previously agreed to permit defeated candidates to stand for the executive as if they were still MPs and he was gratified to be top of the poll again in the constituency section, perhaps from a sympathy vote for the loss of his constituency. He received the highest vote he had had in twenty years.

Benn suffered what he could only describe as bereavement at losing his constituency and was in tears much of the time he was reading the letters of support.[19] Pam Tatlow used the same figure of speech: 'He was devastated. He couldn't believe it. He was like someone in mourning.'

Part of his free time he spent in travelling, to Hiroshima in August

1983 for the World Peace Conference and to Cuba in October with Caroline. He worked on his archives and waited for a constituency.

Financially Tony Benn was as well off as if he had stayed in the Commons, for his redundancy payment reflected his long service. He also immediately received an offer from the *Guardian* to write a weekly column. He enjoyed rediscovering his family and acquainting himself with new members. His first grandchild, Michael, was born on 7 October 1981 to Hilary Benn and Sally Clark. Tony Benn did not tire of noting the joys of being a grandfather in his diary.

He realised, at the age of fifty-eight, with no constituency and with the Labour Party in disarray, what his father must have felt like in 1935 in the same situation and at the same age. The memory of his father's later achievements reassured him, for William Wedgwood Benn was still active in politics twenty-five years after that defeat at the polls.

34

Chesterfield and the Miners' Strike

The first intimation that there might be a new constituency for Benn came from the unlikely quarter of Michael Cocks, who met Benn at Bristol station while both were on their way to speak at a memorial meeting for a Labour Party official. Perhaps out of a sense of guilty obligation, Cocks gave Benn the inside information that the MP for Chesterfield, Eric Varley, would be resigning his seat to take up a job in industry. When he arrived home Benn called Arthur Scargill, who encouraged him to be ready to respond when asked to be nominated. That evening, on 11 November 1983, the Executive Committee of Chesterfield Labour Party heard from their member, the former Secretary of State for Energy and then for Industry, that he was to become chief executive of the Coalite company, and that they must therefore look for a new MP.

Chesterfield CLP had not yet undergone the radicalisation which had been experienced by most CLPs in the late 1970s and early 1980s. It was still dominated by the old guard, who tended to be conservative. Of the younger and more radical element, Tom and Margaret Vallins and Derbyshire miners' leader Peter Heathfield were on the executive, though Heathfield was obliged to give his primary support to an NUM candidate.

That night, with the small cluster of left-wingers talking about the possible candidates in the Vallins' house opposite the Labour club, Tony Benn's name was suggested and Tom Vallins called him there and then, at 12.20 a.m., to see if he was interested. Benn was, and soon set his own network in operation, calling Dennis Skinner, MP for the nearby town of Bolsover, and one of Benn's few allies on the NEC, and Ken Coates, who lived in another nearby town, Matlock, for a rundown on the constituency.

Tom and Margaret Vallins with a few others set about producing a programme for the next few weeks to promote Benn as a candidate. They managed to obtain the most precious item imaginable in the circumstances: a list of the delegates to the GMC which would select the candidate. Now they could seek nominations from the unions, affiliated organisations and branches whose delegates made up the selection conference.

Margaret Vallins said, 'We had to get him here to let him speak to people. We knew if we did that he would be in. We had to keep the press at bay until people had been allowed to see him for themselves. When they did meet him people would say, "We didn't think he was like that." '[1]

Tom Vallins and Bas Barker, of Chesterfield Trades Council, set up trade union campaign meetings to which all candidates for nomination were invited, though principally they were aimed at allowing trade unionists to meet Benn. He visited Chesterfield for the first time on 1 December, finding himself in familiar territory as far as the press was concerned, for they followed his every move. His Chesterfield supporters used a variety of ruses to foil the reporters, having cars speed off in different directions so that it was not known which one he was in, and spreading false rumours about where he was going to be.

After midnight on Friday, 7 January 1984, Tom Vallins called Benn to tell him he had not been shortlisted by the Executive Committee. Despite having thirteen nominations, more than anyone else, the right wing on the executive had edged him out. They had used a familiar procedure where there are multiple votes: they each cast some of their five votes for their favoured candidates, and the rest for candidates who had no chance. This left Benn with only the votes from his supporters, who were in the minority, and no second-, third-, fourth- or fifth-choice votes from the right wing.

At once there was frantic lobbying in Chesterfield for the GMC, which had to ratify the executive's decision at a meeting the following Sunday, to reject it. Many of the delegates at that meeting, including those who were far from being Benn supporters, were angry at the way the nominations had been manipulated. The ruse thus backfired, for the GMC rejected their executive's list and added Benn's name. He came out of it as a wronged man for whom justice had been achieved by the action of popular democracy. If Benn had employed an image-maker, they could not have dreamed up a more attractive position for him. The presence of the press in large numbers outside the meeting also added to the feeling in Chesterfield Labour Party that they were the centre of attention and it was Benn's involvement that had put them there.

The following week the same people convened for the selection. The 127 delegates believed they were in for a long meeting and came with flasks of coffee and sandwiches, for once inside the room they had to stay until a candidate was selected. Outside in the swirling snow a vast crowd of media people waited; one photographer climbed a tree hoping he could grab a picture of the meeting through the window.

Benn was up against an exceptionally strong team. Chief among them were Bill Flannagan, leader of the Labour Group on Chesterfield Council; Cliff Fox, leader of the Labour Group on North-East Derbyshire County Council, who was sponsored by the NUM; and Philip Whitehead, a television producer and MP for Derby North until 1983, when he had lost his seat.

They drew lots to decide who would speak first and Benn found himself in sixth position. This was a stroke of luck, because it gave the impression that all the other speakers were build-ups to the big event. One delegate had a fit while Benn was speaking and had to be carried out, an event which might perturb any orator. The man had to be placed in a side room with the door open so that he could, nominally, take part in the meeting, or he would have lost his precious vote.

Benn gave a clear, straightforward speech and the meeting moved to a ballot. The first round showed the shape of the meeting: it was Fox, Whitehead, Benn. This meant that the NUM-sponsored local man was in the lead, followed by Whitehead, favoured by the right wing, and Benn for the left. The second ballot produced the same result. The NUM delegates were under instructions not to switch their votes to another candidate until after the third ballot but clearly the result would be the same as the first two. They then swapped to Benn. The final voting figures were Benn 64, Whitehead

435

36 and Flannagan 27. Because the total of the other two did not reach Benn's figure, he was the outright winner.

The following six weeks were among the most active of Benn's life. He was determined to see as many individual voters as he possibly could, the only way to overcome the negative image he had been given over the years. His personal approach worked. As Tom Vallins said, 'Once you've got Tony to a group of people he made them relax. After ten or twelve minutes you would see them warming.' But winning the election voter by voter makes for a great many minutes of socialising. Just one day for which there is a record, 5 February, a month from the poll, Benn was canvassing from 10 a.m. till 11 p.m. The Benn campaign also had to neutralise the press. Their plan was to avoid the daily press conferences which are a standard procedure in by-elections. In Chesterfield, the primary relationship would be between the candidate and the voters. The media would be there as onlookers; they would not be allowed to set the agenda. In the end even the *Daily Mail* correspondent was obliged to concede that 'Mr Benn has fought a brilliantly low-key campaign entirely on his own terms.'[2]

At the end of the campaign, 50 per cent of Chesterfield people had seen Benn and he had spoken to meetings with a total attendance of 15,000. The Benn family lent a hand. Joshua Benn, a member of the Labour Party Computer Advisory Group (later called Computing for Labour), was able to computerise the canvass data from one ward, making it the first computerised parliamentary by-election. Caroline Benn and Margaret Vallins set up a women's canvassing team which canvassed places which had never been canvassed before. This organisation later formed the basis for the Chesterfield women's support group in the miners' strike.

There was considerable tension between the local Labour Party and the full-time officials from Walworth Road who had arrived to run the campaign as is customary in by-elections. The antagonism was never more evident than when Peter Tatchell visited, travelling at his own expense, to volunteer to do some canvassing. He was unceremoniously ordered out by one of the Walworth Road officials. When he stood his ground they conceded and had him whisked off to a far corner of the constituency and told not to show his face outside the committee rooms. The ward where he was placed needed canvassers, however, so they encouraged him to go out and meet the voters. Only a few recognised him and they were pleased to see him.[3] When Benn found out what had happened he made a point of telling the media that he was delighted Tatchell had been there and would be glad to have him back. Senior party members arrived to lend a hand, including Neil Kinnock, Roy Hattersley and Denis Healey.

Polling day saw one of the most extreme press attacks on Benn in his entire career. The *Sun* printed a full-page article headed 'Benn on the Couch' in which they purported to establish whether Benn really was 'raving bonkers'. They had given information on Benn to an American psychiatrist who allegedly reported that 'He is greedy for power, and will do anything to satisfy his hunger . . . a man driven by his own self-interest and thinking of himself as God-like . . . [a] Mr Nobody type character'.[4] The psychiatrist, later tracked down by a television programme, judged himself to have been 'lied to and misquoted'.[5] Several Labour MPs, including Michael Foot, complained to the Press Council, which later censured the newspaper.

The eventual vote was 24,633 for Benn against a Liberal vote of 18,369. Benn had a majority of 6264, lower than Varley's majority because the hard-fought campaign had brought out more Tory and Liberal voters. The record number of candidates – seventeen, most of them joke candidates or single-issue campaigners – may well have encouraged more voting than had taken place previously. The Liberal vote was doubled and the Tory vote halved, but Benn had not merely held the Labour vote, he had increased it, achieving 752 more votes than Eric Varley in 1983.

A week after the election Tony Benn had his opportunity to prove his worth to his new constituency. Chesterfield people who had any doubts that Benn was anything more than a 'media politician' learned differently in the following year of crippling hardship for the miners, during which Benn, as NUM official John Burrows said, 'was always there at your shoulder when you needed him, geeing the lads up. He was our closest ally on the picket line. I couldn't speak too highly of him.'[6]

The strike was sparked by the convergence of a number of issues, not least the need for Margaret Thatcher to prove she could succeed where Heath had failed. This personal consideration only gave the issue more spice, however, for the deep and underlying reason was a genuine conviction among hard-line monetarist Tories that Britain's fortunes could not be reversed until the government had 'dealt with' the unions. It would be called class war by the left and sound management by the right but the effect was the same.

Beating the rest of the unions, but leaving the miners intact, would be cowardly and ineffective. The miners were the backbone of the trade union movement: if they could be brought down, the battle was won. The conflict was not entered into without thought and careful planning. In February 1981 extra state money was quickly found to avert a miners' strike over pit closures, the very issue over which the 1984–5 strike was fought. The time was not right. At this stage only James Prior's 1980 Trade Union Act was in place. This contributed to union democracy by permitting public money to be used for strike and leadership ballots, made closed shop agreements far more difficult and outlawed secondary picketing. That was not enough to beat the miners. Norman Tebbit's 1982 Act was the key: this took away the immunity of trade unions for financial loss caused by a strike. Now unions could be fined heavily for conducting 'unlawful' strikes.

While both sides expected a battle over closures, the strike actually came about through a foolish National Coal Board decision, taken at local level, to close Cortonwood pit in South Yorkshire. This led the National Union of Mineworkers to put into action a contingency plan which had previously been agreed at their conference, that a national strike should be called to prevent a pit-closure scheme. The failure to call a national strike ballot lost the miners' leadership a great deal of support, including that of Neil Kinnock and others in the Labour leadership, and gave a justification for those miners, particularly in Nottinghamshire, who did not wish to strike. It could be argued that the Labour leadership would have given scant support whatever the circumstances, and that Nottinghamshire would have disobeyed even an instruction based on a national strike ballot, but the task of undermining the strike need not have been made so easy.

As far as Tony Benn was concerned these were his people and he had to fight for them, regardless of the national issues. He would be up at 4.00 a.m. to do the round of the picket lines, taking soup and good cheer to the men at nearby collieries. He was particularly welcome at times of high tension, because police behaviour was more restrained when a senior politician was observing. He toured the country speaking for the miners, addressing 211 meetings in their support in the year of the strike. He visited the USA, Canada and Italy encouraging international support and collecting donations.

In Parliament he was one of a phalanx of Labour MPs arguing that the government had engineered the dispute to assault the unions; criticising police conduct; attacking the penal bail conditions imposed by magistrates' courts on arrested pickets; pointing out the involvement of the armed forces in supplying facilities used in the policing of mining communities; accusing the government of telephone tapping; and of slowing down the processing of applications for welfare benefits for miners' families to put pressure on them to return to work. He raised the question of the British Embassy in Oslo demanding information from a Norwegian trade union about the extent of its support for the NUM and later called for an amnesty for miners who had been imprisoned during the strike.

The strike transformed British politics. Miners' support groups around the country, particularly in the relatively prosperous south, 'adopted' a mining community and collected money and supplies for them. Cultural stereotypes were challenged as north and south met. Most significantly, the role of women in traditional industrial communities was changed beyond recognition as the women's support groups took command of the home front and became involved in politics, often for the first time. Chesterfield Women's Action Group ran the main distribution network, distributing food parcels to thirty-four other centres in North Derbyshire.

On the middle ground stood the TUC and the Labour Party, whose members often showed individual sympathy to the miners' cause but were not prepared to countenance any industrial action in their support. Collieries in Nottinghamshire, Warwickshire and Leicestershire continued to produce coal. Coal was still being shipped in from abroad. There were no power cuts.

The government too had those who wished to make a display of solidarity, and right-wing figures funded legal actions by working miners against the NUM. The union was subject to other actions under trade union legislation, the net result of which was the sequestration of its assets. This led to a financial paralysis, eased only by some exceptionally creative accounting. Nor was the government prepared to be caught out by flying pickets or mass picketing. The new trade union laws were augmented by new national co-ordinating powers for the police. Cars of pickets would be stopped hundreds of miles from their destination and turned back; on the picket lines police fought miners with a ferocity unparalleled in the recent past.

The enduring image of the miners' strike was of mounted police charging relentlessly into miners at the Orgreave coking depot at Rotherham on 18 June 1984. Police in full riot gear crashed through the crowds of miners, lashing out with truncheons in a spectacle which was criticised as 'suspending the rule of law to maintain public order'. Prosecution cases against each of the ninety-five people charged with offences that day collapsed and South Yorkshire police paid half a million pounds in damages and costs to thirty-nine miners who were injured.[7] Orgreave was just the most infamous example. Violence was widespread during the strike and was by no means limited to the police: attacks on working miners by strikers resulted in manslaughter on one occasion.

Moral questions about the violence aside, the most important issue was whether it was strategically advisable to continue to use the weapon of the mass picket when it was ineffective in achieving its objectives, resulted in a terrifying level of casualties and damaged the miners' cause in the public mind by associating them with intimidatory tactics. It was as if Arthur Scargill, unable to achieve a victory, decided to have a massacre instead, driving the troops in wave after wave, day after day, towards an incomparably better-armed and organised enemy, as if it were hoped that the magnitude of the sacrifice alone would bring active support from the rest of industry.

Ken Coates urged Benn to use his influence with Arthur Scargill to change the strategy. Benn would not, and did not regret his decision later. He said, 'I have no doubts about it at all. Arthur was one of the few trade union leaders I have ever met in my life who wasn't looking for a peerage – he was trying to defend his members. He was a tough character, and his leadership of the miners was very strong. It was a consolidated campaign and you had to back them. When there's a dispute it comes to the point: who's side are you on? That was the basic argument.'[8]

The heroic nature of the struggle seemed to have overturned Benn's political judgement. He had always tended to romanticise the working class. Now his own constituency was part of the very aristocracy of labour. He represented miners who were fighting for the survival of their communities and suffering greater hardships than the country had seen since the war. Once he arrived late at a meeting of left-wingers in the House of Commons and said, 'I've just been with the miners – they are like Greek gods.' Ken Coates agreed they were nice young lads and had had more sunshine than they were used to.[9]

Coates urged a political campaign to unify the country behind the miners' cause. He wanted to change the nature of the debate from one of industrial militancy to a household question. He said, 'The political instrument was to set fire to Thatcher's tents behind her lines, to make a major crusade in the country about fuel poverty and the need to connect the dispute with welfare, with the relief of hypothermia, the distribution of all this coal to the poor.'[10] Benn's failure to support this initiative at the NEC caused the cooling of one of the most valuable, and stabilising, political friendships of his life. Coates's scheme may have seemed idealistic but it was a model of realism compared to Tony Benn's proposal for a general strike 'to protect free trade unionism'.[11]

At the end of the year-long strike the miners agreed to return to work, proudly flying their banners and marching behind their bands. On 5 March 1985 Benn joined the miners and their wives at 5 a.m. to march to Markham Colliery. 'It was an extraordinary day,' he wrote. 'I felt drained of all emotion by the end of it because every emotion swept through me like a gale – tragedy, wanting to weep at seeing these people who had sacrificed so much having to go back without having won, then tremendous pride that they could go back with their banners high and not give any sort of impression that they were beaten, which they are not of course. Then a feeling of hope and dignity as we stood there and applauded as they all went into the colliery.'[12]

One of Benn's greatest leadership qualities was his strength in defeat. In the difficult days after the strike, he told them all was not lost. 'We can look back with pride at what has been done,' he said to the Durham Miners' Gala, 'confident that future generations will commemorate the heroes of Saltley and Orgreave just as now we celebrate the Tolpuddle Martyrs and the Chartists.' Nor could it be claimed that the cause for which the strike took place, the prevention of pit closures, was ill judged. Between the end of the strike and 1991 the Coal Board closed 105 pits and made 134,400 men redundant. No protection was given by the government to the miners who had worked through the strike, or to the breakaway union which was formed during it.

The underlying reason for the success of the Thatcher government in the strike was that the nation was no longer reliant on British-mined coal for fuelling power stations. One of the reasons for the push toward nuclear power was to reduce national reliance on the truculent and well organised mine workers.

As someone who had been responsible for energy longer than any other minister – taking some responsibility for it in all three of his cabinet posts – Benn contributed weightily to the debate over nuclear power and, in particular, the inquiries over which system to use for the new series of reactors. Officials at the Department of Energy still wanted to commission Pressurised Water Reactors which were an American development, pointing to the success of the French nuclear industry which had pushed ahead with PWRs and had nearly 70 per cent of its electricity produced by nuclear power as against less than 20 per cent in the UK.

Benn argued that the true cost of nuclear power had never been made explicit because so many of the costs were carried in the defence budget, which resulted from the tie up between the civil and military uses of nuclear power. The government was eventually obliged to hold an inquiry into the commissioning of a Pressurised Water Reactor at Sizewell in Suffolk. Benn worked closely with the National Union of Mineworkers in 1983 in preparing evidence for the inquiry, an activity which, incidentally, stood him in good stead with leading figures in the NUM when he needed them when he was fighting to be selected at Chesterfield.

At the Sizewell inquiry Benn argued that the building of a coal-fired power station was cheaper and with lower construction costs and less environmental damage, especially when decommissioning occurs, than a nuclear station.

The station did go ahead, and six years later he gave evidence at a similar inquiry into the siting of another PWR at Hinkley Point in Somerset.

He was not restrained in his verbal evidence to the Hinkley Point inquiry, saying that for eight years in the various departments he headed, 'I was told time and time again by my officials, Secretary of State, Minister of Technology, "We understand your feelings but, of course, you have got to face the harsh reality that nuclear power is cheaper." It was a lie. I hate to use plain language in this way. I was lied to time and again because the true economics of this was known from the beginning. I ask myself, "Why did they lie to the Minister?" They lied to the Minister because they wanted the Minister to go on saying this was an atoms for peace programme when actually it was an atoms for war programme. The whole basis of this has been nuclear weapons from the beginning. I blame myself very seriously for being so trusting, but I did not appreciate the full implications at the time.'[13]

While the behaviour of some civil servants may have been Machiavellian in concealing the truth in order to enlist the idealistic young Tony Benn in the pro-nuclear cause, the fact was that he needed little encouragement to promote nuclear power and neither did the civil servants. The civil servants also were seized with enthusiasm for a bright, cheap, clean future for civil nuclear power and in their enthusiasm they submerged the realities in their own minds and their own reports. They too were victims of hope.

35

'Speaking Out for Socialism in the Eighties'

Chesterfield was undergoing a dramatic radicalisation. Eleven days after Benn's election the constituency had had its annual general meeting and the old guard were voted out, Tom Vallins taking over as constituency secretary and John Burrows as president (chair). After the miners' strike, Tony Benn ensured that the party maintained the momentum of political action. John Burrows said in 1991, 'Before Tony came, political activity was limited to supporting candidates for election. It was going through the motions of running the party. He has transformed political activity in Chesterfield beyond belief. It has been one long round of political debate, always led by Tony.'[1]

The new politics in Chesterfield centred on three initiatives. The Community Defence Campaign used the tactics evolved during the strike to give support to others who were perceived to be under threat – hospital workers, teachers and print workers. An International Committee developed the contacts made during the strike and stimulated support for trade unionists in places which formerly generated little interest in Chesterfield, such as South Africa and El Salvador. Most remarkably, for a constituency Labour Party, they produced the Chesterfield Declaration, which set out the long-term aims and objectives of the party, starting with the stirring assertion of 'The right to life, free from fear, oppression, ignorance, preventable ill-health or poverty'. It was produced after a series of meetings at which Chesterfield people discussed their own experiences and aspirations. Copies were sent to every constituency Labour Party in the country and many of them set about examining their own aims and objectives. It was a typical Benn combat strategy: the revisionists had taken the conference and Walworth Road, he would launch ideological guerrilla warfare in the constituencies.[2]

He was, as ever, an exemplary constituency MP. As Bas Barker said, 'His weakness is he doesn't know how to say no. Anyone can come with the most outlandish problem under the sun and he says, "Leave it with me." You've got to make some selection.'[3] Most of Benn's cases were of common hardship which he could do little to alleviate.

Benn needed a strong base. The defeat of the miners and the triumphant progress of the Tory right made his former colleagues re-examine their political positions. The break with Tony Benn was ratified in an article in *New Socialist* in May 1985 called 'Bennism without Benn'. Benn wrote in his diary, 'What in effect the article says is that Ken Coates, Michael Meacher, Tom Sawyer, Stuart Holland, Frances Morrell have all deserted me and I am now alone with Dennis Skinner and the headbangers.'[4] That is a fair résumé.

What had been the 'Bennite' left, grouped around the Labour Co-ordinating Committee, began to move towards a less confrontational relationship with the leadership and a pragmatic attitude to some Thatcher policies. Frances Morrell had already argued elsewhere that the alternative economic strategy (which she had helped to create) was no longer a viable remedy, and Ken Coates, later to be a Member of the European Parliament, was arguing for a more creative relationship with Europe involving alliances with European socialists. In a rare expression of bitterness Benn described it as 'the final repudiation by the fair-weather friends'.[5]

Typically, Benn reacted to the erosion of support and distancing of his friends with no compromise or admission of defeat. He set about building a power structure elsewhere which would keep the flame burning. The group he now worked with – though he was never much of a team man, to put it mildly – was the Campaign Group. This was set up in 1981 and at that time was based on the Benn supporters for the deputy leadership. It would also work with others outside Parliament, including members of the European Parliament. Another initiative to keep the flame alive was the Independent Left Corresponding Society, a broadly based left-wing think tank meeting in Benn's home from late 1985. The mock nineteenth century name was invented by Benn, though the idea for the society came from Ralph Miliband. Other members included Tariq Ali, Robin Blackburn, Jeremy Corbyn and Hilary Wainwright. It was an informal group, 'trying to carry the socialist message over the very dark years of Thatcherism', according to Benn.[6]

His speeches over the second half of the 1980s have a revivalist air, with titles like 'Socialist Renewal', 'Reviving Socialism' and 'Reestablishing the Left'. It says a great deal for Benn's diligence that this superlative orator was still, after forty years of public speaking, taking meticulous care with his speeches. His speech to the Durham Miners' Gala in July 1987, for example, was written out, typed, with salient points marked out in three colours of ink, then sealed in plastic to prevent rain damage.

Benn's instinct when under attack was to change the nature of the debate. This was the impetus behind the publication of his diaries. His feeling was that Neil Kinnock's Labour Party was offering nothing more than the failed Wilson and Callaghan governments had offered – no alternative to capitalism but a promise to make it work in a somewhat ameliorated manner. He wished to demonstrate why those Labour governments had been so disappointing. His express intention was to 'intervene' in political life with the diaries. 'If I don't do it soon it will be of only historical interest,' he wrote.[7]

Crossman had shown the way, publishing his diary despite efforts in the courts to suppress it. The civil service attempted to have diarists and memorialists sign a memorandum (as recommended by the Radcliffe Report on the Crossman affair) agreeing that they would not publish without first submitting the manuscript to the Cabinet Office. Roy Jenkins, Peter Shore and Tony Benn agreed between themselves not to sign it.

With his love of anniversaries, Benn had determined in advance that on his sixtieth birthday in April 1985 he would decide whether to publish the diaries. With this in mind he had invited the Rowntree Foundation to look at his archives and they gave him a grant of £20,000 for transcribing the diaries and putting some order into the massive number of files covering his speeches, his periods in government and his Labour Party work which now occupied the entire basement of the house in Notting Hill and a number of sheds at Stansgate.

He had already decided to publish the diaries when, coincidentally, Richard Cohen of Hutchinson wrote asking him if they might publish them. By October 1985 they had reached agreement and Benn looked round initially for someone to organise the task of transcription. Chris Mullin, who had edited *Arguments for Socialism*, suggested Ruth Winstone, who arrived in December 1985 for a temporary sojourn and started reducing the ten million words of existing typescript from the 1960s and untranscribed tapes to a standard typescript on a word processor.

She remained to take charge of the whole project, editing what became a series of five books published between 1987 and 1992. It was apparent as the tapes were transcribed that as the 1970s wore on Benn had become more voluble in his diary dictation. Volume 1 had to be reduced to a third of its original manuscript length; Volume 3 needed to go down from 1,750,000 words to just over 300,000 words. It was an onerous task, because a great deal of the diary concerned accounts of meetings, and a detailed exposition of who said what at an NEC subcommittee twenty years ago is of limited interest even to the politically enthusiastic, and the selection of what was to be published was discussed in detail between the diarist and his editor.

The first volume, dealing with the period 1963–7, was published in 1987. Reviewers tended to come from the field of politics or political comment and to have known Benn for many years. They were therefore inclined to criticise the man rather than the work. The diaries as a whole made a significant impact in the academic world which it is not possible to assess in the short term. They covered a longer period of high office than any published twentieth-century diaries. By the time the fifth volume was published, they encompassed almost thirty years of political life, including the writer's periods in office during both Labour governments from the beginning to the end. Neither Castle nor Crossman was so long in office.

While the diaries were being edited, the Benn Archives were made available to researchers, a development which also helped to increase the penetration of Benn's ideas. He said, 'The undefended frontier of the establishment is the recent past, because the historians haven't begun to distort it and the media have forgotten the arguments. You turn up with your troops where they're least expecting you.'[8] He described the period during which his work centred on the basement office as the happiest and most productive of his life.

Alongside the enforced remoulding of trade unions came the government's increasing encroachment on the powers of local authorities. In particular, Labour councils were obliged to dismantle the public services they had themselves built up. The symbol of council resistance came to be Liverpool, where councillors had decided to allow the council to go bankrupt rather than make cuts. At the 1985 Labour Party conference Neil Kinnock denounced the campaign, which, he said, 'had ended with the grotesque chaos of a Labour council hiring taxis to travel around a city handing out redundancy notices to its own workers'.

Eric Heffer walked off the platform as Kinnock was speaking. Less conspicuously, Benn too left, unable to bring himself to stay and hear the leader attacking his own members. Outside the hall he saw a woman delegate crying and asked her what was the matter. 'I can't understand what they've done to our party,' she said. Benn told her not to worry but then he too began to cry, moved by her distress, and he had to turn away for he was giving no comfort.[9] At the same conference Tony Benn failed, for the first time, to top the poll for the constituency section of the NEC. He came third.

For several years the Labour leadership was preoccupied with rooting out heresy and expelling dissidents from the party. In Parliament, the House of Lords as a whole proved to be a more effective opposition than the Labour front bench in the Commons. One of the contributory aspects of the pre-eminence of Thatcherism was this weakness of the opposition. Another factor was that Neil Kinnock was not a very adept parliamentarian and was not apparently even very interested in Parliament. Before becoming leader he had only two jobs: a year as parliamentary private secretary to Michael Foot, who described him as 'one of the worst PPSs in history', and opposition education spokesman from 1979 to 1983. During one year of his tenure of this position he had the tenth-worst attendance record of any British MP.[10] This was because, in the year after he had led the abstentions against Benn at the conference of 1981, he spent

virtually all his time travelling the country addressing meeti⌐
bid for hearts and minds in the Labour Party.

Kinnock always looked uncomfortable when facing Thatc⌐
well he might. She outclassed him in every respect. As Benn ⌐ ⌐⌐⌐,
'The Labour Party is totally inadequate in the House of Commons.
Neil Kinnock yaps like a little dog at her heels and she kicks him
aside.'[11] Benn and Thatcher make an interesting comparison, for
both were the candidates of the constituencies. Benn was anyway
able to respect her for her single-mindedness in carrying out her
policies and for having always stood for her principles: 'people think
she says what she means and sticks to it and that is very important
in politics'.

The Tory grandees looked with disdain at the shopkeeper's daughter from Grantham who was so insistent that everything should be
changed. There is a parallel in the attitude of the trade union leaders
to Tony Benn. How dare he tell them what to do, or appeal to their
members over their heads? Thatcher would tell her supporters in
the Conservative clubs around the country just what she intended
to do and they would cheer her to the echo, just as Benn would
address rallies of enthusiastic supporters.

Thatcher's solutions to the problems of Britain, moreover, were
no more profound than Benn's. Such well promoted initiatives as
privatisation of nationalised industries and the sale of council houses
did less than nothing to address the real problems: under-investment
in industry and a shortage of affordable housing. Indeed, such gesture politics may have contributed to decline in that they diverted
attention from genuine issues.

During the 1980s Benn introduced a series of Bills to stimulate
interest in various topics and to show how it would be possible to
change the law. During the controversy over the abolition of the
Greater London Council he introduced the Rights of Londoners
Bill which gave back Londoners the right to elect a city-wide council.
He introduced the Northern Ireland (Termination of Jurisdiction)
Bill, based on the Act terminating the British Mandate in Palestine.
There was a Miners' Amnesty (General Pardon) Bill to relieve
miners of any penalties suffered as a result of actions undertaken in
the strike. The Democratic Oaths Bill would replace oaths of loyalty
to the monarch with an oath to British democracy. The Common

Ownership of Land Bill nationalised all large tracts of land and another Bill disestablished the Church of England. However remote the possibility that the legislation he put forward would be passed, even under a Labour government, the campaigning purpose was served of making the hoped-for changes almost tangible. With a Bill to hold, a radical change seemed less improbable.

In his fourth decade in the Commons Benn was one of the most highly skilled parliamentarians, some would say the best in the House. Making full use of these skills, he scored a significant victory over the Zircon affair. This concerned a documentary made by the BBC about the secret development of the Zircon spy satellite. The film implied that its makers had access to technical details about the satellite. This led to police raids to discover the identity of the informant who had supplied journalists with sensitive military information. BBC chiefs had already decided not to screen the film and an injunction was obtained to stop it from being shown to private audiences. One proposed audience was composed of MPs in the House of Commons. The Speaker made the error of ruling that an injunction which prevented a video of the film being shown elsewhere also applied to the House of Commons.

The government put forward a motion supporting the Speaker. An opposition amendment endorsed the Speaker's ruling though with reservations: it would prevent from seeing the film even the Public Accounts Committee and the Defence Select Committee, which should not have been denied access to material which might assist them in their work of public scrutiny. During the debate Benn questioned whether it was right for any government to engage in major military projects without telling Parliament. 'Is it right that ministers should be able to go to any court and use the magic words "national security" as the basis for a court injunction? In a democracy it is for the House and electors to decide what is in the national interest.'[12]

Benn submitted a manuscript amendment recommending that the whole matter be referred to a Privileges Committee. The opposition and the government both backed down and allowed Benn's amendment to go through. As the Speaker wrote to him later, 'It is often claimed by the uninformed that speeches in Parliament have no impact and are unlikely to influence events. I am keeping a list of

450

those who in my time as Speaker have, by powerful argument, changed the course of a debate. Your *admirable* speech yesterday will always be an example to be quoted.'[13]

Thatcher's star was in the ascendant and no scandals, over *Belgrano* or Westland or *Spycatcher*, or the unsavoury behaviour of some of her ministers, seemed to alter her trajectory. This was confirmed by the June 1987 election, at which the Conservatives were returned with an overall majority, albeit reduced, of 102 seats.

The Labour campaign was conducted with exceptional skill by the new media managers at Walworth Road. The most important decision was to follow the route taken in the Chesterfield by-election and abandon the fixed routine of London press conferences as requiring too much time and effort which was not justified by the coverage they could expect from the press. Instead, the Labour campaigning team set the pace by organising 'photo-opportunities' around the country with brief on-site interviews for the media. Benn called it the most professional Labour campaign since 1959, which was praise indeed.[14]

The problem for Labour was that, despite the lacklustre performance of Thatcher and her team, she was still seen as a real leader and, despite the presidential-style promotion of Neil Kinnock, he was not.

Labour votes held up in the northern strongholds and in Scotland and Wales but the more prosperous and densely populated areas of the Midlands and the south stayed Conservative. Benn's vote in Chesterfield had held, at 24,532. The Liberal vote was down by more than 2000 votes and the Conservatives were still in third place, as they had been at the by-election. Benn's majority had gone up to 8577. He noted that in areas where 'hard-left' candidates stood, their majorities increased. Kinnock's response was to resume his assault on the hard left to make Labour more electorally popular.

The Liberals and SDP held no superlative attraction for the voter – they had won one seat less than they had in 1983 – but they again split the anti-Conservative vote, still a major factor in Thatcher's vast majority. It was these votes Kinnock was aiming to claw back by urging the Labour Party to the right. The two centre parties concluded that they would do better together, and in August 1987 the membership voted to merge. David Owen carried on with a dwindling band of personal followers until even he had to call it a day when the SDP candidate polled fewer votes than the representative of the Monster Raving Loony Party in a by-election in May 1990.

The disconsolate Labour Party leaders went through a detailed post-mortem, demonstrating a very different approach to that of Callaghan, who had explicitly refused Benn's attempt to talk about their defeat in 1979.[15] The campaign could not be faulted, so it must be the policies that were wrong. They had to look at what the public wanted from a political party, 'what the demand is' as one leading light put it, and then they must supply that demand.[16] Thus was the Policy Review born, an attempt to engage the public and party members in a debate on policy, something which in itself was not alien to proposals Benn had long been making about public involvement.

Benn said he did not in any way object to a policy review which actually looked at policy. He said, 'What was lacking about it was a depth of analysis. Instead of saying, "Let's look again at where we are and what's happening. How can we say relevant things about the rapidly changing circumstances in which we live?", it was, "What were we saying that we can drop, that will move us towards the centre and make us more acceptable?" It was a PR exercise.'[17]

It was in the aftermath of electoral defeat that the Independent Left Corresponding Society decided they must challenge the right-wing ideas of the Labour Party. They called together others of similar mind to a meeting in July 1987 at the Africa Centre in London where it was decided that there should be a socialist conference and that it should be held in Chesterfield.

The conference was held over 24 and 25 October 1987. It was open to socialists who were not Labour Party members and was no public-relations exercise; it was aimed at a hard ideological policy review. As Benn said in his introductory speech, 'Socialists must take a closer look at the moral base of their beliefs; at questions of class in a technological society; strengthen the democratic challenge to all unaccountable power; and re-establish solidarity and internationalism as the foundations of our work.' The conference became an annual event, moving to other northern venues after 1988.

452

For some Benn was a dinosaur of the left, full of outdated ideas which would never again secure an election victory. For others, including those who had previously supported him but whose current interest led them to cleave to Kinnock, he was making uncomfortably accurate statements about the betrayal of principle for short-term media advantage.

Benn received sixty-nine votes in the election for the shadow cabinet in 1987, not enough to be in but only fifteen short of entry. It was not that he hankered after a shadow cabinet place – he already had more government experience than any shadow cabinet member – but he wanted to show he was still in the game.

The next step for the left had to be to challenge the leadership. The current leadership had failed to win the election; a leadership challenge was only really viable when there was no new general election in the offing; the left needed a rallying point; and anyone with an opposing idea to the prevailing orthodoxy had a moral obligation to put it to the test.

As usual, Benn pondered long over whether to contest the leadership, and Caroline Benn advised against: he had given enough. He confided to Chris Mullin that all those who loved him thought it was a bad idea, and Mullin said he could include him in that.[18] It would be a strain and there would be calumny heaped upon him but, as he wrote at the end of the year, 'The old war horse in me sniffs the gunpowder, and prepares for battle.'[19] Arthur Scargill urged him to stand at the beginning of January 1988, as did the former Labour Party general secretary Jim Mortimer. Eric Heffer said to Benn on 11 January that they should stand together, and pressure from members of the Campaign Group for Benn to stand increased through the first quarter of the year.

Benn's own mind was made up by Kinnock's equivocation over support for the health service workers in February 1988. The light of political sense had failed, Benn felt, when the NEC was hostile to support for the National Health Service strike. His judgement was correct: this strike proved to be one of the staging posts in the demise of Thatcherism. The public and even the media sided with the strikers and the government was obliged to give in.

At two acrimonious meetings held on the subject, some members of the Campaign Group opposed the leadership challenge. Finally, on 23 March 1988, with Benn stepping outside so that the vote could take place in his absence, the Group voted by only two to one in favour. Four women – Clare Short, Jo Richardson, Joan Walley and Margaret Beckett – resigned from the Group over the leadership, arguing that politics should not be about who was the leader, which was an outdated, macho approach to public life. Benn's response was that an election was an opportunity to put the issues and encourage questioning of current policies. Winning and actually being leader were not the point. The Group nominated Benn for leader and Eric Heffer as deputy. The deputy leader's post, currently occupied by Roy Hattersley, was also being contested by John Prescott, the former seaman who was MP for Hull East. Neil Kinnock merely said that the candidature would 'end in massive defeat for those who have put their self-indulgence above the interests of the party and of democratic socialism'.[20] Benn would argue that elections are the essence of democracy: 'the idea that an election is a bad thing is a dangerous argument'.[21]

The uncertainties and the consultations about candidature meant that it was not until the end of March that Benn declared himself. The delay was a serious mistake. It was too late to obtain backing from certain unions, who had already reached their decision, including most of the unions whose federation made up the National Union of Mineworkers. Arthur Scargill said that by the time Benn's candidature was announced, 85 per cent of mining unions had already made their nominations.[22]

Benn spent the next six months touring the country addressing meetings and giving interviews. The effortless answers, the facts at the fingertips, were of course the result of diligent practice. He wrote out the answers to forty questions he expected to be asked in the course of the campaign like 'Didn't the 1981 contest lose the Labour Party the 1983 election?' and 'Aren't you too old to be taken seriously?' To the latter question the answer notes ran, 'No. Same age as the Prime Minister. Far younger than Callaghan or Foot when elected. 17 years younger than Churchill when he retired. Mitterrand at 71 is standing for 7 more years. Reagan is still President in his mid-70s.'[23]

At this time, strongly influenced by conference decisions being amended by the Policy Review, he started attacking the leadership for its 'consensus' thinking. All the parties were now in favour of NATO, the Common Market and an economy dominated by market forces, Benn said. There was less choice than ever before. He could see the signs that there would soon be even less choice because Neil Kinnock was about to back down on unilateral nuclear disarmament.

When the leadership election took place at the conference in Blackpool that year it became clear how little support the left now had. Even in what had been Benn's stronghold, the constituencies, the result was miserable. Out of 586 constituencies, he won 112. His most disappointing vote was in the trade union section where he had 0.3 per cent; the constituencies gave him 5.1 and the PLP 5.8. He received 11.3 per cent overall against Neil Kinnock's 88.6. Hattersley also won outright, with 66.8 per cent to John Prescott's 23.7 per cent and Eric Heffer's 9.5 per cent. No one had expected the Benn challenge to be successful but the heaviness of the defeat was shocking. Benn had used the leadership campaign to put the message across, and it had been decisively rejected.

Still, Benn was used to encouraging faith in the face of disaster. As he said to one meeting, 'I dare say that the General Secretary of the Scribes and Pharisees announced in Jerusalem in AD 32 "What's the point in following a leader who gets crucified?" That may have been the birth of the new realism for all I know.'[24]

The Labour Party defence review team which planned to reverse the unilateral nuclear disarmament policy in April 1988 produced a report so secret its drafts could only be read in shadow Foreign Secretary Gerald Kaufman's room with him present, or elsewhere in the presence of his researcher, who then returned the copy. When the NEC came to accept the policy reviews on 8 and 9 May 1988, Neil Kinnock made a clear and explicit personal repudiation of unilateralism. From the teenager who had denounced his hero Aneurin Bevan for renouncing the same creed to the party leader had been a long road for Kinnock, but at last he had come home.

The 1989 party conference saw the publication of the policy reviews. Benn dramatically intervened in the defence debate to oppose nuclear weapons. 'This is not a choice between unilateral and multilateral disarmament,' he said. 'The Policy Review would commit this party to the Trident which has nine times the firepower of the Polaris. The NEC wants us to accept unilateral nuclear *re-armament.*' He said Britain had never possessed a truly independent nuclear deterrent for it was under American control; Britain didn't need it, couldn't use it and couldn't afford it.

Finally he turned to the historic event in the minds of many delegates, the last renunciation of a non-nuclear policy: 'I heard Aneurin Bevan thirty-two years ago today about his need to be clothed in the conference chamber. I heard him speak, spoke in the debate myself. We have never been invited to the top table in disarmament talks in that whole period. It doesn't give you a place at the conference table, it doesn't guarantee a Labour victory: the last Labour government supported nuclear weapons; Jim committed a billion pounds and we lost the election. Who would believe us if we said we were changing our policy to win votes? Who would believe us on that or anything if that was the basis of our policy? Comrades, we cannot say what we do not believe. We need a vision.'

His plea was not entirely unsuccessful. Although the vote over unilateralism was lost, another motion he was speaking in favour of, that Britain's defence spending should be cut to bring it into line with the European average, was passed, to the embarrassment of the leadership.

At the end of conference week the leadership attempted to jetti-son the commitment, agreed at three previous conferences, for a common age of consent for homosexuals and heterosexuals. 'The gays and lesbians issue is costing us dear among the pensioners,' Patricia Hewitt, Neil Kinnock's press secretary, had warned in a confidential memorandum.[25] The policy review had therefore replaced the phrase 'full equality' for gays with 'greater equality'. Conference changed it back. Later that month Benn brought in a Sexual Offences Amendment Bill to give full equality to homo-sexuals, a means of putting pressure on Neil Kinnock and the National Executive to attend to the conference decision.

At the election of the National Executive, only Benn and Skinner of the hard left were elected, Benn in fourth place. Ken Livingstone, former leader of the GLC, lost his seat. By now many former colleagues had left the Campaign Group. It was assumed that there was no preferment under Neil Kinnock's leadership for Campaign Group members. Benn did not criticise them. He said, 'I have always had to remember that I have had a marvellous political career with all the fruits of office. It was easy for me at my age to be free to say and do things which would be controversial. But, for people at the beginning of their lives, association with me was a barrier to their advance. It has never caused any bitterness – people had to move on.'[26]

Tony Benn and Dennis Skinner would second each other's motions on the NEC and maintain a resistance to expulsions of left-wingers and what they saw as the more excessive opportunism of the leadership. But they were always in a minority of two. The association between Benn and Skinner was not as strong as their united position on the NEC implied. Skinner was rather more of a doctrinaire socialist than Benn; he would lay down the line which divided perdition from salvation and almost challenge an audience to dare to step across it. Benn would encourage people to find an inner strength from the contemplation of the achievements of socialism; he would urge them to show solidarity and courage in the face of those who would attempt to break their morale. It was rather like the difference between a Methodist and a Congregationalist preacher.[27]

For all the arm-twisting methods of the Labour Party under Neil Kinnock, it did fight its way to recovery, scoring an exceptional success in the European elections in 1989, with forty-five seats to the Tories' thirty-two, an election which gave the socialist group the largest number of seats in the European Parliament. The residual Labour Party opposition to Europe was largely dispelled by this refreshing taste of electoral success. The enormity of the task of winning elections again required firm measures, and history may well judge Kinnock as the man who reformed the party when that was the most urgent task, after the SDP split.[28]

Tony Benn's criticism of the leadership was more playful, free from the bitterness which had characterised it during the years of government. He would delight in using his voluminous archives to pick out a choice tit-bit of left-wing rhetoric from the leader's early days, or some other item from the past to show how the present leaders had moved to the right. He wrote his own version of the campaign song 'Face the Challenge – Make the Change' (which was also the title of the Policy Review). His first verse went:

> Miss the challenge – change your mind
> Labour leads now from behind
> We can run the status quo
> If you doubt it OUT YOU GO.

It ended,

> Pink and harmless we must be
> If we want a victory.

The collapse of the Soviet empire and of some of the East European dictatorships at the end of 1989 gave heart to the rebellious. Some Conservatives attempted the old trick of comparing the Labour Party with the oligarchies of Eastern Europe. One of them came top of the ballot for back-bench debating time and chose for his subject the future of socialism, which gave the House of Commons in December 1989 five hours of ideological debate, a matter of delight for Tony Benn. He scorned the simplicities of their analysis. Did the Tories honestly believe, he said, 'that what happened in Warsaw was because Poles were longing for a poll tax, that people in Uzbekistan are yearning to sell off their water supply, that there is an almost irresistible demand for the YTS [Youth Training Scheme] in Romania, or that they need more homeless people in East Berlin to prove the wisdom of market forces, or that they are longing to have the Tsar back?

'If Mr Gorbachev announced that his son was to succeed him, as the system that we have here in Britain, would that be a democratic gain? If the supreme Soviet divided itself into two, half by patronage and half by heredity, as in Britain, would that be a great gain? . . . Does the hon. Gentleman honestly believe that the people in Warsaw, East Germany and Hungary have demanded their human rights only because we had a cruise missile on hire purchase from Washington?'[29]

At least, Benn said, it was the end of the cold war, which he had regarded as the greatest barrier to progressive ideas. Now he could convert Russia to socialism. He attended the founding conference of the Socialist Party in Moscow in June 1990, remarking that they had a shared experience with Labour: 'Once any government comes to power that calls itself socialist, it doesn't want anybody else to talk about socialism.'[30]

36

The Benn Renaissance

The introduction of the poll tax was the most foolhardy single action taken by any post-war government on the British mainland. In essence it was an attempt to oblige local authorities (many of which were unwilling) and magistrates' courts (all of which were overworked) to impose on the nation a piece of ideological dogma with which not even all members of the Conservative cabinet agreed.

It had at its root the Conservative manifesto pledge to replace the rating system of local authority finance, though no specific proposal had been mooted. Margaret Thatcher's personal decision, against the advice of the better informed, was for a standard tax per head of the population. This ensured that all residents contributed equally towards the cost of council services – indeed, the tax bore no relationship to ability to pay. Those with large properties were far better off than they had been under the rating system, a property tax, and they were better off in direct proportion to the size of their homes. It was therefore as much a piece of legislative class warfare as the inheritance tax.

Understandably, all Labour supporters opposed it, as did a large number of Conservative supporters. The question was: what should be done about it? National government so controlled local government finance that resistance was impossible from that quarter – the town halls would do what they were told. Tony Benn clearly and unequivocally said that the only correct response was civil disobedience. He would not pay the tax. He would not even register for it, which was an offence in itself.

The principle of conscience being above the law had been moulded and refined by Benn since the imprisonment of the Pentonville Five had led him to enunciate it first in 1972, though he traced this conviction back to his Old Testament studies in childhood. He had it incorporated in the Chesterfield Declaration:

> We assert the right of all people to follow their own conscientious beliefs even if it involves them in breaking the law; and that while there may be a legal obligation to obey the law there is no moral obligation to obey unjust laws; but we also know that those who break the law on moral grounds may face punishment for their beliefs, and the final verdict on their actions will rest with the public and with history.[1]

A Young Conservative in North Kensington saved the council and the bench the embarrassment of having Benn in court by registering his and Caroline Benn's name. Benn still refused to pay the tax, and found himself in demand again as he had not been for years, to address Anti-Poll Tax Federation meetings. 'Many of our most precious religious and political rights in this country were won by conscientious law-breaking which compelled Parliament to make the necessary concessions to justice,' he declared in March 1990.[2]

The Labour Party leadership urged compliance with the law, arguing that the only way to get rid of the poll tax was by winning the next general election and revoking the legislation. All over the country there were demonstrations at the town halls, including invasions of the council chambers. Neil Kinnock denounced such demonstrators as 'toytown revolutionaries' and accused the twenty-eight Labour MPs who refused to pay the tax of luxurious self-righteousness.[3]

The massive poll-tax rally in Trafalgar Square on 31 March 1990 witnessed a stunning demonstration of the way the spirit of radicalism had spread from Eastern Europe, where television nightly showed scenes of mass demonstrations and the overthrow of authoritarian regimes. All the speakers, including Benn, referred to Eastern Europe, with a guest speaker from Romania underlining the message as Benn sat puffing his pipe between the Landseer lions. When he was called on to speak the organiser mentioned that he must leave early for his birthday celebration with his family. The crowd sang 'Happy Birthday', an affectionate tribute it would be difficult to imagine being given to any other Labour politician.

In Whitehall (which leads to Trafalgar Square) there had been conflicts, even before Benn's departure, between demonstrators and police. As the rally concluded, after Benn had left, the fighting turned into serious violence, rioting and looting, which continued until 8 p.m. Benn was later to remark that he was not in favour of setting buildings on fire as a solution to any problem, but it was undeniable that 'things change when people do things'.[4]

Margaret Thatcher refused to budge, despite the desperation in the ranks of her own back-benchers. Unrest over the poll tax formed, with the negative approach to Europe, the most easily identifiable element of the background to her fall. Underlying it was what Tony Benn called 'the way Britain has become a grimy Third World type of country'. The body blow was struck by the resignation from Thatcher's cabinet at the beginning of November 1990 of Sir Geoffrey Howe, the last surviving member of her 1979 cabinet excepting herself. Within weeks the former chancellor John Major had replaced her as Prime Minister.

Major's attitude to Europe was more relaxed than Thatcher's and later, having declared the poll tax 'uncollectable', he all but abolished it – as a face-saver he reduced it to a negligible level. Benn and others who had been withholding the payment on moral grounds now paid up, their battle won, though they still argued for an amnesty for those who could not pay. By the end of the revolt over the poll tax, in March 1991, fourteen million people had not paid.[5]

On 2 August 1990 the Iraqi army invaded Kuwait, a small but immensely rich neighbouring oil state which had supported Iraq in her eight-year war against Iran. The United Nations Security Council condemned the invasion that day. The Iraqi army then gathered on the border of Saudi Arabia, a land which Iraqi President Saddam Hussein claimed was not legitimately ruled. He was clearly going to invade, so the first deployment of troops (under a UN resolution) was made to prevent this. The US went in first, quickly followed by Britain and other Western and Arab countries.

Tony Benn had seen before the sort of sabre-rattling which accompanied this deployment of troops. He knew by their protestations of virtue that George Bush and Margaret Thatcher were gearing up for a war. Despite their rhetoric – the talk of democracy, of protecting the innocent, of standing up to an aggressor – the

461

reason for the impending war was to protect oil supplies from the Middle East. The West had to safeguard one of the major sinews of its economy. Additionally, if Saddam was not stopped now, he would invade further countries, including Israel, until the West had to step in at a later date when a military operation would be far more difficult.

Benn tacitly accepted the Arab agenda: that this crisis could be the occasion for a settlement of the outstanding problems which had distressed the Middle East since the Second World War. He argued for continued sanctions to dislodge Iraq from Kuwait, a measure the United Nations Security Council had imposed shortly after the invasion. The Iraqi regime then increased tension by taking hostage all Westerners in Kuwait and Iraq. Troop deployments by the US built up steadily day by day. Benn and others who were alarmed at the escalation and still saw a chance of peace through negotiation formed the Committee to Stop War in the Gulf. It involved traditional peace groups like CND, Christian organisations, ecological interests, some of the traditional left and Third World organisations. As the campaign moved under way, it became clear that it also included people for whom the agenda was not only negative: opposition to the war, but positive: victory to Iraq.

From the start of the Gulf debate at the Labour Party conference that October Benn was standing, holding his agenda, indicating his wish to speak. To increasingly angry shouts from conference delegates, the chair, Jo Richardson, failed to call him. As was so often the case throughout his life, this mean action aimed at him rebounded on its perpetrators. He was surrounded outside the conference hall by media people who expected him to be angry. He was courteous and uncomplaining and was able to repeat for a large audience the message he had hoped to give the conference. He was frustrated that the US seemed to be working on its own agenda which would inevitably lead to full-scale war, while negotiation and discussion had not been tried. It was a view shared by Edward Heath, who was invited to Iraq to talk with Saddam Hussein. He pleaded for the release of the hostages, thirty-three of whom were released to fly back with him.

The Iraqi Ambassador in London asked to see Benn on 6 November and invited him to visit Baghdad. Benn was one of a number of elder statesmen – Willy Brandt was also to go – who had spoken out against war at home and were invited to Iraq to discuss the situation. Benn pondered the difficulties of the journey for a time – not least the cost of travel. The opportunities for ignominious failure were great. Aside from the difficulties of travel in a hostile country in which he did not speak the language, there was the question of what he might return with. Would he even meet Saddam Hussein? He eventually decided to go after a particularly bellicose speech in the House of Commons by Margaret Thatcher on 7 November (she left office during the Gulf crisis). He felt he had to take a translator and confidant, and accepted the assistance of Paul Lalor, a student of Arabic who was familiar with Baghdad.

Once he had made the decision he courteously called Neil Kinnock's office to tell him. By chance, a features reporter for a Radio 4 programme was seeing Benn that morning to interview him on another matter and therefore found himself in the middle of an international news story. Benn's visit was thus the lead story on BBC radio's *World at One*, the best possible time to gain maximum coverage in other media. As soon as the broadcast went out the telephone calls from the relatives of hostages began. The callers were often in tears begging for any hint of help. Tony Benn's secretary, Kathy Ludbrook, organised the appeals from the families of hostages and those in hiding in Kuwait. Benn had been assured by the Iraqi Ambassador that he would not leave Baghdad 'empty handed', so it was clear they would permit some hostages to leave with him.

Unlike Heath, who said he was going only for humanitarian reasons and could not negotiate, Benn explicitly said he was going because diplomatic negotiations had not taken place and he would discuss alternative possibilities for a settlement. Politically, he said he wanted to build a bigger platform in Britain from which he could warn of the danger of war.

Soon the Benn office was swamped with letters, 30,000 over the period of the Gulf Crisis, which several volunteers helped with. The letter-writers, evenly distributed in age, came from a wide range of class and education. Two broad strands emerged: people in the Labour Party who felt that Benn was a remaining representative of the moral role the party should adopt; and Christians, particularly

Quakers, who felt they must give support to a man who spoke about peace with no hint of cynicism.

He loved being the centre of attention, fighting a great humanitarian cause with almost all the powers in the country ranged against him. He appealed for messages of support from statesmen abroad, many of whom he had known in his Movement for Colonial Freedom days. Among those who responded were Nelson Mandela, Kenneth Kaunda, Julius Nyerere, Pierre Trudeau and François Mitterrand. King Hussein of Jordan, whom Benn had previously met, offered the hospitality of his palace when Benn was in his country. The Indian Embassy in Baghdad undertook to provide him with accommodation and office facilities – the British Embassy did not wish to host an unofficial visit of this nature. He took with him copies of all of his Gulf speeches, which Saddam Hussein's office were to be given in advance so that the President would know how harshly he had spoken about the Iraqi regime, to which he had no intention of giving any support, explicitly or tacitly.

He left on 18 November 1990. There was a series of meetings with leading Iraqi politicians and with hostages, then Benn was called upon by Saddam Hussein's principal interpreter and taken to 'a modest little villa' on the outskirts of Baghdad. He had been told wherever he went that he must speak his mind with Saddam, because the President would be hearing things from Benn which none of his own advisers would dare tell him. It would also be helpful for the advisers, nine of whom were present at the meeting, to be able to refer back to the arguments Benn had put in their later comments to the dictator.

He found Saddam intelligent and willing to listen. Benn had prepared the brief of what he was to say to him with great care, rewriting it each day to take account of new information. After initial courtesies they entered three hours of discussion, during which each man made a statement and had it translated. There were three basic arguments. The first was that the hostages would not protect him from war; in fact holding them was more likely to provoke an attack. Benn said, 'I have not come pleading for my quota of hostages. I have come to try to persuade you to restore freedom of movement to all foreign nationals.' If they were released they would become 'ambassadors for peace'. Saddam said he would consider the argument.

The next point was that Saddam could not expect even friends of Iraq to accept four different interpretations of the status of Kuwait. A year before it was a friendly neighbour, then an unfriendly neighbour, then in August (after the invasion) it had a new, friendly government, and now Saddam had declared it had always been part of Iraq and was the nineteenth province of Iraq. Saddam Hussein said he had not wanted to invade Kuwait, but the Kuwaitis had moved the border northwards, taking some of his territory. He denied an intention to take over more countries in the Middle East.

Finally Benn argued that complying with the United Nations resolution demanding that Iraq withdraw from Kuwait would leave Saddam in a morally superior position to request the implementation of another UN resolution, for Israel to withdraw from the Palestinian 'occupied territories'. Saddam Hussein had argued that the issues should be linked. Saddam's answer was that, even if he did withdraw, how could he be sure the US would not attack anyway? He would like to withdraw, he said, but it would damage the morale of his troops so much that if America were to attack after the withdrawal, they would not be fit to defend themselves. But if you withdraw now, insisted Benn, the American troops will all be demanding of their commander that they should be home for Christmas.[6]

Benn did return with some hostages, and the following month Saddam Hussein ordered that freedom of movement should be restored to all foreign nationals, which liberated not only the hostages but also the Westerners in hiding in Kuwait.

Less than two weeks after Benn's visit, on 29 November, the UN Security Council voted to use force against Iraq unless she withdrew from Kuwait. Benn and other activists kept up pressure on the Allies to justify their position at every stage, stressing the consequences of going to war. He forced a Commons debate at which forty-one Labour MPs and three Welsh Nationalists voted against the government line, which was supported by the Labour front bench. Edward Heath and Denis Healey were also alarmed at the possibility of war and at the limited diplomatic effort to avert it. In particular they stressed the ecological catastrophe which could be caused by all-out war in the Gulf. Benn concentrated on the number of casualties which could be anticipated. All urged that sanctions should be given time to work.

It would have placed an exceptional strain on the Allies to have kept half a million troops in the Arabian desert for another year while sanctions took time to work. The military were not prepared to take the risk. Saddam tried every means, short of withdrawing from Kuwait, to avert the war. It was to no avail. Around midnight on 17 January 1991 the Allies launched a massive attack against Iraqi positions in Iraq and Kuwait. Benn was up all night, giving interviews, watching the news and sending out faxed press releases. 'The horror, barbarity and obscenity of war being done in our name came through for those who had eyes to see and ears to hear,' he said at a press conference at Westminster that day.[7]

Massive Allied bombardment of military and strategic targets in Iraq caused casualties running, some sources would say, into hundreds of thousands. There was severe damage to the non-military infrastructure like the water and sewage systems and power plants. Saddam Hussein ordered the pumping of oil into the waters of the Gulf, creating the biggest oil slick in history, and ecological disaster. His engineers had also mined the Kuwaiti oil wells, which were fired late in the war, the smoke from them putting some parts of the area into a permanent twilight. He fired missiles at Israel, not a party to the conflict, hoping to draw her in and split the Arab states from the UN coalition. Finally, Iraq's forces crushed by air, the Allies went in by land, meeting little resistance. There was a cease-fire on 28 February. Benn noted sourly that Labour's National Executive had voted by thirteen to five against calling for a cease-fire thirteen hours before even George Bush agreed to one.

There was some possibility that Benn would be damaged electorally by his opposition to the war. John Burrows in Chesterfield remarked that it had lost him popularity among people who felt that a criticism of the war was in some way a criticism of the people fighting it.[8] Benn was unperturbed. He said, 'I opposed the Suez war, I opposed the Falklands war, I opposed the Libyan bombing and I opposed the Gulf war and I never believed that any of those principled arguments lost a single vote – indeed, I think they gained support, though that was not why you did it. What has been lacking in Labour politics over a long period is a principled stand.'[9] Even if they could not agree with him wholeheartedly, a large number of people were pleased that someone was speaking out for all their reservations about the war. Benn fulfilled his function as conscience of the nation. Few agreed with him one hundred per cent, but few felt there was no truth at all in what he was saying.

After the cease-fire with the West, George Bush called on Saddam Hussein's enemies inside Iraq, the Kurds and the Shi'ites, to rise up against him. This they duly did and were ruthlessly crushed by the Iraqi army, the rebels receiving no military assistance from the Allies. The failure of the West to help these people was shocking to those who had believed that the war had had something to do with justice. Benn and others in a letter to the *Independent* wrote, 'This does not represent an incomprehensible change of heart or line by Washington. In reality, the "non-interference" policy, ridiculous coming from a power that has just laid waste to Iraq and still occupies a large slice of it, is consistent with the US approach before and after the Gulf crisis. This has been based solely on Washington's strategic interests.'[10]

The great fear for George Bush and his advisers had been that they might become involved in a war like Vietnam, with a small anti-war movement at home growing into a majority of the population as the television daily showed Americans dying in a futile war in a part of the world where they had long since ceased to be wanted. Bush had to finish the war quickly, and to do that he had to order the massive use of firepower to destroy the Iraqi infrastructure. When the UN force did go in, it faced virtually no resistance at all – the enemy had been destroyed on the ground, and hungry and terrified Iraqi soldiers were giving themselves up to unarmed Western journalists. It may be that much of the destruction of Iraq, the 'overkill' on bombing raids, was stimulated by fears of another Vietnam. Tony Benn and the anti-war movement may have done more harm than good to Iraqi civilians.

There were attributes of the Benn personality which were more fashionable by the 1990s than they had been during the whole of the rest of the century. They were the feminine, caring side of his nature: the man who was not ashamed to cry; the opposition to war at any cost; his respect for living things to the point of vegetarianism. He and Caroline had become vegetarian after Hilary Benn had impressed upon him that if grain were not being grown and fed to animals it could be grown for people and there would be sufficient to feed everyone in the world. He had long been aware of the issues. As early as 1972 he had been saying that the people of the future would be as horrified by the exploitation of animals as they now were about the exploitation of other humans.[11] He fitted easily into the 'New Age', always alert to spiritual values as long as they were not codified by an administrative hierarchy. Teetotalism was no longer a characteristic which would set him apart from others, drinking to excess having ceased to be socially acceptable. He was also the image of a 'new man' as far as his grandchildren were concerned, only too pleased to share in the care of them.

Even in his sixties, his appeal was still to youth. Talented young people volunteered to work in his office for nothing but expenses. Many of them seemed destined to have successful careers in public life themselves. Theses were written about his influence, and fiction writers scavenged parts of his career or personality to incorporate into their work. Two writers who worked with him produced novels which owed something to the understanding of Westminster politics they had learned from him. They were Brian Sedgemore's *Mr Secretary of State* (1979) and the far better novel *A Very British Coup* (1982) by Chris Mullin, which was made into a successful television drama series in 1988. In it a left-wing Labour leader becomes Prime Minister only to face an effective *coup d'état* by the civil service and MI5. A stage play, Howard Brenton's *13th Night* (1981), has a Bennite character cast in the role of a modern Macbeth.

The publication of his diaries, and his obvious depth of experience, made him sought after by television documentary makers and academics from all over the world. He frequently took part in television discussion programmes, but also received more airtime than any other politician in programmes which were based on his life and work. In Britain two lengthy programmes for national television were made about his diaries; he hosted a series of discussion programmes and a documentary was made about his leadership bid, with a full programme discussing it the next day. All these programmes were on independent television, for the BBC had never felt able to make a documentary about Benn which did not have a political commentator intervening.

He was given the BBC establishment accolade of an appearance on *Desert Island Discs*. After it the presenter, Sue Lawley, was so kind as to allow him to have a copy of his BBC obituary. 'I thought at least when I'm dead they'll say something like "this interesting man" and so on. Not at all, every media myth was in it. At least when you're dead you expect to be correctly reported, so I photocopied it, corrected it and sent it to Michael Checkland [Director General of the BBC] with a note saying, "As I won't be here when this is broadcast I thought you might be interested in factual accuracy." '[12]

He experienced the usual problems brought by exceptional fame, that people would project on to him their impression of what they thought he ought to be doing if he were running true to their image of him. His former cabinet colleague Joel Barnett criticised Benn for 'his desire to show his solidarity with working people by always insisting on drinking tea out of a mug'. The idea that Benn might use mugs because they contain more tea than cups, and that he likes tea, could not be countenanced in the face of a complex, psychopolitical interpretation.[13]

To let one other example serve for many: a columnist in a serious magazine criticised Benn for 'putting political commitment before aesthetic merit' in his choice of records on *Desert Island Discs*. In fact his choice was almost entirely personal and included a nonconformist hymn ('To Be a Pilgrim'), a song by his boyhood friends Flanders and Swann, the music played at his brother's funeral and at his own wedding, and the composition called 'Madrigal' by Stephen Benn played at Rosalind Benn's funeral and at Stephen's wedding and which Benn wished to have played at his own funeral.[14] At the risk of labouring the point: much of what was said about Tony Benn even after he had been in public life for forty years was not only untrue, it was self-evidently untrue.

Political longevity had its advantages. When the thirty-year rule governing official records released papers on Suez, revealing the lies told by the Eden cabinet, Benn noted that the only member of that government who was still in office was Lord Hailsham, who was 'always lecturing us on the need for higher standards in public life'.[15]

So Benn asked the Prime Minister to suspend the Lord Chancellor while the extent of his personal complicity was investigated.

There were also pleasures. He was outside the South African Embassy when Nelson Mandela was freed, which meant he was one of the few people (perhaps the only person) who had been demonstrating in protest when Mandela was imprisoned twenty-six years before and in celebration when he was freed. 'I've never been kissed by so many people,' he said of the crowd outside the Embassy. He met Nelson Mandela himself when he came to London in July 1990 and gave him a copy of the motion he had proposed in 1960 for sanctions against South Africa, before Mandela was even imprisoned.

His work on the Gulf war had delayed Benn's presentation of the Commonwealth of Britain Bill, which to some extent was the result of four or five years of work, since the historian Peter Hennessy had suggested that he compile his various Bills into one. In a larger sense the fifty-two-clause Bill which emerged on 24 June 1991 was the result of a whole life spent promoting radical reform.

Benn had long argued for constitutional reform and seen people's eyes glaze over. Now he could not find anyone who did not agree that reform was necessary. Constitutional change was in the air. A liberal group called Charter 88, the Liberal Democrats and the Institute for Public Policy Research had constitutional proposals, while both front benches were promoting the idea of a Bill of Rights in different forms.

None were as wide ranging as Benn's, which proposed a presidency, an elected second chamber, equal male and female representation in both Houses, votes at sixteen, the restoration of autonomy to local government, reform of the honours system, the return of all powers ceded to NATO and the European Community to Parliament, disestablishment of the Church of England, parliamentary oversight of the intelligence services, the termination of British jurisdiction in Northern Ireland, freedom of information and a Charter of Rights including the right to a home, work, medical care and education.

It was classic Benn, marrying exceptional parliamentary skill with visionary promise. His next action was classic too: because the Bill included the abolition of the House of Lords and the monarchy, he thought he should tell the Queen it was nothing personal, so he sent it to the Palace to explain and received a letter thanking him for his courtesy.

There was widespread interest in the Bill from abroad, where it did not seem quite so normal and straightforward to have a country governed by a monarch whose powers were exercised by a Prime Minister; where the monarch was head of the Church; and half the Parliament was either hereditary or appointed by the monarch.

Coverage in the serious newspapers was complimentary. It was lauded by Bernard Levin, far indeed from being an uncritical admirer of Benn: 'Mr Benn's principal aim is to put back into the hands of the elected Parliament the democratic power that has been stolen, piece by piece, since the end of the Second World War, by all the governments we have had in that period.'[16] The one constitutional reform Benn did not support was proportional representation, which he believed would unacceptably increase the power of party leaders; would break the close link between MPs and their constituencies; and would increase the trading of matters of principle for short term gain in the House of Commons.

Benn's energy showed no signs of flagging in the 1990s, nor his political perception of losing its relevance. At various celebrations to mark his forty years in Parliament he tried to put his experience in perspective. Forty years before his election was before the Russian Revolution, forty years before that was the Paris Commune, forty years before that was the Great Reform Act, 'which is 160 years ago, but it is only four times my political life. One hundred and sixty years before that there was a republic in England. You realise that the whole of modern history is just a blip. It gives you patience to understand that you have to go through a decade of difficulty, and things will improve again.'

37

An Assessment

Michael Foot believed that at some point Tony Benn had lost interest in the present, and had 'turned his brilliantly agile, inventive faculties to the future'. 'Foot is here referring to the period of the 1974–79 Cabinet but at other points in his sour essay on Benn in *Loyalists and Loners* he approaches a deeper understanding. This presents Benn the diarist, the architect of great social schemes which have no hope of success but which sound attractive on the platform and seem visionary in the records. It is quite possible to see Benn, the man who loved influence more than power, as someone who traded practical achievement here and now for an illustrious place in the history books. This is Benn as Faustian hero in reverse – wagering wealth and power for immortality. There is some truth in this. Benn has a strong sense of history and, in particular, an understanding of the reverence the Labour movement has for the rebels of the past, while giving position and power to the conformists of the present. Benn's archive and diary keeping show that, from childhood, he had a sense of the importance of his life in terms of history. Throughout his very public life is a classical appreciation of the obligations of elected service and the dignity of statesmanship.

Like all attempts to wrap up Benn in a neat, psychological package, this analysis is insufficient. This is partly because a great deal of Benn's achievement throughout his career was straightforward and practical, from the modernisation of the Post Office to the negotiations to obtain 25 per cent of North Sea Oil for Britain. It was direct public service with bankable results. The two failures of his ministerial career, the Industry Bill and the alternative economic strategy, were likewise practical measures, though certainly guided by idealism, which Benn worked as hard as anyone to see put into practice.

His constitutional reforms were similarly practical. To date, Tony Benn's three greatest achievements are the Peerage Act, the referendum over Europe and the democratisation of the Labour Party. They are achievements whose effects were felt at the time. While each of them related to a phase in Benn's career, they were not mere personal triumphs. Far from it. In each case others gained more than he did: Alec Douglas-Home became Prime Minister after renouncing the peerage; the pro-Common Market lobby won; and in the case of the reform of the Labour Party, which he did not instigate but to which he decisively contributed, an election under the new rules meant Neil Kinnock was the only person who could attract sufficiently wide support.

Benn is loyal to principles in politics, not people. He invariably therefore made allies and lost them, but his arguments with the leaders of the Labour Party took this beyond the boundaries of reasonableness. To have argued with one leader may be regarded as a clash of personalities; to have argued with two, a principled difference of opinion. Tony Benn had bitter disagreements with his leaders from Gaitskell through Wilson, Callaghan and Foot to Kinnock. It was not for nothing that one of his favourite images was of the Old Testament prophets challenging the power of the kings. He taunted the establishment with exquisite political skill, and could only expect them to attack back. His life resembles more a quest for martyrdom than a struggle for power.

Benn's refusal to behave as everyone else did, to settle down and climb the political ladder, belied every instinct in Harold Wilson. If Benn did not become more right wing as he got older, if he did not sacrifice all in his lust for the highest office, there must be something wrong with him. 'He immatures with age', was a frequent Wilson remark.

More helpfully, from the point of view of history, is the Wilson comment that Benn was brilliantly able but lacked judgement.[2] Of course, a complaint that someone lacks judgement means he did not decide to do what the speaker would have done given the same circumstances. Presuming Benn wanted to be leader, he made some disastrous mistakes which severely damaged his chances. He would have been the clear favourite had he been the centre-left candidate. Clearly a left-left candidate was not going to win without changing the rules of the election. It would have been simpler just to be a little more appealing to the PLP. But the problem with these statements is that the premise is faulty. Benn did want to be leader, but not at any price. He was rather more like Coriolanus than Macbeth. He would be leader if they would acquiesce in his judgement, he would not bend his principles to them. Not for the power brokers in the Labour Party, nor for the media, nor even for the electorate would he betray the deepest lesson he had learned from his father: to do what he believed was right, no matter if it left him alone in the world.

On a more mundane level, Benn is criticised as being out of touch. One reason is that, licentiousness and avarice not being prominent in his make-up, he has difficulty recognising these qualities as motivating factors in others. Rather more significantly, he does not sufficiently credit personal interest as a motive among his colleagues or the electorate. Similarly, he never seems to have comprehended the deep loathing which second-rate politicians have for the truly gifted. He was frustrated by the grumblers and the manipulators of politics, not by others of his own stature.

Still, like so many people whose lives are worth study, he has the disadvantages of his virtues. His invincible determination against impossible odds was truly heroic when pitted against the constitution in the peerage case, or in the fight to obtain a referendum. It is less admirable in his refusal to accept the verdict of the referendum, his continuing stand against the Economic Community when others have come to terms with it. By the late 1970s, the Common Market was a dead issue, but Benn would compulsively dig it up, shake it by the collar and try to revive it, to the irritation of his colleagues and the disdain of the voters. Benn believed the movement of decision-making powers to Brussels was an outrage to parliamentary democracy so blatant that it must be opposed. For the vast majority of members of the public, who have not grown up in its environs, Westminster is as distant as Brussels.

The dynamic energy of Benn is impressive, but so often it is turned to minor issues which he would have been better advised to let pass by. Somehow he never seems to be satisfied, his restless

nature always luring him to what is frequently seen as mere queru-
lousness. The incessant opposition is wearying even to read about.
The published comments of his former colleagues attest it was no
more enjoyable to sit through at meetings.

If such behaviour made him friends in some quarters, they were
not remarkable for their solidarity when he needed them. The great
disaster of his ministerial career was his failure to convince his own
colleagues, or even the Labour movement, to rally to his industrial
policy. His Industry Act would have done no harm and might
have helped, if only a little, had it been operated with conviction.
Admittedly it was crisis management, a desperate attempt to stop
the inexorable decline of manufacturing industry in Britain which
continued whichever government was in power. Yet it was better
than the failure to manage crises which preceded and followed
Benn's tenure of office. In the end, Benn never worked under his
own Industry Act; all the supposedly radical things he did, for which
he was so viciously publicly pilloried, were performed under the
legislation of the previous Conservative government.

The analysis of society Benn offers says that the principles by
which social structures are set up, be they ever so lofty, are
invariably betrayed by the abuse of power. The greatest abuse is
that of patronage. Benn said, 'If you are accountable always to the
person above you to promote you or marginalise you, then clearly
there will be an enormous pressure to respond to that structure. If
on the other hand you are accountable to the people who elected
you then it's a different pressure. There is a corrective element in
democracy which corrects that tendency to corruption.[3]

This is the reason Tony Benn spent so much of his life arguing
about democracy, framing new constitutions, and writing a diary
which describes how principles are undermined by the exercise of
power. His belief in the almost spiritual power of democracy to
cleanse and renew society leads him to quote often from his friend
Reinhold Niebuhr's saying, 'Man's capacity for evil makes democracy necessary, man's capacity for good makes democracy possible.'

Benn's great continuous achievement is the endurance of his
challenge to authority. With calmness, politeness and eloquence he
repeated the message of popular democracy from the peerage case

to the Commonwealth of Britain Bill. He gave people faith in their own power to bring about change.

The personal achievement is as great. It is that, despite the unjustifiably cruel attacks on him by the press, the excoriation of erstwhile colleagues, and a decline in his support even within the Labour Party, he retains his gaiety and humanity. He was always true to himself, and no sacrifice made a stone of his heart.

Appendix

Books and Pamphlets by Tony Benn

Books

The Regeneration of Britain (Gollancz, 1964)
Speeches by Tony Benn (Spokesman Press, 1974)
Arguments for Socialism (Jonathan Cape, 1979)
Arguments for Democracy (Jonathan Cape, 1981)
Parliament, People and Power (Verso, 1982)
(ed.), *Writings on the Wall* (Faber & Faber, 1984)
Out of the Wilderness: Diaries, 1963–67 (Century Hutchinson, 1987)
Fighting Back: Speaking Out for Socialism in the Eighties (Century Hutchinson, 1988)
Office Without Power: Diaries, 1968–72 (Century Hutchinson, 1988)
Against the Tide: Diaries, 1973–76 (Century Hutchinson, 1989)
Conflicts of Interest: Diaries, 1977–80 (Century Hutchinson, 1990)
The End of an Era: Diaries 1980–90 (Hutchinson, 1992)

Pamphlets

The Privy Council as a Second Chamber (Fabian Society, 1957)
New Politics (Fabian Society, 1970)
Workers' Control (Institute for Workers' Control [IWC], 1973)
Industrial Democracy (IWC, 1974)
The Common Market (IWC, 1974)
Ten-Year Industrial Strategy (IWC, 1975)
Labour and the Slump (IWC, 1975)
New Course for Labour (IWC, 1976)
The Levellers (IWC, 1976)

Tony Benn

Industry, Technology and Democracy (IWC, 1978)
The Right to Know (IWC, 1978)
Why America Needs Democratic Socialism (IWC, 1978)
The Need for a Free Press (IWC, 1979)
Prospects (IWC, 1979)
The Case for a Constitutional Premiership (IWC, 1979)
Democracy and Human Rights (Haldane Society, 1979)
The Case for a Constitutional Civil Service (IWC, 1980)
The Case for Party Democracy (IWC, 1980)
European Unity (IWC, 1980)
The Falklands War (IWC, 1982)
Trade Unionism: A Strategy for the Eighties (IWC, 1983)
The Sizewell Syndrome (Spokesman Press, 1984)

Abbreviations

Attempts have been made to keep abbreviations to a minimum, but the following occur with such regularity in the text and the references it was felt the use of abbreviations would be the least tiresome option.

BA   Benn Archives – situated at Tony Benn's home in Notting Hill, London, and at the family's house in Stansgate, Essex.

BD   Benn Diaries

CLP   Constituency Labour Party

EC   Executive Committee – managing body of a CLP.

GMC   General Management Committee – decision-making body of a CLP. In the late 1980s referred to as a GC.

IV   Personal interview with author.

NEC   National Executive Committee – the Labour Party's ruling body.

PLP   Parliamentary Labour Party – the organisation including all Labour Members of Parliament and peers.

TB   Tony Benn. The use of these letters at the beginning of a reference means an article which Benn wrote himself, rather than one in which he is quoted.

References

1. Childhood and Family

1   IV Lady Stansgate 15 June 1989
2   TB A Radical in Politics; *The Times*, 7 May 1977
3   *Dictionary of National Biography*
4   Ibid; and Higgins, S., *The Benn Inheritance* (London, 1984)
5   Benn, William Wedgwood, *In the Side Shows* (London, 1919)
6   Higgins, S., op. cit.
7   Ibid.
8   IV Lady Stansgate 15 June 1989
9   Ibid.
10 While it is possible to trace Tony Benn's ancestry, whether it is profitable in telling the story of his life is questionable. Taking the principle of Occam's Razor: if the manner and bearing of Tony Benn are explicable in terms of his upbringing and his immediate family, why complicate the issue by going further back into the past?
11 IV Lady Stansgate 15 June 1989
12 IV David Benn 4 July 1989
13 IV Lady Stansgate 15 June 1989
14 Ibid.
15 Ibid.
16 Ibid.
17 ITV network programme *It's My Belief*, 21 July 1989; c.f. TB *Arguments for Socialism* (London, 1979)
18 IV Lady Stansgate 15 June 1989
19 Ibid.
20 IV David Benn 4 July 1989
21 TB *Isis* 4 June 1947. It was customary for *Isis* to print a biographical profile of incoming presidents of the Union, and for it to be written by the subject in the third person.

References

2. Westminster School

1 IV Tony Benn 29 June 1989
2 IV Neville Sandelson 13 June 1989
3 Letter to author 12 June 1989, from school archivist John Field
4 IV Neville Sandelson 13 June 1989
5 Ustinov, P., *Dear Me* (London, 1977)
6 IV Donald Swann 12 June 1989
7 IV Patrick MacMahon 20 June 1989
8 UFPF minutes book, Westminster archive
9 IV Tony Benn 29 June 1989
10 Ibid.
11 Ibid.
12 Hansard 22 July 1971
13 IV Neville Sandelson 13 June 1989
14 IV Tony Benn 29 June 1989
15 Ibid.
16 Field, J., *The King's Nurseries* (London, 1987)
17 IV David Benn 4 July 1989
18 IV Lady Stansgate 15 June 1989
19 IV Tony Benn 29 June 1989
20 Field, J., op. cit.
21 IV Tony Benn 29 June 1989
22 IV Lady Stansgate 15 June 1989
23 IV Tony Benn 13 September 1989

3. The Oxford Union and War Service

1 IV Tony Benn 29 June 1989
2 IV Patrick MacMahon 20 June 1989
3 Walter, D., *Playground of Power* (London, 1984)
4 IV Tony Benn 13 September 1989
5 Minutes of Oxford Union Debating Society
6 Oxford Magazine 28 January 1943
7 Oxford Magazine 20 May 1943
8 Seaman, L. C. B., *Post-Victorian Britain 1902–1951* (London, 1967)
9 IV Tony Benn 13 September 1989
10 Oxford Magazine 11 March 1943

11   Speech to Oxford Union 4 March 1943; BA Speeches 1946–50
12   IV Tony Benn 13 September 1989
13   Ibid.
14   The Mashona and the Matabele; BA Speeches 1946–50
15   Ibid.
16   IV Tony Benn 13 September 1989
17   Ibid.
18   Ibid.
19   IV Lady Stansgate 15 June 1989
20   BD 18 June 1965
21   IV Tony Benn 30 October 1989
22   Quoted in Higgins, S., *The Benn Inheritance* (London, 1984)
23   TB 'Memoir of a Brother in Arms' *The Guardian* 9 June 1984
24   IV Tony Benn 30 October 1989
25   TB *Isis* 4 June 1947
26   IV Tony Benn 13 September 1989
27   IV David Benn 4 July 1989
28   IV Tony Benn 13 September 1989
29   Ibid.

4. Touring the USA

1   IV Bill Allchin 28 July 1989
2   *Isis* 5 March 1947
3   Oxford Magazine 27 February 1947
4   IV Kenneth Harris 22 August 1989
5   Walter, D., *The Oxford Union Playground of Power* (1984) for an accurate representation.
6   *Isis* 4 June 1947
7   Ibid.
8   BA Speeches 1946–50
9   Impressions of a Visit to America, 4 May 1948; BA Speeches 1946–50
10   IV David Butler 1 October 1990. Butler visited on the day it occurred.
11   Harris, K., *Travelling Tongues* (1949)
12   Impressions of a Visit to America, op. cit.
13   IV Kenneth Harris 22 August 1989
14   Impressions of a Visit to America, op. cit.
15   IV Kenneth Harris 22 August 1989
16   Ibid.
17   Ibid.

18 *The Seven Ages of Man*, BBC 18 October 1947; BA Speeches 1946–50
19 Impressions of a Visit to America, op. cit.
20 *Isis* 4 June 1947
21 Proops, M., *Daily Mirror* 29 March 1951

5. Caroline Benn

1 IV Caroline Benn 18 December 1989
2 Ibid.
3 IV Kenneth Harris 22 August 1989
4 IV Tony Benn 12 September 1989
5 IV Caroline Benn 18 December 1989
6 TB to Anthony Crosland 14 January 1949, Crosland Papers 9/1;
   London School of Economics
7 The House Magazine 18 July 1986
8 IV Tony Benn 13 September 1989
9 IV Kenneth Harris 22 August 1989
10 IV Caroline Benn 18 December 1989
11 Ibid.
12 TB to Anthony Crosland 14 January 1949
13 IV Tony Benn 13 September 1989
14 IV Derek Holroyde 13 September 1989

6. Into Parliament with Bristol South-East

1 *Bristol Evening Post* 26 January 1950
2 Lord Jenkins of Hillhead, letter to author, 20 June 1989
3 IV The Rt Revd Mervyn Stockwood 9 June 1989
4 Ibid.
5 Bristol South-East Labour Party EC minutes 1933–53
6 IV Herbert Rogers 7 June 1989
7 IV Tony Benn 12 September 1989
8 Bristol South-East selection conference speech 2 November 1950; BA
   Speeches 1946–50
9 IV Cyril Langham 27 July 1989
10 *Manchester Guardian* 3 November 1950
11 *Observer* 5 November 1950
12 IV Rt Revd Mervyn Stockwood 6 June 1989
13 IV Tony Benn 25 September 1989

14 Clement Attlee to TB 24 November 1950
15 *Bristol Evening World* 17 November 1950
16 *Western Daily Press* 27 November 1950
17 IV Rt Revd Mervyn Stockwood 9 June 1989
18 IV Celia Roach 17 November 1989
19 IV Tony Benn 25 September 1989
20 IV Ian Mikardo 24 November 1989
21 Heeley Young Socialist, July–August 1952
22 IV Cyril & David Langham 27 July 1989
23 IV Tony Benn 25 September 1989
24 BBC radio script of tribute to Stafford Cripps, BA Speeches 1951. The texts of all Benn's speeches and interviews which are quoted in this book can be taken to come from the 'Speeches' files of the Benn Archive, filed under the year of delivery.
25 IV the Rt Revd Mervyn Stockwood 9 June 1989

7. New Boy at the House

1 *Daily Express* 1 January 1951
2 Parliament from the Back Benches, LSE political seminar, 5 February 1952
3 Ibid.
4 BBC radio interview, TB with his father 21 July 1951
5 Hansard 7 February 1952
6 *Daily Herald* 19 January 1951
7 Hansard 10 May 1951
8 BA Letter, John Carvel to TB 11 May 1951
9 IV Tony Benn 25 September 1989
10 Memorandum on the working of the Postmaster General's directive March 1956
11 IV Michael Bowen 15 November 1989
12 IV Caroline Benn 18 December 1989
13 IV Tony Benn 27 November 1989
14 Ibid.
15 BA Benntapes spool No 1
16 IV Tony Benn 27 November 1989
17 IV Tony Benn 30 October 1989 'It makes me shudder when I look back on it,' he remarked.
18 *Revue Français de Science Politique* Vol 11 No 2 April–June 1952
19 Ibid.

20 *Bristol Evening World* 16 October 1951
21 IV Lord Mishcon 11 November 1989
22 IV George and Frances Easton 7 June 1989
23 *Bristol Evening World* 25 May 1955
24 IV Caroline Benn 18 December 1989
25 Sked, A., and Cook, C., *Post-War Britain: A Political History* (London, 1979)
26 Bristol City Archive, Bristol South-East Labour Party EC minutes 1933–53. The minutes were referring to Benn as Rt Hon., the designation for a Privy Councillor, as Stafford Cripps was. Benn could be referred to as The Hon. as the eldest son of a Lord. Ward Labour Parties tended to use this exalted designation when announcing his appearance to open fetes.
27 Parliament from the Back Benches, LSE political seminar, 5 February 1952
28 IV Lady Stansgate 15 June 1989
29 *Bristol Evening Post* 28 November 1970
30 IV Bert and Celia Roach November 1989. Bert Roach was later to be an election sub-agent for Benn though he could play no great part in politics because he was excluded as a civil servant – in fact a sales superintendent in Post Office Telephones. Celia Roach was a Labour councillor from 1963 until 1985.
31 IV Irving and Joyce Rogers 26 July 1989
32 *Daily Express* 26 January 1952
33 IV Irving and Joyce Rogers 26 July 1989
34 Ibid.
35 IV Tony Benn 25 September 1989. The Bristol South-East General Management Committee minutes are missing from the archive for the years 1946–57.
36 IV Cyril and David Langham 27 July 1989
37 IV Tony Benn 25 September 1989
38 Ibid.
39 BD 7 November 1956
40 IV Tony Benn 25 September 1989
41 IV Tony Benn 30 October 1989
42 Poole Labour Party; 20 December 1951
43 BBC radio script of tribute to Stafford Cripps; BA Speeches 1951
44 BBC Interview, Lord Stansgate and Tony Benn 21 July 1951
45 IV Tony Benn 25 September 1989

8. The Cold War and Colonial Freedom

1   IV Tony Benn 30 October 1989
2   Dalton, H., *The Political Diary of Hugh Dalton 1918–40, 1945–60* (London, 1986)
3   Dutfield, M., *A Marriage of Inconvenience* (London, 1990) is a well documented, if racy, account of the early years of the marriage including the staggering callousness with which the British authorities attempted to stop the marriage occurring at all. Unfortunately the book stops short at the beginning of Khama's exile from Bechuanaland.
4   Hansard 27 March 1952. The Commonwealth had been in uproar over the case. Benn was correct, as in terms of pure self interest Britain would have done better to please the emergent black African nations than South Africa which was anyway soon to leave the Commonwealth. Benn did not know, however, about the uranium, and it is still impossible to tell to what extent the uranium negotiations affected the Seretse Khama affair, as British and South African files on the matter are closed.
5   Hansard 27 March 1952
6   TB, As I See It, *Bristol Evening World* 18 June 1957
7   Cocks, M., *Labour and the Benn Factor* (London, 1989)
8   *Bristol Evening World* 9 May 1955
9   IV Tony Benn 27 November 1989
10 IV Anthony Sampson 2 August 1989
11 TB *Bristol Evening World* 21 November 1952. The version quoted is from the original copy, before sub-editing.
12 Cincinnati Women's International Forum, September 1952
13 *Lincoln Echo* 19 January 1951
14 *Daily Herald* 3 December 1952
15 1953 constituency report
16 *Daily Herald* 5 April 1954
17 *Bristol Evening Post* 3 May 1954
18 Hansard 5 April 1954
19 Hansard 8 April 1954. Previous quotations from Hansard of 5 April or Keesing's Contemporary Archives.
20 IV Tony Benn 25 September 1989
21 Hansard 12 July 1955
22 BBC North American Service 18 August 1953
23 TB A Blow at British Justice, *Reynolds News* 27 June 1954. The

McCarran Internal Security Act (1950) placed numerous restrictions on Communists in the US.

24 Hansard 30 July 1954
25 *Bristol Evening World* 17 February 1954
26 *Bristol Evening World* 13 February 1954
27 *Bristol Evening World* 19 February 1954
28 IV Tony Benn 30 October 1989
29 TB As I See It, *Bristol Evening World* 28 July 1954
30 Lords Hansard 2 May 1950
31 *The Times* 18 January 1954

9. A First Assault on the Peerage

1 *Daily Express* 19 December 1954
2 BD 18 December 1956
3 *Sunday Mirror* 20 March 1955
4 Book in Progress – Part 1 Chapter 6 of unfinished book by TB on peerage. A great deal of peerage information used in this and the following chapters comes from a series of interviews conducted by David Butler with Tony Benn (and one with Caroline Benn) in 1961–2 as part of the Nuffield College Oral History Project. The reference for this material will be 'Nuffield' with the number of the interview. In this case Nuffield 4.
5 Lords Hansard 26 April 1955
6 IV Tony Benn 30 November 1989
7 Bristol City Council minutes 8 February 1955
8 BD 7 November 1956
9 *Tribune* 1 February 1957
10 Hansard 12 February 1958
11 BD 18 December 1956. The unpopularity courted by the peerage campaign is demonstrated by the drop in Benn's vote for a shadow cabinet place, from 63 in 1954 to 38 in 1955.
12 Hansard 8 June 1956
13 'Taper', *The Spectator* 26 July 1957
14 TB As I See It, *Bristol Evening World* 25 July 1957
15 'Taper', *The Spectator* 2 August 1957
16 Hansard 29 July 1957
17 TB As I See It, *Bristol Evening World* 28 November 1957

10. The Suez Campaign

1   *Daily Express* 18 December 1953
2   IV Tony Benn 30 October 1989
3   Discussion on Conservative Party Conference, BBC Light Programme,
    7 October 1955
4   Mikardo, I., *Back-Bencher* (London, 1988)
5   BD 5 November 1956 (Benn is recalling the 2 August event)
6   Gaitskell, H., *The Diary of Hugh Gaitskell 1945–56* (London, 1983)
7   The Suez Crisis, statement 18 August 1956
8   Hansard 13 September 1956
9   BD 29 October 1956
10 BD 31 October 1956
11 Horne, A., *Macmillan 1894–1956* (London, 1989)
12 Telegram Ben-Gurion to TB et al. 3 November 1956
13 *Cambridge Daily News* 3 November 1956
14 BD 3 November 1956
15 Original of Gaitskell's speech in BA
16 BD 8 November 1956
17 BD 23 November 1956
18 BD 5 November 1956
19 Hansard 5 November 1956
20 BD 5 November 1956
21 Hansard 9 November 1956
22 Ibid.
23 Hansard 19 November 1956
24 BD 4 December 1956. The 'Suez Group' were right-wing Tories.
25 TB, As I See It, *Bristol Evening World* 4 April 1957
26 TB, As I See It, *Bristol Evening World* 19 March 1959

11. Front Bencher

1   *Reynolds News* 23 June 1957
2   Paraphrased from 'Introducing Wit', TB's contribution to the National
    Union of Students Debating Handbook, 3 July 1958
3   Hansard 7 May 1957
4   TB, As I See It, *Bristol Evening World* 28 November 1957
5   Hansard 9 May 1957

6   Foot, M., *Aneurin Bevan 1945–1960* (London, 1973)
7   Mikardo, I., *Back-Bencher* (London, 1988)
8   Labour Party Annual Report 1957
9   IV Tony Benn 30 October 1989
10 Ibid.
11 Ibid.
12 BA Speeches 1956
13 Straight From Conference; BBC Light Programme 8 October 1955
14 *Any Questions?* BBC Light Programme 19 October 1956
15 Horne, A., *Macmillan 1957–1986* (London, 1989)
16 IV Caroline Benn 18 December 1989
17 TB Terror on the Streets of London, *Reynolds News* 7 September 1958
18 TB As I See It, *Bristol Evening World* 4 September 1958
19 TB On Marriage, *News Chronicle* 2 April 1956
20 *Bristol Evening Post* 22 September 1959
21 *New Statesman* 22 June 1957
22 *TV Times* 13 January 1956
23 *TV Times* 30 August 1957
24 TB, The TV Election, for Labour Organiser. Manuscript dated 16
    June 1955
25 *Forward*, 27 March 1958
26 TB, Draft Plan for General Election Broadcasting, presented to Campaign Committee, 14 November 1958
27 Ibid.
28 Bristol South-East Labour Party GC Minutes, 11 September 1959
29 *Bristol Evening Post* 7 October 1959
30 Crossman, R., *The Backbench Diaries of Richard Crossman* (London, 1981)
31 IV Tony Benn 30 October 1989
32 *Daily Sketch* 25 September 1959
33 *Daily Mail* 21 September 1959

12. Breaking with Gaitskell

1   IV Tony Benn 30 October 1989
2   *Bristol Evening News* 28 September 1959
3   IV Tony Benn 30 October 1989
4   Healey, D., *The Time of My Life* (London, 1989)
5   Labour Party NEC Minutes, 16 March 1960

6 Crossman, R., *The Backbench Diaries of Richard Crossman* (London, 1981)

7 Foot, M., *Loyalists and Loners* (London, 1986)

8 Hansard 10 December 1959

9 Ibid.

10 *Observer* 4 October 1959

11 Horne, A., *Macmillan 1957–1986* (London, 1989)

12 TB, As I See It, *Bristol Evening World* 5 February 1960

13 Crossman, R., *The Backbench Diaries of Richard Crossman* (London, 1981)

14 *News Chronicle* and *Daily Telegraph* reports 18 March 1960

15 Goodman, G., *The Awkward Warrior* (London, 1979)

16 IV Tony Benn 27 November 1989

17 Ibid.

18 Ibid.

19 *Daily Herald* 3 October 1960

20 *Bristol Evening Post* 4 October 1960

21 IV Tony Benn 30 November 1989

22 Bristol South-East Labour Party GC Minutes 3 October 1960

23 Bristol South-East Labour Party GC Minutes 16 October 1960

24 *The Times* 17 October 1960

25 TB letter to Bert Peglar 28 October 1960

26 Bristol South-East Labour Party GC Minutes 7 November 1960

27 TB, A Radical in Politics, *The Times* 7 May 1977

28 IV Tony Benn 27 November 1989

29 Ibid.

13. Expelled from the Commons

1 Sergeant-at-Arms to TB 1 December 1960

2 Lecture at New College, Oxford, 19 May 1961

3 Nuffield 1

4 Nuffield 6

5 Ibid.

6 Ibid.

7 Ibid.

8 Ibid.

9 TB to Harold Macmillan 2 December 1959

10 Nuffield 5. Macmillan's biographer, Alistair Horne, tells me (letter to author 26 April 1990) that Macmillan did not take the actions he did

in order to keep Hailsham out; Hailsham was 'outstandingly loyal' and Macmillan was a firm supporter of his until 1963.

11 Nuffield 2
12 Nuffield 5
13 Bristol South-East EC minutes 1954–70
14 Lecture at New College, Oxford, 19 May 1961
15 IV Herbert Rogers 7 June 1989
16 *The Times* 2 March 1961
17 Nuffield 7 ·
18 TB As I See It, *Bristol Evening World* 26 January 1962
19 TB *Sunday Dispatch* 12 May 1961
20 TB This Man Jack is Fearless, *Bristol Evening Post* 27 February 1961
21 Nuffield 8
22 BA The Bristol Campaign, Documents
23 Hansard 31 March 1961
24 Nabarro, Sir G., *NAB 1 – Portrait of a Politician* (Oxford, 1969)
25 Nuffield 8
26 Bristol South-East GMC minutes 1957–63
27 TB to Hugh Gaitskell 8 December 1960
28 Nuffield 7
29 Keesing's Contemporary Archives, 13–20 May 1961
30 Report of the Committee of Privileges 14 March 1961
31 Lecture at New College, Oxford, 19 May 1961
32 Garter Principal King at Arms to TB 15 December 1960
33 Hugh Gaitskell to TB 8 December 1960. The 'Officers' were those of the PLP: the Leader, Deputy Leader and Chief Whip.
34 TB to Hugh Gaitskell 8 December 1960
35 Hansard 13 April 1961
36 BD 25 March 1963
37 Howard, A., Member for the Queen's Bench, *New Statesman* 14 July 1961 and Pannell's letter of 21 July which was written to spare his leader's blushes and implies uncompromising support for the Benn cause. The facts in this letter are accurate but the truth has escaped through the holes between them.
38 Nuffield 7
39 Ibid.
40 Hansard 13 April 1961
41 Ibid. The Tory dissenters in the divisions on the Benn case hurt Butler personally, particularly because they were his own former young admirers, including Julian Critchley, Christopher Chataway, James

Prior and Peter Tapsell. Anthony Howard in his life of Butler gives the figure of 22 Tory dissenters.

42 IV Lord Home of the Hirsel 27 February 1990. Anecdotal evidence suggests Butler's position changed on this issue according to who was putting pressure on him.

14. Challenging the Constitution

1 The colourful eighteenth-century radical John Wilkes was elected five times for Middlesex, defying the refusal of the House to allow him to take his seat because of charges against him arising from his attacks on the government. In the middle of the nineteenth century the Jewish banker Lionel Rothschild was elected six times for the City of London before being allowed to take his seat when the Oaths Bill was passed, no longer requiring an oath on the Christian faith. Later that century the radical and freethinker Charles Bradlaugh was elected four times for Northampton before he was allowed to affirm rather than swearing on the Bible.

2 Bristol South-East GMC minutes 1957–63

3 *Bristol Evening Post* 20 April 1961

4 Nuffield 8. Benn remarked that Crossman had also opposed Hailsham's attempt to stay in the Commons in 1950, 'So here was an issue on which Dick was consistent, I suppose one should be grateful for that.'

5 BA The Bristol Campaign, Documents

6 Agent's report in BA The Bristol Campaign, Documents; and BA The Benntapes 1961

7 Lecture at New College, Oxford, 19 May 1961

8 Nuffield 9

9 BA The Bristol Campaign, Documents

10 Nuffield 9

11 Ibid.

12 Ibid. and contemporary newspaper accounts.

15. *The Election Court*

1 Nuffield 9. Benn was impressed with the effect of forcing the Establishment to go to the full extent of their powers. The next time he was returned he resolved he would use force to enter – as Bradlaugh had.
2 Hansard 8 May 1961
3 Michael Zander to Caroline Benn, undated but obviously mid-May 1961
4 Michael Zander to TB 10 May 1961
5 Nuffield 9
6 Lecture at New College, Oxford, 19 May 1961
7 Nuffield 10
8 IV Michael Zander 22 March 1990
9 Ibid.
10 *Guardian* 29 July 1961
11 Zander, M., 'How to Lose a Title', *Town* Magazine September 1963. I am indebted to Professor Zander for access to his private papers on the peerage case and for advice.
12 Keesing's Contemporary Archives
13 Barbara Castle to TB 15 May 1962
14 Sir Edward Boyle to TB 13 February 1962. Few others were in a position to be equally generous, though Edward and Lois Sieff also gave the Benns £500 and attempted to insist it was to be used for their living expenses in this difficult time.
15 Bristol South-East EC minutes 1954–70
16 Higgins, S., *The Benn Inheritance* (London, 1984)

16. *Political Limbo*

1 Herbert Rogers to Len Williams 9 August 1961
2 Nuffield 11
3 The Labour Party Conference Report, Blackwell 1961
4 The NEC minutes at the 1 October 1961 meeting which discussed the issue are bland, merely noting that if their decision were questioned, 'the Deputy General Secretary give a full explanation of the constitutional position'.
5 Nuffield 11
6 The Labour Party Conference Report, Blackpool 1961

7   *Time and Tide* 4 May 1961
8   Nuffield, Caroline Benn, 1 February 1962
9   Ibid.
10 *Daily Mail* 13 January 1961
11 IV Tony Benn 12 March 1990
12 IV Michael Bowen 15 November 1989
13 BBC Light Programme, *Any Questions?* 1 May 1964
14 BBC Home Service, Conference, 11 April 1963
15 Sir William Haley to TB 11 December 1961
16 BBC Light Programme, *Any Questions?* 30 March 1962
17 BA The Benntapes 1962–4
18 Bristol South-East GMC minutes 1957–63
19 TB to Hugh Gaitskell 12 May 1961
20 IV Tony Benn 15 September 1989

17. Back Victorious

1   BD 18 January 1963
2   Nuffield 18, on 19 December 1961, recording a meeting held on the previous day. Truly contemporary history. Benn actually said 'a £3000 bill' which may have been the sum which remained to be paid off. I have altered it to reflect, more or less, the figure at the end of the election court. This was made up of: £1000 for Ashurst, Morris and Crisp (though all the work had been done by the £15 a week Michael Zander) which they later reduced by a quarter; and the £7518 bill for St Clair's solicitors which Benn later had reduced by £2300 on appeal to a 'taxing master', an event at which he again represented himself. The Tories explained that they needed a very expensive counsel because, with the defendant representing himself, he would doubtless need the assistance of an experienced man on the other side.
3   IV Tony Benn 13 March 1990
4   Nuffield 19
5   BD 20 January 1963
6   BA 'The Book' Chapter 7
7   TB to Charles Pannell 13 July 1962
8   BD 21 July 1963
9   *Western Daily Press* 29 May 1963
10 BD 15 May 1963
11 BD 13–15 August 1963 where a long letter to Caroline Benn was used as an account of the events.

12   TB to Herbert Rogers 26 August 1963
13   *Bristol Evening Post* 21 August 1963

18. The Tories in Decline

1   Pannell, C., Letter to *The Times* 4 May 1961
2   *Sunday Dispatch* 27 November 1960. William Douglas-Home was well acquainted with the issues, being the brother of the future Sir Alec Douglas-Home.
3   IV Tony Benn 13 March 1990
4   Nuffield 20
5   Macleod, I., What Happened?, *The Spectator* 17 January 1964. He states that this was the situation at lunchtime the day before Home went to the Palace to kiss hands.
6   *Daily Mirror* 20 October 1963. Home renounced six titles and some have remarked that as he actually had seven, but never renounced the Earldom of Dunbar, he sat for his entire period as Prime Minister as a peer.
7   IV Lord Home of the Hirsel 28 February 1990. He also remarked that he thinks he was probably wrong to renounce. He would not have done it had not his son been prepared to take on the Earldom and thereby maintain continuity. He had been a Hailsham supporter until Blackpool. Rab Butler had not asked him about his intentions despite their friendship.
8   BD 24 October 1963
9   Hansard 24 October 1963. In fact the seriously ill Macmillan had based his advice on speedy consultations with the Conservative Party. Home was the first choice of the Cabinet and the Lords backed him two to one; the 300 Tory backbenchers supported him by a narrow margin and the constituencies seemed to support Hailsham first and Butler second. Horne, A., op. cit.
10   Outline for a Post Office Development Programme 30 October 1963; ideas also used in his *Guardian* column 19 June 1964.
11   BD 17 July 1964
12   NEC Home Policy Committee Report on Honours and Awards, January 1964
13   BD 8 June 1964
14   BD 25 May 1964
15   BD 23 October 1964
16   BD 16 November 1964

17 IV David Butler 1 October 1990
18 IV Tony Benn 12 June 1990
19 BD 20 February 1963
20 Horne, A., *Macmillan 1957–86* (London, 1989)
21 TB *Sunday Citizen* 10 February 1963
22 TB *Sunday Citizen* 7 July 1963
23 TB *Sunday Citizen* 23 June 1963

19. The Modernising Postmaster General

1 BD 19 October 1964
2 IV Kenneth Harris 22 August 1989
3 Sampson, A., *Anatomy of Britain* (London, 1962)
4 *Post & Times-Star*, Cincinnati, 21 April 1965
5 TB, The Labour Beacon, 30 January 1965
6 *Daily Worker* 4 December 1964
7 *Evening Standard* 4 March 1965
8 *Daily Mail* 4 August 1965
9 BA The Benntapes 1964–66
10 IV Donald Wratten 16 August 1990
11 BA The Benntapes 1964–66
12 Castle, B., *The Castle Diaries 1964–70* (London, 1984)
13 BD 21 October 1964
14 Crossman, R., *The Diaries of a Cabinet Minister, Vol 1* (London, 1975)
15 Wilson, H., *The Labour Government 1964–70* (London, 1971)
16 *Guardian* 14 June 1965
17 Hansard 10 November 1964
18 Bevins, R., Letter to *The Times* 12 November 1964
19 *The Times* 31 March 1965
20 Castle, B., *The Castle Diaries 1964–70* (London, 1984)
21 *Guardian* 1 July 1965
22 IV Tony Benn 12 June 1990
23 BD 15 April 1965
24 *The Economist* 24–30 April 1965
25 BD 1 June 1965
26 BD 20 June 1965
27 *Observer* 6 June 1965
28 *Daily Express* 27 June 1965
29 BD 12 October 1965
30 IV Charles Morris 19 June 1990

31 BD 24 May 1965
32 BD 30 November 1964
33 BA Premature obituary transcript and letter from BBC 22 February 1965
34 Falkender, M., *Downing Street in Perspective* (London, 1983)
35 Wilson, H., *Final Term – The Labour Government 1974–1976* (London, 1979)
36 *Evening Standard* 4 March 1965
37 IV Kenneth Harris 22 August 1989 and BD 16 September 1965
38 Buchanan, B., *The New Observer* 27 February 1965
39 IV Caroline Benn 18 December 1989
40 Wilson, H., *The Labour Government 1964–1970* (London, 1971)
41 Williams, M., *Inside Number 10* (London, 1972)
42 BD 29 September 1965

20. Stamps and Pirates

1 Castle, B., *The Castle Diaries 1964–70* (London, 1984)
2 BD 3 June 1967
3 IV Charles Morris 19 June 1990
4 IV Donald Wratten 17 August 1990
5 BD 7 December 1964
6 To the Annual Conference of National Federation of Sub-Postmasters 9 May 1966
7 BD 10 March 1965
8 IV Charles Morris 19 June 1990
9 BD 11 March 1965
10 BD 29 June 1965
11 D. Mitchell to D. Wratten 12 October 1965, copy filed in BD
12 BD 2 November 1965
13 Ibid.
14 Hansard 18 May 1966
15 BA The Benntapes 1964–66
16 *The Times* 27 July 1965
17 BA The Benntapes 1964–66
18 Dr Ernest Claxton as reported in the *Sun*, 6 December 1965
19 Hansard 15 December 1965
20 Hansard 10 November 1964
21 ITA dinner 16 September 1965
22 BA The Benntapes 1964–66

23 Crossman, R., *The Diaries of a Cabinet Minister, Vol 1* (London, 1975)
24 IV Tony Benn 12 June 1990 and BA The Benntapes 1964–66
25 BA Post Office Numbered Minute 84
26 *Daily Telegraph* 13 December 1965
27 Hansard 2 June 1966. The debate on the pirates actually took place at 5 a.m. as part of an all-night sitting so the events on Radio City were not literally on the day of the debate.
28 IV Tony Benn 12 June 1990
29 Ibid.
30 BD 4 April 1966
31 Ibid.
32 BA Post Office Numbered Minute 89. There was some discussion as to whether there should be three corporations: telecommunications, mail and banking.
33 Browne, A., *Tony Benn* (London, 1983)
34 IV Tony Benn 12 June 1990

21. Technology Evangelist

1 Brown, G., *In My Way* (London, 1971)
2 BD 30 June 1966 and Wilson, H., *The Labour Government 1964–1970* (London, 1971)
3 Crossman, R., *The Diaries of a Cabinet Minister, Vol 1* (London, 1975)
4 Wilson, H., *The Labour Government 1964–1970* (London, 1971)
5 BD 4 July 1966. Benn frequently inspired this almost desperate devotion in people he worked with and among members of the Labour Party. It would be cloying to give further examples.
6 Fords, Dagenham, 7 September 1966, speech on the occasion of the production of the millionth Cortina.
7 Opening the Engineering Industry Board's regional office 9 September 1966
8 Dinner of the International Reinforced Plastics Conference, 24 November 1966
9 This theme was used for a BBC television lecture and a subsequent *Listener* article of 5 June 1969
10 European Organisation for Quality Control 6 June 1967
11 BD 5 August 1966
12 BD 30 July 1966
13 BD 11 July 1966

14 BD 5 August 1966. Clarke is always known familiarly as Otto though sometimes referred to by his first name, Richard.
15 IV Tony Benn 25 September 1990
16 IV Sir Bruce Williams 20 July 1990
17 Ibid.
18 IV Anthony Sampson 2 August 1989
19 Crossman, R., *The Diaries of a Cabinet Minister, Vol 2* (London, 1976)
20 IV Lord Lever of Manchester 17 February 1990
21 Crossman, R., *The Diaries of a Cabinet Minister, Vol 3* (London, 1977)
22 BD 22 November 1968
23 BD 18 September 1966
24 Wilson speech to PLP 2 March 1967, quoted in Butler, D. & G., *British Political Facts 1900–1985* (London, 1986)

22. The Common Market and Concorde

1 Castle, B., *The Castle Diaries 1964–70* (London, 1984)
2 BA notes to Chequers meeting 30 April 1967
3 IV Tony Benn 25 September 1990
4 *Observer* 27 November 1966, in a forward-looking article
5 Annual Dinner of Society of British Aerospace Companies 28 June 1967. The Mintech press release of the speech puts it more delicately: 'Successive Ministers of Aviation secured victory after victory in the battle for a share of the public purse.'
6 Hansard 25 April 1968 and reports in the *Telegraph* and *The Times* of following day
7 IV Tony Benn 25 September 1990
8 Castle, B., *The Castle Diaries 1964–70* (London, 1984)
9 *Daily Express* 12 December 1967
10 BD 11 July 1969
11 Central Office of Information film interview at Filton, 21 March 1969
12 Hansard 27 November 1968
13 IV Ken Binning 18 July 1990
14 The first planned test boom, along 'boom alley' up the West of the UK, was cancelled, but there was presumptive distress: there were claims that cows had aborted, foundations had shifted and glasshouses had been shattered.
15 *Bristol Evening Post* 4 October 1967
16 BD 5 September 1967. Lord Zuckerman remembers 'the Chancellor

looking dubious, Healey in a corner and the Foreign Secretary didn't
know what it was about.'

17 IV Tony Benn 25 September 1990
18 Institute of Contemporary British History seminar on Mintech 14 Feb-
    ruary 1990. I am indebted to Dr Richard Coopey, who organised this
    seminar, for many of the facts about Mintech which have been quoted
    in these chapters.
19 IV Tony Benn 25 September 1990
20 Institute of Contemporary British History seminar on Mintech 14 Feb-
    ruary 1990. The transfer of the Atomic Weapons Research Establish-
    ment to the Ministry of Defence was announced on 5 August 1971.
    Benn protested that nuclear weapons research and production should
    not be under a defence minister who would also be responsible for the
    strategy and possible use of the weapons.
21 IV Sir Bruce Williams 20 July 1990
22 Ibid.
23 *Private Eye* August 1967
24 Waugh, A., *The Spectator* 3 January 1969
25 Lord, M. *Bristol Evening Post* 21 October 1968

23. Radical Clarion

 1 Crossman, R., *The Diaries of a Cabinet Minister, Vol 2* (London, 1976)
 2 IV Tony Benn 25 September 1990
 3 BD 6 February 1968 and, BA, Benn's handwritten note to Wilson of
    the same date.
 4 *Daily Mirror* 13 May 1968
 5 BD 3 April 1968
 6 BD 1 April 1968
 7 BD 9 April 1968
 8 BD 2 November 1968
 9 Harlech TV Broadcast 7 June 1968
10 BD 14 June 1968
11 *The Enthusiasts*, Central Office of Information film, April 1967
12 Quoted in Cosgrave, P., *The Lives of Enoch Powell* (London, 1989)
13 Foot, P., *The Rise of Enoch Powell* (London, 1969). He gives details
    which show that similar stories about immigrants were common at the
    time, generally sharing features related to defecation and sex. Some
    were even more bizarre, the 'naked immigrant up a tree' for example.

14 BD 21 April 1968. Powell's parents were schoolteachers, but their parents were working class. He was a brigadier at 32.
15 IV Tony Benn 25 September 1990
16 From Parliamentary to Popular Democracy, Annual Conference, Welsh Council of Labour 25 May 1968
17 *Sunday Express* 26 May 1968
18 *Daily Telegraph* 27 May 1968
19 *Newsweek* 10 June 1968
20 *Industrial Society* 27 November 1968
21 *Young Fabians* 5 November 1968
22 Bristol South-East GMC minutes 1963–70
23 Castle, B., *The Castle Diaries 1964–70* (London, 1984)
24 BD 8 October 1968
25 BD 21 June 1967
26 Report to Bristol South-East CLP 6 March 1968
27 January 1970 paper to Management Committee
28 Johnson, P., *New Statesman* 25 October 1968
29 *Guardian* 22 October 1968

24. Technology Turns Sour

 1 BD 10 December 1969
 2 Castle, B., *The Castle Diaries 1964–70* (London, 1984)
 3 *Face the Press*, Tyne-Tees TV 6 February 1969
 4 Harlech Television 7 June 1968
 5 Hansard 11 December 1969
 6 Directors of Research Associations lunch 13 December 1966
 7 IV Tony Benn 25 September 1990
 8 Crossman, R., *The Diaries of a Cabinet Minister, Vol 3* (London, 1977)
 9 BD 16 April 1969
10 BD 17 June 1968
11 BBC West Region 8 February 1969
12 BD 3 April 1968
13 *Sunday Times* 12 October 1969. This was a highly accurate remark. The leaders Labour did get in a decade or so were Foot and Kinnock, from the generation above and below Benn.
14 *Focus on Youth*, Tyne-Tees TV 10 October 1969
15 *Bristol Evening Post* 10 November 1969
16 BD 19 October 1969
17 IV Lord Lever of Manchester 17 February 1990

18 TB, Yesterday's Men at Mintech, *New Statesman* 24 July 1970
19 BA speeches files: 9 December 1968
20 *Daily Mirror* 6 June 1970
21 *Daily Mirror* 4 June 1970
22 The time was right for such interventions. Jeremy Thorpe, speaking in Orpington on the same night, said Powell was not only unchristian but evil. His remarks were reported alongside Benn's in the first edition only of the *Daily Sketch* for 4 June 1970. The second edition dropped Thorpe's quotes to make room for reaction to Benn's speech.
23 *The Times* 5 June 1970
24 BD 5 June 1970
25 Cocks, M., *Labour and the Benn Factor* (London, 1989)
26 Patrick Cosgrave remarks (op. cit.) that Cyril Osborne and Duncan Sandys had been 'energetic' in discussing racial issues. Benn's intervention stopped forays into this territory.
27 IV Tony Benn 25 September 1990
28 BD 16 January 1974
29 Steed, M., 'The Results Analysed', in Butler, D., and Pinto-Duschinsky, M., *The British General Election of 1970* (London, 1971). When the National Front offered the electors a clear choice on the issue of race alone, their vote in individual constituencies in national elections was derisory.

25. 'Citizen Benn'

1 Crosland, S., *Tony Crosland* (London, 1982)
2 BD 21 June 1970
3 David Butler interview 17 December 1971. I am profoundly indebted to Dr Butler for permitting me access to this archive.
4 There is a considerable difference in the 'Prime Minister stakes' between Conservatives and the main opposition even if we make up for Labour's small size during the first decades of the century and imply a continuity between Liberal and Labour governments. Adding the two Liberal PMs would still leave Labour and Liberal with exactly half the number of Prime Ministers compared with the Tories. Lloyd George's Liberal–Conservative coalition is excluded from this sum.
5 BD 10 June 1975
6 *Sunday Express*, 'Mister Zero' 31 October 1971 and *Sunday Express* as quoted in *Daily Mirror* 3 August 1972

7   BD 4 November 1971. 'Sea-green incorruptible' is, of course, Carlyle's description of Robespierre.
8   David Butler interview 17 December 1971
9   BD 8 December 1971
10 BD 8 November 1972
11 BD 6 August 1971
12 Neil Kinnock to TB 16 September 1970
13 The Role of Women in Society, Yorkshire Labour Women's rally, Rotherham 5 June 1971. Benn may have been the first leading politician of either gender to declare himself in support of women's liberation.
14 BD 24 July 1970
15 Bristol South-East GMC minutes 1970–76. It was an uphill task. This was 3 December 1970. The minutes for 4 October 1973 show that Herbert Rogers, 'had secured the services of two young ladies to take over the job of Young Women's Organiser'.
16 BD 3 July 1971
17 Business International Chief Executive Officer's Roundtable on Corporate Leadership for Survival in a Turbulent World, Trinidad, 24 January 1972
18 BBC Radio 4 1 June 1971
19 Hansard 4 November 1970. He was echoing a remark made by Benn when he announced 'safeguards against the support of lame ducks' on 1 February 1968.
20 *Bristol Evening Post* 23 September 1970
21 The *Sunday Times* 28 February 1971
22 IV Lord Lever of Manchester 17 February 1990
23 TB Press release 7 May 1973. He had already, on 30 November 1970, warned the House that those who bought public sector businesses should not assume they would receive compensation at market value when a future Labour government repossessed them.
24 BD 9 May 1973 and press reports
25 *Christian Science Monitor* 31 July 1971
26 BD 2 August 1971
27 *Sunday Times* 1 August 1971 and other press reports
28 Freeman, A., *The Benn Heresy* (London, 1982)
29 IV Ken Coates 23 December 1990
30 Ibid.
31 IV (telephone) Eric Heffer 20 February 1991
32 IV Tony Benn 21 February 1991

33 Fletcher, R., in *Tribune* 7 May 1971. Benn wrote for *Tribune* occasionally but did not join the group at this time.
34 *Sunday Times* 23 July 1972
35 Labour's Debt to Judaism, Poale Zion Dinner, 21 October 1972
36 TB Press Release 4 August 1972
37 BD 31 July 1972
38 *Daily Mirror* 3 August 1972

26. Party Chairman

1 Benn remarked on the absence of destitution in his diary on 10 September 1971. The world was still ignorant of the great famine in China between 1959 and 1961, which had been the subject of an astonishingly efficient censorship operation by the Chinese government.
2 BD 26 June 1973
3 NEC minutes 28 February 1973
4 IV Caroline Benn 21 March 1991
5 BD 21 June 1972
6 *Any Questions?* BBC Radio 4 27 November 1970
7 BD 11 November 1970
8 IV Tony Benn 25 September 1990
9 *Sunday Mirror* 27 January 1974
10 IV Neville Sandelson 13 June 1989
11 IV Bert and Celia Roach 17 November 1989
12 IV Cyril and David Langham 27 July 1989
13 Sicco Mansholt to TB 12 April 1972
14 Speech at Bristol 20 September 1972
15 IV Tony Benn 18 February 1991
16 BD 2 August 1972
17 The Incredible Shrinking Anthony Wedgwood Benn, *Daily Mirror* 6 April 1973
18 BD 7 May 1977
19 *Labour Weekly* 10 November 1978
20 *Daily Telegraph* 4 October 1972
21 Labour Party conference report 1972. He actually said 'Transport House', not 'Thomson House', but all reports of the speech corrected this slip. Taverne won the election as a Democratic Labour candidate but lost the seat in 1974.
22 Statement by Harold Wilson 9 October 1972
23 BD 20 June 1973

24 Labour Party Conference Report 1973

25 Hansard 29 January 1973

26 Davies' flat in London was bombed on 31 July 1971 without injury.

27 BD 8 September 1973

28 BD 3 May 1974. Family history made him wary of the libel laws. In 1910 John Benn (Tony Benn's grandfather) lost a libel action brought by the manufacturers of a tramway system that had been rejected by the London County Council and about which John Benn had made comment. He was ordered to pay £12,000 and the second general election of 1910, in which both John and William Wedgwood Benn stood, was held while there were bailiffs in the family home. 'The fear that the lawyers might get involved was burned into my mind from a very early age,' said Tony Benn. 'I have always fought everything politically, I don't want anything to do with the law.' IV Tony Benn 18 February 1991

29 For example in *Workers Press* 20 September 1974

30 *Socialist Worker* 8 March 1975

31 Bristol Trades Council 20 December 1973

32 BD 2 January 1974

33 Castle, B., *The Castle Diaries 1974–76* (London, 1980)

34 David Butler interview 12 January 1974

35 King, C., *The Cecil King Diary 1970–4* (London, 1975). The meeting took place on 18 October 1972.

36 IV Cyril and David Langham 27 July 1989

37 *Daily Mail* 7 January 1974

27. *'The Wedgie Man'*

1 BD 7 March 1974

2 Castle, B., *The Castle Diaries 1974–76* (London, 1980)

3 Ibid.

4 IV Joe Ashton 26 February 1991

5 BD 26 March 1974

6 IV Tony Benn 18 February 1991. The upside down map, which made the British Isles resemble Italy 'with all the poverty concentrated at the bottom' had been a fitting in his office in the later years of Mintech. It does not seem to have been up for long in the Department of Industry.

7 Castle, B., *The Castle Diaries 1974–76* (London, 1980)

8 BD 10 June 1974

9   Healey, D., *The Time of My Life* (London, 1989)

10 BD 20 November 1974

11 Healey, D., op. cit.

12 BD 11 April 1974

13 Part, A., *The Making of a Mandarin* (London, 1990)

14 Ibid.

15 BD 21 January 1975

16 Castle, B., *The Castle Diaries 1974–76* (London, 1980)

17 Ibid.

18 *The Times* 27 June 1974

19 *Birmingham Post* 9 November 1974

20 *Sunday Times* 1 December 1974

21 David Butler interview 8 October 1974

22 IV Jack Jones 8 March 1991

23 *Daily Telegraph* 4 January 1975

24 *Sunday Telegraph* 12 January 1975, a day on which there were also positive pieces about Benn in the *Sunday Times* and *The People*.

25 *Daily Mail* 18 February 1975

26 Castle, B., *The Castle Diaries 1974–76* (London, 1980)

27 IV Jeremy Bray 17 August 1990

28 IV Ian Mikardo 24 November 1989

29 Part, A., *The Making of a Mandarin* (London, 1990)

30 BD 13 January 1975

31 *Daily Express* 9 May 1975

32 Allegations of great wealth were a time-honoured method of undermining leading socialists: Keir Hardie and Stafford Cripps were similarly credited with riches, and Nye Bevan was claimed to drive close to his constituency in a Bentley and finish the journey wearing a cloth cap and driving a Morris Minor.

33 IV Caroline Benn 21 March 1991

34 *Guardian* 22 August 1974

35 'Yorick', *The Ugly Face of Mr Wedgwood Benn* (London, 1974)

36 IV Michael Ivens 28 January 1991

37 Foot, P., *Who Framed Colin Wallace?* (London, 1989)

38 Wright, P., *Spycatcher* (New York, 1987); *Twenty Twenty* Television, MI5's Official Secrets; Channel 4 TV (UK) February 1985

39 *New Statesman* 20 February 1981

40 TB to *New Statesman* 18 February 1981

41 BD 30 June 1974

42 BD 29 July 1975

43 *Twenty Twenty* Television, MI5's Official Secrets; Channel 4 TV (UK) February 1985
44 IV Joshua Benn 2 May 1991
45 Ibid.
46 *Miami Herald* 29 December 1977

28. *Wilson Attacks*

 1 BA Speeches 1974 file. Minute of 1 June 1974
 2 Castle, B., *The Castle Diaries 1974–76* (London, 1980)
 3 Harold Wilson to TB 4 July 1974
 4 Castle, B., *The Castle Diaries 1974–76* (London, 1980)
 5 Stewart to Roy Williams 28 December 1974
 6 Callaghan, J., *Time and Chance* (London, 1987)
 7 BA Speeches file, March 1975, draft declarations. Two other cabinet ministers were anti-Market, Eric Varley and William Ross.
 8 Childs, D., *Britain Since 1945* (London, 1986)
 9 David Butler interview 1 June 1975
10 Castle, B., *The Castle Diaries 1974–76* (London, 1980)
11 Foot, M., *Loyalists and Loners* (London, 1986)
12 Castle, B., *The Castle Diaries 1974–76* (London, 1980)
13 BA cassette of speech 30 May 1975
14 *Daily Mail* 4 June 1975
15 *Evening Standard* 6 May 1975
16 Castle, B., *The Castle Diaries 1974–76* (London, 1980)
17 BD 11 May 1975
18 *Evening Standard* 27 May 1975
19 IV (telephone) Francis Cripps 23 March 1991
20 BD 6 July 1975
21 Hollingsworth, M., *The Press and Political Dissent* (London, 1986)
22 IV Joe Ashton 26 February 1991
23 IV Lord Lever of Manchester 17 February 1990
24 David Butler interview 23 July 1975
25 *Sun* and *Daily Telegraph* 10 June 1975
26 BD 9 June 1975, all following quotations from the same source unless otherwise indicated.
27 Castle, B., *The Castle Diaries 1974–76* (London, 1980)
28 IV Joe Ashton 26 February 1991
29 IV Tony Benn 27 November 1989
30 IV Eric Heffer (telephone) 20 February 1991

31 IV Joe Ashton 26 February 1991
32 IV Ian Mikardo 24 November 1989
33 Castle, B., *The Castle Diaries 1974–76* (London, 1980)
34 IV Michael Meacher 28 February 1991
35 Foot, M., *Loyalists and Loners* (London, 1986)
36 IV Jack Jones 8 March 1991. Jack Jones insists his concern was that Benn should not be sacked, not that he should not be moved from Industry, which is Benn's diary version of Jones' television statement of 6 June 1975.
37 Haines, J., *The Politics of Power* (London, 1977)
38 Falkender, M., *Downing Street in Perspective* (London, 1983)
39 BD 11 June 1975. The children bore up to the experience with the resolution of those inured by previous exposure. Melissa Benn remarked that this day was not so remarkable; through the whole period the house was 'besieged'. Similarly, Joshua Benn said this was not the first time he had been followed to school by the press.

29. Secretary of State for Energy

1 Harold Wilson to TB 4 February 1976
2 BD 5 December 1970
3 IV Joe Ashton 26 February 1991
4 Reports of Durham Miners' Gala 17 July 1976
5 BD 7 October 1976. His prediction was half right, the Labour Party was more than ten years in opposition.
6 BD 16 October 1977
7 LBC radio 29 February 1976
8 TB, The Levellers and the English Democratic Tradition; Nottingham 1976
9 Lord Brockway to TB 23 April 1977
10 *The Times* 21 June 1977
11 *Talking Politics* BBC Radio 4, 3 September 1977
12 BD 26 December 1976
13 *Newsday*, BBC 2 TV 16 February 1976
14 *Guardian* 10 July 1975
15 Fenton, J., 'Inside Mr Benn', *New Statesman* 10 June 1977
16 Whitehead, P., *The Writing on the Wall* (London, 1985)
17 IV Tony Benn 9 April 1991
18 Healey, D., *The Time of My Life* (London, 1989)
19 IV Lord Kearton 24 April 1991

20 Ibid.
21 David Butler interview 22 December 1978
22 IV Frances Morrell 13 December 1990
23 Nuclear Power – The Case for a Pause 2 May 1977
24 BD 3 July 1978. The first reactor at Dungeness actually began production only in 1983.
25 IV Tony Benn 25 September 1990
26 BD 26 February 1970
27 IV Tony Benn 18 February 1991
28 Ibid.
29 IV Tony Benn 9 April 1991
30 Sir Bruce Williams 20 July 1990
31 IV Lord Kearton 24 April 1991
32 IV Joe Ashton 26 February 1991
33 IV Sir Bruce Williams 20 July 1990
34 BD 13 February 1976
35 Whitehead, P., in Hennessy, P., and Seldon, A. (eds), *Ruling Performance* (Oxford, 1987)
36 *New Statesman* 27 May 1977
37 Bristol South-East GMC minutes 1976–79
38 BD 24 January 1979
39 BD 3 October 1977
40 BD 5 October 1977
41 *New Society* 16 June 1977
42 IV Tony Benn 9 April 1991
43 BD 25 October 1977
44 *Newsday*, BBC2 TV 18 February 1978
45 IV Melissa Benn 12 February 1991
46 IV Michael Meacher 28 February 1991
47 IV Frances Morrell 13 December 1990
48 BD 1 March 1978
49 Bristol South-East GMC minutes 1976–79. Herbert Rogers stayed defiant, at the following meeting he proposed a motion of no confidence in the chair, which only he and his friend Joyce Perham voted for.
50 Bristol South-East GMC minutes 1976–79
51 David Butler interview 26 April 1979
52 IV Tony Benn 13 June 1991
53 Benn Diaries, Granada TV programme on Channel 4 (UK) 29 September 1989
54 BD 21 December 1978

55 Morrell, F., *From the Electors of Bristol* (Nottingham, 1977)
56 IV Irving and Joyce Rogers 26 July 1989

30. The Battle for the Labour Party

 1 Quotes from raw copy for *Daily Mirror* story 20 July 1979
 2 BD 8 May 1979
 3 Press statement 10 May 1979
 4 BA Book in Progress file, 1964
 5 *New Statesman* 13 August 1976
 6 Press Gallery Lunch 14 February 1977
 7 BD 5 July 1979
 8 BD 20 August 1978
 9 Conversation with TB 12 December 1990
10 IV Tony Benn 12 June 1991
11 BD 13 June 1980
12 Whitehead, P., *The Writing on the Wall* (London, 1985)
13 Labour Party Conference Report 1980
14 IV Joe Ashton 26 February 1991
15 Labour Party Conference Report 1980
16 IV Tony Benn 12 June 1991
17 BD 2 October 1980

31. The Deputy Leadership Election

 1 IV Neville Sandelson 13 June 1989
 2 *Sunday Times* 12 April 1981
 3 IV Tony Benn 16 April 1991
 4 *Panorama*, BBC TV 22 June 1981
 5 BD 13 April 1981
 6 BD 30 April 1981
 7 Foot, M., *Loyalists and Loners* (London, 1986)
 8 Healey, D., *The Time of My Life* (London, 1989)
 9 Ibid.
10 Harris, R., *The Making of Neil Kinnock* (London, 1984)
11 IV Michael Meacher 28 February 1991
12 Hughes, R. A. C., *Guillain-Barré Syndrome* (London, 1990)
13 *Sun* 10 September 1981
14 *The Times* 25 September 1981; correction on 26

15 Mullin, C., '*The Times* and the "Stansgate Trust" – anatomy of a smear', *Tribune* 23 October 1981
16 IV Chris Mullin 27 June 1991
17 Ibid.
18 IV Joshua Benn 2 May 1991
19 IV Joe Ashton 26 February 1991
20 IV Ian Mikardo 24 November 1989
21 *New Statesman* 22 October 1976
22 IV Chris Mullin 27 June 1991
23 BA TB recommendations to the Prime Minister 8 April 1976
24 Radice, G., 'Denis Healey', *The Independent Magazine* 2 December 1989
25 *Labour Herald* 9 October 1981
26 BD 27 September 1981
27 This issue is an example of Benn's refusal to stand by and allow others to be attacked. At the 1982 conference he appeared at the Labour Campaign for Gay Rights meeting to which he had previously apologised for being unable to attend. At the last minute he turned up, saying, 'I am here by courtesy of the *News of the World*. When I read it, I cancelled something else to show my solidarity.'
28 BD 16 December 1981
29 *Guardian* 17 December 1991
30 Bristol South-East GMC minutes 1979–83

32. The Falklands War

1 *New York Post* 5 April 1984
2 CND rally 24 October 1981
3 BD 4 July 1977
4 BD 6 April 1982
5 Hansard 7 April 1982
6 Ibid.
7 IV Tony Benn 12 June 1991
8 Hansard 29 April 1982
9 BD 24 February 1983
10 TB to Michael Colvin 17 April 1985
11 IV Pam Tatlow 16 November 1989
12 BD 7 May 1983

33. Defeat in Bristol

1   Bristol South-East GMC minutes 1979–83
2   IV Dawn Primarolo 16 April 1991
3   Cocks, M., *Labour and the Benn Factor* (London, 1990)
4   Ibid.
5   BA Report of meeting held at the Dragonara Hotel on 23 November
    1981
6   IV Pam Tatlow 16 November 1989
7   BD 7 May 1983
8   IV Dawn Primarolo 16 April 1991
9   IV Cyril and David Langham 27 July 1989
10 IV George and Frances Easton 7 June 1989
11 BD 9 June 1983
12 IV Dr Robert Glendinning 27 July 1989
13 Higgins, S., *The Benn Inheritance* (London, 1984)
14 IV Dr Robert Glendinning 27 July 1989
15 BD 6 June 1983
16 IV Herbert Rogers 7 June 1989
17 IV Tony Benn 12 June 1991
18 *Mail on Sunday* 25 September 1983. Kinnock later wrote to Benn
    saying he had been misrepresented and the remark had been *wouldn't*
    not *couldn't* and he had made the remark in response to allegations
    of extremism against Benn. BD 28 March 1983.
19 BD 17 June and 31 December 1983

34. Chesterfield and the Miners' Strike

1   IV Margaret Vallins 19 March 1991
2   Quoted in *New Socialist* May/June 1984
3   IV (telephone) Peter Tatchell 30 May 1991
4   *Sun* 1 March 1984
5   *World in Action*, Granada TV 5 March 1984
6   IV John Burrows 18 March 1991
7   *The Independent* 20 June 1991
8   IV Tony Benn 12 June 1991
9   IV Ken Coates 23 December 1990
10 Ibid.
11 Speech at St Ives reported in full in *Socialist Action* 14 December 1984

12   BD 5 March 1985
13   TB evidence to Hinkley Point C Inquiry 7 April 1989

35. 'Speaking Out for Socialism in the Eighties'

1   IV John Burrows 18 March 1991
2   Turner, C., *Campaigning for Socialism: The Chesterfield Experience* (Chesterfield, 1986)
3   IV Bas Barker 18 March 1991
4   BD 24 April 1985
5   TB Converation 28 May 1991
6   IV Tony Benn 12 June 1991
7   BD 1 April 1986
8   IV Tony Benn 3 July 1991
9   BD 1 October 1985
10   Harris, R., *The Making of Neil Kinnock* (London, 1984)
11   BD Review of 1988
12   Hansard 27 January 1987
13   The Speaker to TB 28 January 1987
14   Hughes, C., and Wintour, P., *Labour Rebuilt: The New Model Party* (London, 1990)
15   BD 9 May 1979
16   Hughes, C., and Wintour, P., op. cit.
17   IV Tony Benn 3 July 1991
18   IV Chris Mullin 27 June 1991
19   BD 31 December 1987
20   Hughes, C., and Wintour, P., op. cit.
21   Godwin, N., and Krishnamma, Suri., *Comrades and Friends*, Channel 4 TV (UK) 11 December 1989
22   Ibid.
23   BA The Campaign for Socialism – Questions That May be Asked
24   Godwin, N., and Krishnamma, Suri., op. cit.
25   Hughes, C., and Wintour, P., op. cit.
26   IV Tony Benn 3 July 1991
27   This comparison is drawn from a meeting at which Benn and Skinner both spoke, Lambeth Against the Witch-hunt; Lambeth Town Hall 30 May 1991
28   The SDP split can be compared to other party rifts: the Conservatives over Corn Law Reform in 1846 and the Liberals over Home Rule for

Ireland in 1886. In both cases it took twenty years before the parties were fully recovered.

29 Hansard 15 December 1989
30 *Campaign Group News* July 1990

36. The Benn Renaissance

1 Chesterfield Labour Party, Aims and Objectives
2 Memorial Lecture on Democracy and Socialism, Barkingside 8 March 1990
3 *Guardian* 10 March 1990
4 Institute of Contemporary British History conference, London School of Economics 3 April 1990
5 Local Government Information Unit figures for 15 March 1991 for England, Scotland and Wales. Northern Ireland was never poll taxed.
6 IV Tony Benn 3 July 1991
7 *Independent* 18 January 1991
8 IV John Burrows 18 March 1991. Benn rather resembled John Bright agitating against the Crimean War in the 1850s. Ruth Winstone remarked on the resemblance and stuck on the wall of the office the famous 'angel of death has been abroad throughout the land' quotation from Bright. It was also a reminder of what happened to Bright, for he lost his Manchester seat in the next election.
9 IV Tony Benn 12 June 1991
10 *Independent* 5 April 1991
11 *Any Questions?* BBC Radio 4 7 April 1972
12 IV Tony Benn 25 September 1990
13 Barnet, J., Eric Heffer Obituary; *Independent* 28 May 1991
14 *Independent Magazine* 21 January 1989
15 BD 1 January 1987
16 *The Times* 3 June 1991

37. An Assessment

1 Foot, M., *Loyalists and Loners* (London, 1986)
2 BD 3 November 1974
3 IV Tony Benn 3 July 1991

Index

Note: In this index the abbreviation TB throughout refers to Tony Benn

Index

Basnett, David 411

BBC: broadcasts in twenty-two languages on the Beveridge Report, 30; TB works as producer for 56–8; rules regarding political broadcasts 90; and the Suez crisis 123–5; and TB's title 203; *That Was the Week That Was* 257; radio and television licence fees 258; 1960s policy re popular music 259, 260, 263; and TB's 1968 speech on role of broadcasting 297–8; Richard Crossman's 1968 speech on broadcasting 298; Zircon spy satellite documentary 450–51; TB and the 468–9; obituary for TB 469

Beagle Aircraft Company 278

Bechuanaland, Seretse Khama case 91–3

Beckett, E. F. 103

Beckett, Margaret 454

Ben-Gurion, David 4, 121–2

Benn, Sir Anthony (Elizabethan courtier) 2

Benn Brothers (family publishing firm) 7, 8, 54, 56

Benn, Caroline (wife of Tony Benn): background 51; gains place at Oxford University summer school 1948 51; social commitment 51–2; gains first-class degree at Vassar 52; at Oxford 52; meets and becomes engaged to Tony Benn 52–3; abandons academic plans 53; takes MA degree course at Cincinnati University 53; curiosity about TB and his parents' names 54–5; marriage in Cincinnati to TB 55; Lake Michigan honeymoon 55; first English home 55–6; post-grad. course at University College 56; expects first child 77; move to larger flat 78; son Stephen born 78; and TB's unsocial working hours 78; comes to terms with British politics 82; surveillance of, under Aliens Restriction Act 97; birth of three more children 97; and TB's peerage battle 109, 201; visit to Israel 116; visit to Cincinnati 138; involvement in politics 138–9; social life 138–9; on Tony Crosland 139; and South Africa's racial policy 155: TB's resignation from NEC at 1960 party conference 159; and 1961 election campaign 187, 188; listens to debate on TB's request to speak from bar 191; the press and 200–201, 357–8, 368–9; simple lifestyle 202; children's education 220; suggests title for Labour's 1964 manifesto 225; and the 1965 Budget incident 236–7; views on education 242;

writings of 242–3; works for National Extension College 243, 303; and the Open University 258–9; work for comprehensive education 289, 303; extends work in education 326; at TB's meeting after he loses Industry Dept 371; influence on TB's political thinking 381; and TB's speech at 1977 party conference 390; on result of 1981 deputy leadership election 417; travels of, with TB 431; works in the Chesterfield campaign 436; and the 1988 leadership contest 453

Benn, David (brother of Tony Benn): on teetotalism 5; on Sir Ernest Benn 8; birth 10; on his father 13; contracts bovine tuberculosis 14; evacuated to Scotland 22, 23; moves with mother and TB to Oxted 24; on TB's war service 38; works for BBC 57–8; at 1951 Oxford Union debate 96–7; and the Suez campaign 127, 130; world travels of 163; and TB's peerage 212; as TB's next-door neighbour 317

Benn, Sir Ernest (uncle of Tony Benn), 2, 7–8, 105

Benn, Glanvill (cousin of Tony Benn) 54

Benn, Hilary (son of Tony Benn): service in local government 86, 401; birth 97; support for TB 194; involvement with TB's career 289; at Sussex University 326; marriage to Rosalind Retey 326; and press harassment 368; sporting injury 369; and TB's loss of Industry Dept 371, 372; speaks at 1978 Labour Party conference 394; gains seat on Ealing Council 401; death of Rosalind 401–2; as adviser to TB 407–8; son Michael born 432

Benn, Sir John (paternal grandfather of Tony Benn), 5, 14, 239

Benn, Joshua (son of Tony Benn): birth 97, 138; relationship with father 269; involvement with TB's career 289; at Holland Park School 326; press harassment 357, 368, 369, 376; discovers tapping of TB's phone 360; rigs up alarm system 361; love for electronics 401; and 1981 deputy leadership ballot 416; computerises data in Chesterfield campaign 436

Benn, Revd Julius (great-grandfather of Tony Benn) 198

Benn, Julius (great-great uncle of Tony Benn) 402

Index

Benn, Margaret (mother of Tony Benn), (later Lady Stansgate): background 2, 3–4; character 4; learns Hebrew 4; Hebrew University library named after her 4; meets and marries William Wedgwood Benn 5; husband's teetotalism demand 5; birth of sons Michael and Tony 5–6; gift of religion to her sons 6; member of League of the Church Militant 6; watches husband resign his seat 7; Mediterranean cruise 7–8; home is flooded 9; on TB as a child 9; on son David 10; on TB's childhood political ambition 11; on family mealtimes 12; birth of fourth child (stillborn) 14; fire at London home 23, constituency work during husband's war service 23; teaches theology 24; moves to Oxted 24; and death of son Michael 35; joins Congregationalists 162–3; and TB's peerage battle 166; continuing religious interests of 326–7

Benn, Melissa (daughter of Tony Benn): birth 93, 97; Seretse Khama godfather to 93; relationship with father 269; involvement with TB's career 289; feminist interests 316–17, 392; at Holland Park School 326; discovers father's telephone is tapped 360; as supporter of TB 371; press harassment 376; works as journalist 401

Benn, Michael (brother of Tony Benn): birth 5; at Westminster School 15–16; love of rowing 16, 19; school evacuates to Lancing College 17, 20; joins RAF 21, 22; gets his wings 25–6; maintains contact with school 26; death in plane crash 35–7, 38; letters of 36; spiritual leadership of 36

Benn, Michael (grandson of Tony Benn), birth of 432

Benn, Rosalind (daughter-in-law of Tony Benn); marriage to Hilary Benn 326, tragically early death of 401–2, 469

Benn, Stephen (son of Tony Benn): birth 78; mother takes him to his first public meeting 82; and father's peerage 212–13; support for TB, 194, 371, 272; press harassment 201; involvement in TB's career 289; at Keele University 326; Ph.D studies and work in Washington 401; musical compositions of 402, 469; as adviser to TB 407

Benn, Tony (Anthony Neil Wedgwood), first political memories 1; origin of Christian names 1–2; birth of 5–6; teetotalism 5, 34–5, 48, 383, 468; religious background 6, 10–11; sent to country during 1926 General Strike 8; Uncle Ernest a major influence on him 8; flooding of Grosvenor Road home 9; family moves to Scotland 9; return to London 10; called James by his family 10, 20; first school 10, 11; early political ambition 11; works in father's office 12; diary- and note-keeping habits 12, 220–22, 283–4, 350; relationship with parents 12–13, 104–5; inveterate list-maker and record-keeper 13–14; campaigns for Westminster Labour candidate in 1935 election 14; at Westminster School 15–26; joins Scouts and Air Training Corps 17; academic achievement 18, 19–20; joins Debating Society 18, 19–20; claims never to have heard of the Levellers 18–19; love of rowing, boxing and fencing 19; condemnation of English public schools 21; Westminster School's moves around the country during Second World War 21, 24; evacuated to Oban 22; Civil Defence work 22; hears of bomb damage to London home 23; experience of the Blitz 23–4; joins Home Guard 24; moves to Oxted 24; father's elevation to the peerage 25; relationship with brother Michael 26; joins Labour Party at age seventeen 26; ambitions 26; foot operation 27–8; reticence about minor illness 27–8; at Oxford University 27–32, 40–54; friendship with Patrick MacMahon 27, 28; member of Oxford Union 28–9, 31, 41–9; first speeches 28–9, 31; joins university air squadron 28; calls for nationalisation 30–31; oratorical style 31–2, 48–9, 84–5; shows tendency to stand for election 32; joins RAF 32; in South Africa for training, 32–5; on Fascism 33; writes essay 'The Matabele and the Mashona' 33–4; on treatment of blacks in Africa 33–4; pipe-smoking habit 34, 138; and brother Michael's death 35–7; gets his wings and is posted to Egypt 37; visits kibbutz in Palestine 37–8; hears Churchill's election speech while on homeward-bound ship 38; returns to family 38; work during July 1945 election 38–9; sought as parliamentary candidate before being eligible 38; hears election